MODERN DRAFTING
An Introduction to CAD

MODERN DRAFTING
An Introduction to CAD

James D. Bethune

Boston University, College of Engineering

Bonnie A. Kee

Martin Marietta Missile Systems

PRENTICE HALL, Englewood Cliffs, N.J. 07632

Bethune, James D.
    Modern drafting : an introduction to CAD / James D. Bethune,
Bonnie A. Kee.
        p.   cm.
    Includes index.
    ISBN 0-13-591058-7
    1. Mechanical drawing.   2. Computer graphics.   I. Kee, Bonnie A.
II. Title.
T353.B456 1989
604.2′4′0285—dc19   88-12408
                                                       CIP

Editorial/production supervision and
    interior design: Ed Jones
Cover design: Joel Mitnick Design Inc.
Manufacturing buyers: Peter Havens and Robert Anderson
Page layout: Charles Pelletreau

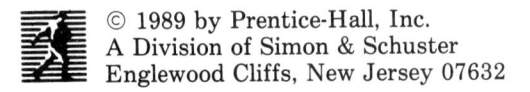

© 1989 by Prentice-Hall, Inc.
A Division of Simon & Schuster
Englewood Cliffs, New Jersey 07632

All rights reserved. No part of this book may be
reproduced, in any form or by any means,
without permission in writing from the publisher.

Printed in the United States of America

10 9 8 7 6 5 4 3 2 1

ISBN 0-13-591058-7

PRENTICE-HALL INTERNATIONAL (UK) LIMITED, *London*
PRENTICE-HALL OF AUSTRALIA PTY. LIMITED, *Sydney*
PRENTICE-HALL CANADA INC., *Toronto*
PRENTICE-HALL HISPANOAMERICANA, S.A., *Mexico*
PRENTICE-HALL OF INDIA PRIVATE LIMITED, *New Delhi*
PRENTICE-HALL OF JAPAN, INC., *Tokyo*
SIMON & SCHUSTER ASIA PTE. LTD., *Singapore*
EDITORA PRENTICE-HALL DO BRASIL, LTDA., *Rio de Janeiro*

To Kendra

*To Mom, Dad,
and Brother Jim*

CONTENTS

PREFACE   *xiii*

1 INTRODUCTION   1

    1-1   Computer Graphic Systems   2
    1-2   Computers   2
    1-3   Screens   4
    1-4   Input Devices   5
    1-5   The Binary System   6
    1-6   Glossary of Computer Graphic Terms   8
            Problems   9

2 MATHEMATICAL CONCEPTS   12

    2-1   Introduction   13
    2-2   Units   13
    2-3   Conversions   14
    2-4   Screen Units   14
    2-5   Rectangular Coordinate System   17
    2-6   Rotated Rectangular Coordinate System   19
    2-7   Polar Coordinate System   20
    2-8   Three-Dimensional Coordinate System   21
    2-9   Absolute and Relative Axis Systems   23
            Problems   25

3 BASIC TWO-DIMENSIONAL CONSTRUCTIONS 29

3-1 Introduction 30
3-2 Horizontal Lines 30
3-3 Vertical Lines 32
3-4 Combining Horizontal and Vertical Lines 35
3-5 Slanted Lines 37
3-6 Circles 39
3-7 Arcs 42
3-8 Fillets and Rounds (Corners) 42
3-9 Irregular Curves 44
3-10 Sample Problems 44
Problems 46

4 GEOMETRIC CONSTRUCTIONS 59

4-1 Introduction 60
4-2 Perpendicular Bisect of a Line 60
4-3 Line Perpendicular to Another Line through a Given Point 61
4-4 Line Divided into Equal Parts 63
4-5 Line Tangent to a Circle through a Given Point on the Circle 65
4-6 Line Parallel to Another Line 67
4-7 Triangles 68
4-8 Squares 70
4-9 Pentagons 72
4-10 Hexagons 74
4-11 Octagons 77
4-12 Arcs Tangent to Arcs 79
4-13 Corners 82
4-14 Ellipses 85
4-15 Parabolas 85
Problems 86

5 BASIC CONCEPTS OF DIMENSIONING 98

5-1 Introduction 99
5-2 Conventions and Definitions 99
5-3 Slanted Features 103
5-4 Circular Features 104
5-5 Arcs 106
5-6 Angles 107
5-7 Dimensioning Small Distances 109
5-8 Repetitive Hole Patterns 109

Contents ix

- 5-9 Multiple Hole Patterns 111
- 5-10 Chamfers 114
- 5-11 Knurls 114
- 5-12 Rounded Ends 115
- 5-13 Slotted Holes 116
- 5-14 Keys and Keyseats 116
- 5-15 Countersinks 117
- 5-16 Counterbores 118
- 5-17 Spotfaces 118
- 5-18 Counterdrills 119
- 5-19 Irregular Features 119
- 5-20 Double Dimensions 121
- 5-21 Locating Dimensions on a Drawing 122
  Problems 122

6 ORTHOGRAPHIC VIEWS 128

- 6-1 Introduction 129
- 6-2 Three Views of an Object 130
- 6-3 Computer Applications of Orthographic Views 132
- 6-4 Hidden Lines 136
- 6-5 Choosing a Front View 138
- 6-6 Normal Surfaces 140
- 6-7 Slanted Surfaces 141
- 6-8 Oblique Surfaces 143
- 6-9 Rounded Surfaces 150
- 6-10 Cylinders 152
- 6-11 Holes 154
- 6-12 Irregular Shapes 156
- 6-13 Sheet Metal Objects 161
- 6-14 Castings 162
- 6-15 Three-Dimensional Coordinate Systems and Orthographic Views 163
  Problems 165

7 SECTIONAL VIEWS 185

- 7-1 Introduction 186
- 7-2 Section Lines 186
- 7-3 Cutting-Plane Lines 191
- 7-4 Multiple Sectional Views 195
- 7-5 Broken-Out Sectional Views 196
- 7-6 Revolved Sectional Views 197
- 7-7 Rotated Sectional Views 197
- 7-8 Removed Sectional Views 198

- 7-9 Half-Sectional Views 198
- 7-10 Thin Sectional Views 198
- 7-11 Ribs and Webs 200
- 7-12 Holes 200
  - Problems 201

8 AUXILIARY VIEWS 211

- 8-1 Introduction 212
- 8-2 True-Length Lines and Planes 212
- 8-3 Primary Auxiliary Views 215
- 8-4 Partial Auxiliary Views 223
- 8-5 Auxiliary Views of Rounded Shapes 224
- 8-6 Auxiliary View of an Oblique Surface 229
  - Problems 237

9 BASIC CONCEPTS OF TOLERANCES 249

- 9-1 Introduction 250
- 9-2 Bilateral Tolerances 250
- 9-3 Unilateral Tolerances 251
- 9-4 Limit Dimensions 252
- 9-5 Angular Tolerances 252
- 9-6 Tolerance Accumulation 252
- 9-7 Tolerance Studies 254
- 9-8 Sample Problem 255
- 9-9 Limits and Fits 258
- 9-10 Basic Hole and Basic Shaft Systems 261
- 9-11 Tolerance Symbols 262
- 9-12 Fit Tolerances in Inches 265
- 9-13 Fit Tolerances in Millimeters 267
- 9-14 Basic Shaft System Sample Problems 268
- 9-15 Surface Finish 269
- 9-16 Surface Finish Symbols 271
- 9-17 Inspection of Toleranced Dimensions 274
- 9-18 Dual Dimensioning 274
  - Problems 276

10 THREADS AND FASTENERS 290

- 10-1 Introduction 291
- 10-2 Terms and Definitions 291
- 10-3 Thread Depths and Lengths 294
- 10-4 Screws and Bolts 297
- 10-5 Nuts 300

Contents　　　　　　　　　　　　　　　　　　　　　　　　　　　　　　　　xi

  10-6 Assembled Fasteners 301
  10-7 Design Guidelines 302
  10-8 Washers 304
  10-9 Setscrews and Studs 305
  10-10 Keys 307
  10-11 Rivets 308
  10-12 Springs 309
  10-13 Building a Reference Library 309
     Problems 321

11 PRODUCTION DRAWINGS   **330**

  11-1 Introduction 331
  11-2 Assembly Drawing 331
  11-3 Detail Drawings 334
  11-4 Drawing Title Assignment 336
  11-5 Title Blocks 337
  11-6 Parts Lists (Bills of Materials) 338
  11-7 Drawing Revisions 340
  11-8 Drawing Zones 342
  11-9 Drawing Notes 345
  11-10 Printers and Plotters 346
     Problems 347

12 THREE-DIMENSIONAL DRAWINGS: PICTORIALS **351**

  12-1 Introduction 352
  12-2 Three-Dimensional Axis Systems 352
  12-3 Three-Dimensional Coordinate Values 354
  12-4 Axis Orientation 355
  12-5 Right Rectangular Prisms 357
  12-6 Cylinders 358
  12-7 General Prisms 360
  12-8 Pyramids 361
  12-9 Cones 363
  12-10 Spheres 364
  12-11 Combining Geometric Shapes 364
  12-12 Modifying Three-Dimensional Geometric Shapes 365
  12-13 Rounded Three-Dimensional Surfaces 368
  12-14 Preparing Three-Dimensional Drawings from Orthographic Views 369
  12-15 Three-Dimensional Windowed Drawings 374
  12-16 Three-Dimensional Drawings Created Using Two-Dimensional Systems 376
  12-17 Exploded Drawings 378
     Problems 378

APPENDICES

A Standard Thread Sizes 398
B Wire and Sheet Metal Gages 400
C Paper Sizes 400
D Fit Tolerances 401
E Standard Twist Drill Sizes 410

INDEX   412

PREFACE

This book is a generic approach to computer-aided drafting. It does not rely on any single computer graphic system, but considers all systems to be powerful new tools that enable drafters and designers to produce drawings quickly and accurately. It is the authors' contention that the principles and techniques developed over the years to create correct, easy-to-understand drawings are directly applicable to computer-aided drafting. ANSI drafting standards are followed throughout the book. Consideration is given to both large and small systems.

Drafting principles are presented and explained with heavy emphasis on orthographic views, layout techniques, dimensioning, tolerancing, assembly, and detail drawings. The book often presents board techniques alongside the equivalent computer techniques so that students can better understand how computers interpret and apply these techniques to create drawings.

The book uses a highly visual approach, with many illustrations, photographs, and sample problems. All material is presented in a step-by-step format. Each chapter includes many exercise problems. Instructors should find ample material to help students apply and practice the material presented in the chapters.

Several people deserve special thanks for their help in preparing this book, among them, Sally Fischer, who typed the manuscript, and Sue Angell, Debbi Herman, and Diane Cotter, who did the bulk of the inked line drawings, working from our pencil originals. Thanks also to our editor, Ed Moura, who led the project, and our production editor, Ed Jones, who brought the whole thing together.

Please send any comments, corrections, and questions to us via Prentice Hall. We value and sincerely appreciate them.

James D. Bethune
Bonnie A. Kee

1
INTRODUCTION

1-1 COMPUTER GRAPHIC SYSTEMS

Computer graphic systems are made from several components: a computer, a screen, a keyboard, and a device to input to the screen, such as a light pen, mouse, or thumbscrews. The size, capacity, and accuracy of these individual components determine the overall quality and capabilities of the system. Figure 1-1 shows a typical computer graphic system.

1-2 COMPUTERS

The principal component of any computer graphic system is a *computer*. The computer drives the entire system. Its memory capacity, speed of processing, and overall size will determine the capability and speed of the system.

Computers are, in general, rated by their *memory* capacity. Memory can either be *permanent*, called ROM (read-only memory), or *intermediate*, called RAM (random access memory). ROM is built into the computer and cannot be erased. A computer that has "built-in BASIC" has the fundamentals of the language BASIC stored in its ROM.

RAM memory is the memory used for most on-the-screen work. That is, as drawings are created, the computer is probably operating in its RAM mode. After a drawing is complete, it is transferred into a file and saved. It is important to mention that once the computer is turned off, that is, the power is off, the RAM will be wiped clean. Any work not filed correctly will disappear.

FIGURE 1-1 Computer graphics system. (Courtesy of Apple Computer Inc.)

Computers derive their memory capacity from *chips*. Chips are pieces of silicon with integrated circuits comprised of thousands of small switches, transistors, resistors, and capacitors etched into their surface. A single chip about $1\frac{1}{2}$ in. long and $\frac{1}{2}$ in. wide will contain about 100,000 functions.

Most computer companies do not manufacture their own chips; they purchase them from individual companies specializing in chip manufacture. The rivalry between chip manufacturers is intense. Each company continually tries to produce chips that are smaller, with larger capacity, that operate faster, and can be sold at a lower price. Figure 1-2 shows a computer chip.

Chips are combined into larger circuits called *boards* or *cards*. Figure 1-3 shows a board from a computer. One edge of a board is fitted with metal strips that slide into receptacles within the computer.

Many smaller computers can be upgraded — given greater memory or operating capabilities — by adding boards. For example, a "color board" will give a computer the ability to understand and process color commands.

Computer memory capacity is specified by the number of memory locations available. A 64K computer has 64,000 memory locations; a 256K has 256,000 locations. The term *Meg*, short for the prefix *mega*, meaning millions, is also used to identify memory capacity. A 40-Meg memory has 40,000,000 memory locations.

Graphics work in general requires large amounts of memory both for the software used to create the drawing packages and for the actual drawings. Unfortunately, large memory capacity usually costs large amounts of money. However, as chips become more powerful, the ability of smaller systems to create more detailed and accurate graphics increases.

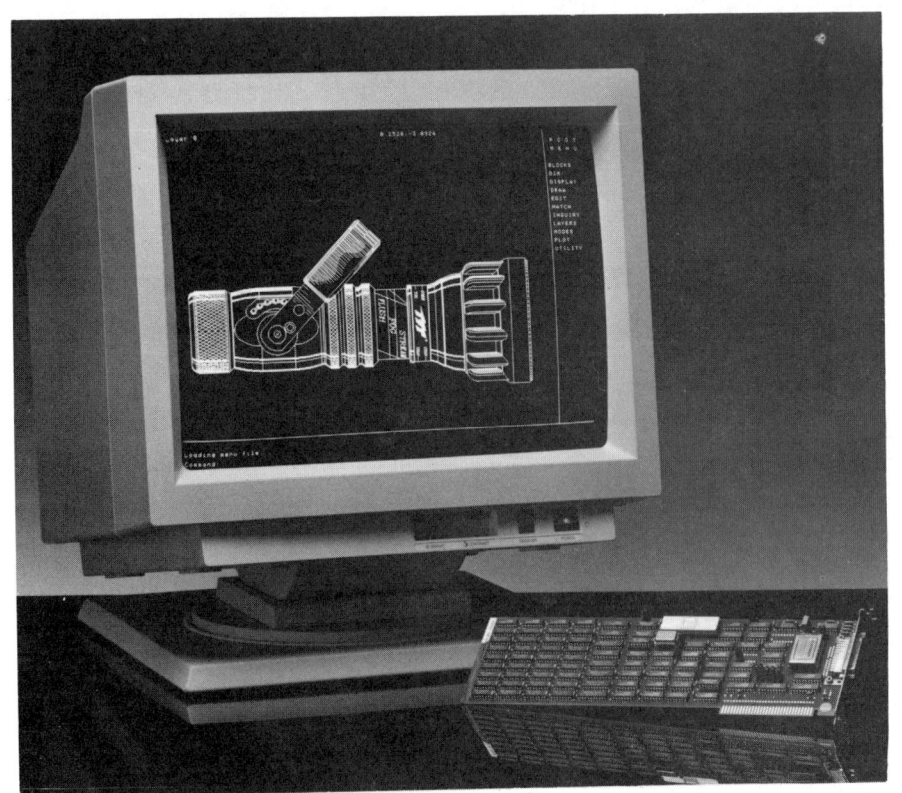

FIGURE 1-2 Computer chip.

FIGURE 1-3 Computer circuit board. (Courtesy of IGC Inc., 1568 Ocean Ave., Bohemia, NY 11716.)

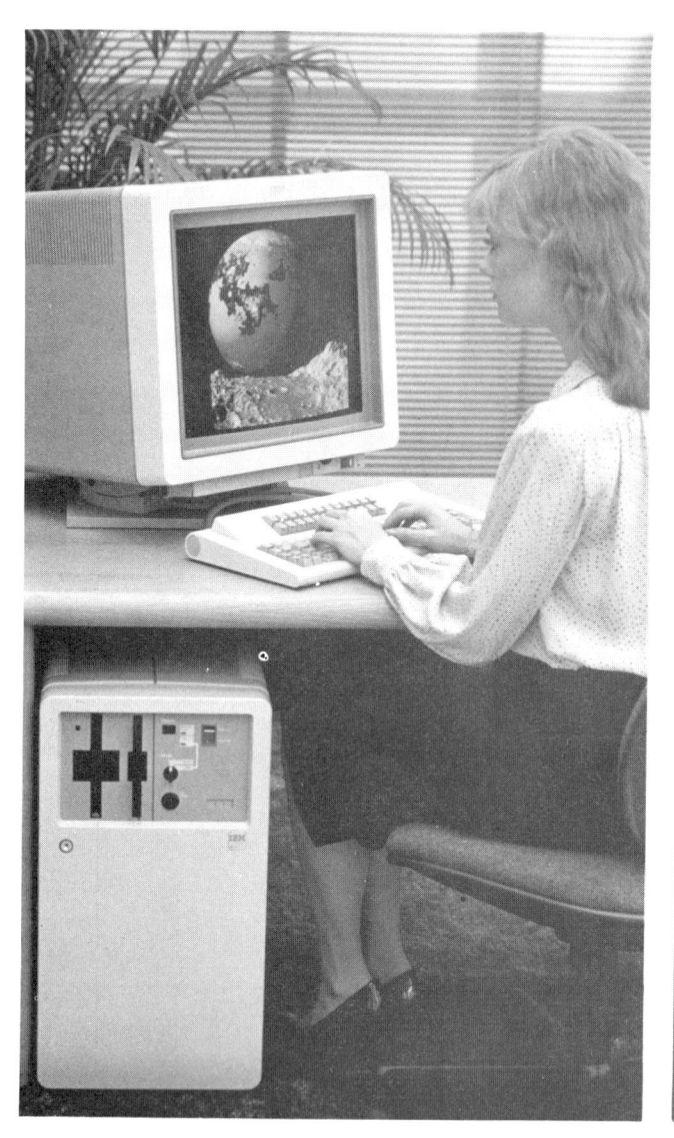

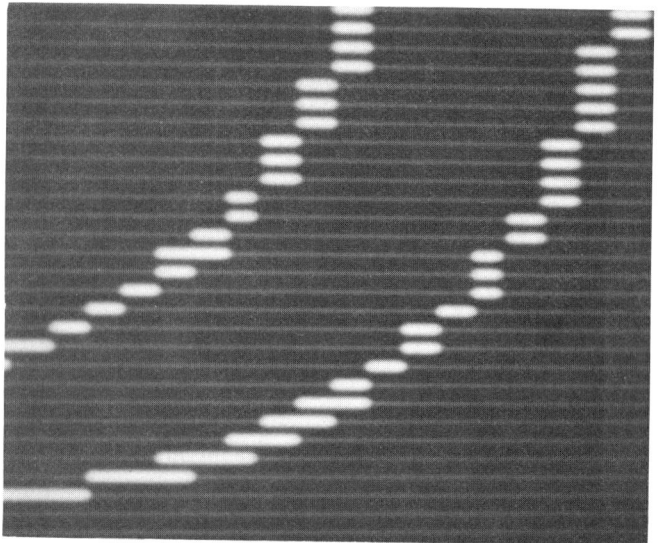

FIGURE 1-4 Computer that stands on the floor near a workstation. (Courtesy of International Business Machines Corporation.)

FIGURE 1-5 Comparison of high- and low-resolution screens.

Systems with large memories require a space larger than is convenient for desktop computers. Figure 1-4 shows a computer stored in a small box located beside an operator's desk or workstation.

1-3 SCREENS

Computer *screens*, also called *visual display units* (VDUs), are rated by the number of *pixels* they contain. A pixel is like a small dot on the screen that is turned on or off to create the screen picture. The more pixels within a screen, the better the resolution (clarity) of the screen. A high-resolution screen might have 640 × 400 pixels, that is, a pattern consisting of 640 pixels from left to right of the screen and 400 pixels from top to bottom. A low-resolution screen might have a pixel rating of 320 × 200. Figure 1-5 shows a comparison between the graphics produced by high-resolution and low-resolution screens.

Sec. 1-4　Input Devices

1-4　INPUT DEVICES

In addition to keyboards, other devices are used to input information into the computer. The system shown in Figure 1-6 shows the use of a *light pen;* Figure 1-7, a *mouse* (in the operator's right hand), and Figure 1-8, *thumbscrews.* All these devices are used to control a screen cursor, which, in turn, is used to input information into the computer.

FIGURE 1-6　Light pen.

FIGURE 1-7　Mouse. (Courtesy of International Business Machines Corporation.)

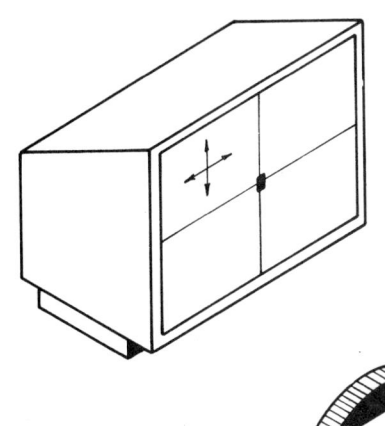

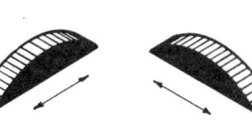

FIGURE 1-8　Devices used to control the screen cursor.

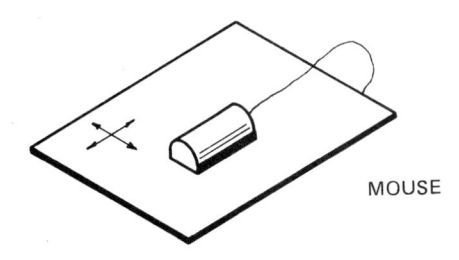

LIGHT PEN

THUMB SCREWS

MOUSE

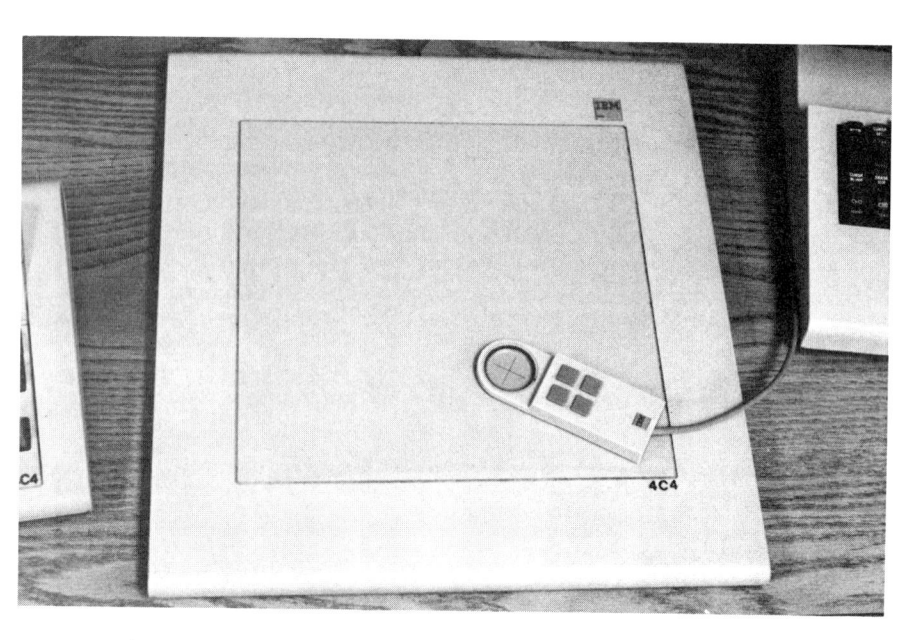

FIGURE 1-9 Digitizing board.

Another input device that is used in combination with a mouse or similar device is a *digitizing board*. Figure 1-9 shows a digitizing board. The digitizing board has small sensors embedded within its surface. A mouse is used to activate these sensors and to pass the location onto the computer. Shapes can be electronically traced and defined in numerical or digital information, which, in turn, can be processed by the computer.

1-5 THE BINARY SYSTEM

The *binary system* is a numerical system that expresses all numbers and letters in terms of just two values, 1 and 0. The number 5186 could be expressed in binary code as 0010 0100 0100 0010. The letter S could be expressed as 0101 0011.

The binary system is well suited to integrated circuits used in computer chips, because the switches within the chip are either open or closed, or the equivalent of the 0 and 1 coding required by the binary system. The drawback to the binary system is the extremely large size of the numbers. For example, in standard base 10, 5186 is expressed using four numbers, but 16 numbers, 0001 0100 0100 0010, are required to express 5186 in binary.

Individual switches within chips are called *bits*. Bits can be combined to create outputs as shown in Figure 1-10. The two bits (switches) shown are capable of producing four combinations. The four combinations are expressed numerically in the table shown. Three bits can be used to generate 8 combinations, and 4 bits, 16 combinations (Figure 1-11). Bits are combined into larger combinations called *bytes*. There are 8 bits in a byte.

Figure 1-12 shows how switches can be used to generate various output combinations. In example 1, switch A is open, producing a 0 output; B and C are closed, producing 1 outputs; and D is open, producing a 0 output. The result is equivalent to a binary number of 0110. In example 2, the switches are combined to produce a 1101 output.

Figure 1-13 shows some numbers to the base 10 (standard numbers) and their binary equivalents.

Sec. 1-5   The Binary System

TWO ON-OFF SWITCHES

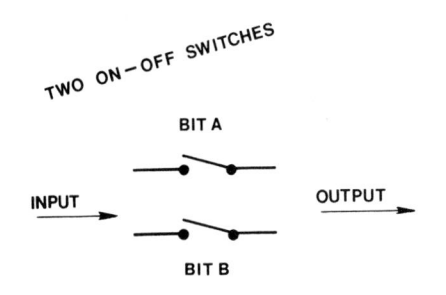

INPUT → BIT A / BIT B → OUTPUT

NUMERICAL EQUIVALENT

A	B	OUTPUT
0	0	0
0	1	1
1	0	1
1	1	1

FIGURE 1-10 Two ON-OFF switches will produce four possible combinations and could generate one of the four outputs shown.

3 INPUTS

A	B	C
0	0	0
0	0	1
0	1	0
0	1	1
1	0	0
1	0	1
1	1	0
1	1	1

4 INPUTS

A	B	C	D
0	0	0	0
0	0	0	1
0	0	1	0
0	0	1	1
0	1	0	0
0	1	0	1
0	1	1	0
0	1	1	1
1	0	0	0
1	0	0	1
1	0	1	0
1	0	1	1
1	1	0	0
1	1	0	1
1	1	1	0
1	1	1	1

FIGURE 1-11 Three inputs will produce eight combinations, and four inputs will produce 16 combinations.

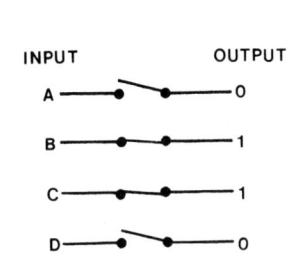

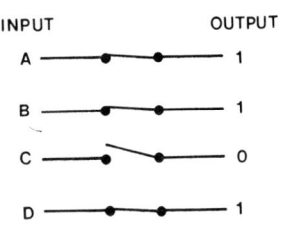

① INPUT — OUTPUT
A —•— 0
B —•— 1
C —•— 1
D —•— 0

② INPUT — OUTPUT
A —•— 1
B —•— 1
C —•— 0
D —•— 1

FIGURE 1-12 Two examples of how ON-OFF switches can be arranged to produce different output combinations.

BINARY	DECIMAL EQUIVALENT
0 0 0	0
0 0 1	1
0 1 0	2
0 1 1	3
1 0 0	4
1 0 1	5
1 1 0	6
1 1 1	7

FIGURE 1-13 Some sample binary numbers and their equivalent decimal values.

1-6 GLOSSARY OF COMPUTER GRAPHIC TERMS

Following is a glossary of terms commonly used when working with computer graphic systems.

Algorithm Any special method used to solve a problem. The word usually refers to the mathematical equations used by a computer to perform specific functions.

Analog A circuit that works on voltage values rather than numbers.

Blanking Erasing all information within a window.

Batch Processing Data processing that requires no interaction from the user.

Bit The smallest piece of digital information.

Buffer A location within the computer memory that serves as a temporary holding area until information is recalled.

Byte Eight bits combine to form a byte.

Character A number, letter, decimal point, punctuation mark, and so on. A normal line of written text has about 80 characters.

Chip A piece of silicon that contains one or more integrated circuits.

Clipping Erasure of all or part of an element.

Digital System A system that handles information in discrete pieces such as numbers.

Element A line or arc drawn on the screen.

EPROM ROM that can be erased and/or programmed.

Error Message Computer message to the user that appears on the screen and tells the user what error has been made.

Floppy Disk A flexible disk that is used to store data. Information can be transferred from a floppy disk to the computer's RAM, or from the RAM to the floppy disk.

Gate A simple ON–OFF switch.

Hard Copy The drawings or text printout produced by a computer system via a printer or plotter.

Hardware The physical components that form a system: the computer, screen, printer, and so on.

Image Processing The overall process of generating pictures on a computer.

Integrated Circuit A series of very small circuits etched into a piece of silicon.

Interactive A system that receives, processes, and returns data to a user. Systems that have good interactive capabilities are called "user friendly."

Local Area Network A system that links together terminals or computers.

LSI (large-scale integration) An LSI system contains about 1000 gates.

Memory Computer circuits that retain information.

Microcomputer Any small computer that contains only a few circuit boards. Some microcomputers contain only one chip.

Microprocessor That part of the computer that processes digital information.

Chap. 1   Problems

Mode   A point where two or more lines intersect.

Modem   A device that enables the computer to receive and transmit information over telephone lines.

Monochromatic Screen   A screen that displays only one color, usually white or green.

Number Crunching   A slang term that refers to a computer's ability to complete mathematical operations quickly.

On-Line   A computer or terminal that is in an operational mode.

Operator   A person using a computer.

Painting   Asking the computer to reproduce a known drawing on the screen.

Panning   Moving across a drawing that is larger than the screen.

Pixel   A single display element on a raster screen that can be varied in color and intensity.

Primitive   A basic command to the system. Usually, a single word that cannot be used for any other purpose. For example, if the word DRAW is a primitive within a given system, it cannot be used as a file name.

Program   A set of instructions used to command computer operations.

RAM (random access memory)   The temporary computer memory.

Raster Screen   A screen made with pixels that are activated by a horizontally scanning beam. A TV screen is a raster screen.

Resolution   A determination of the clarity and distinguishability of pictures on a screen.

ROM (read-only memory)   The permanent memory of a computer.

Software   The programs that control computer operations.

Time Sharing   A system whereby a large computer is linked to individual terminals that, in turn, share access to the main computer.

User   A person operating a computer.

VLSI (very large scale integration)—VLSI systems usually contain over 50,000 gates.

Window   A specific rectangular area within a drawing. It is used to define a specific area of a drawing so that the area can be worked on.

Zooming   To isolate and enlarge a specific area of drawing.

PROBLEMS

P1-1   Given the switching arrangement shown in Figure P1-1, determine the output in binary numbers and state the equivalent base 10 number.

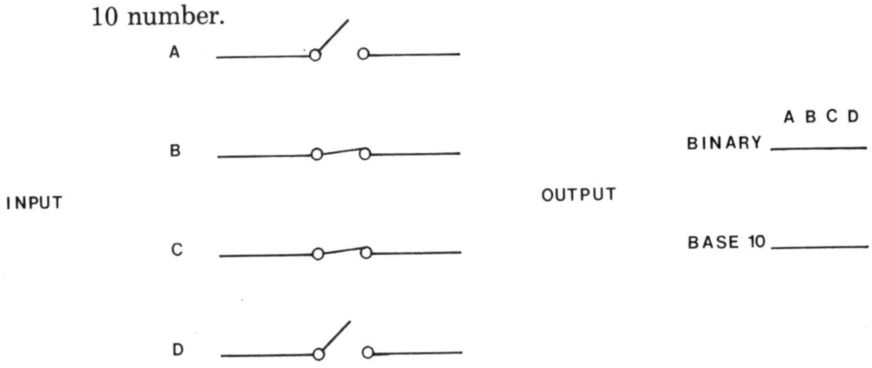

FIGURE P1-1

P1-2 Given the switching arrangement shown in Figure P1-2, determine the output in binary numbers and state the equivalent base 10 number.

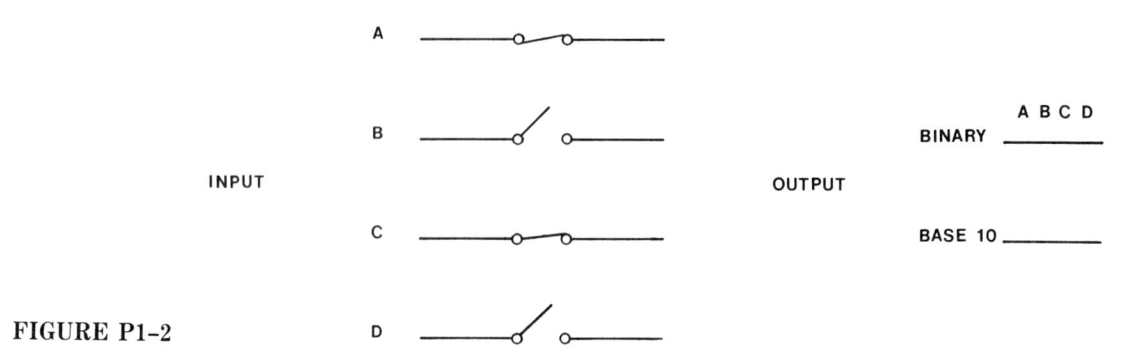

FIGURE P1-2

A B C D
BINARY _____

BASE 10 _____

P1-3 Sketch the appropriate switching arrangement that will yield the outputs listed in Figure P1-3.

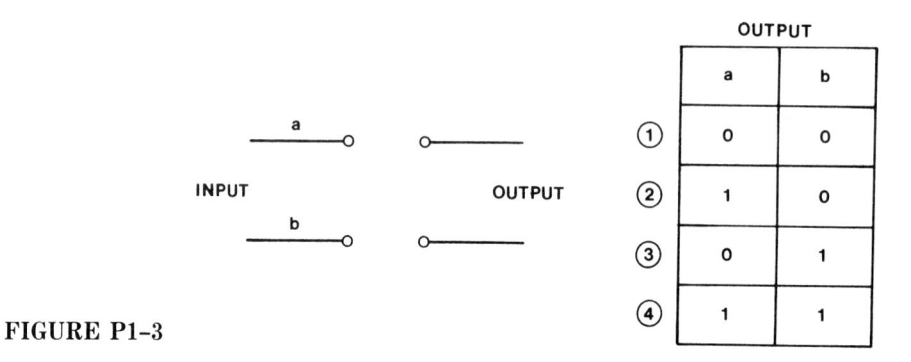

	OUTPUT	
	a	b
①	0	0
②	1	0
③	0	1
④	1	1

FIGURE P1-3

P1-4 Sketch the appropriate switching arrangement that will yield the outputs listed in Figure P1-4.

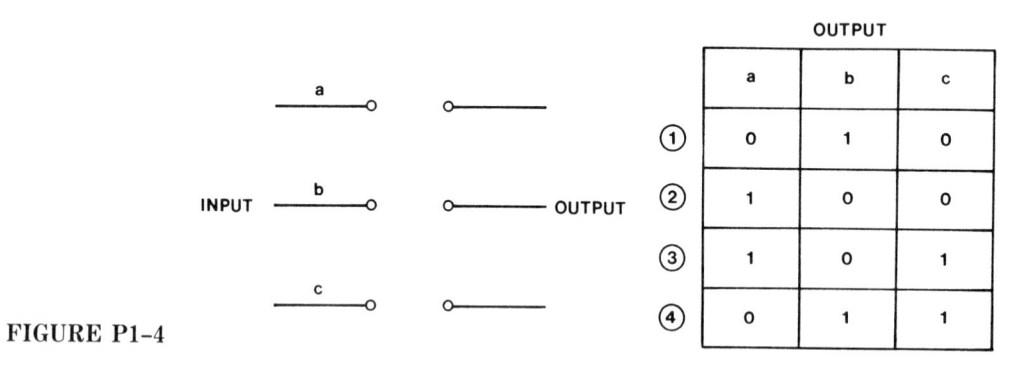

	OUTPUT		
	a	b	c
①	0	1	0
②	1	0	0
③	1	0	1
④	0	1	1

FIGURE P1-4

P1-5 Sketch the appropriate switching arrangement that will yield the outputs listed in Figure P1-5.

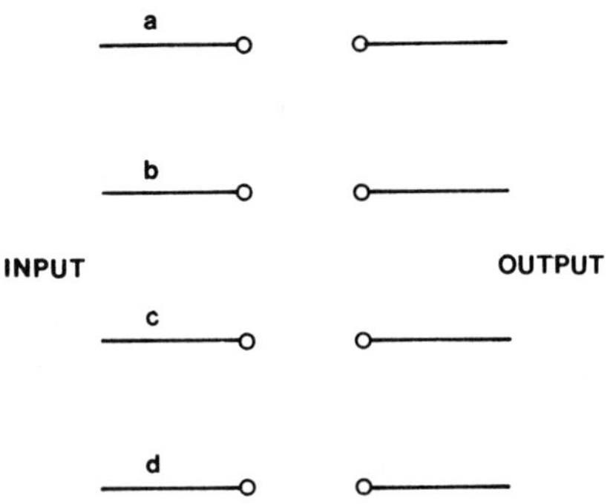

	OUTPUT			
	a	b	c	d
①	1	0	0	1
②	1	1	0	1
③	1	0	0	0
④	0	1	1	0

FIGURE P1-5

2
MATHEMATICAL CONCEPTS

IBM 3270-PC/G Graphics Workstation. (Courtesy of International Business Machines Corporation.)

2-1 INTRODUCTION

In this chapter we introduce and review the mathematical concepts essential to the understanding and operation of computer graphic systems. English, metric, and screen units are covered together with six different types of coordinate systems: rectangular, rotated, polar, three-dimensional, and absolute versus relative.

2-2 UNITS

A *unit* is a basic measurement of length. It is the standard for other measurements. Technical drawing uses two basic units of measure, the millimeter as defined by the Système International d'Unités (SI units), and the inch as defined by U.S. Customary units.

The *metric system* is based on the meter. The meter is officially defined as 1,650,763.73 wavelengths of light as emitted from a transition state of a kryton 86 atom.

A meter is divided into larger and smaller units based on multiples of 10. This makes conversion between units easy. All that is required is a shift in the decimal point. The standard units of a meter are as follows.

$$0.001 \text{ meter} = 1 \text{ millimeter}$$
$$0.01 \text{ meter} = 1 \text{ centimeter}$$
$$0.1 \text{ meter} = 1 \text{ decimeter}$$
$$10 \text{ meters} = 1 \text{ decameter}$$
$$100 \text{ meters} = 1 \text{ hectometer}$$
$$1000 \text{ meters} = 1 \text{ kilometer}$$

All measurements on technical drawings are made using millimeters. Figure 2-1 lists various subunits of a meter together with their conversion factors (multiples of a meter) and their abbreviations.

UNIT	Multiple of a meter	ABBREVIATION
meter	1	m
nanometer	10^{-9}	nn
micrometer	10^{-6}	μm
millimeter	10^{-3}	mm
centimeter	10^{-2}	cm
decimeter	10^{-1}	dm
decameter	10^{1}	dam
hectometer	10^{2}	hm
kilometer	10^{3}	Km
megameter	10^{6}	Mm

FIGURE 2-1 Multiples of a meter.

FIGURE 2-2 Multiples of an inch.

UNIT	MULTIPLE OF AN INCH	ABBREVIATION
INCH	1	IN.
FOOT	12	FT
LINK	12	LINK
YARD	36	YD
ROD	198	ROD
CHAIN	1,200	CHAIN
MILE	63,360	MI

Technical drawings, done using English units, are based on an inch. An inch is defined as 0.0254 meter exactly.

Small measurements can be specified using fractions of an inch ($\frac{1}{4}$, $\frac{1}{2}$, $\frac{3}{4}$, etc.) or decimal inches (0.25, 0.50, 0.75, etc.). Larger measurements are defined using the units shown in Figure 2-2. All measurements on technical drawings are made using inches.

2-3 CONVERSIONS

Inches are converted to millimeters by multiplying the inch value by 25.4.

$$\text{inches} \times 25.4 = \text{millimeters}$$

For example,

$$3 \text{ in.} \times 25.4 = 76.2 \text{ mm}$$
$$0.50 \text{ in.} \times 25.4 = 12.7 \text{ mm}$$

Millimeters are converted to inches by dividing by 25.4.

$$\frac{\text{millimeters}}{25.4} = \text{inches}$$

For example,

$$\frac{15 \text{ mm}}{25.4} = 0.59 \text{ in.} \qquad \frac{31.5 \text{ mm}}{25.4} = 1.24 \text{ in.}$$

2-4 SCREEN UNITS

Computer graphic screens are divided into distances called *screen units*. The length of a screen unit is in turn derived from the screen's pixel size. (The word *pixel* derives from the term "picture element.") High-resolution screens can have 400 pixels vertically and 700 horizontally. Low-resolution screens can have as few as 40 pixels vertically and 60 horizontally.

Pixel size is not fixed, as with an inch or a millimeter, but varies according to the screen's capability. Figure 2-3 shows a line 50 pixels long drawn on a low-resolution screen. Figure 2-4 shows a line 50 pixels long drawn on a high-resolution screen. Note the difference in their lengths.

Pixel size will affect the clarity and accuracy of the picture presented on the screen. Figure 2-5 shows a circle drawn using a low-resolution screen, that is, one with large pixel units. Note the sharp edges.

Sec. 2-4 Screen Units 15

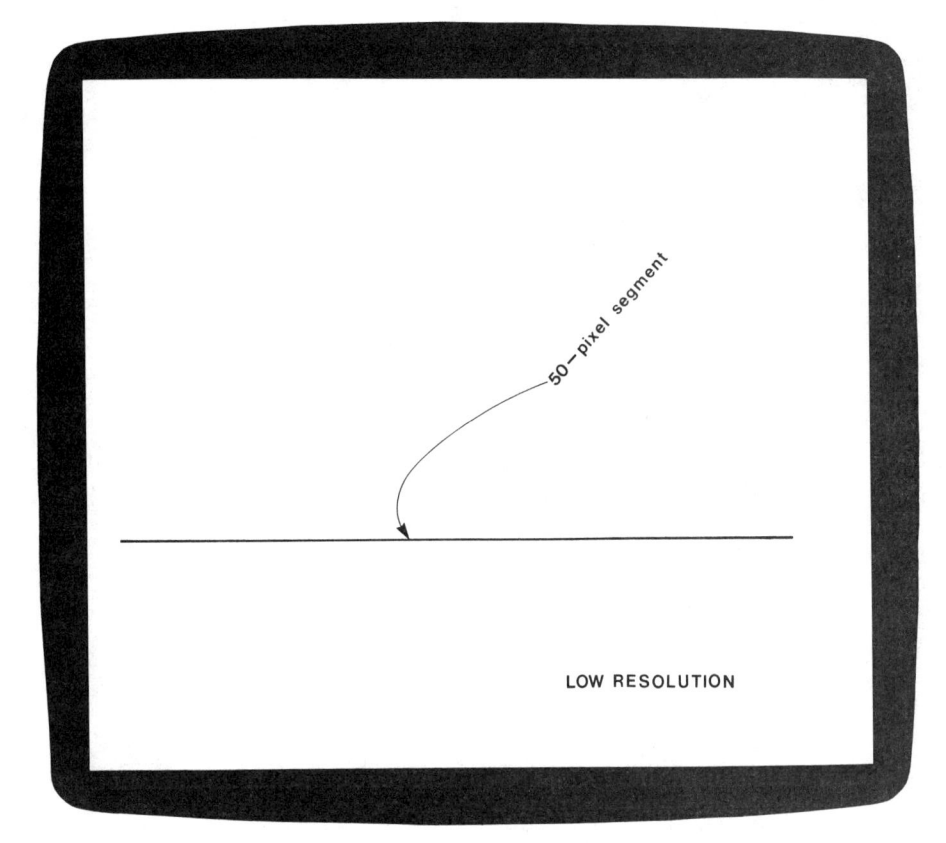

FIGURE 2-3

LOW RESOLUTION

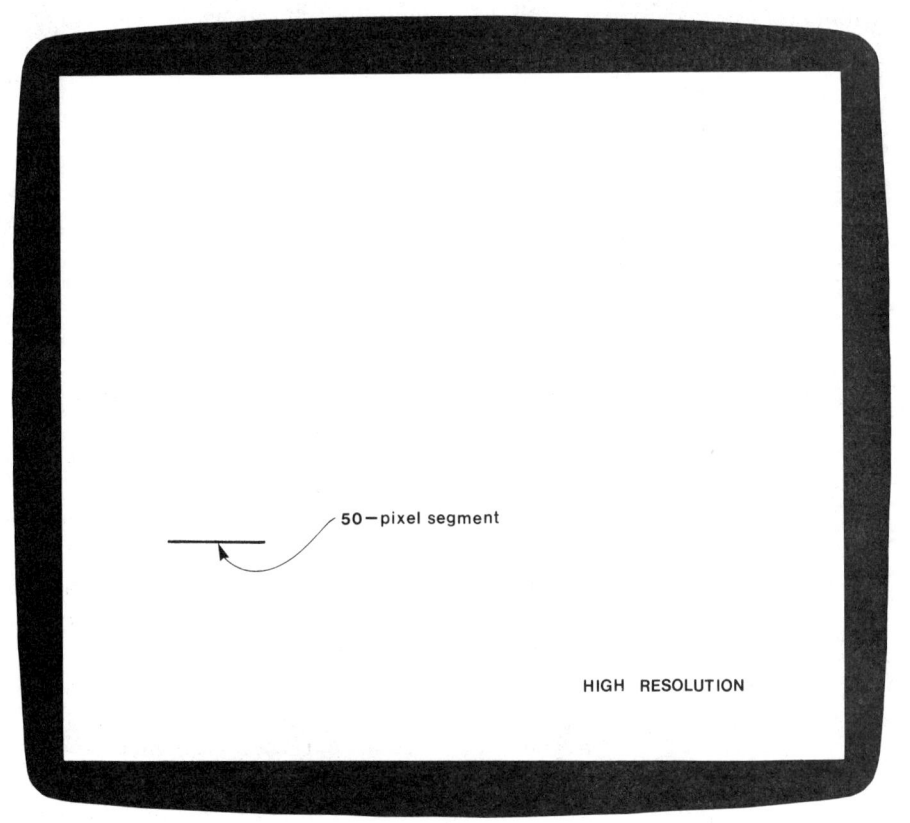

FIGURE 2-4

HIGH RESOLUTION

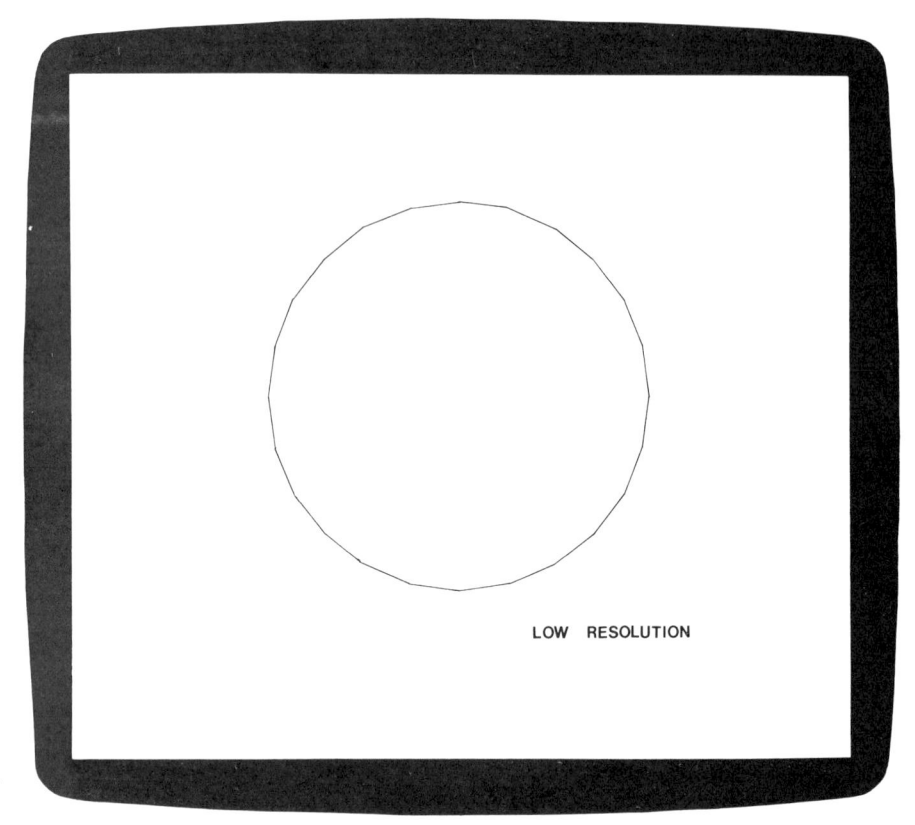

FIGURE 2-5 Circle drawn on a low-resolution screen.

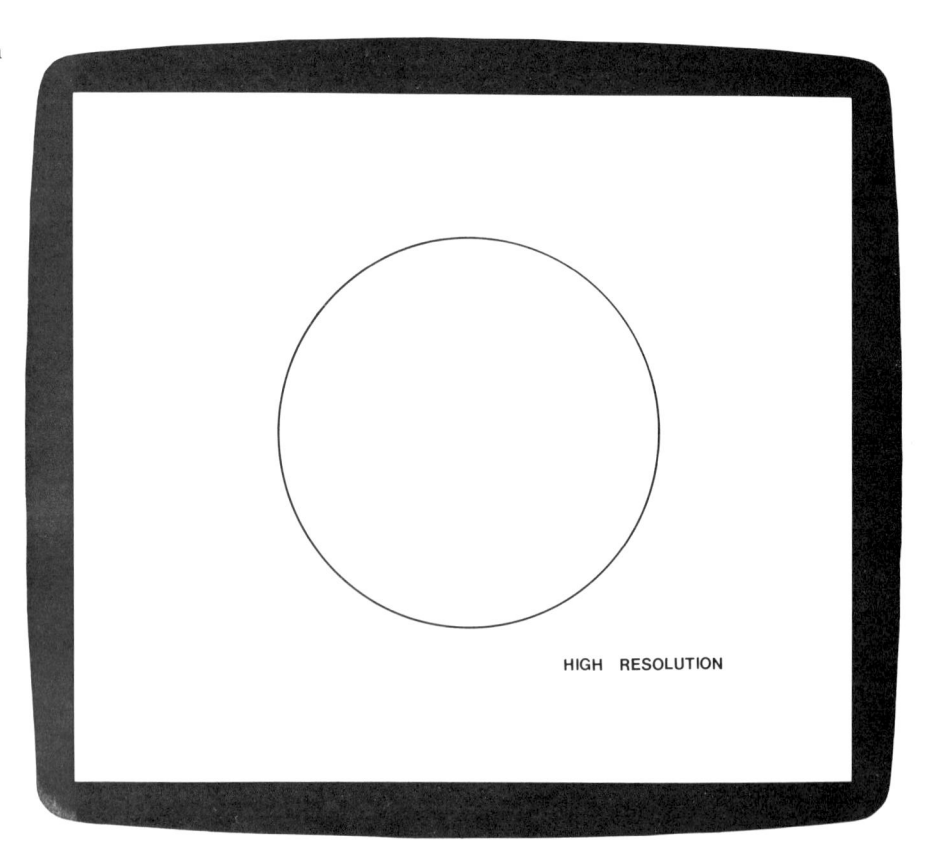

FIGURE 2-6 Circle drawn on a high-resolution screen.

Sec. 2-5 Rectangular Coordinate System

Figure 2-6 shows the same circle drawn on a high-resolution screen, that is, with very small pixel units. Note the smoothness of the curve.

Some computer systems have the ability to vary screen unit size by a viewing window command. This command changes the working size of the screen and allows the operator to work on small details or large overall drawings.

Some computer systems work exclusively in screen units and produce drawings and dimensions using screen units. Drawings done in screen units must be converted into either inches or millimeters if they are to be used as working drawings in manufacturing. An exception would be a system where a machine is linked directly to the computer graphic system, but even in this situation the screen units must be related to inches or millimeters for practical applications of the finished parts.

2-5 RECTANGULAR COORDINATE SYSTEM

A *rectangular coordinate system* is defined by two perpendicular lines, one horizontal and one vertical, that intersect at a point. The lines are called *axes*. The horizontal axis is the X *axis*, the vertical axis is the Y *axis*, and the point of intersection is the *origin* (Figure 2-7). A rectangular coordinate system uses both positive and negative X and Y values. X values located to the right of the origin are positive, X values located to the left of the origin are negative. Y values located above the origin are positive, Y values located below the origin are negative.

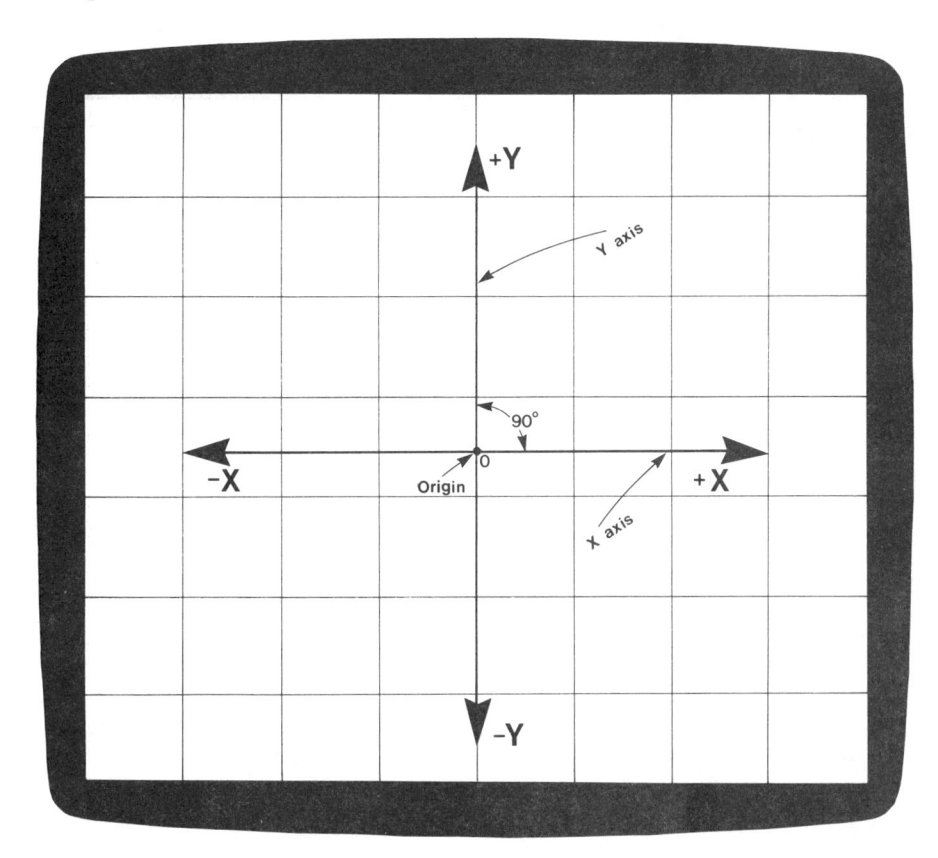

FIGURE 2-7 XY coordinate axis system.

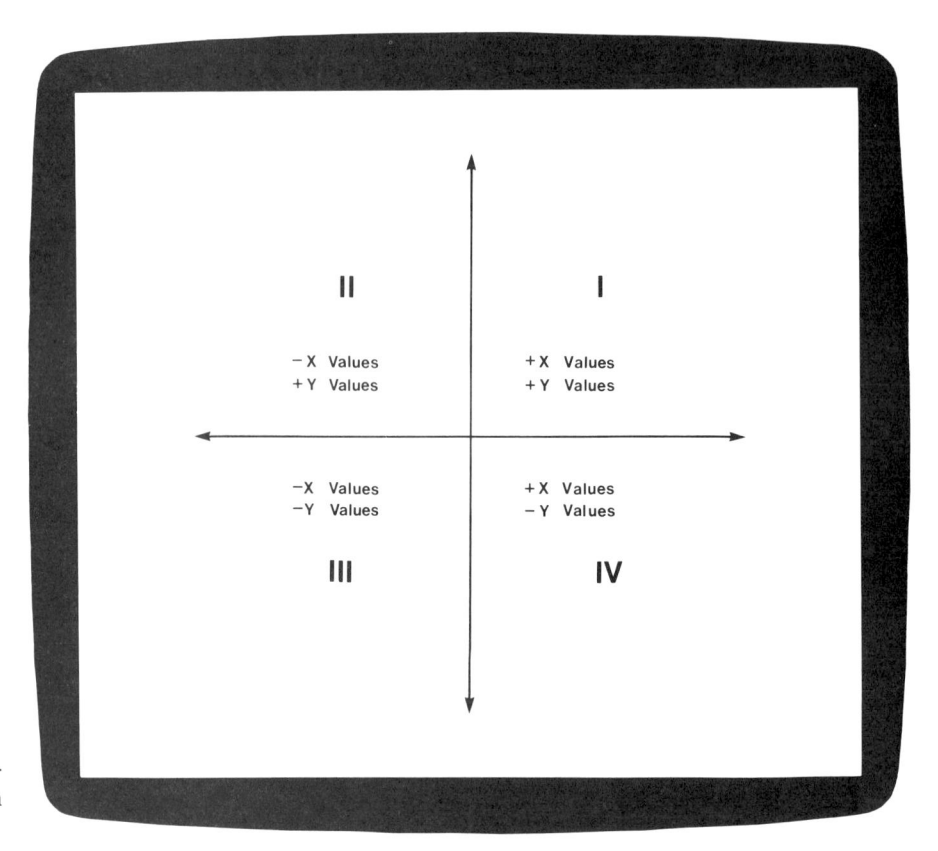

FIGURE 2-8 Coordinate values in the four quadrants of an XY coordinate system.

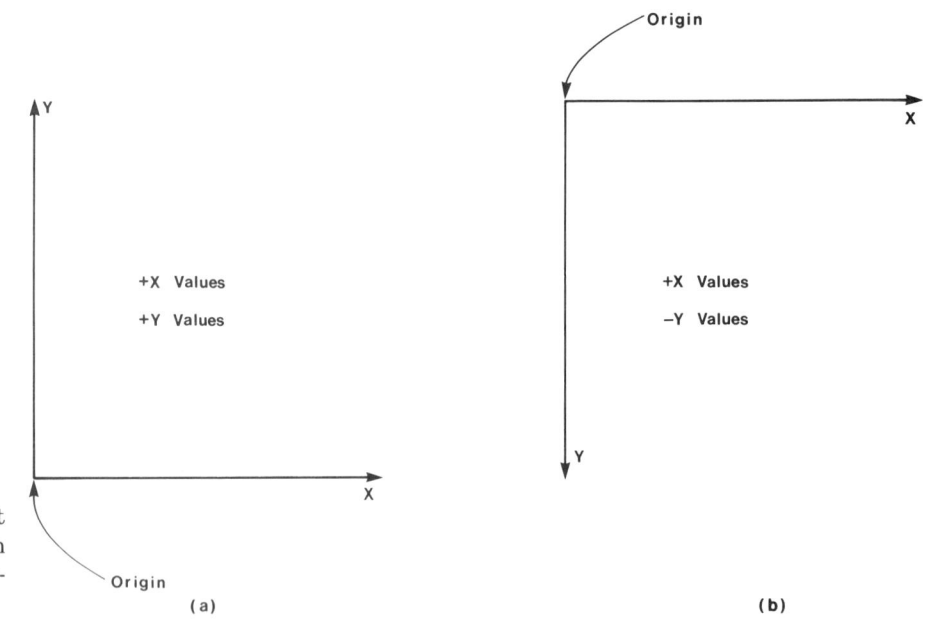

FIGURE 2-9 Each quadrant on an XY coordinate system may be used as a separate coordinate system.

A rectangular coordinate system is divided into four *quadrants* (Figure 2-8). Each quadrant may stand alone as a separate coordinate system. For example, in Figure 2-9a the first quadrant is used to locate values with positive X and positive Y values. In Figure 2-9b the fourth quadrant is used to locate values with positive X and negative Y values. The second and third quadrants are for $(-X, +Y)$ and $(-X, -Y)$ values, respectively.

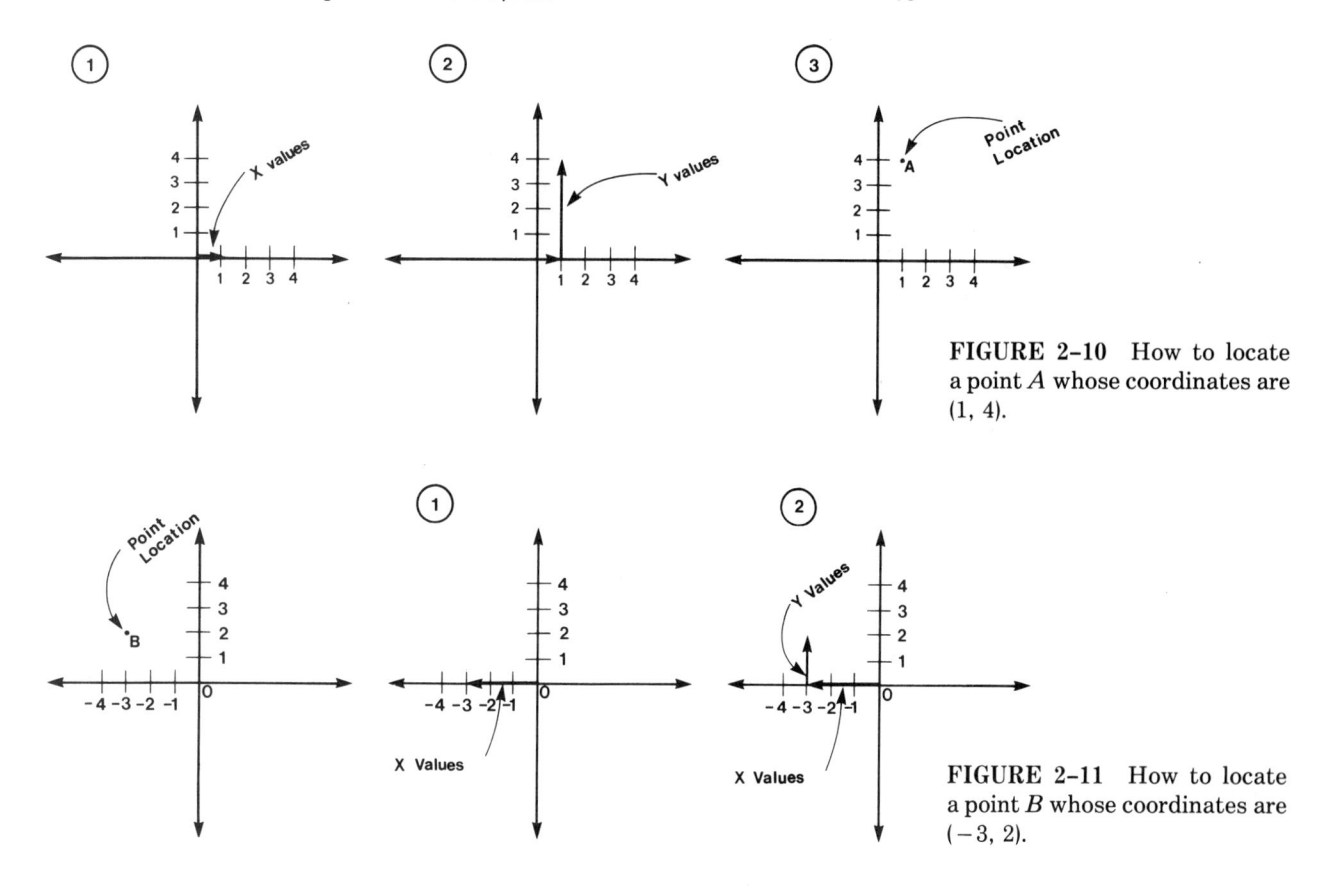

Sec. 2-6 Rotated Rectangular Coordinate System   19

FIGURE 2-10 How to locate a point A whose coordinates are (1, 4).

FIGURE 2-11 How to locate a point B whose coordinates are (-3, 2).

A location on a rectangular coordinate system is defined using an X and a Y value. The location is called a *point* and the X and Y values are the *coordinates* of the point. Coordinates are written in the form (X, Y). The first coordinate, the X value, is the horizontal distance from the origin. The second coordinate, the Y value, is the vertical distance from the origin. An X and a Y value are sufficient to locate any point in a rectangular coordinate system if the system is two-dimensional or planar.

Figure 2-10 shows how to locate a point A whose coordinate values are (1, 4). In step 1, move horizontally 1 unit to the right of the origin. This defines the X value. In step 2, move vertically upward 4 units from the distance marked off in step 1. This defines the Y value. In step 3, mark the location of the point (1, 4). Define the point as A.

Figure 2-11 shows how to find the coordinates of a point given its location relative to a known axis system. In step 1, count to the left from the origin along the horizontal axis to find the X coordinate value. (This is the negative X direction. The X value is -3.) In step 2, count upward from the origin along the vertical axis to find the Y coordinate value. The Y value is 2. It is acceptable to omit the positive sign when writing coordinates. A number with no sign stated is assumed positive.

2-6 ROTATED RECTANGULAR COORDINATE SYSTEM

A *rotated rectangular coordinate system* is a two-axis coordinate system turned through a specified angle. The 90° intersection of the two axes does not change. Figure 2-12 shows an axis system rotated 45°.

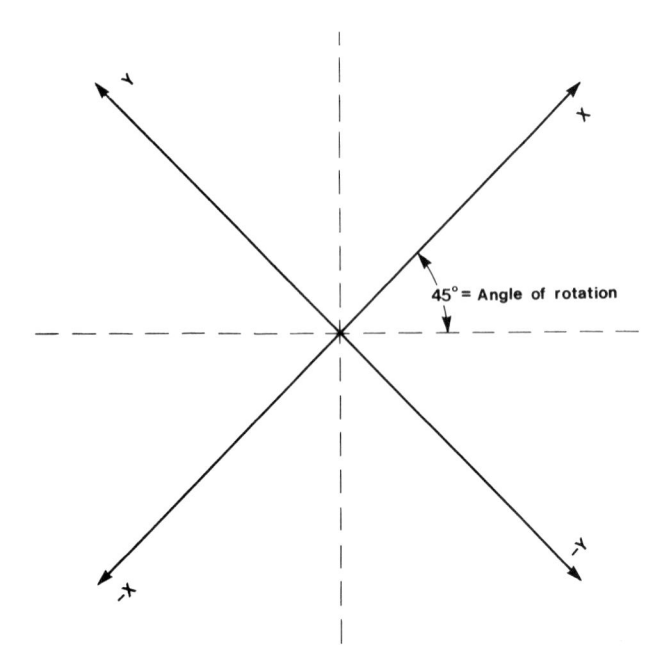

FIGURE 2-12 Rotated axis system.

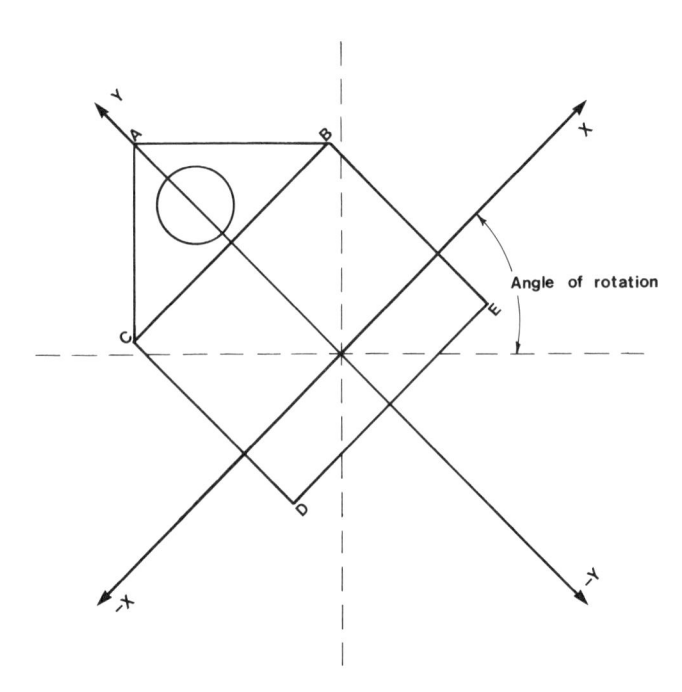

FIGURE 2-13 Example of an object drawn on a rotated axis system.

In computer-aided drafting, rotated coordinate systems are used for convenience. If the major portion of a drawing is constructed at an angle, it is easier to work with a rotated coordinate system than to reference values constantly back to a horizontal/vertical axis.

Figure 2-13 shows a figure constructed on a rotated axis system. The point coordinates relative to the rotated axis are $A(0, 2)$, $B(1, 1)$, $C(-1, 1)$, $D(-1, 1)$, and $E(1, -1)$. These values are measured directly from the rotated axis and need not be referenced to the horizontal/vertical axis.

Rotated rectangular coordinates are particularly useful when drawing auxiliary views. Auxiliary views are discussed in Chapter 8.

2-7 POLAR COORDINATE SYSTEM

FIGURE 2-14 Polar coordinate system.

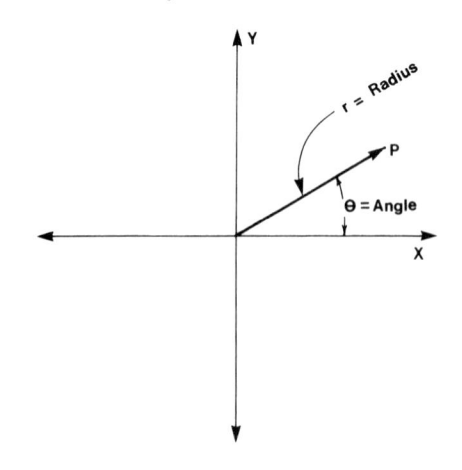

Polar coordinates locate a point using a radius and an angular value reference to an XY axis (Figure 2-14). Polar coordinates are most useful when working with circular or cylindrical shapes. They can also be used for dimensioning, as shown in Figure 5-27.

Polar coordinates are written in the form (r, ϕ) where r is the radius value and ϕ is the angular value. A polar coordinate of (12, 45) would mean a radius equal to 12 linear units and an angle of 45°. The linear units may be inches, millimeters, or screen units. The angular values are always measured in degrees.

Figure 2-15 shows how to locate a point C given the polar coordinates (5, 30), where 5 is defined in screen units. In step 1, a line 30° to the horizontal is drawn. In step 2, 5 screen units are measured along the 30° line defining the location of point C.

Negative polar coordinate values are interpreted differently by different computer graphic systems. Some systems permit only positive inputs; that is, they will not understand and process negative values. If

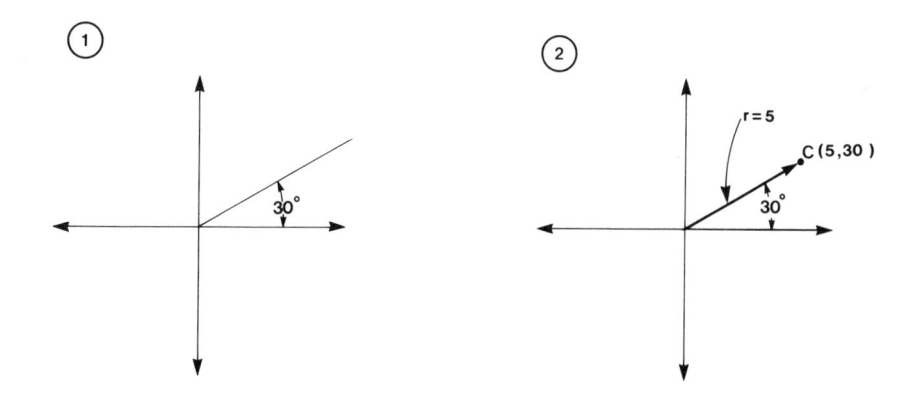

Sec. 2-8   Three-Dimensional Coordinate System   21

FIGURE 2-15 How to locate a point C whose polar coordinates are (5, 30).

point C of Figure 2-15 were to be located 30° below the horizontal, the polar coordinates using a positive-value-only system would have to be (5, 330). The counterclockwise direction is normally considered the positive angular direction; clockwise direction is negative.

Negative radius values are located in some systems by reflecting a negative value 180° from a positive value. For example, a polar coordinate of (−5, 30) would result in the reflected location shown in Figure 2-16, 180° from the positive 5 location. The actual degree value for the reflected point would be 210°.

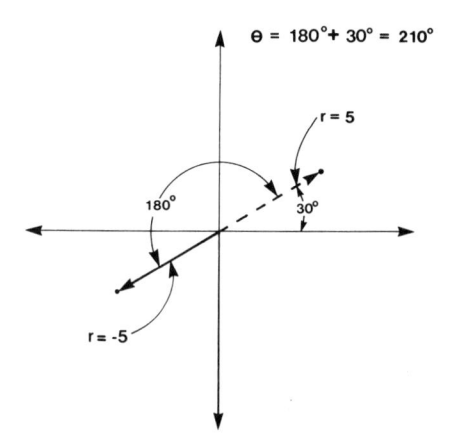

Figure 2-17 shows another example of a point located using negative polar coordinate values. The value (5, 330) could be equivalent to the value (−5, 150) if the computer system reflects negative values.

Polar coordinate values can be changed to linear XY values using the formulas shown in Figure 2-18. If a computer system does not accept polar coordinates, it is sometimes possible to use these equations, stored in subroutines, to work with polar coordinate values by using their rectangular equivalents.

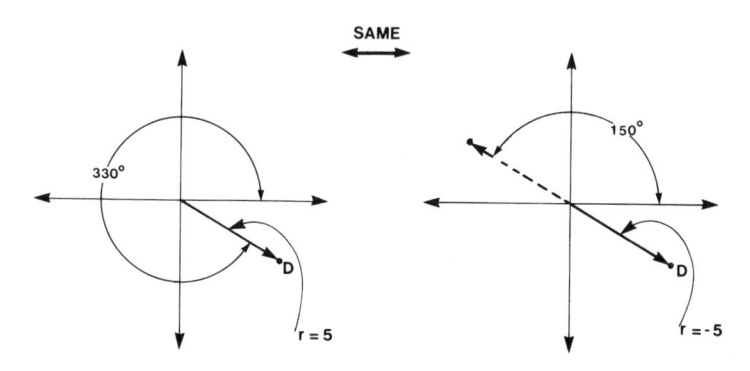

FIGURE 2-16 Some computer graphic systems reflect negative linear values of polar coordinate inputs.

FIGURE 2-17 Two different coordinate values which locate a point in the same place.

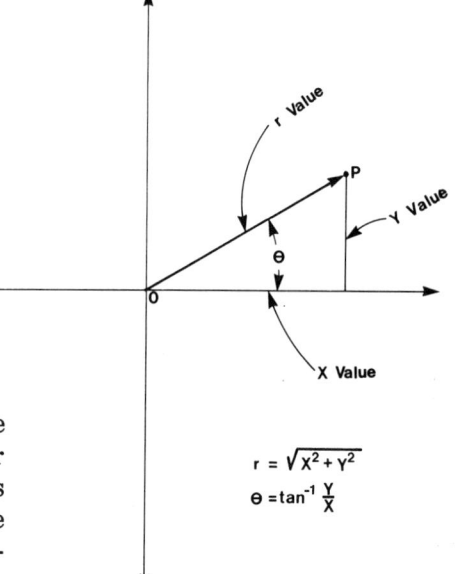

FIGURE 2-18 Formulas for converting between linear and polar coordinates.

$$r = \sqrt{X^2 + Y^2}$$
$$\theta = \tan^{-1} \frac{Y}{X}$$

2-8 THREE-DIMENSIONAL COORDINATE SYSTEM

A three-dimensional rectangular coordinate system is defined by three axis lines: a horizontal (X), a vertical (Y), and a third line perpendicular to the plane formed by the horizontal and vertical lines (Z). All three axes lines intersect at 90° to each other. The point of intersection is called the origin (Figure 2-19). X values located to the right of the origin are positive, X values located to the left of the origin are negative. Y values

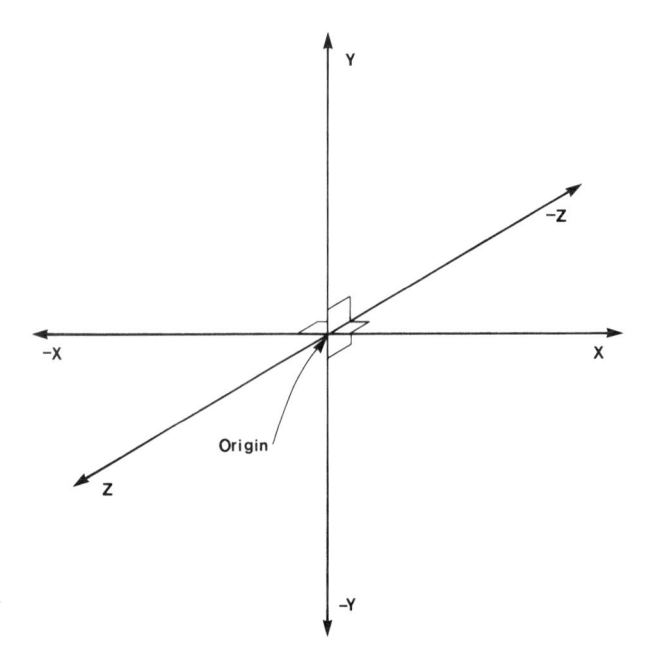

FIGURE 2-19 Three-dimensional XYZ coordinate system.

located above the origin are positive, Y values located below the origin are negative. Z values located in a direction out of the page are positive, Z values located in a direction into the page are negative.

Any point on a three-dimensional system is defined using three coordinate values. The three values are written in the form (X, Y, Z). The first coordinate is the horizontal distance from the origin, and the third is the distance "out of the page" from the origin.

Figure 2-20 shows how to locate a point, Q, whose coordinates are (1, 2, 3). In step 1, move horizontally 1 unit to the right of the origin. This defines the X value. In step 2, move vertically upward 2 units from

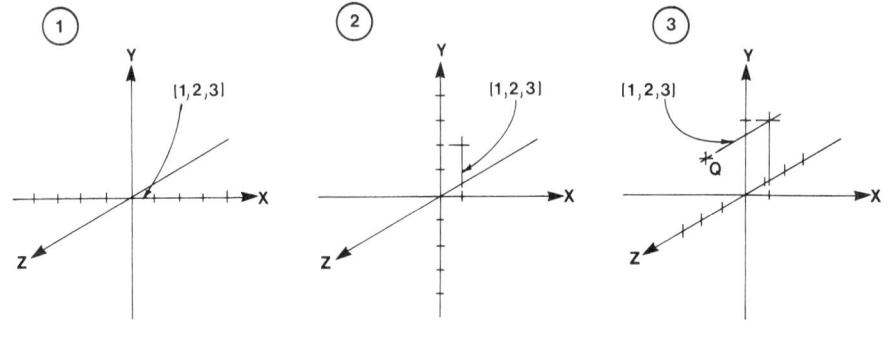

FIGURE 2-20 How to locate a point on a three-dimensional XYZ axis system whose coordinates are (1, 2, 3).

FIGURE 2-21 How to locate a point on a three-dimensional XYZ axis system whose coordinates are (-4, 1, -6).

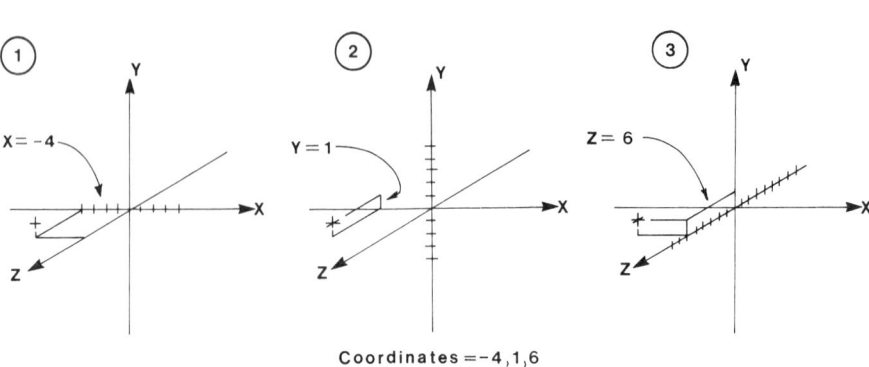

Coordinates = $-4, 1, 6$

Sec. 2-9   Absolute and Relative Axis Systems

the distance marked off in step 1. This defines the Y axis. In step 3, move out of the page (parallel to the Z axis) 3 units. This defines the Z axis. Label the point $(1, 2, 3)$ by the letter Q.

Figure 2-21 shows how to find the coordinates of a point given its location relative to the given axis. In step 1, count horizontally 4 units to the left from the origin to find the X coordinate. This is the negative X direction, so the X value equals -4. In step 2, count vertically upward 1 unit from the origin to find the Y coordinate. The Y value equals 1. In step 3, move into the page 6 units; this is the negative Z direction, so the Z value equals -6. The coordinates for point B are $(-4, 1, -6)$.

2-9 ABSOLUTE AND RELATIVE AXIS SYSTEMS

The *absolute axis system* of a computer graphic system is the basic reference system built into the computer by the manufacturer. All calculations and transactions done by the computer are made in reference to the absolute axis system.

Most computer manufacturers set the origin location for the absolute system in the center of the screen. This is why, when a system is first turned on, the cursor, which represents the origin, appears in the center of the screen (Figure 2-22).

The absolute axis never moves but remains fixed in the predetermined location. Other axis systems, called *relative axis systems*, can be created by moving the original axis. In fact, the absolute axis system does not move, but disappears from the screen and the newly created relative system appears (Figure 2-23).

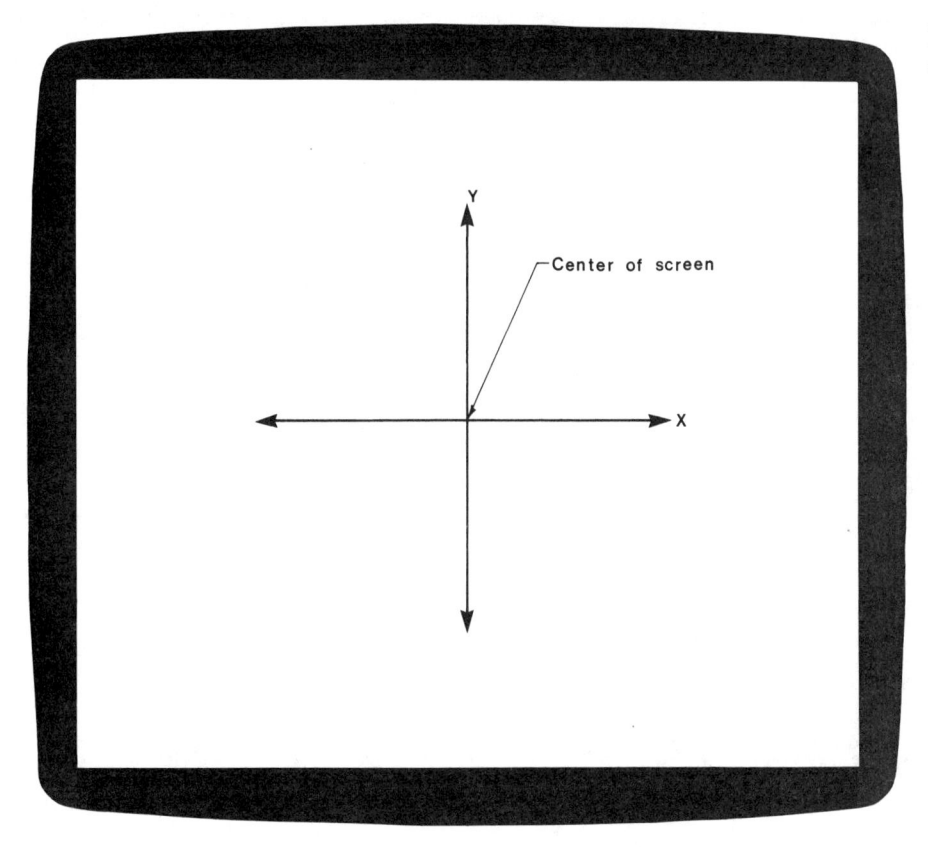

FIGURE 2-22   Absolute coordinate system.

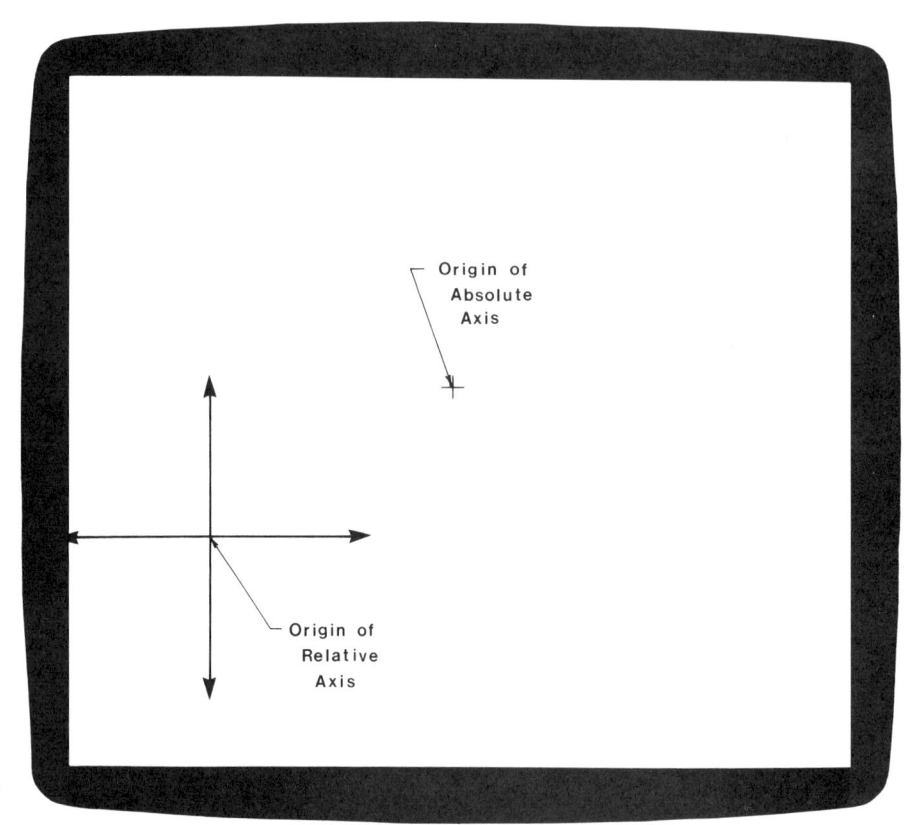

FIGURE 2-23 Relative coordinate system.

FIGURE 2-24 Relative coordinate system.

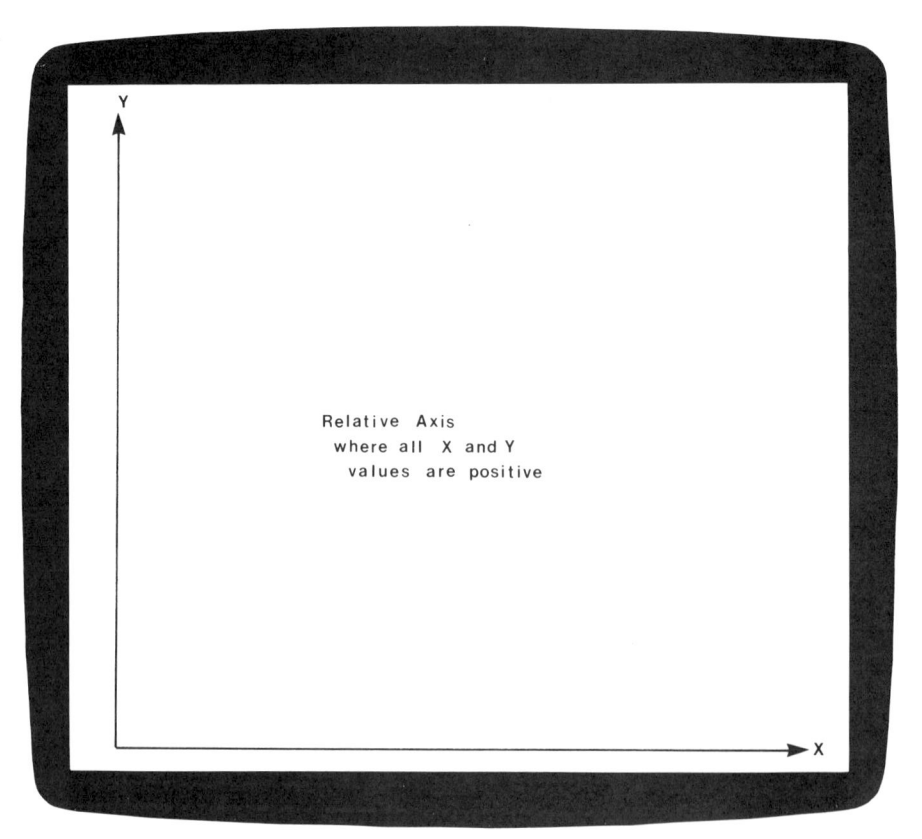

Relative axis systems are set up for the convenience of the user. In Figure 2-24 a relative axis system is located in the lower left corner of the screen. This means that the screen essentially shows only the first quadrant of the axis system and all input values for X and Y coordinates will be positive.

Some computer graphic systems allow several axis systems to exist on the same screen. This is helpful when working with multiple orthographic views and is discussed in Section 6-15.

PROBLEMS

For Problems P2-1 through P2-4, draw an XY axis system. Locate the origin in the center of the screen. Add the following points and, if possible, label each point with its letter and coordinate values. This exercise can be done using graph paper.

P2-1 All values are in inches.
- (a) (2, 2)
- (b) (−2, 2)
- (c) (2, −2)
- (d) (−2, −2)
- (e) (1, 4)
- (f) (4, −1)
- (g) (2, −3)
- (h) (−1, −1)
- (i) (−1, 4)
- (j) (−3, 1)

P2-2 All values are in millimeters.
- (a) (50, 50)
- (b) (−50, 50)
- (c) (50, −50)
- (d) (−50, −50)
- (e) (25, 100)
- (f) (100, −25)
- (g) (50, −75)
- (h) (−25, −25)
- (i) (−25, 100)
- (j) (−75, 25)

P2-3 All values are in inches.
- (a) (1.50, 3.25)
- (b) (0.50, −2.13)
- (c) (−2.25, −1.00)
- (d) (−1.75, 0.88)
- (e) (3.13, 1.44)
- (f) (3.75, −2.75)
- (g) (−1.38, 3.50)
- (h) (−2.63, −1.75)
- (i) (0.13, 0.56)
- (j) (−0.63, −0.44)

P2-4 All values are in millimeters.
- (a) (40, 82)
- (b) (12, −65)
- (c) (−65, −25)
- (d) (−35, 20)
- (e) (82, 33)
- (f) (91, −62)
- (g) (−37, 81)
- (h) (−72, −31)
- (i) (3, 5)
- (j) (−13, −9)

For Problems P2-5 through P2-8, list the points shown in Figures P2-5 through P2-8 along with their respective coordinates. For example, point A in Figure P2-5 would be listed as

1. A (2, 8)

FIGURE P2-5

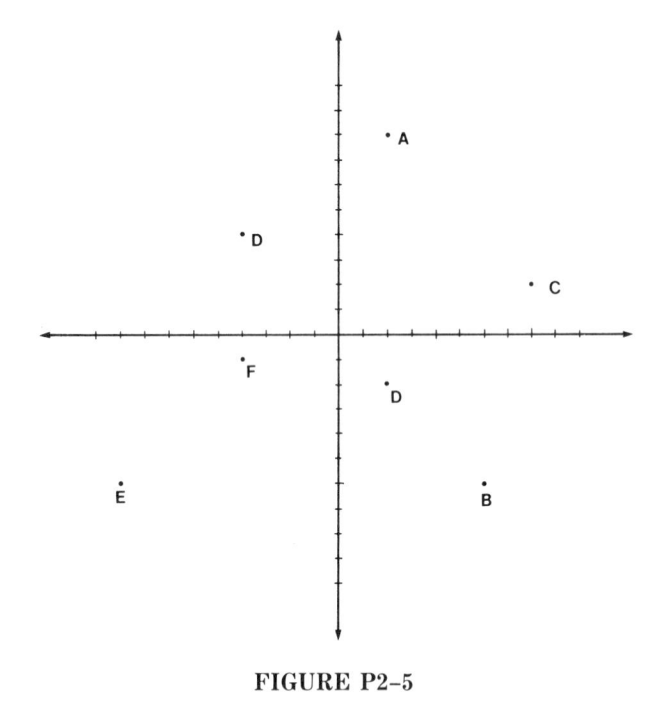

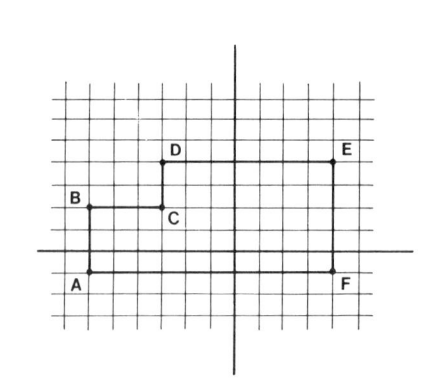

FIGURE P2-6

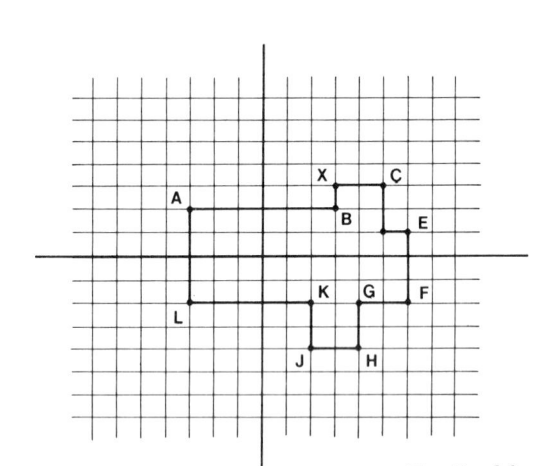

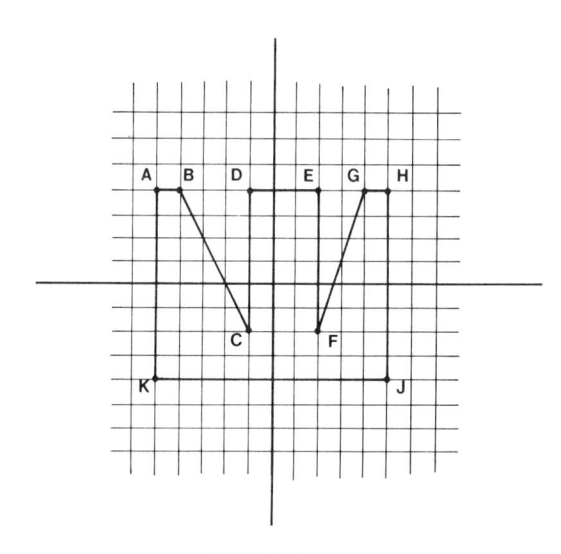

FIGURE P2-7

FIGURE P2-8

For Problems P2-9 through P2-12, draw an XY axis system. Locate the origin at the center of the screen. Add the following points and, if possible, label each point with its letter and coordinate values.

P2-9   All values are in inches and degrees (polar coordinates).

    (a) (2, 45)   **(f)** (3, 100)
    (b) (2, 135)   **(g)** (1, 150)
    (c) (2, 225)   **(h)** (3, 200)
    (d) (2, 315)   **(i)** (1, 250)
    (e) (1, 30)   **(j)** (3, 330)

P2-10   All values are in millimeters and degrees (polar coordinates).

    (a) (50, 45)   **(f)** (75, 100)
    (b) (50, 135)   **(g)** (25, 150)
    (c) (50, 225)   **(h)** (75, 200)
    (d) (50, 315)   **(i)** (25, 250)
    (e) (25, 30)   **(j)** (75, 330)

Chap. 2 Problems

P2-11 All values are in inches and degrees (polar coordinates).
   (a) (1.5, 30)
   (b) (−1.0, 55)
   (c) (2.3, −40)
   (d) (0.75, 160)
   (e) (−2.15, 200)
   (f) (3.25, 327)
   (g) (−1.80, 15)
   (h) (4.13, 227)
   (i) (−0.30, 160)
   (j) (2.60, 290)

P2-12 All values are in millimeters and degrees (polar coordinates).
   (a) (37, 30)
   (b) (−25, 55)
   (c) (62, −40)
   (d) (20, 160)
   (e) (−73, 200)
   (f) (88, 327)
   (g) (−42, 15)
   (h) (107, 227)
   (i) (−8, 160)
   (j) (74, 290)

For Problems P2-13 and P2-14, list the points shown in Figures P2-13 and P2-14 along with their respective polar coordinates. Approximate the location of points not directly on a grid intersection. For example, point A in Figure P2-13 would be listed as

  1. A (5, 90)

P2-15 Figure P2-15 shows 10 points. List the points and their coordinate values relative to both axis systems: the absolute system and the system rotated 45° counterclockwise. For example, point A would be listed as

Point	Absolute	Rotated
1. A	(2, 5)	(5, 2)

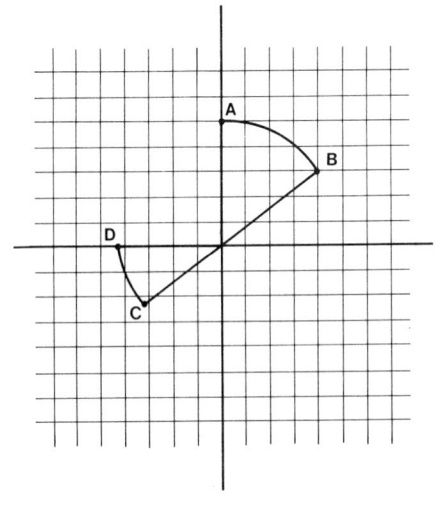

FIGURE P2-13

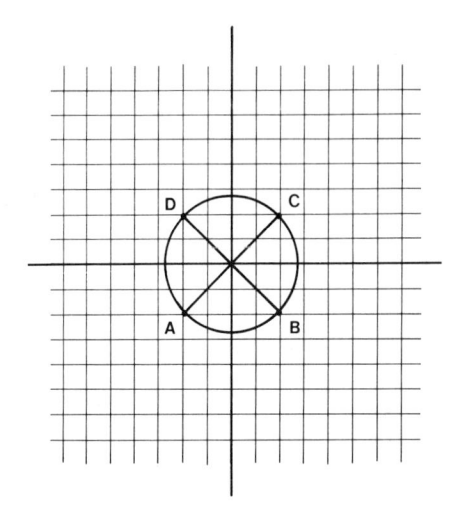

FIGURE P2-14

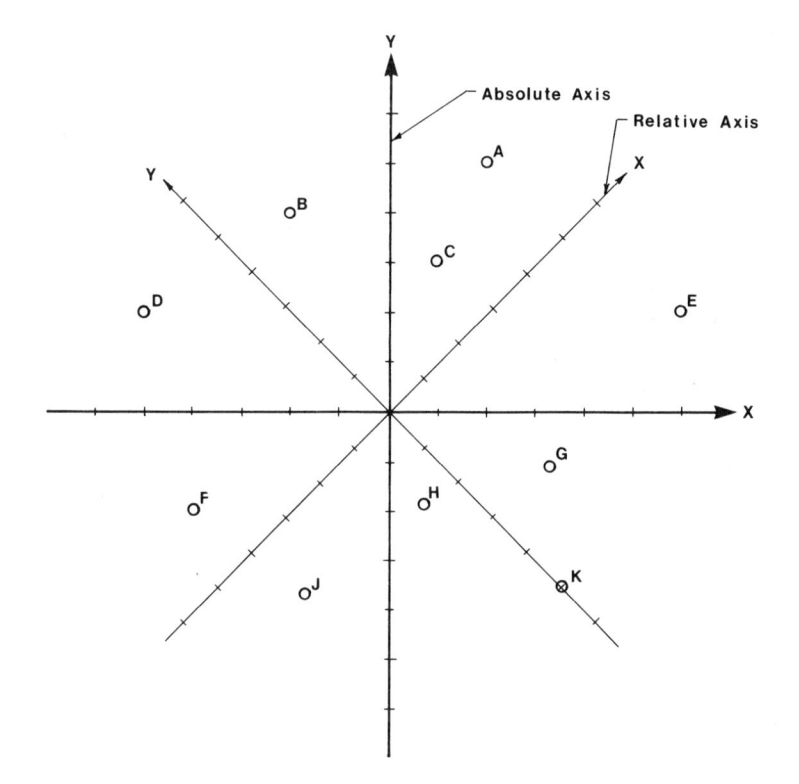

FIGURE P2-15

P2-16 Figure P2-16 shows 10 points. List the points and their coordinate values relative to both axis systems: the absolute system and the relative system. For example, point A would be listed as

Point	Absolute	Relative
1. A	(1, 5)	(9, 11)

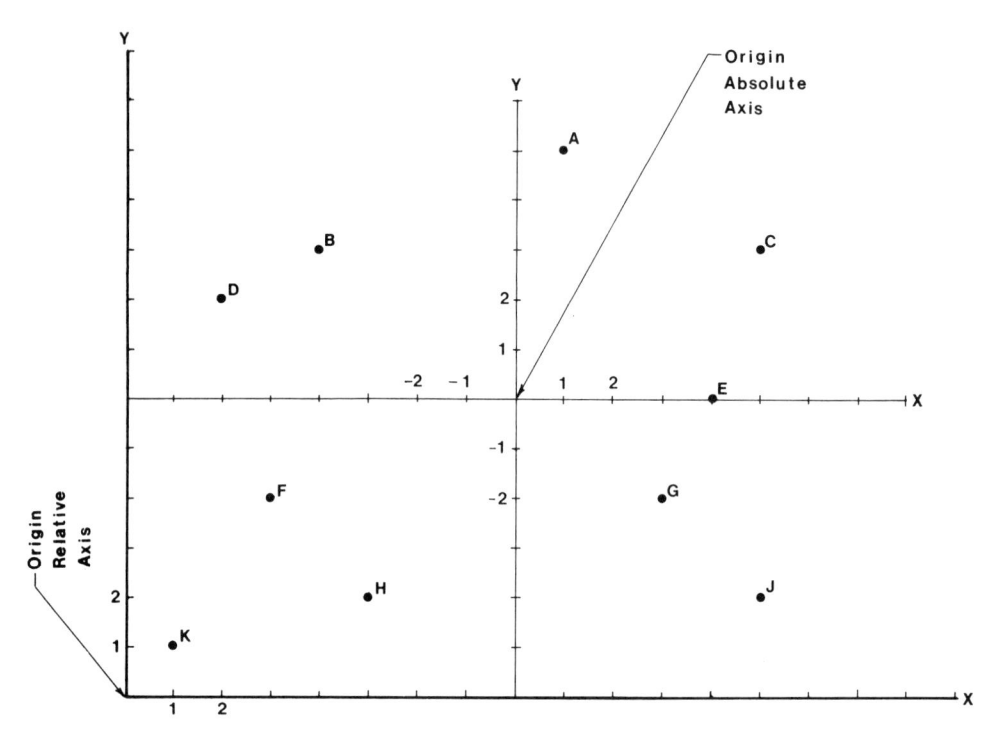

FIGURE P2-16

P2-17 The following points and coordinate values are based on an absolute coordinate system whose origin is at the center of the screen. List the points with their coordinate values relative to the absolute coordinate system and with their coordinates relative to a relative coordinate system whose origin is located at $(-7, -6)$ from the origin of the absolute system.

(a) (1, 1)   (f) $(-2, -3)$
(b) $(2, -1)$ (g) $(1, -5)$
(c) (3, 3)   (h) $(5, -2)$
(d) $(-2, 2)$ (i) $(-2, 1)$
(e) $(-5, -1)$ (j) $(-5, 2)$

3
BASIC TWO-DIMENSIONAL CONSTRUCTIONS

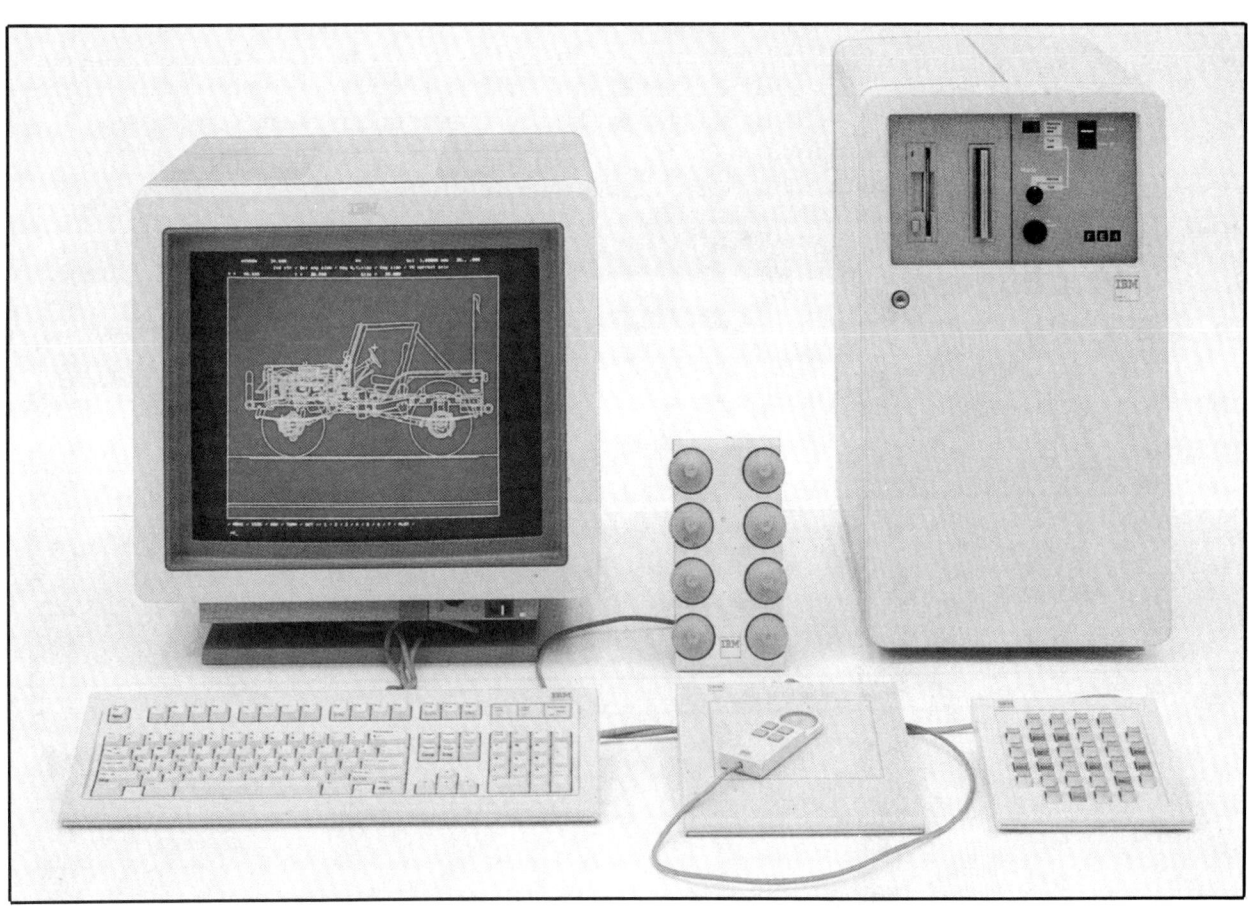

IBM 5080 display. (Courtesy of International Business Machines Corporation.)

3-1 INTRODUCTION

In this chapter we explain how to draw basic two-dimensional shapes, including horizontal, vertical, and slanted lines, as well as, arcs, circles, and irregular shapes. We also explain how to combine these shapes to form planes.

3-2 HORIZONTAL LINES

There are three ways to draw horizontal lines using a computer graphic system: a line of infinite length through a point, a line from a known point with a specified length and direction, and a line from one known point to another known point. The input format for these three methods varies from system to system, and not all systems can utilize all three methods, but in general, these three methods apply.

Horizontal lines of infinite length may be drawn by specifying only a Y-axis value. A horizontal line has only a Y-axis value.

Figure 3–1 shows three horizontal lines: one at $Y = 3$, one at $Y = 0$, and one at $Y = -3$. These lines are of infinite length, so they run completely across the screen.

FIGURE 3-1 Horizontal lines of infinite length.

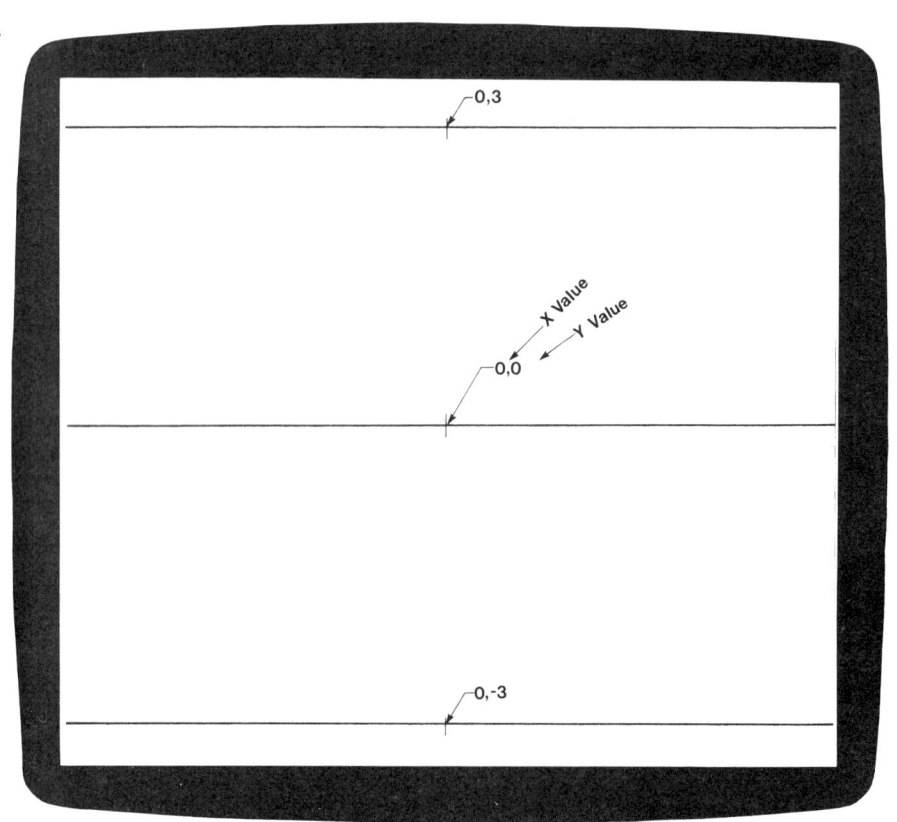

Sec. 3-2   Horizontal Lines

Figure 3-2 shows a horizontal line drawn between two known points. The input coordinates of the two points are (−3, 3) and (3, 3). The system would then be instructed to draw a line between these two points. Figure 3-3 shows four horizontal lines, each drawn between two

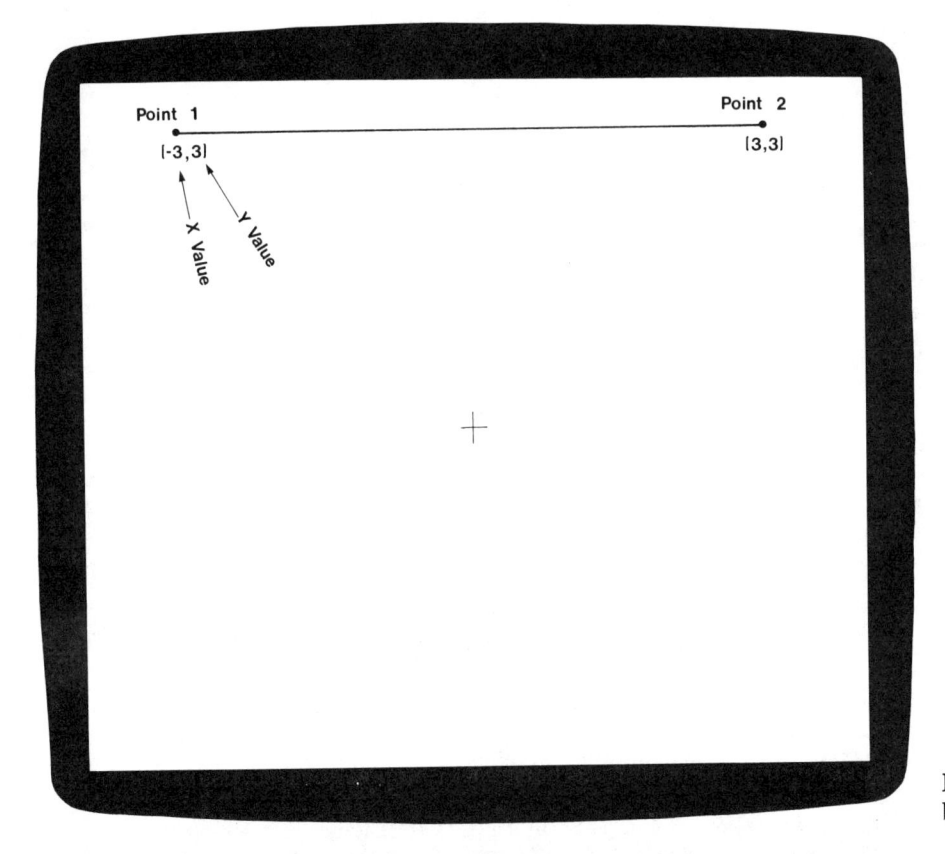

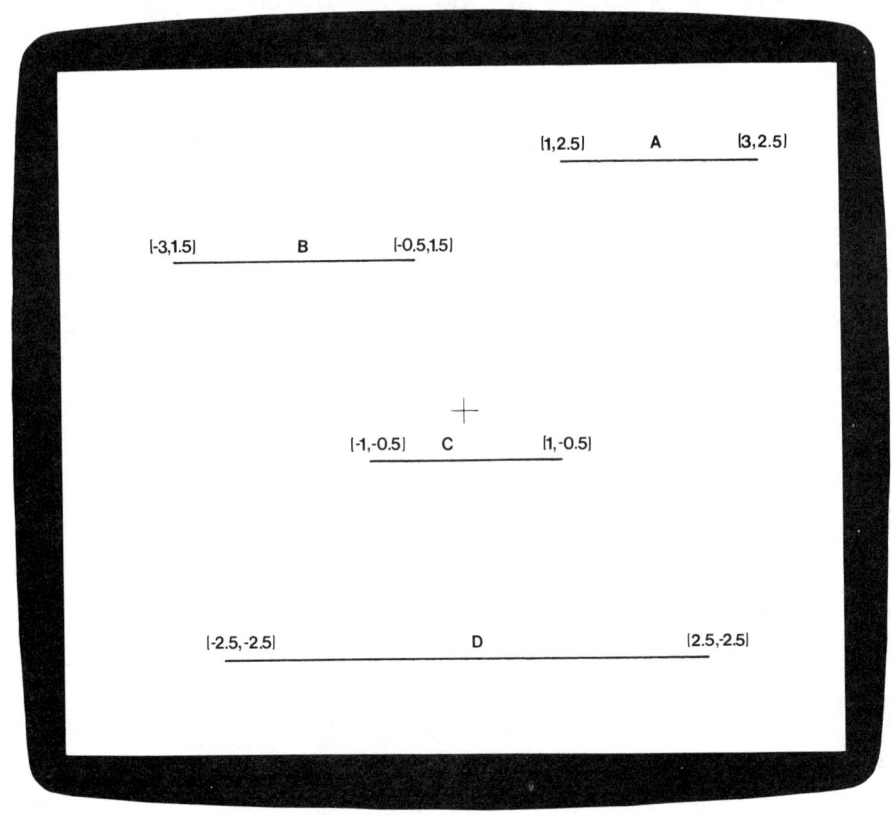

FIGURE 3-2 Horizontal line between two known points.

FIGURE 3-3 Horizontal lines between two known points.

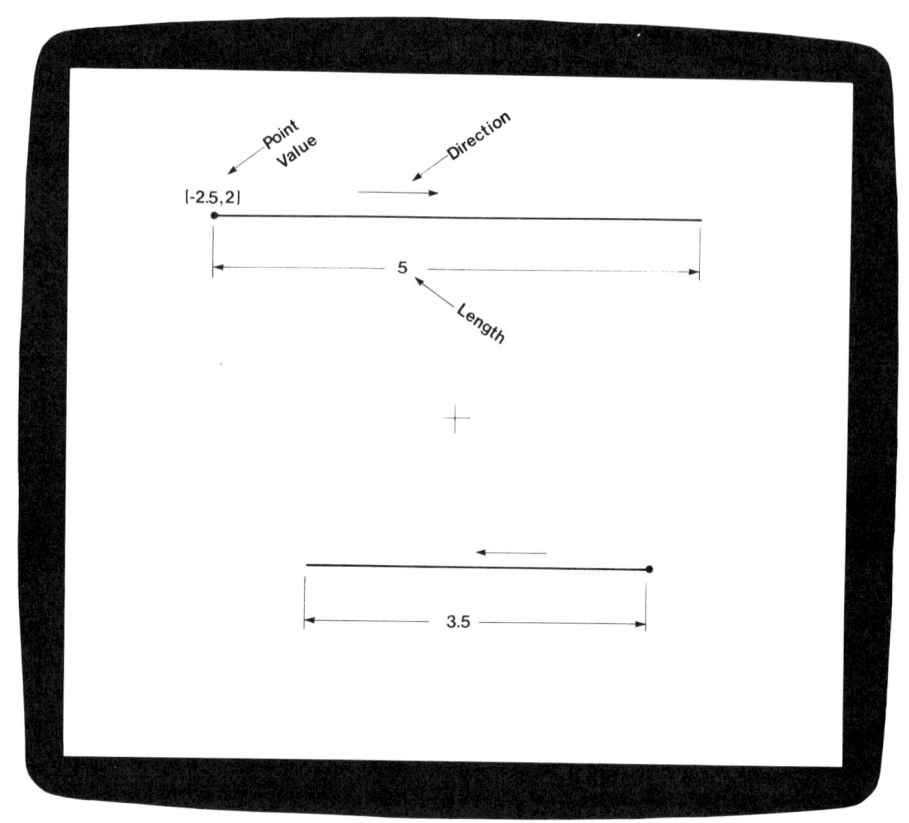

FIGURE 3-4 Horizontal lines created by specifying a point, a length, and a direction.

given points. Note that the Y value is the same for both points on a horizontal line.

Horizontal lines can also be drawn by specifying the location of one point, a length, and a direction. Figure 3-4 illustrates the procedure. First a point of location (−2.5, 2) is defined, then a length of 5 is entered, and finally, a direction to the right of the point is specified. Specifying a point, length, and direction gives an accurate line of known length that can be incorporated into a drawing.

3-3 VERTICAL LINES

There are three ways to draw vertical lines using a computer graphic system: a line of infinite length through a point, a line from one known point to another known point, and a line from a known point with a specified length and direction. The format for the required inputs varies with each individual system, and not all systems can operate with all three methods, but in general, these methods apply.

Vertical lines of infinite length have an X value but no Y value. The Y value is implied to be 0. Figure 3-5 shows three vertical lines: one at $X = 3$, one at $X = 0$, and one at $X = -3$. These lines are infinite, so they can run completely across the screen. Figure 3-6 shows a vertical line between two points (2, 2) and (−2, −2.5). First the coordinate values for the points would be entered, then the system would be instructed to draw a line between the two points. Figure 3-7 shows four vertical lines. Each was drawn between two given points. Note that the X value is the same for all points on the given vertical line.

Vertical lines can also be drawn by specifying the location of one point, a length, and a direction. Figure 3-8 illustrates. First a point (2, −3)

Sec. 3-3 Vertical Lines

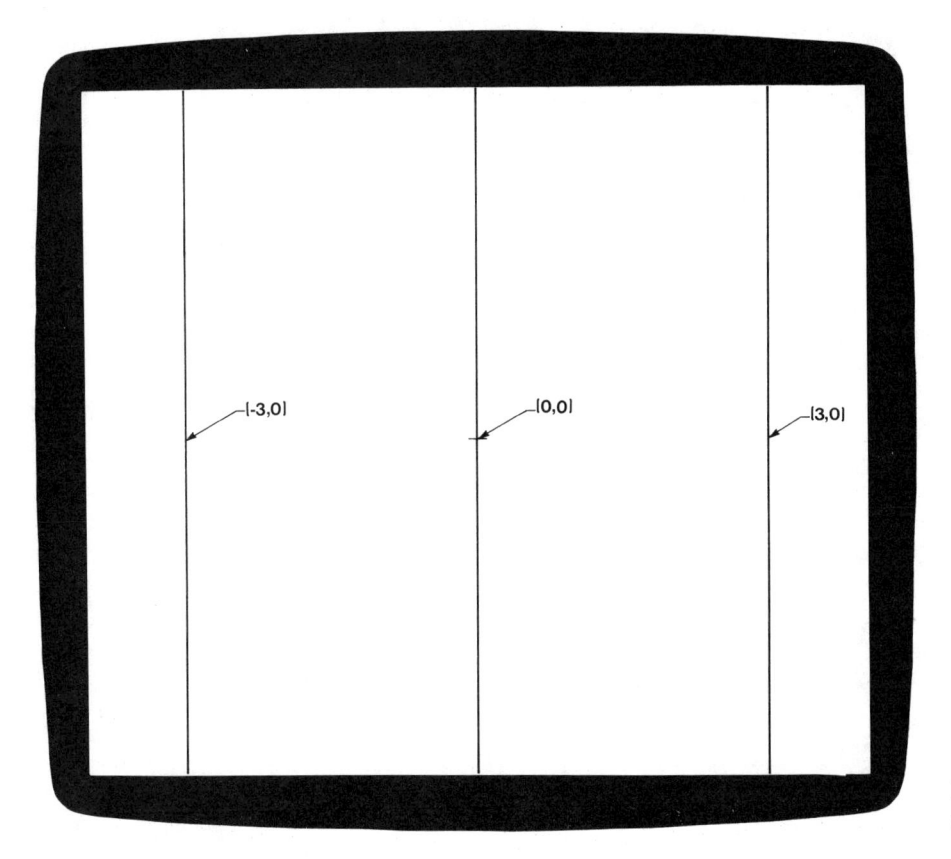

FIGURE 3-5 Vertical lines of infinite length.

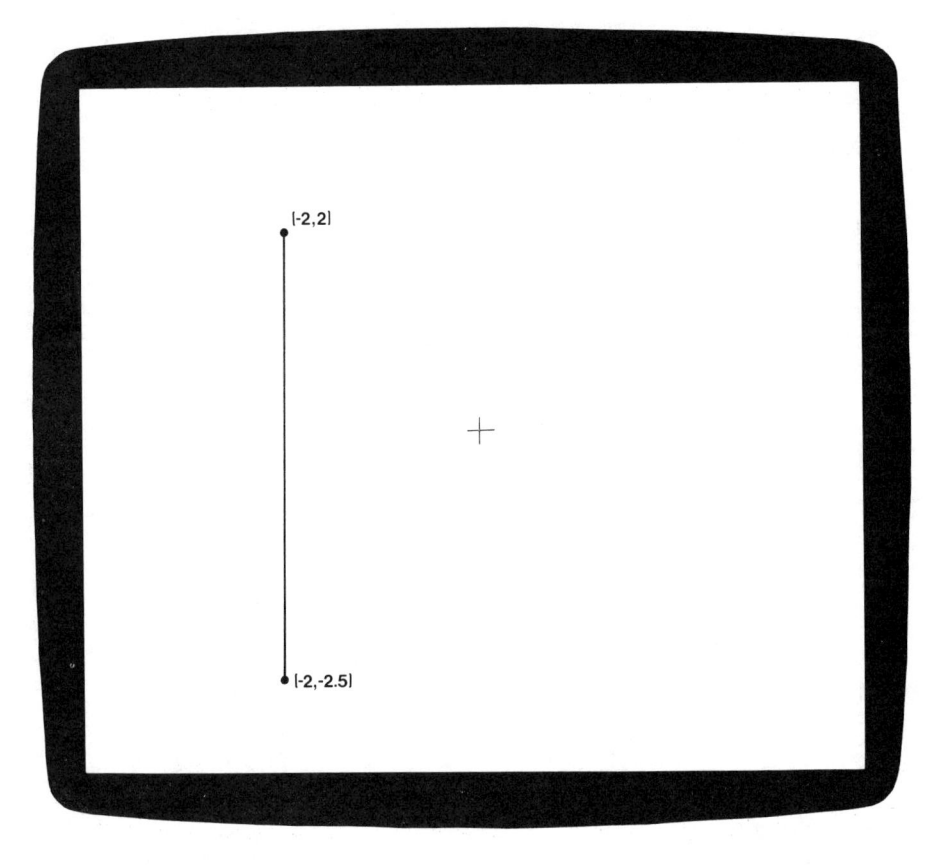

FIGURE 3-6 Vertical line between two known points.

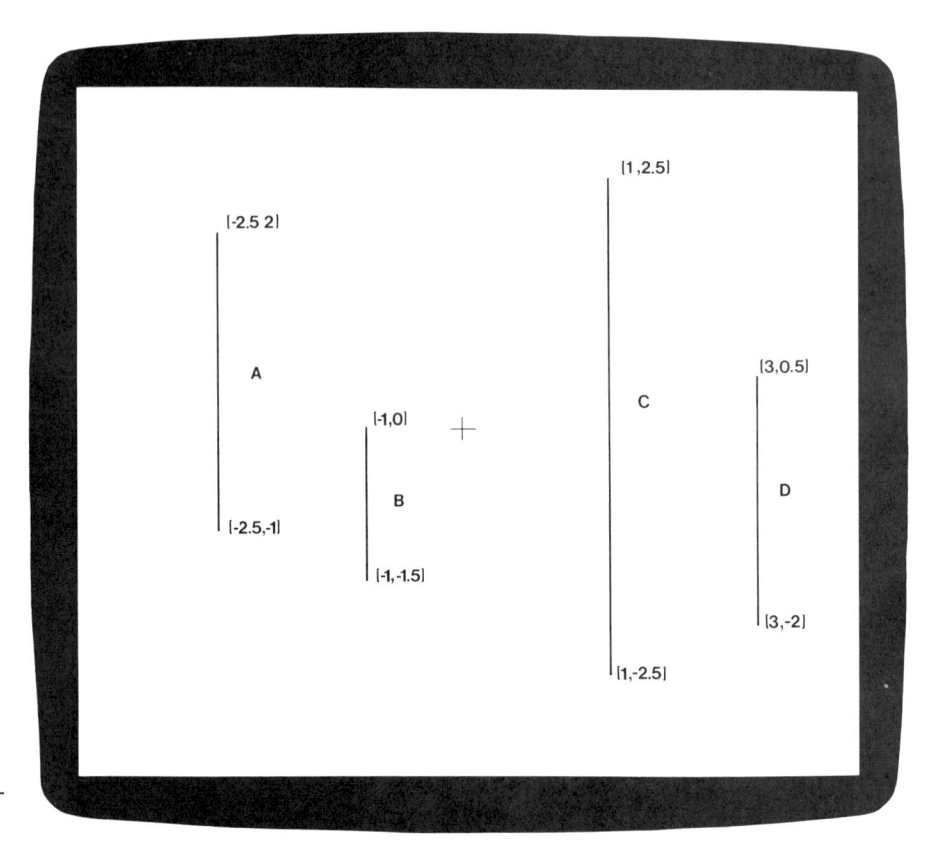

FIGURE 3-7 Vertical lines between two known points.

FIGURE 3-8 Vertical lines created by specifying a point, a length, and a direction.

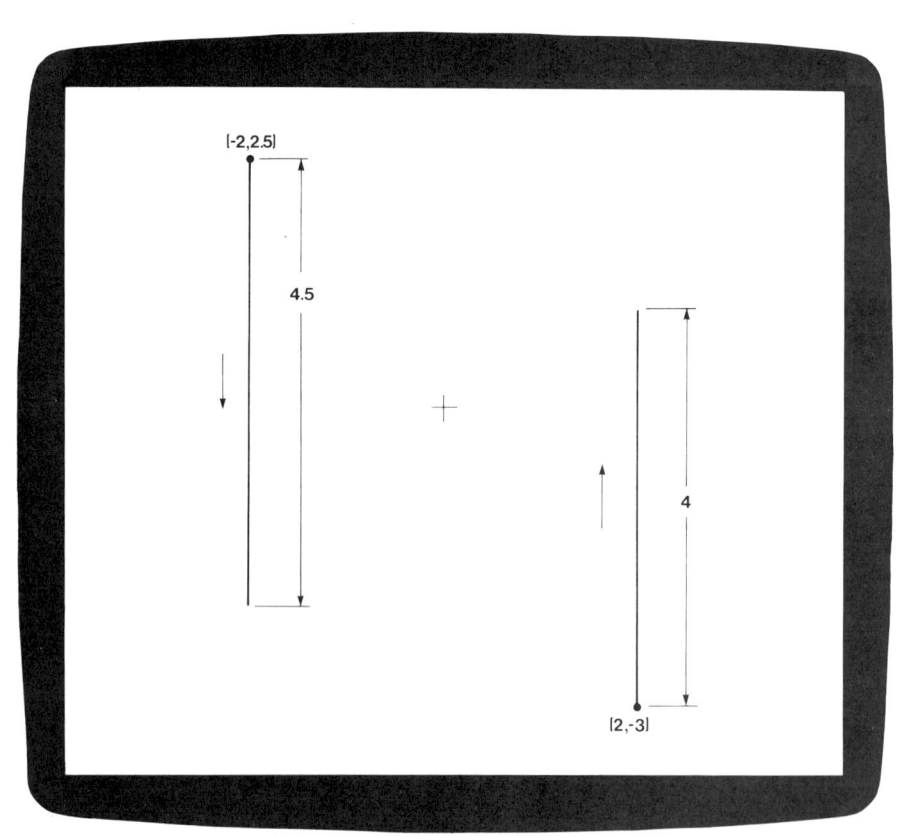

3-4 COMBINING HORIZONTAL AND VERTICAL LINES

Horizontal and vertical lines may be combined to form shapes as shown in Figures 3-9 and 3-10. In Figure 3-9 the lines were drawn using lines between known points. Figure 3-10 was drawn giving each line a point, a length, and a direction.

Rectangular shapes can be created using lines of infinite length. Excess line length (the part of each line that extends beyond the needed length) can be erased or trimmed to create the desired final shape. The term "trim" refers to erasing part, but not all, of a drawn feature.

Figures 3-11 and 3-12 are more complex shapes that combine horizontal and vertical lines. Figure 3-11 was created using point-to-point lines and Figure 3-12 use lines specified using a point, length, and a direction.

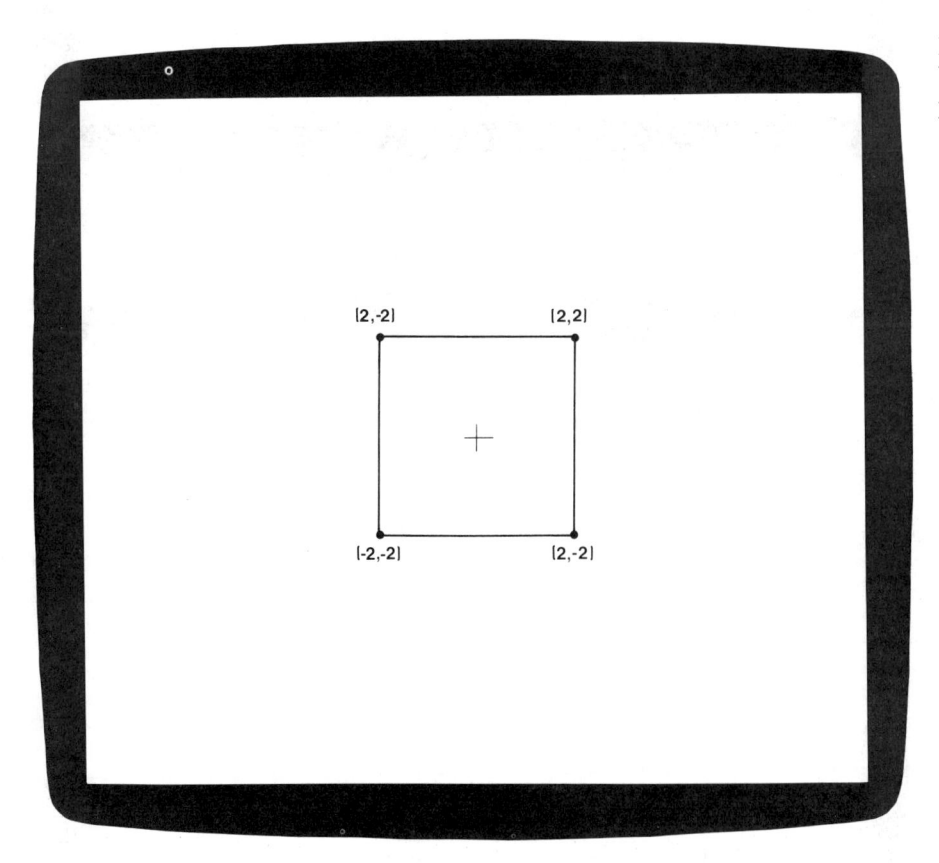

FIGURE 3-9 Shape formed by lines drawn between known points.

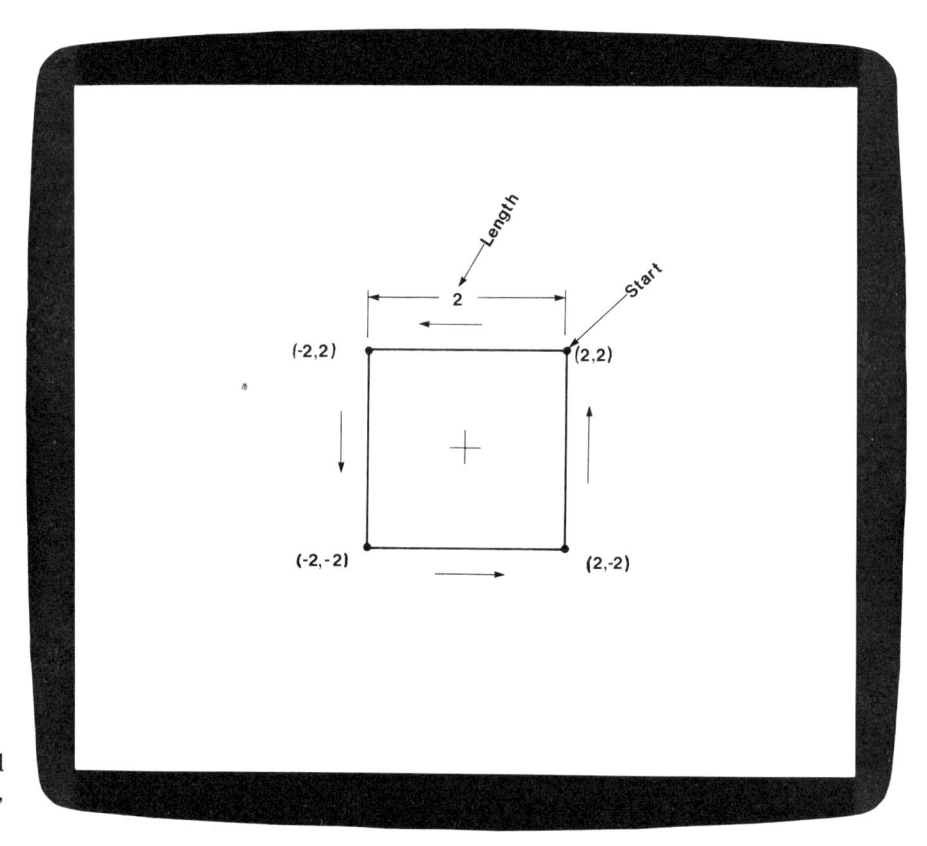

FIGURE 3-10 Shape formed by lines specified using a point, a length, and a direction.

FIGURE 3-11 Point-to-point lines.

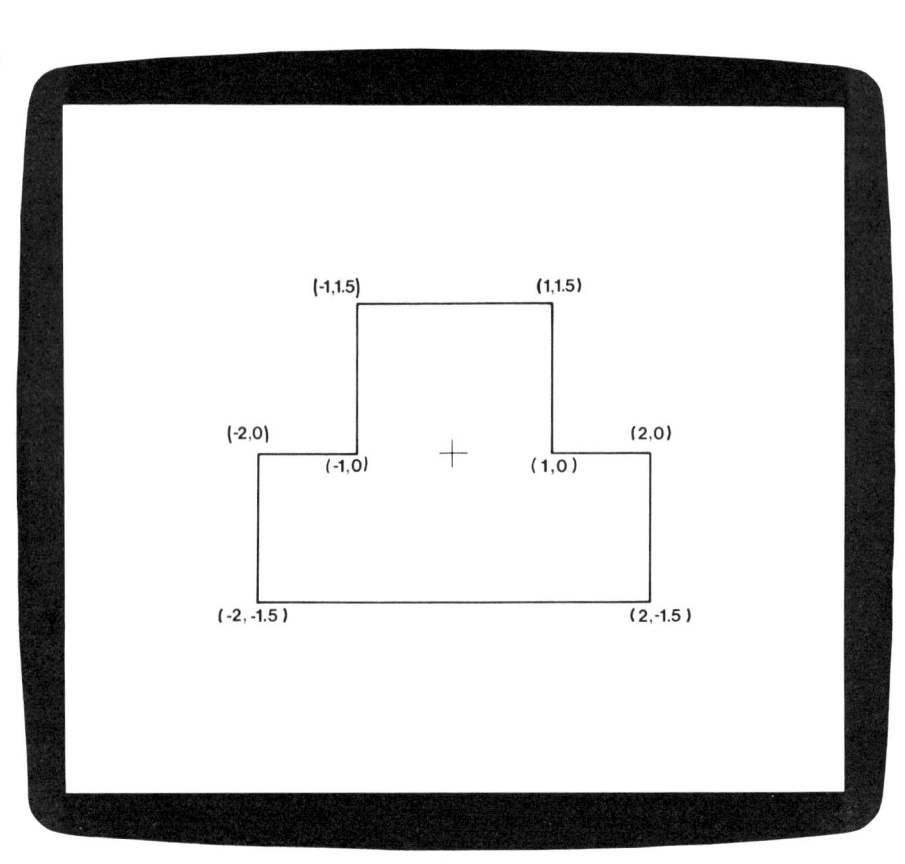

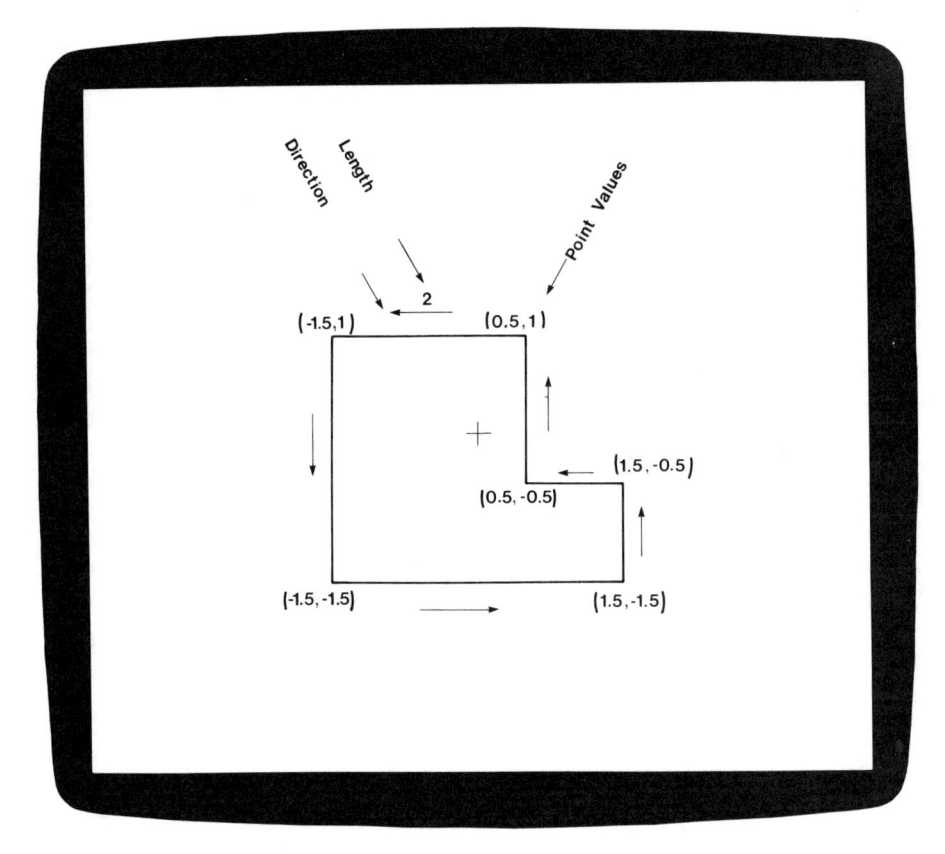

FIGURE 3-12 Point, length, and direction lines.

3-5 SLANTED LINES

Slanted lines can be drawn in one of two ways: point to point and by specifying a point location length and angle. Figure 3-13 shows two slanted lines drawn between known points. This method uses only linear inputs; that is, the points are defined in terms of the XY axis. No angular values are used.

Figure 3-14 shows a slanted line drawn by defining a point location, a length, and an angle. The angle was defined in degrees with the counterclockwise direction as positive. (Angular values as used in computer graphic systems were discussed in Section 2-7.) Most technical drawings use angular and linear dimension rather than only linear dimensions. However, many numerically controlled machines require point-to-point type inputs, so both systems are important.

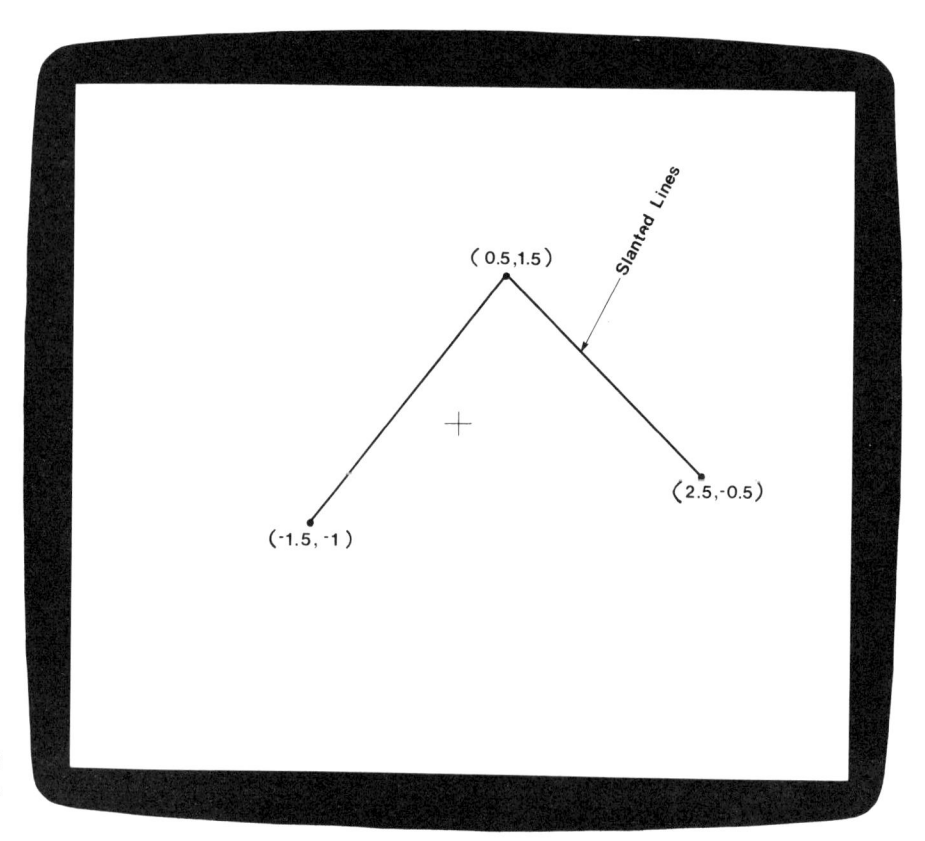

FIGURE 3-13 Slanted lines created by joining known points.

FIGURE 3-14 Slanted line created by defining a point, line length, and angle.

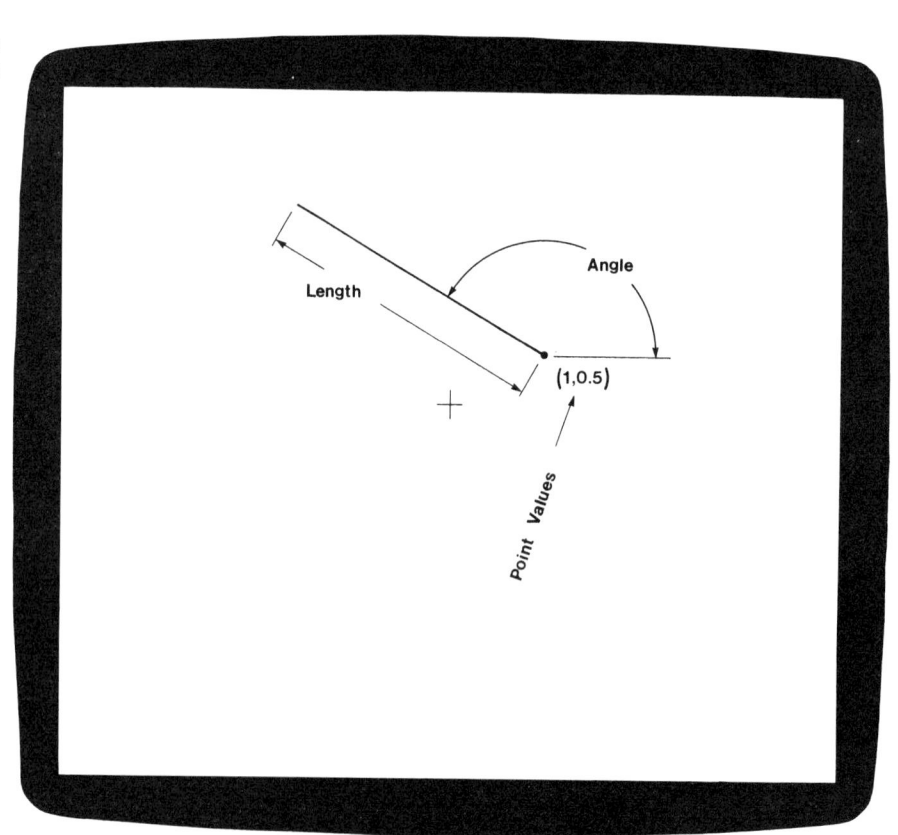

Sec. 3-6 Circles

3-6 CIRCLES

Circles are drawn by specifying a centerpoint location and a size. The location is given by defining a point location and the size by defining a radius or diameter depending on the system. In Figure 3-15 a circle was drawn around the screen centerpoint (0, 0) using a radius value of 0.75.

Circles drawn by computer graphic systems are not pure mathematical shapes. (They are not exactly equal to the loci of all points about a centerpoint at a constant radius.) They are a series of short straight lines. The more straight lines, the smoother the circular shape. This is referred to as a screen resolution. The higher the resolution, the smoother the circle.

Systems that draw circles as a series of straight lines require a series of inputs specifying a distance and an angle. The procedure is to create a series of interconnected lines that appear as a circle. For example, in Figure 3-16, a distance of 10 screen units and an angle of 15° were used to create a circle. Figure 3-17 shows a photograph of a circle drawn this way using an Apple IIe computer working in LOGO.

The total value of the angles used to draw the circle shown in Figure 3-16 must equal 360°. Therefore, the distance and 15° angle must be repeated 24 times to form a complete circle. The diameter size of the circle is controlled by the distance input.

Figure 3-18a shows three circles. Each has a different centerpoint location and size. The input for each was an X value, a Y value, and a radius value. Figure 3-18b shows a circle drawn on a very high-resolution screen (Tektronix-618 using an IBM 8084 system working with CADAM).

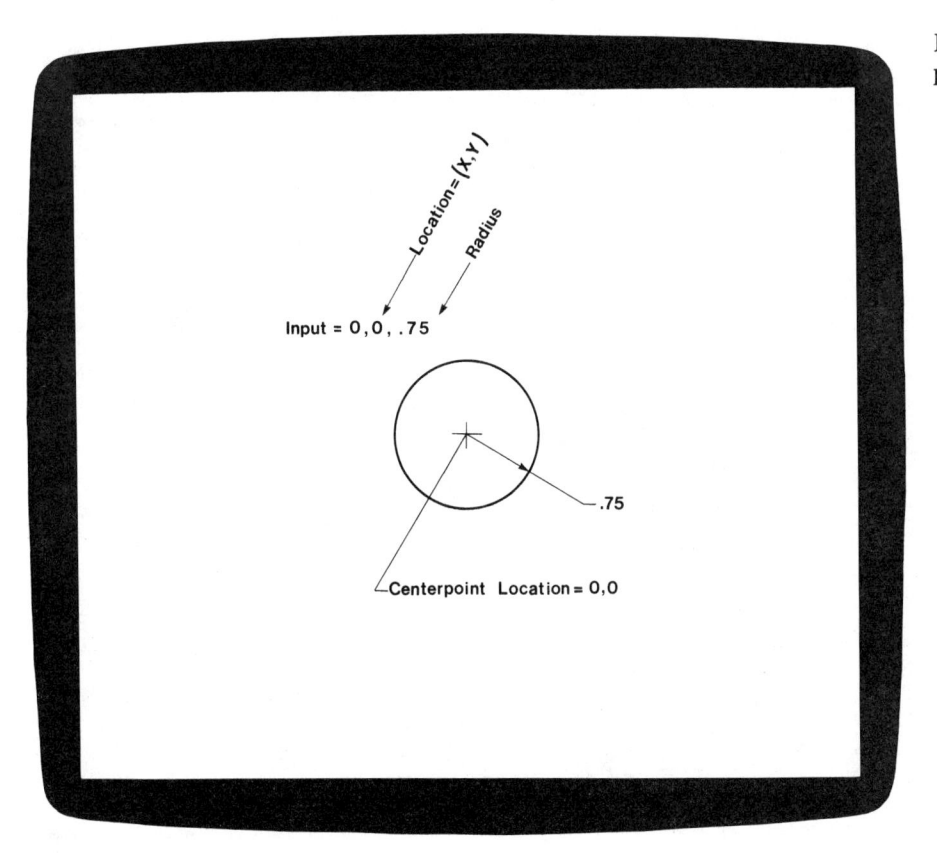

FIGURE 3-15 Circle with inputs for location and radius.

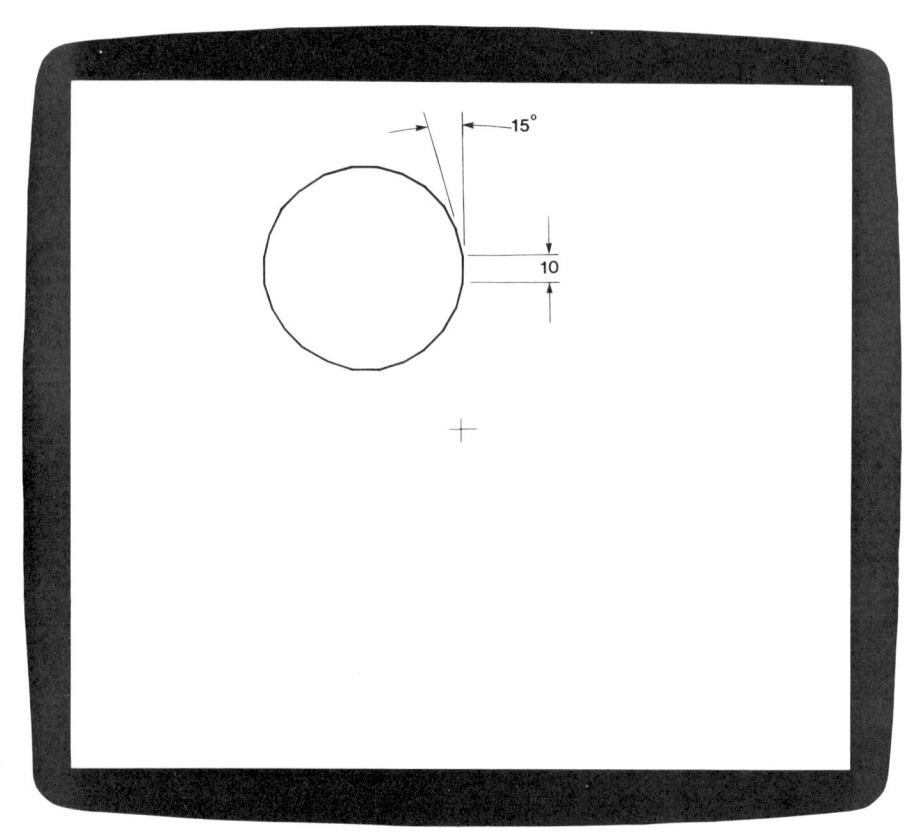

FIGURE 3-16 Circle formed by short straight-line segments.

FIGURE 3-17 Circle formed using short straight-line circles (Apple IIe computer).

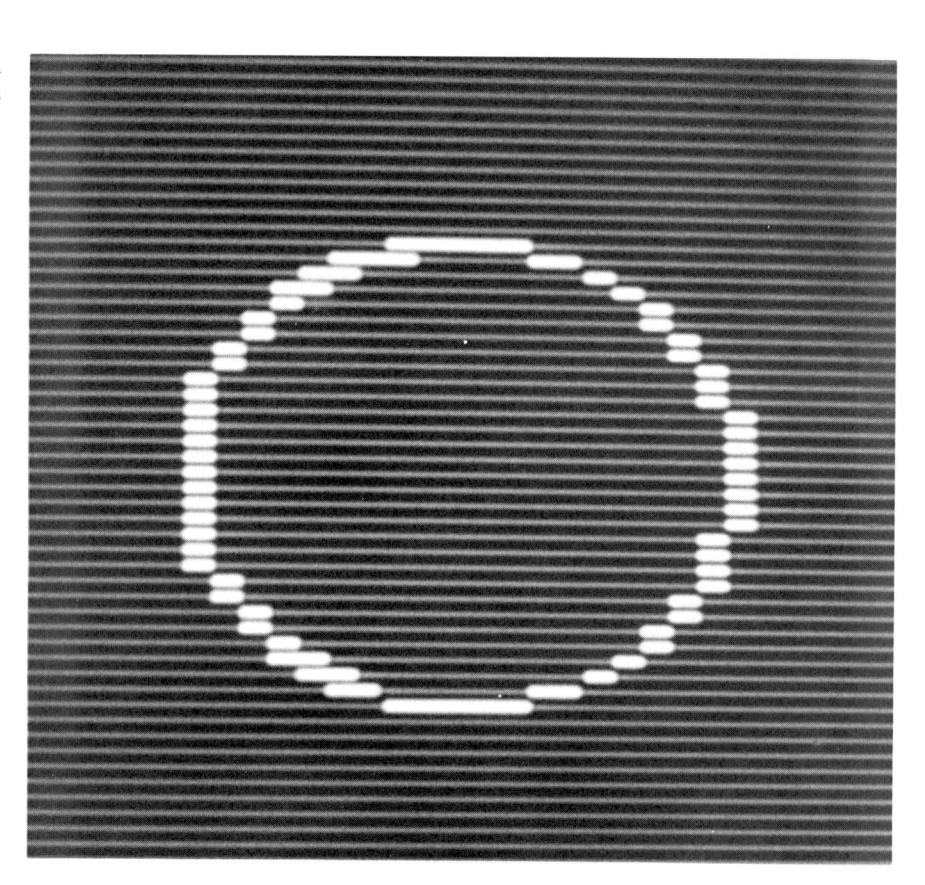

Sec. 3-6 Circles

(a)

(b)

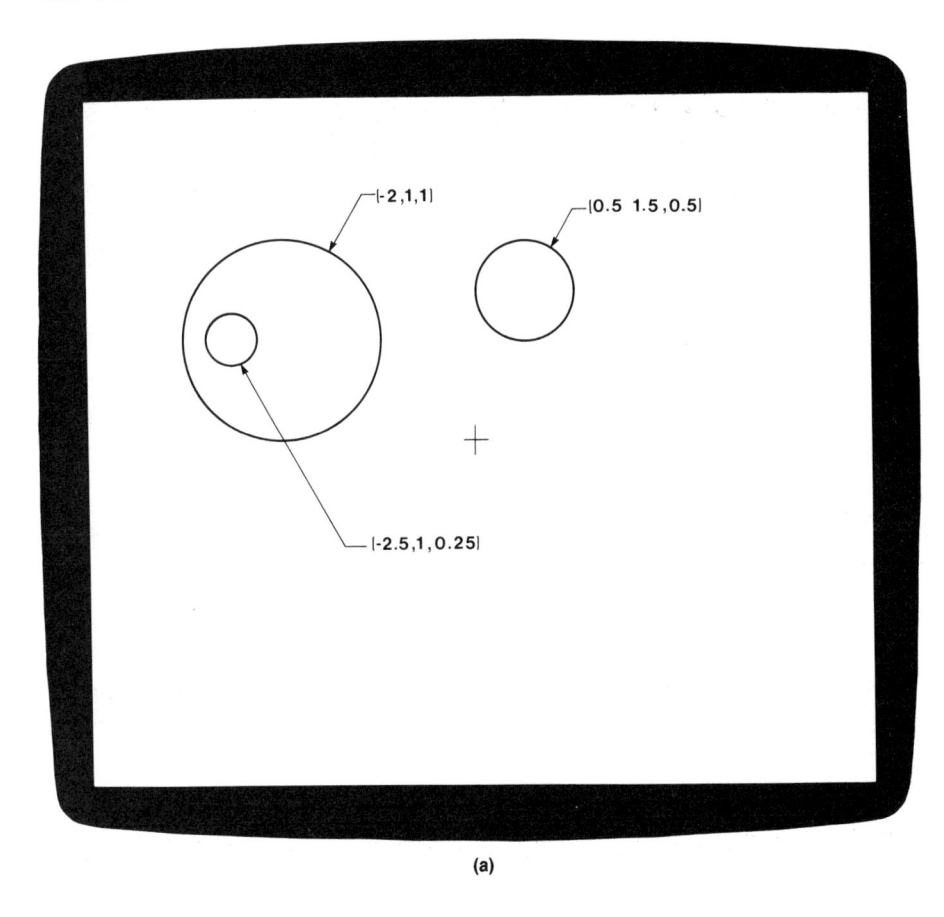

FIGURE 3-18 (a) Three different circles with their inputs.

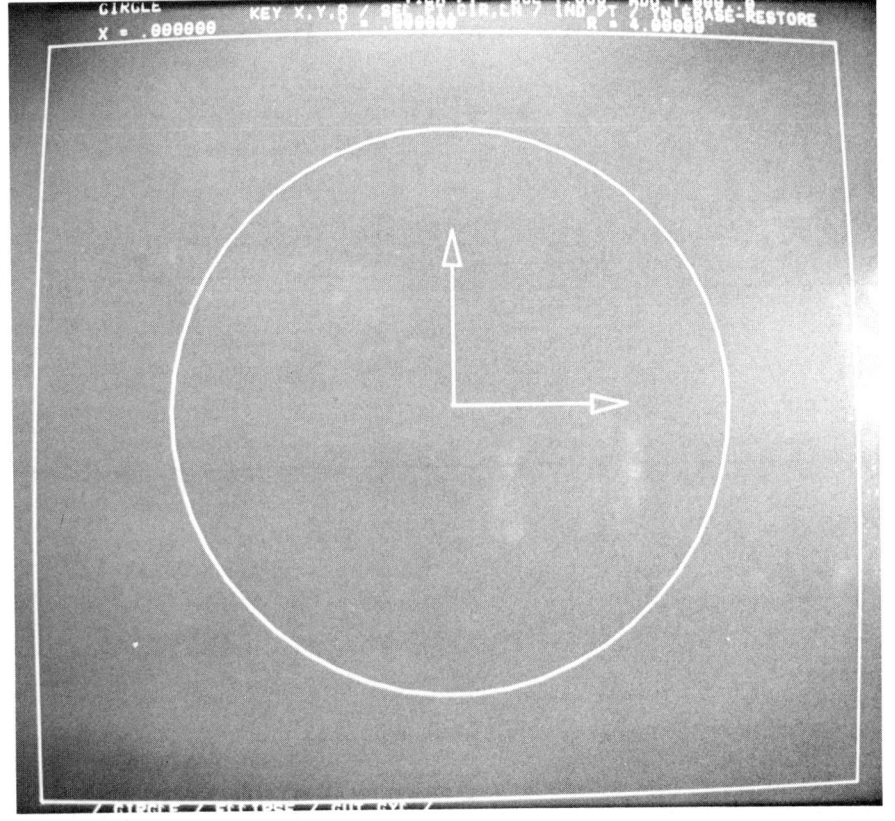

FIGURE 3-18 (b) Circle on a high-resolution screen.

3-7 ARCS

Arcs, as interpreted by computer graphics systems, are considered parts of circles. The inputs required are location, radius, and arc length. The arc length may be specified in degrees or by first drawing a circle and then erasing that portion of the circle that is not needed.

Erasing part of a circle is called *trimming*. To trim a circle, it must first be divided into segments. The arc would be considered one segment, and the remainder of the circle a second segment.

Figure 3-19 shows two arcs: one defined using degrees, the other using starting and end points. The arc centerpoint is located using X, Y coordinates. Each also uses a radius input. In general, arcs are defined using a radius value, circles using a diameter value.

Figure 3-20 shows an arc created by interconnecting lines and angles. The length of the arc is controlled by limiting the number of lines. A complete circle would require a total angle input of 360°. The arc in Figure 3-20 has a length of 90°, so the total angular input must equal 90°. In this example, this means six angles of 15° each.

FIGURE 3-19 Two different methods for drawing an arc.

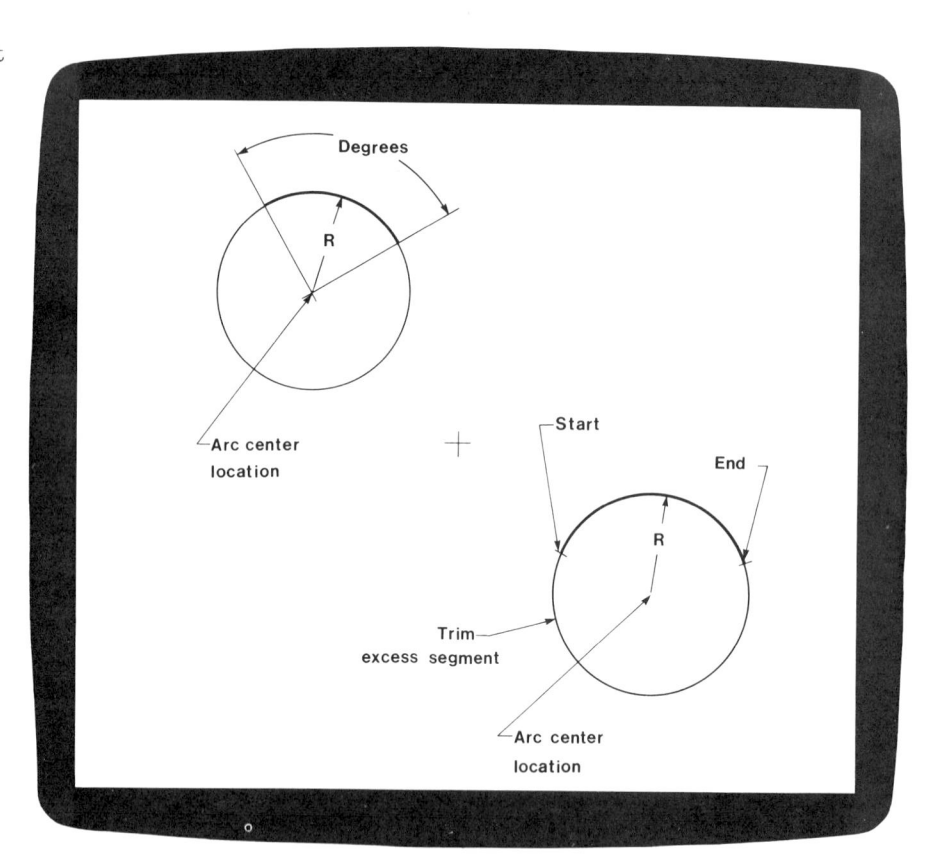

3-8 FILLETS AND ROUNDS (CORNERS)

A *fillet* is a concave arc and a *round* is a convex arc (Figure 3-21). They are often referred to as *corners*, particularly if they are 90° arcs. Many computer systems have a separate function specifically to create fillets and rounds.

Sec. 3-8 Fillets and Rounds (Corners)   43

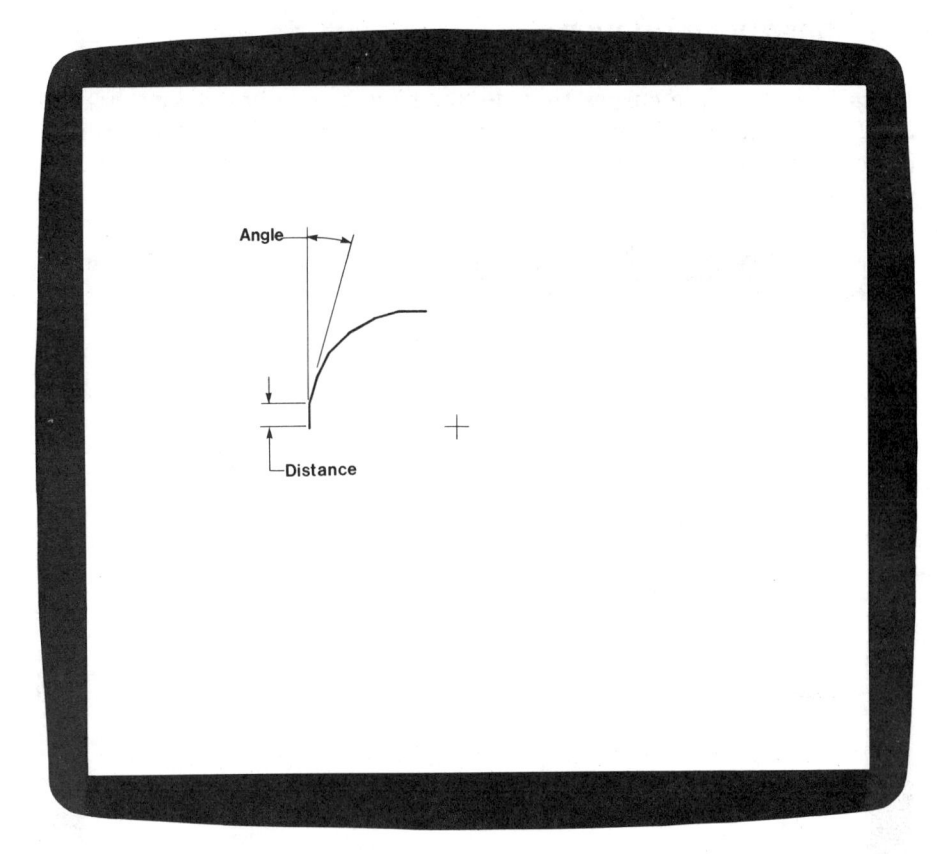

FIGURE 3-20 A 90° arc created by short straight-line segments.

Fillets and rounds are drawn by adding arcs between straight-line corners and then erasing the square corner beyond the arc. Figure 3-21 shows how this process works. The shape is first drawn square, that is, as if it were constructed entirely of straight lines; then the corners are added. Some systems will automatically erase the excess straight lines, whereas others require line trimming. Centerlines through the arc centerpoint can be used to help define the beginning and end of the arc for trimming purposes.

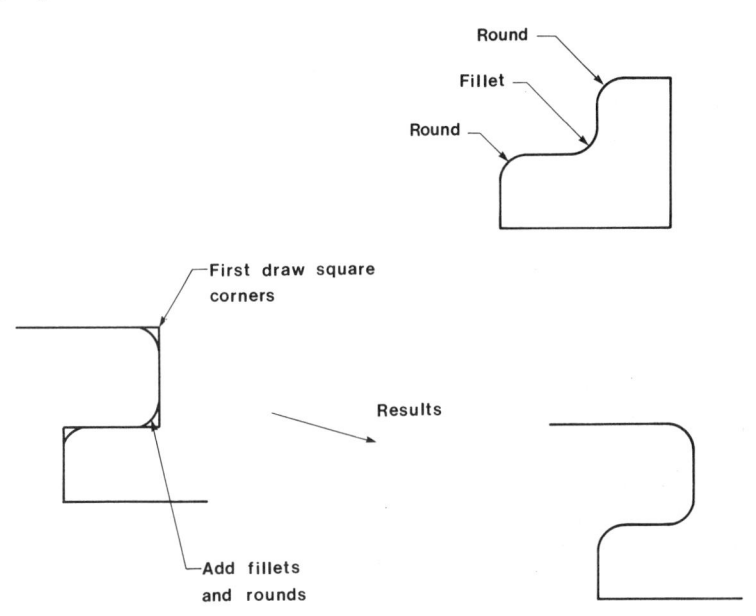

FIGURE 3-21 Fillets and rounds.

3-9 IRREGULAR CURVES

Irregular curves are curves that do not have a constant radius. Figure 3-22 shows an irregular curve. Irregular curves are defined using a series of point locations, then constructing a smooth line between the points.

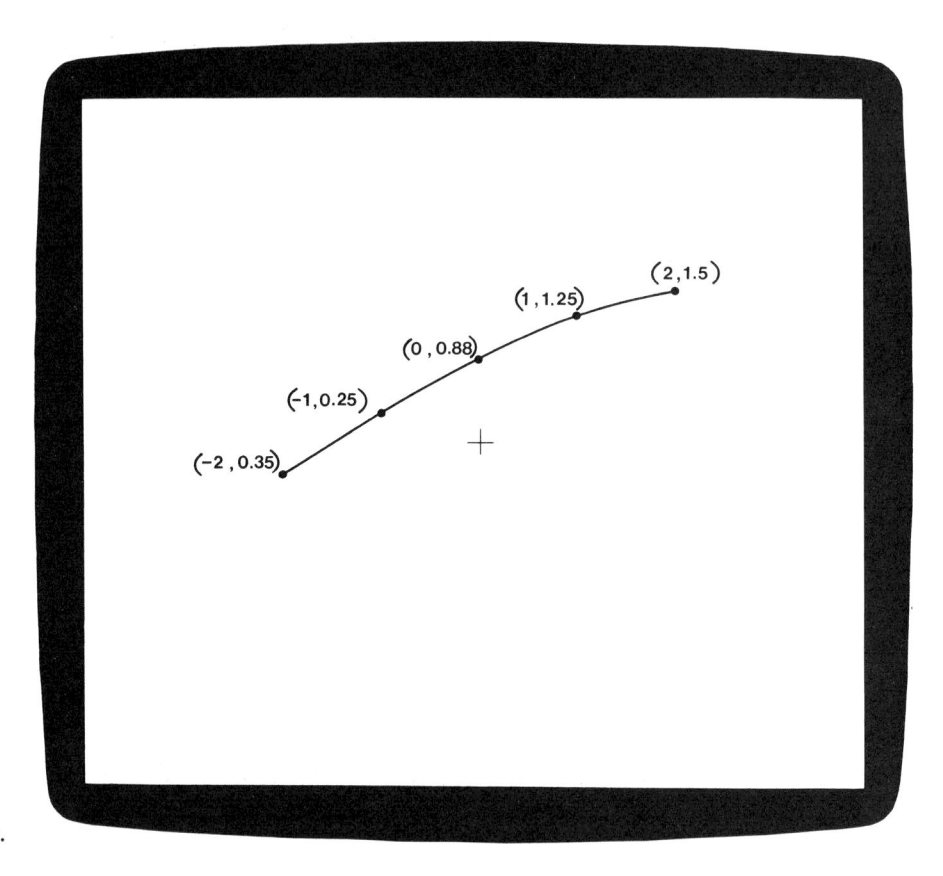

FIGURE 3-22   Irregular curve.

Computer graphic systems call an irregular curve drawn between known points a *spline*. Splines may be opened or closed. Figure 3-23 shows an example of each.

Points for irregular curves are inputed either randomly, using a digitizer, or by defining the locations in relationship to an X, Y axis (coordinate value of each point).

3-10 SAMPLE PROBLEMS

Figure 3-24 shows a shape that is made up of several different shapes: horizontal lines, vertical lines, and a circle. Shape 1 was drawn using point inputs, and shape 2 was drawn using point location, length, and distance inputs.

Figure 3-25 is a shape drawn by combining horizontal lines, vertical lines, an arc, a circle, and two corners (fillets). It is typical of shapes used in technical drawing.

Sec. 3-10 Sample Problems   45

FIGURE 3-23 Open and a closed spline.

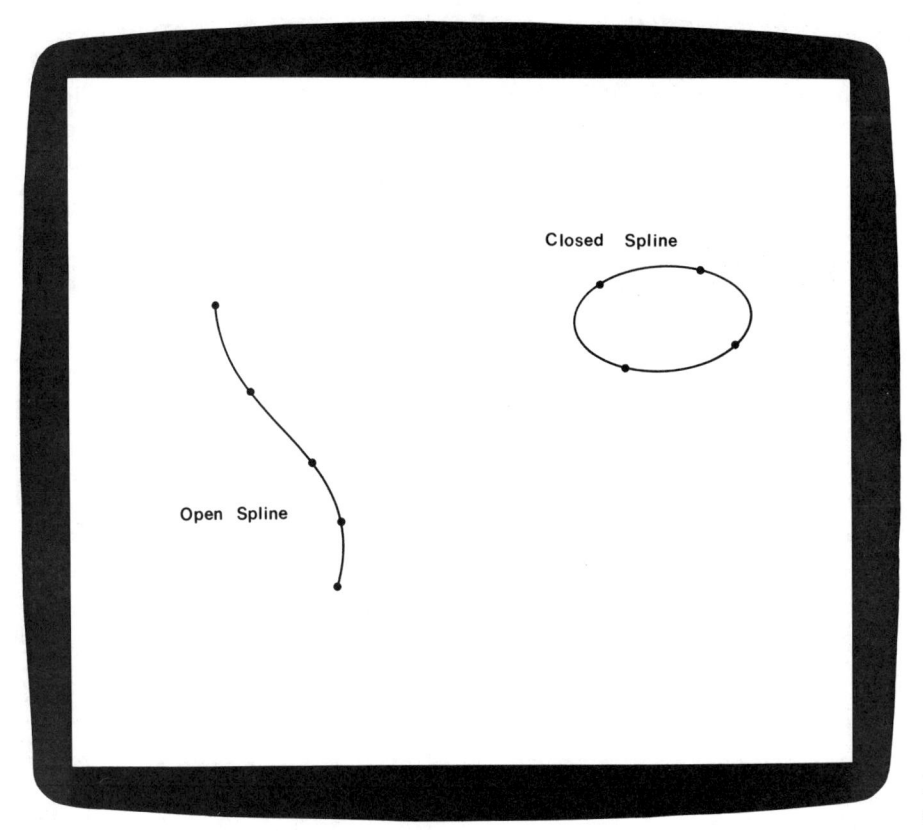

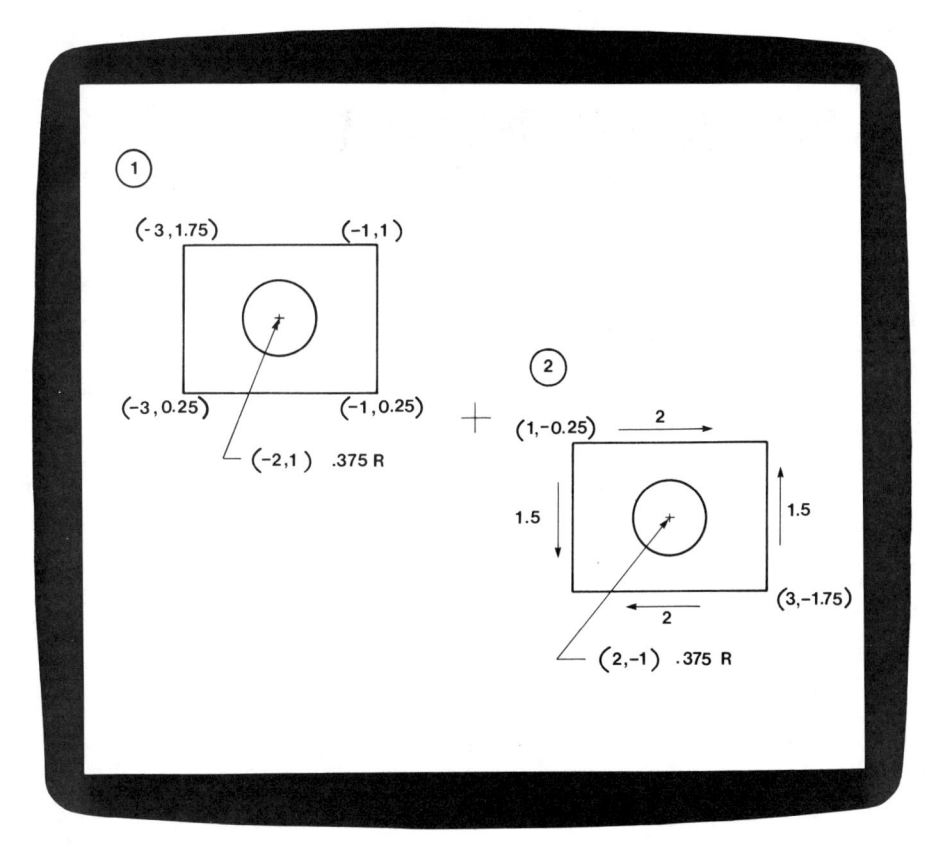

FIGURE 3-24 Two shapes made by combining lines and circles.

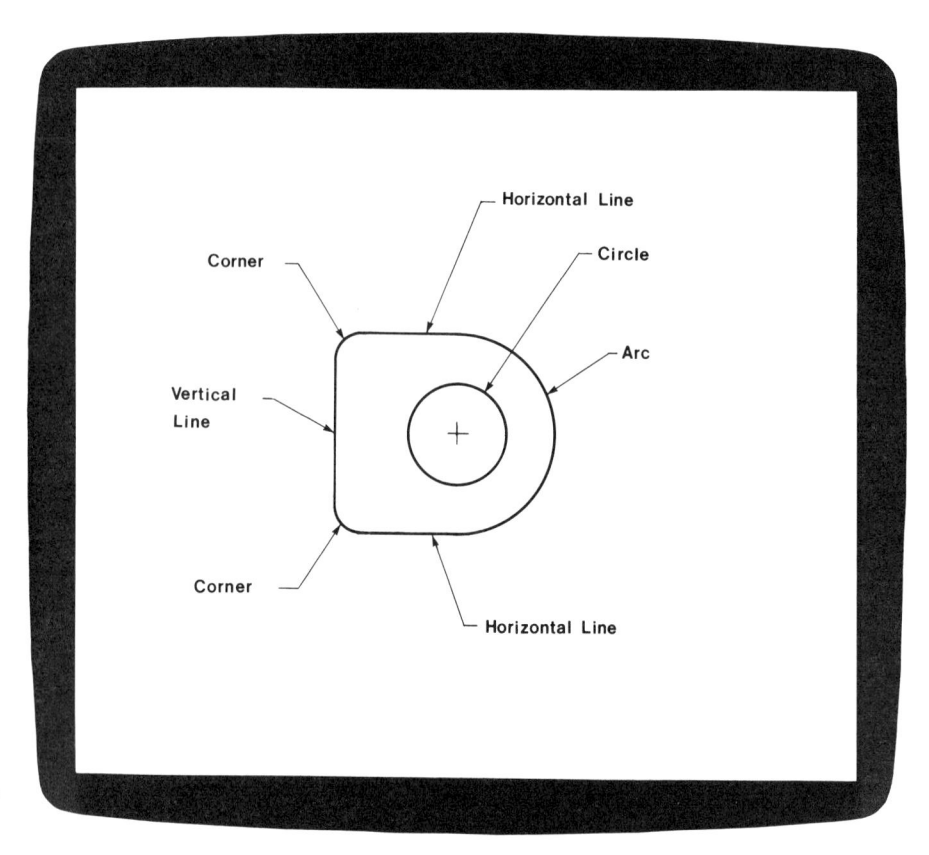

FIGURE 3-25 Shape made by combining other basic shapes.

PROBLEMS

P3-1 Draw the following horizontal lines. All measurements are in inches.
   (a) Infinite length at (0, 4)
   (b) Infinite length at (0, −2.5)
   (c) From (−3, 2) to (5, 2)
   (d) From (−3, −3) to (5, −3)
   (e) From (−2.5, 2.5) and toward the right 4 in.
   (f) From (1.75, −0.50) and toward the left 2.5 in.

P3-2 Draw the following horizontal lines. All measurements are in millimeters.
   (a) Infinite length at (0, 100)
   (b) Infinite length at (0, 60)
   (c) From (−75, 50) to (125, 50)
   (d) From (−75, −75) to (125, −75)
   (e) From (−60, 60) and toward the right 110 mm
   (f) From (45, −13) and toward the left 75 mm

Chap. 3 Problems

P3-3 Draw the following vertical lines. All measurements are in inches.
  (a) Infinite length at (3, 0)
  (b) Infinite length at (−2, 0)
  (c) From (−2.5, 2) to (−2.5, −2)
  (d) From (2, 1.5) to (2, −2.5)
  (e) From (−0.5, 2) and toward the bottom 4 in.
  (f) From (1, 1.3) and upward 3 in.

P3-4 Draw the following vertical lines. All measurements are in millimeters.
  (a) Infinite length at (75, 0)
  (b) Infinite length at (−50, 0)
  (c) From (−60, 50) to (−60, −50)
  (d) From (50, 38) to (50, −63)
  (e) From (−13, 50) and toward the bottom 105 mm
  (f) From (25, 33) and upward 75 mm

P3-5 Draw the following slanted lines. All measurements are in inches.
  (a) From (−2, 1) to (0, 2)
  (b) From (−2.5, −2.5) to (2.5, 0.5)
  (c) From (0.5, 3) to (0, 0)
  (d) From (−1.5, −0.5) to the right 3 in. at 15° below the horizontal
  (e) From (0.5, −2.0) upward 4 in. at 20° to the right of vertical

P3-6 Draw the following slanted lines. All measurements are in millimeters.
  (a) From (−50, 25) to (0, 50)
  (b) From (−62, −62) to (62, 13)
  (c) From (13, 75) to (0, 0)
  (d) From (−33, −13) to the right 75 mm at 15° below the horizontal
  (e) From (13, −50) upward 100 mm at 20° to the right of the vertical

P3-7 Draw the following circles. All measurements are in inches.
  (a) At (0, 0) with radius = 1.00
  (b) At (−1, 0) with diameter = 4.00
  (c) At (2, 2) with radius = 0.50
  (d) At (2, −0.5) with diameter = 0.50
  (e) At (1.5, 1) with radius = 1.25
  (f) At (1, −2) with diameter = 1.50

P3-8 Draw the following circles. All measurements are in millimeters.
  (a) At (0, 0) with radius = 25
  (b) At (−25, 0) with diameter = 100
  (c) At (50, 50) with radius = 13
  (d) At (50, −13) with diameter = 13
  (e) At (38, 25) with radius = 33
  (f) At (25, −50) with diameter = 40

P3-9 Draw the following irregular curves. Each curve is defined using five points. All measurements are in inches.

(a) Curve 1

Point	Coordinates
1	(−3, 0)
2	(−2, 1.2)
3	(−0.5, 2.3)
4	(0.7, 2.7)
5	(2, 3)

(b) Curve 2

Point	Coordinates
1	(−3, 0)
2	(−1, 1)
3	(0.3, 1.4)
4	(1.5, 1.3)
5	(2.7, 0)

(c) Curve 3

Point	Coordinates
1	(−2, 2.5)
2	(−1.3, 2.6)
3	(−0.5, 0.6)
4	(0, 0)
5	(0.6, −1)

(d) Curve 4

Point	Coordinates
1	(−1.2, −2)
2	(−1, −1.3)
3	(−0.6, −0.5)
4	(0, 0)
5	(1, 0.4)

P3-10 Draw the following irregular curves. Each curve is defined using five points. All measurements are in millimeters.

(a) Curve 1

Point	Coordinates
1	(−75, 0)
2	(−50, 30)
3	(−13, 58)
4	(18, 68)
5	(50, 75)

(b) Curve 2

Point	Coordinates
1	(−75, 0)
2	(−25, 25)
3	(8, 36)
4	(38, 32)
5	(68, 0)

(c) Curve 3

Point	Coordinates
1	(−50, 62)
2	(−33, 66)
3	(−13, 16)
4	(0, 0)
5	(16, −25)

(d) Curve 4

Point	Coordinates
1	(−30, −50)
2	(−25, −33)
3	(−16, −13)
4	(0, 0)
5	(25, 10)

Chap. 3 Problems

P3-11 Draw Figure P3-11. All coordinate values and dimensions are in inches.

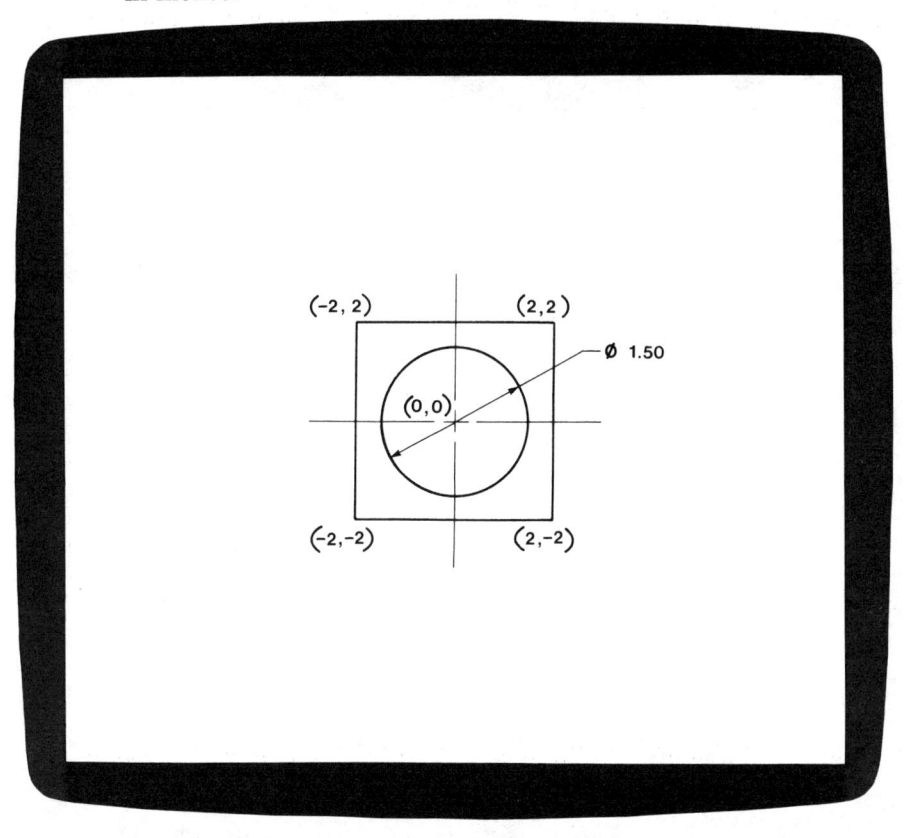

FIGURE P3-11

P3-12 Draw Figure P3-12. All coordinate values are in millimeters.

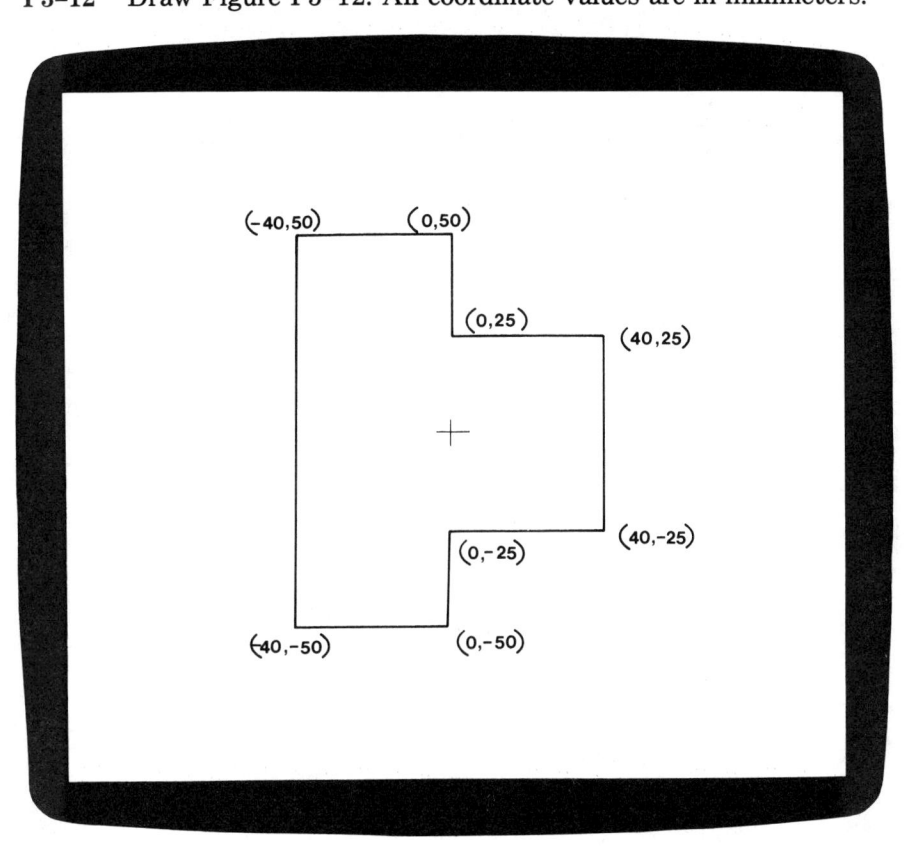

FIGURE P3-12

P3-13 Draw Figure P3-13. All coordinate values and dimensions are in millimeters.

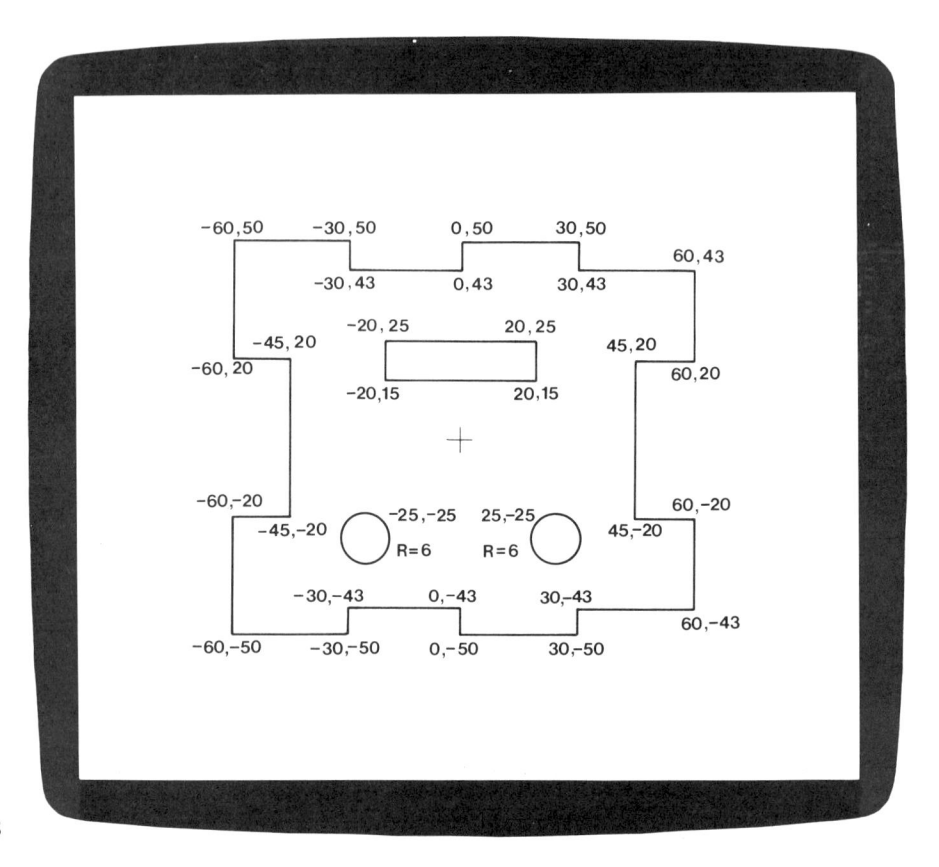

FIGURE P3-13

P3-14 Draw Figure P3-14. All coordinate values are in inches.

FIGURE P3-14

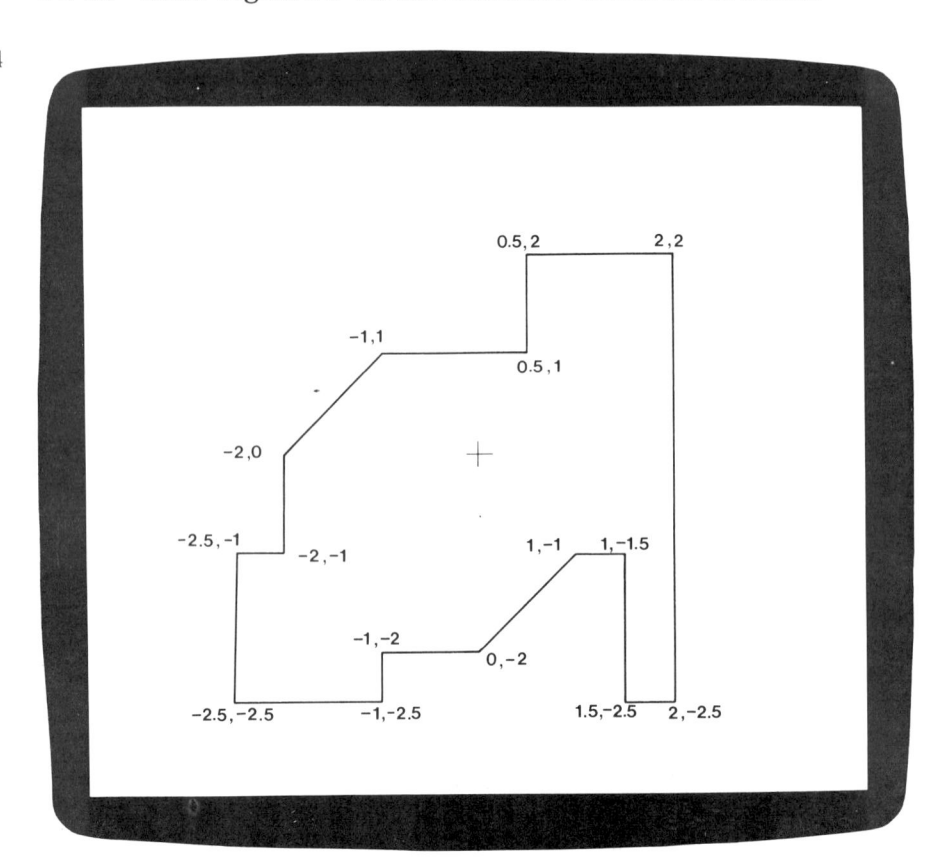

Chap. 3   Problems   51

P3-15   Draw Figure P3-15. All dimensions are in millimeters. Each corner of the figure is identified by a number. The coordinate values for each numbered corner are listed below.

Point	Coordinates	Point	Coordinates
1	−75, 60	29	30, −40
2	−60, 60	30	40, −25
3	−45, 53	31	12, −25
4	−45, 35	32	12, −43
5	−25, 35	33	−12, −43
6	−35, 17	34	−12, −25
7	−15, 17	35	−40, −25
8	−15, 47	36	−30, −40
9	15, 47	37	−30, −50
10	15, 17	38	−40, −50
11	35, 17	39	−60, −60
12	25, 35	40	−75, −60
13	45, 35	41	−75, −50
14	45, 53	42	−65, −50
15	60, 60	43	−65, −30
16	75, 60	44	−52, 30
17	75, 50	45	−52, 30
18	65, 50	46	−65, 30
19	65, 30	47	−65, 50
20	52, 30	48	−75, 50
21	52, −30	49	−40, 9
22	65, −30	50	−15, 9
23	65, −50	51	−15, 0
24	75, −50	52	15, 0
25	75, −60	53	15, 9
26	60, −60	54	40, 9
27	40, −50	55	40, −15
28	30, −50	56	−40, −15

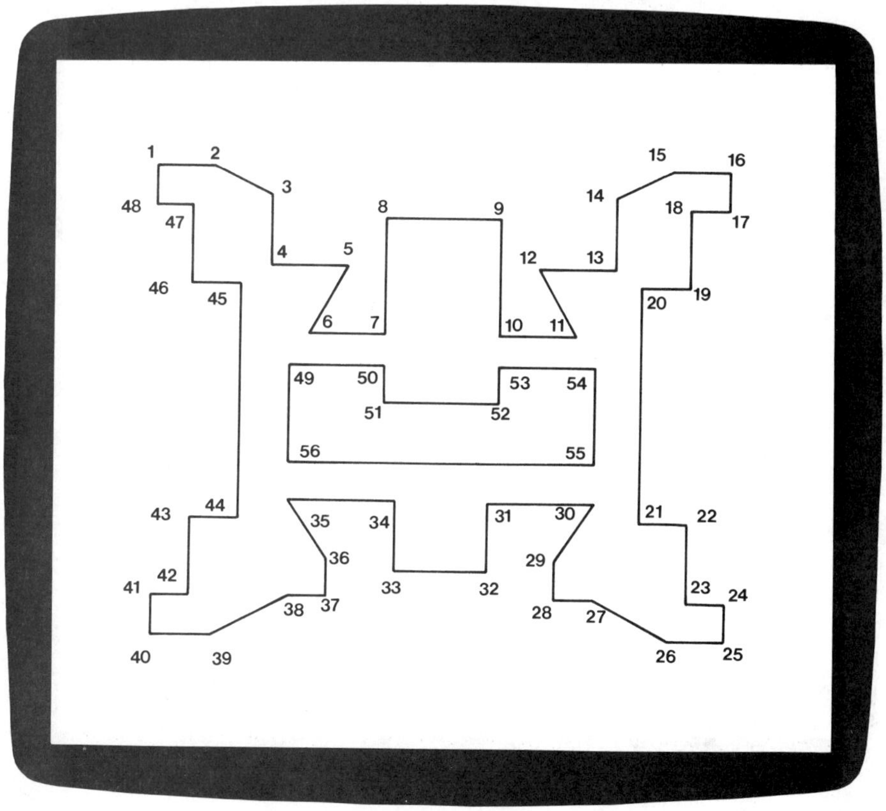

FIGURE P3-15

For Problems P3-16 through P3-19, draw Figures P3-16 through P3-19 based on the coordinate and dimension information given. The dimensional units are as noted below.

P3-16 Millimeters   **P3-18** Inches
P3-17 Millimeters   **P3-19** Millimeters

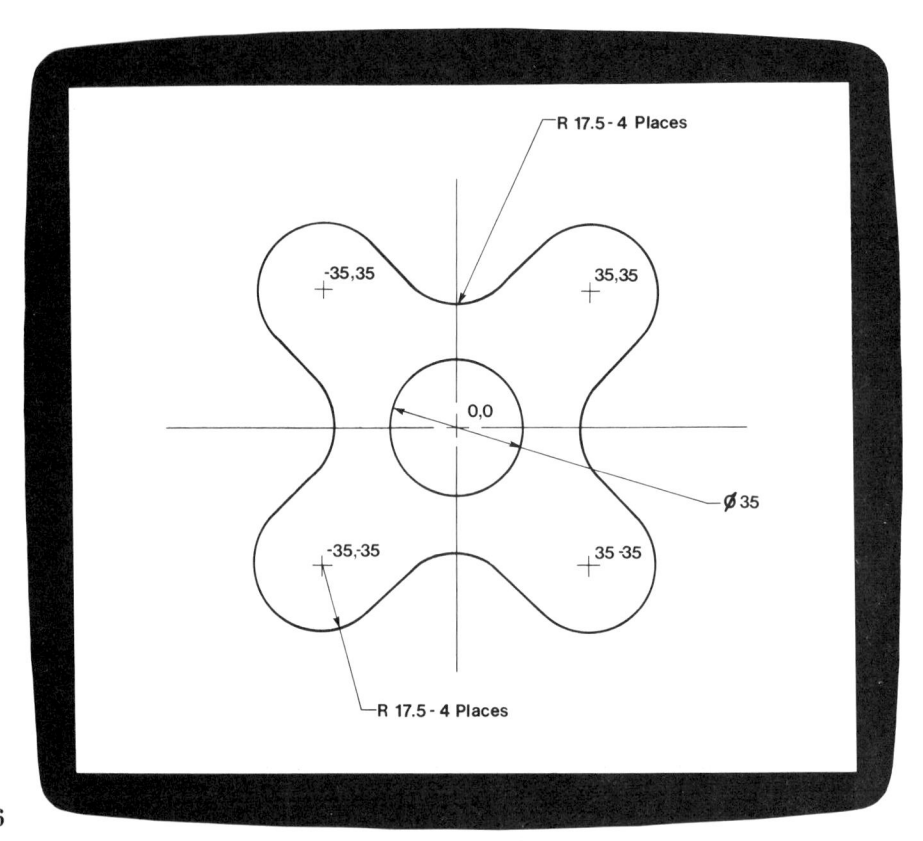

FIGURE P3-16

FIGURE P3-17

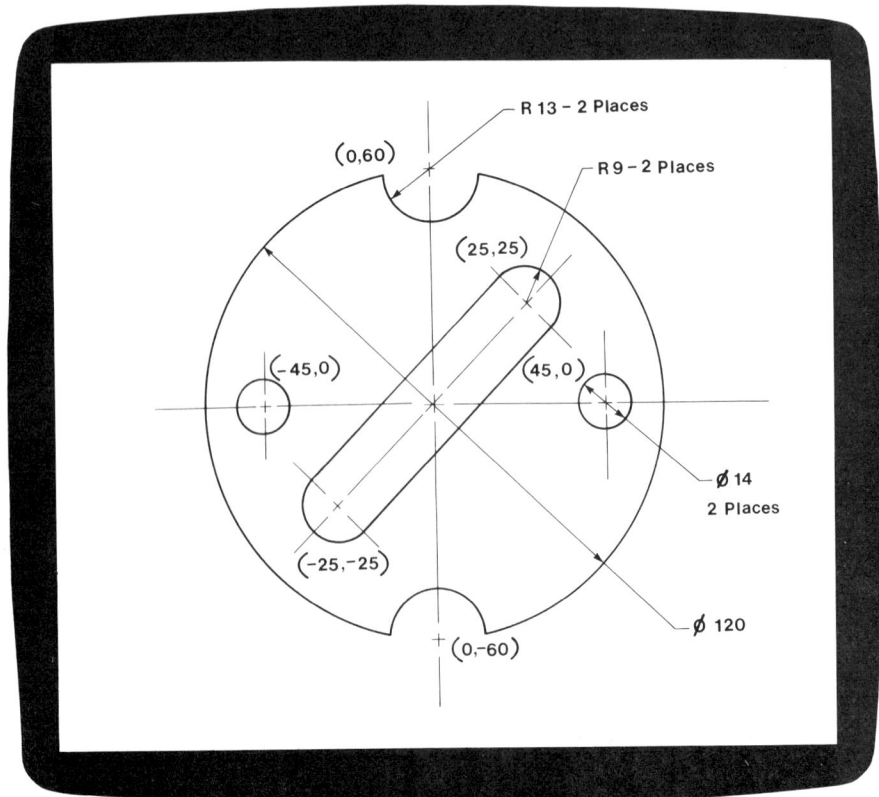

Chap. 3 Problems

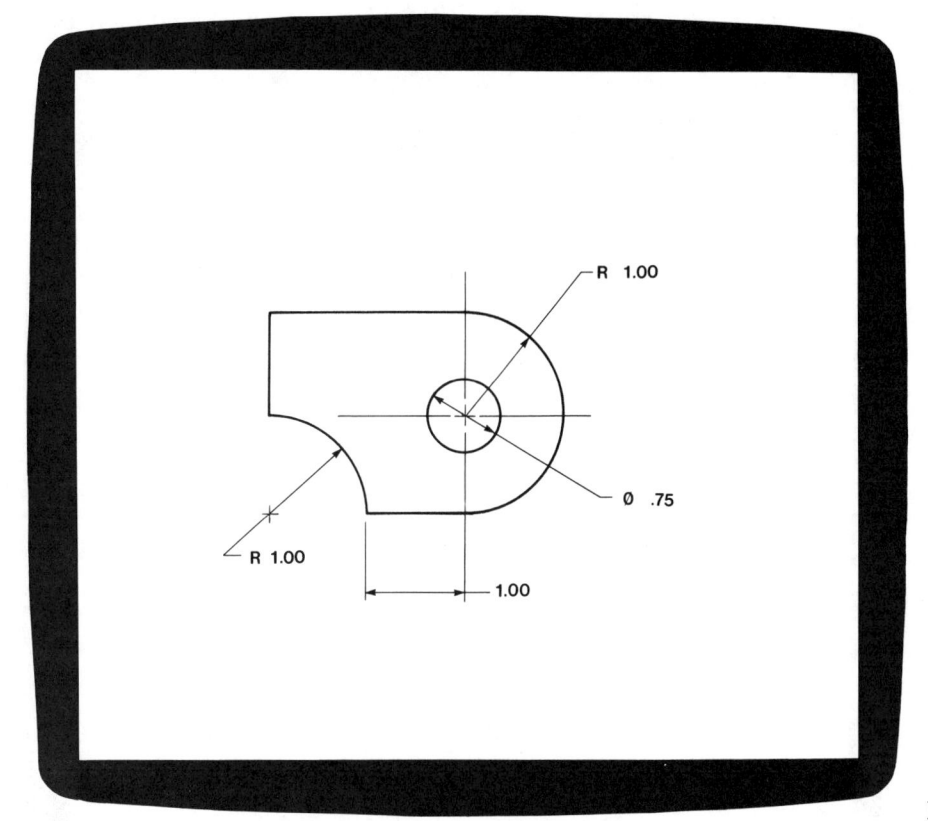

FIGURE P3-18

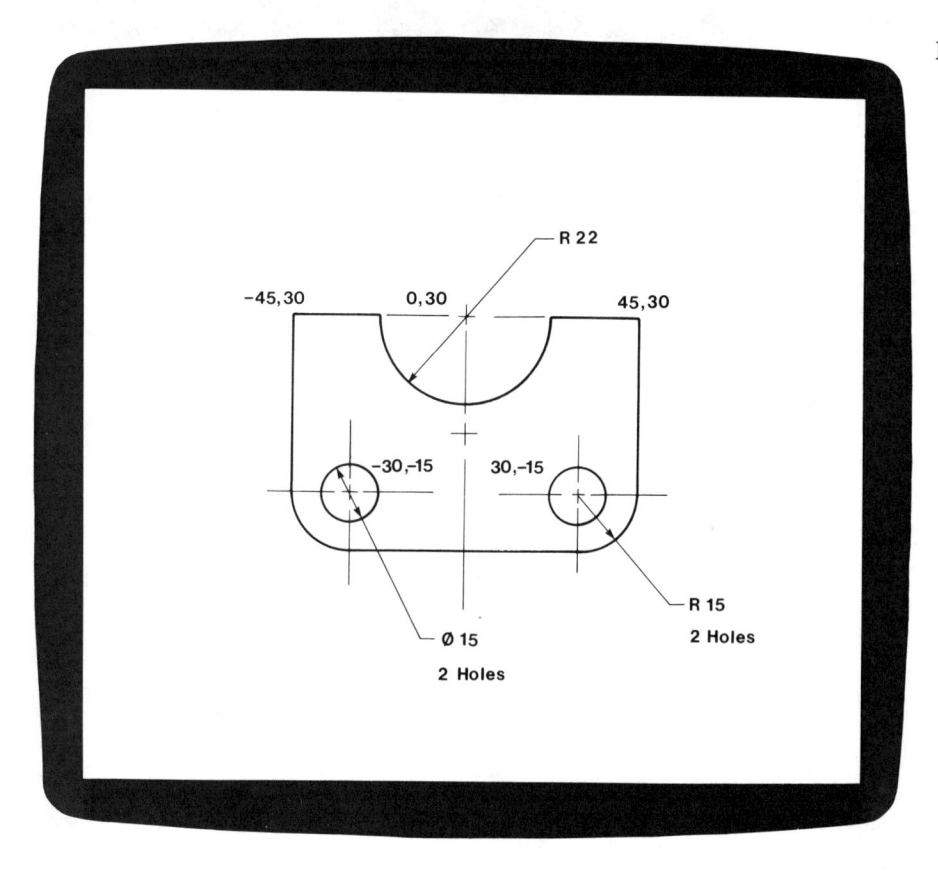

FIGURE P3-19

P3-20 Start with the defined a point location (−2, −1.50) and construct Figure P3-20. The values next to each line are the line's length expressed in inches.

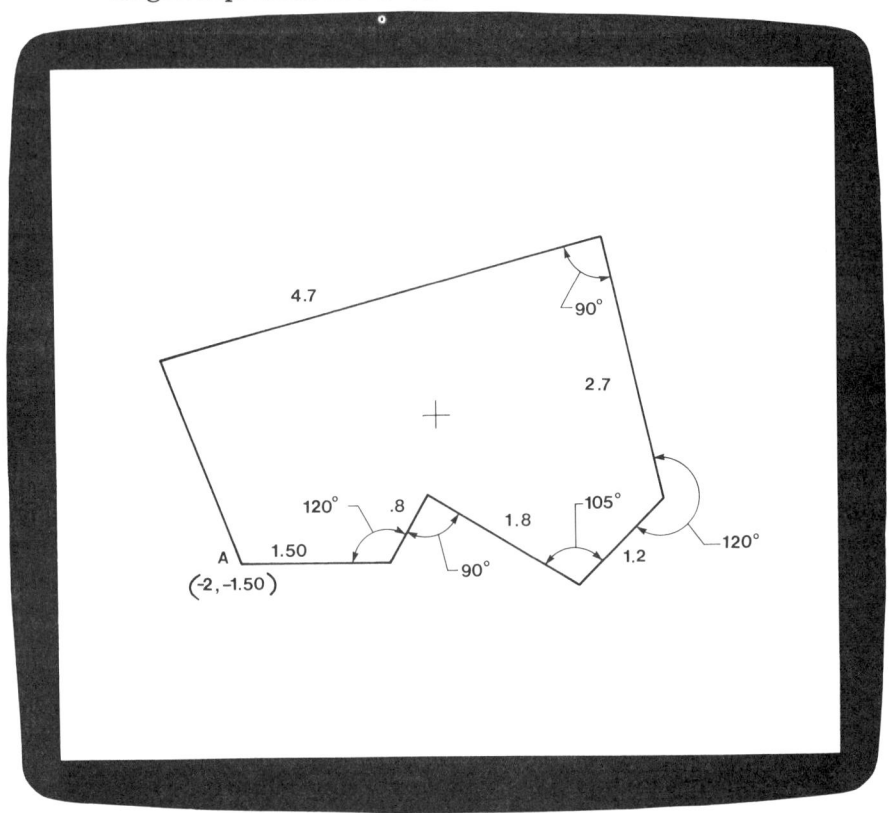

FIGURE P3-20

P3-21 Start with the defined a point location (−65, −60) and construct Figure P3-21. The values next to each line are the line's length expressed in millimeters.

FIGURE P3-21

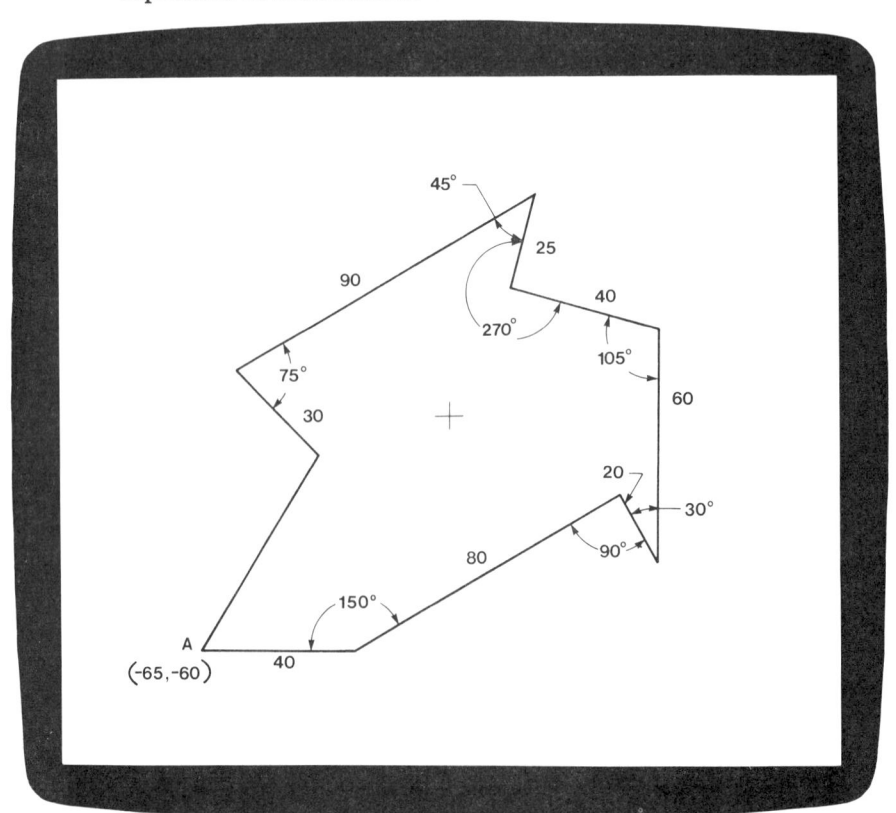

Chap. 3 Problems 55

P3-22 Draw Figure P3-22. All coordinate and dimensional values are in inches.

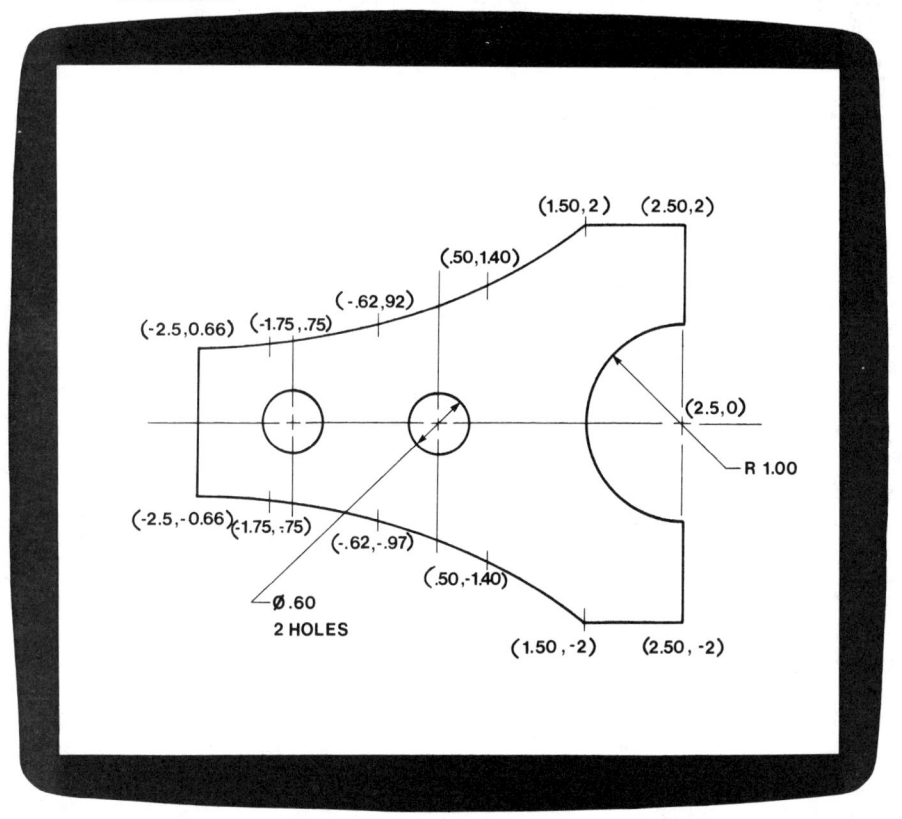

FIGURE P3-22

P3-23 Draw the CAM shown in Figure P3-23 based on the information given. Each point on the outer surface is defined using polar coordinates. All radius dimensions are in millimeters.

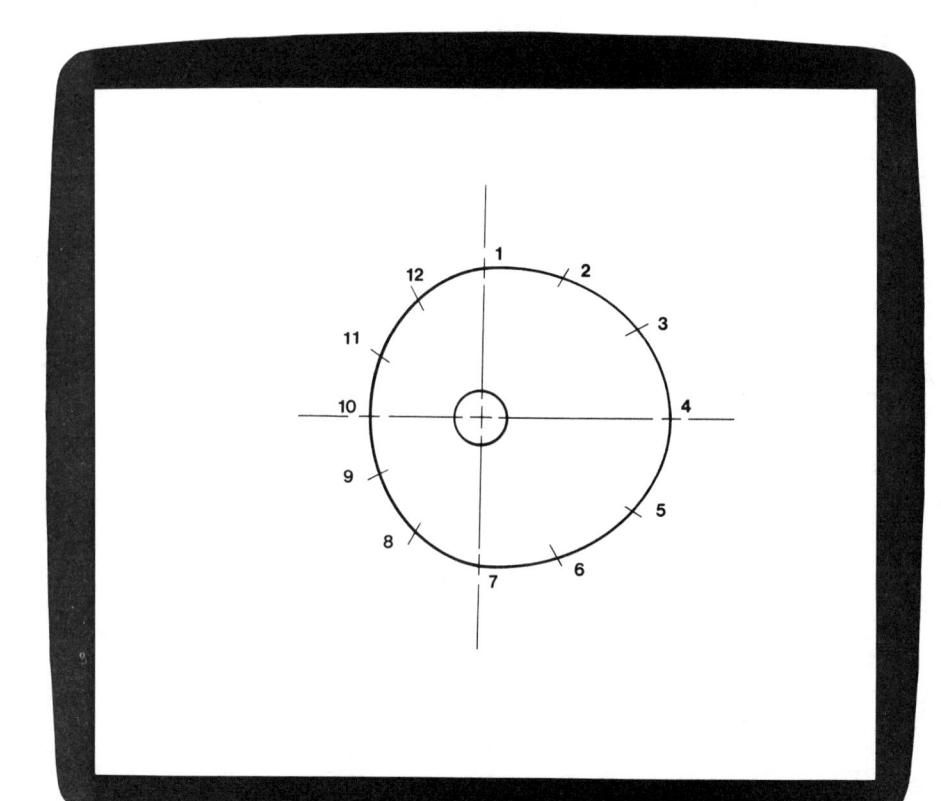

FIGURE P3-23

Point	Angle	Radius
1	0	38.25
2	30	42.0
3	60	46.6
4	90	49.0
5	120	46.6
6	150	42.0
7	180	38.5
8	210	34.0
9	240	30.8
10	270	30.0
11	300	30.8
12	330	34.0

For Problems P3-24 through P3-28, redraw Figures P3-24 through P3-28 using the dimensions given. The dimensional units are as noted below.

P3-24	Inches	P3-27	Millimeters
P3-25	Millimeters	P3-28	Millimeters
P3-26	Millimeters		

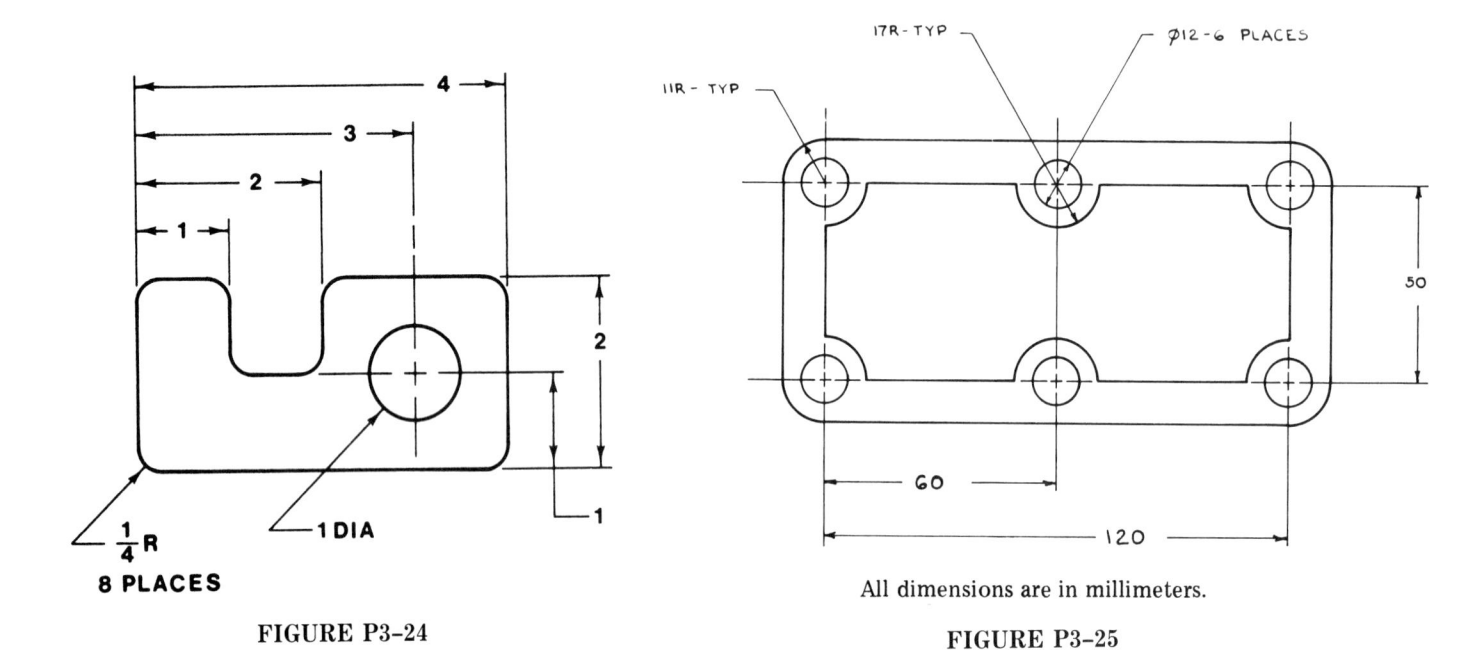

FIGURE P3-24

All dimensions are in millimeters.

FIGURE P3-25

All dimensions are in millimeters.

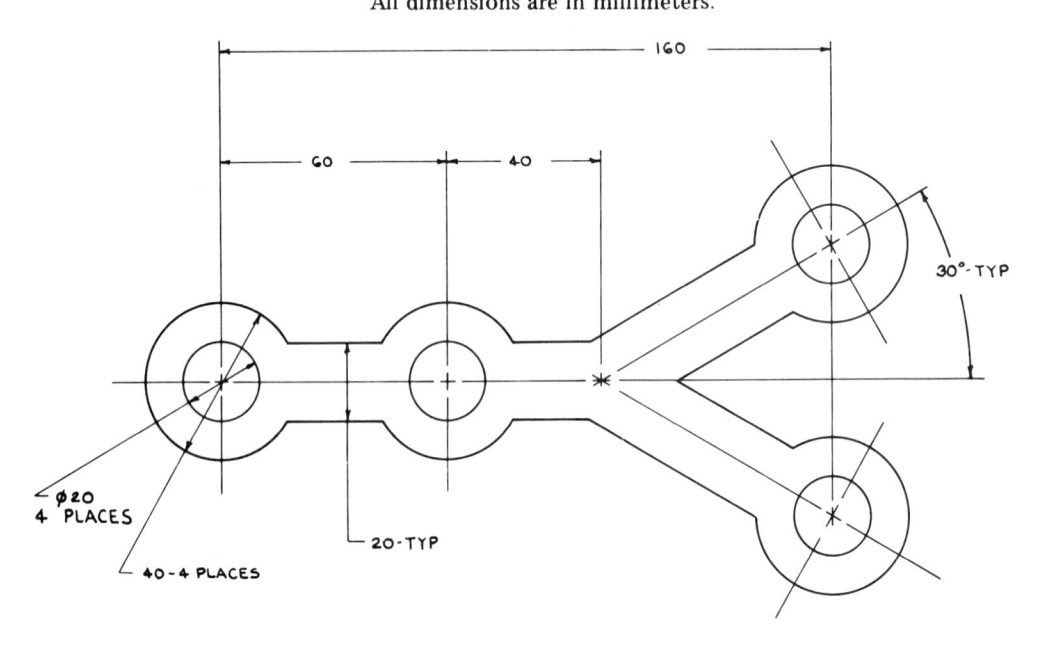

FIGURE P3-26

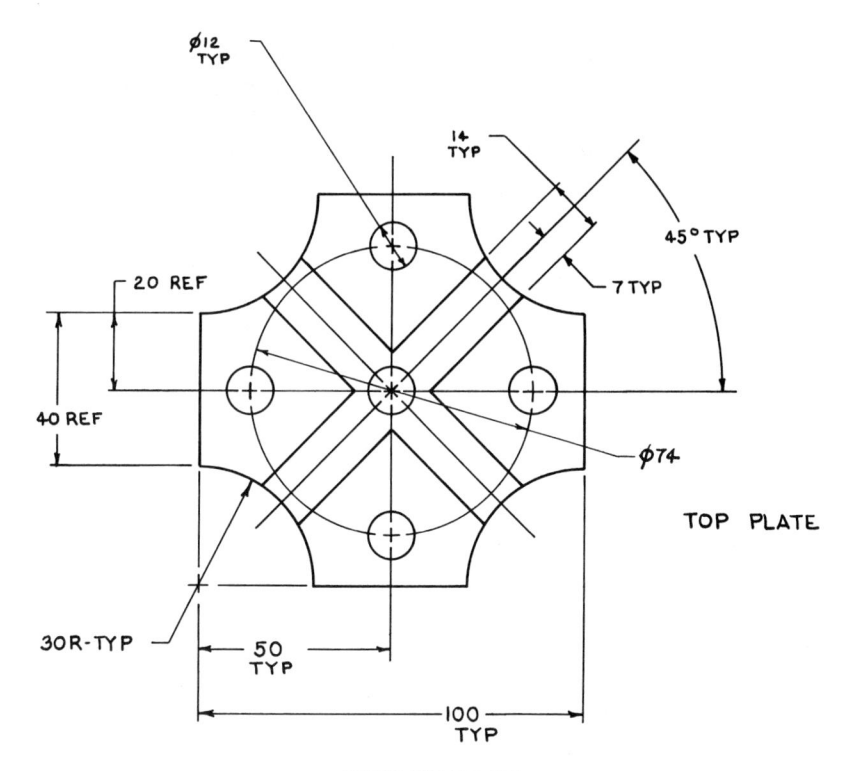

FIGURE P3-27

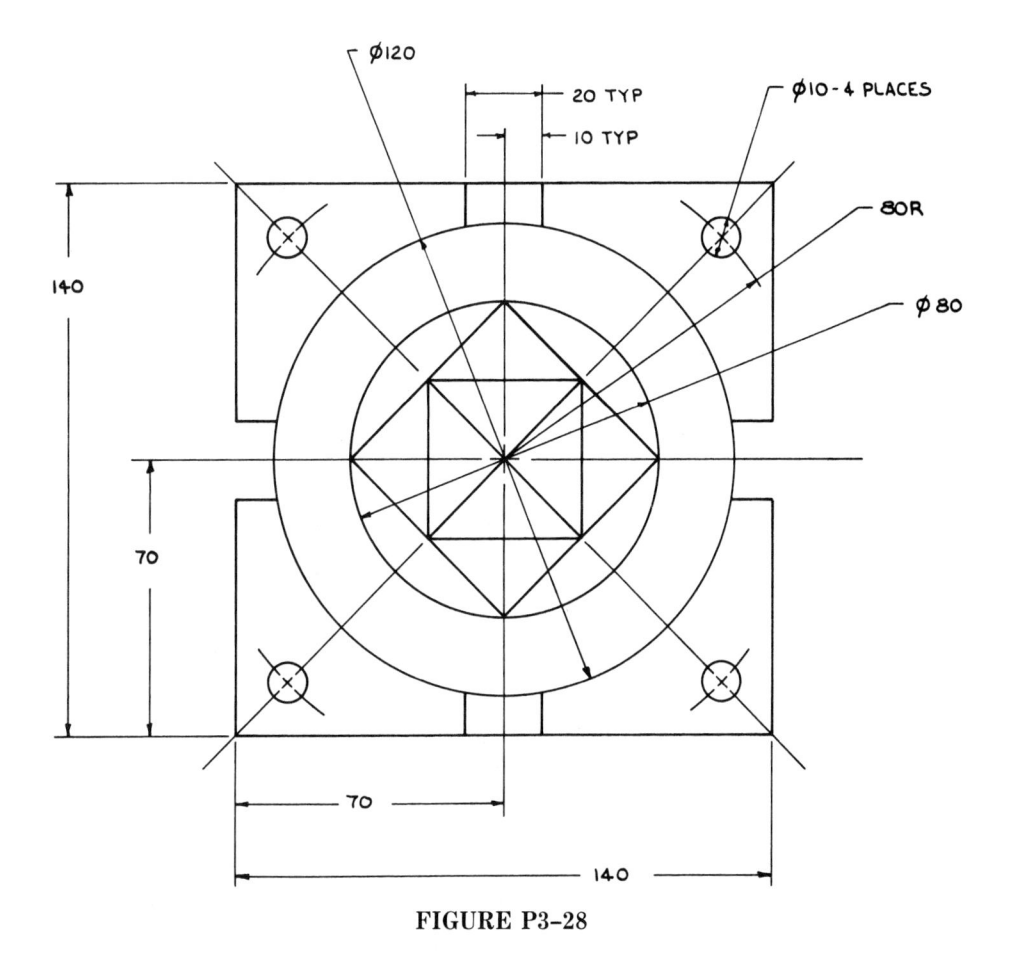

FIGURE P3-28

58 Basic Two-Dimensional Constructions Chap. 3

For Problems P3-29 and P3-30, redraw Figures P3-29 and P3-30 using the dimensions given. After completion, measure the distances specified in the charts and list their values. Use the system's measuring capabilities to measure the distances. The dimensional units are as noted below.

P3-29 Millimeters **P3-30** Inches

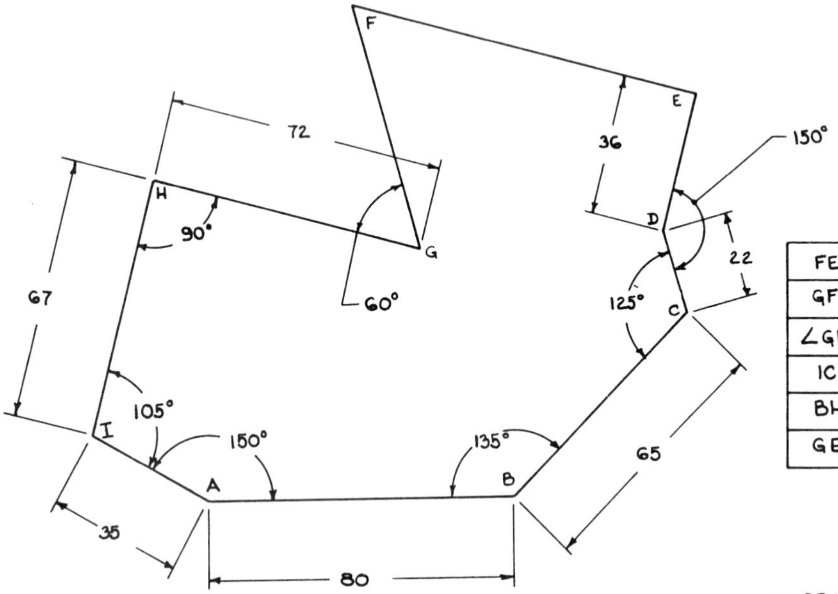

FE	
GF	
∠GFE	
IC	
BH	
GE	

FIGURE P3-29

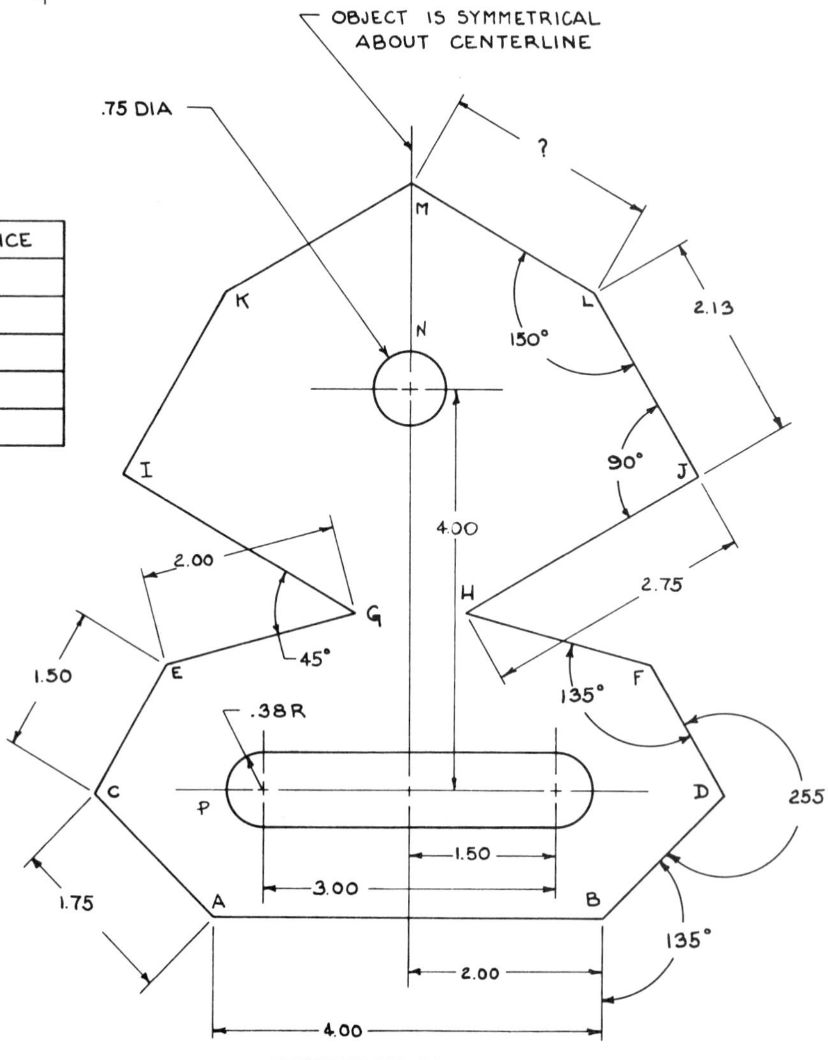

LINE	DISTANCE
LM	
AJ	
GH	
NP	
BK	

FIGURE P3-30

4
GEOMETRIC CONSTRUCTIONS

Unisolid Systems. (Courtesy of McDonnell Douglas Systems Company, St. Louis, Mo.)

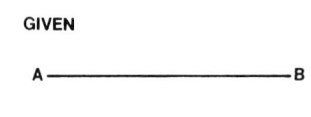

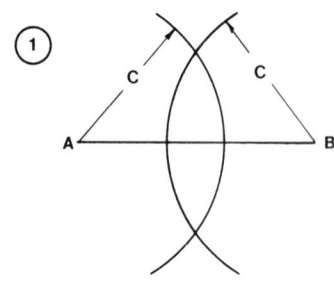

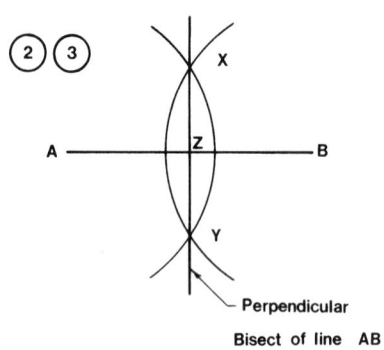

FIGURE 4-1 How to bisect a line: classical method.

FIGURE 4-2 How to bisect a line: computer method.

4-1 INTRODUCTION

In this chapter we present geometric constructions in two different ways: classical construction methods drawn using a straightedge, compass, and so on, and computer methods based on the drawing capabilities of most computer graphic systems. Many computers have geometric construction capabilities built into their permanent memories. Others require additional software, and still others can use their existing capabilities to mimic the classical methods.

4-2 PERPENDICULAR BISECT OF A LINE

Figure 4-1 shows the classical construction method for drawing a perpendicular bisect of line. The procedure is as follows:

1. Given a line AB, draw two equal arcs of any radius C greater than $\frac{1}{2}AB$ using points A and B as centerpoints.

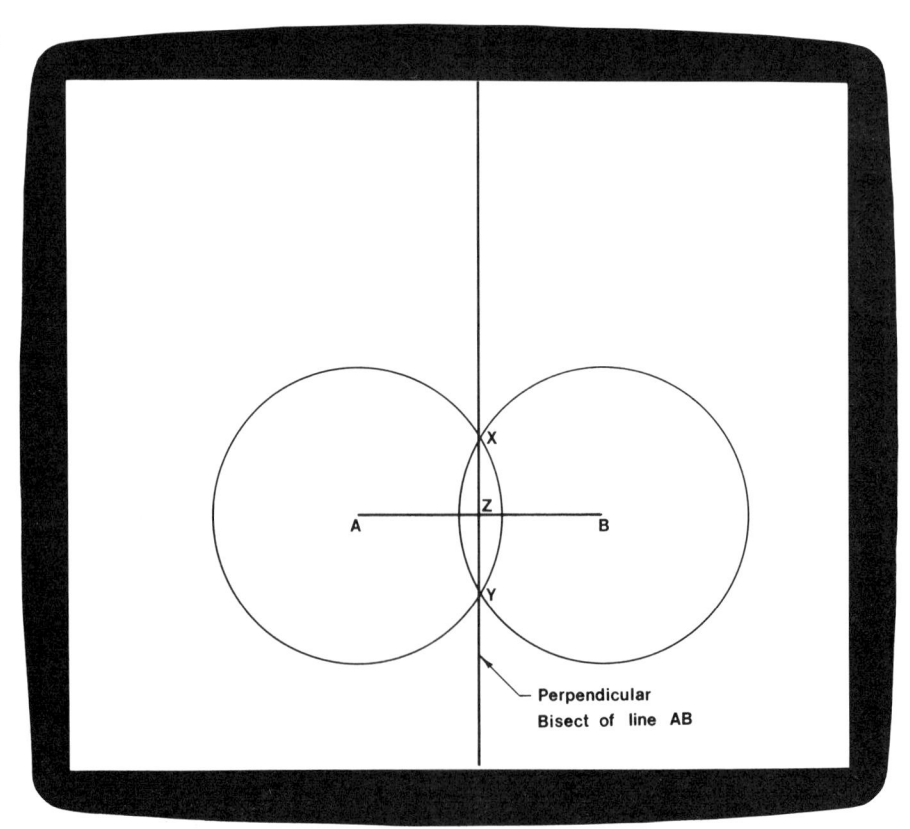

Sec. 4-3   Line Pependicular to Another Line through a Given Point   61

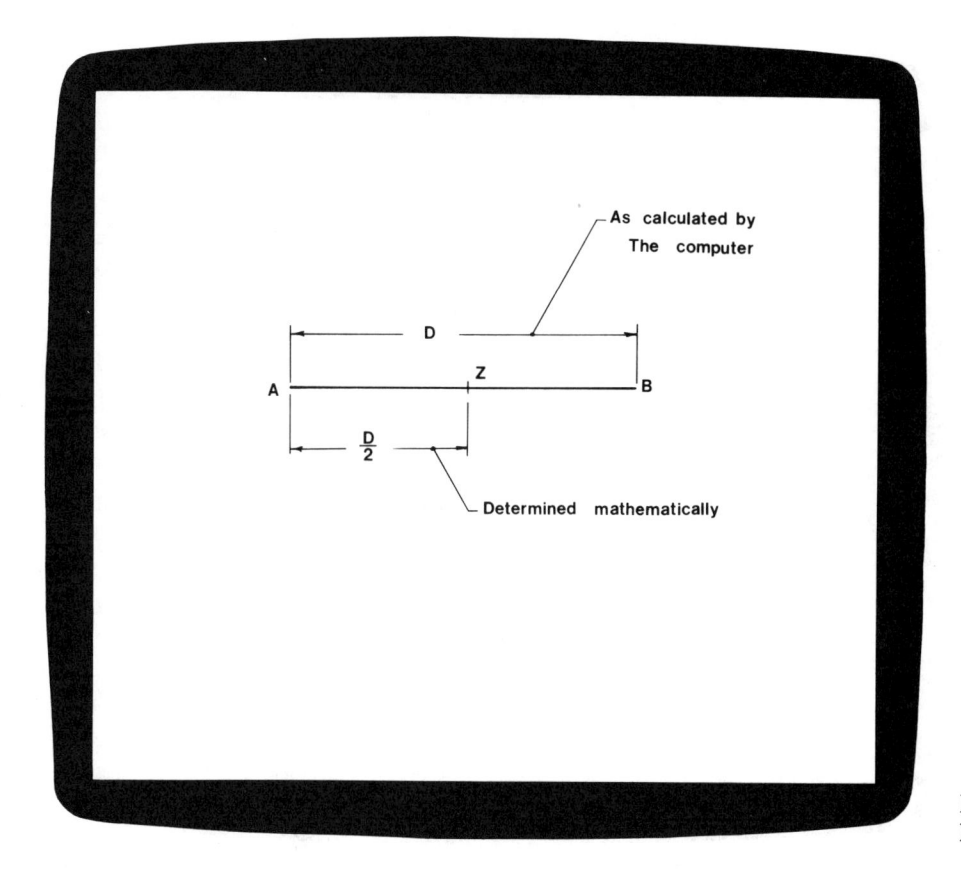

FIGURE 4-3   How to bisect a line using mathematics.

2. Label the intersection of the two arcs X and Y as shown.
3. Draw a line XY. Label the intersection of line XY and AB as Z.

Line XY is perpendicular to line AB and line AZ equals line ZB.

Figure 4-2 shows the method outlined in Figure 4-1 drawn using a computer graphic system. The procedure is the same except that the arcs have been replaced by circles.

Another method used by some computer graphics systems to determine the perpendicular bisect of a line is to have the computer first calculate the length of the line. The calculated distance can then be divided mathematically and used to define the distance to the line's bisect point (Figure 4-3).

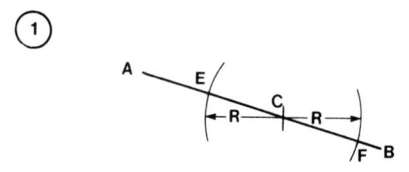

Section 4-3 explains how to draw a line perpendicular to a line through a given point.

FIGURE 4-4   How to draw a line perpendicular to a line through a given point: classical method.

4-3 LINE PERPENDICULAR TO ANOTHER LINE THROUGH A GIVEN POINT

Figure 4-4 shows the classical construction method for drawing a line perpendicular to another line through a given point. The procedure is as follows:

1. Given a line AB and a point C on line AB, draw two equal arcs of any length R through line AB using point C as the centerpoint. Label the intersection points E and F as shown.

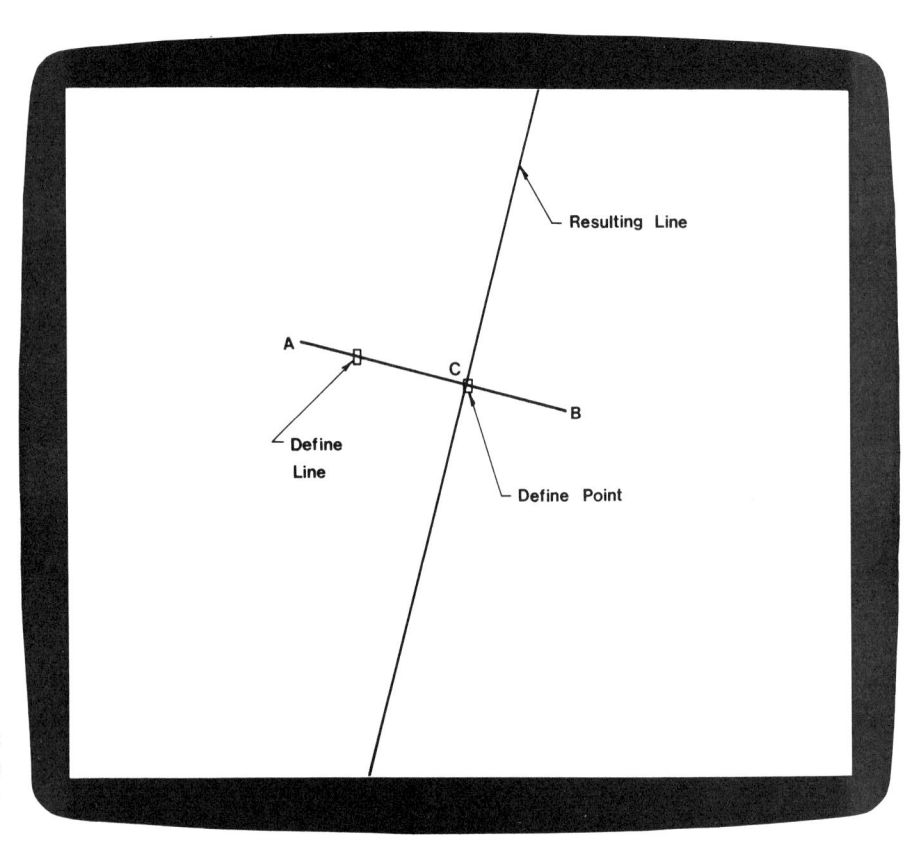

FIGURE 4-5 How to draw a line perpendicular to a line through a given point: computer method.

FIGURE 4-6 How to draw a line perpendicular to a line through a given point: computer method.

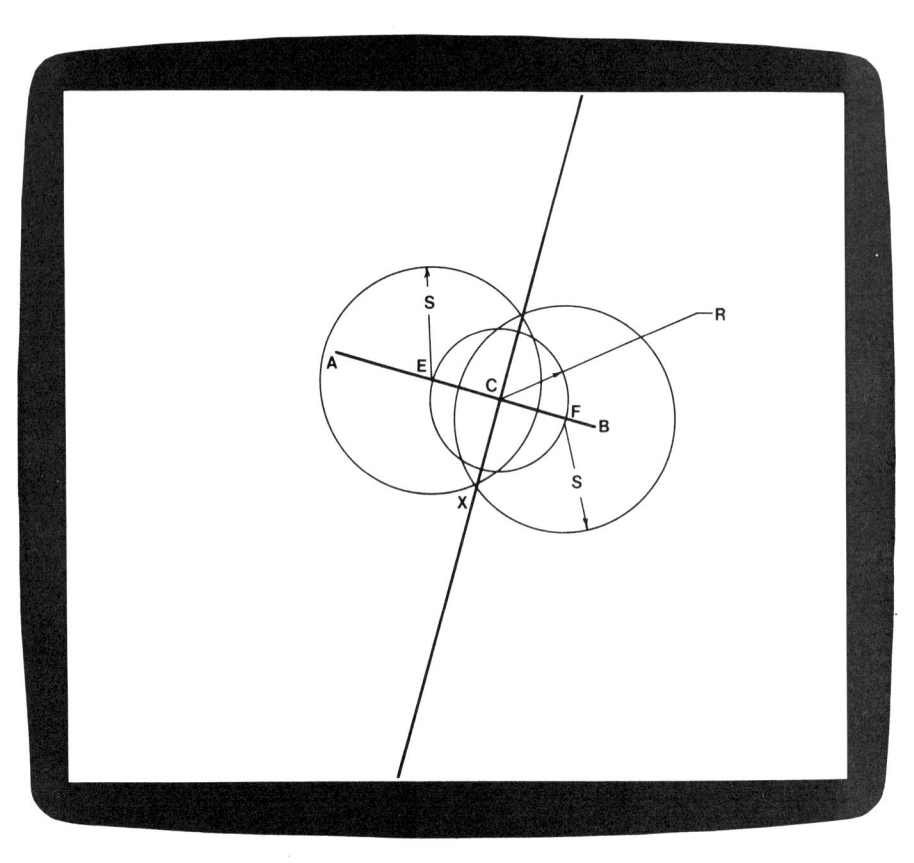

2. Draw two equal arcs of any length S using points E and F as centerpoints. The two arcs must intersect each as shown. The intersection of arcs S is defined as point X. Line CX is the perpendicular to line AB through point C.

Figure 4-5 shows how a computer graphic system with built-in geometric construction capabilities might be used to construct a line perpendicular to another line through a given point. Line AB and point C are inputted into the computer, which has been set to the correct mode. The result is a line of infinite length through point C perpendicular to line AB.

Figure 4-6 shows the classical construction of Figure 4-1 drawn using a computer graphics systems. The construction requires the computer to draw only lines and circles, and to be able to recognize accurately an intersection of lines as a point. The procedure is as follows:

1. Given a line AB and a point C on line AB, draw a circle of any radius R using point C as the centerpoint. Label the intersection points of the circle with the line as E and F.
2. Draw two circles of radius S using points E and F as centerpoints. The two circles or radius S must intersect. Define the intersection of the two circles below line AB as point X. Line CX is perpendicular to line AB through point C.

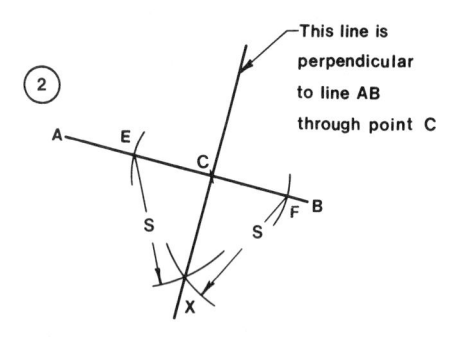

FIGURE 4-4 (cont.)

4-4 LINE DIVIDED INTO EQUAL PARTS

Figure 4-7 shows the classical construction method for dividing a line into equal parts. The procedure is as follows:

1. Given line FG and the requirement to divide the line into five equal parts, draw another line through point F at any acute angle relative to line FG.
2. Define equal-length spaces along the line drawn in step 1. The number of spaces must equal the number of divisions required. In this example five equal spaces are required.
3. Draw line G-5 as shown.
4. Draw lines parallel to line G-5 through each of the spaces defined in step 2. The intersection of these lines with line FG will divide line FG into the required number of equal spaces.

Figure 4-8 shows a mathematical solution possible on some computer graphic systems. Any line can be divided into any number of parts by dividing the total length of the line by the total number of parts required. In the example shown, line FG is divided into five equal parts. The length of one line segment equals FG/5.

Figure 4-9 shows the classical construction of Figure 4-7 drawn using a computer graphic system. The procedure is as follows:

1. Given line FG, draw another line through point F at any acute angle relative to line FG. In the example shown, a horizontal construction line was drawn. Horizontal and vertical lines are easily drawn using computers, so are used most frequently.

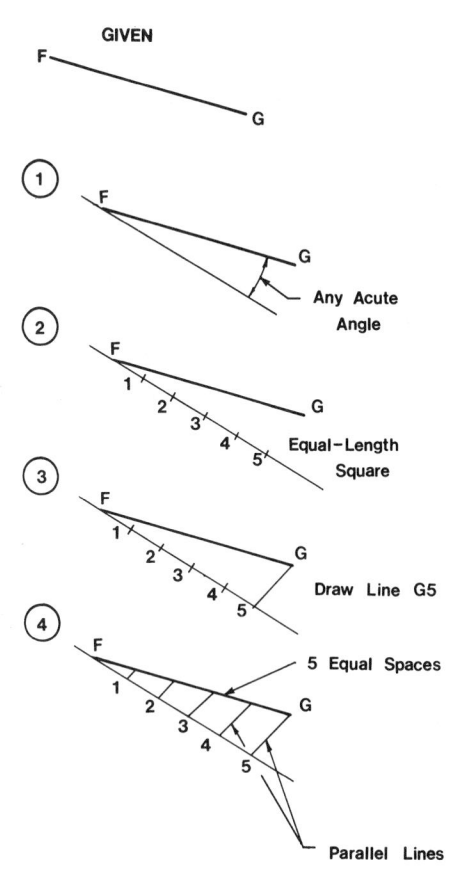

FIGURE 4-7 How to divide a line into equal parts: classical method.

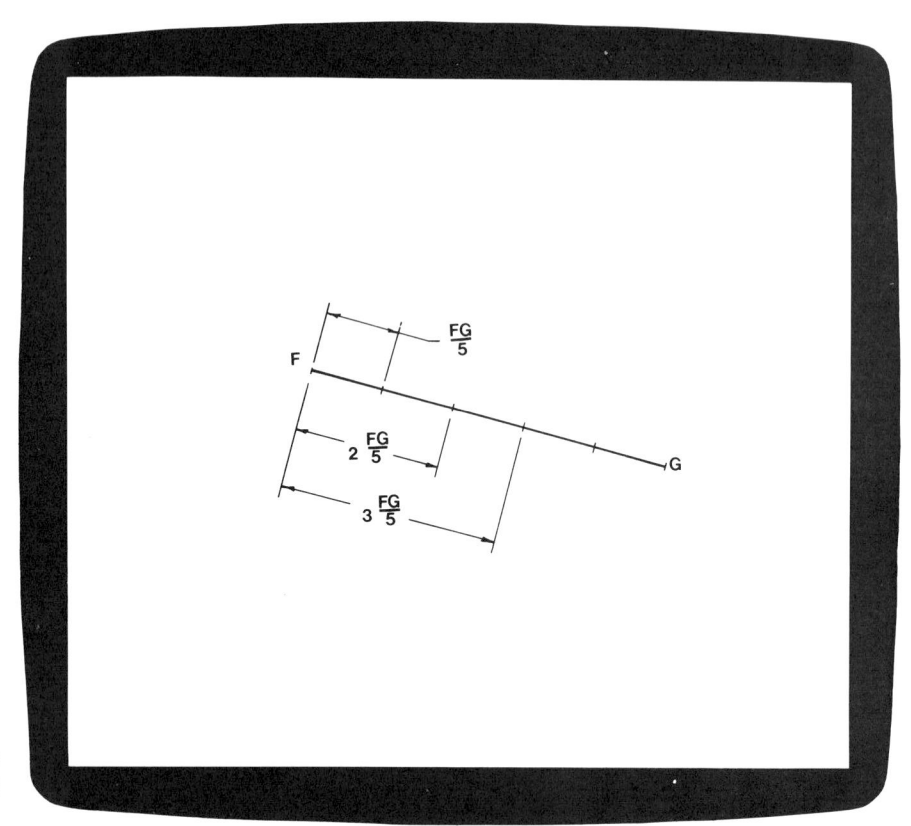

FIGURE 4-8 How to divide a line into equal parts using mathematics.

FIGURE 4-9 How to divide a line into equal parts: computer method.

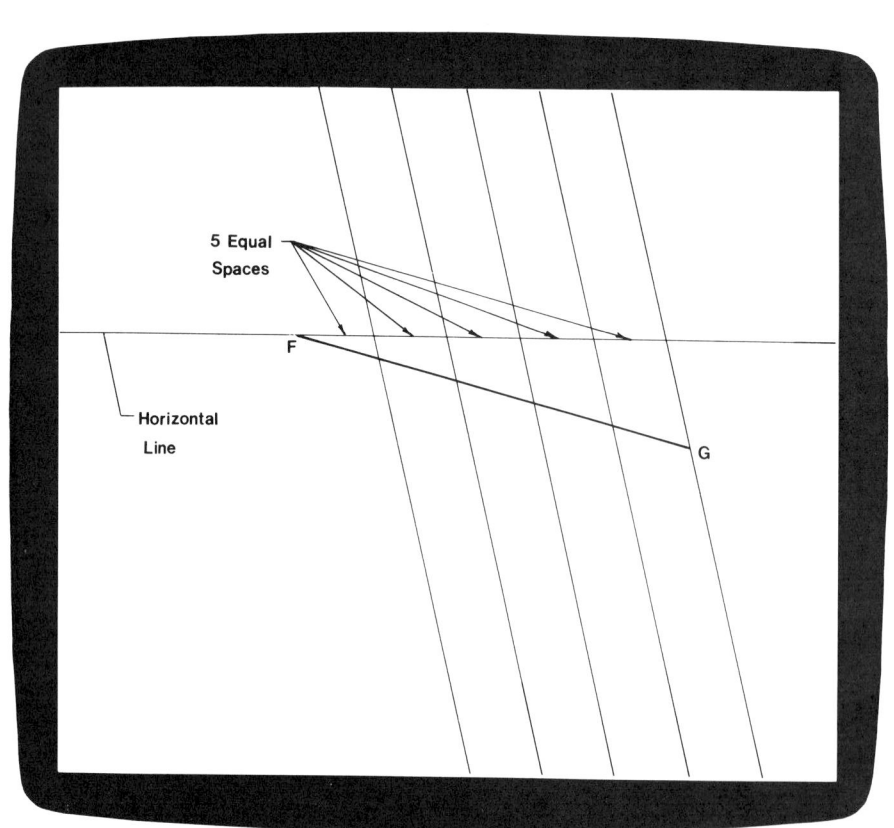

Sec. 4-5 Line Tangent to a Circle through a Given Point on the Circle 65

2. Define equal-length spaces along the line drawn in step 1. In the example shown, the spacing was specifying distances from point F of 10, 20, 30, and 40, respectively.
3. Draw line G-5 as shown.
4. Draw lines parallel to line G-5 through each of the spaces defined in step 2. Computer graphics systems usually have the ability to measure lengths and angles with extreme accuracy, so the angle between line G-5 and the horizontal construction line was determined using the computer's measuring capability and then used as an input value for the direction of other lines. A parallel-line function could also be used, if available.

The intersections of the lines drawn in step 4 will divide line FG into the required number of equal parts.

4-5 LINE TANGENT TO A CIRCLE THROUGH A GIVEN POINT ON THE CIRCLE

Figure 4-10 shows the classical construction method for drawing a line tangent to a circle through a given point on the circle using a 45° triangle and a straightedge (T-square). The procedure is as follows:

1. Given a circle and a point T on the circle, align a straightedge with the centerpoint of the circle and point T as shown.
2. Hold the straightedge in place and slide the 45° triangle so that the opposite leg from that aligned in step 1 intersects point T. This leg is tangent to the circle and intersects point T. Draw a line using the triangle edge as a guide.

Figure 4-11 shows a line tangent to a circle through a given point drawn using a computer graphics system. The construction is based on

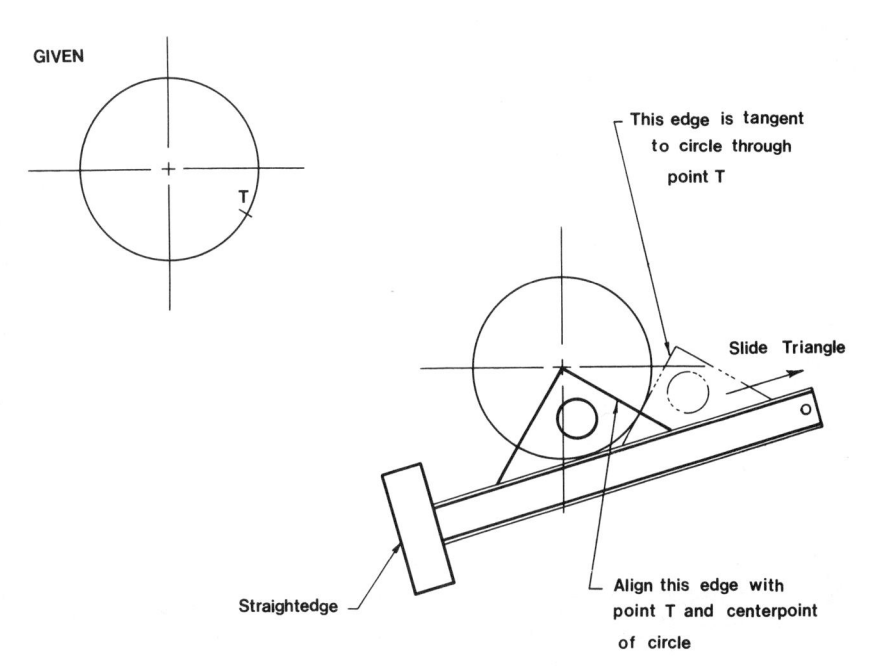

FIGURE 4-10 How to draw a line tangent to a circle through a given point: classical method.

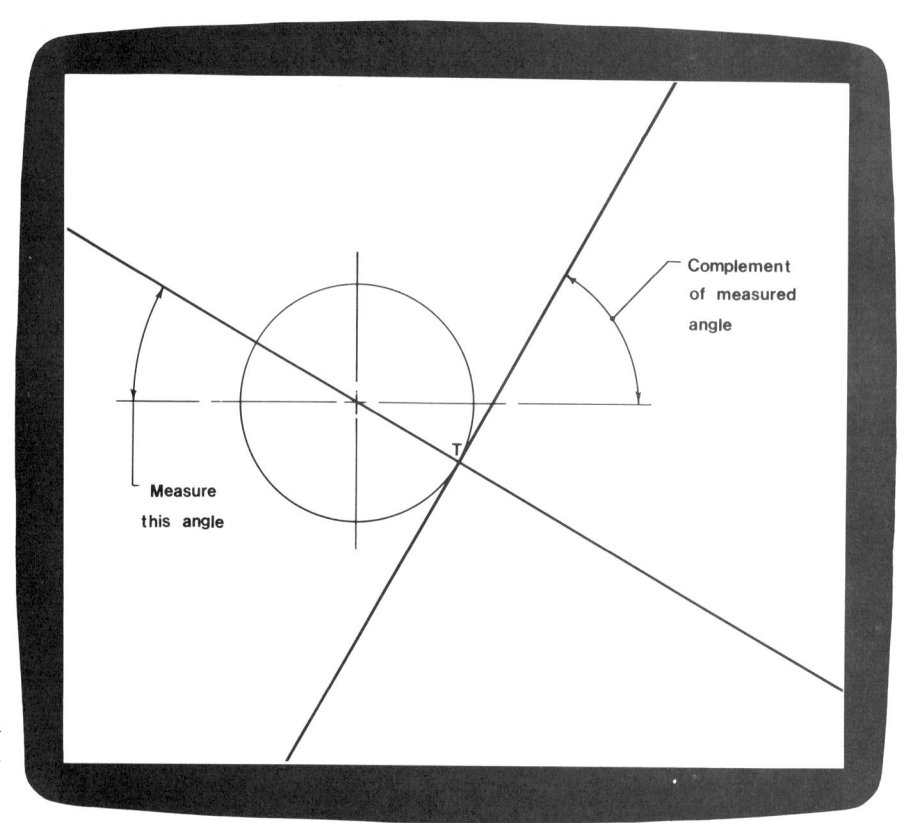

FIGURE 4-11 How to draw a line tangent to a circle through a given point: computer method.

FIGURE 4-12 How to draw a line tangent to a circle through a given point: computer method.

Sec. 4-6   Line Parallel to Another Line

the system's ability to measure angles accurately. The procedure is as follows:

1. Draw a line through the centerpoint of the circle and the point.
2. Measure the angle between the line drawn in step 1 and the horizontal axis of the circle. Define the complement of the angle. Use the complementary angle as an input to draw a line through the known point.

Figure 4-12 shows another computer method. The procedure is as follows:

1. Draw a line through the centerpoint of the circle and the given point.
2. Apply the procedure outlined in Section 4-2.

4-6 LINE PARALLEL TO ANOTHER LINE

Figure 4-13 shows the classical construction method drawing a line parallel to a given line. The procedure is as follows:

1. Given a line *JK*, set a compass for length *D* where *D* is the distance between the parallel lines and draw two arcs as shown. The centerpoint for each arc is located anywhere on line *JK*.
2. Draw a line tangent to the two arcs. This line is parallel to line *JK* at a distance *R*.

Some computers have standard functions that enable parallel lines to be drawn directly. The results are illustrated in Figure 4-14. Line *JK*

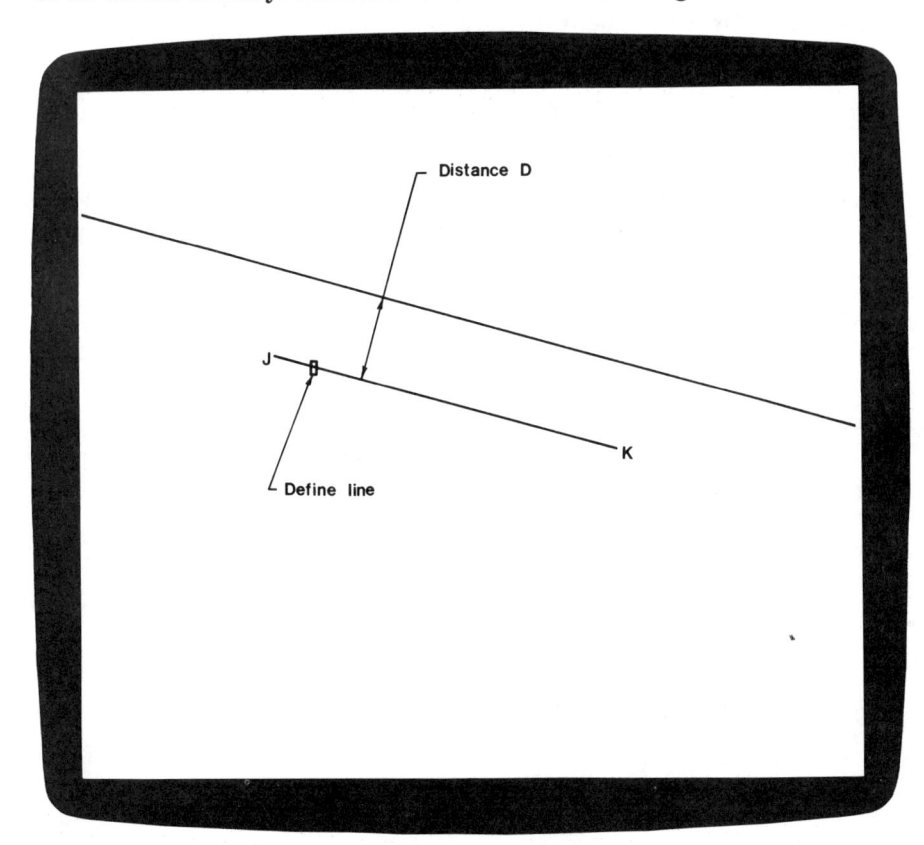

FIGURE 4-13 How to draw a line parallel to a given line: classical method.

FIGURE 4-14 How to draw a line parallel to a given line: computer method.

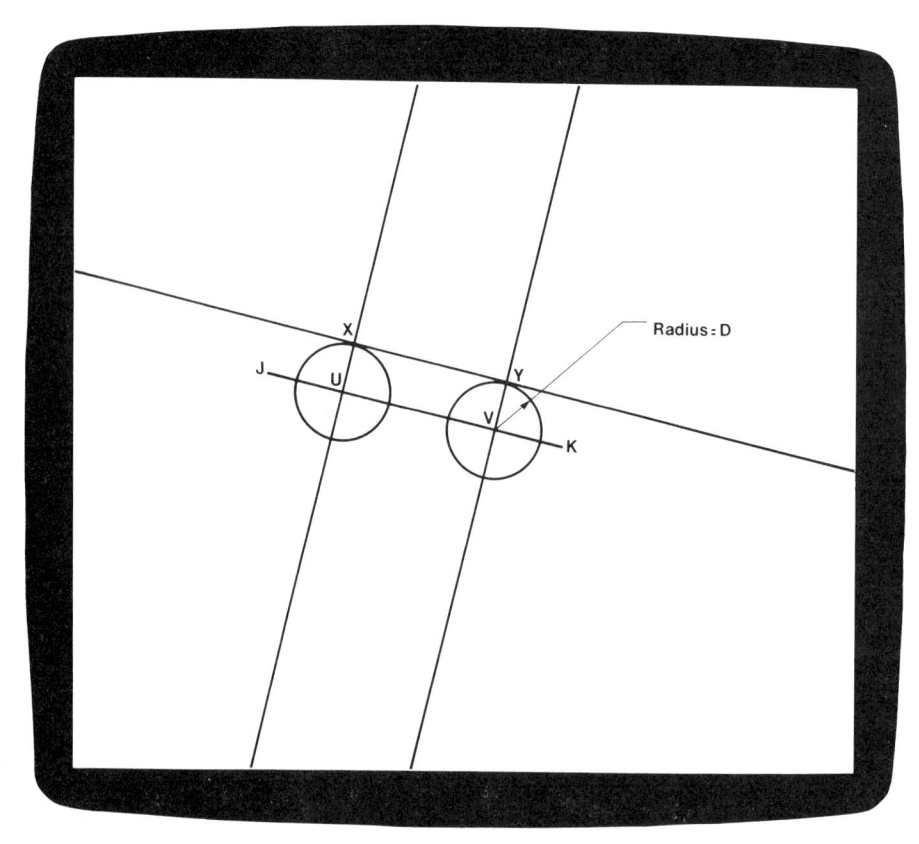

FIGURE 4-15 How to draw a line parallel to a given line: computer method.

is identified and the required distance D inputted (usually via the keyboard). The approximate location of the parallel line is indicated. The result is a line parallel to JK at a distance D.

Figure 4-15 shows a method for drawing parallel lines using a computer graphic system. The procedure is as follows:

1. Draw two circles of radius D whose centerpoints are located on line JK. Label the centerpoints as U and V.
2. Draw lines, perpendicular to line JK, through points U and V.
3. Label the intersections of the two perpendicular lines drawn in step 2 with the circles as points X and Y. Draw a line through points X and Y. This line is parallel to line JK at a distance D.

4-7 TRIANGLES

There are several different construction methods used to draw triangles where the classical method is identical to that used by computer graphic systems. For example, in Figure 4-16, three points are located and then joined using straight lines to form a triangle. Figure 4-17 defines a triangle by giving two lengths and the angle between them. Figure 4-18 defines a triangle by giving the length of one side and two angles.

Figure 4-19 shows the classical method for drawing a triangle given only the length of each side. The procedure is as follows:

1. Draw one side. Define the line as TS.
2. Draw an arc of length equal to one of the other given leg lengths using point T as a centerpoint.

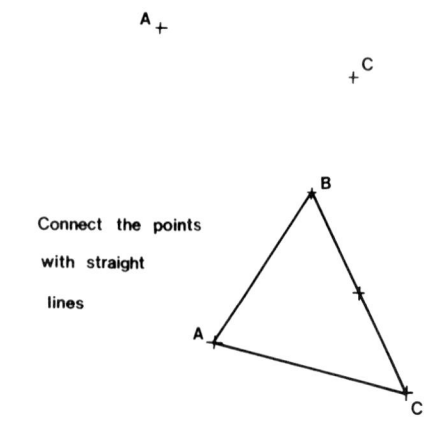

FIGURE 4-16 How to draw a triangle given three points.

Sec. 4-7　Triangles

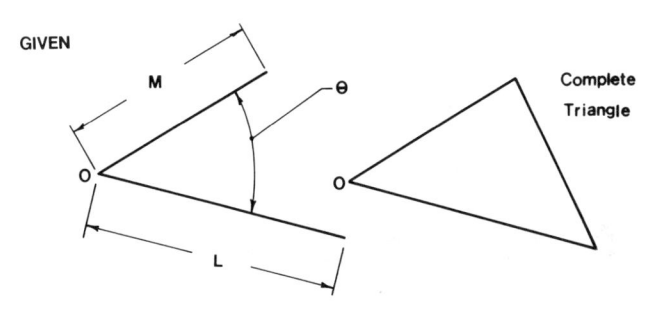

FIGURE 4-17 How to draw a triangle given two legs and the angle between the legs.

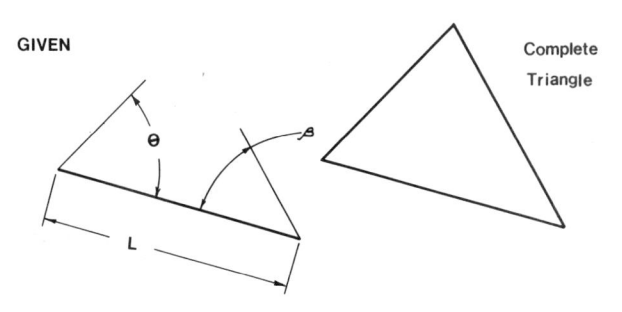

FIGURE 4-18 How to draw a triangle given a leg and two adjacent angles.

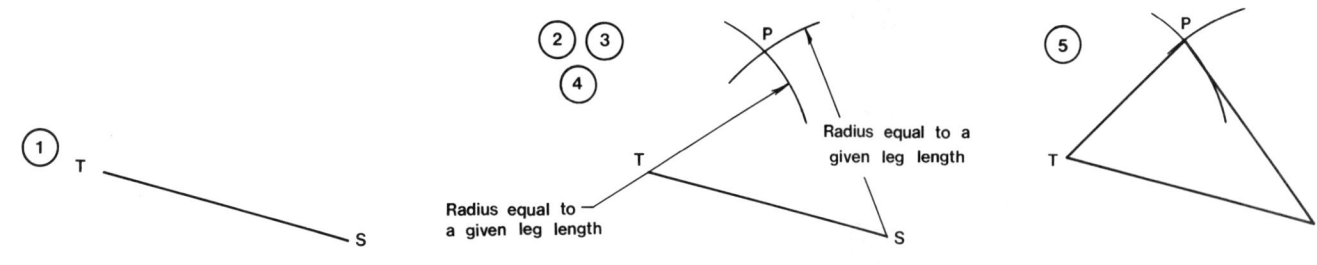

FIGURE 4-19 How to draw a triangle given three legs: classical method.

3. Draw a second arc of length equal to the length of the remaining defined leg using point S as centerpoint.
4. Define the intersection of the two arcs as point P. Join points T, S, and P to form the required triangle.

Figure 4-20 shows the method outlined in Figure 4-19 as drawn using a computer graphic system. The only difference between the two methods is that the computer method uses circles instead of arcs.

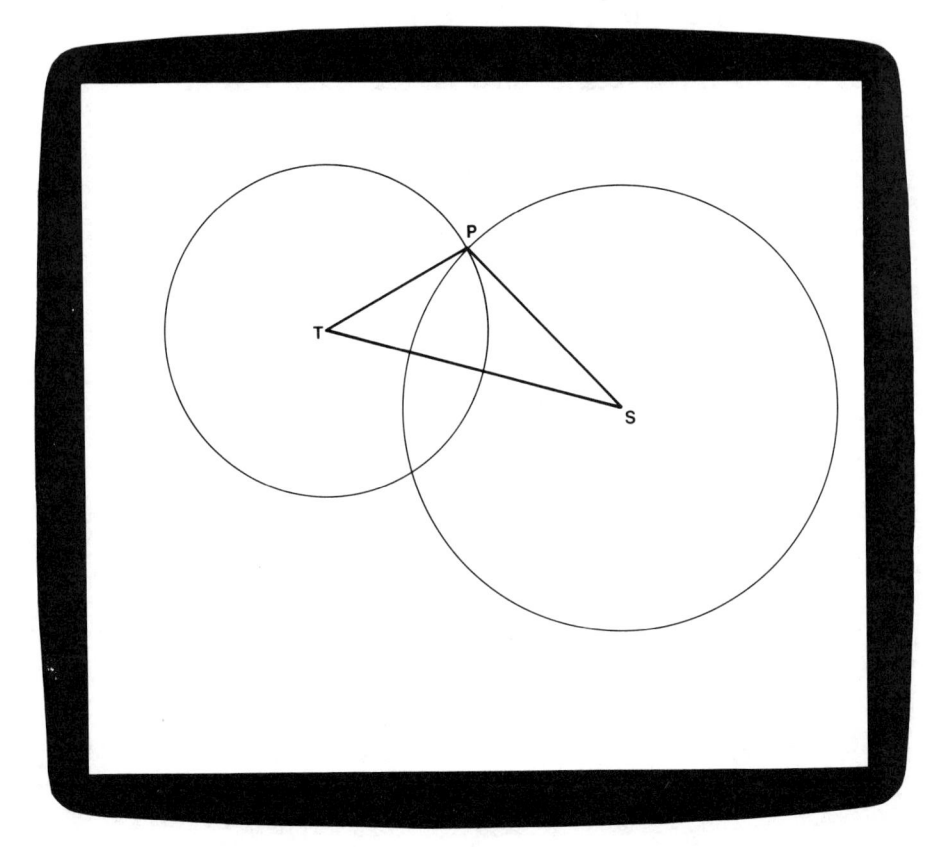

FIGURE 4-20 How to draw a triangle given three legs: computer method.

4-8 SQUARES

There are several different methods that can be used to construct squares. The square in Figure 4-21 was created by first locating the four corner points, then joining them with straight lines.

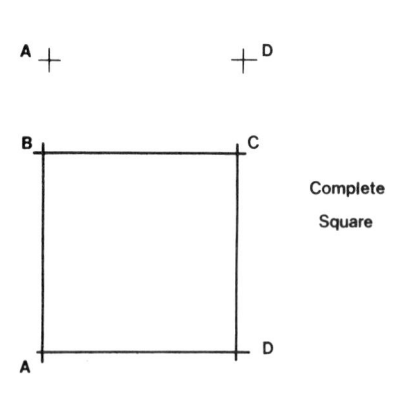

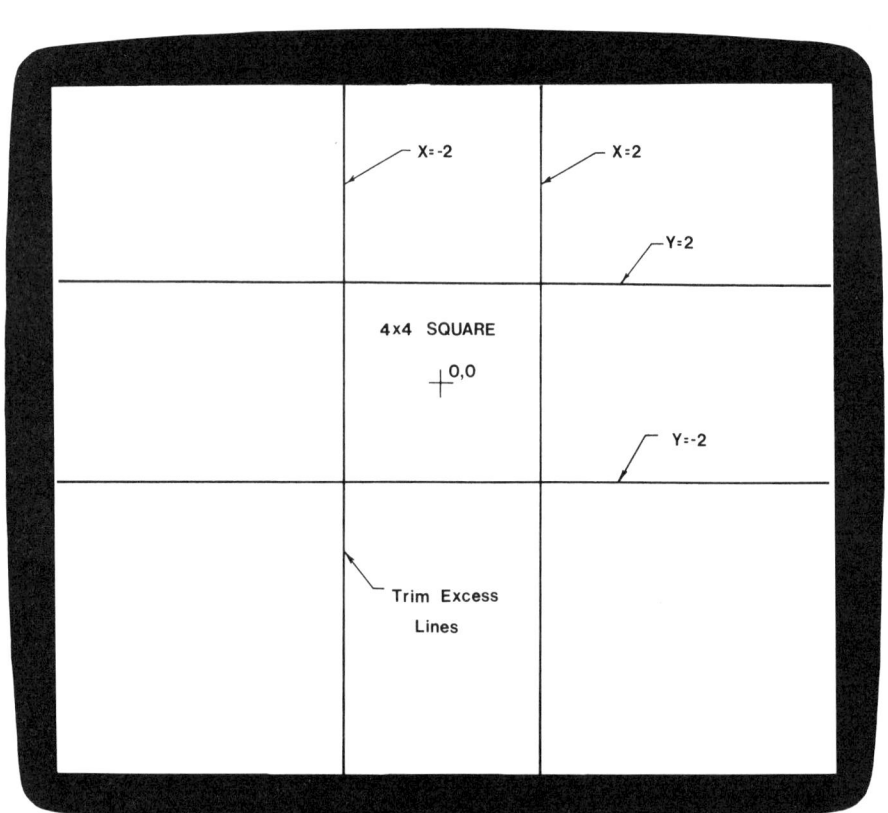

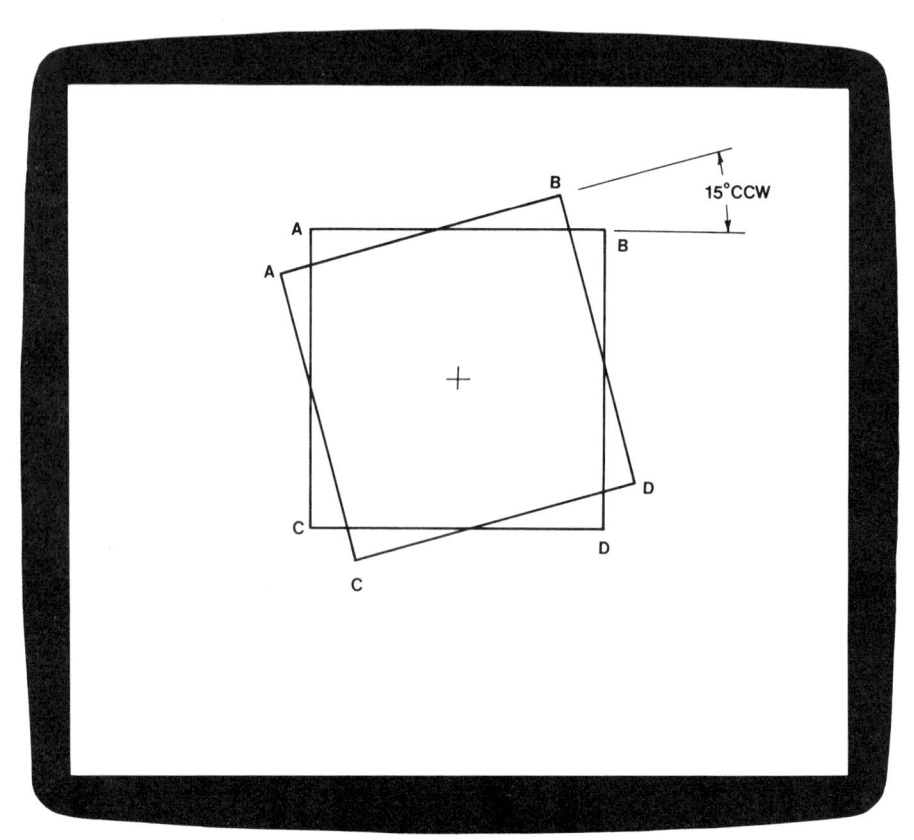

FIGURE 4-21 How to draw a square given four points.

FIGURE 4-22 How to draw a square.

FIGURE 4-23 Square rotated 15° about its centerpoint.

Sec. 4-8 Squares

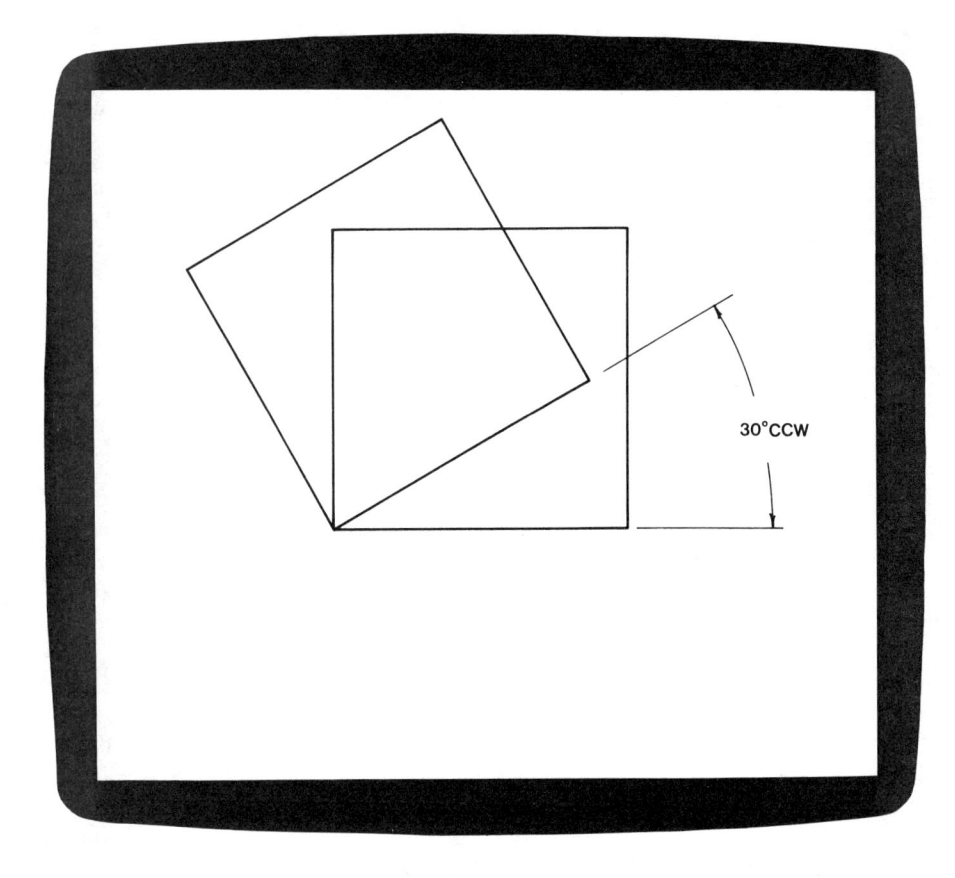

FIGURE 4-24 Square rotated 30° about a corner.

The square in Figure 4-22 was created on a computer graphic system capable of drawing horizontal and vertical lines through given coordinate points. Two horizontal lines of infinite length were drawn through coordinate points $Y = 2$ and $Y = -2$, and two vertical lines were drawn through coordinate points $X = 2$ and $X = -2$. The lines were then trimmed to form a 4 × 4 square.

Once drawn, a square can be rotated into other orientations. Figure 4-23 shows a square rotated 15° counterclockwise about a centerpoint. Figure 4-24 shows a square rotated 30° clockwise about a corner.

Figure 4-25 shows the classical method for drawing a square given the length of a side. The procedure is as follows:

1. Draw one side and label it *EF*.
2. Draw a second side 90° to the first using the method outlined in Section 4-2. Label the line *EH*.
3. Draw two arcs of length equal to *EF* using points *H* and *F* as centerpoints. Define the intersection of the two arcs as point *G*.
4. Draw lines *HG* and *FG* to form a square.

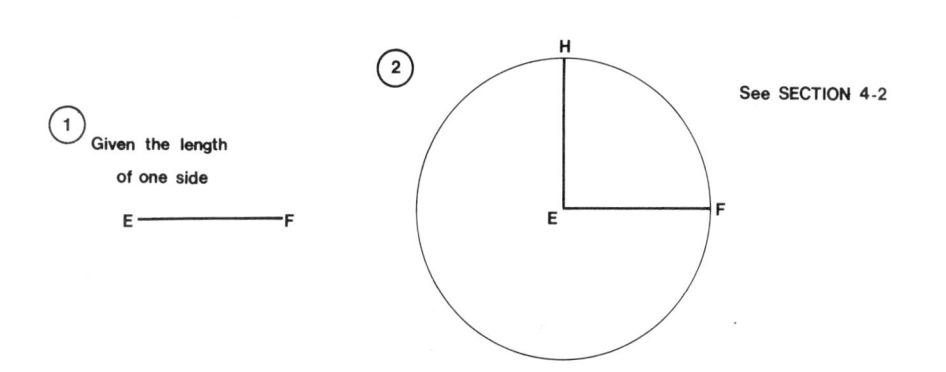

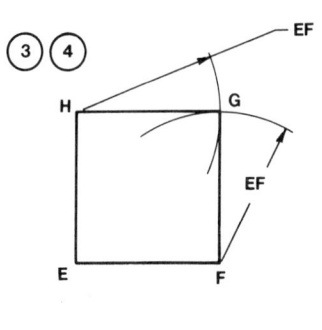

FIGURE 4-25 How to draw a square given the length of one side: classical method.

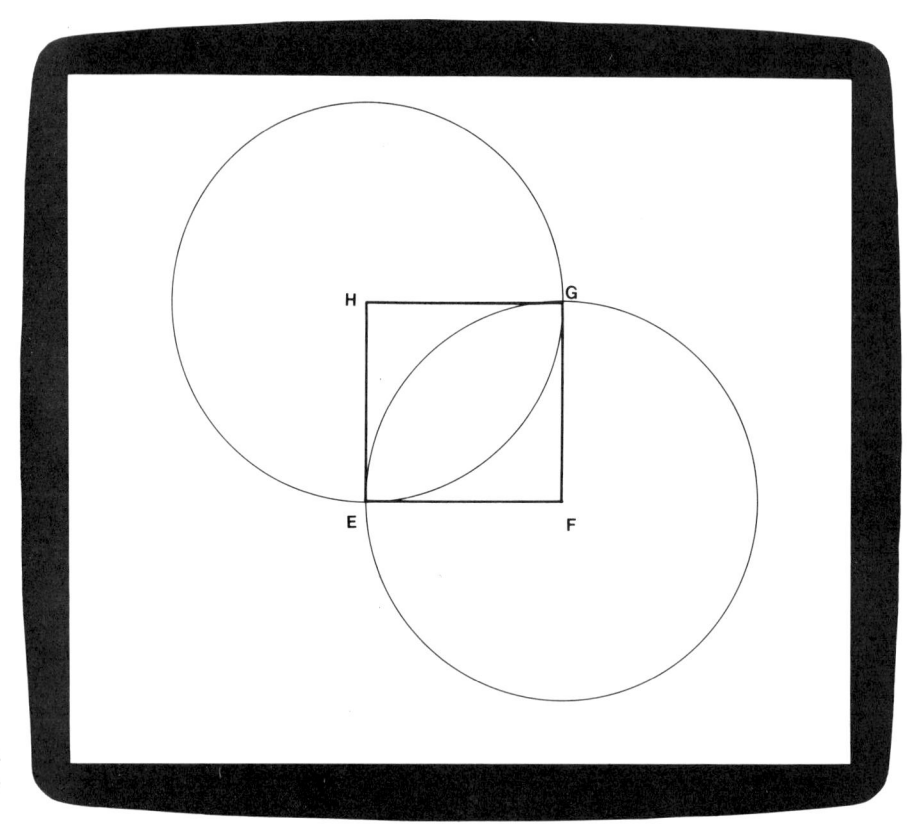

FIGURE 4-26 How to draw a square given the length of one side: computer method.

Figure 4-26 shows the method outlined in Figure 4-25 drawn using a computer graphics system. The only difference is that the arcs drawn in step 3 are replaced by circles. In general, square shapes are more easily drawn using computer graphic systems by defining points or using horizontal and vertical lines, then rotating and moving the square into position.

4-9 PENTAGONS

Figure 4-27 shows the classical construction method for drawing a pentagon. The method inscribes the pentagon within a given circle. The radius of the circle is approximately 0.85 times as long as the length of one of the sides of the pentagon. For example, a pentagon with a leg length of 2.40 has a circle radius equal to 0.85(2.40) or 2.04.

Given a circle in which to inscribe a pentagon, the procedure is as follows:

1. Draw a circle and a perpendicular axis about its centerpoint as shown.
2. Bisect the radius OR and label the bisect point A (see Section 4-2).
3. Draw an arc of length AB with A as the centerpoint so that the arc intersects the horizontal axis as shown. Label the intersection C.
4. Draw an arc of length BC with B as the centerpoint so that the arc intersects the circle. Label the intersection D. The length BD equals the length of each side of the pentagon.

Sec. 4-9 Pentagons

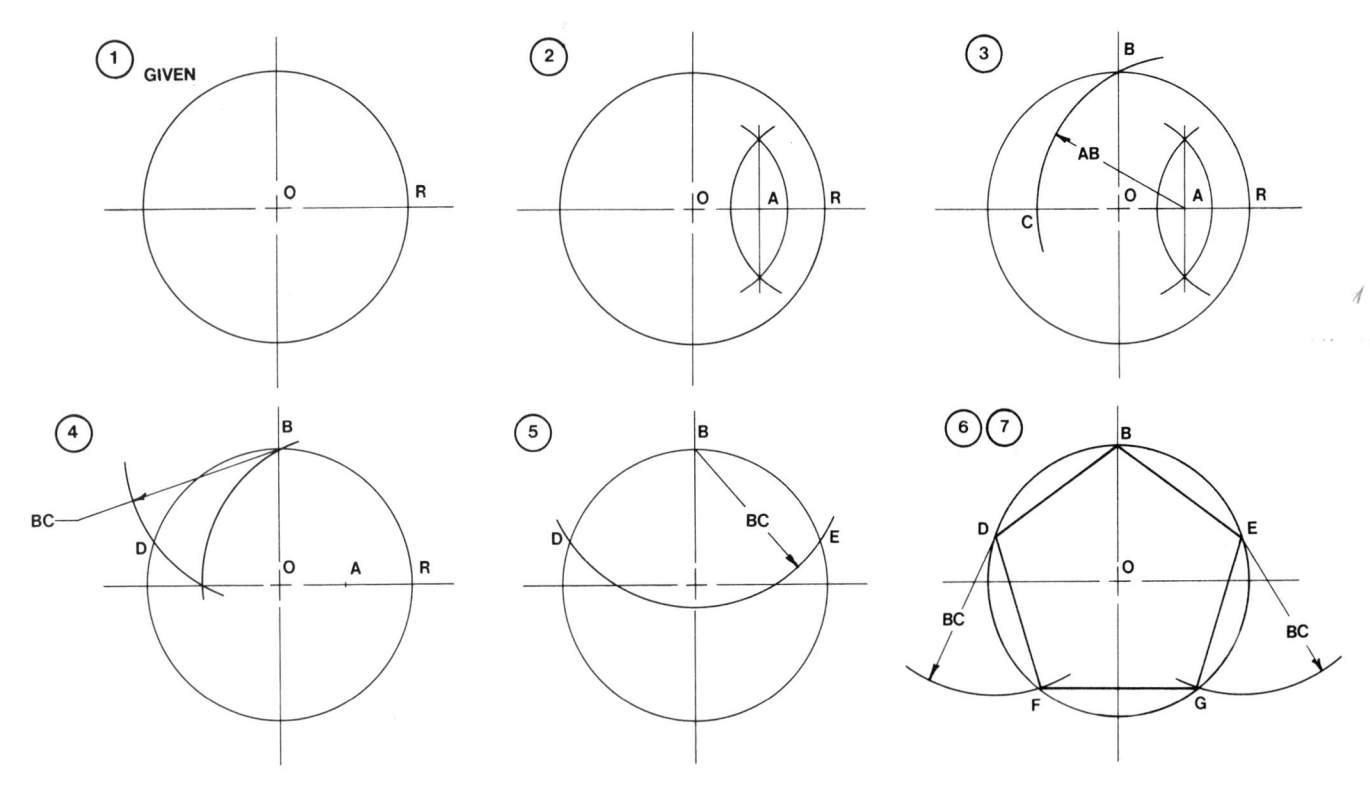

FIGURE 4-27 How to draw a pentagon: classical method.

5. Draw an arc *BD* using point *B* as a centerpoint so that it intersects the circle a second time as shown. Label the intersection *E*.
6. Draw two arcs of length *BD* using points *D* and *E* as centerpoints, respectively. Label the intersections *F* and *G*.
7. Join points *B, D, F, G,* and *E* to form a pentagon.

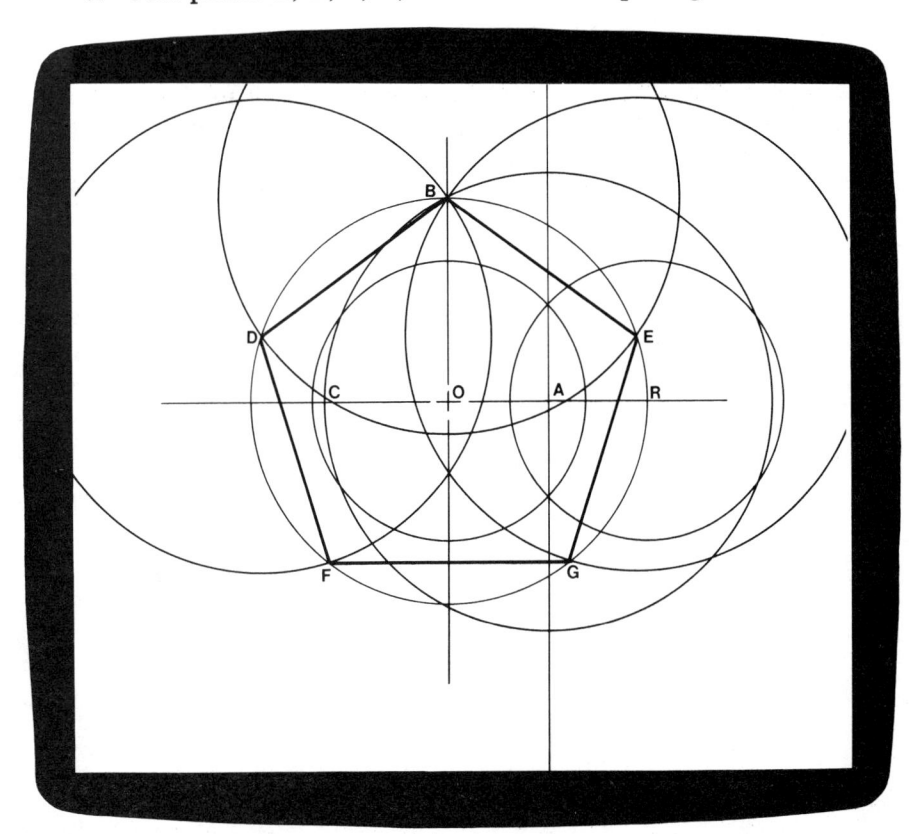

FIGURE 4-28 How to draw a pentagon: computer graphics method.

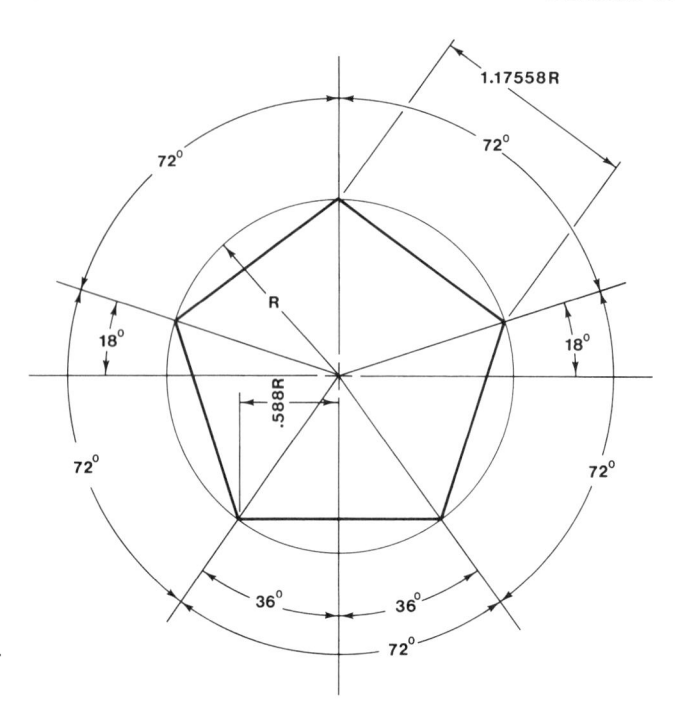

FIGURE 4-29 The mathematical definition of a pentagon.

Figure 4-28 shows the procedure described above drawn using a computer graphic system. The procedure is the same except that circles were used in place of arcs. Once the needed points are established, the construction circles can be erased.

Figure 4-29 gives a mathematical definition of a pentagon. It is sometimes easier to use mathematical inputs rather than to manipulate and erase circles and lines.

4-10 HEXAGONS

The size of a hexagon is defined in one of two ways: the distance across the flats or the distance across the corners. The distance across the flats is the more common way of specifying hexagon size. Hexagon heads on screws, bolts, and nuts are sized by the distance across their flats. Figure 4-30 shows how to interpret the two distances.

FIGURE 4-30 Distances across the flats and across the corners of a hexagon.

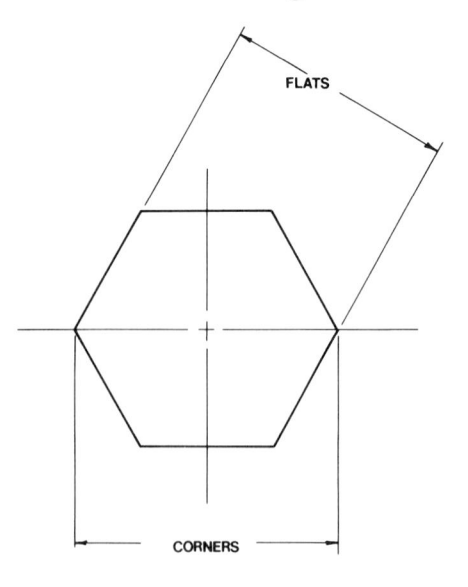

Figure 4-31 shows the classical method of constructing a hexagon of a specific distance across the flats. The procedure is as follows:

1. Draw a circle and a perpendicular axis about its centerpoint as shown. The diameter of the circle should equal the distance across the flats of the desired hexagon.
2. Draw two horizontal line segments tangent to the circle.
3. Draw two line segments 60° to the horizontal, tangent to the circle as shown.
4. Draw two more line segments 60° to the horizontal, tangent to the circle as shown.
5. Erase the excess part of the line segments and darken in the hexagon.

Figure 4-32a and b shows the procedure outlined for Figure 4-31 drawn using a computer graphic system. Thirty-degree lines were added

Sec. 4-10 Hexagons

FIGURE 4-31 How to draw a hexagon for a given distance across the flats: classical method.

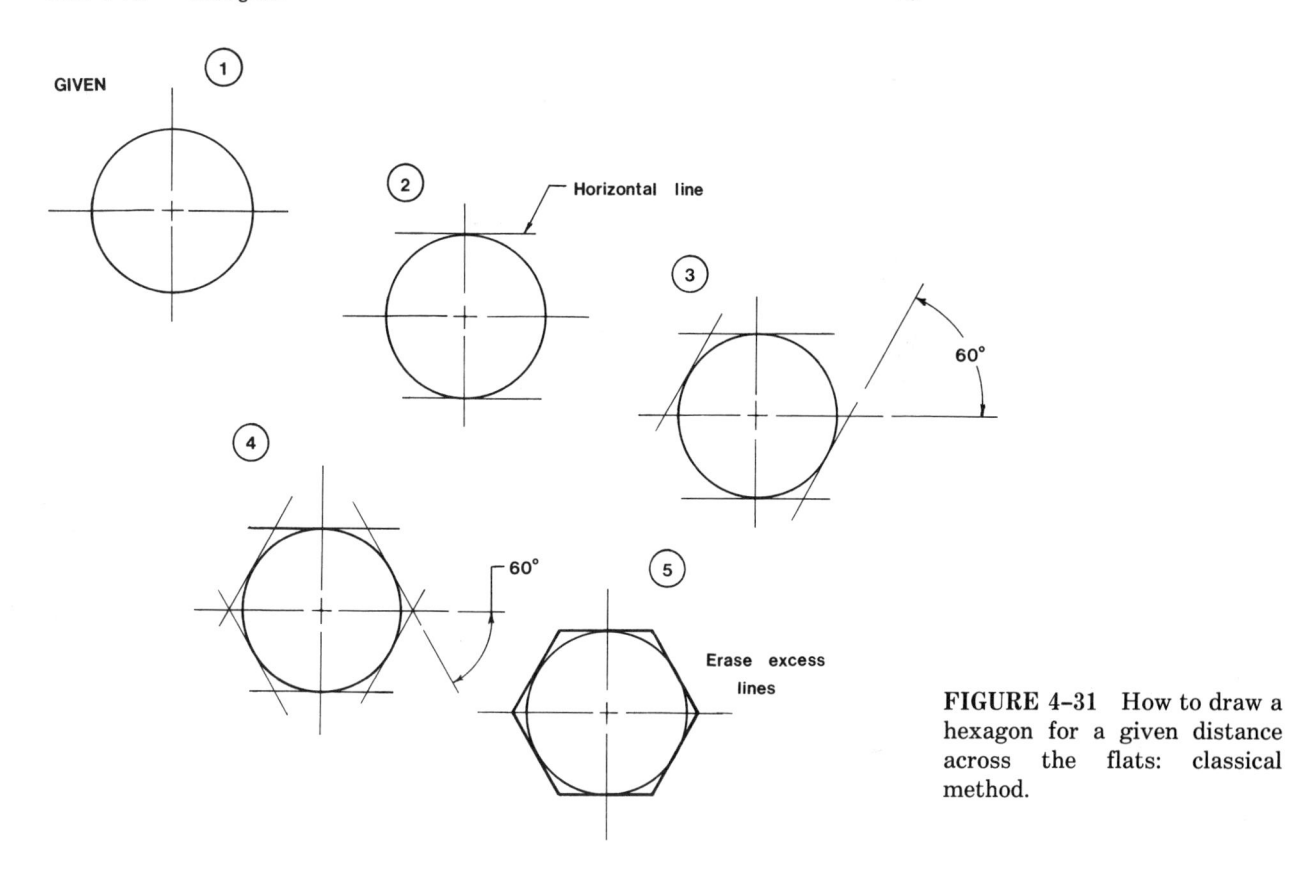

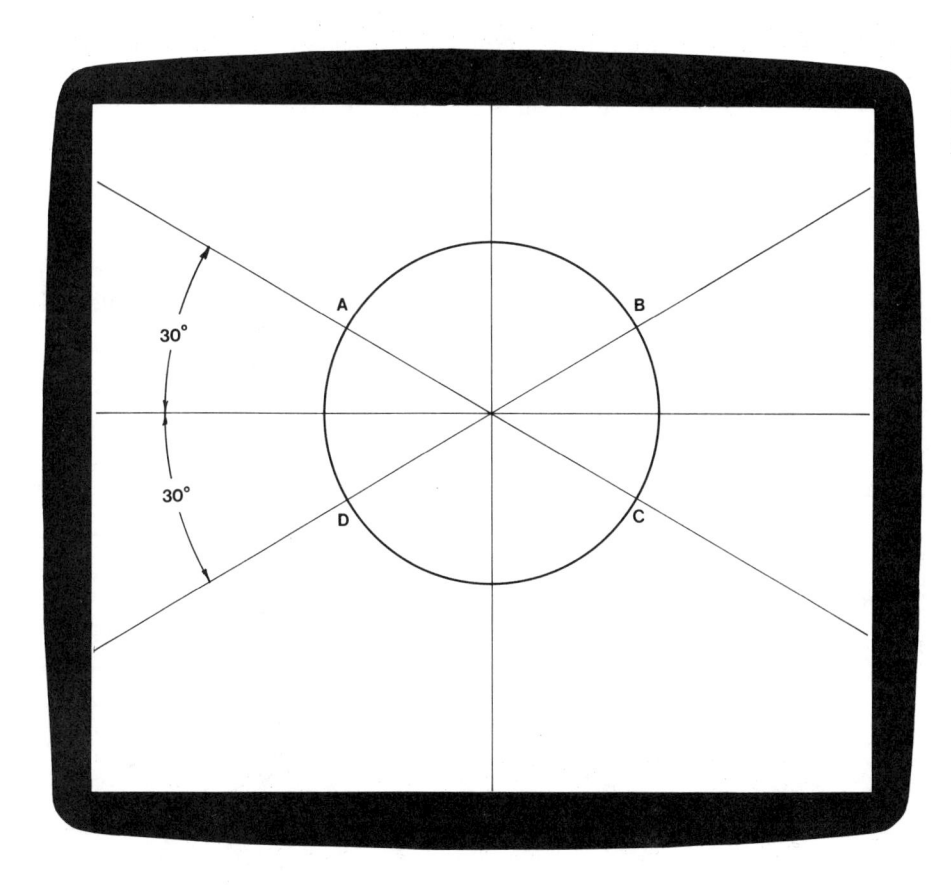

FIGURE 4-32 (a) How to draw a hexagon for a given distance across the flats: computer method.

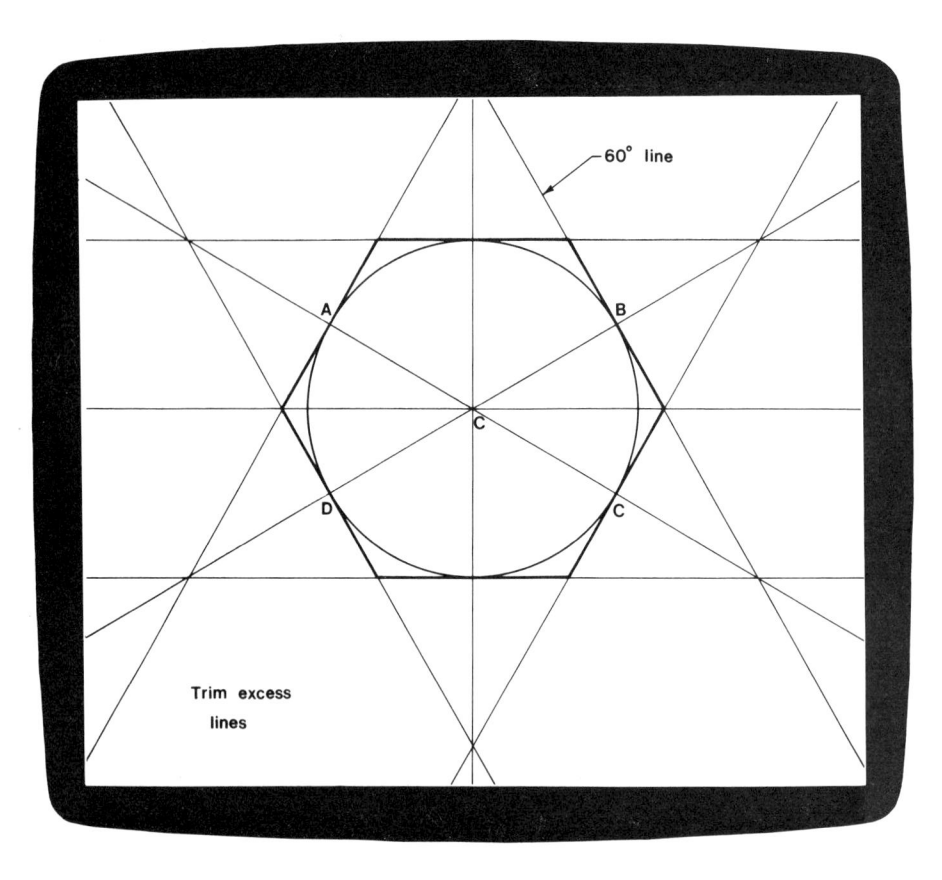

FIGURE 4-32 (b)

to establish points A, B, C, D. Points A, B, C, D were used to define tangency points for the 60° lines. Infinite-length lines were drawn rather than line segments. Once the hexagon shape is established, the lines can be trimmed as needed.

Figure 4-33 shows the classical construction for a hexagon of a specific distance across the corner. The procedure is as follows:

1. Draw a circle and a perpendicular axis about its centerpoint as shown. The diameter of the circle should equal the distance across the corners of the desired hexagon. Label the intersections of the circle and the vertical centerline E and G as shown.
2. Draw arcs of radius EO and GO using points E and G as centerpoints. Label the intersections of the arcs and circle as H, J, K, and L.
3. Draw lines between points EJKGL and H to form the desired hexagon.

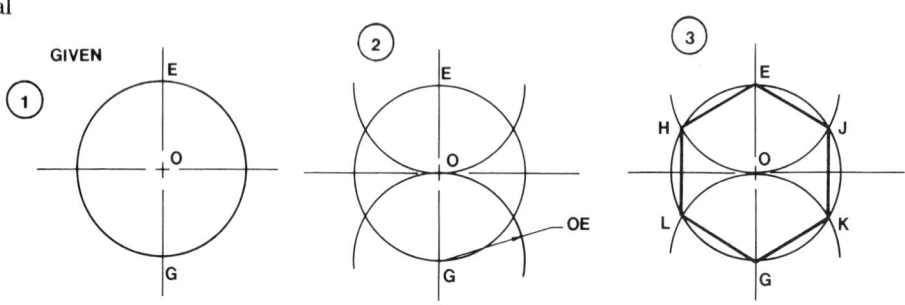

FIGURE 4-33 How to draw a hexagon for a given distance across the corners: classical method.

Sec. 4-11 Octagons

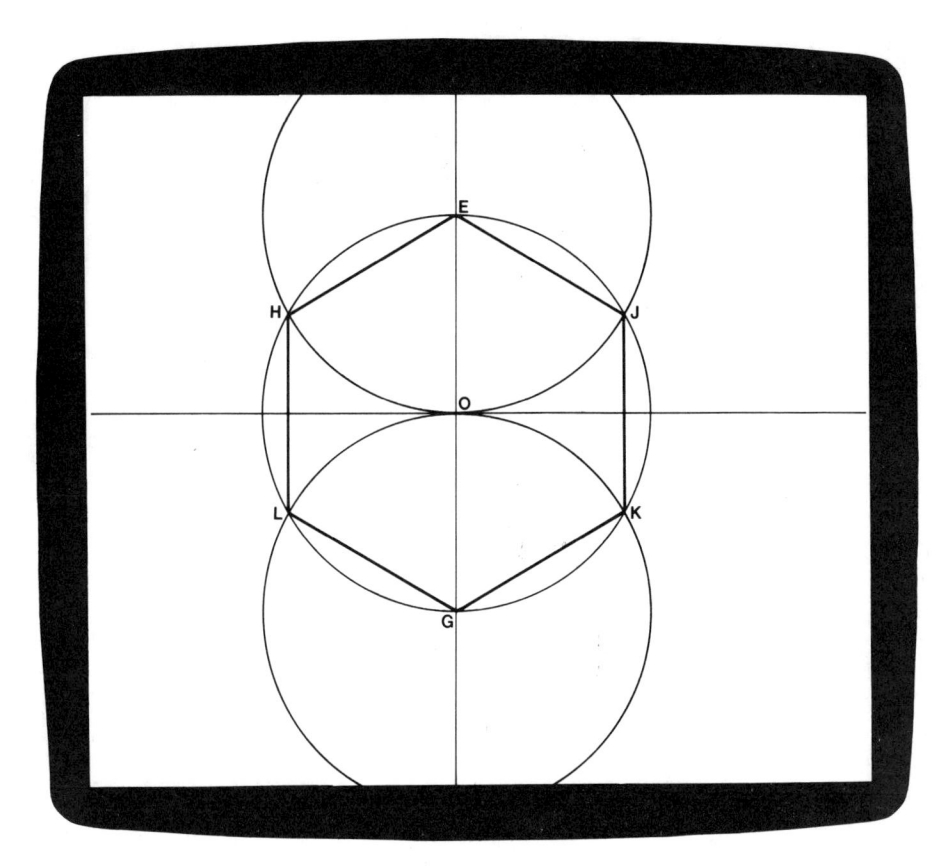

FIGURE 4-34 How to draw a hexagon for a given distance across the corners: computer method.

Figure 4-34 shows the method outlined for Figure 4-33 drawn using a computer graphic system. The method is the same except the arcs were replaced by circles.

4-11 OCTAGONS

Figure 4-35 shows the classical construction method for an octagon. The procedure is as follows:

1. Draw a circle and a perpendicular axis system about its centerpoint as shown. The diameter of the circle should be equal to the distance across the flats of the octagon. Label the intersections of the circle with the axis as *A*, *B*, *C*, and *D*.
2. Draw horizontal line segments through points *A* and *C*, and vertical line segments through *D* and *B*.
3. Draw line segments at 45° to the horizontal and tangent to the circle as shown.
4. Darken in the octagon and erase the excess lines.

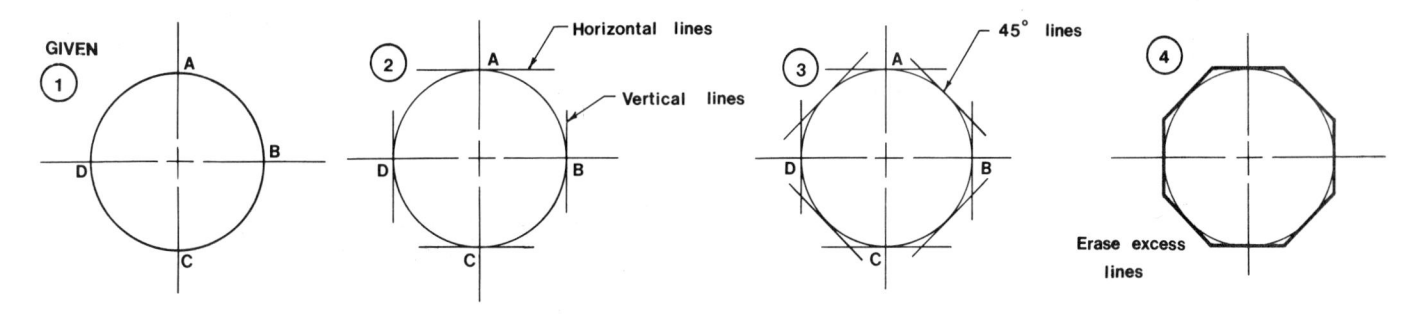

FIGURE 4-35 How to draw an octagon: classical method.

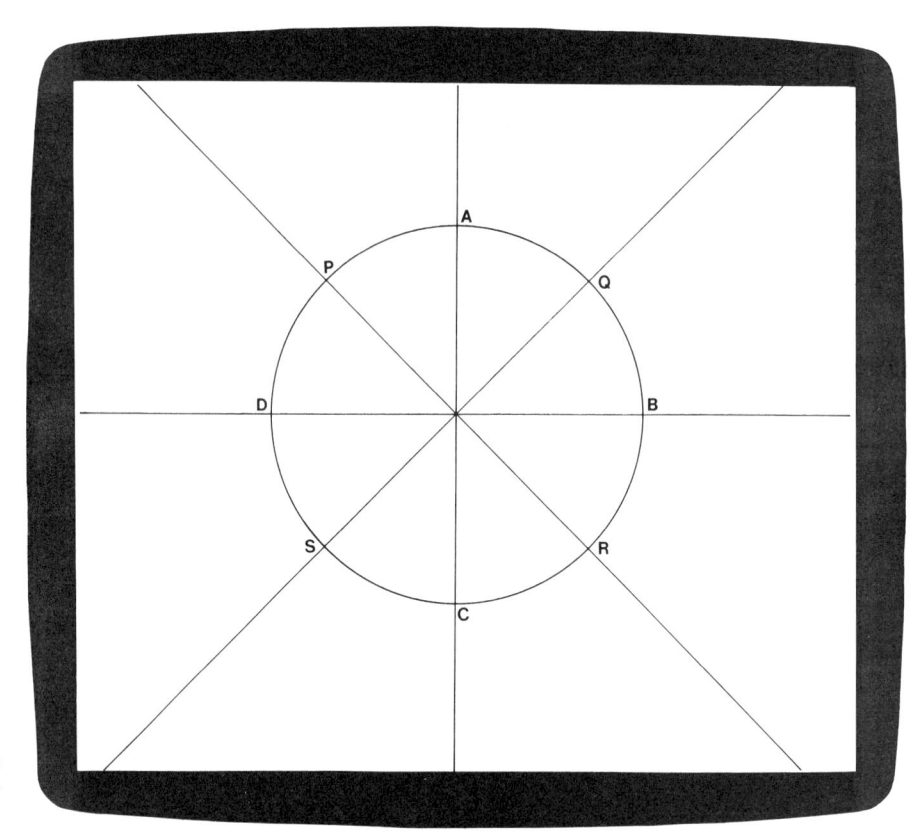

FIGURE 4-36 (a) How to draw an octagon: computer method.

FIGURE 4-36 (b)

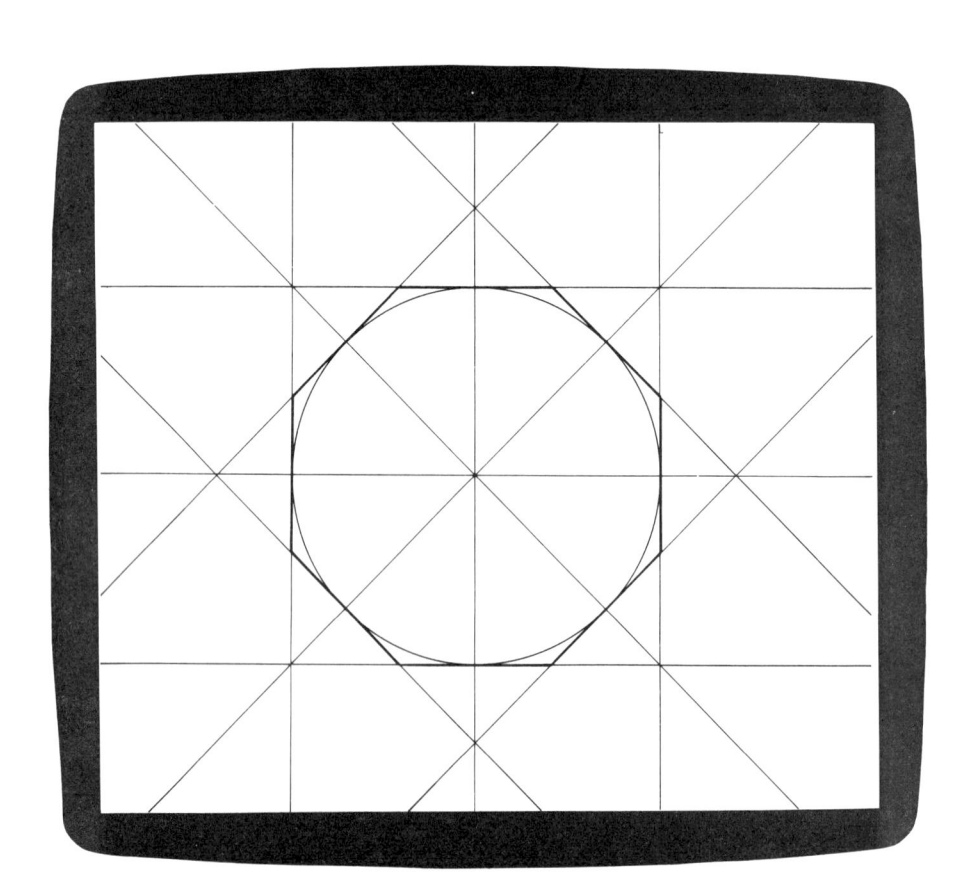

Sec. 4-12 Arcs Tangent to Arcs

Figure 4-36 shows a variation of the method outlined in Figure 4-35 that can be utilized by some computer graphic systems. The procedure is as follows:

1. Draw a circle and a perpendicular axis about its centerpoint as shown in Figure 4-36a. The diameter of the circle should equal the distance across the flats of the octagon. Label the intersections of the circle and axis lines A, B, C, and D.
2. Draw horizontal lines through points A and C, and vertical lines through D and B.
3. Draw lines 45° to the horizontal through the origin of the axis as shown in Figure 4-36a. Label the intersections of the lines through the circle P, Q, R, and S.
4. Draw lines 45° to the horizontal through points P, Q, R, and S as shown in Figure 4-36b. These lines are tangent to the circle.
5. Trim the excess lines.

4-12 ARCS TANGENT TO ARCS

Figure 4-37 shows the classical method for drawing a concaved arc of radius T tangent to two given arcs. The procedure is as follows:

1. Label the centerpoints of the two given arcs A and B as shown. Identify the radii of the arcs as R and S.
2. Draw an arc of radius $R + T$ using point A as a centerpoint.
3. Draw a second arc of radius $S + T$ using point B as a centerpoint.
4. Label the intersection of arc $R + T$ and $S + T$ as point X. Draw an arc of radius T using point X as a centerpoint. The arc will be tangent to the two given arcs.

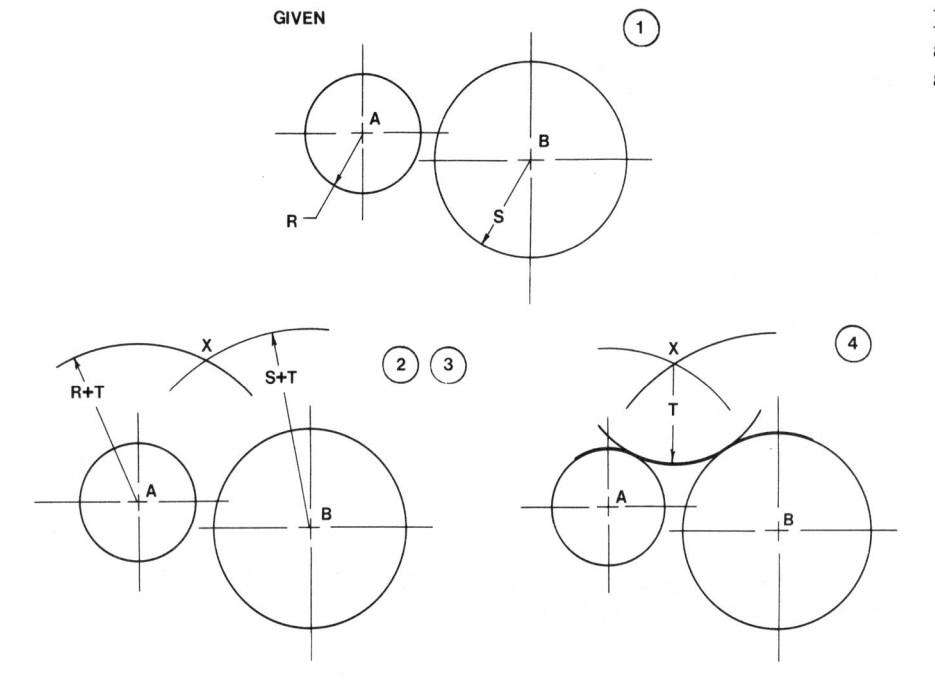

FIGURE 4-37 How to draw an arc tangent to two given arcs: classical method.

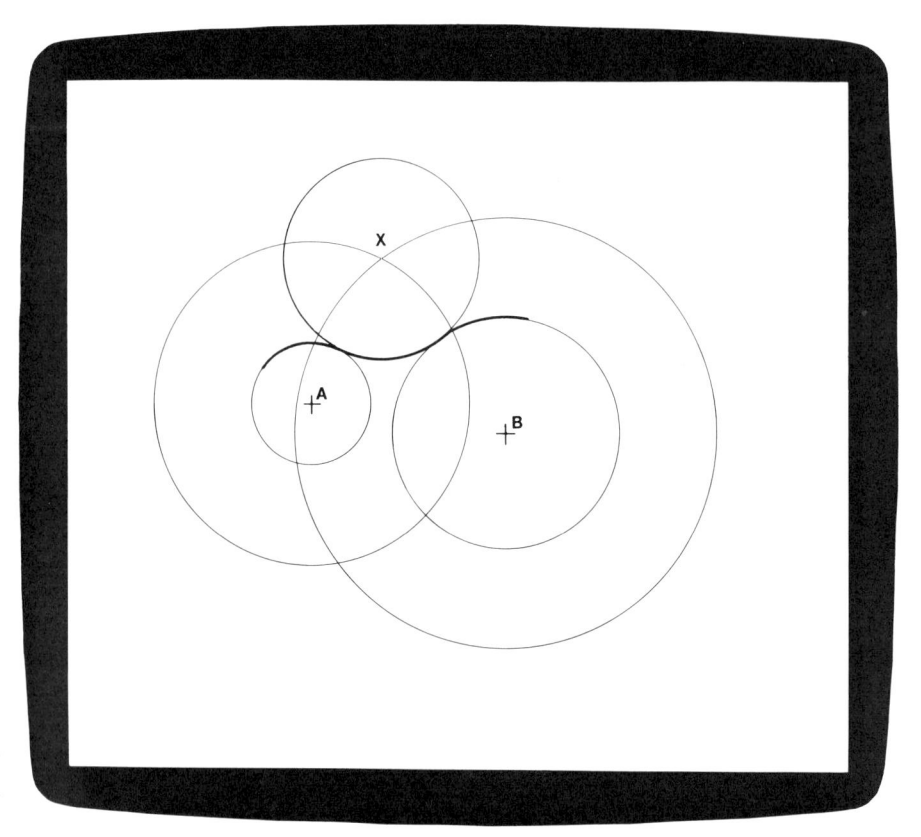

FIGURE 4-38 How to draw an arc tangent to two given arcs: computer method.

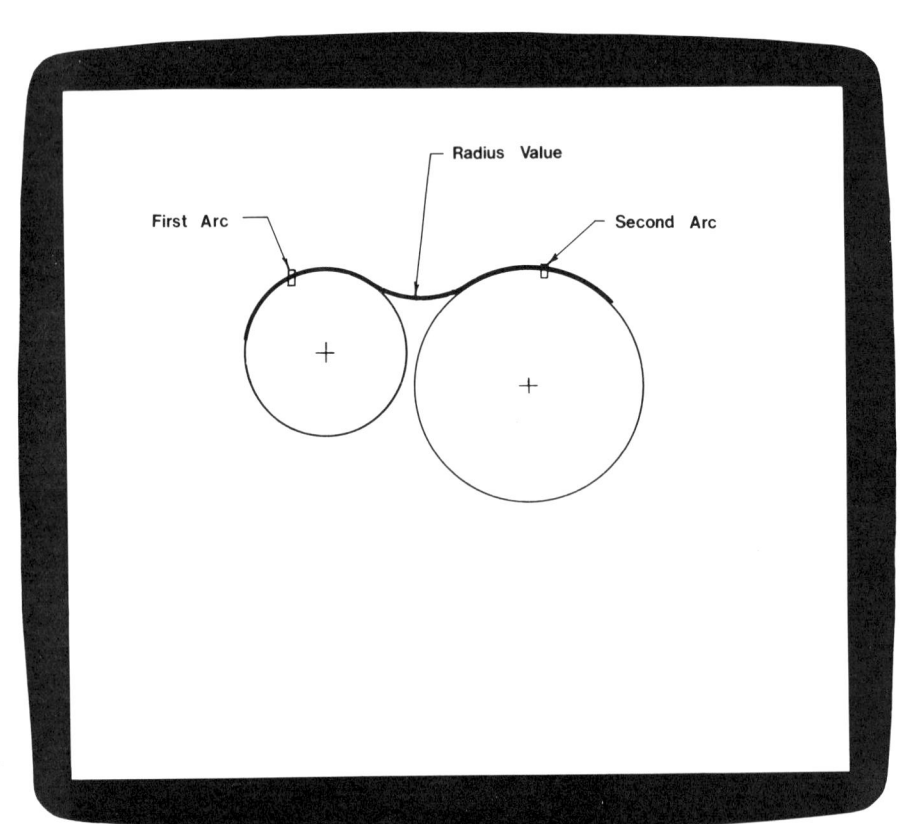

FIGURE 4-39 How to draw an arc tangent to two given arcs: computer method.

Sec. 4-12   Arcs Tangent to Arcs   81

Figure 4-38 shows the method outlined in Figure 4-37 drawn using a computer graphic system. The method is identical except that circles have replaced arcs.

Some computer graphic systems can draw an arc tangent to two arcs directly. The general input format is to identify each of the given arcs as an element using the cursor. The radius of the desired arc is inputted via the keyboard, and an approximate centerpoint location for the arc is indicated. Figure 4-39 illustrates the procedure.

Figure 4-40 shows the classical method for drawing a convexed arc of radius T tangent to two given arcs. The procedure is as follows:

1. Label the centerpoints of the two given arcs as A and B as shown. Identify the radii of the arcs as R and S.
2. Draw an arc of radius $R - T$ using point A as the centerpoint.
3. Draw an arc of radius $S - T$ using point B as the centerpoint.
4. Label the intersection of arcs $R - T$ and $S - T$ as point X. Draw an arc of radius T using point X as the centerpoint. The arc will be tangent to the two given arcs.

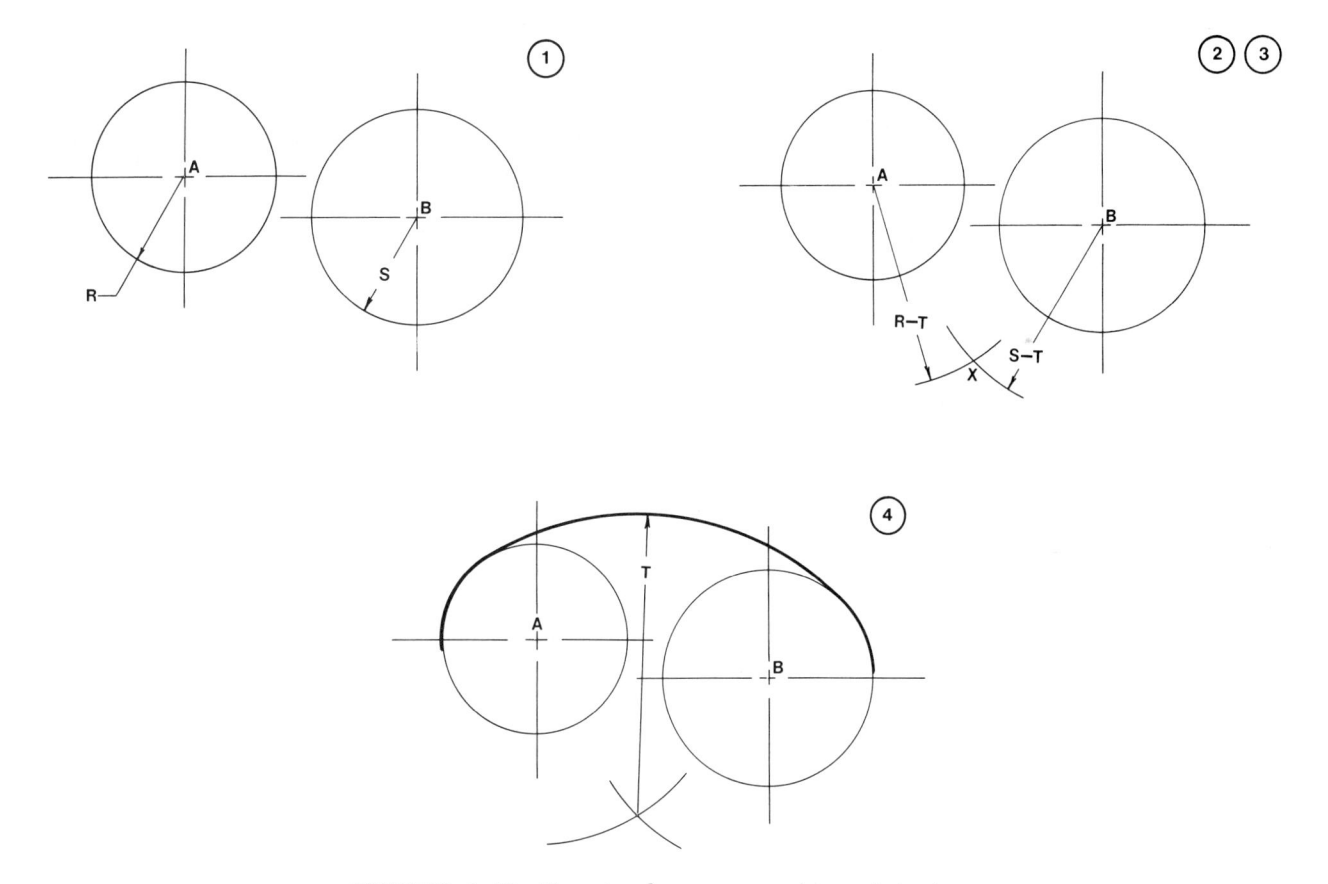

FIGURE 4-40 How to draw an arc tangent to two given arcs: classical method.

Figure 4-41 shows the method outlined in Figure 4-40 drawn using a computer graphics system. The method is identical except that circles have replaced arcs.

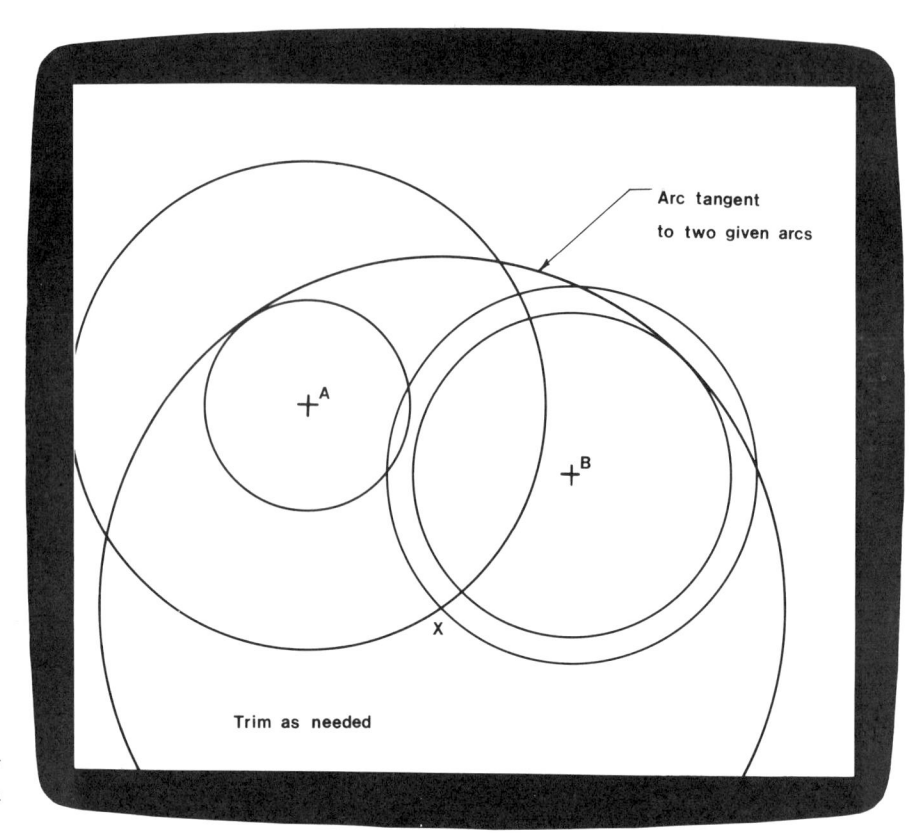

FIGURE 4-41 How to draw an arc tangent to two given arcs: computer method.

4-13 CORNERS

Figure 4–42 shows the classical method for constructing a 90° rounded corner. Assume that the radius for the corner is G. The procedure is as follows:

1. Draw an arc of radius G using the corner intersection as a centerpoint. Label the intersections of the arc with horizontal and vertical lines J and K.
2. Draw two more arcs of radius G using points J and K as centerpoints as shown. Label the intersection of the two arcs point M.
3. Draw the rounded corner of radius G using point M as a centerpoint. Erase all excess lines.

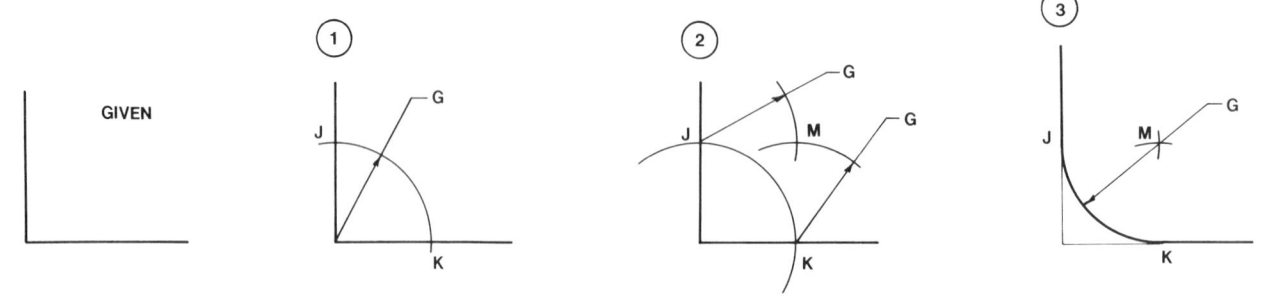

FIGURE 4–42 How to draw a rounded corner: classical method.

Sec. 4-13 Corners

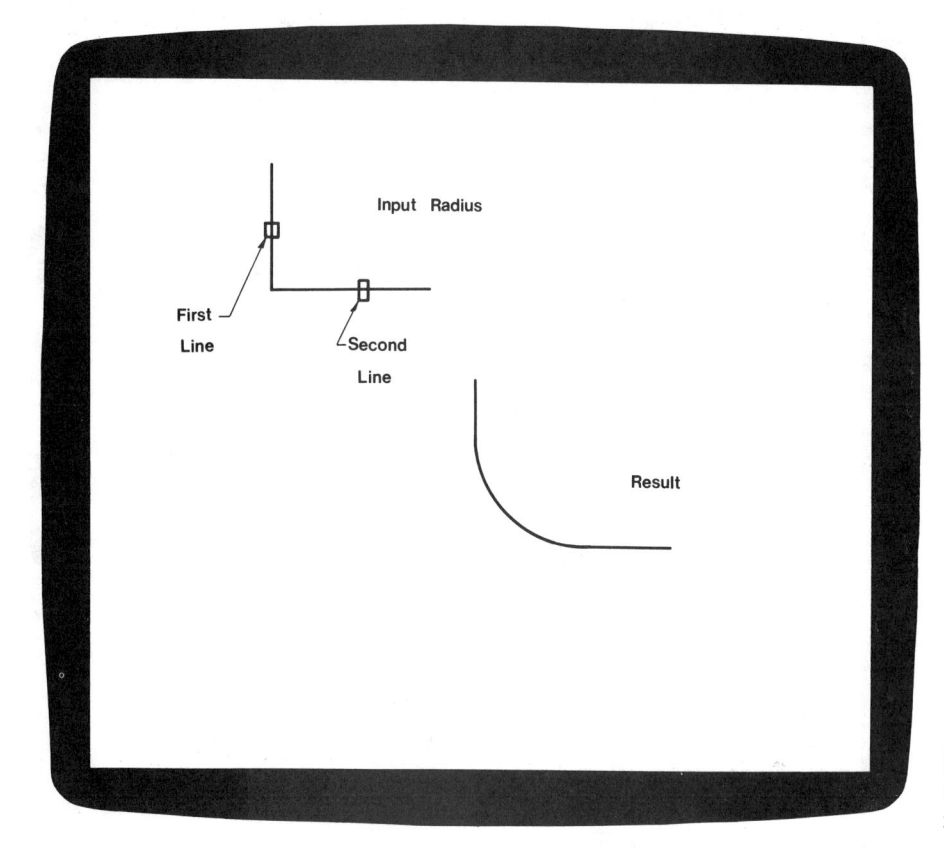

FIGURE 4-43 How to draw a rounded corner: computer method.

Many computer graphic systems draw rounded corners directly given the proper inputs. Generally, these systems require identification of the two lines that define the corner, a radius value, and an approximate centerpoint location. Figure 4-43 illustrates the concept.

It is sometimes difficult to trim the excess lines from a corner when drawing using a computer graphic system. The computer will erase the entire line, not just the portion beyond the corner. Figure 4-44 shows one possible solution to this problem. The procedure is as follows:

1. Draw lines parallel to the lines that define the corner. The distance between the corner lines and the parallel lines should equal the radius of the proposed corner. In this example, the radius of the corner equals G; therefore, the distance between parallel lines should equal G.
2. Trim the corner lines as shown. The lines added in step 1 not only define the centerpoint for the corner, but serve as a way to divide the corner lines into two different parts. The part next to the corner can be trimmed leaving a clear space for the rounded corner.
3. Draw the rounded corner (a 90° arc) using the intersection of the parallel lines added in step 1 as a centerpoint.
4. Erase the lines added in step 1.

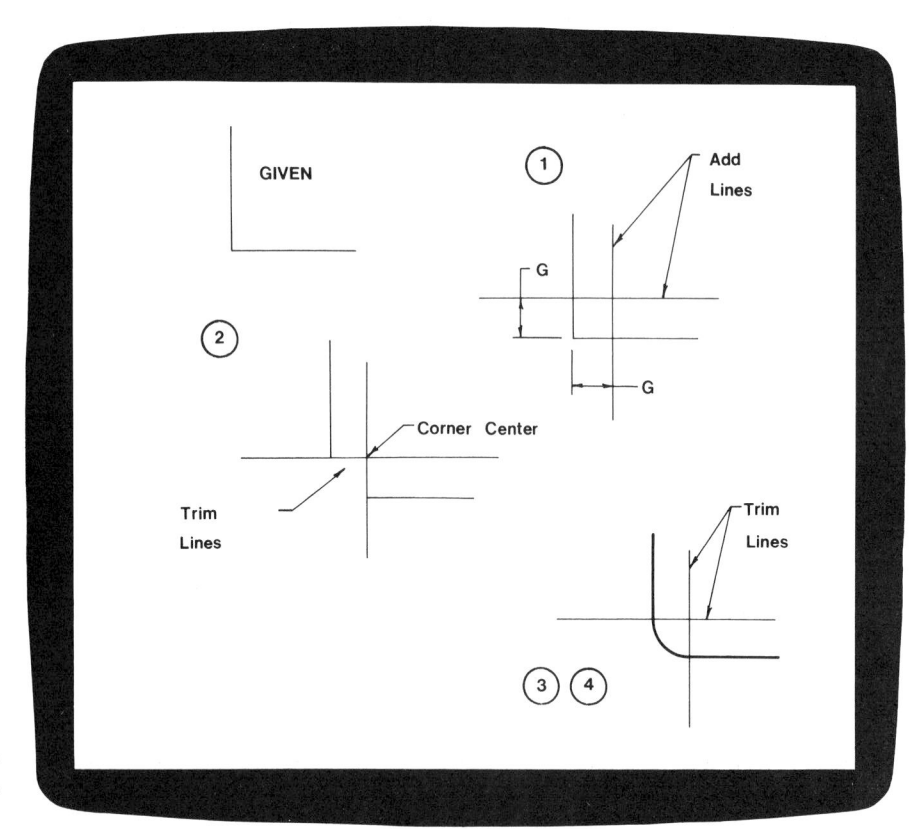

FIGURE 4-44 How to draw a rounded corner: computer method.

FIGURE 4-45 Terms for an ellipse.

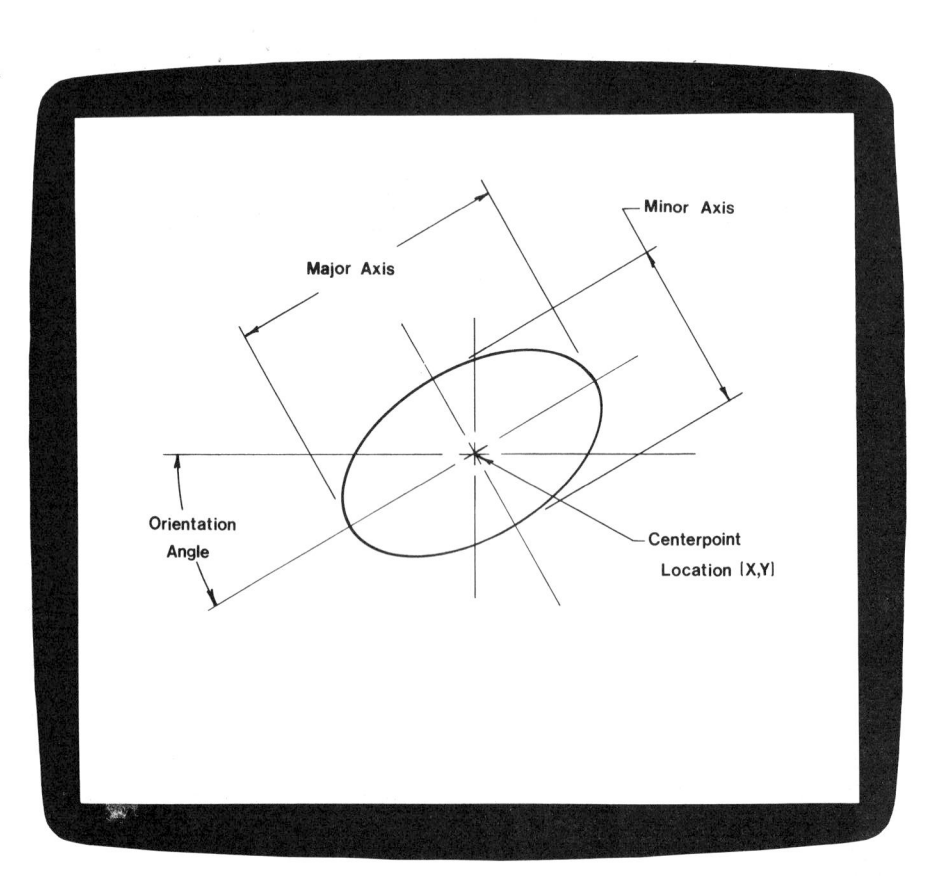

4-14 ELLIPSES

The classical methods for constructing an ellipse are, with one exception, approximate methods. They do not produce mathematically true-shaped ellipses. The one exception is to mathematically derive sufficient points to define the shape accurately, then connect the points with a smooth curve. It is a time-consuming process and difficult unless templates are used.

Some computer graphic systems can draw ellipses directly given the proper inputs. The input requirements are generally the sizes of the major and minor axis, the location of the centerpoint, and the orientation angle. Figure 4-45 illustrates these inputs.

4-15 PARABOLAS

Computer graphic systems usually draw parabolas and other more complex geometric shapes by plotting curves based on the mathematical definition of the shape. For example, the mathematical formula for a parabola about a vertical axis is

$$(X - h)^2 = 4c(Y - k)$$

where h and k are the coordinates of the vertex and c is the focal length. Solving the equation for y yields

$$Y = \frac{(X - h)^2 + 4ck}{4c}$$

This equation can be used to generate X and Y values for a parabolic curve. The values, in turn, can be inputted into the computer to generate a parabolic curve.

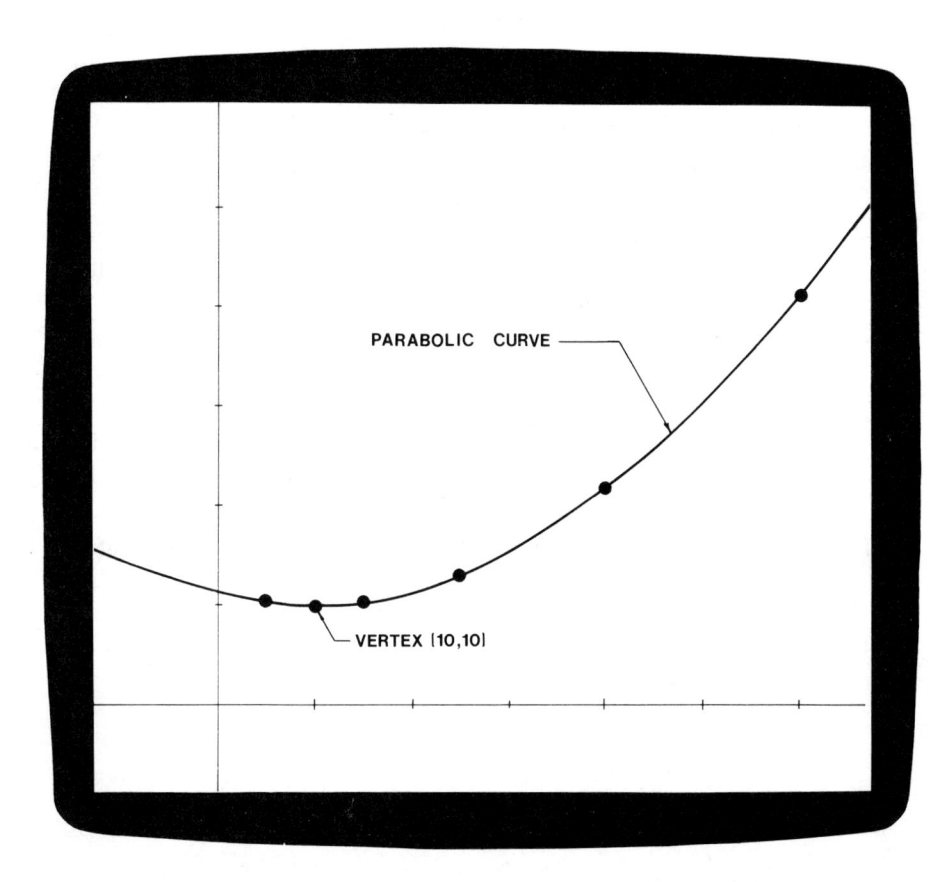

FIGURE 4-46 Parabolic curve.

Figure 4-46 shows this procedure. It was assumed that $c = 20$, $h = 10$, $k = 10$. Various X values were inputted into the equation for a parabola. The following points were derived:

X	Y
5	10.31
10	10.00
15	10.31
25	12.81
40	21.25
60	41.25

The values were plotted and joined by a smooth curve called a *spline*. The result is a parabolic curve.

PROBLEMS

P4-1 Given a line 4.25 in. long that slopes downward from left to right at 30°, bisect it.

P4-2 Given a line 175 mm long that slopes upward from left to right at 70°, bisect it.

P4-3 Given a line AB 3.63 in. long that slopes upward from left to right at 15°, and a point C located 1.00 in. from the right end of the line, draw a line perpendicular to line AB through point C.

P4-4 Given a line AB 215 mm long that slopes downward from left to right at 45°, and a point C located 100 mm from the left end of the line, draw a line perpendicular to line AB through point C.

P4-5 Given a line 4.44 in. long that slopes upward from left to right at 22°, divide the line into five equal parts.

P4-6 Given a line 168 mm long that slopes downward from left to right at 10°, divide the line into three equal parts.

P4-7 Given a circle with a diameter of 3.00 in. and two points located on the circle 1.25 in. above the horizontal centerline, draw lines tangent to each point.

P4-8 Given a circle with a diameter of 162 mm and two points located on the circle 62 mm to the left of the vertical centerline, draw lines tangent to each point.

P4-9 Given a line 5.00 in. long that slopes upward from left to right at 10°, draw a line parallel to the given line at a distance of 1.38 in.

P4-10 Given a line 210 mm long that slopes downward from left to right at 42°, draw a line parallel to the given line at a distance of 75 mm.

P4-11 Given three points $A(1, 10)$, $B(10, 8)$, and $C(4, 3)$, connect the three points to form a triangle.

Chap. 4 Problems

P4-12 Given three points A(6, 12), B(3, 4), and C(16, 6), connect the three points to form a triangle.

P4-13 Given angle of 30° and two legs of lengths 3.25 and 2.88 in. adjacent to the angle, draw a triangle.

P4-14 Given an angle of 37° and two legs of lengths 143 and 98 mm adjacent to the angles, draw a triangle.

P4-15 Given a leg of length 2.00 in. and two angles of 45° and 27° adjacent to the leg, draw a triangle.

P4-16 Given a leg of length 106 mm and two angles of 36° and 42° adjacent to the leg, draw a triangle.

P4-17 Given three legs of lengths 1.62, 2.15, and 2.32 in., draw a triangle.

P4-18 Given three legs of lengths 120, 95, and 105 mm, draw a triangle.

P4-19 Draw a square. Each side must equal 1.88 in.

P4-20 Draw a square. Each side must equal 133 mm.

P4-21 Given a line 2.16 in. long that slopes downward from left to right at 17°, construct a square using the line.

P4-22 Given a line 95 mm long that slopes upward from left to right at 26°, construct a square using the line.

P4-23 Inscribe a pentagon within a 4.00-in.-diameter circle.

P4-24 Inscribe a pentagon within a 265-mm-diameter circle.

P4-25 Construct a hexagon 1.75 in. across the flats.

P4-26 Construct a hexagon 71 mm across the flats.

P4-27 Construct a hexagon 2.36 in. across the corners.

P4-28 Construct a hexagon 86 mm across the corners.

P4-29 Construct an octagon 3.38 in. across the flats.

P4-30 Construct an octagon 160 mm across the flats.

P4-31 Given two circles of radius 1.25 and 2.13 in. whose centerpoints are located on the same horizontal line 4.00 in. apart, draw an arc of radius 1.62 in. that is tangent to both circles.

P4-32 Given two circles of radius 30 and 63 mm whose centerpoints are located on the same vertical line 132 mm apart, draw an arc of radius 44 mm that is tangent to both circles.

P4-33 Given two circles of radius 0.80 and 1.20 in. whose centerpoints are located on the same vertical line 2.60 in. apart, draw an arc of radius 2.40 tangent to both circles.

P4-34 Given two circles of radius 60 and 90 mm whose centerpoints are located on the same horizontal line 70 mm apart, draw an arc of radius 97 mm tangent to both circles.

P4-35 Draw a 1.50- × 2.25-in. rectangle. Add round corners of radius 0.50 in. to each of the four corners.

P4-36 Draw a 45- × 65-mm rectangle. Add round corners of radius 20 mm to each of the four corners.

P4-37 Draw an ellipse with a major diameter equal to 4.50 in., a minor diameter equal to 2.50 in., at an orientation angle of 20° counterclockwise.

P4-38 Draw an ellipse with a major diameter equal to 260 mm, a minor diameter equal to 115 mm, at an orientation angle of 35° clockwise.

P4-39 Draw a parabolic curve about the vertical axis. The vertex is located at $X = 0$, $Y = 15$, and the focal length $C = 0.37$ in.

P4-40 Draw a parabolic curve about the vertical axis. The vertex is located at $X = 0$, $Y = 0$, and the focal length $C = 5$ mm.

For Problems P4-41 through P4-56, redraw Figures P4-41 through P4-56 using the dimensions given. Do not include the dimensions on your drawing. The dimensional units are as noted below.

P4-41	Millimeters	P4-49	Inches
P4-42	Inches	P4-50	Millimeters
P4-43	Millimeters	P4-51	Inches
P4-44	Millimeters	P4-52	Millimeters
P4-45	Millimeters	P4-53	Inches
P4-46	Millimeters	P4-54	Millimeters
P4-47	Millimeters	P4-55	Millimeters
P4-48	Millimeters	P4-56	Millimeters

FIGURE P4-41

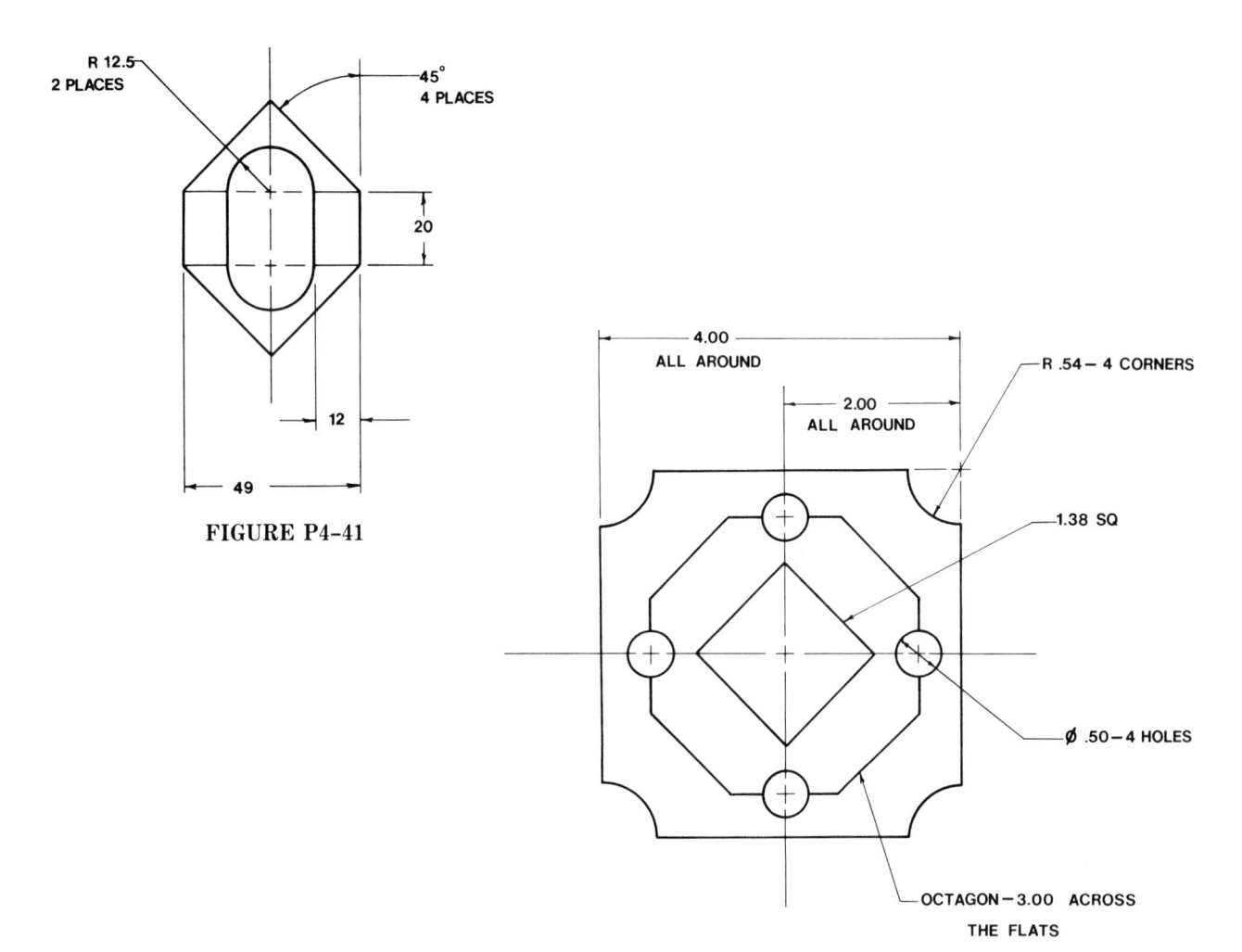

FIGURE P4-42

Chap. 4　Problems

FIGURE P4-43

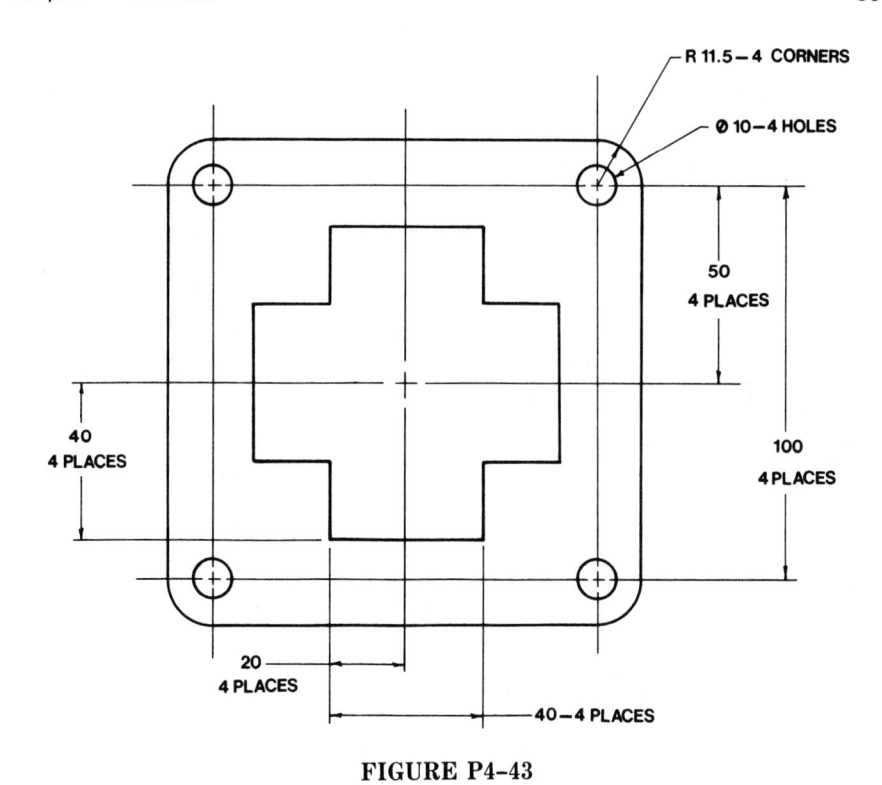

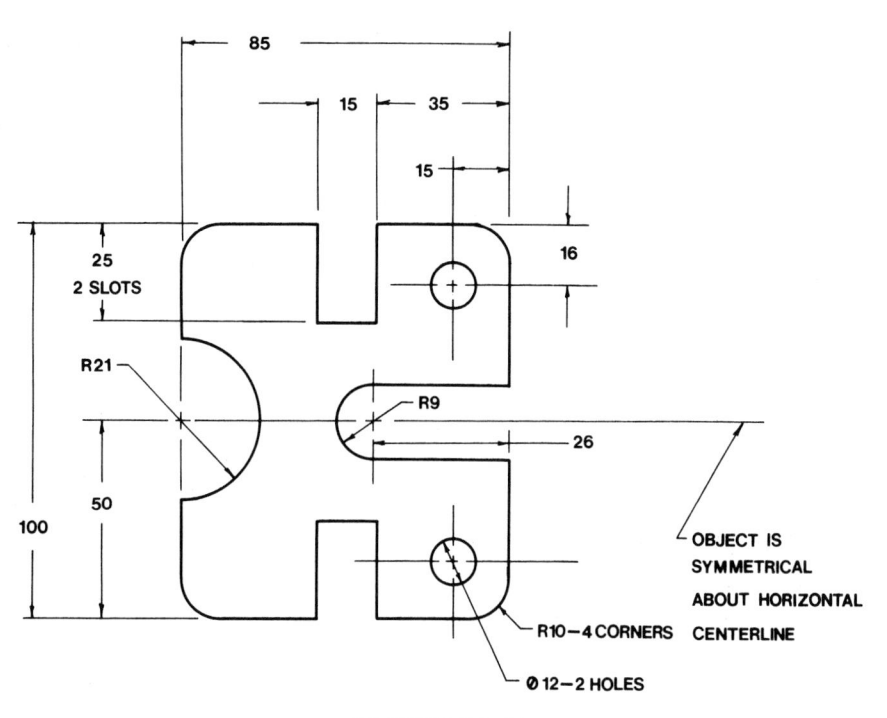

FIGURE P4-44

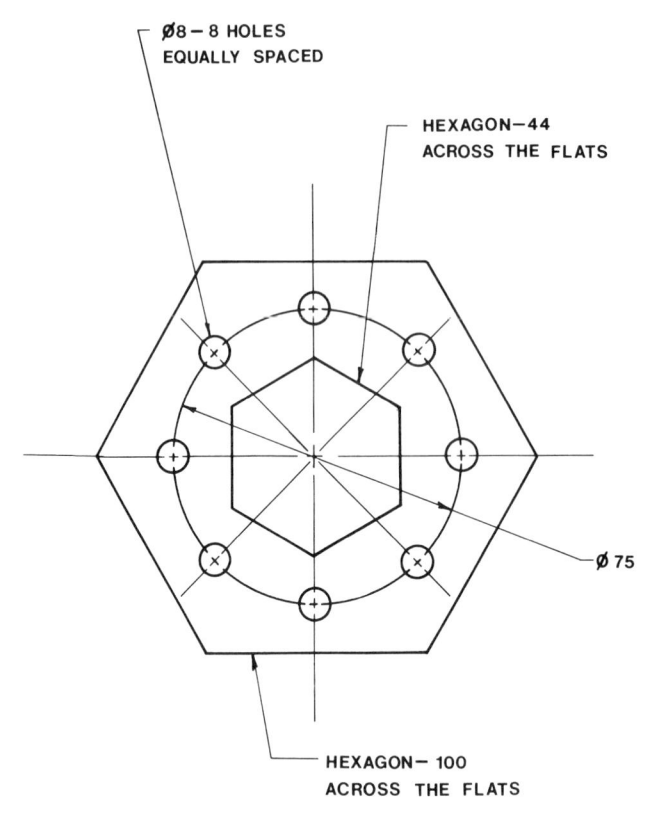

FIGURE P4-45

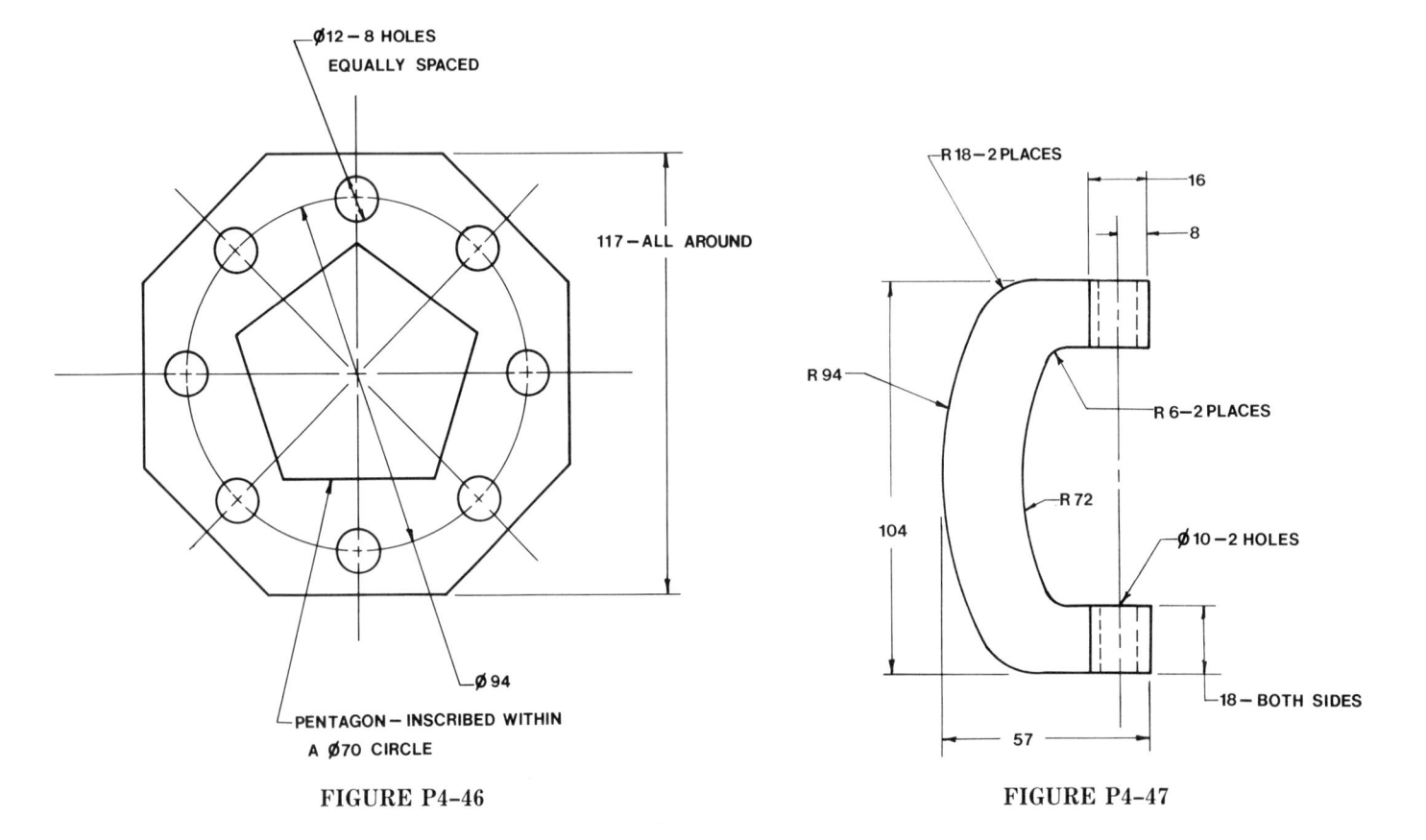

FIGURE P4-46

FIGURE P4-47

FIGURE P4-48

FIGURE P4-49

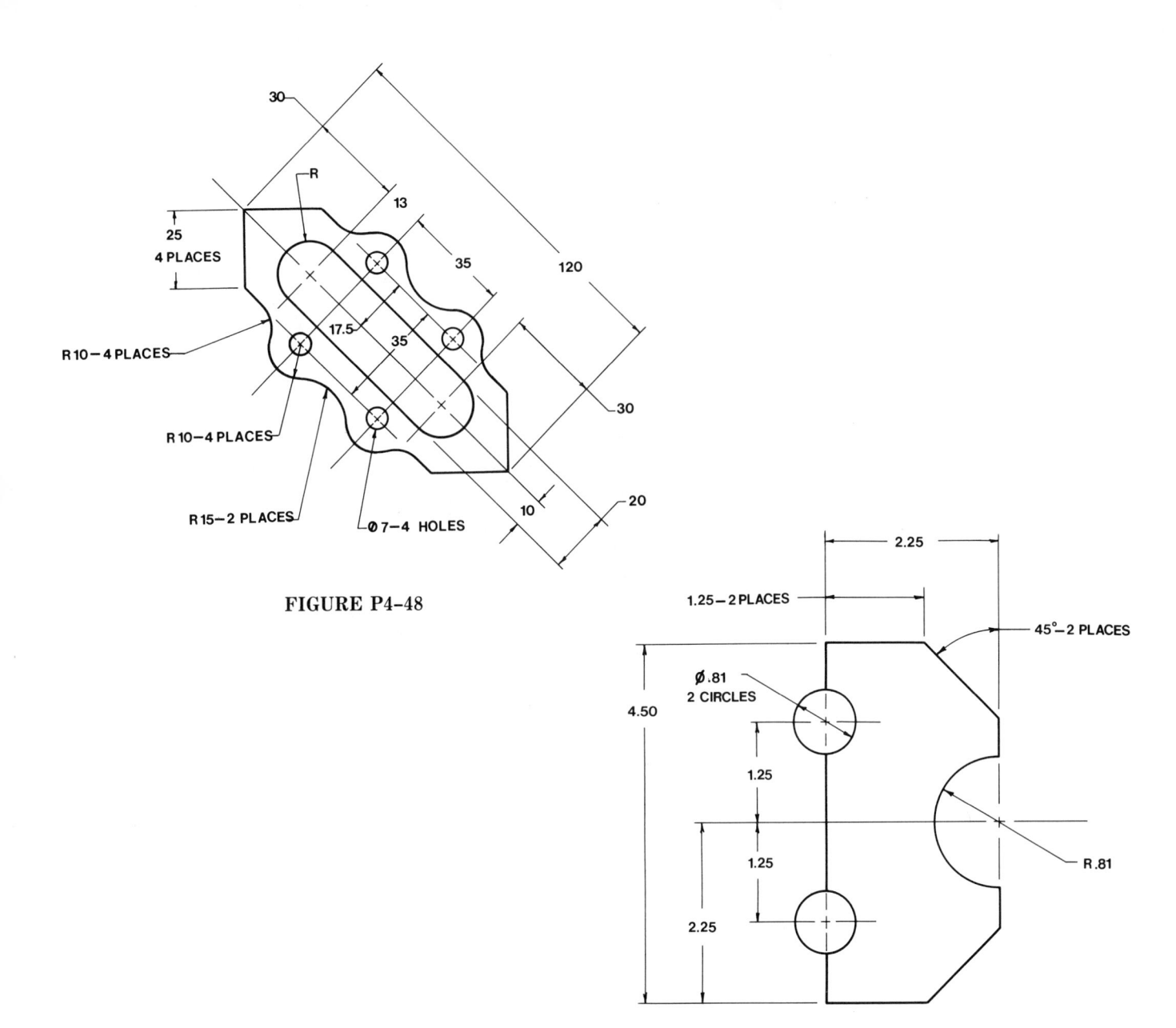

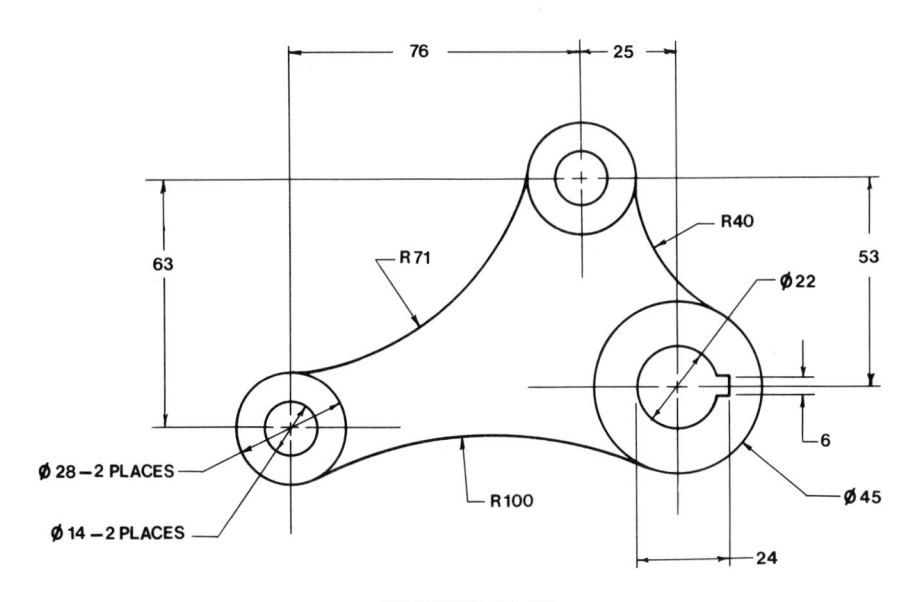

FIGURE P4-50

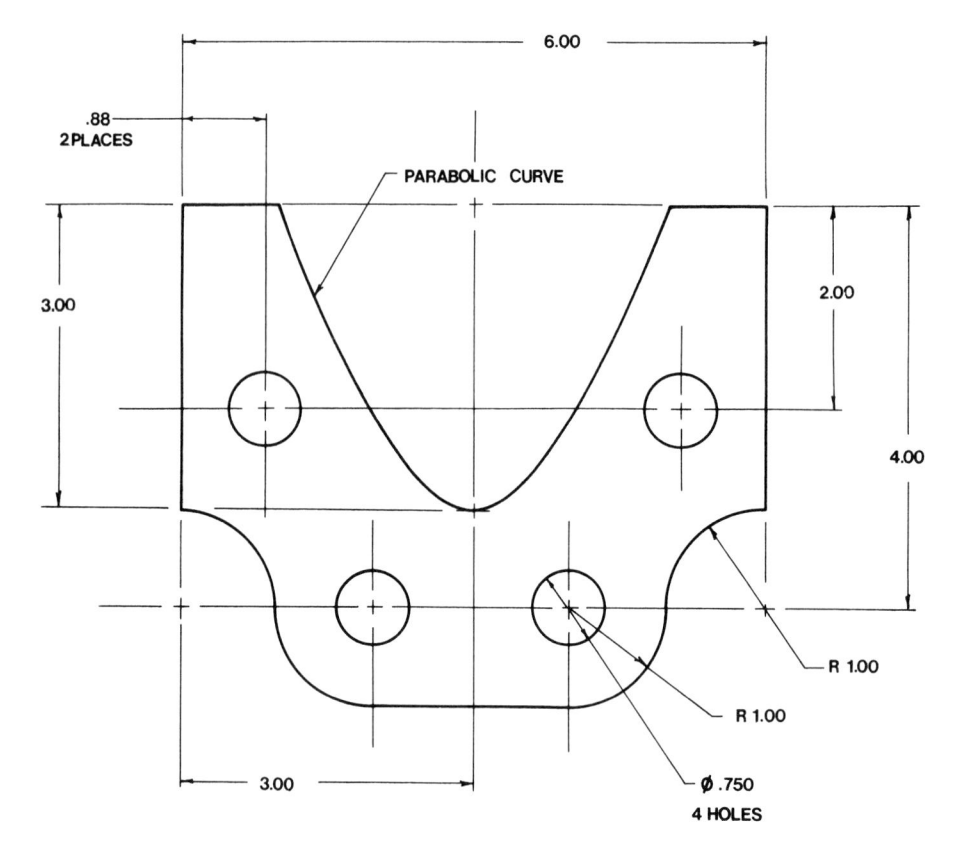

FIGURE P4-51

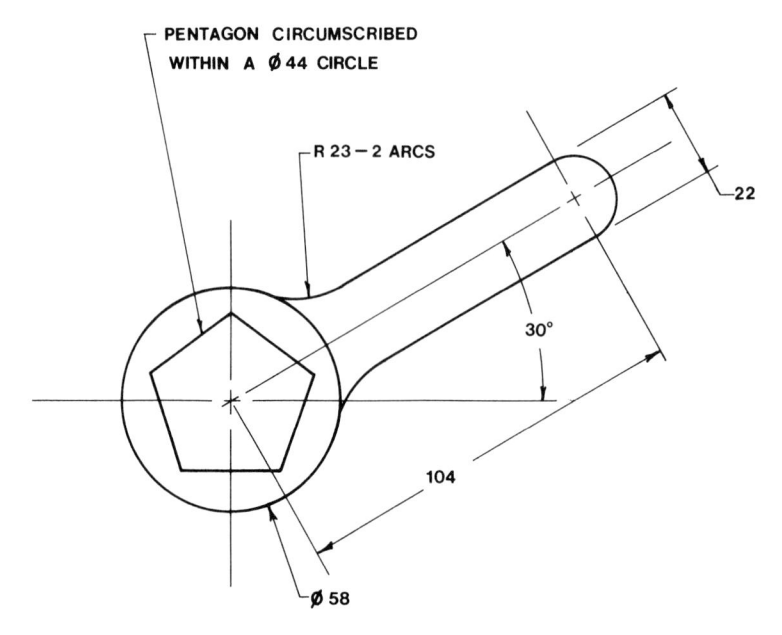

FIGURE P4-52

Chap. 4 Problems

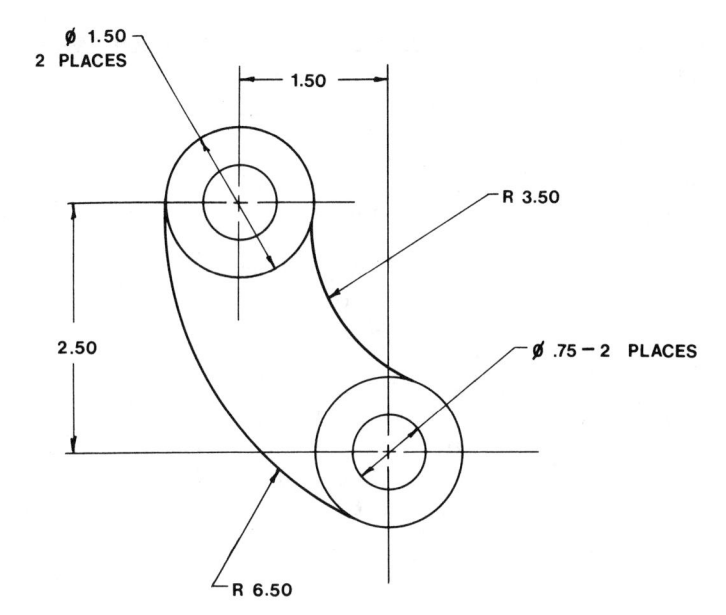

FIGURE P4-53

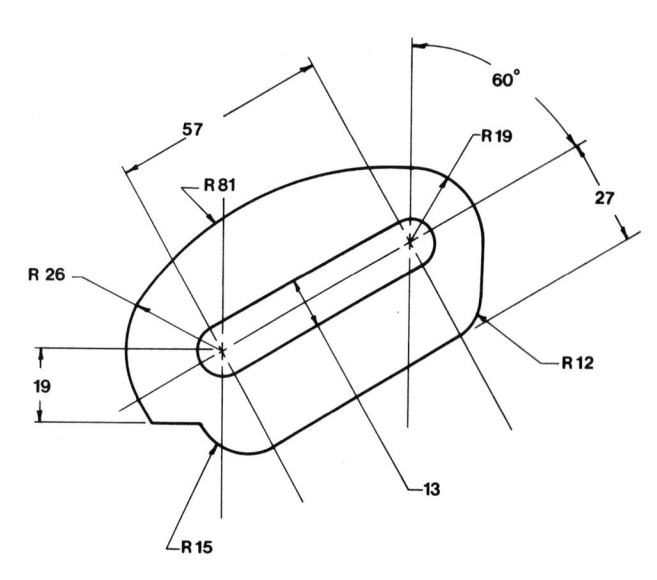

FIGURE P4-54

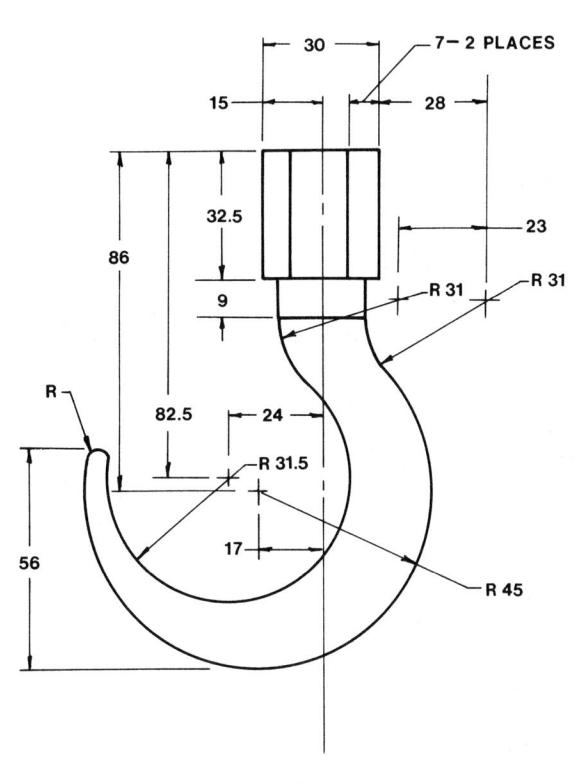

FIGURE P4-55

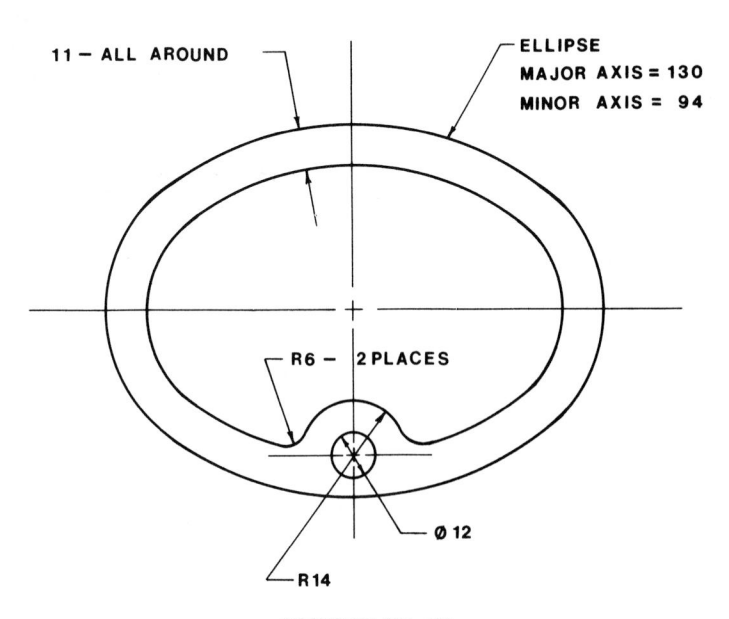

FIGURE P4-56

P4-57 Redraw the curves shown in Figure P4-57. The data point values are noted below. All values are in inches.

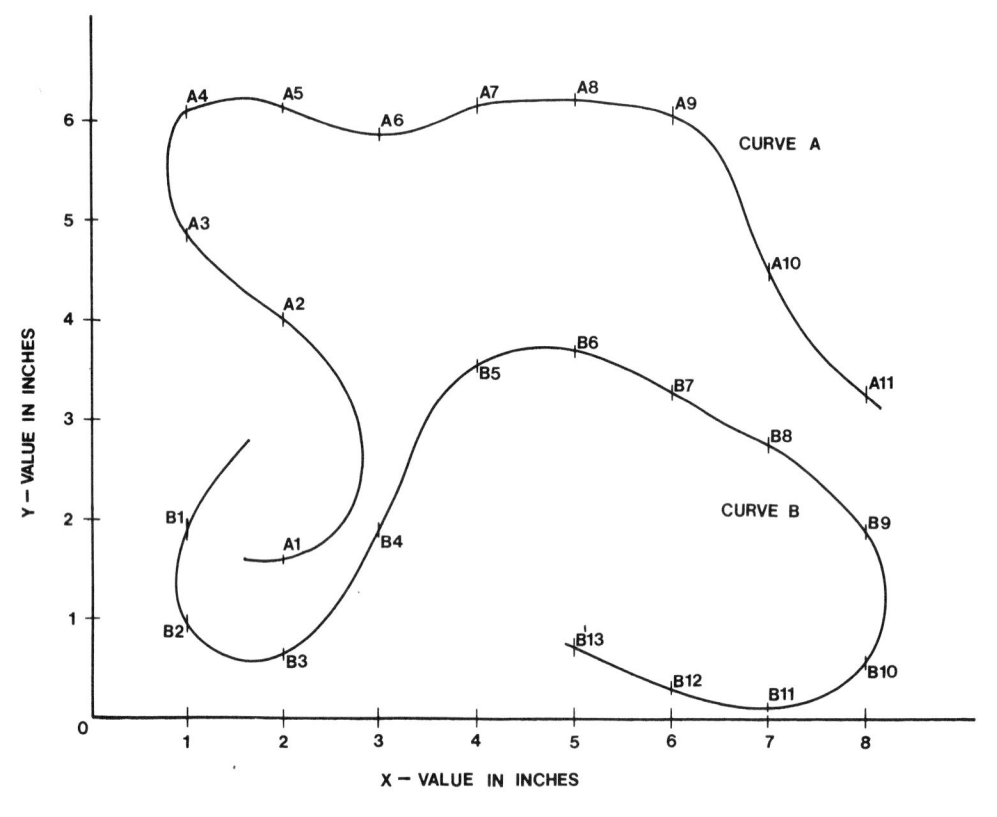

Points	X	Y	Points	X	Y
A1	(2.0,	1.60)	B1	(1.00,	1.90)
A2	(2.0,	4.00)	B2	(1.00,	0.95)
A3	(1.0,	4.85)	B3	(2.00,	0.65)
A4	(1.0,	6.10)	B4	(3.00,	1.90)
A5	(2.0,	6.15)	B5	(4.00,	3.55)
A6	(3.0,	5.85)	B6	(5.00,	3.70)
A7	(4.0,	6.15)	B7	(6.00,	3.25)
A8	(5.0,	6.20)	B8	(7.00,	2.75)
A9	(6.0,	6.05)	B9	(8.00,	1.85)
A10	(7.0,	4.50)	B10	(8.00,	0.55)
A11	(8.0,	3.25)	B11	(7.00,	0.10)
			B12	(6.00,	0.30)
			B13	(5.00,	0.70)

FIGURE P4-57

Chap. 4   Problems

P4-58 Redraw the four curves shown in Figure P4-58. The data point values are noted below. All values are in inches.

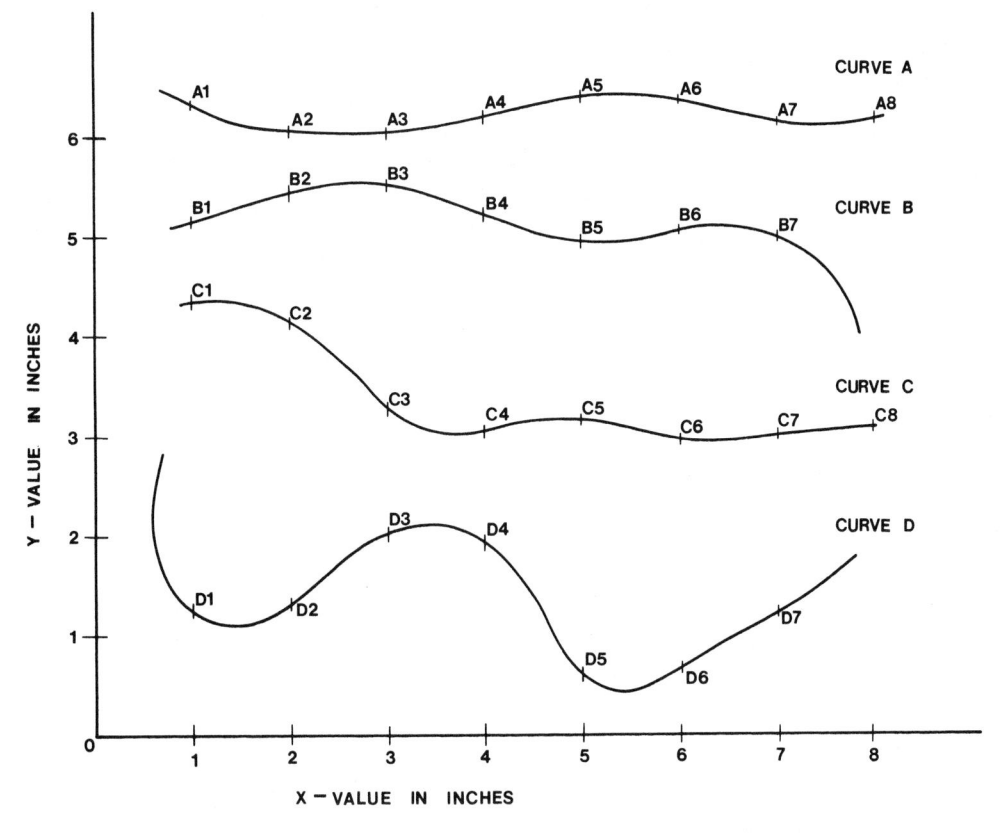

Points	X	Y
A1	(1.00,	6.30)
A2	(2.00,	6.05)
A3	(3.00,	6.05)
A4	(4.00,	6.20)
A5	(5.00,	6.40)
A6	(6.00,	6.35)
A7	(7.00,	6.15)
A8	(8.00,	6.05)

Points	X	Y
B1	(1.00,	5.15)
B2	(2.00,	5.40)
B3	(3.00,	5.50)
B4	(4.00,	5.20)
B5	(5.00,	4.95)
B6	(6.00,	5.05)
B7	(7.00,	5.00)

Points	X	Y
C1	(1.00,	4.30)
C2	(2.00,	4.15)
C3	(3.00,	3.25)
C4	(4.00,	3.05)
C5	(5.00,	3.15)
C6	(6.00,	2.95)
C7	(7.00,	3.00)
C8	(8.00,	3.10)

Points	X	Y
D1	(1.00,	1.25)
D2	(2.00,	1.30)
D3	(3.00,	2.00)
D4	(4.00,	1.95)
D5	(5.00,	0.60)
D6	(6.00,	0.65)
D7	(7.00,	1.20)

FIGURE P4-58

P4-59 Redraw the curves shown in Figure P4-59. The data point values are noted below. All values are in millimeters.

Points	X	Y
A1	(25.4,	140.1)
A2	(50.8,	137.2)
A3	(76.2,	119.4)
A4	(101.6,	81.3)
A5	(127.0,	123.2)
A6	(152.4,	147.3)
A7	(177.8,	147.3)
A8	(203.7,	124.5)
A9	(203.2,	91.44)
A10	(177.8,	71.1)
A11	(152.4,	2.40)

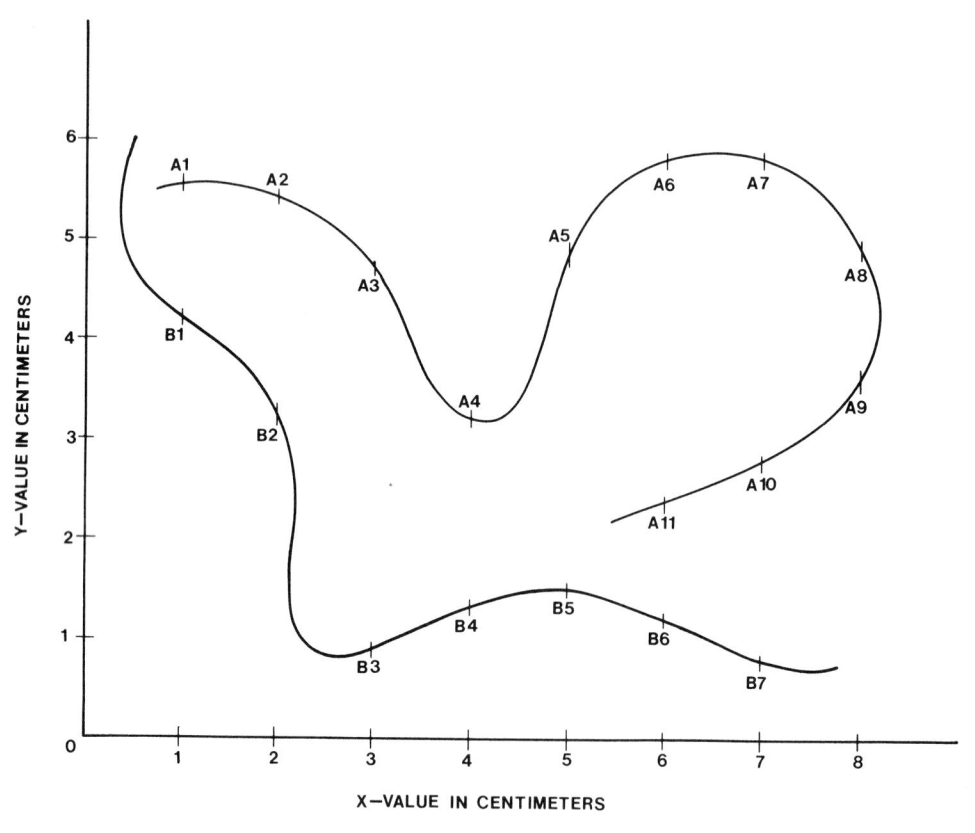

Points	X	Y
B1	(25.4,	106.7)
B2	(50.8,	82.6)
B3	(76.2,	22.9)
B4	(101.6,	33.0)
B5	(127.0,	38.1)
B6	(152.4,	30.5)
B7	(177.8,	20.3)

FIGURE P4-59

P4-60 Redraw the four curves shown in Figure P4-60. The data point values are noted below. All values are in millimeters.

Points	X	Y
A1	(25.4,	139.7)
A2	(50.8,	114.3)
A3	(76.2,	121.92)
A4	(101.6,	140.97)
A5	(127.0,	144.78)
A6	(152.4,	152.4)
A7	(177.8,	167.64)
A8	(203.2,	167.64)

Points	X	Y
B1	(50.8,	94.0)
B2	(76.2,	97.8)
B3	(101.6,	109.2)
B4	(127.0,	132.1)
B5	(152.4,	121.9)
B6	(177.8,	110.5)
B7	(203.2,	109.2)

Points	X	Y
C1	(25.4,	62.23)
C2	(50.8,	58.4)
C3	(76.2,	67.3)
C4	(101.6,	74.7)
C5	(127.0,	71.1)
C6	(152.4,	61.0)
C7	(177.8,	61.0)
C8	(203.2,	58.4)

Points	X	Y
D1	(25.4,	15.24)
D2	(52.8,	24.13)
D3	(76.2,	35.6)
D4	(101.6,	44.5)
D5	(127.0,	44.5)
D6	(152.4,	35.6)
D7	(177.8,	12.7)
D8	(203.2,	20.3)

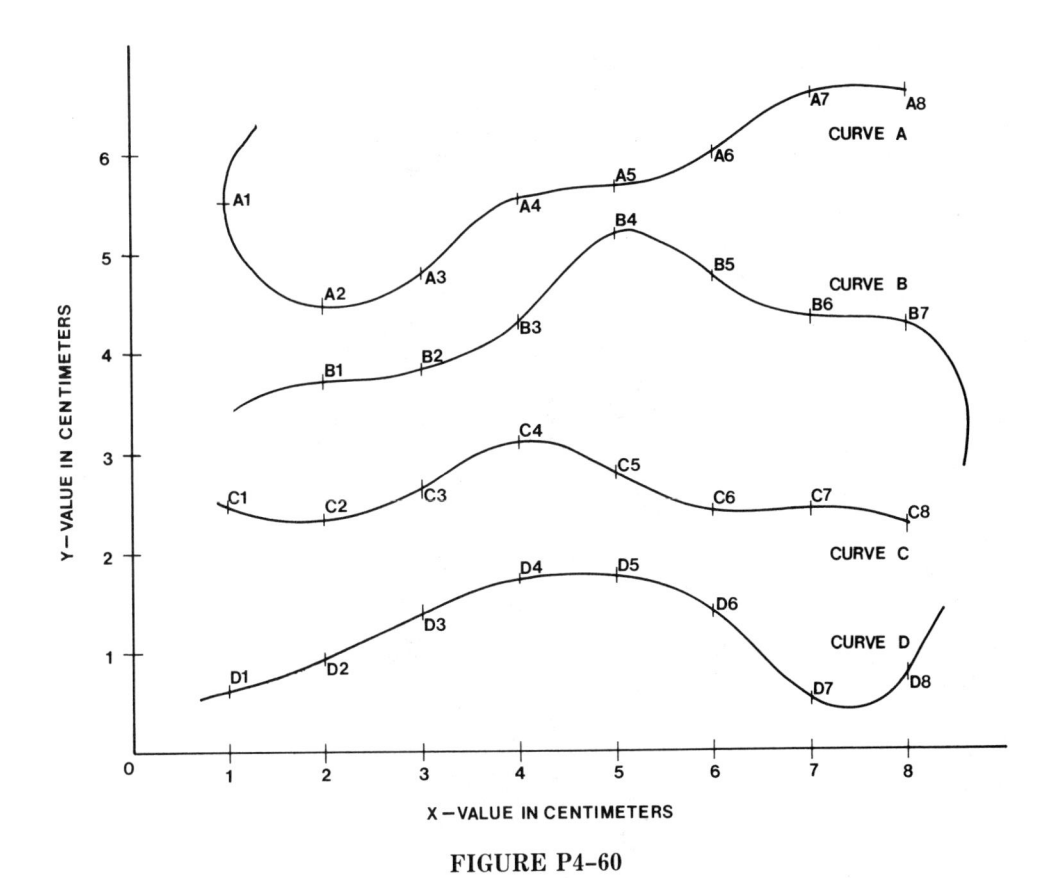

FIGURE P4-60

5
BASIC CONCEPTS OF DIMENSIONING

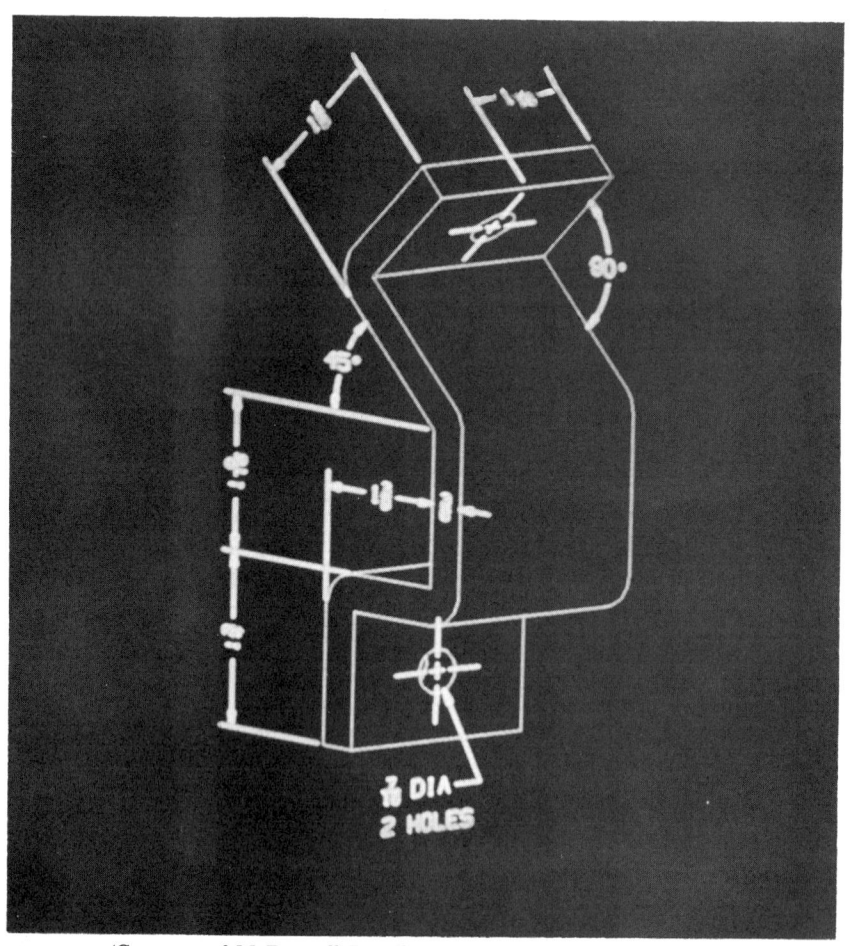

(Courtesy of McDonnell Douglas Manufacturing Industry Systems Company, St. Louis, Mo.)

5-1 INTRODUCTION

This chapter introduces the basic principles of dimensioning. Specifically, the subject matter is written to complement the material presented in Chapters 3 and 4: two-dimensional shapes and geometric constructions.

Dimensioning is presented at this point in the book because of its overall importance in technical drawing. The picture portion of any technical drawing is very important, but correct dimensioning is of equal importance. Correct dimensioning is more than a mathematical definition of the object's shape. Dimensions should also consider tolerance requirements, manufacturing procedures, inspection, and the object's function. An understanding of the interaction of these variables comes from experience and practice, so practice in applying dimensions to drawings should be started early in the learning process. Students are encouraged to apply dimensions to their work so that they can develop skill in applying dimensions to technical drawings.

The conventions presented in this chapter are in accordance with American National Standards Institute, ANSI, Y14.5-1982, "Dimensioning and Tolerancing," published by the American Society of Mechanical Engineers, and Department of Defense documents DOD-D-1000 and DOD-STD-100.

5-2 CONVENTIONS AND DEFINITIONS

Figure 5-1 shows a rectangle with dimensions. No dimensions are located on the part. Dimensions are located off the part, next to the appropriate feature. Extension lines and dimension lines are used to locate the dimensions off the part.

Both extension and dimension lines are drawn thinner than the object lines used to outline the part. Some systems do this automatically, others require a change in line font, and others cannot make line thickness changes. If possible, there should be a line thickness change.

There should be a noticeable gap between the object lines and the extension lines. Most smaller computer graphic systems do not draw a gap but simply continue the lines, at a constant thickness, as shown in Figure 5-1. If possible, the gap should be included.

Dimension lines should be located at least 10 mm from the edge of the part. After the first dimension line, all subsequent dimension lines should be located at least 6 mm from the previous line, as shown in Figure 5-2.

Dimensions can be added to a drawing, using a computer graphics system, by drawing each line individually (a series of horizontal and vertical thin lines), or, if available, by using a dimensioning function. Di-

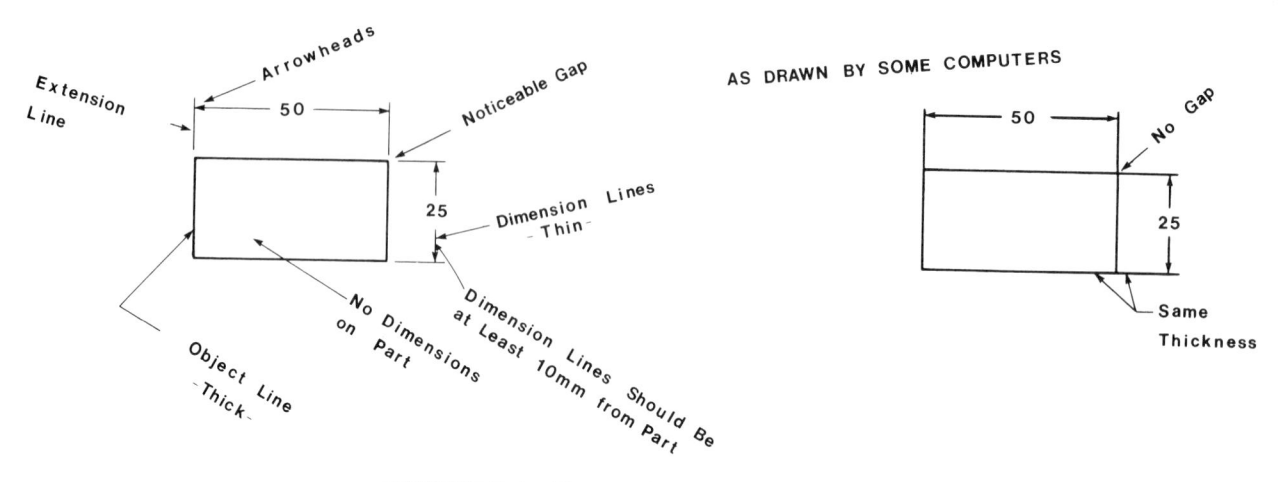

FIGURE 5-1 How to dimension a rectangle.

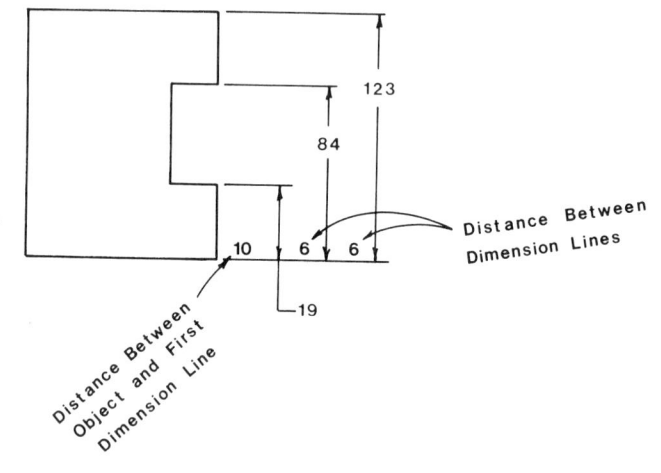

FIGURE 5-2 How to space dimension lines.

mensioning functions require inputs of the starting point for the dimension, an end point for the dimension, and where the value of the dimension is to be located. Figure 5-3a and b shows how these inputs are applied using a horizontal and vertical dimension function, respectively.

To create a horizontal dimension, first indicate the starting point using the cursor. In this example, the vertical edge line of the part is used. Then the end point of the dimension distance is indicated using the cursor; the right edge line was chosen. Finally, a value location is indicated.

Because a horizontal dimension was called for, the system automatically calculates and prints the perpendicular distance between the two indicated points. This means that any points along the two edge lines will result in the same dimension value.

The value location is usually done by eye, that is, not always exactly 10 mm from the part as called for in Figure 5-2. The 10-mm distance is a minimum distance and may be exceeded. Under no circumstances should any part of the dimension touch the edge of the part or appear to be squeezed.

Sec. 5-2   Conventions and Definitions

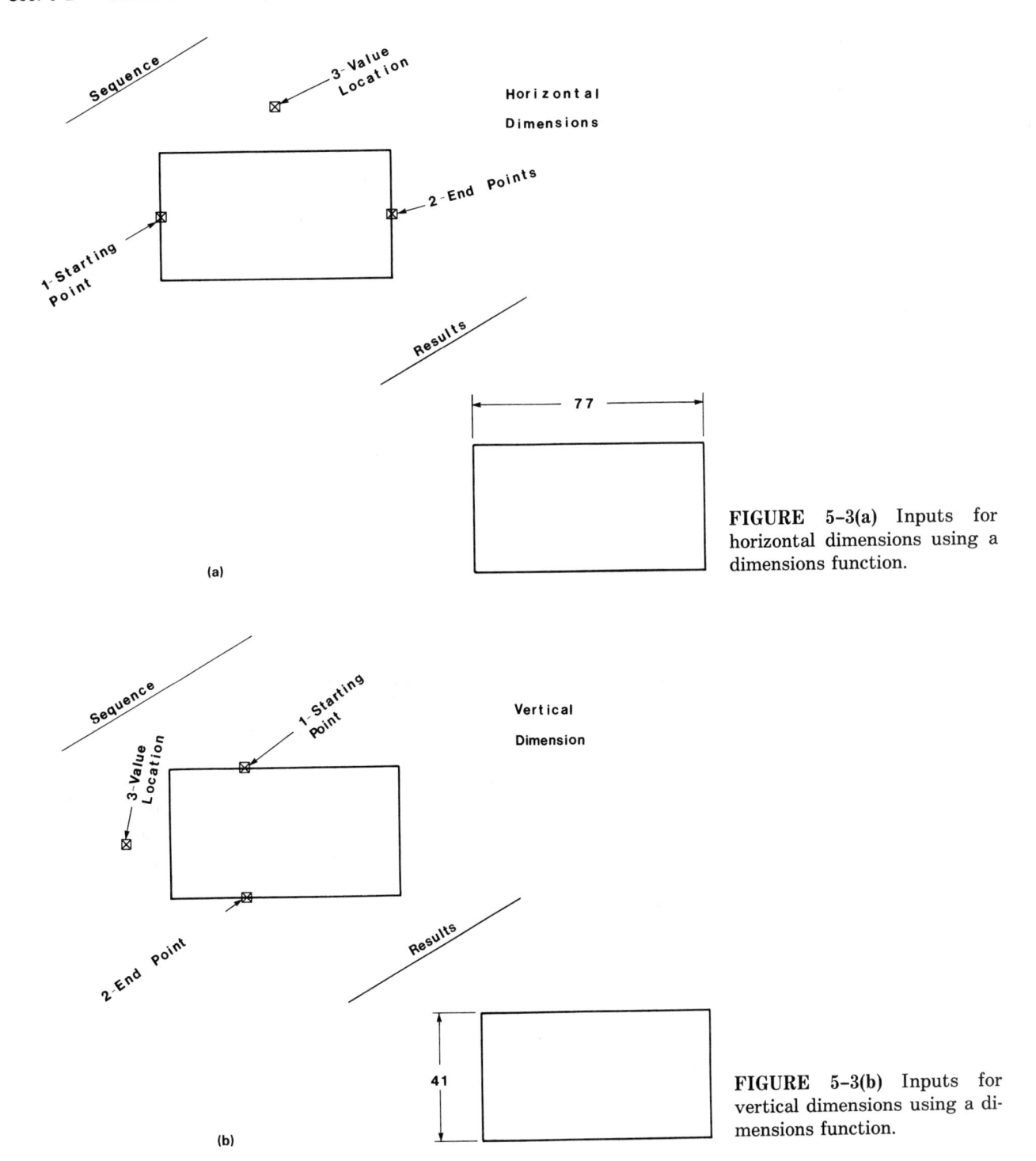

FIGURE 5-3(a) Inputs for horizontal dimensions using a dimensions function.

FIGURE 5-3(b) Inputs for vertical dimensions using a dimensions function.

Dimensions are written on a drawing so that they can be read from the bottom of the drawing. This is called the *unidirectional system* (Figure 5-4). The unidirectional system is preferred to the older *aligned system*, where dimensions were aligned parallel to the feature they were defining.

Dimensions should always progress away from the object according to length. The shorter-distance dimensions are located closer to the object than the longer-distance dimensions. The dimension that defines the

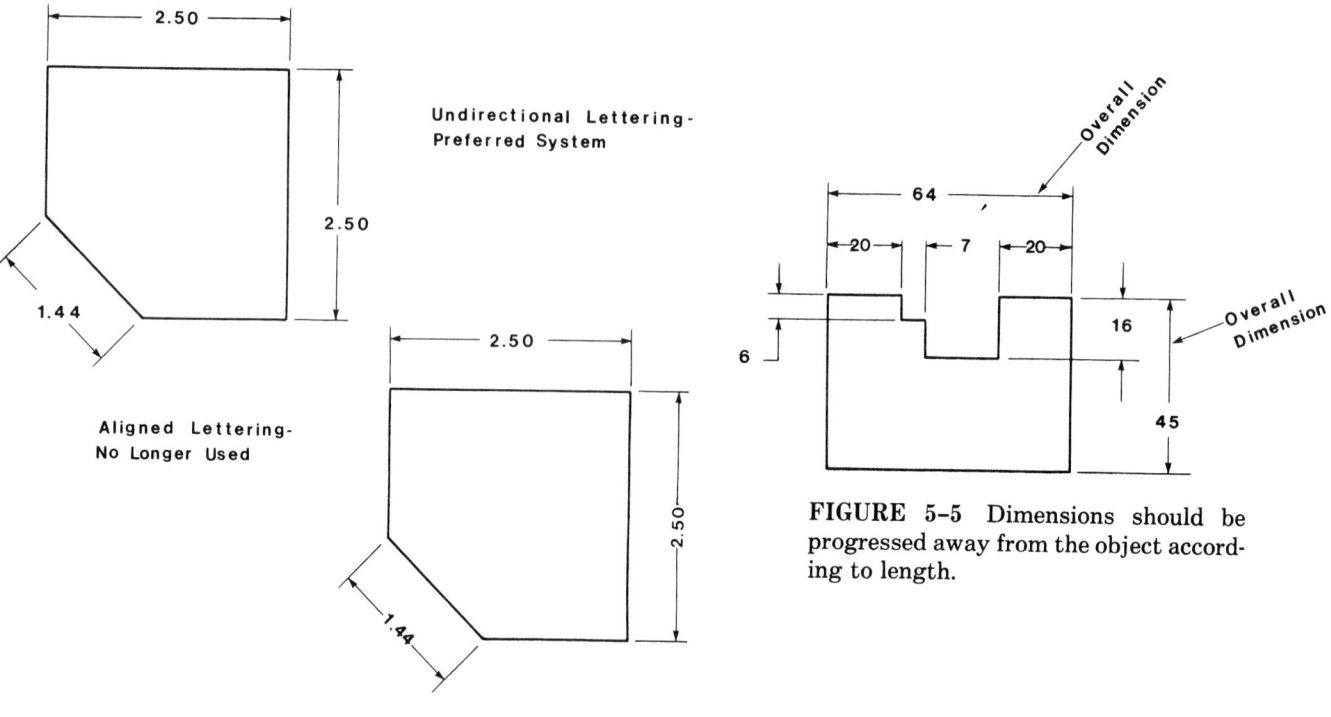

FIGURE 5-4 Unidirectional and aligned dimensioning systems. Unidirectional system is preferred.

FIGURE 5-5 Dimensions should be progressed away from the object according to length.

overall length of a feature is called the *overall dimension* and is always located farthest away from the object (Figure 5-5).

Dimensions should always be staggered relative to one another, as shown in Figure 5-6. This makes the dimensions easier to read and helps prevent interpretation errors.

Crossing extension and dimension lines should be avoided. However, if the crossing is unavoidable, the lines are not broken but drawn through each other. Extension lines *are* broken for arrowheads, as shown in Figure 5-7.

The extension lines used in Figure 5-7 for the overall dimensions need not cross. They may be moved as shown to avoid the crossing. The

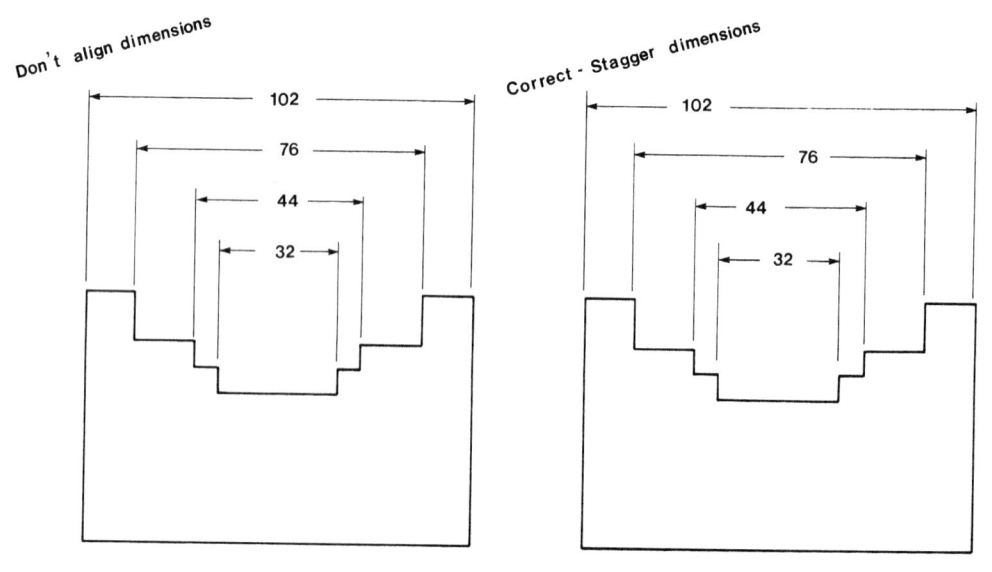

FIGURE 5-6 Dimensions should be staggered for clarity.

Sec. 5-3 Slanted Features

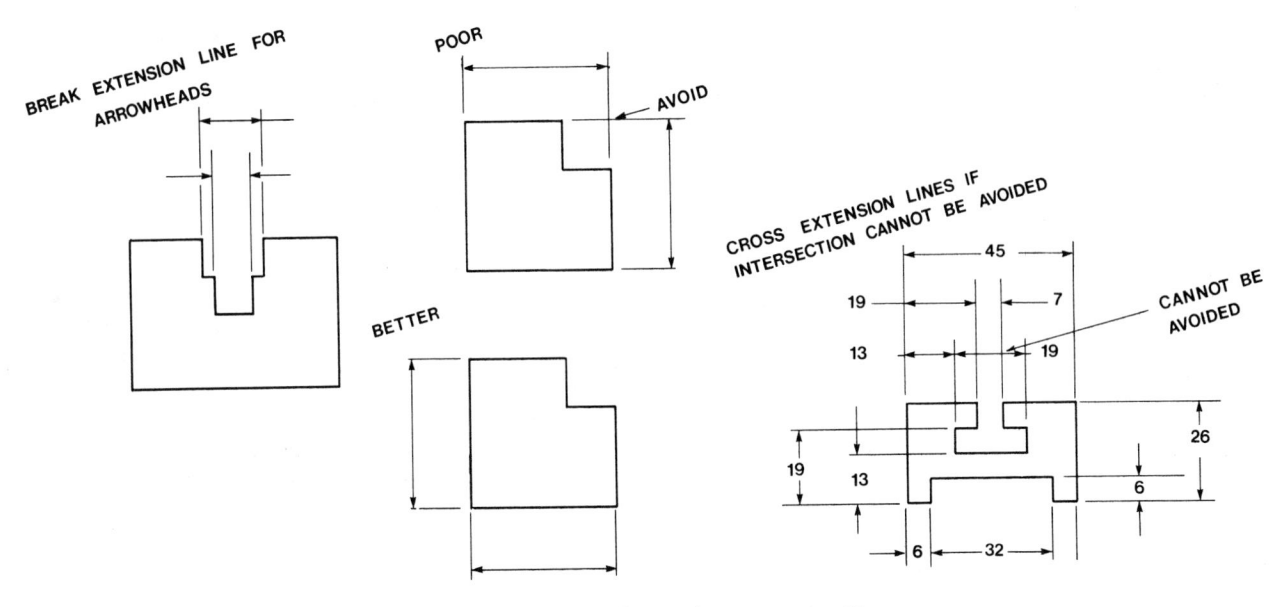

FIGURE 5-7 Avoid crossing extension lines.

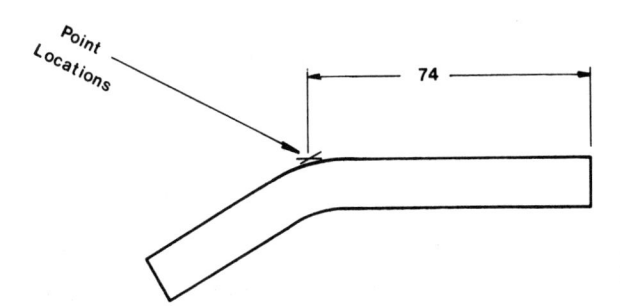

FIGURE 5-8 Locating a point by crossing extension lines.

extension lines used to dimension the T-slot in Figure 5-7 will cross other extension or dimension lines regardless of how they are located, so the crossing is unavoidable. These lines are drawn through each other with no breaks.

A point location may be defined by crossed extension lines as shown in Figure 5-8 if no corners or distinct edges are available to indicate clearly the starting or end points of a dimension. This type of dimensioning is prevalent in bending and casting work.

5-3 SLANTED FEATURES

Slanted features are dimensioned as shown in Figure 5-9. The dimension line should be parallel to the surface it is dimensioning. Note how the dimension lines for the horizontal perpendicular and vertical perpendicular distances are horizontal and perpendicular, respectively.

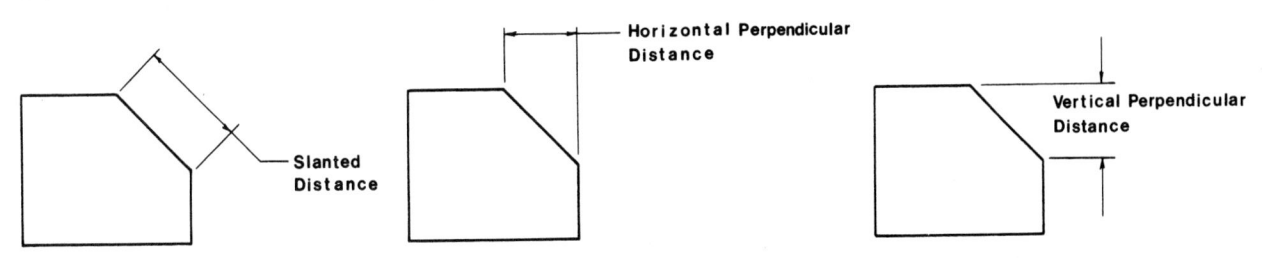

FIGURE 5-9 How to dimension slanted features.

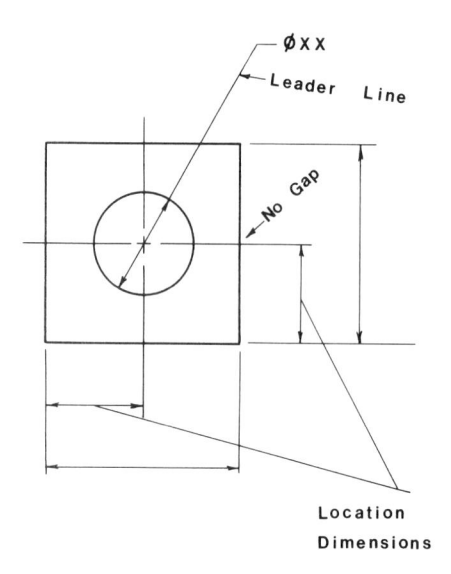

FIGURE 5-10 How to dimension circular features.

Slanted features require more care to dimension using a computer dimensioning function than do horizontal and vertical distances. The starting and end points must be carefully defined and indicated so that the corrected value is calculated and inserted on the drawing.

5-4 CIRCULAR FEATURES

Circular features are dimensioned by a location and a size. The location is defined using extension, center, and dimension lines as shown in Figure 5-10. The location dimensions always indicate the centerpoint of the feature. A centerline may be used as an extension line. No gap is required when a centerline crosses an object line.

The size value for a circular feature in reference to the feature using a leader line is shown in Figure 5-10. The leader line should pass through, or point at, the centerpoint of the feature. It should also end with a short horizontal segment at the end of leader lines. Some computer graphic systems do not include a short horizontal segment at the end of leader lines, but point at the center of the value callout as shown in Figure 5-11.

Figure 5-10 uses the symbol ϕ to specify a diameter. The notation DIA is still used, but the latest ANSI standards call for the ϕ symbol (Figure 5-12).

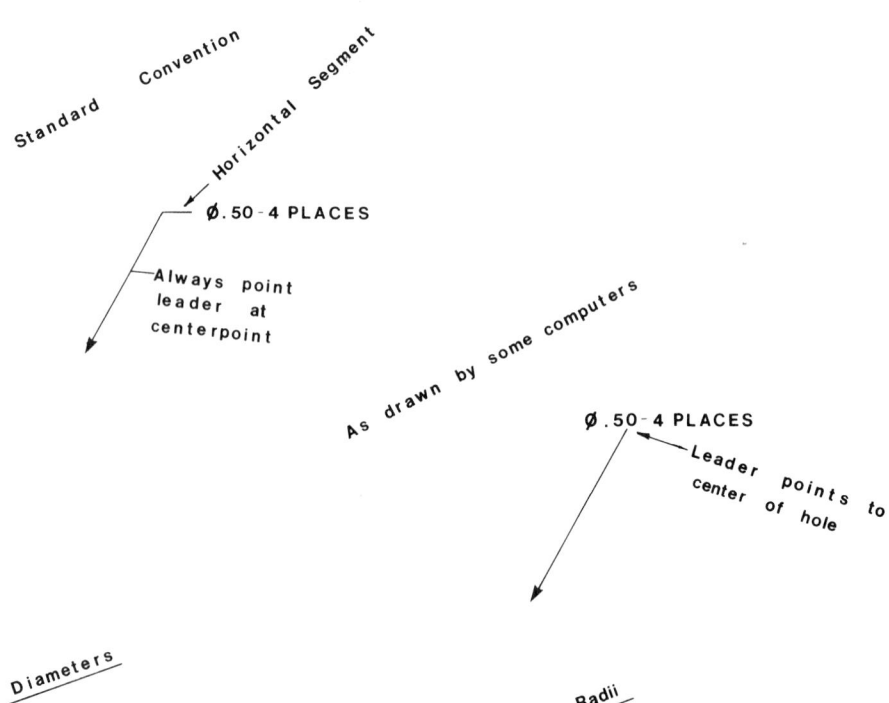

FIGURE 5-11 If possible, include a short horizontal segment at the end of leader lines.

FIGURE 5-12 Older and new symbols for diameter and radius.

Sec. 5-4 Circular Features

The ϕ symbol for diameter has been introduced to help eliminate language dependences in technical drawing. The R notation used to designate radius dimensions should precede the dimension value. The older notation located the R after the value.

Diameter values are specified when the feature is a complete, or almost a complete, circle. Radius dimensions are used for arcs. The general rule is to match the dimension notation to the tool size designations needed to manufacture the feature. For example, holes that will probably be manufactured using a drill should be dimensioned using a diameter, as drill sizes are specified in diameters (a 0.500 drill produces a hole 0.500 in diameter; see Figure 5-13).

Parts that contain several concentric circular features should be dimensioned on the longitudinal view as shown in Figure 5-14. Dimensions on the longitudinal view are easier to follow than those located on a circular view, where it is sometimes confusing to follow the leader lines, particularly when many circles are involved.

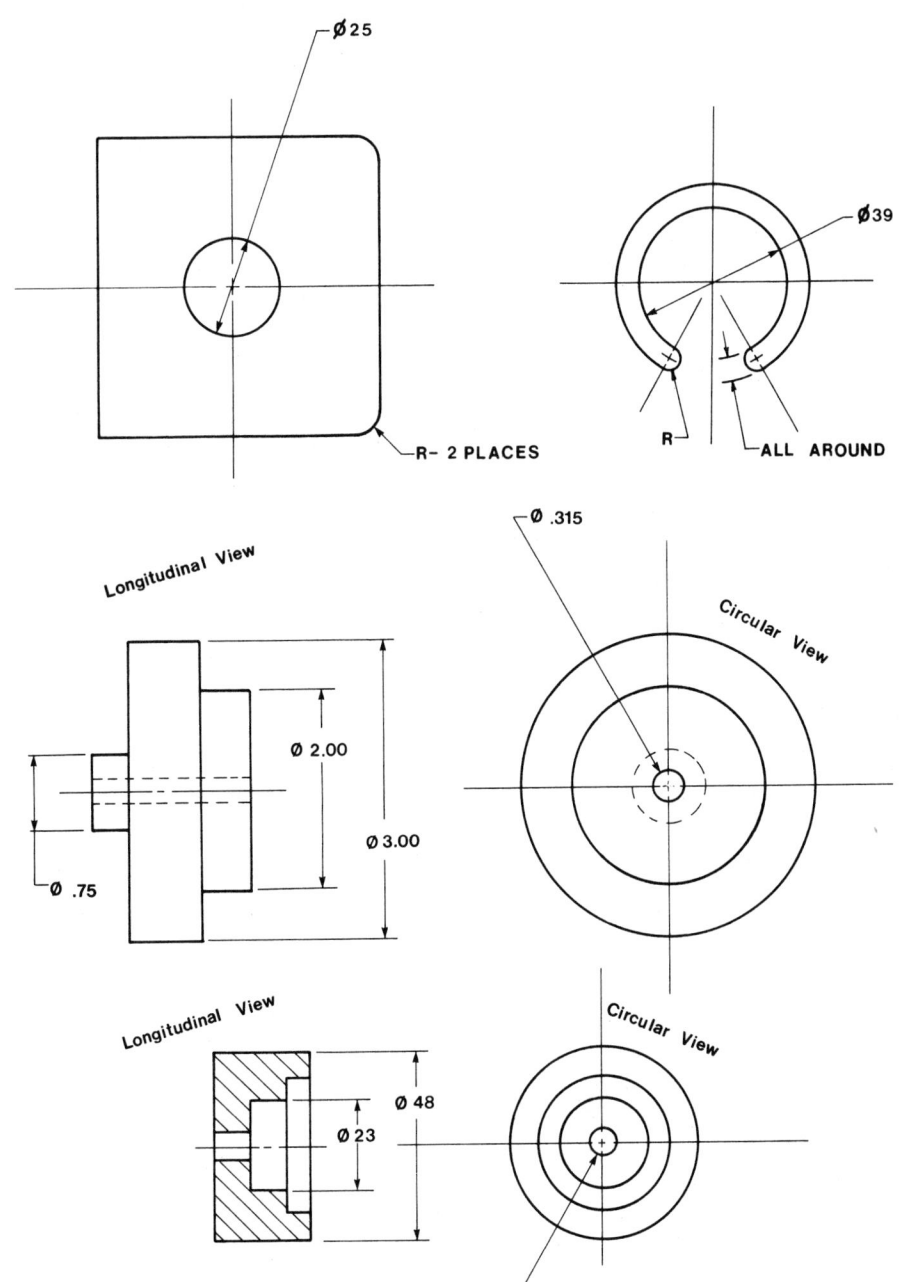

FIGURE 5-13 Use a diameter dimension (∅) when a feature is a complete or almost a complete circle.

FIGURE 5-14 Longitudinal dimensions for circular features.

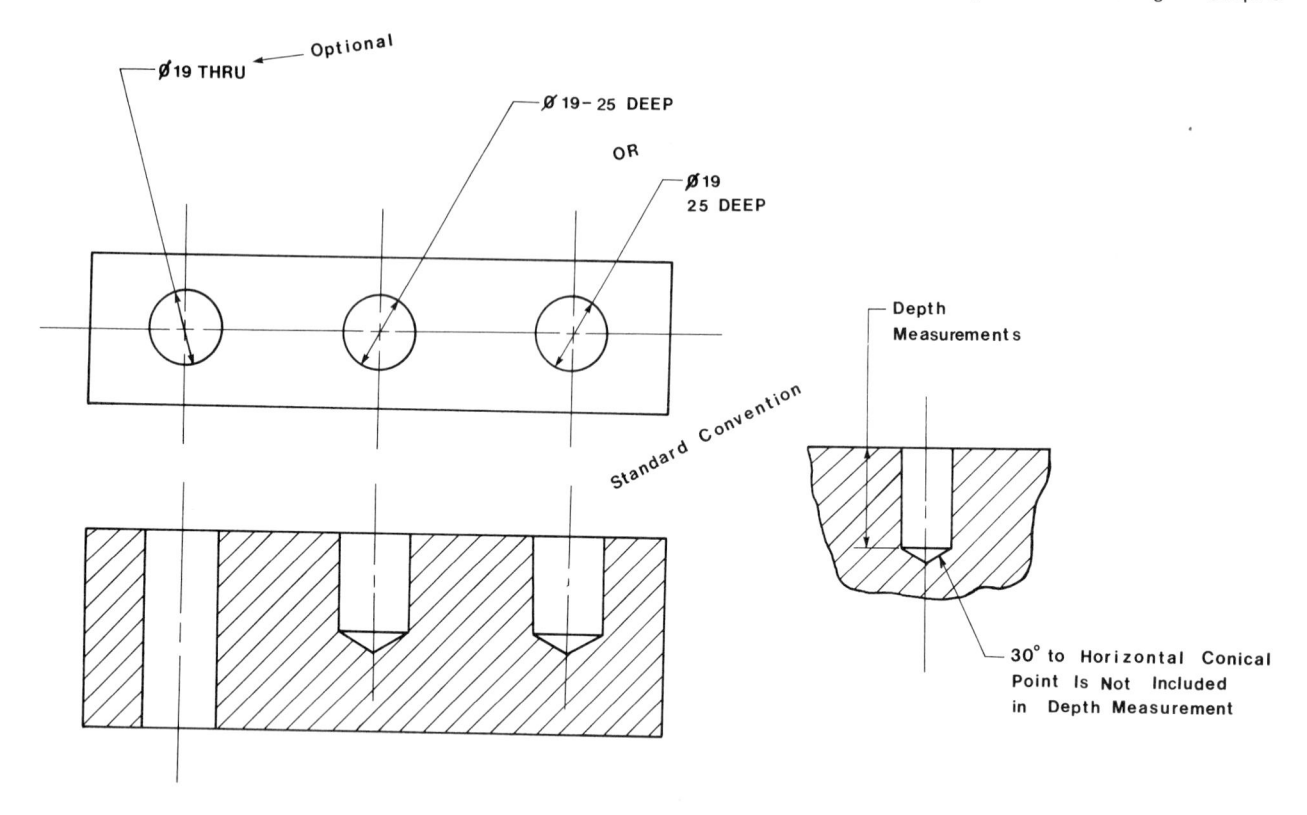

FIGURE 5-15 How to dimension holes.

Holes that go completely through an object need only a diameter dimension. It will be assumed that a hole goes completely through a part unless a specific depth is given. If there is a possibility for confusion, the note THRU may be added after the diameter value, as shown in Figure 5-15.

Depth dimensions are added either to the right or just below the diameter value, as shown in Figure 5-15. The depth of a hole refers to the straight portion of the hole and does not include the conical tip. The slanted lines representing the conical portion of the hole are drawn at 30° to the top surface of the hole. Some computer systems will add the conical shape automatically; others require that it be drawn using slanted lines.

5-5 ARCS

Figure 5-16 shows several different ways to dimension arcs. In general, the centerpoint is not indicated on the drawing. If the centerpoint location for an arc is needed, it is dimensioned as shown in Figure 5-17.

FIGURE 5-16 How to dimension arcs.

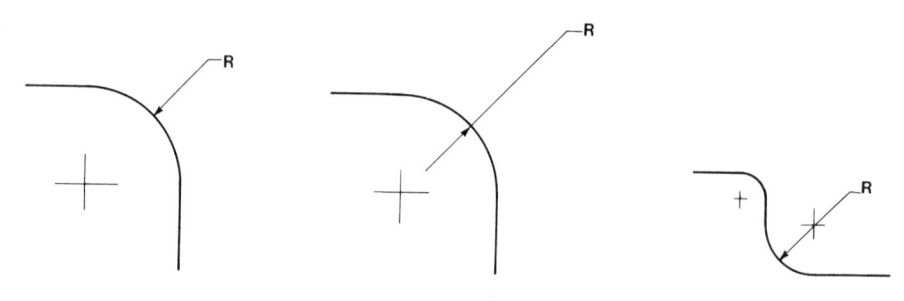

Sec. 5-6 Angles 107

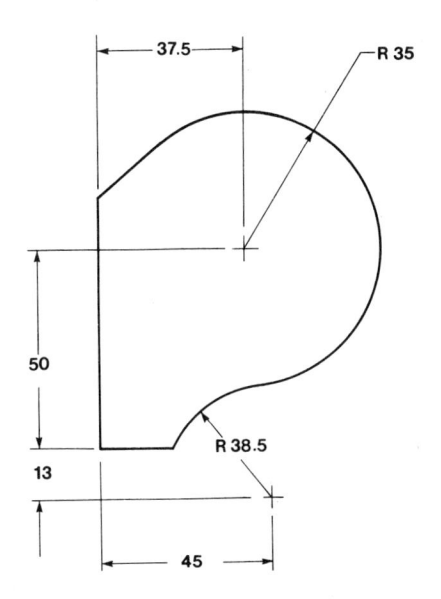

FIGURE 5-17 How to dimension arcs using arc centerpoints.

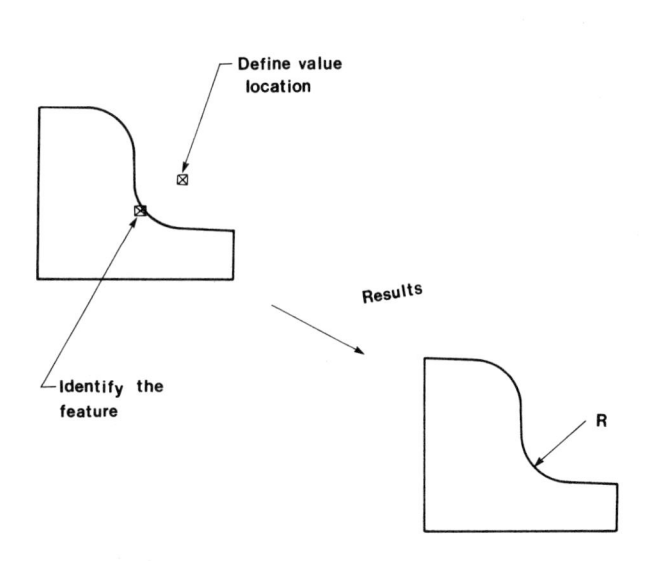

FIGURE 5-18 Inputs required to dimension an arc.

Leader lines may be foreshortened if the centerpoint is either off the drawing or interferes with another part of the drawing.

Arc dimensions are added to a drawing by indicating which arc is to be dimensioned, and then indicating where the dimension value is to be located (Figure 5-18).

5-6 ANGLES

Angles are dimensioned using either angular units (degrees) or linear units (inches or millimeters; Figure 5-19). Angular dimensions can be measured in either degrees and decimal parts of a degree, or in degrees, minutes, and seconds. Figure 5-20 shows several different ways to place angular units on a drawing.

Computer graphic systems must have a reference surface or edge identified to start measurements. Note in Figure 5-21 how a different sequence of inputs will result in a different degree value. From a mathematical standpoint the angles may simply be complementary and therefore almost interchangeable. From a tolerance and manufacturing standpoint, the different angles may result in different-sized parts. For

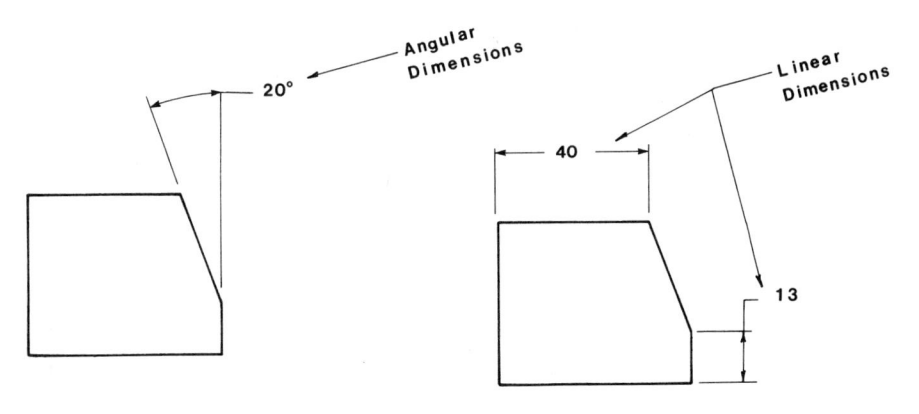

FIGURE 5-19 How to dimension angles.

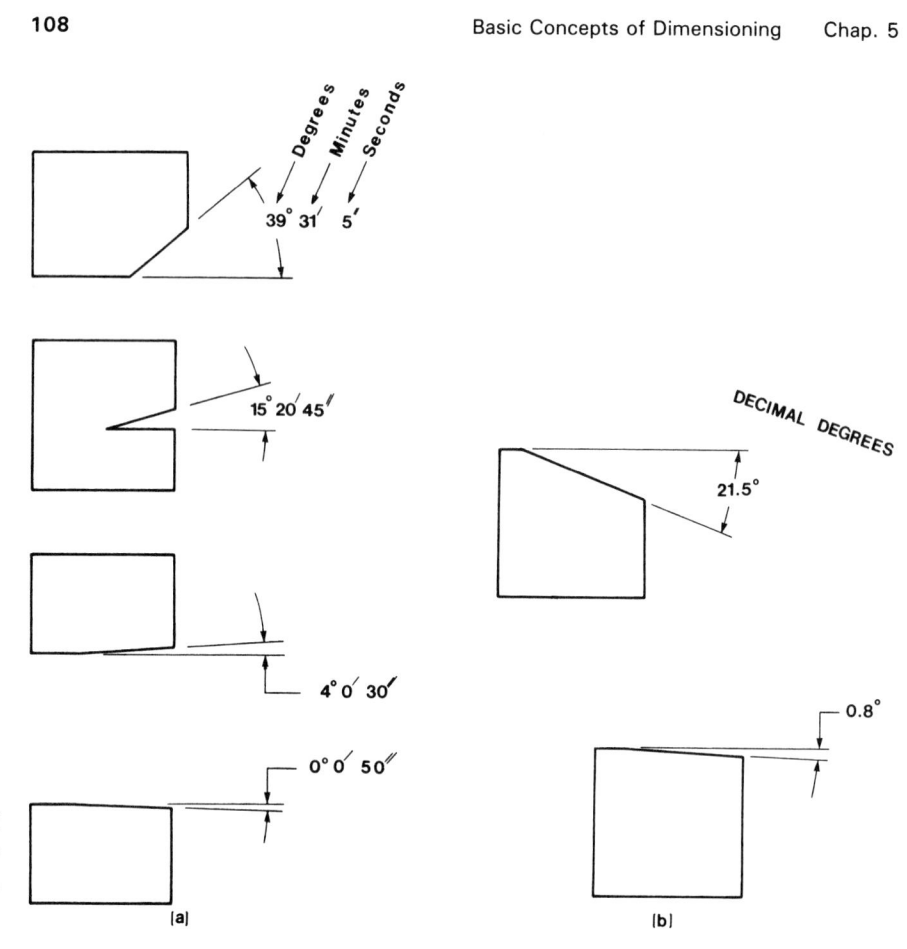

FIGURE 5-20 Examples of angular dimensions using (a) degrees, minutes and seconds, and (b) decimal degrees.

FIGURE 5-21 Cursor input sequence will affect the resulting dimension value.

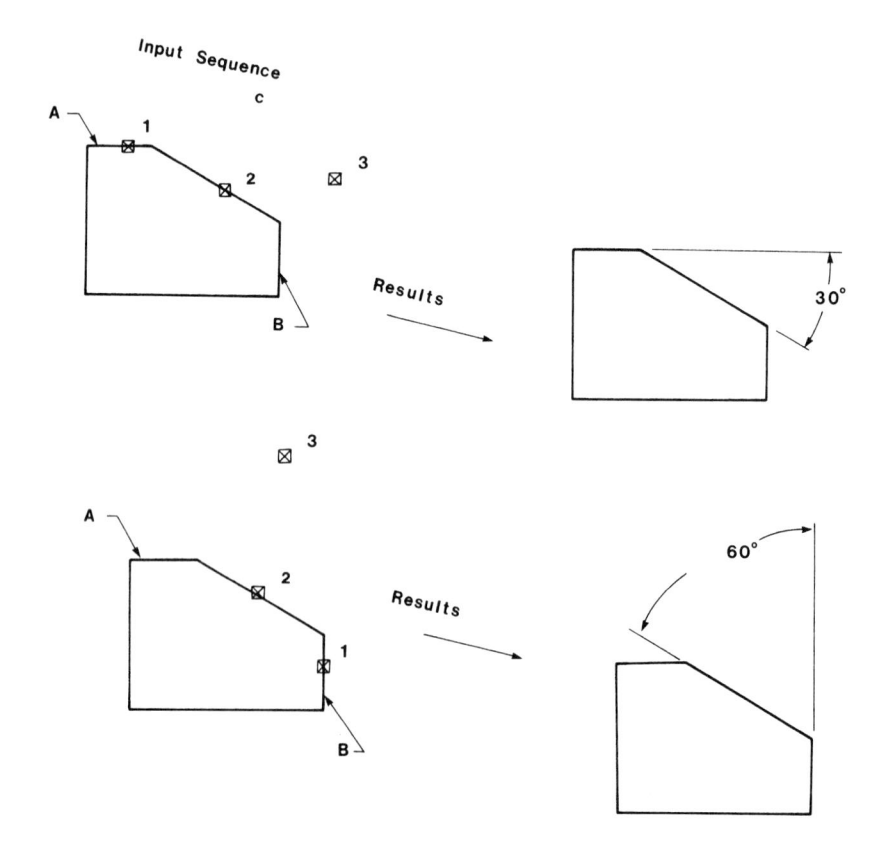

example, if surface A were a very smooth surface and surface B a very rough surface, it would be very difficult to check the accuracy of the 60° angle. If the parts had to interfere with other parts, it would be very important for the angle to be manufactured accurately. Inaccuracies resulting from measurements from rough surfaces might result in some parts not fitting properly. As with linear measurements, angular measurements should not touch or be squeezed next to the part or other dimensions.

5-7 DIMENSIONING SMALL DISTANCES

Figure 5-22 shows two different methods for dimensioning a surface that contains several small distances. Method 1 relates each distance in sequence and is called the *chain system*. The very small distances are referenced to the appropriate size callout using leader lines. The dimensional values were not squeezed into the small distance and do not touch or interfere with other dimensions. Method 2 references most dimensions back to the left edge of the part that serves as a datum or baseline surface. This method is called the *baseline method*.

Computer graphic systems must be used carefully when dimensioning small distances. Systems could place one dimension directly over another if dimension location is not considered carefully. The leaders, as used in the chain method, would have to be drawn and located individually as separate lines and values. The baseline method is somewhat easier, but still must be applied carefully.

Figure 5-23 shows two examples of dimensioning small distances. The problem is to indicate that the two slots are to be centered about their centerlines. Just because a centerline is drawn in the middle of a slot is not sufficient to assure that the slot will be centered. Tolerances could cause variations. Note in example 2 how the extension lines were broken about the arrowheads. In both examples, extension and dimension lines crossed without breaks because the crossings were unavoidable.

5-8 REPETITIVE HOLE PATTERNS

Repetitive hole patterns are very common. Figure 5-24 shows several different ways to dimension a repetitive hole pattern. Method 1 uses a shortened notation form to present the dimensions. The dimension 4 × 25 (= 100) means that five holes are located 25 units apart, starting from the centerline of the first hole. The dimension 13 on the right end of the part means that the hole distances would be measured right to left.

The notation (= 100) means that the total distance is 100 units. It is enclosed in parentheses because it is only a reference dimension. It is not to be inspected. If the total distance is something other than 100, the part can still be accepted if the four values of 25 each are within limits. The hole diameters are given in the notation 5 × ϕ6. This means five holes of diameter 6 each. The (25) value is also a reference dimension and is not to be inspected. It is only included to help clarify the other dimension.

Method 2 is the baseline method. All dimensions are referenced to a single datum surface or baseline. The baseline system helps eliminate

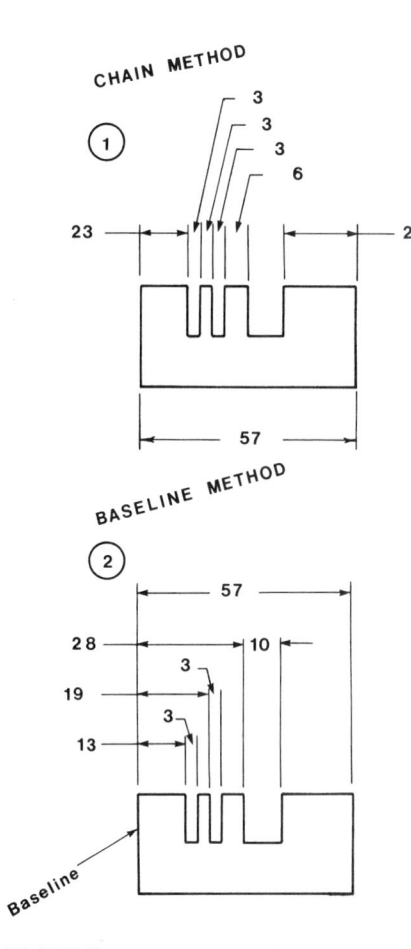

FIGURE 5-22 Examples of how to dimension very small distances.

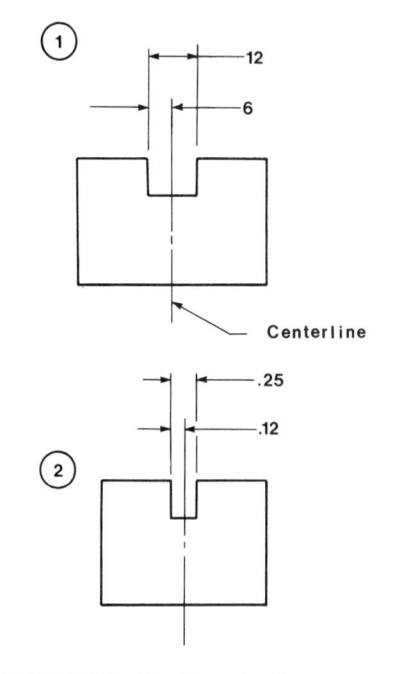

FIGURE 5-23 How to dimension slots about a centerline.

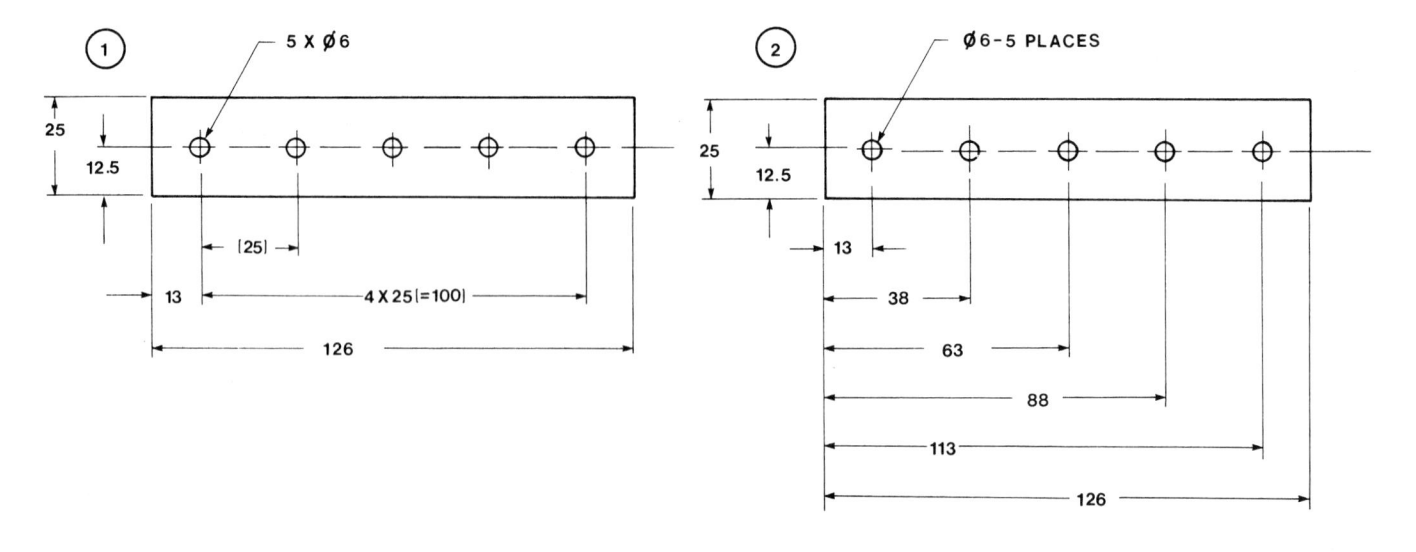

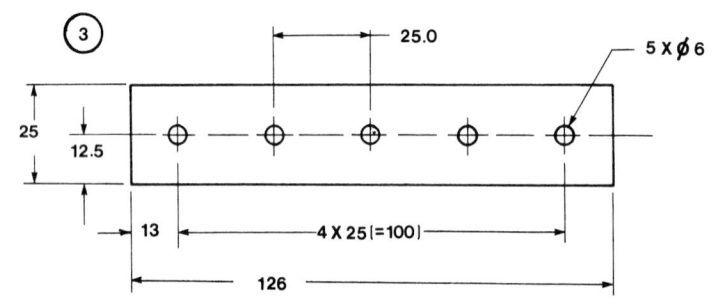

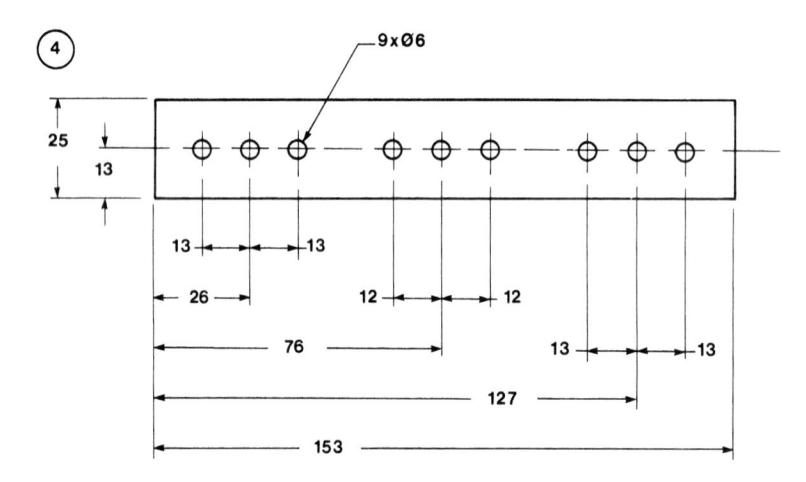

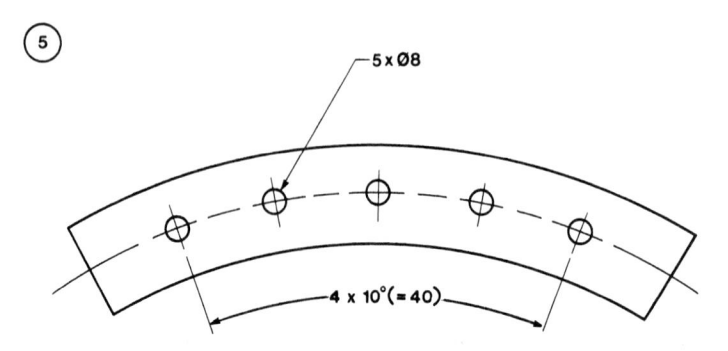

FIGURE 5-24 How to dimension hole patterns.

Sec. 5-9 Multiple Hole Patterns 111

tolerance buildup as each dimension is independent of any other. Tolerance buildup is like making an error in the first question of an exam and then having that error carry through the exam, making every other answer wrong.

The baseline method is difficult to use when preparing drawings by hand. It is easy to forget to dimension a feature, which would mean that all the dimension and extension lines would have to be erased back to the point of omission so that the omitted dimension can be added. Also, any feature changes could require the drafter to redraw the entire drawing. Computer graphics systems, with their ability to erase cleanly and to move dimensions around easily, are well suited for the baseline method. The baseline method not only eliminates tolerance buildup but is very compatible with numerically controlled machines that utilize table surfaces as datums. Some systems allow for direct input from the computer graphics system memory to the machine.

Method 3 is similar to method 1 but assures that a specific distance between the second and third holes is maintained. This method is useful for parts that must interface with other parts.

Method 4 shows how to dimension a smaller repetitive pattern within a larger pattern. The three-hole pattern is dimensioned within itself, and then the group is referenced back to a baseline. This type of dimensioning is common when a large part must interface with several smaller independent parts.

Method 5 shows the same method shown in method 1 but as applied to angular measurements. The notation 4 × 10° means five holes located 10° apart. The other notations are interpreted as they were in method 1.

5-9 MULTIPLE HOLE PATTERNS

Parts that contain many different-sized holes within a small area are dimensioned using one of the methods shown in Figures 5-25 to 5-27. Figure 5-25 shows the rectangular dimensioning systems without dimen-

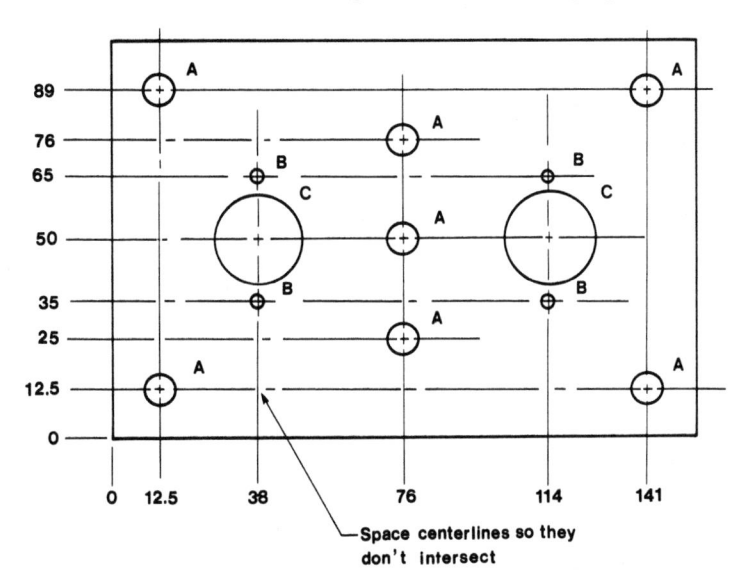

SIZE SYMBOL	A	B	C
HOLE DIA	8.5	4.0	28

FIGURE 5-25 Rectangular dimension system without dimension lines.

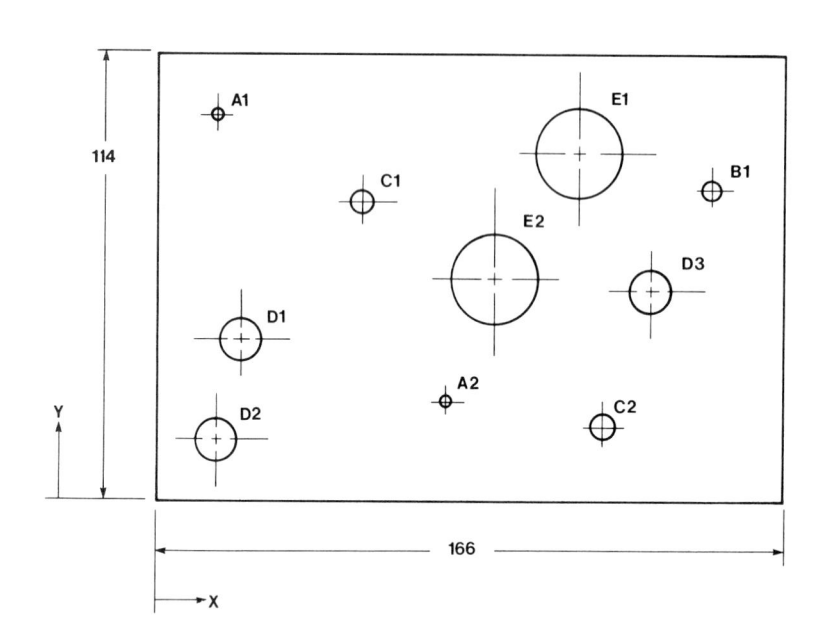

HOLE	DIAMETER	QTY
A	3.5	2
B	6.0	1
C	7.0	2
D	11.0	3
E	23.0	2

HOLE	FROM	X	Y
A1	X,Y	11	98
A2		76	25
B1		146	80
C1		54	76
C2		118	19
D1		22	41
D2		16	16
D3		131	54
E1		111	89
E2	X,Y	89	57

FIGURE 5-26 Rectangular coordinate system.

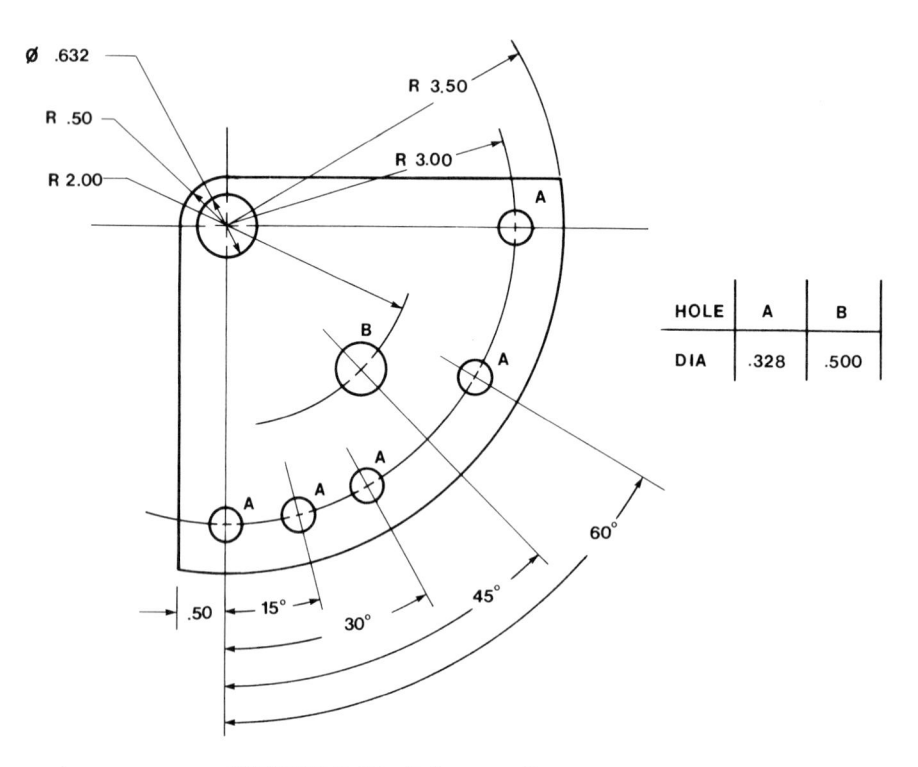

HOLE	A	B
DIA	.328	.500

FIGURE 5-27 Polar coordinate system.

Sec. 5-9 Multiple Hole Patterns

sion lines. The location of each hole is defined as a distance from the corner (0, 0). The distance value for each centerline from the 0, 0 corner is written along the horizontal and vertical axes as shown. Values that are close together are staggered for clarity. Each hole is assigned a letter, written, if possible, to the upper right of the hole. The assigned letters are referenced to a hole diameter value in a table. Any tolerance values needed would also be included in the table.

Centerlines are drawn in a rectangular system without lines so they do not touch when they cross. This is done by arranging the dashes and spaces of the centerline pattern so that there is always a gap when they intersect.

Figure 5-26 shows the rectangular coordinate system. Each hole is assigned a letter and a number. Holes of common diameter have a common letter, but each hole has a separate number. The hole letters are referenced to a diameter-value chart as shown. The hole numbers are referenced to an XY coordinate system. The XY coordinate system is defined on the body of the drawing along with the overall dimensions and any other appropriate dimensions.

Figure 5-27 shows a polar coordinate dimensioning system. Polar coordinate systems locate holes using a radial distance and an angular value. Many machines have worktables that can be rotated and are calibrated in terms of angles. Polar coordinate dimensions are helpful when locating a large number of holes located on the same radius. Hole diameter values can be listed in a chart as shown in Figure 5-27, or they may be dimensioned individually.

Figure 5-28 shows two ways to dimension hole patterns. Each pattern contains two patterns of three holes each. If the difference in hole size is obvious (method 1), only a single leader line referencing one hole is needed. The size dimension would include the qualifier 3 HOLES.

If the difference in the hole sizes is not obvious (method 2), that is, the holes are similar in size, one of the hole patterns can be identified by a letter. Each hole in the pattern would have an identifying letter written next to it and the size would be qualified by the notes 3 HOLES, and INDICATED followed by a letter.

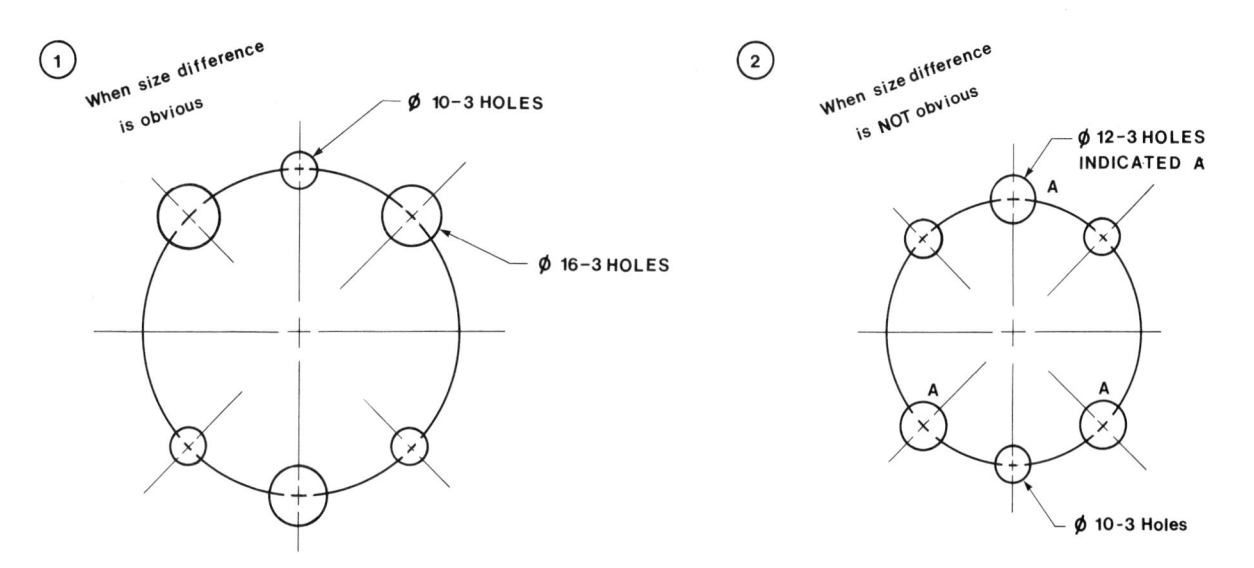

FIGURE 5-28 How to dimension hole patterns.

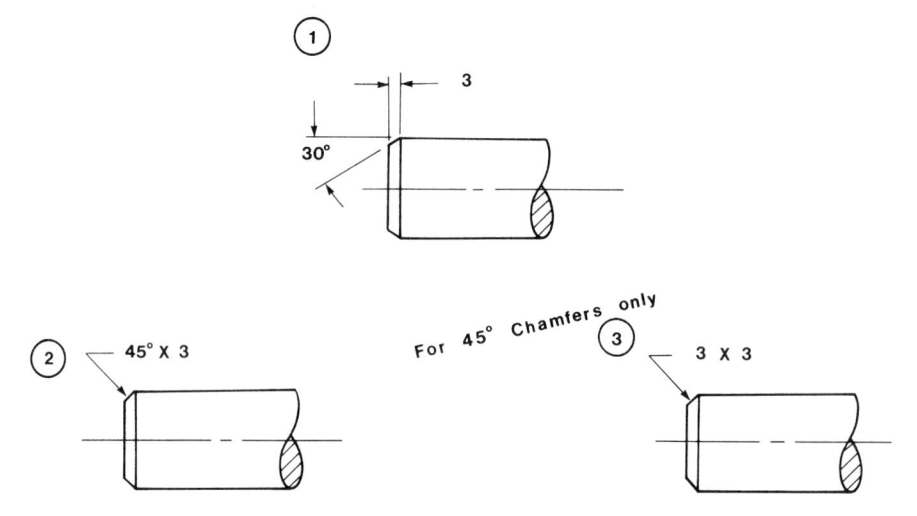

FIGURE 5-29 How to dimension chamfers.

5-10 CHAMFERS

Chamfers are angled surfaces usually added to the ends of shafts or fasteners to eliminate sharp edges and to help make it easier to assemble the parts. Chamfers may be made at any angle, although 45° is most common.

Figure 5-29 shows three different chamfer notes. Note 1 defines the chamfer using an angle and a distance. Each dimension is drawn separately. Note 2 combines the angle and distance. Some companies require that the word CHAMFER be added after this type of note. Note 3 gives only a distance and can only be used for 45° chamfers.

5-11 KNURLS

Knurls are patterns cut into objects that make it easier to grip the object. Knurls can also be added to shafts before the shafts are fitted into a hole, to help ensure a stronger, more permanent fit. Figure 5-30 shows how to define and call out a knurl. The shaft diameter is given along with the length to be knurled and the depth of the knurl. The note FULL KNURL is added to the length because the edges of the knurl pattern may not form completely. The portion of the knurl that is not fully formed is not counted as part of the knurl length.

The distance from the end of the shaft is given if necessary. Knurls that start at the end of the shaft do not need this dimension, and the full knurl distance can be measured directly from the shaft end. There

FIGURE 5-30 How to dimension a knurl.

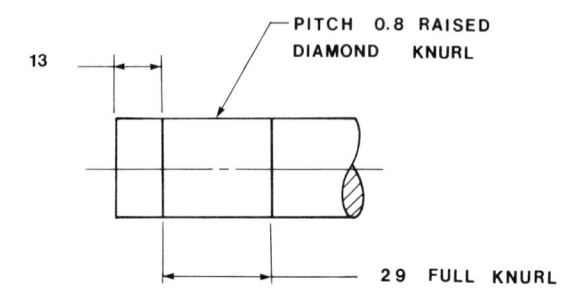

Sec. 5-12   Rounded Ends   115

FIGURE 5-31 Example of a diamond knurl and a straight knurl.

are two types of knurls: diamond and straight. Figure 5-31 shows each type. The depth of a knurl is defined in terms of pitch.

5-12 ROUNDED ENDS

Shapes with rounded ends are very common on technical drawings. Figure 5-32 shows several different types of rounded ends and shows how to dimension each.

Fully rounded ends, ends of 180°, are dimensioned by giving the two overall lengths and the note R—2 PLACES (method 1). No value is assigned to the R dimension. The implication is that it will be fitted within the stated overall dimensions and tolerances. Partially rounded ends are dimensioned by giving the two overall lengths and a radius value (method 2). The centerpoints are drawn but are not located. It is assumed that the edge of the rounded corner will align with the overall dimension that defines the end of the part. The circular extension lines used for the radius dimension prevents crossed extension lines and makes the dimensions easier to read. Rounded corners are dimensioned by giving two overall dimensions and a radius value (method 3). Extension lines must be broken to clear arrowheads.

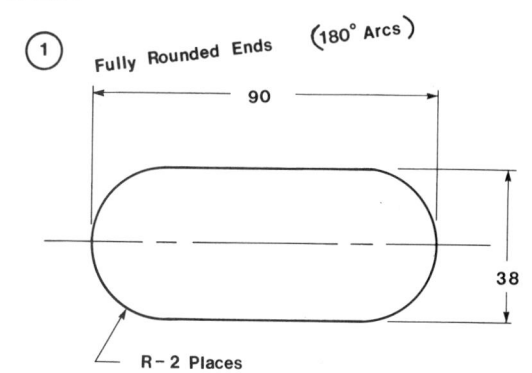

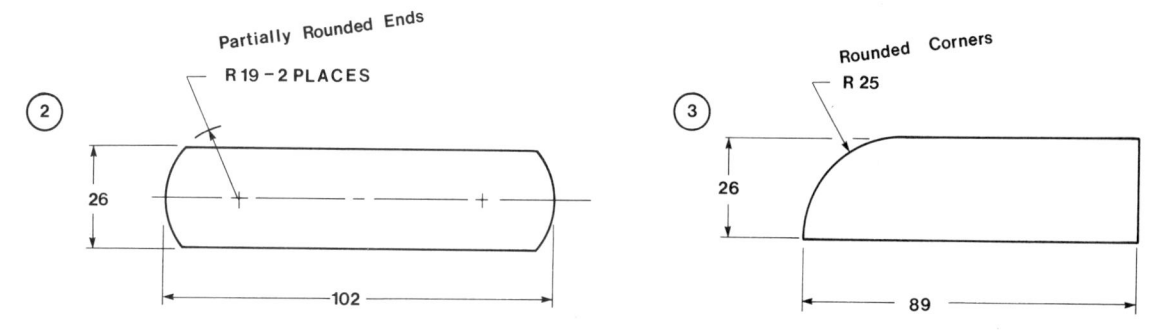

FIGURE 5-32 How to dimension objects with rounded ends.

5-13 SLOTTED HOLES

There are three ways to dimension slotted holes, as shown in Figure 5-33. Method 1 locates the two centerpoints for the rounded corners. This method is used when the slot is manufactured by drilling two holes and cutting away the material between them.

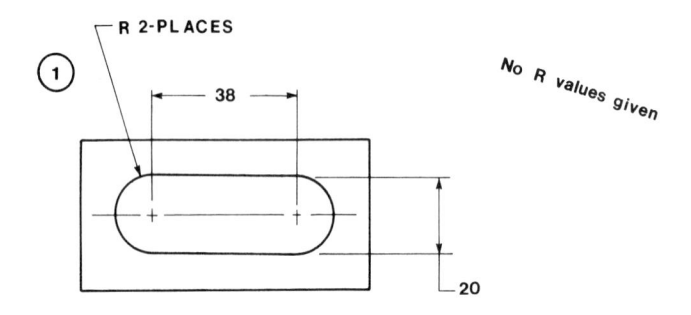

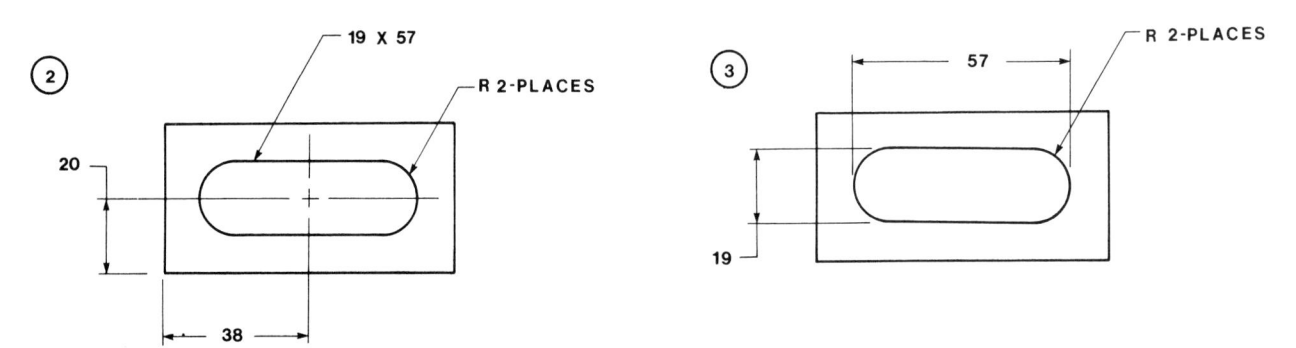

FIGURE 5-33 How to dimension slotted holes.

Method 2 gives the overall dimensions in note form and a single centerpoint location. This method is useful when using punches or other single-action manufacturing techniques.

Method 3 gives the two overall dimensions using extension lines as shown. No radius value is given for any of the three methods. Each method assumes that the radius will be aligned with the stated overall dimensions.

5-14 KEYS AND KEYSEATS

Keyseats are dimensioned as shown in Figure 5-34. The depth of a keyseat is given by stating a distance from one real surface to another real surface. Note in Figure 5-34 how the depth dimension given from a point on the centerline requires a measurement from a theoretical point. There is no real point on the part. Whenever possible, dimensions should always be referenced to real surfaces and edges.

Keyseat lengths are dimensioned as shown. If a keyseat runs the entire length of a part, no length dimension is required. The end of a keyseat which does not run the entire length of a part is always rounded because the cutting tool is rounded. The radius is equal to the depth of a keyseat.

Sec. 5-15 Countersinks 117

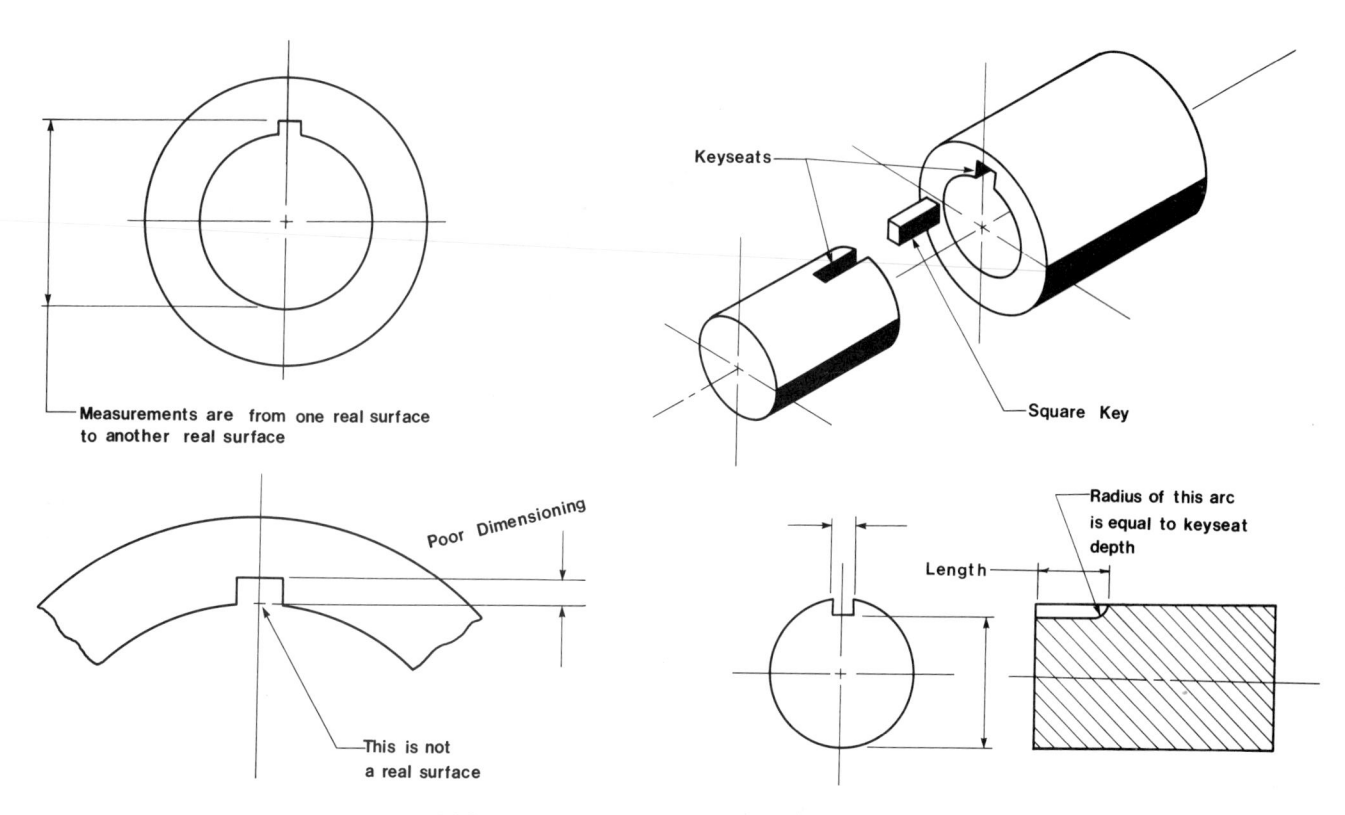

FIGURE 5-34 How to dimension keyseats.

5-15 COUNTERSINKS

Countersinks are dimensioned as shown in Figure 5-35. The dimension note is referenced to the circular view. The information in the dimension note is given in the sequence required for manufacture. First, the hole size is given followed by any depth requirement. No depth is specified if the hole goes completely through the part, although the word THRU may be added to ensure clarity.

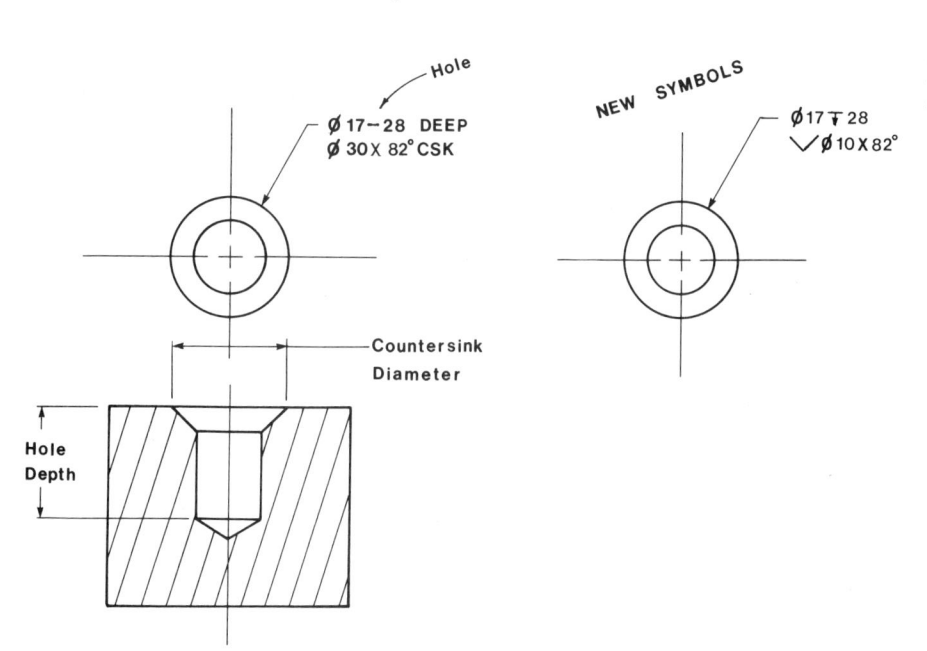

FIGURE 5-35 How to dimension a countersunk hole.

A countersink size is given as a diameter. A countersink is manufactured by marking the required diameter on the top surface of the part and then advancing the cutting tool into the part until it matches the mark. The countersink size, usually 82°, is added to the note. Countersinks will always be cut at 82° unless specified otherwise. Representations of countersinks are drawn at 90°, 45° per side, rather than 82°.

Figure 5-35 also shows some symbols for dimensioning countersink holes. These symbols are designed to help eliminate language barriers in reading technical drawings and for compatibility with computer graphic systems. The symbols are presented in ANSI Y14.5-1982.

5-16 COUNTERBORES

Counterbores are dimensioned as shown in Figure 5-36. The dimension note is referenced to the circular view. The information in the dimension note is given in the sequence required for manufacture. First, the hole size is given followed by any depth requirement. No depth is specified if the hole goes completely through the part, although the word THRU may be added to ensure clarity.

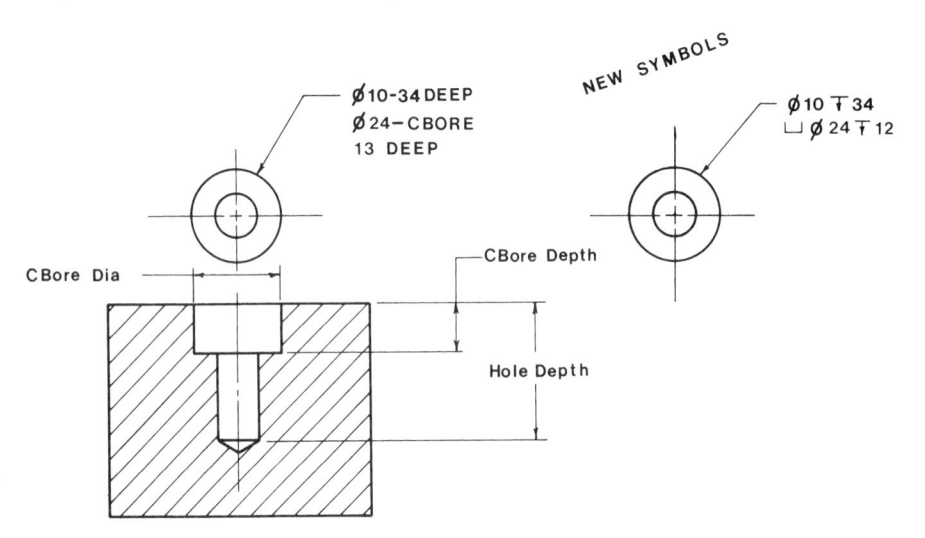

FIGURE 5-36 How to dimension a counterbored hole.

Next, the counterbore size is given, followed by a depth. Sometimes it is advantageous to define the counterbore depth from the surface opposite the counterbore. In such cases the depth size is not included as part of the counterbore note, but is referenced directly to the part using extension lines.

Figure 5-36 also shows symbols for dimensioning counterbores as presented in ANSI Y14.5-1982.

5-17 SPOTFACES

Spotfaces are dimensioned as shown in Figure 5-37. Spotfaces may be dimensioned without a depth requirement. A spotface with no depth requirement is cut just deep enough to create a smooth, machine-quality surface. A sand casting, which has a rough, dark surface, would have a spotface cut into the surface just deep enough to produce a smooth shiny surface.

Sec. 5-19   Irregular Features   119

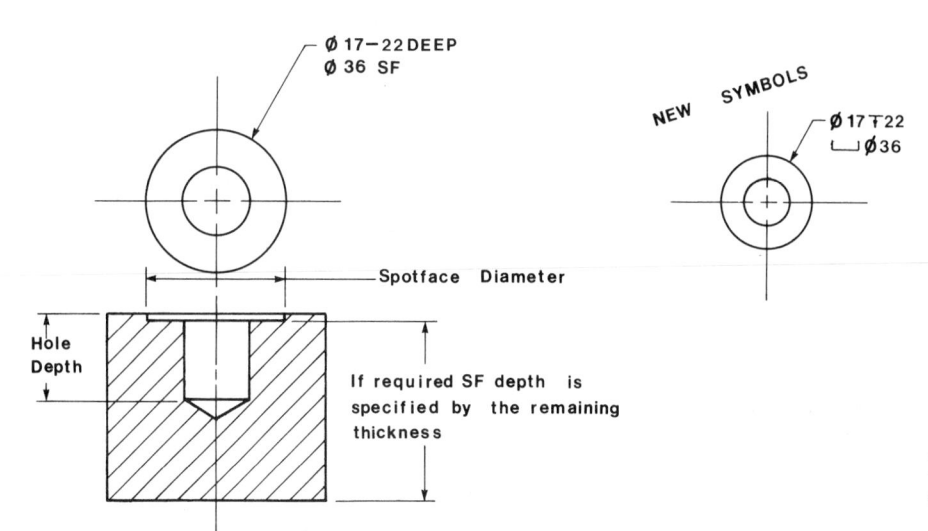

FIGURE 5-37 How to dimension a spotface.

If a depth requirement is necessary, it may be called out in one of two ways. It may be included as part of the spotface note followed by the word DEEP, or it may be added directly to the drawing using extension lines.

5-18 COUNTERDRILLS

A *counterdrill* is a combination counterbore and countersunk hole. It is dimensioned as shown in Figure 5-38. The callout note is always referenced to the circular view of the counterdrilled hole. The callout note is set up to match the manufacturing sequence.

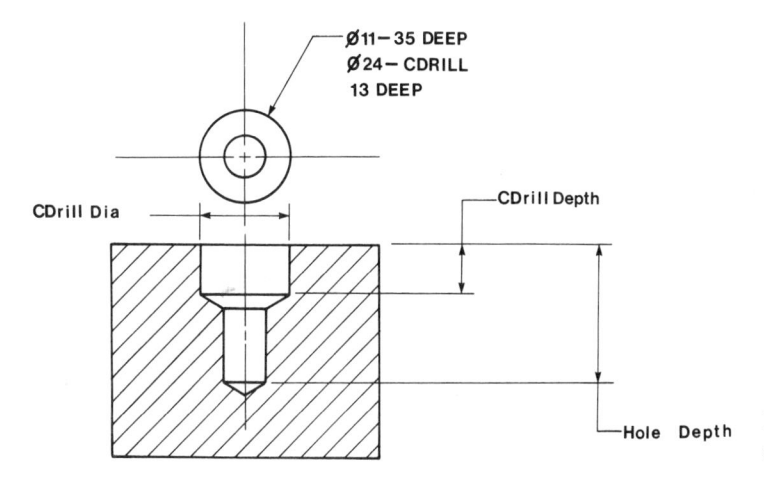

FIGURE 5-38 How to dimension a counterdrilled hole.

5-19 IRREGULAR FEATURES

Irregular shapes are shapes that are neither straight nor of constant radius. There are several ways to dimension irregular shapes.

Figure 5-39 shows the *tabular outline method*. First a coordinate system is defined using an *X* and *Y* axis. Then several points along the shape are marked and labeled using numbers. A chart is then set up to

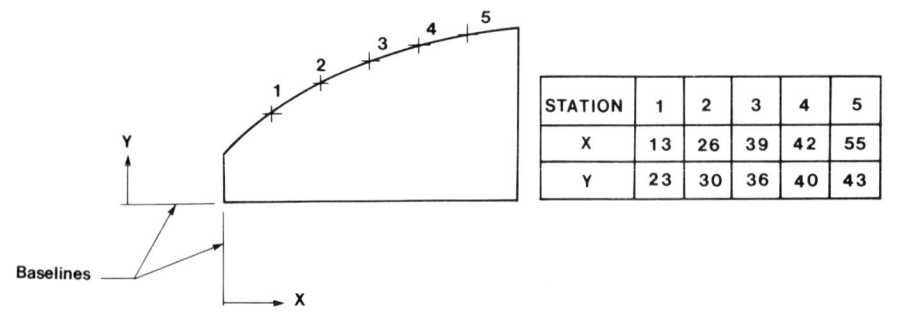

FIGURE 5-39 Tabular outline method for dimensioning irregular features.

STATION	1	2	3	4	5
X	13	26	39	42	55
Y	23	30	36	40	43

reference the point numbers to their distances from the XY axis. The more points used, the more accurate the definition of the shape.

Figure 5-40 shows the *coordinate method*. It is very similar to the baseline method described in Section 5-8. In the coordinate method, points are marked and labeled. The points are dimensioned directly to the baseline using extension lines.

An irregular shape made from a series of interconnected arcs is dimensioned as shown in Figure 5-41. Arc centerpoints are not located directly. Each arc radius is defined and the overall dimensions are given. It is assumed that each arc aligns directly with the arcs or lines adjacent to it. Instructions on how to draw an arc tangent to another arc or a straight line are given in Section 4-12.

Figure 5-42 shows how to dimension a symmetrical irregular feature. This method may only be used when the shape is perfectly symmetrical. Points are marked along the shape and referenced to the centerline and to another line perpendicular to the centerline. In the example shown in Figure 5-42, the bottom edge of the part serves as the second reference line.

FIGURE 5-40 Coordinate method for dimensioning irregular features.

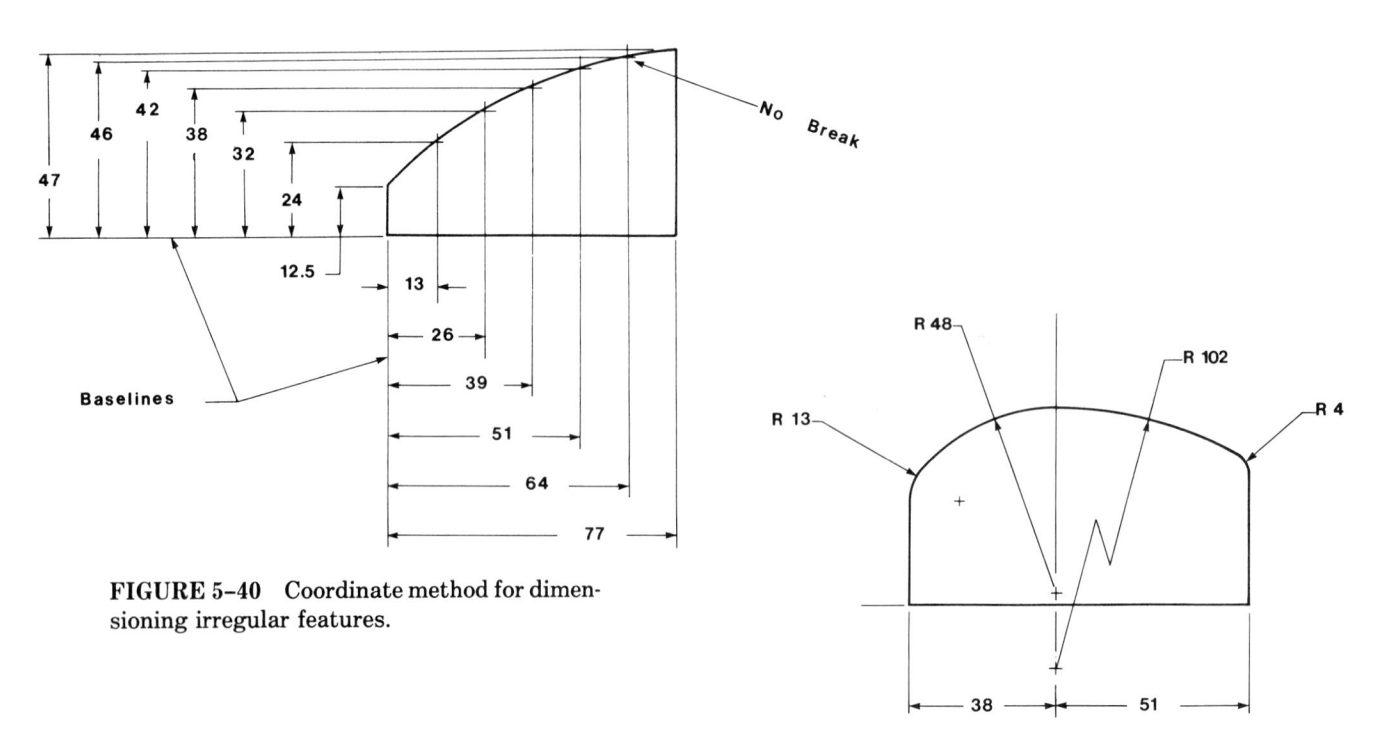

FIGURE 5-41 How to dimension interconnected arcs.

Sec. 5-20　Double Dimensions 121

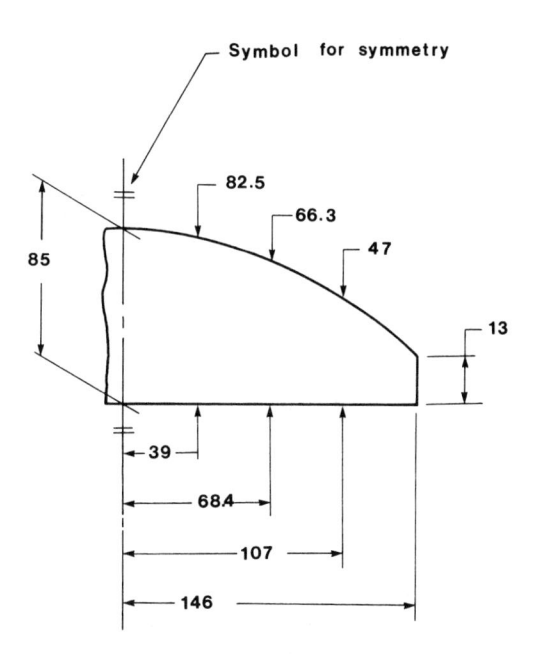

FIGURE 5-42 How to dimension a symmetrical irregular feature.

5-20 DOUBLE DIMENSIONS

Any feature or combination of features may only be dimensioned *once*. One dimension ensures clarity in dimensions and prevents tolerance errors. For example, in Figure 5-43, the top edge of the part is dimensioned using two 1.00 dimensions. The bottom surface is dimensioned using a 2.00 dimension. Mathematically the two 1.00 dimensions and the 2.00 are equal, but not when considering tolerances. If each value has an assigned tolerance of ± 0.02, at their maximum value each number could be 1.02, for a total of 2.04, and still be considered within acceptable limits. The 2.00 dimension could be as great as 2.02 or 0.02 less than the combined 2.04 dimensions. The numbers refer to the same surface, so there would be confusion as to what length is the true acceptable maximum.

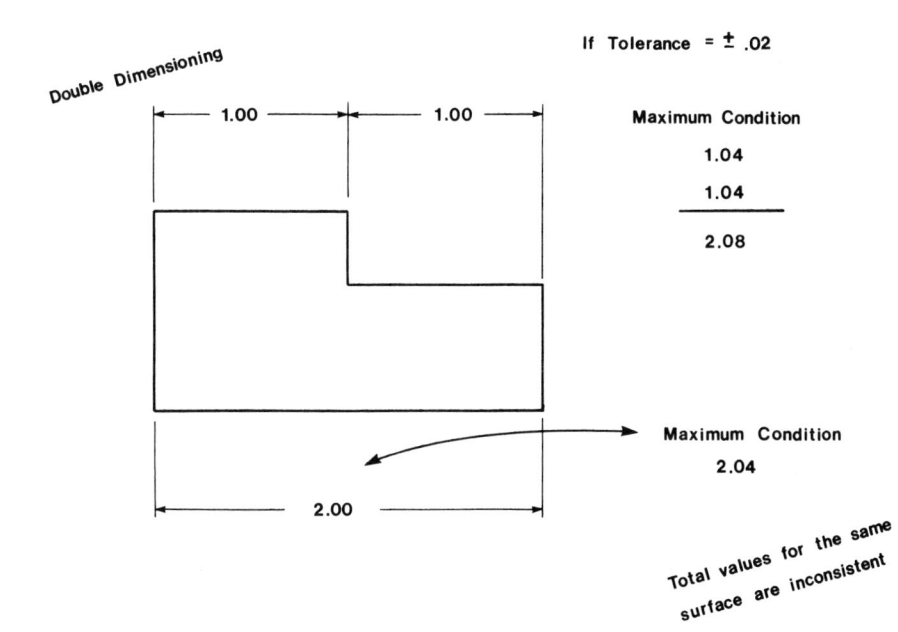

FIGURE 5-43 Example of double dimensioning. Double dimensioning is unacceptable.

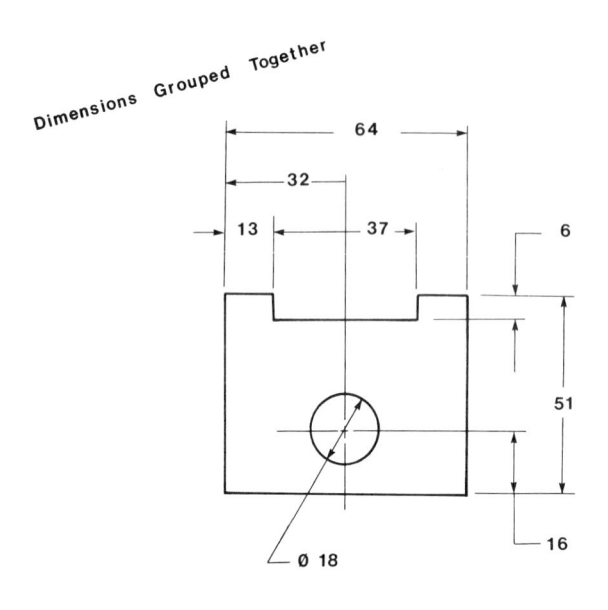

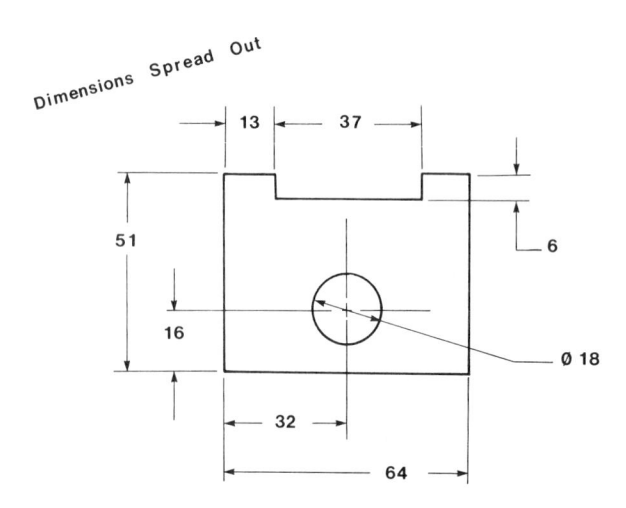

FIGURE 5-44 How to locate dimensions on a drawing.

5-21 LOCATING DIMENSIONS ON A DRAWING

There are two ways to locate dimensions on a drawing; keep all dimensions together, or spread them evenly around the drawing. Placing dimensions together prevents the reader from having to search the drawing for a particular dimension, but can appear cluttered. Spreading the dimensions evenly around the part makes the drawing appear neater and more balanced, but may require the reader to hunt for a particular dimension (Figure 5-44).

PROBLEMS

P5-1 Redraw the object shown in Figure P5-1 and insert the following dimensions.

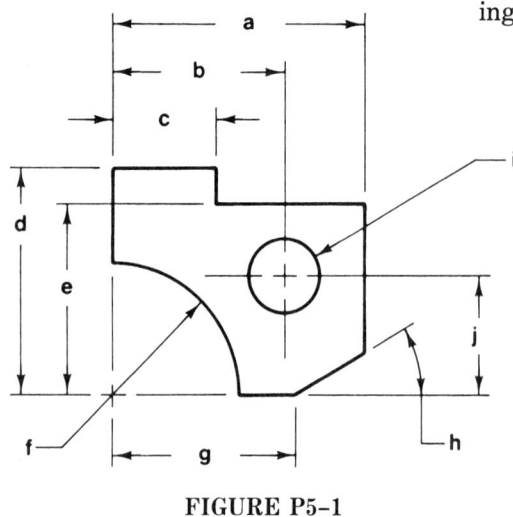

a. $2.75 \begin{array}{c} +0.01 \\ -0.02 \end{array}$
b. 1.88 ± 0.01
c. 1.130 ± 0.002
d. 2.38 ± 0.01
e. $2.000 \begin{array}{c} +0.003 \\ -0.002 \end{array}$
f. $1.38R \begin{array}{c} +0.00 \\ -0.01 \end{array}$
g. $2.00 \begin{array}{c} +0.05 \\ -0.00 \end{array}$
h. $30° \pm 5°$
i. 0.750 ± 0.001
j. 1.25 ± 0.03

FIGURE P5-1

P5-2 Redraw Figure P5-2 using the dimensions and tolerances listed below. Add the dimensions and tolerances in the appropriate places. All values are in inches.

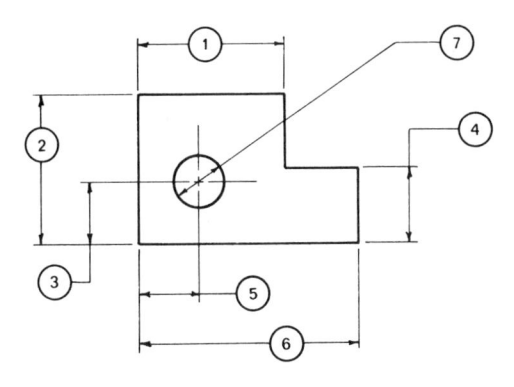

1. 1.50 ± 0.02
2. 1.50 ± 0.03
3. 0.63 ± 0.01
4. 0.75 ± 0.02
5. 0.63 ± 0.01
6. 2.25 ± 0.01
7. 0.500 ± 0.001

FIGURE P5-2

P5-3 Redraw Figure P5-3 using the dimensions and tolerances listed below. Add the dimensions and tolerances in the appropriate places. All values are in inches.

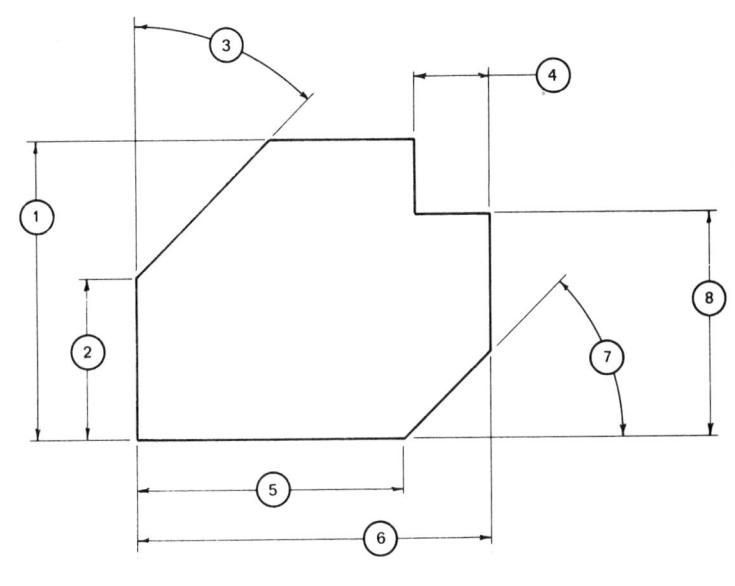

1. $3.002 \atop 2.999$
2. $1.630 {}^{+0.001}_{-0.003}$
3. 45° ± 3°
4. 0.75 ± 0.02
5. $2.754 \atop 2.749$
6. 3.50 ± 0.01
7. 45.0° ± 0.5°
8. $2.250 {}^{+0.000}_{-0.005}$

FIGURE P5-3

P5-4 Redraw Figure P5-4 using the dimensions and tolerances listed below. Add the dimensions and tolerances in the appropriate places. All values are in millimeters.

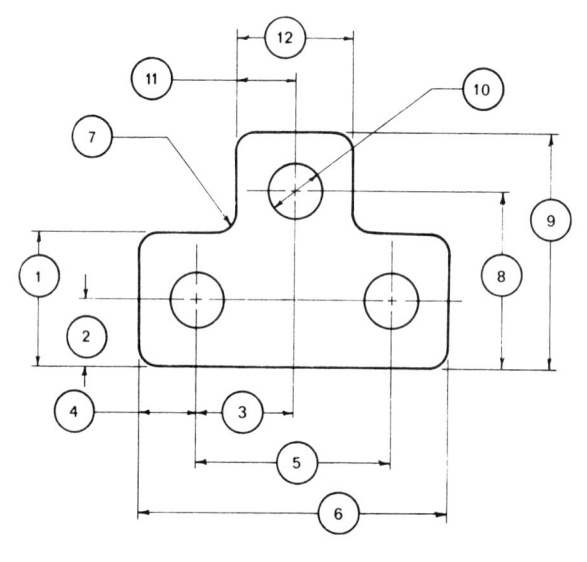

1. 34 ± 0.1
2. 17 ± 0.05
3. 25 ± 0.03
4. 15 ± 0.5
5. 50 ± 0.03
6. 80 ± 1.0
7. R5 ± 0.1 ALL AROUND
8. 45 ± 0.5
9. 60 ± 0.5
10. $\phi\,^{14.02}_{13.99}$ – 3 HOLES
11. 15 ± 0.1
12. 30 ± 0.1

FIGURE P5-4

P5-5 Redraw Figure P5-5 using the dimensions and tolerances listed below. Add the dimensions and tolerances in the appropriate places. All values are in inches.

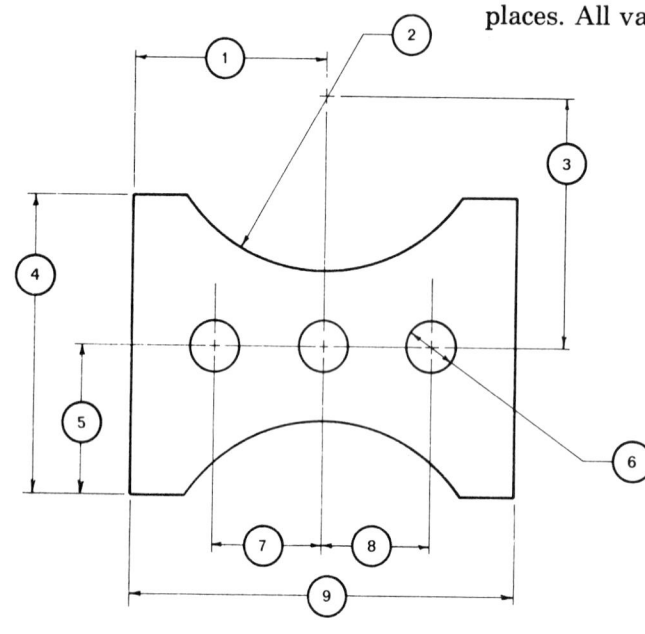

1. 2.00 ± 0.02
2. R1.75 ± 0.05
3. 2.50 ± 0.01
4. $\begin{array}{c}3.02\\3.00\end{array}$
5. $\begin{array}{c}1.51\\1.49\end{array}$
6. $\phi\,^{0.500}_{0.497}$ – 3 HOLES
7. 1.250 ± 0.001
8. 1.250 ± 0.001
9. 4.000 ± 0.04

FIGURE P5-5

P5-6 Redraw Figure P5-6 using the dimensions and tolerances listed below. Add the dimensions and tolerances in the appropriate places. All values are in inches.

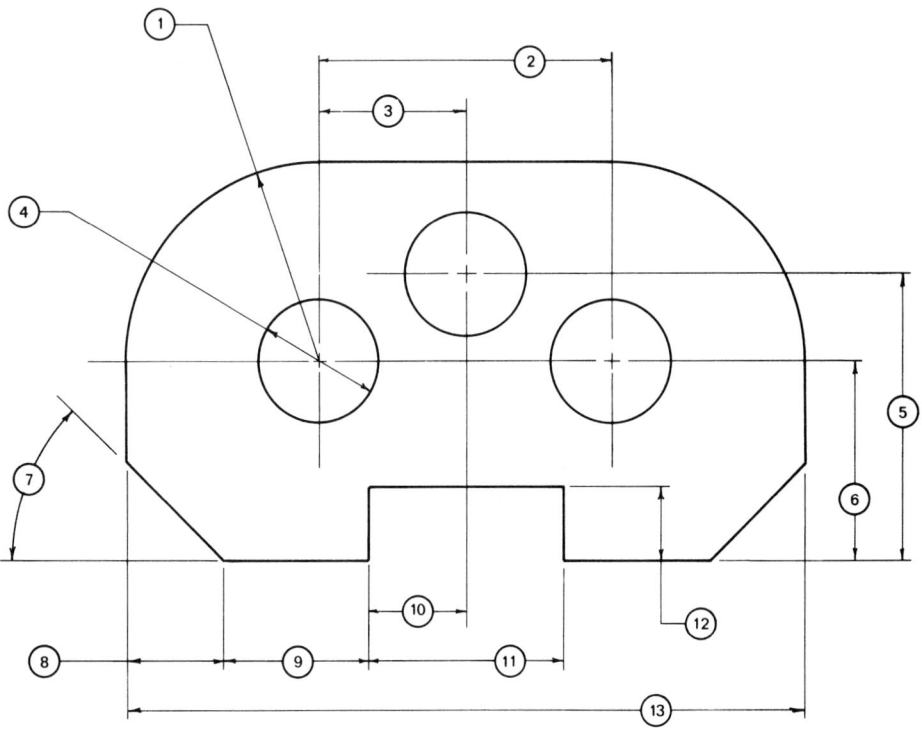

1. R2.00 ± 0.05
2. 3.002
   2.999
3. 1.501
   1.498
4. 1.250 ± 0.001
5. 2.875 ± 0.002
6. 2.000 ± 0.002
7. 45.0 ± 0.2° − BOTH SIDES
8. 1.00 ± 0.01
9. 1.50 ± 0.01
10. 1.000 ± 0.002
11. 2.003
    1.999
12. 0.750 ± 0.005
13. 7.00 ± 0.01

FIGURE P5-6

P5-7 through P5-11 Redraw and dimension each shape or object shown in Figures P5-7 through P5-11. Each square on the grid pattern is $\frac{1}{4}$ per side.

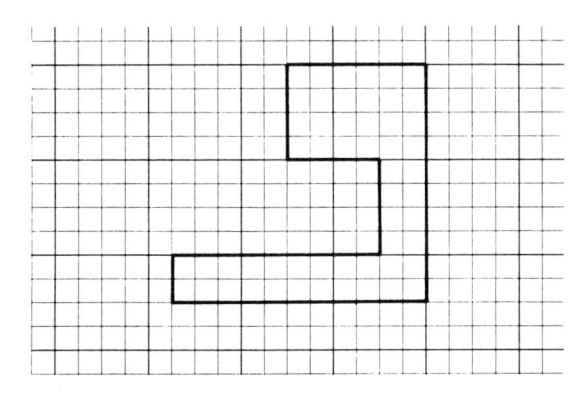

FIGURE P5-7

FIGURE P5-8

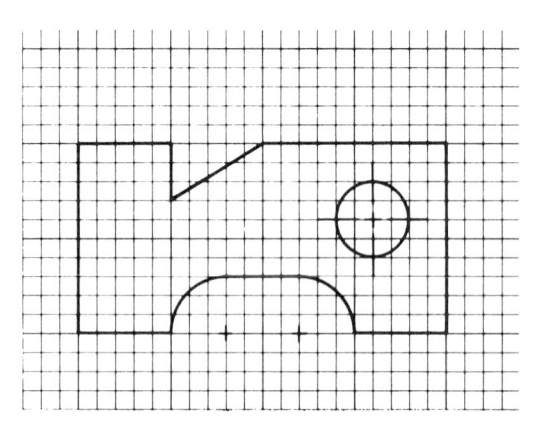

FIGURE P5-9

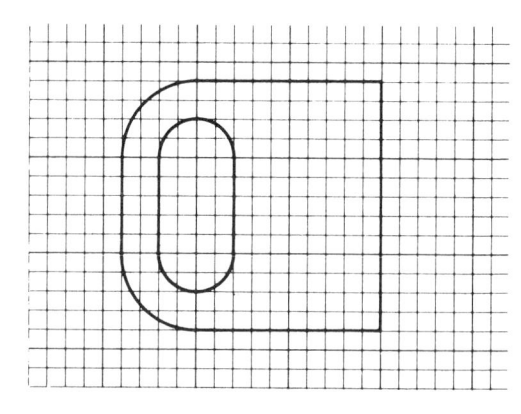

FIGURE P5-10

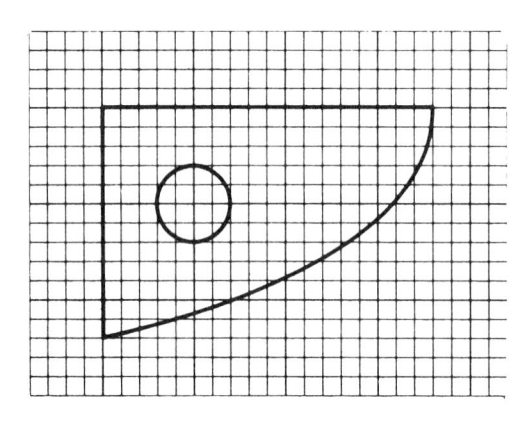

FIGURE P5-11

P5-12 Dimension the chassis surface shown in Figure P5-12 twice, once using the baseline system and once using the coordinate system.

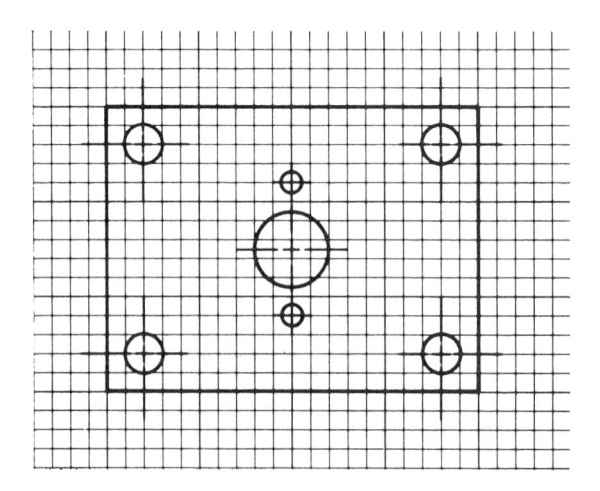

FIGURE P5-12

P5-13 through P5-24 In Figures P5-13 to P5-24, each shape is shown at scale: $\frac{1}{2}$ = 1. Redraw the shape full size by measuring each drawing and multiplying the distances by 2. Add appropriate dimensions.

Chap. 5   Problems

Figures may be measured using either inches or millimeters. If inches are used, measure to the nearest $\frac{1}{32}$ or 0.03 in. If millimeters are used, measure to the nearest millimeter (scale: $\frac{1}{2} = 1$).

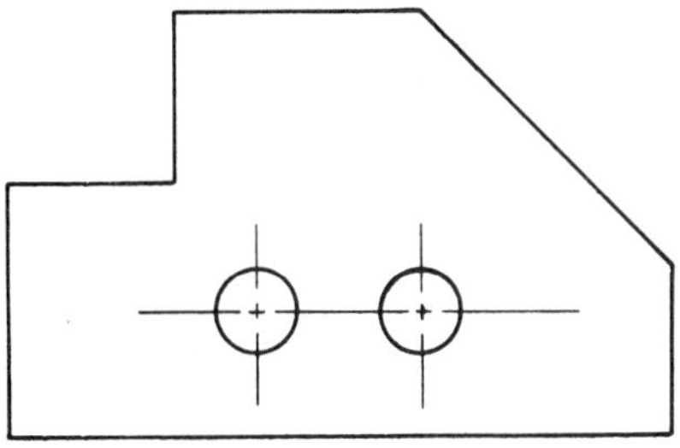

FIGURE P5-13

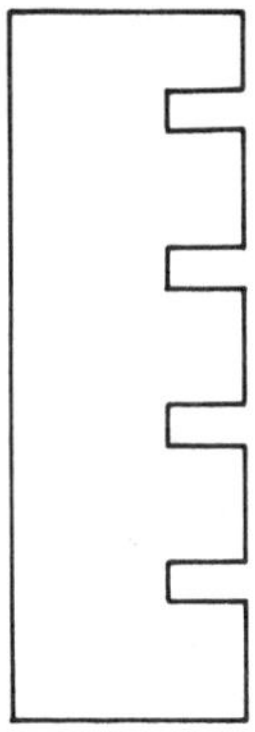

FIGURE P5-14

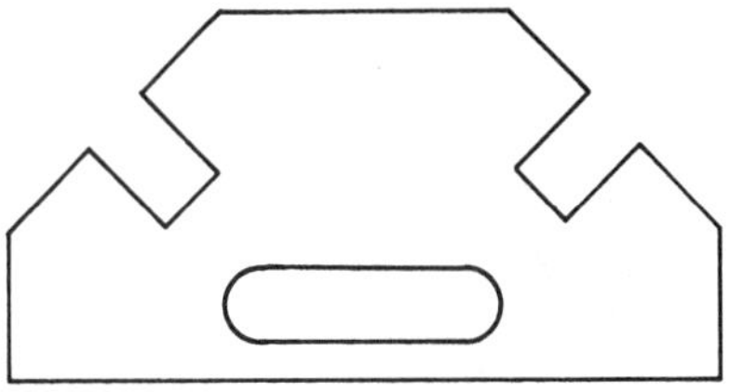

FIGURE P5-15

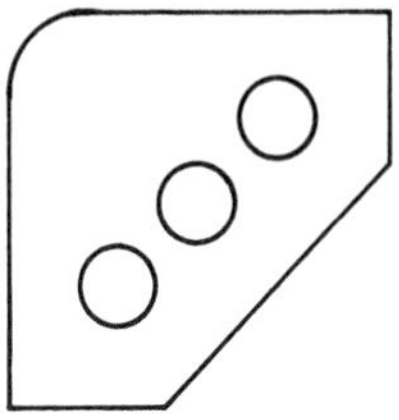

FIGURE P5-16

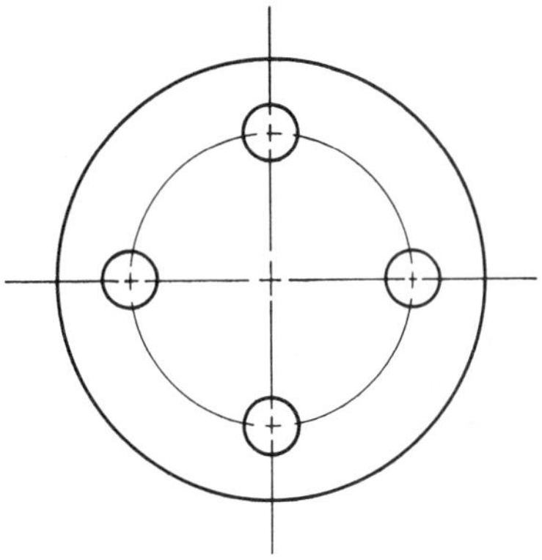

FIGURE P5-17

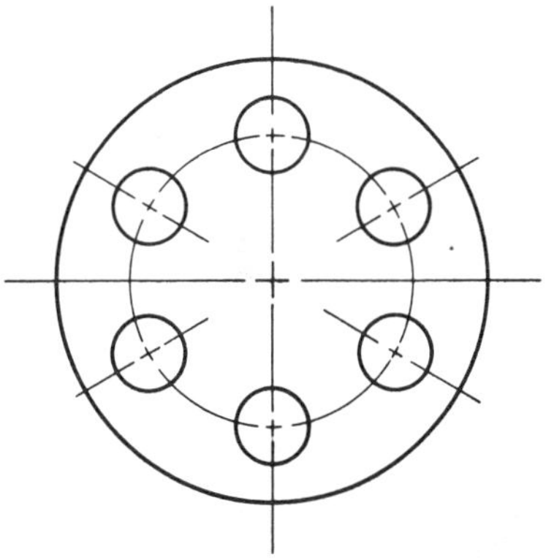

FIGURE P5-18

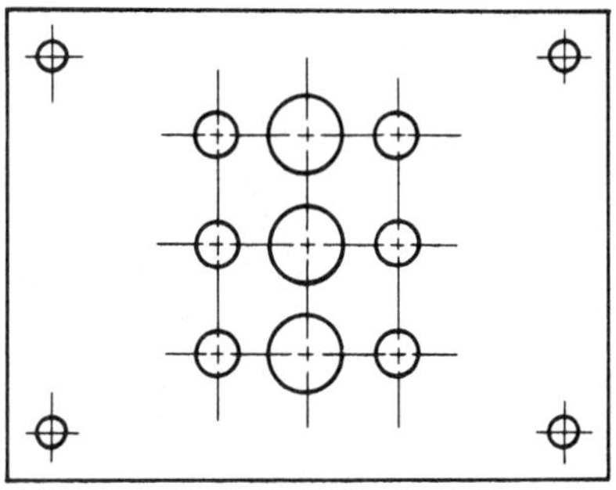

FIGURE P5-19

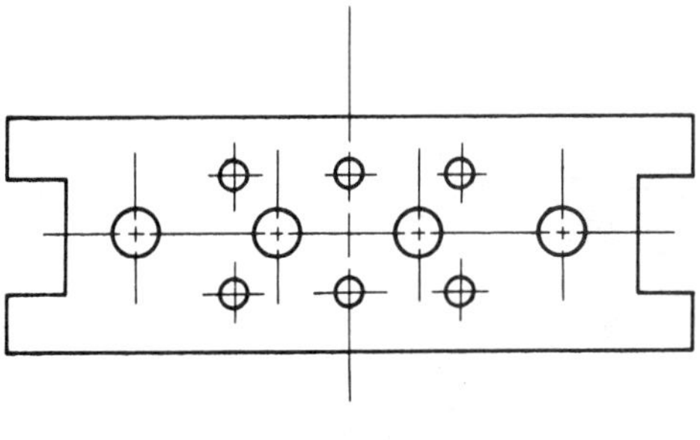

FIGURE P5-20

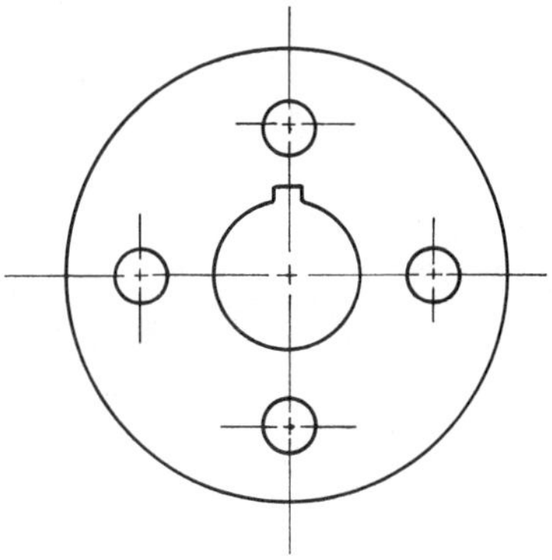

FIGURE P5-21

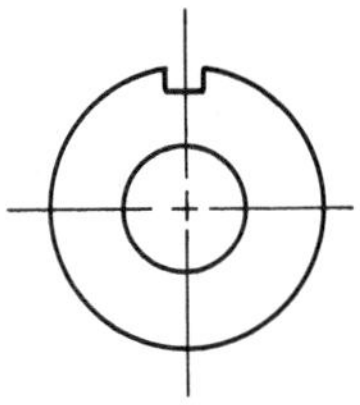

FIGURE P5-22

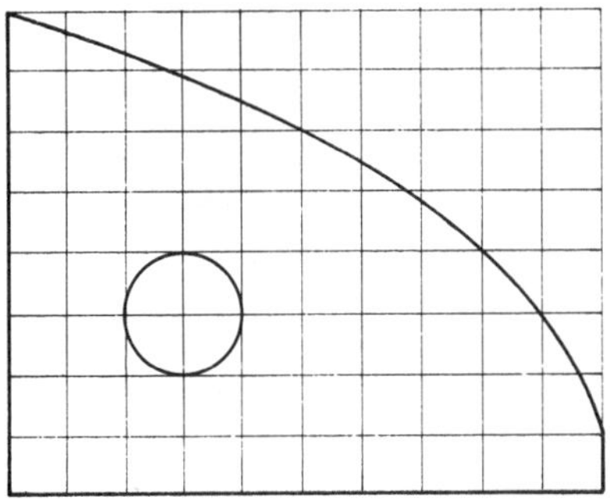

FIGURE P5-23

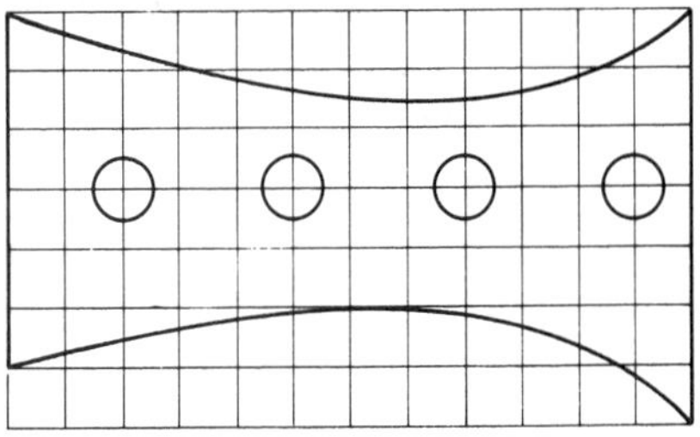

FIGURE P5-24

6 ORTHOGRAPHIC VIEWS

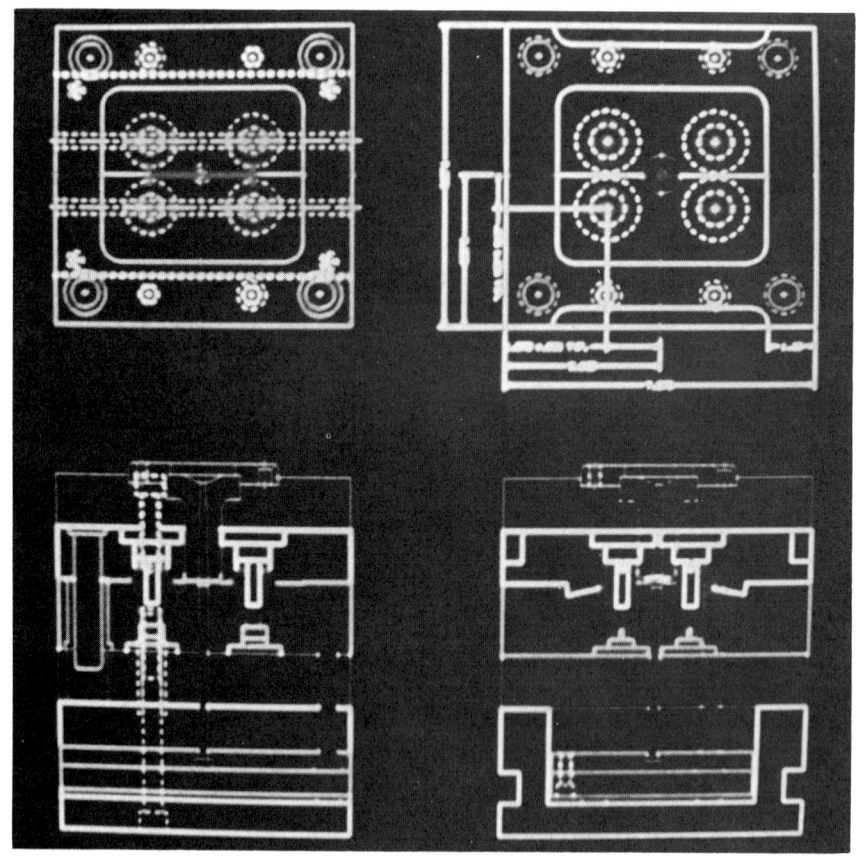

(Courtesy of McDonnell Douglas Manufacturing Industry Systems Company, St. Louis, Mo.)

6-1 INTRODUCTION

Orthographic views are two-dimensional drawings of an object taken at fixed angles relative to the object. Figure 6-1 shows an object and one possible orthographic view of the object.

The orthographic view shown in Figure 6-1 shows the height and width of the object, but not the depth. There is no information concerning the depth of the object on the given orthographic view. Additional orthographic views, taken at other angles around the object, are needed to define the shape completely, including depth.

The two-dimensional limitations of orthographic views mean that line 1-2, which represents one of the edges of the object shown in Figure 6-1, appears as a point (corner) in the orthographic view. This point is an *end view* on line 1-2. Plane A in Figure 6-1 appears as a line in the orthographic view. The line is an end view of the plane.

The concept of end views may be visualized by holding a sheet of paper and rotating it until the plane of the paper is directly in line with your line of sight. If the sheet of paper is aligned directly behind the edge, the sheet will appear as a single edge line. The paper edge is the same as an orthographic view taken in line with the plane of the paper (Figure 6-2).

FIGURE 6-1 Orthographic view of an object.

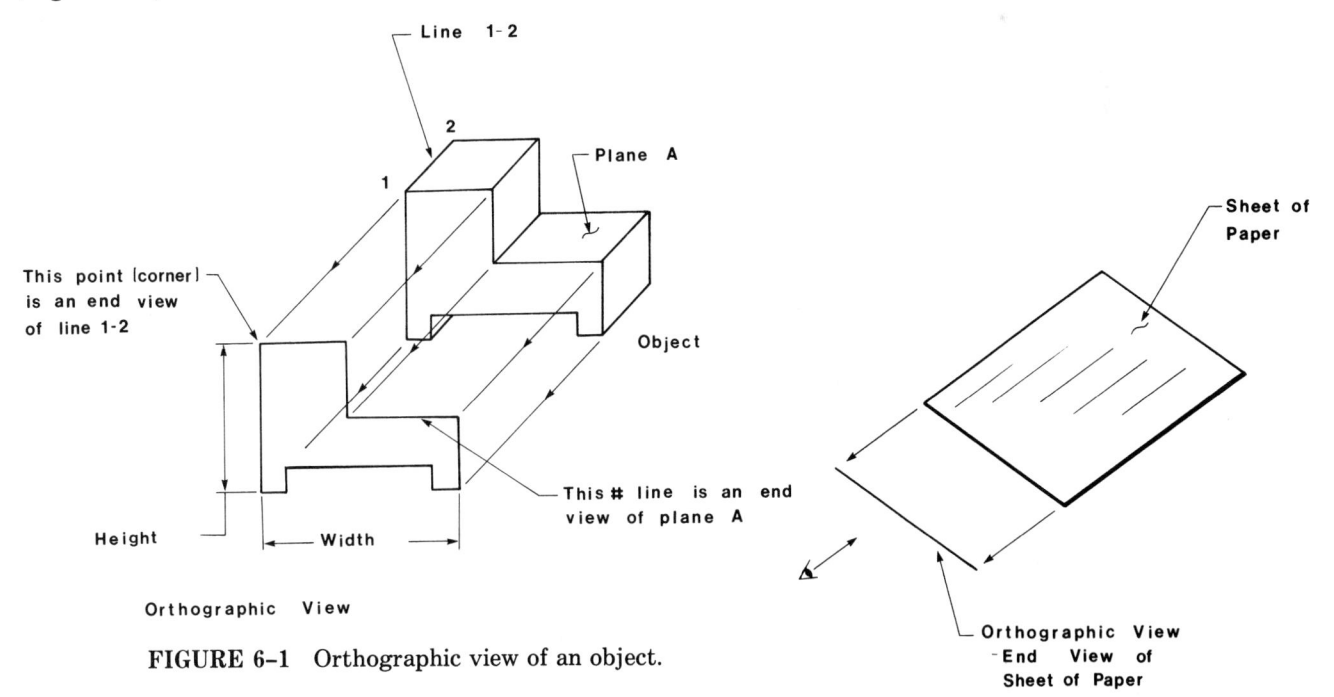

FIGURE 6-2 The end view of a plane is a straight line.

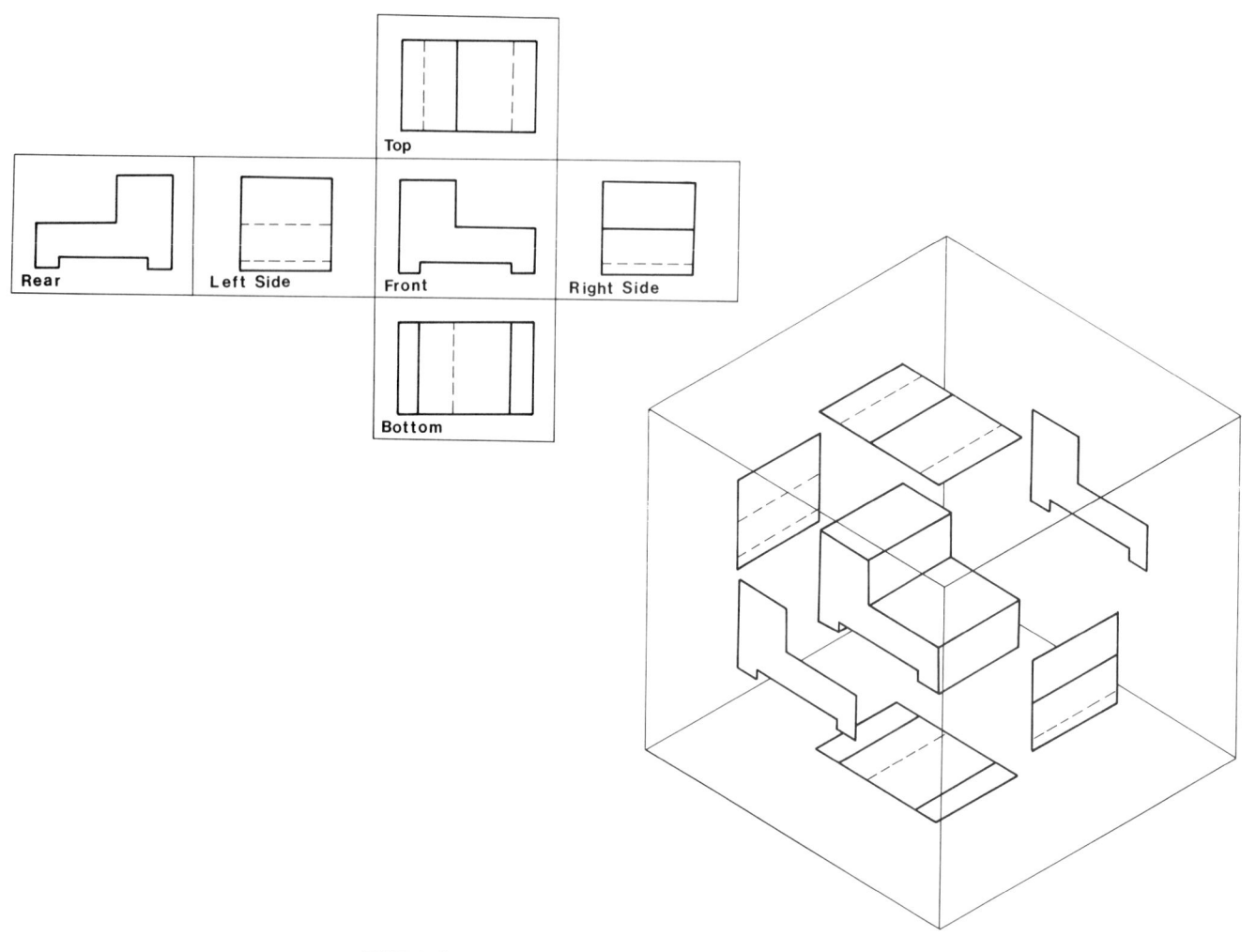

FIGURE 6-3 Six orthographic views of an object.

Orthographic views may be taken at any angle to an object. Assume that the object were within a box as shown in Figure 6-3, and that an orthographic view was projected from the object to each face of the box. The box faces could then be unfolded to produce the six views shown. Each of the six views was taken at 90° to every other. In this chapter we explain how orthographic views are generated, how they relate to one another, and how they are interpreted.

6-2 THREE VIEWS OF AN OBJECT

Standard drafting convention calls for three orthographic views to define an object: a front, top, and right-side view. Some objects may require more than three views, and some fewer, for complete shape definition, but the primary approach to defining an object using orthographic views should always be three views.

Figure 6-4 shows an object and the front, top, and right-side views of the object. The location of the three views, relative to each other, is critical. The top view must be located directly over the front view, and the right-side view directly to the right of the front view. Each view of

Sec. 6-2 Three Views of an Object   131

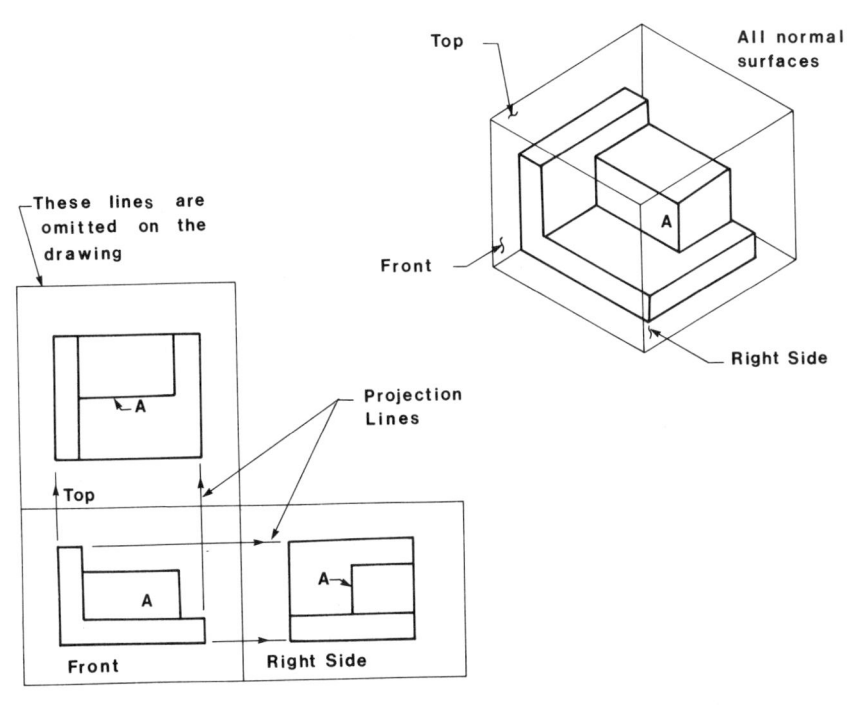

FIGURE 6-4 Standard three orthographic views of an object; front, top, and side.

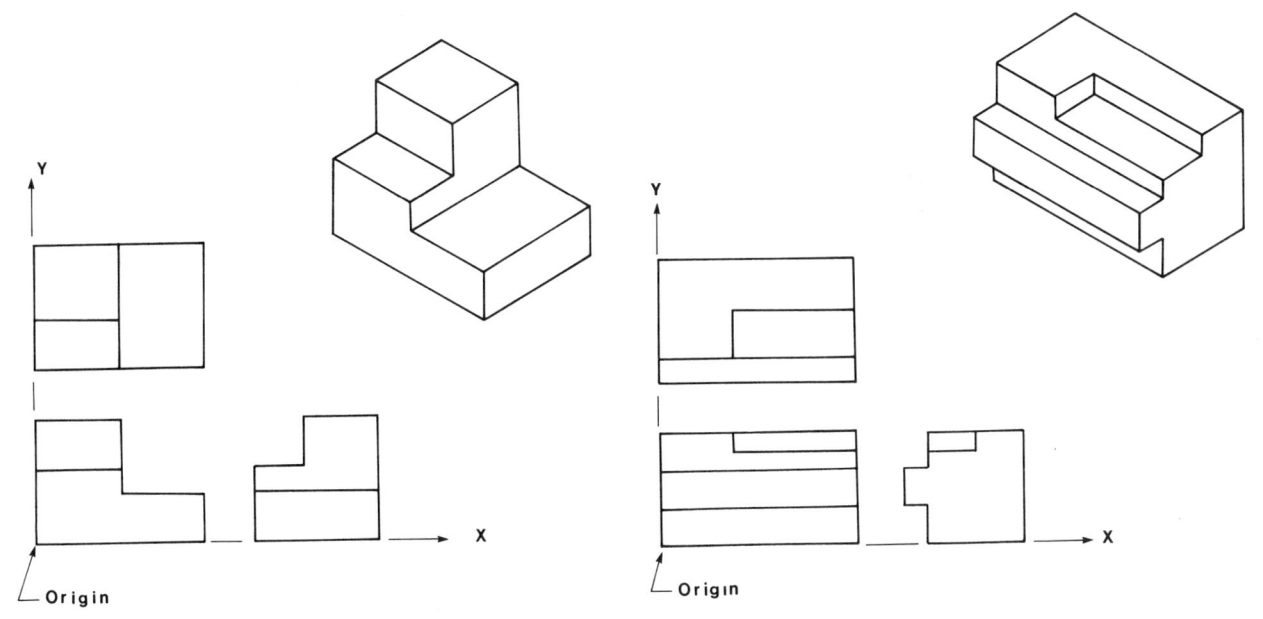

FIGURE 6-5 Object and three orthographic views of the object.

FIGURE 6-6 Object and three orthographic views of the object.

a feature must be directly aligned with the same feature in the other orthographic views. For example, the top view of surface A in Figure 6-4 is located directly over the front view of surface A. The right-side view of surface A is located directly to the right of the front view. Projection lines have been added in Figure 6-4 to help accent the alignment. Figures 6-5 and 6-6 are further examples of objects and three orthographic views of the objects.

6-3 COMPUTER APPLICATIONS OF ORTHOGRAPHIC VIEWS

Orthographic views are drawn on a computer graphic using one of several different methods, depending on the system's capability. One system is first to position the front view relative to the XY axis. The other two views are then aligned with the front view along the XY axis system. The front view defines the height and length of the object (Figure 6-7). The top view defines the object's length but is coupled with the depth measurements. The side view shares the height values with the front view, but in addition, includes the depth values.

The distance between views is usually equal. This helps give the drawing a more organized appearance. The distances between views need not be the same, and if extra space is needed for dimensions, the distances may be increased. A good rule of thumb is about 1.00 in. or 25 mm between views.

A consistent distance between views is helpful when using a computer graphic system. The distance can be treated as a constant and can be factored into the view locations. For example, in Figure 6-7 the overall values for length, height, and depth are known. The distance between views is also known. This means that coordinate points used to define the top and side views can be taken directly from given dimensions by adding the value of the distance between the views. For example, C_x equals the length value plus the distance between the views. C_x defines the distance from the origin to the left edge of the side view.

Point A in the side view can be defined relative to the origin by adding the dimensional value 16 to the constant C_x. This is equal to the

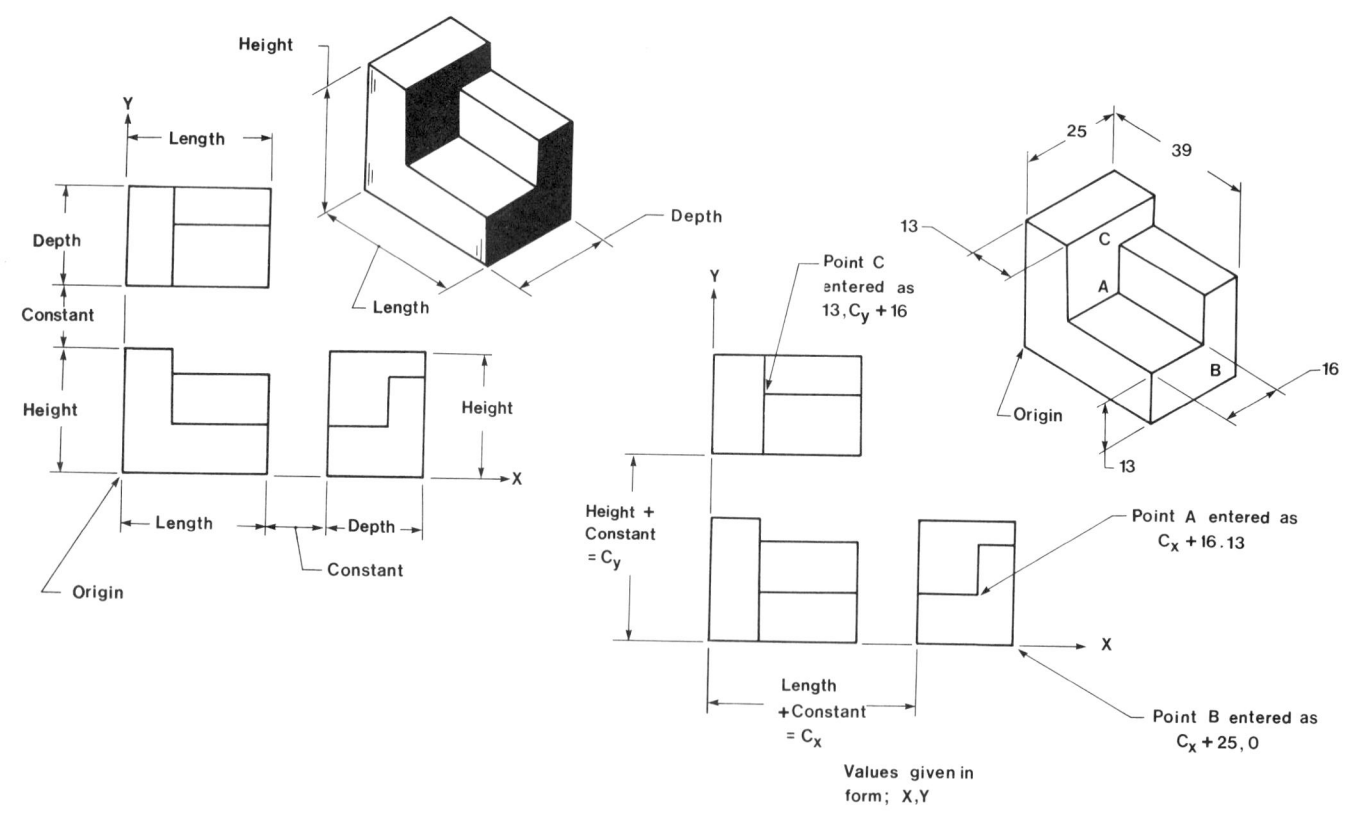

FIGURE 6-7 How to locate orthographic views relative to an XY axis system.

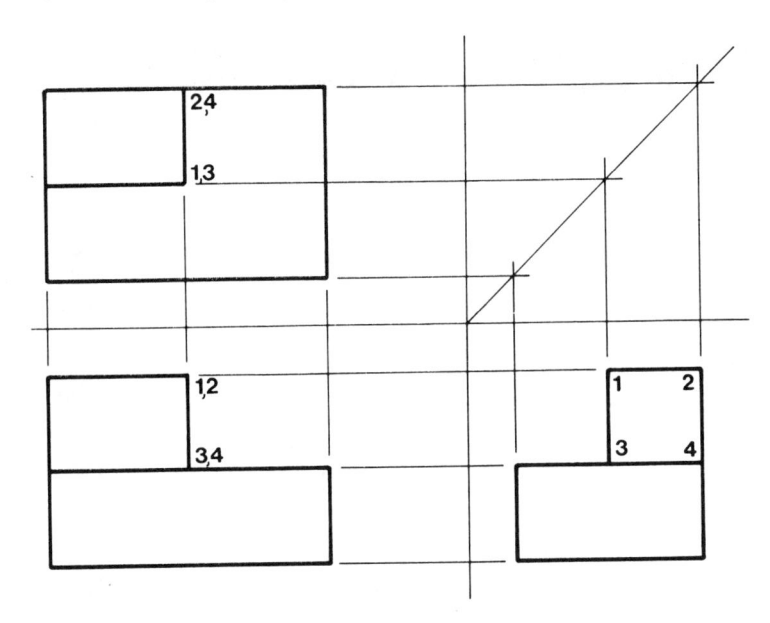

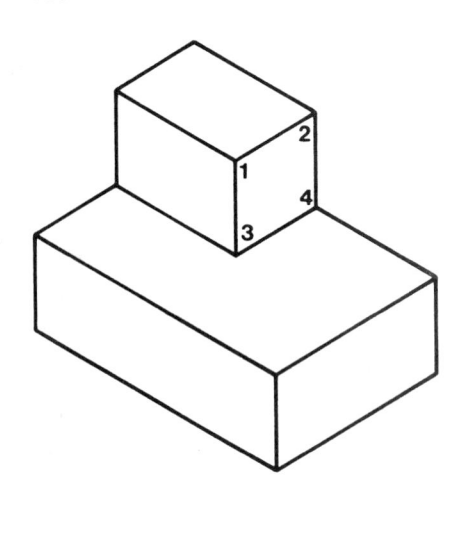

Sec. 6-3   Computer Applications of Orthographic Views   133

FIGURE 6-8 An example of projection between the side and top view using a 45° miter line.

length of the object plus the distance between views. The final coordinate value becomes $C_x + 16, 13$ (x, y). Values for the top view are found in a similar manner, using a constant C_y equal to the height of the object plus the distance between views. Point C would have the coordinate values $(10, C_y + 16)$. The values for C_x and C_y can be added to the computer's memory and utilized while preparing the orthographic views.

It is possible on some computer graphic systems to project information from the side view to the top view using a 45° miter line as shown in Figure 6-8. This technique is used extensively in on-the-board drafting. The procedure is as follows and is illustrated in Figure 6-9.

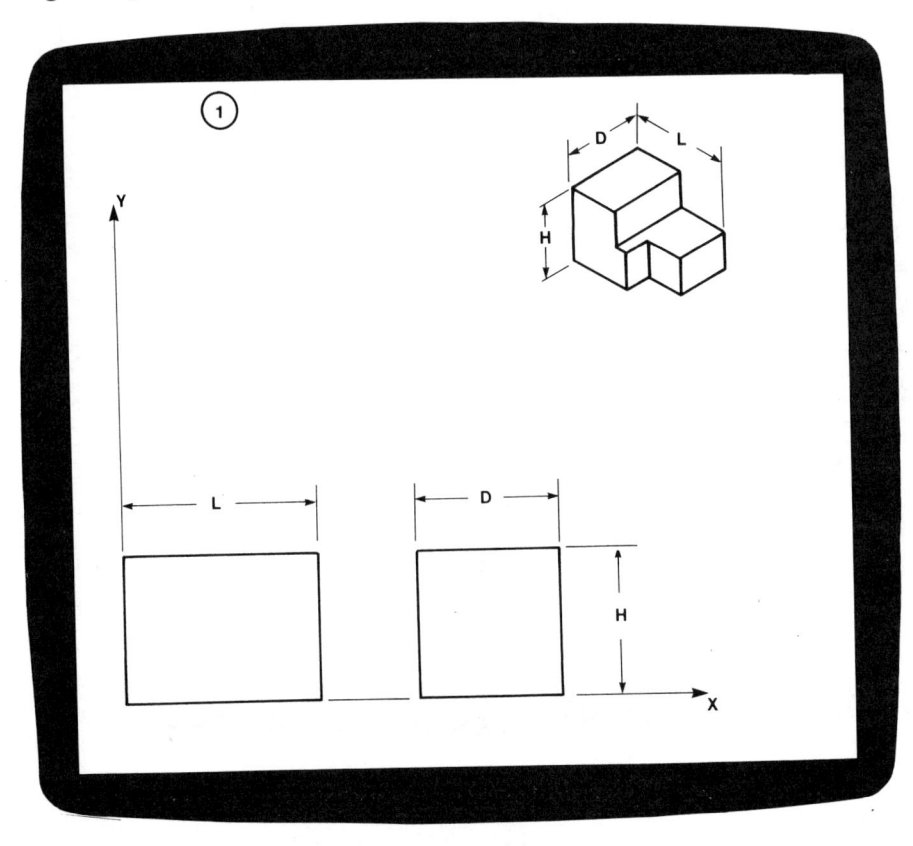

FIGURE 6-9 How to use a 45° miter to project between views.

134 Orthographic Views Chap. 6

FIGURE 6-9 (cont.)

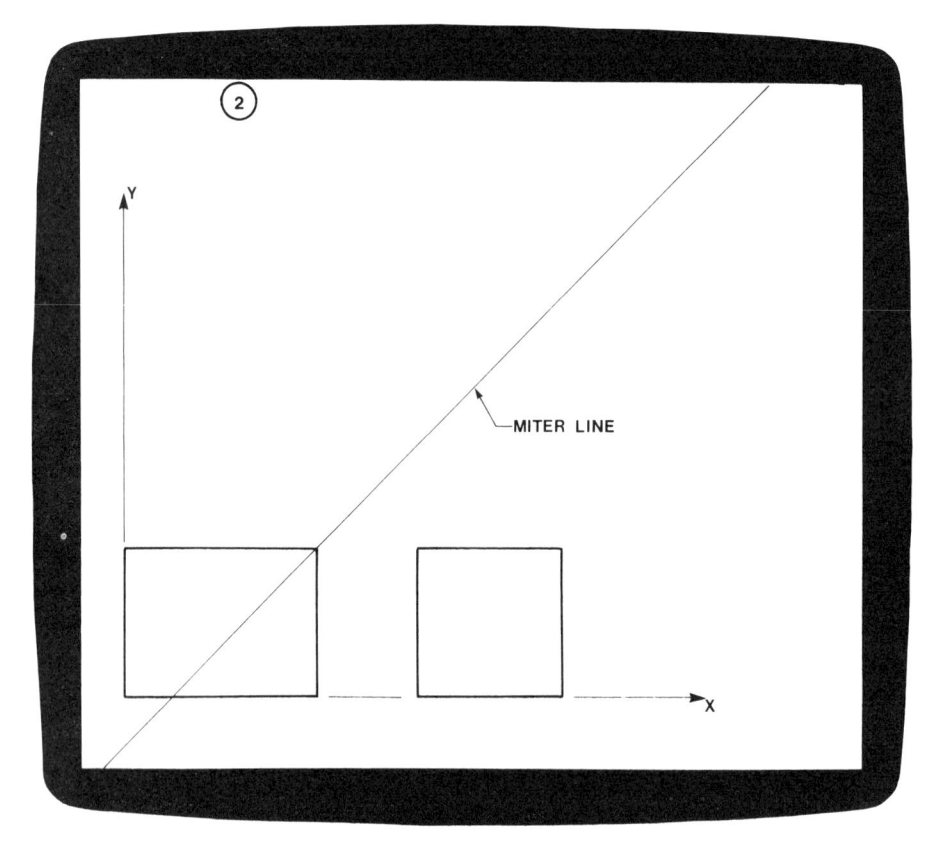

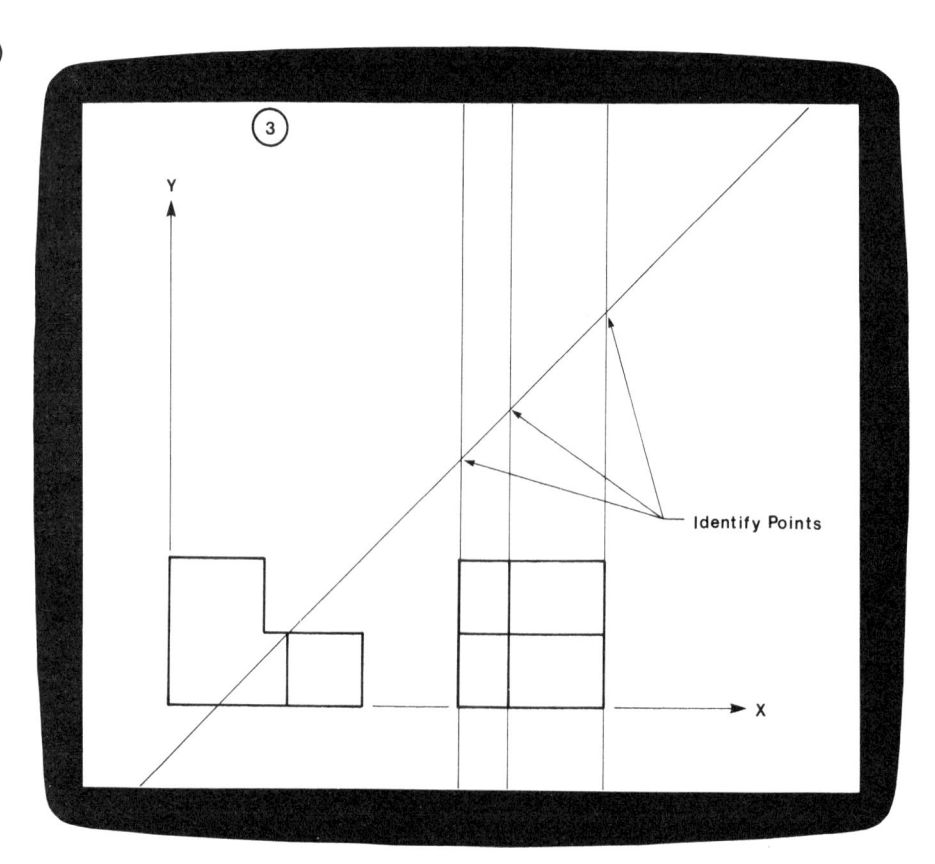

FIGURE 6-9 (cont.)

Sec. 6-3 Computer Applications of Orthographic Views 135

FIGURE 6-9 (*cont.*)

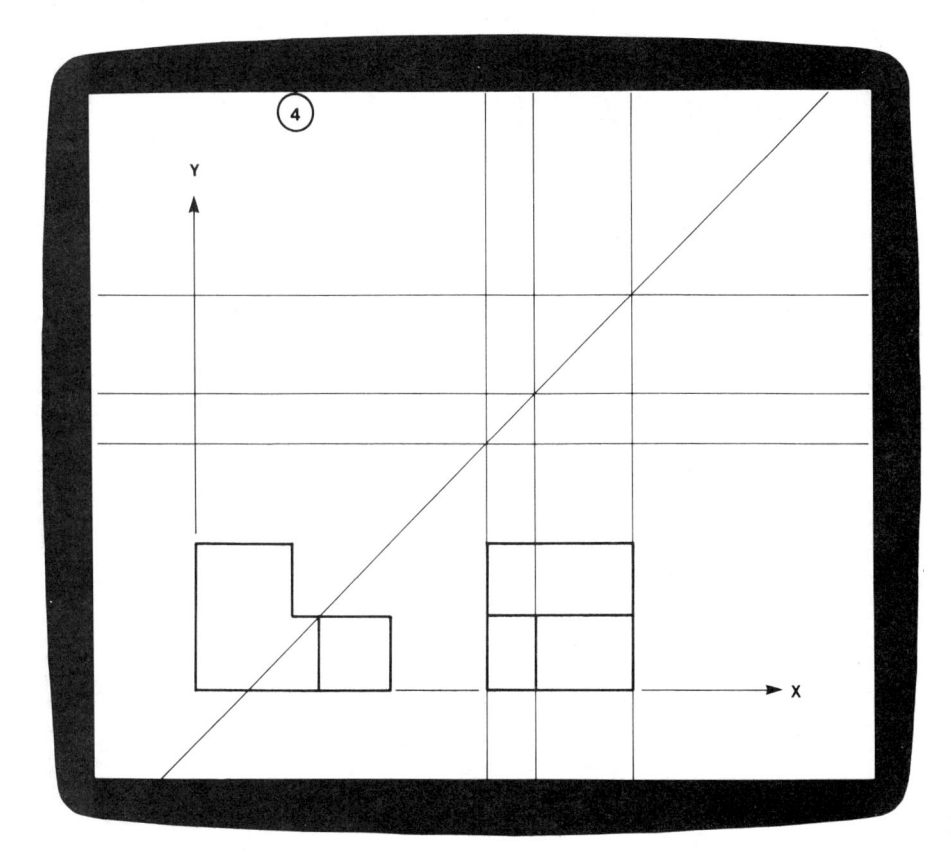

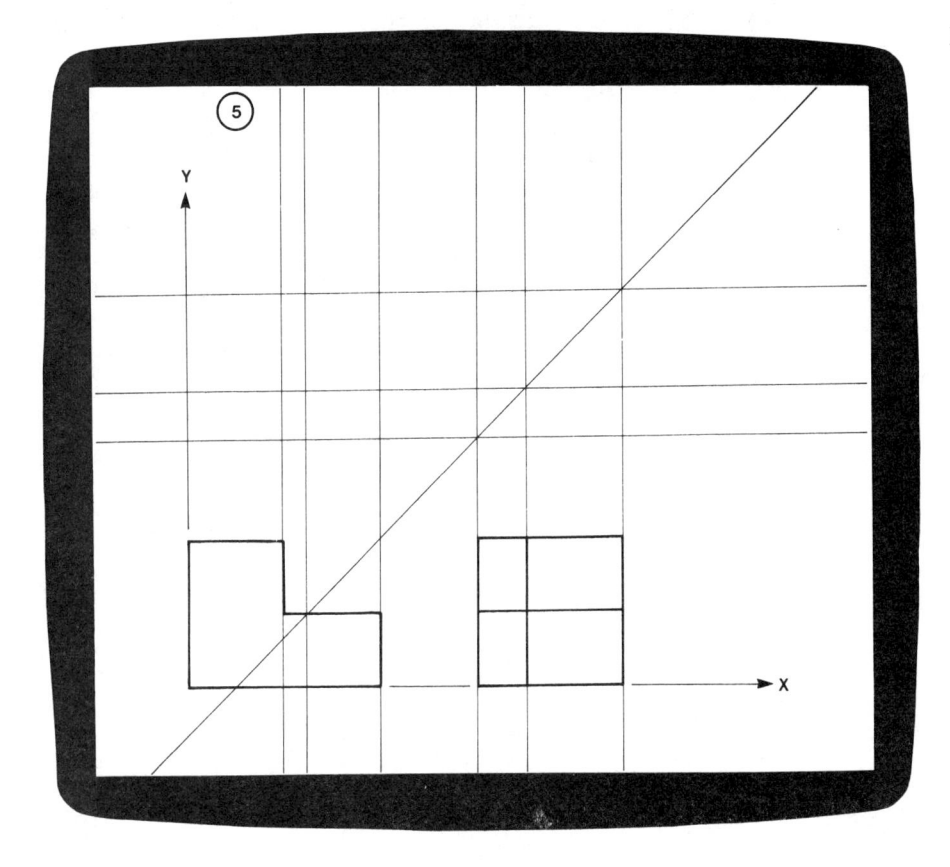

FIGURE 6-9 (*cont.*)

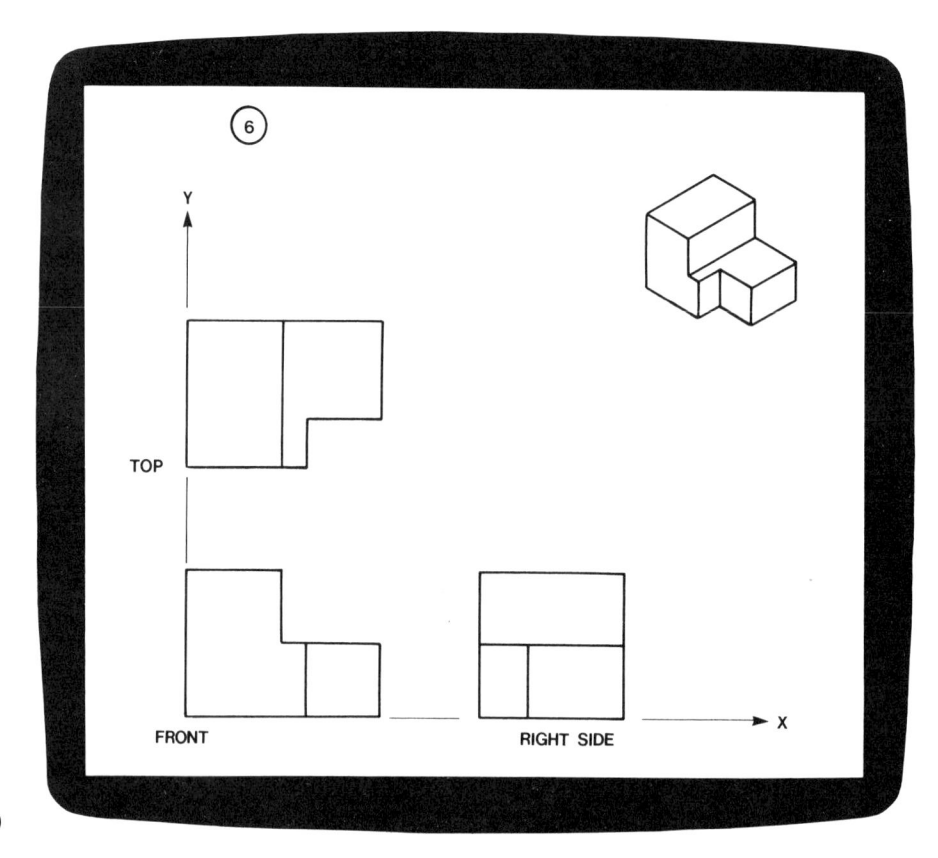

FIGURE 6-9 (cont.)

1. Draw the front and side views as if the object were a rectangular prism using the given overall dimensions.
2. Draw a 45° line through the top right corner of the front view. This line is the miter line.
3. Complete the front and side views and draw vertical lines through all the corners in the side view so that they intersect the miter line. Define the intersection points. (*Note:* This method is dependent on the accurate location of these intersection points. Some systems can define a point by identifying two intersecting elements; others need specific coordinate inputs. If a cursor or light pen is used to locate the points by eye, the locations may not be accurate. It is suggested that if the points are to be located by eye, the drawing scale be increased to its maximum size before trying to define the points, so as to minimize location errors.)
4. Draw horizontal lines through the intersection points of step 3.
5. Draw vertical lines through all corners in the front view. The intersection of these lines with the horizontal lines of step 4 will define the lines in the top view.
6. Erase all excess lines and change all needed lines to their correct thickness and font.

6-4 HIDDEN LINES

Hidden lines are lines that represent features not directly visible. Figure 6-10 shows an object and orthographic views of the object. The ortho-

Sec. 6-4　Hidden Lines

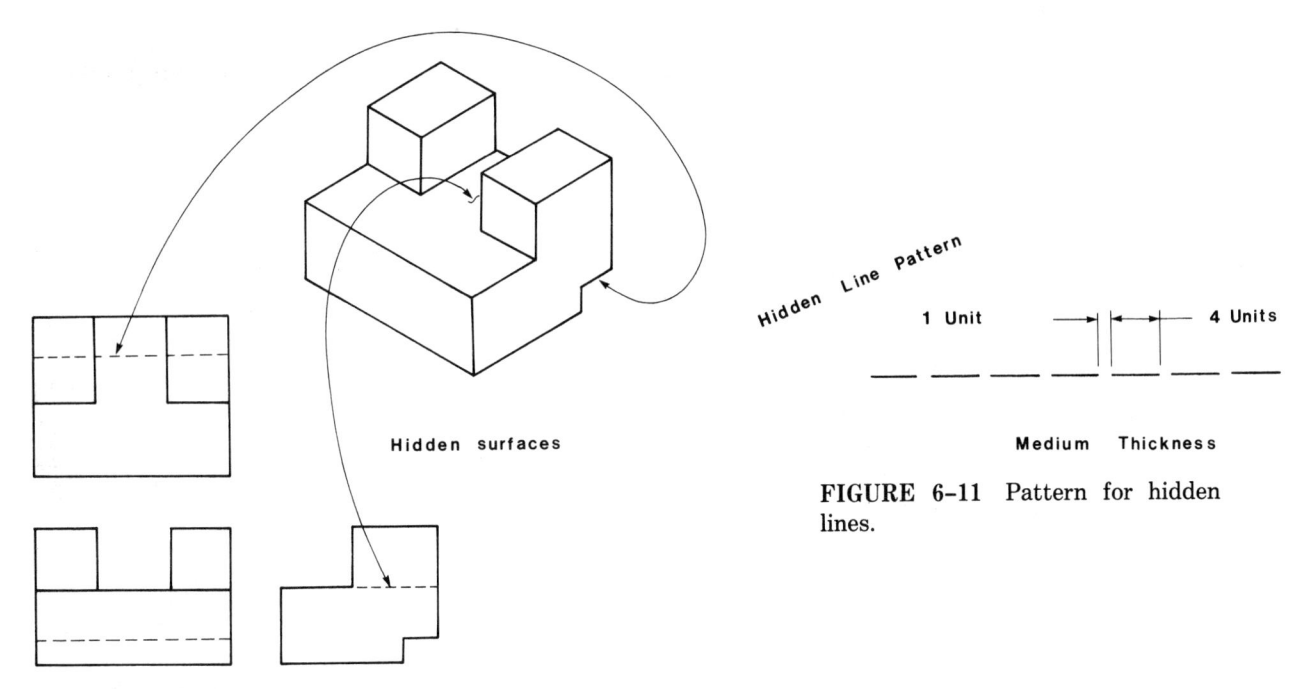

Hidden surfaces

FIGURE 6-10 Hidden lines are used to represent features that are not directly visible.

FIGURE 6-11 Pattern for hidden lines.

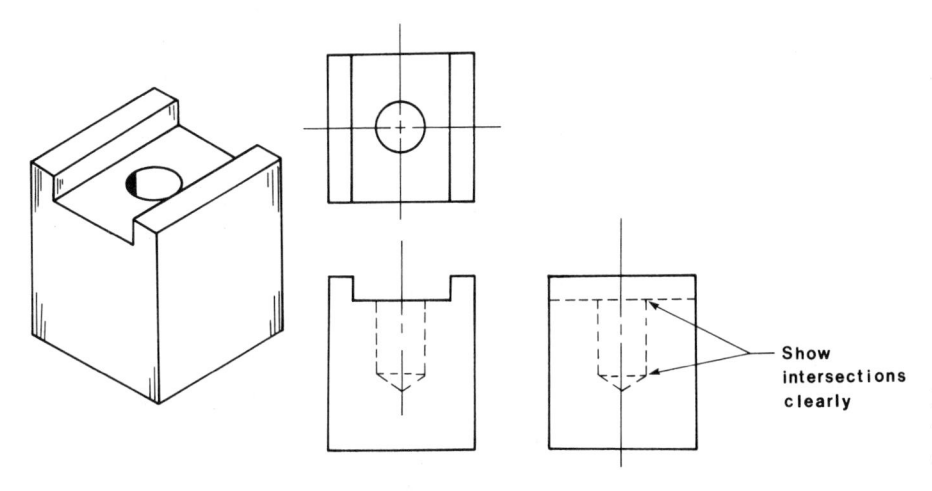

FIGURE 6-12 Corners and intersections must be shown clearly.

graphic views contain hidden lines. The hidden line in the top view represents the cutout that runs across the back bottom corner of the object. The hidden line in the front view also represents the cutout. The hidden line in the side view represents the slot that runs from front to back in the top center of the object.

Hidden lines are drawn using the pattern shown in Figure 6-11. The lines are approximately 4 units long separated by a space 1 unit long. Most computers are already programmed to create hidden lines to this specification. It is usually done by inputting a hidden-line font from a menu or by first drawing the line as a solid line and then changing it to a hidden-line pattern.

Hidden lines are drawn using a medium thickness. Not all computer systems have the capability to distinguish between line thickness, but whenever possible, hidden lines should be drawn at a medium thickness.

Corners and other intersections should be shown clearly, even if hidden lines are used (Figure 6-12). This convention is sometimes difficult

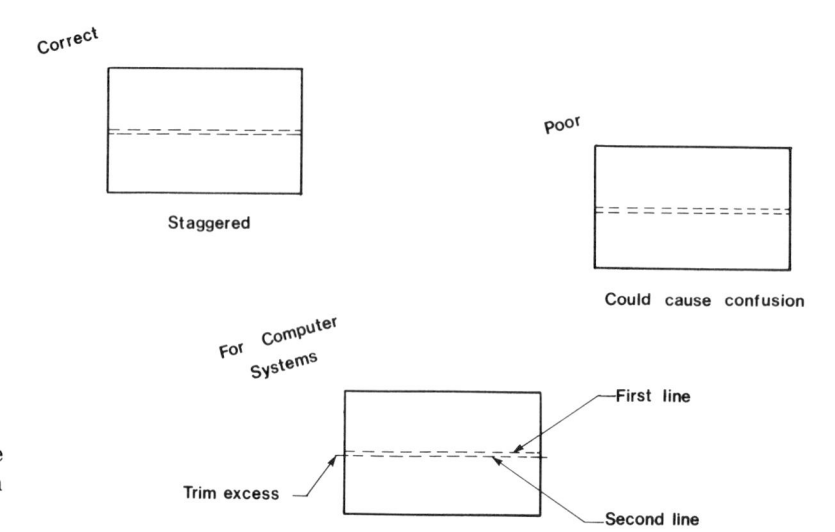

FIGURE 6-13 Stagger the spacing of close parallel hidden lines to ensure clarity.

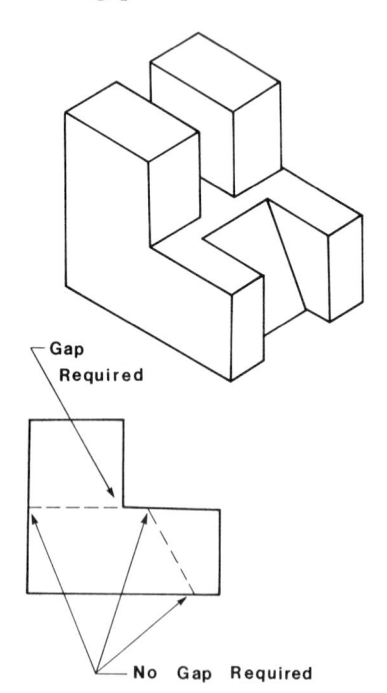

FIGURE 6-14 Object lines should never run directly into hidden lines. The two types of lines should be separated by a small gap.

to follow when preparing drawings using a computer graphic system. Computers draw hidden lines at a predetermined fixed line length and spacing distance. This makes it difficult to assure correct intersections. Drafters often vary the pattern slightly to assure clear corners and intersections. If possible, always show all hidden intersections clearly.

Parallel hidden lines that are very close together should be staggered to prevent confusion (Figure 6-13). This convention is also difficult to achieve on a computer system that uses predetermined line and spacing distances. Staggering can be created by starting one of the lines at some point beyond the actual starting point and then trimming any excess. In Figure 6-13, the second line was intentionally drawn beyond the needed limits to create the staggering effect. The excess can be trimmed.

Object lines should never run directly into a hidden line (Figure 6-14). A small gap is required to help distinguish between the two types of lines. Gaps are needed *only* when a hidden line is directly aligned with an object line. Hidden lines that intersect object lines at any other angle do not require a gap. If a computer system does not allow for gaps, they should be added by trimming.

6-5 CHOOSING A FRONT VIEW

The front view of three-view drawing should give the clearest picture of the object's overall shape. The other views should complement the front view to form a complete shape definition, but the front view should be the view that gives the best overall shape definition.

Front views are sometimes called *plan views* or *profile views*. These names help convey the intent of the front view. In Figure 6-15, two sets of orthographic views are shown of the same object. Both contain correct orthographic views, but which has the best front view?

Example 2 is the best view because it gives the better overall shape definition. The front view in Example 1 tells very little about the object. Without the other views, the front view of Example 1 is almost meaningless, whereas the front view of Example 2 gives a good idea of the object's shape.

Figure 6-16 shows another example of a good front view. In this example, the front view initially appeared as the top of a pictorial view.

Sec. 6-5 Choosing a Front View 139

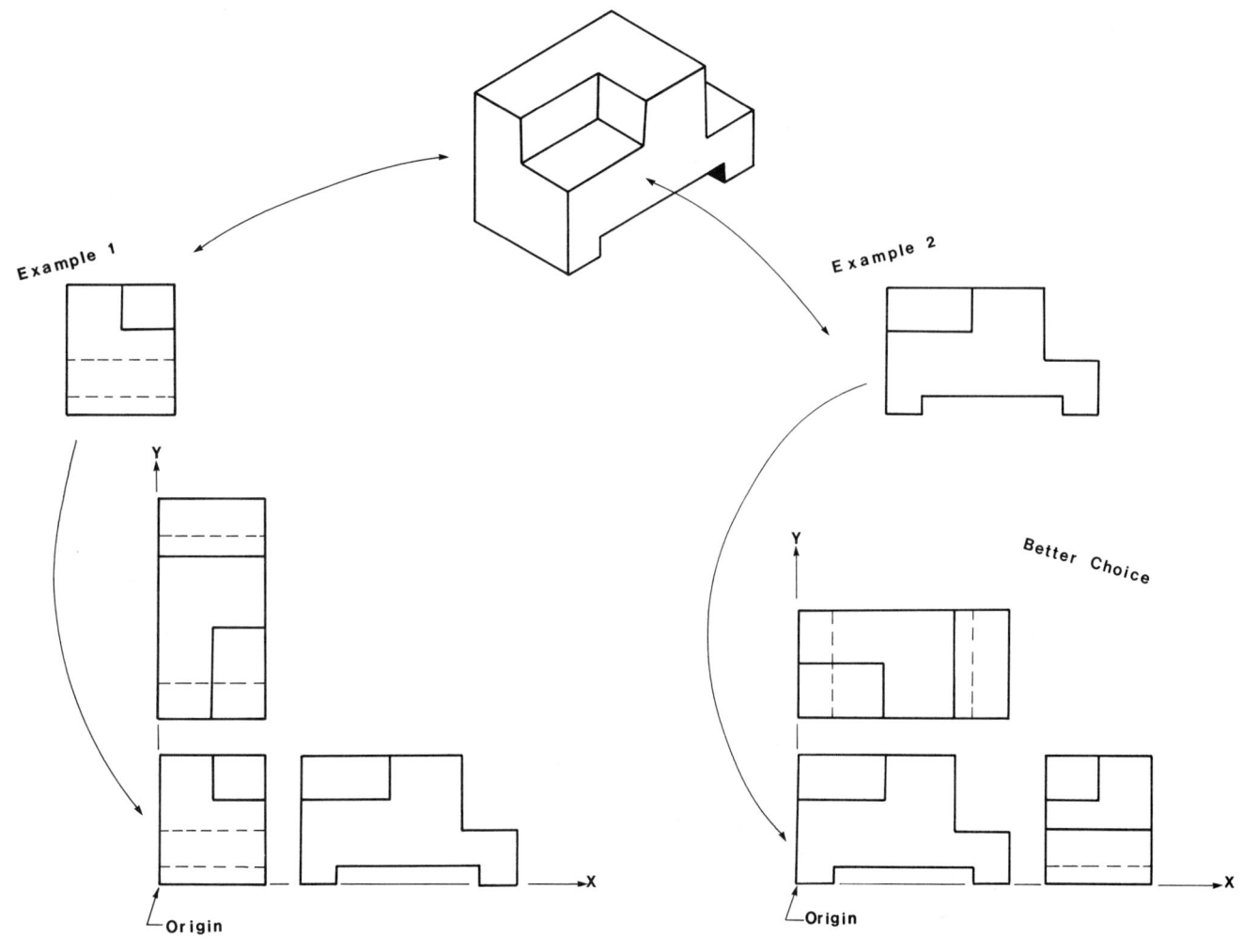

FIGURE 6-15 Choose a front view that gives the best overall picture of the object's shape.

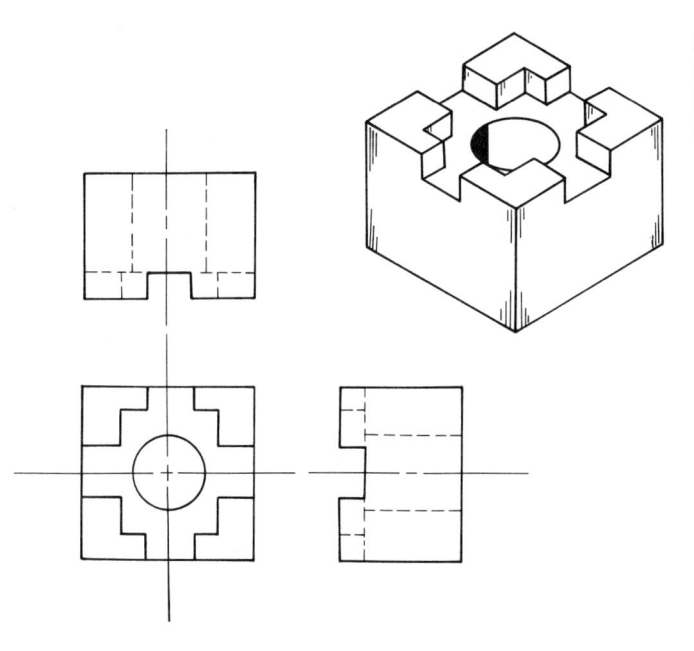

FIGURE 6-16 Example of a front view that most clearly defines the overall shape of the object.

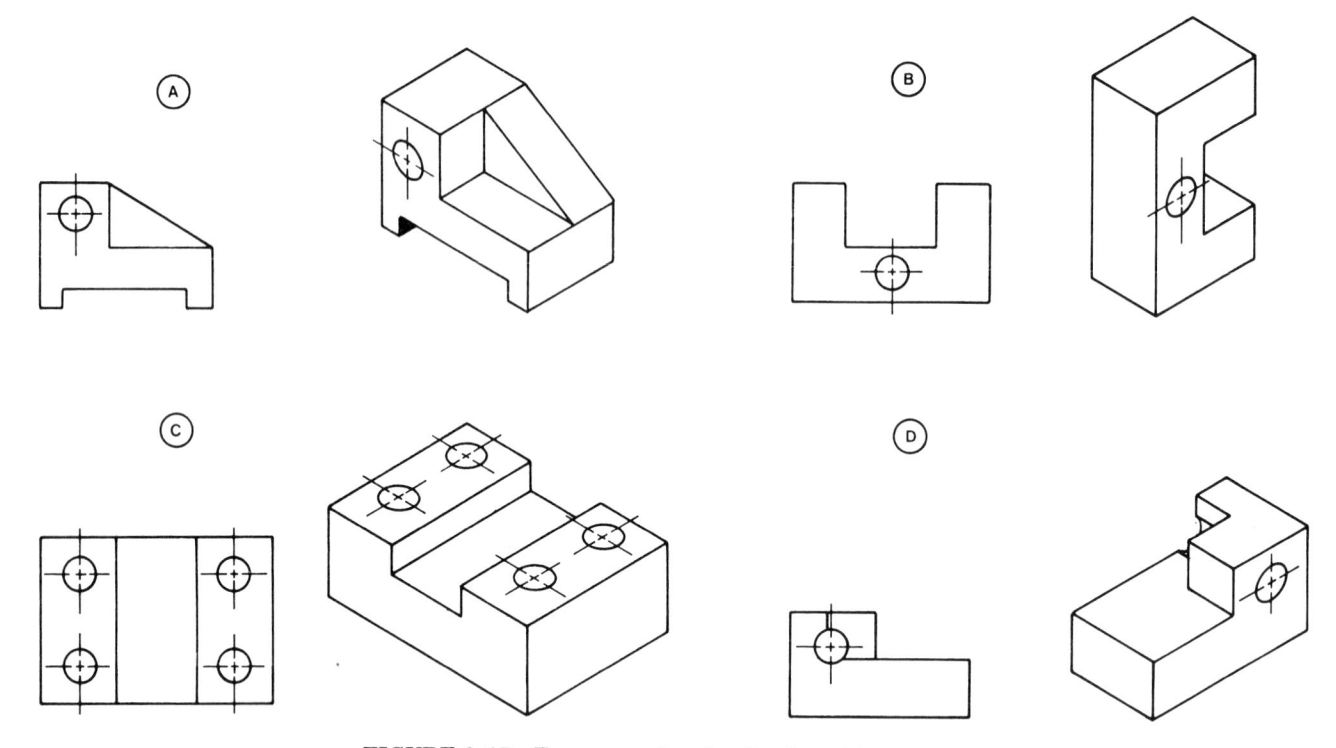

FIGURE 6-17 Four examples of well-selected front views.

This view was chosen because it expresses the most detail. The hole is clearly shown and the shape of the features surrounding the hole are shown in profile. Figure 6-17 shows four more examples of objects and correct front views of the objects.

6-6 NORMAL SURFACES

Normal surfaces are surfaces located 90° from each other. A normal angle is a 90° angle. Figure 6-16 shows an object that contains only normal surfaces. (All illustrations in this chapter, up to this point, have also contained only normal surfaces.)

FIGURE 6-18 Normal surfaces are located 90° from each other. All surfaces are true length and shape.

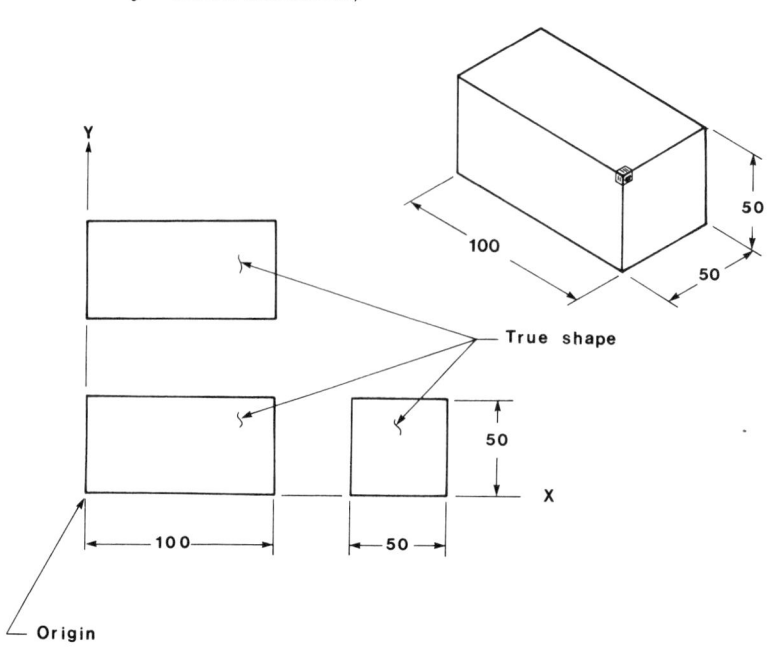

Sec. 6-7 Slanted Surfaces 141

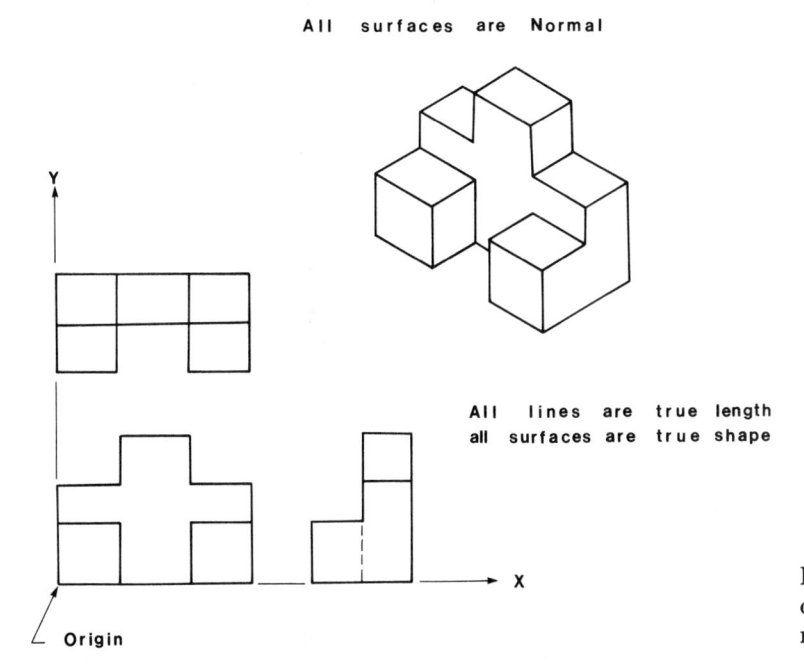

FIGURE 6-19 Example of an object that contains only normal surfaces.

All lines in orthographic views of objects that contain only normal surfaces are *true length* and all surfaces are *true shape*. This means that the front view of the object shown in Figure 6-18 is drawn as a rectangle 50 × 100 mm as specified by the given dimensions. Similarly, the side view is drawn as a square, 50 × 50 mm.

All lines in Figure 6-18 are either parallel or perpendicular to the X and Y axes. Figure 6-19 shows another object that contains only normal surfaces. Note again that all lines are parallel to either the X or Y axis. All lines are true length and all surfaces are true shape.

6-7 SLANTED SURFACES

Slanted surfaces are surfaces drawn at an angle to the XY axis. Figure 6-20 shows an object that contains a slanted surface. The front view shows a profile of the slanted surface (an end view of the surface). The

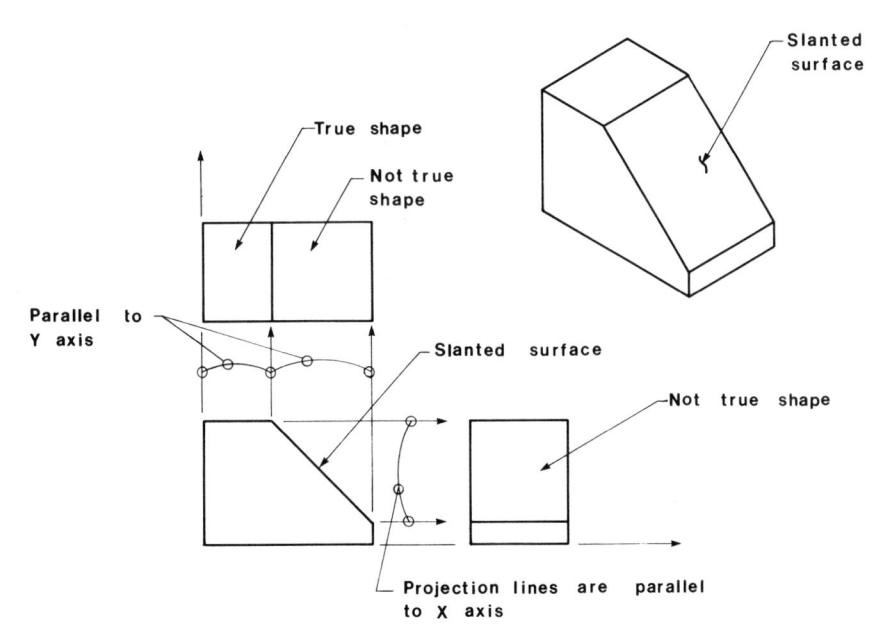

FIGURE 6-20 Object that contains a slanted surface.

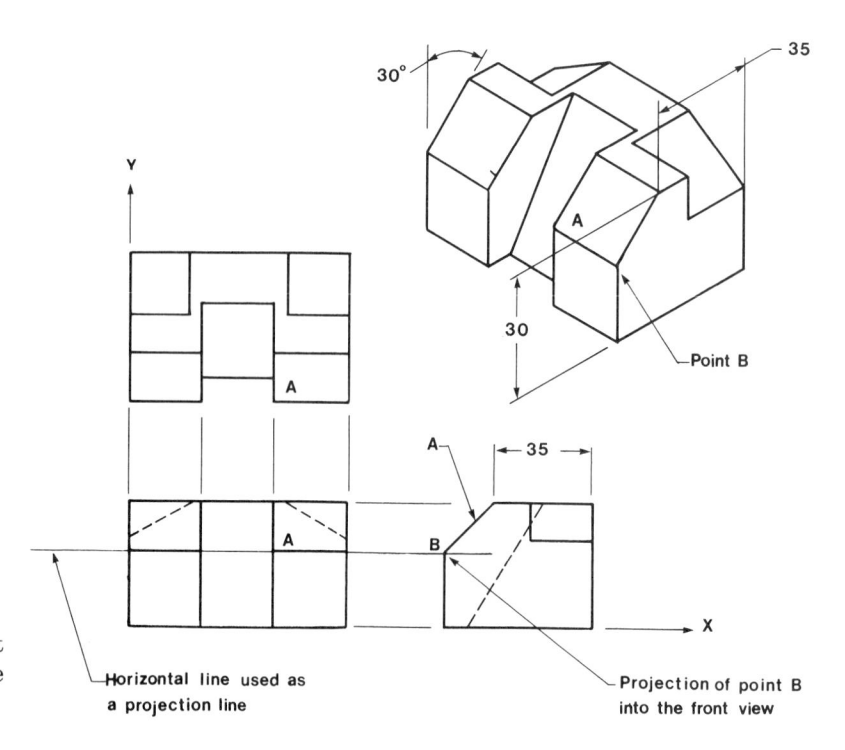

FIGURE 6-21 How to project point *B* from the side to the front view.

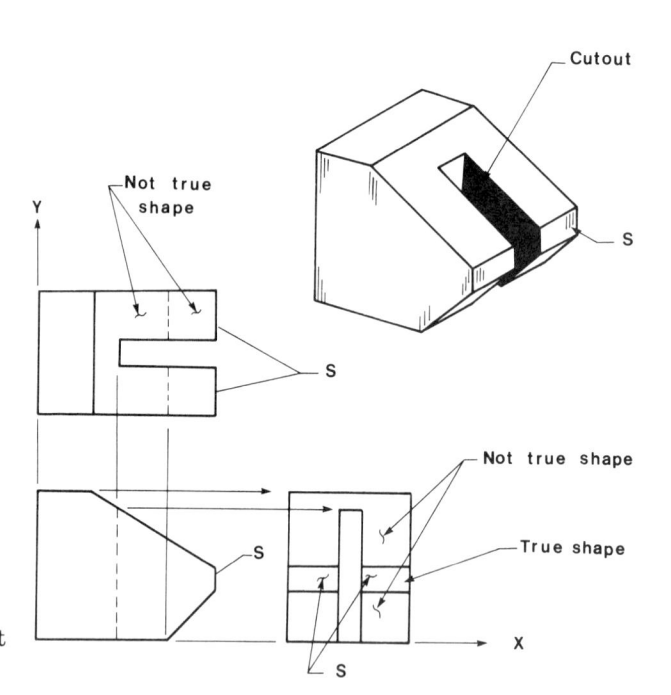

FIGURE 6-22 How to project information between views.

surface appears as a rectangle in both the top and side views, but these rectangles are *not* true shapes. Both are foreshortened from their actual size. The size on the slanted surface in the top and side view is determined by projection.

Projection lines are parallel to either the *X* or *Y* axis as shown. This ensures that the views will be aligned as required by standard convention. Projection lines are useful when preparing orthographic views of

Sec. 6-8 Oblique Surfaces 143

more complex objects. For example, in Figure 6-21 the surface labeled
A is a slanted surface. The dimensions define the slant as 30° to the
vertical and the overall height is 30 mm. This information is sufficient
to draw the side view but not the front view. The vertical distance of
point B from the top surface is needed. This distance could be calculated
but is more easily determined by projection. Because the front and side
views are aligned, the vertical distance can be projected using a horizontal line of unlimited length through point B in the side view, across the
front view. Projection lines are primarily construction lines, but serve,
in part, to define object lines. The excess may be trimmed, leaving only
those lines required for a correct front view.

Figure 6-22 shows another example of an object with slanted surfaces. The front view was chosen because it gives a true picture of the
various angles involved in the object's shape. The top and side views of
the slanted surfaces are not true shapes. The intersection of the cutout
with the slanted surfaces was found by projection. Note that surface S
is shown in true shape in the side view because its front view is parallel
to the Y axis (it is a surface normal to the XY axis).

6-8 OBLIQUE SURFACES

Oblique sufaces are surfaces that are not aligned with either the X or
the Y axis. Figure 6-23 shows an object with an oblique surface. None
of the orthographic views show an end view of the oblique surface, and
none of the views show the true shape.

Oblique surfaces are sometimes difficult to draw using orthographic views because they are difficult to visualize. Orthographic views
of oblique surfaces rely heavily on projection for their development.

Figure 6-24 shows a comparison between projection lines used to
create orthographic views on the drawing board and projection lines used
when working with a computer graphic system. Projection between the
front and side views and between the front and top views is as explained

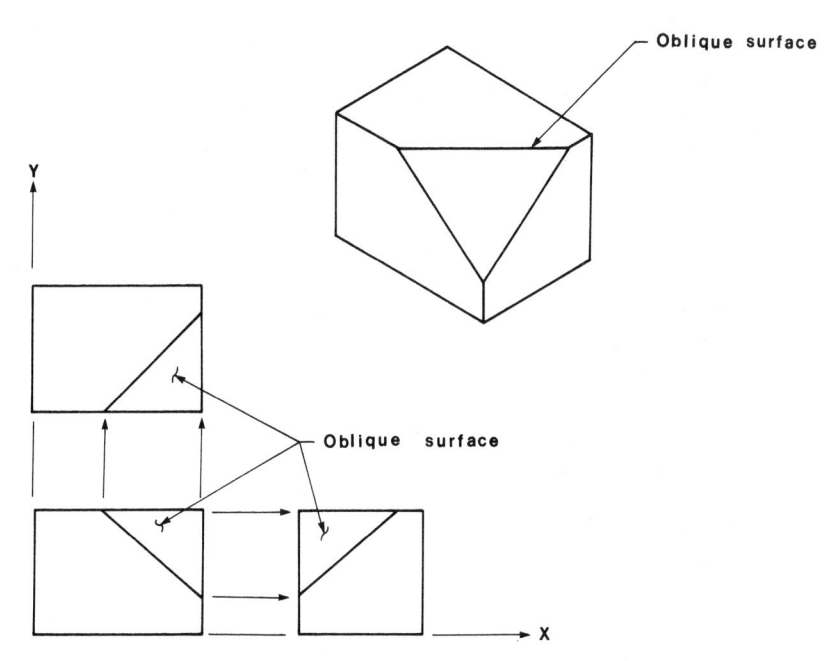

FIGURE 6-23 Example of an object that contains an oblique surface.

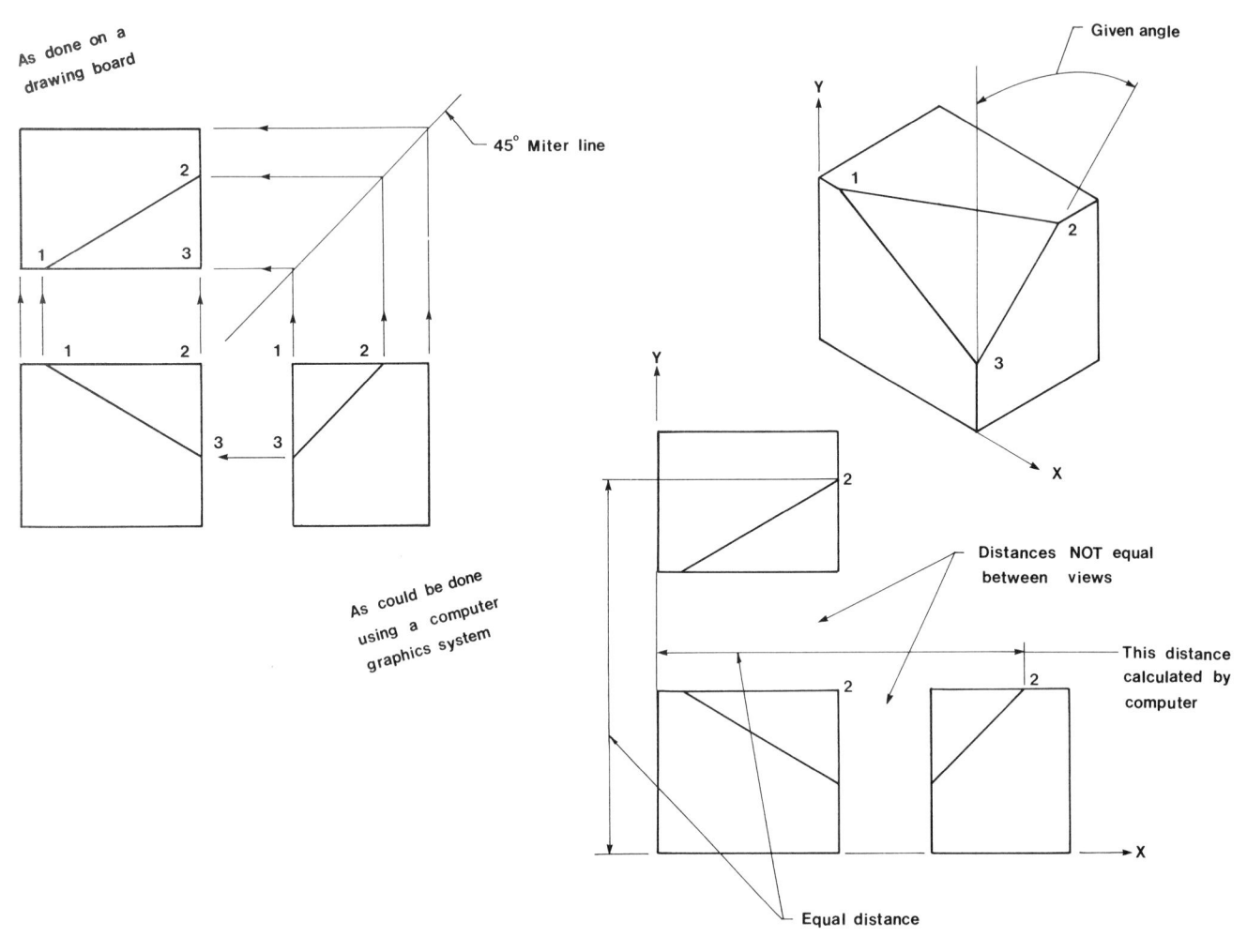

FIGURE 6-24 Projecting an oblique surface between orthographic views.

in Section 6-7. There is very little difference between the procedure used on the drawing board and that used on a computer. Projection lines between the front and top views and between the front and side views are simply vertical and horizontal lines, respectively. However, there is a difference in projection techniques when projecting between the top and side views.

On-the-board projection techniques require the addition of a 45° miter line as shown in Figure 6-24. The 45° miter line allows projection lines to "turn the corner" between the two views. Vertical projection lines from the side view define the location for equivalent vertical projection lines when they intersect the miter line, and vice versa. This technique can be used on a computer graphic system as shown in Figures 6-8 and 6-9.

For example, point 2 in Figure 6-24 is defined using an angle. This angle is drawn in the side view because that is where, according to the view orientation, it appears as true shape. But how is the location of point 2 determined for the view? Computers reference all points to an axis system and are very good at calculating, with extreme accuracy, the location of any point relative to that axis. The computer can calculate the distance from the Y axis to point 2. How this is done varies from

Sec. 6-8 Oblique Surfaces 145

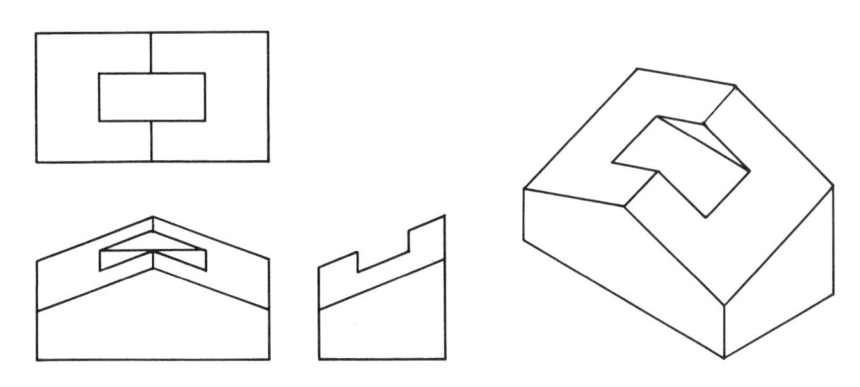

FIGURE 6-25 Object that contains oblique surfaces.

system to system, but one simple approach is to ask the system to create a horizontal dimension from the Y axis to point 2. Once that value has been determined, record it and erase the dimensional configuration. Ask the computer to locate a new point from the X axis equal to the determined value. This can be done by drawing a new horizontal line at a distance from the X axis equal to the determined value. Once the location of point 2 has been defined in the top view, the horizontal line can be erased. This technique is the computer equivalent to on-the-board projection using a miter line.

This technique differs from that presented in Figure 6-7. Here the distance between the views is *not* equal. Distances from individual points to the reference axis are equal. Figure 6-25 shows another example of an object that contains oblique surfaces.

A computer can be used to project information between views using techniques similar to those used when creating drawings on a drawing board. Figures 6-26 and 6-27 illustrate these techniques.

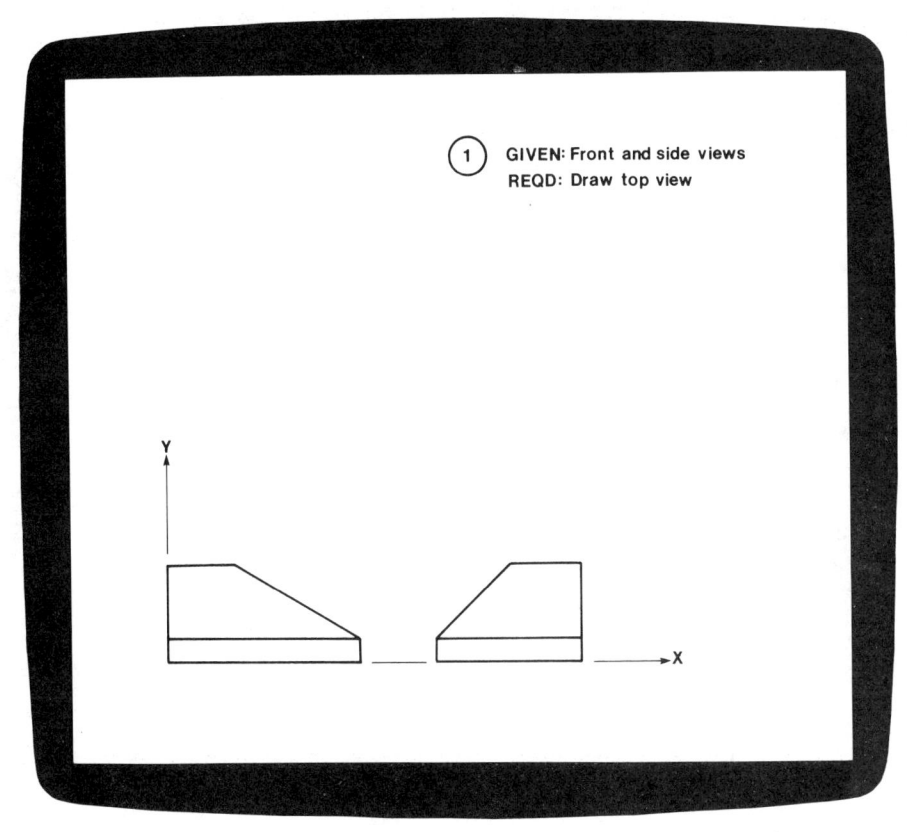

FIGURE 6-26 How to create a top view from given front and side views using a computer graphics system. The distance between views is equal.

In Figure 6-26 we are given the front and side views of an object and asked to draw the top view. In addition, we are required to keep the distance between the views equal. The procedure is as follows:

1. Draw the front and side views on the screen using the lower left corner of the front view as the origin.
2. Draw unlimited-length vertical lines through all corners and feature intersections in the front view.
3. Establish two reference planes, distances C_x and C_y from the origin as shown in the figure. Measurements can be taken in the side view and transferred to the view via the two reference planes. The distances can be derived using the dimensioning technique presented in Figures 6-7 and 6-9.
4. Add the appropriate lines.
5. Trim all unnecessary lines and points.

This method is easiest to use on systems that allow new reference planes to be established. Systems limited only to an XY axis would be required to reference all values to the Y axis using C_x plus the dimensional value, then convert the C_x value to a C_y value and reference the C_y value plus the dimensional value to the X axis. The procedure is easier if we allow the distances between the views to be unequal, thereby listing $C_x = C_y$.

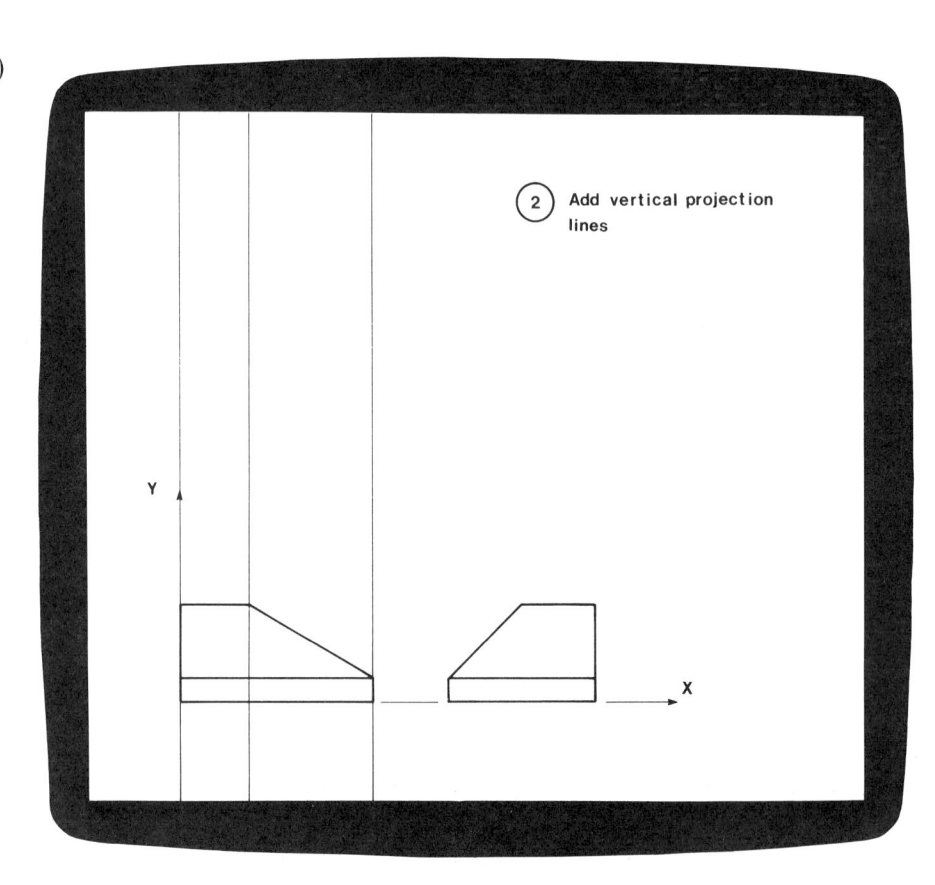

FIGURE 6-26 (*cont.*)

Sec. 6-8   Oblique Surfaces   147

③ Add horizontal lines for top view

Distance between views is equal

Establish new reference planes

Depth

C_y

Depth

C_x

X

FIGURE 6-26 (*cont.*)

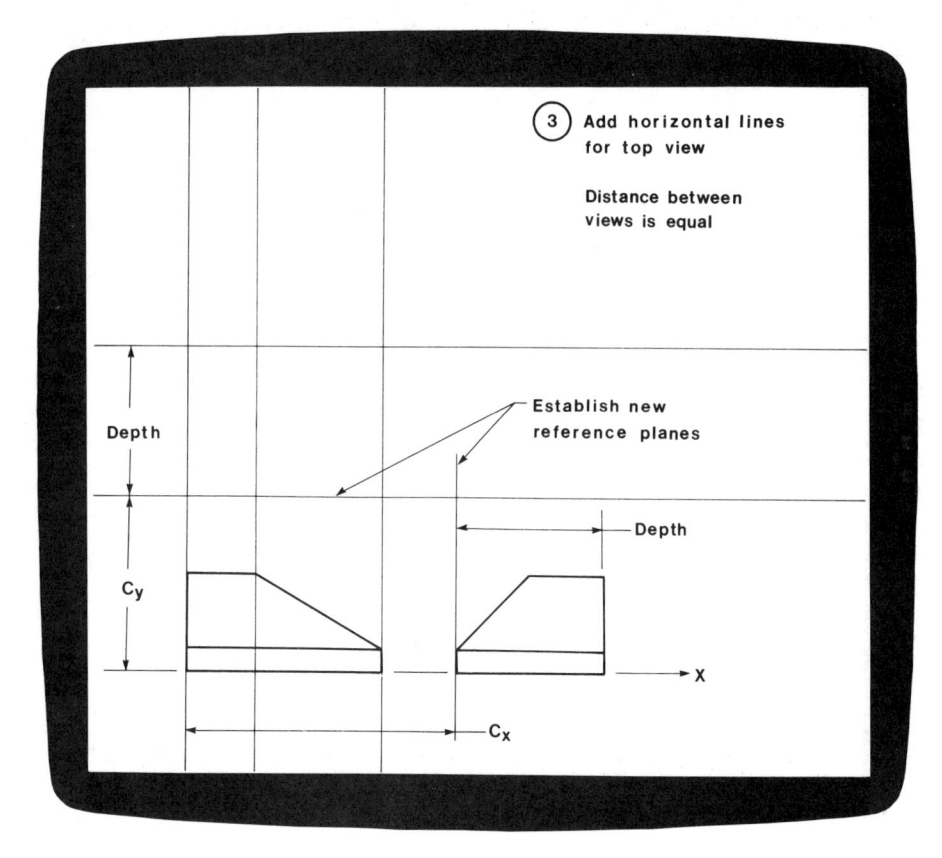

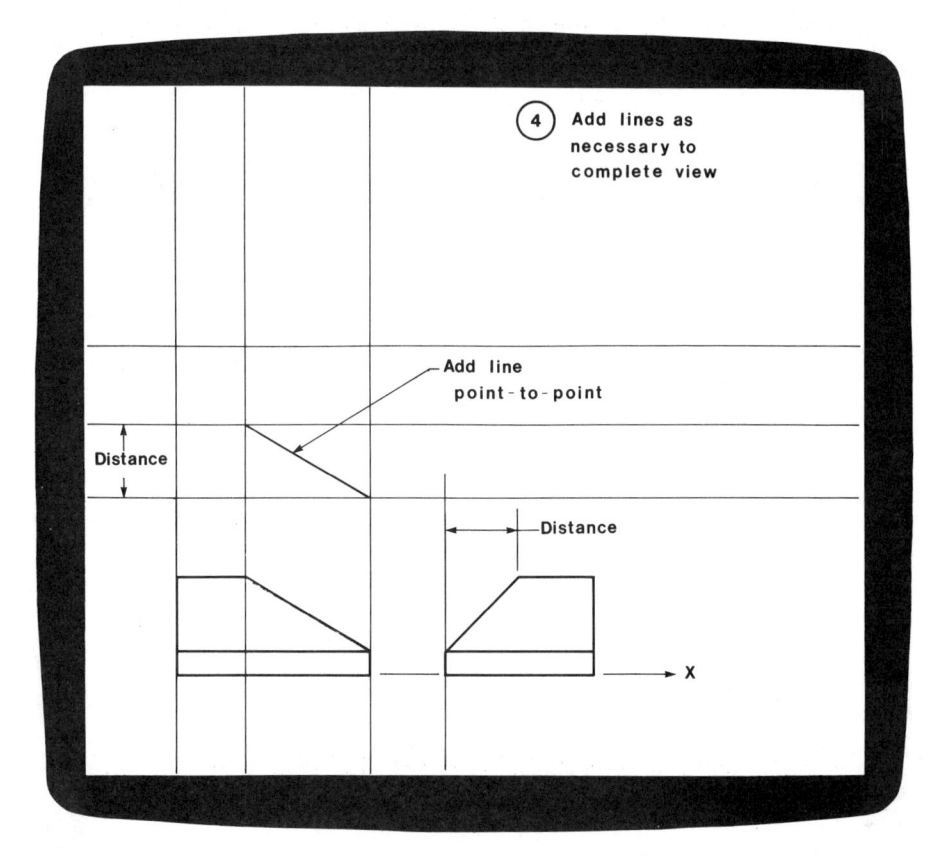

FIGURE 6-26 (*cont.*)

④ Add lines as necessary to complete view

Add line point-to-point

Distance

Distance

X

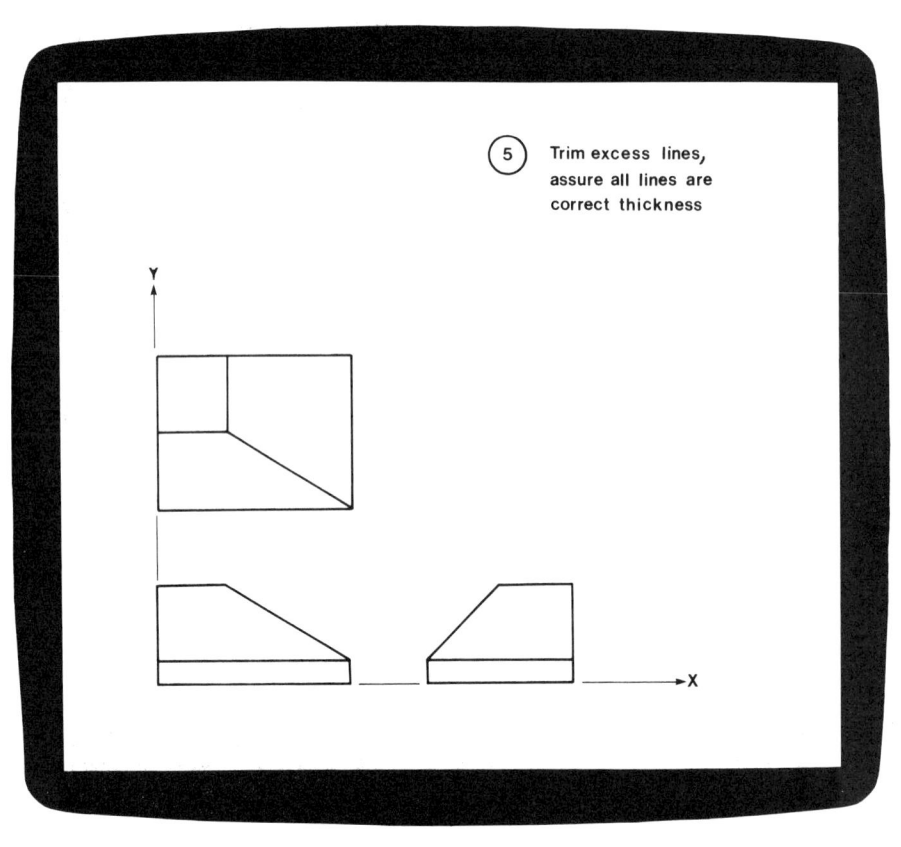

FIGURE 6-26 (cont.)

FIGURE 6-27 How to create a top view from given front and side views using a computer graphics system. The distance between views need not be equal.

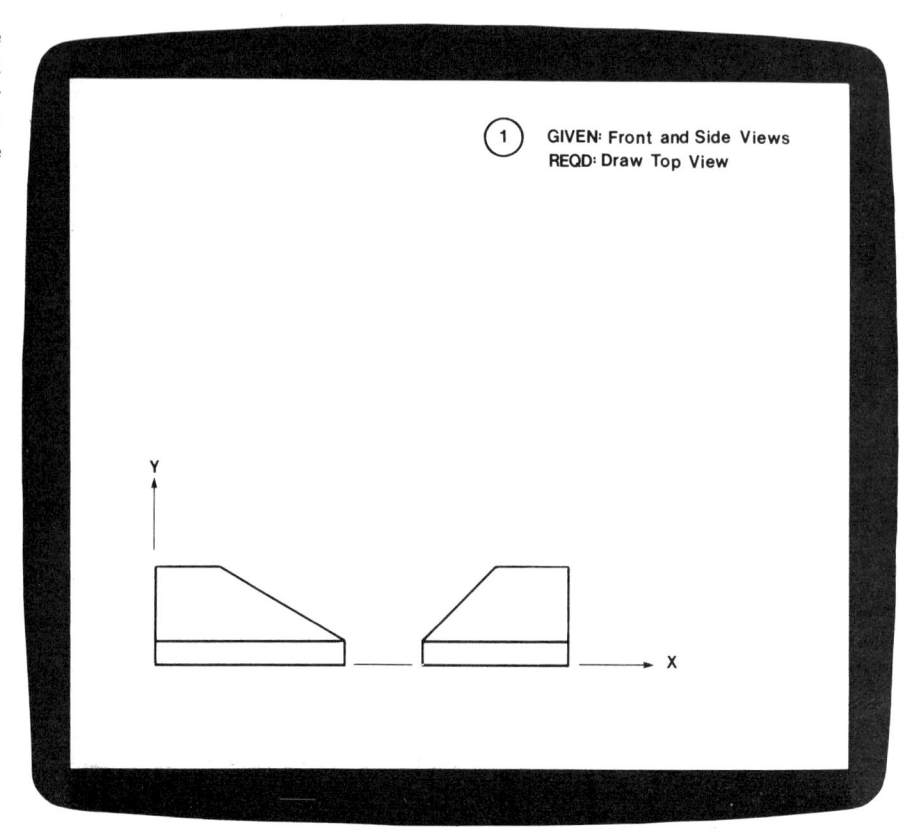

Figure 6-27 shows how to create a top view from front and side views where the distance between views is not equal. The procedure is as follows:

1. Draw the front and side views so that the lower left corner of the front view is located on the origin.

Sec. 6-8   Oblique Surfaces   149

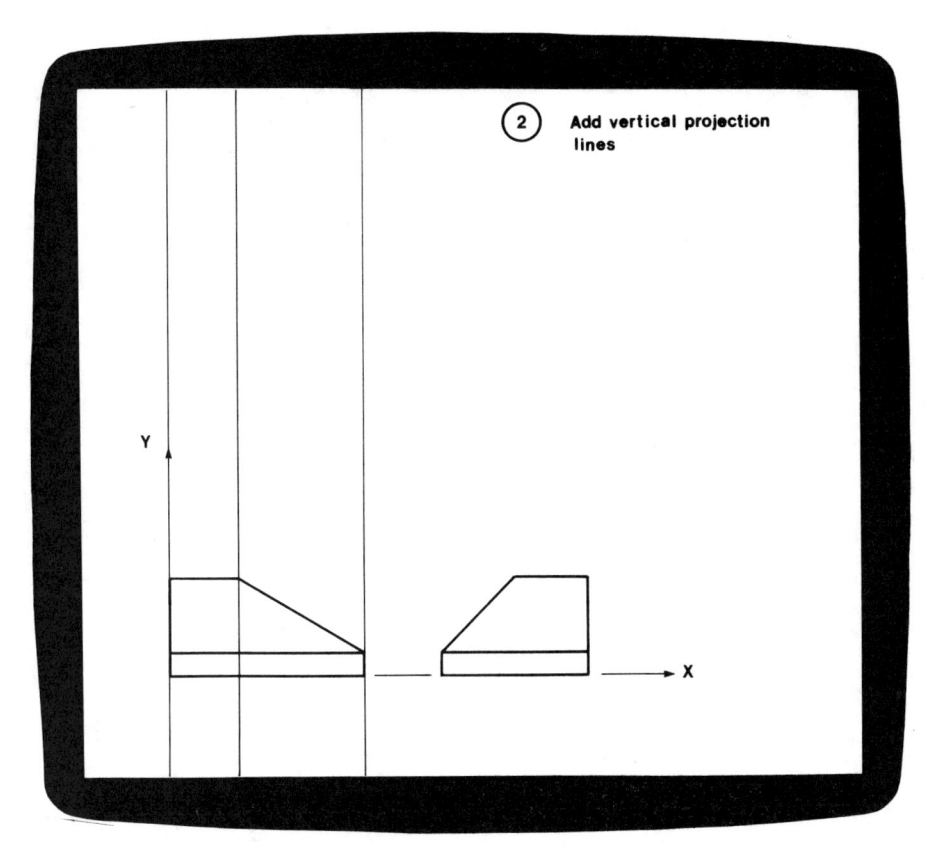

FIGURE 6-27 (*cont.*)

2. Draw unlimited-length vertical lines through all corners and feature intersections in the front view.
3. Reference all features in the side view to the Y axis using the dimensioning technique shown in the figure.
4. Add any necessary lines and trim any lines not needed.

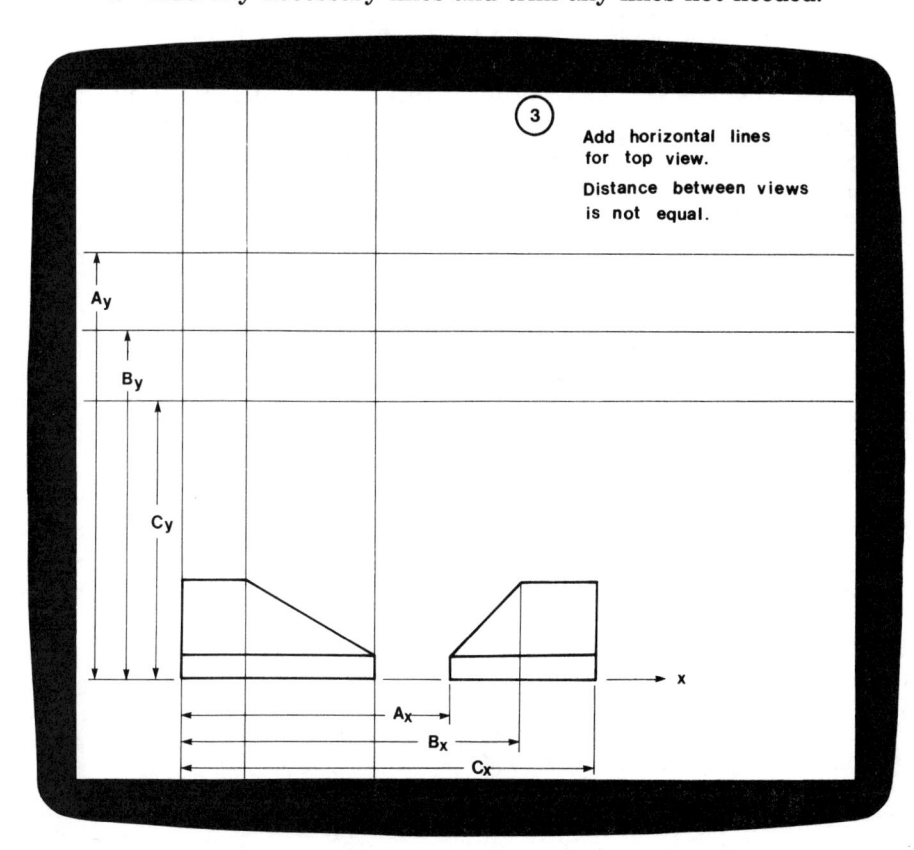

FIGURE 6-27 (*cont.*)

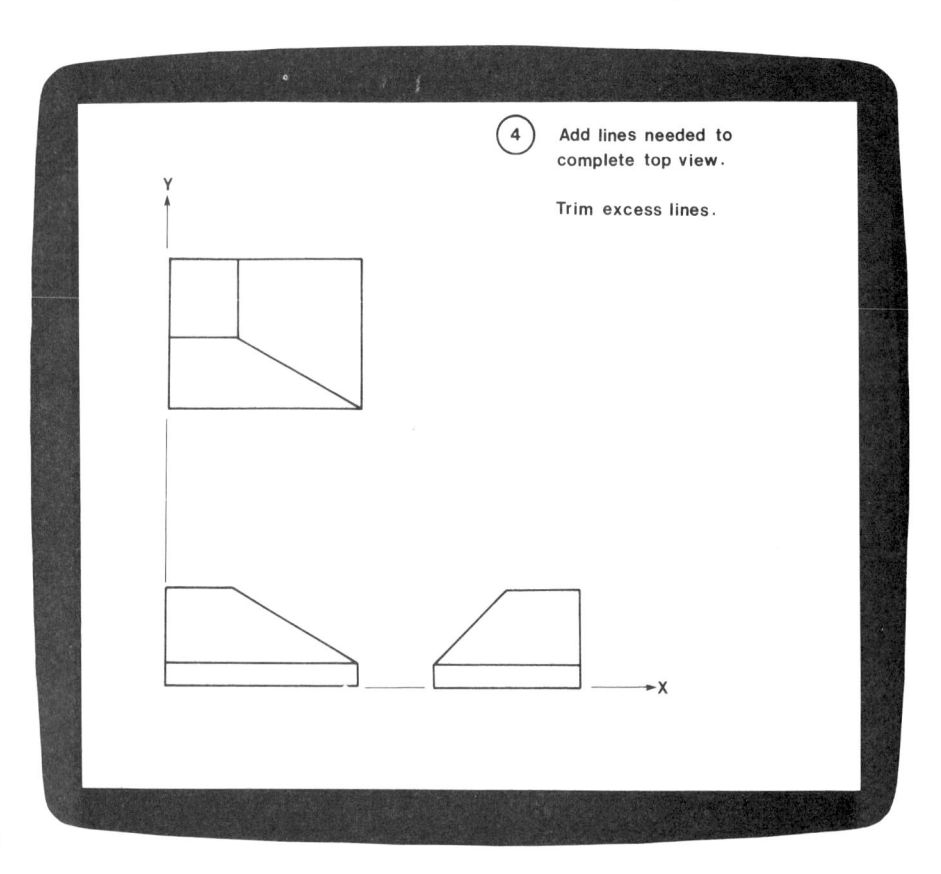

FIGURE 6-27 (cont.)

6-9 ROUNDED SURFACES

Rounded surfaces are surfaces whose end view is an arc of constant radius. Figure 6-28 shows an object that contains a rounded surface. Note how the top and side views show the rounded surface as a rectangle. There is no indication in these views that the surface is round.

Figure 6-29 shows a convex rounded surface. The rounded surface becomes tangent (blends smoothly into) to both the vertical and horizontal surfaces of the object. There is no edge line between the two surfaces. This means that the top and side views will appear rectangular with no indication of the shape of the rounded surface and with no edge line to show where the two surfaces become tangent.

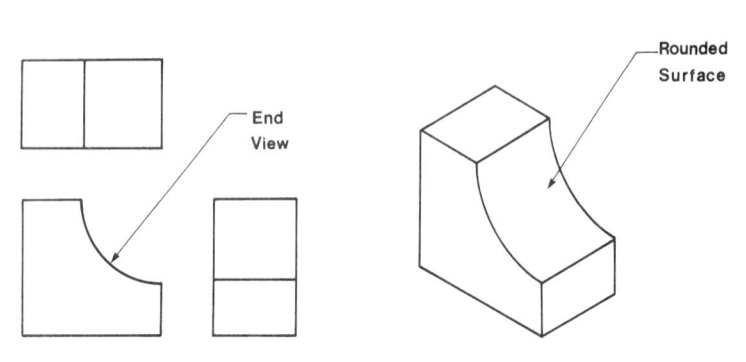

Figure 6-30 shows five sets of orthographic views that contain rounded surfaces. In object 1 of Figure 6-30, two rounded surfaces are separated by a short vertical surface. This vertical section must be represented in the top view by an object line. In object 2 there is no vertical surface. The rounded surfaces are separated by a slanted surface. In this example there would be no object line in the top view.

FIGURE 6-28 Object with a rounded surface.

Sec. 6-9   Rounded Surfaces

FIGURE 6-29 Object with a convex rounded surface.

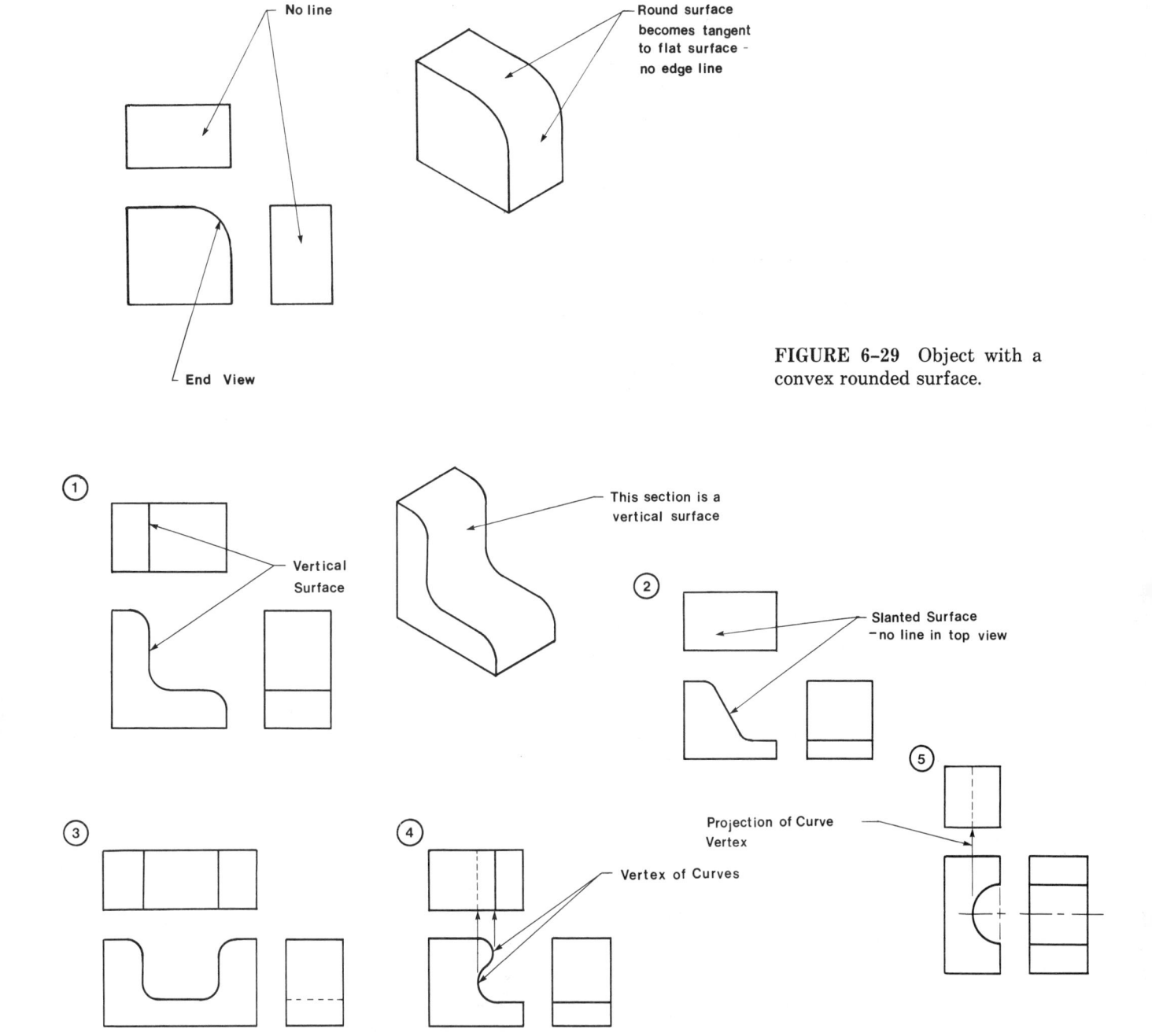

FIGURE 6-30 Five sets of orthographic views that contain rounded surfaces.

Object 3 is similar to object 1. The flat horizontal surface appears as a hidden line in the side view.

Object 4 in Figure 6-30 shows two rounded surfaces, one concave and one convex. The vertices of both curves are represented in the top view. The concave curve vertex is represented by a hidden line because it is not directly visible.

Object 5 in Figure 6-30 contains a circular cutout. The top view of the object contains a hidden line which represents a vertex (the deepest point) of the curve. The hidden line location is found by first drawing the curve, then projecting its vertex into the top view.

6-10 CYLINDERS

Three views of a cylinder are shown in Figure 6-31. The side view is a circle and both the front and top views are rectangular. The width of the front and top views are equal to the diameter of the circle. If the cylinder were elliptical in shape, the front and top views would still be rectangular, but of different sizes.

Figure 6-32 shows cylinders with different kinds of surfaces. Cylinder 1 has a surface cut above the longitudinal centerline. The top view

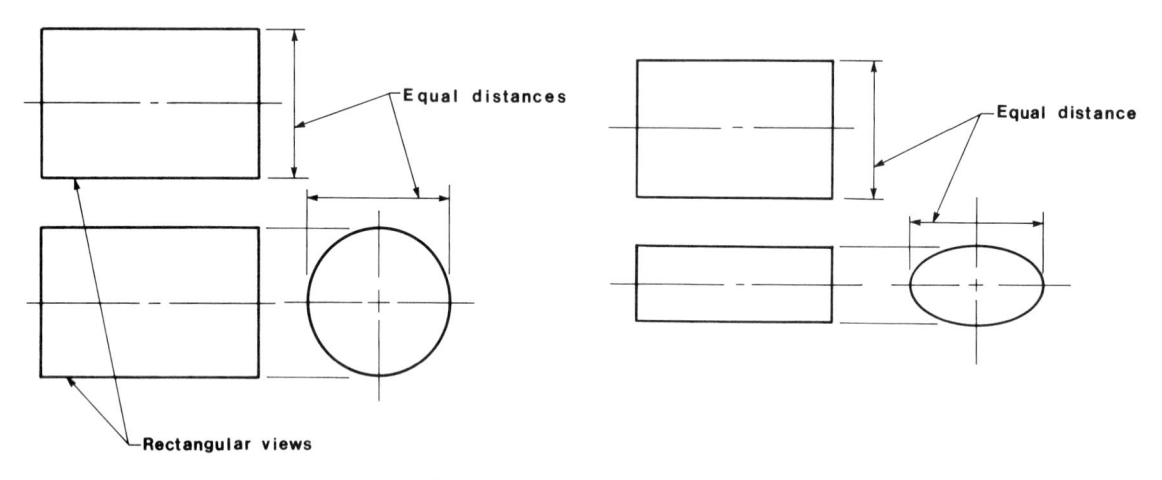

FIGURE 6-31 Three views of a cylinder.

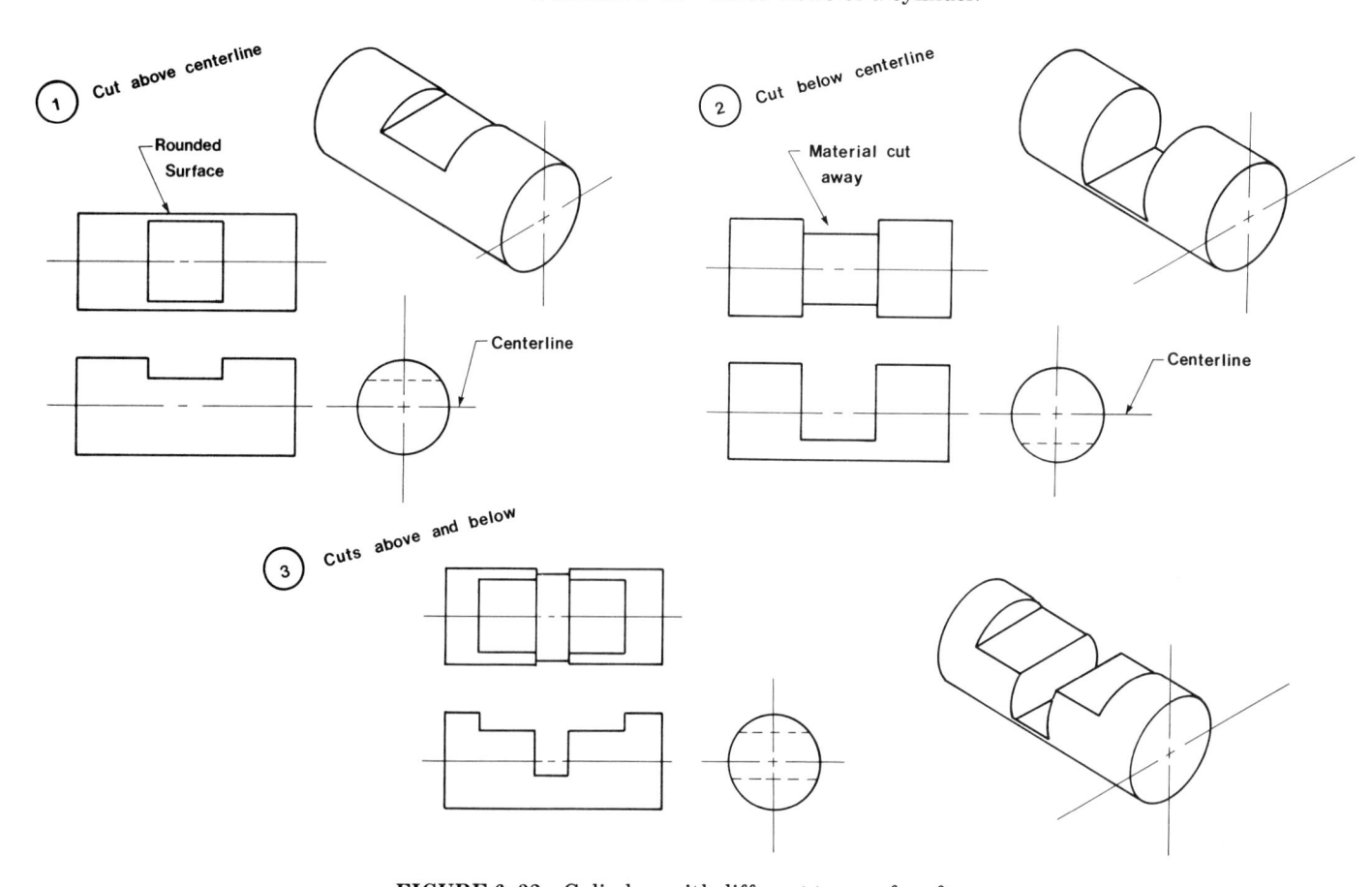

FIGURE 6-32 Cylinders with different types of surfaces.

Sec. 6-10 Cylinders 153

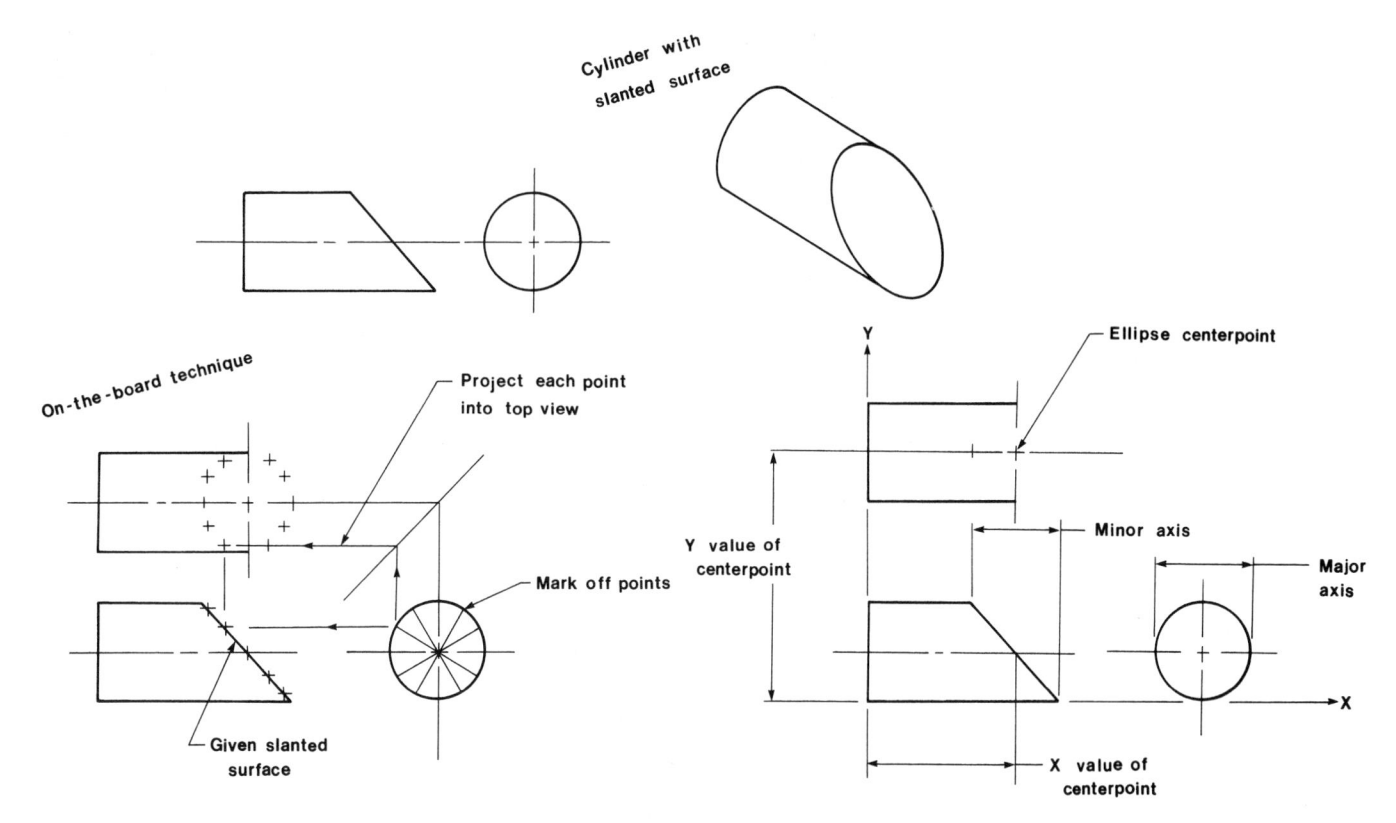

FIGURE 6–33 Cylinder with a slanted surface.

of this cylinder shows two rectangles. The smaller rectangle is the flat cut surface and the larger rectangle is the rounded surface of the cylinder.

Cylinder 2 has a surface cut below the centerline. This means that material has been cut away, so the surface width is narrower than the cylinder's. The top view is as shown.

Cylinder 3 has surfaces cut both above and below the centerline. Note how the cuts affect the top view.

Figure 6-33 shows a cylinder with a slanted surface cut. The side view is still circular, but the top view contains an ellipse. On-the-board techniques require that this elliptical shape be generated by a series of points located by projection from the front and side views.

Computers are usually programmed to draw elliptical shapes given either the major and minor axis or the major axis or the major axis and an angle of rotation. Figure 6-34 shows the definition of these terms. Note that if the major axis remains constant, the elliptical shape projected becomes narrower as the angle of rotation increases.

The major and minor diameters of the ellipse needed to complete the top view of Figure 6-33 are determined from information on the other two views. The major axis is equal to the diameter of the circular view. The minor axis is the perpendicular distance across the front view of the slanted surface as shown. The perpendicular distance can be determined by using the computer to calculate it using the dimensioning technique explained in Figure 6-7 and then inputting the value as the minor diameter of the ellipse.

The centerpoint for the ellipse in the top view can be determined by using the computer to calculate the distance from the intersection of the cylindrical centerline with the slanted surface in the front view from

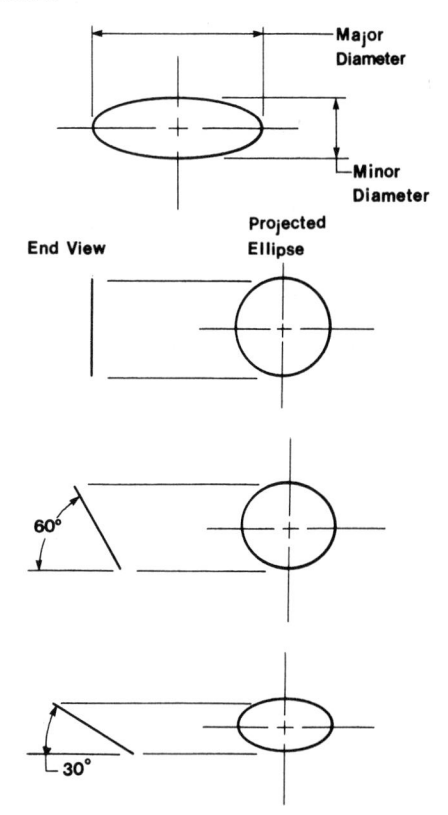

FIGURE 6–34 Definition of the major and minor diameters of an ellipse.

the origin, then using this distance as the X coordinate value for the centerpoint location in the top view. The Y value will be equal to the distance from the top view centerline to the X axis.

6-11 HOLES

Holes are drawn in orthographic views as shown in Figure 6-35. Holes *always* require a centerline. Holes that do not go completely through an object should always include a 30° conical tip as shown. The conical portion of a hole is not included in the depth value but is added to the depth value. Holes perpendicular to slanted surfaces are drawn as shown in Figure 6-36. Elliptical shapes are generated in the side and front views. The ellipse in side view has a major diameter equal to the diameter of the hole. The minor diameter is found by projecting the foreshortened

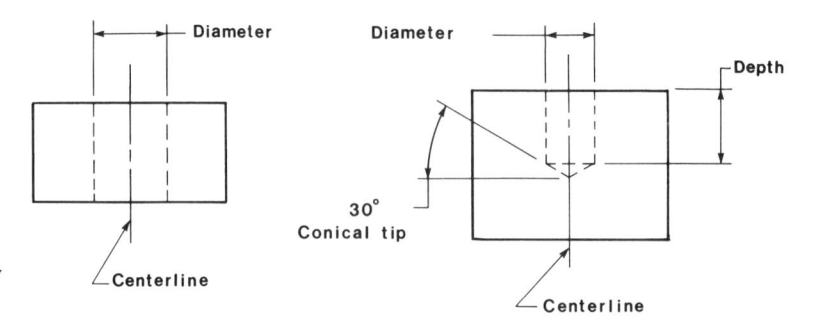

FIGURE 6-35 How to draw holes in orthographic views.

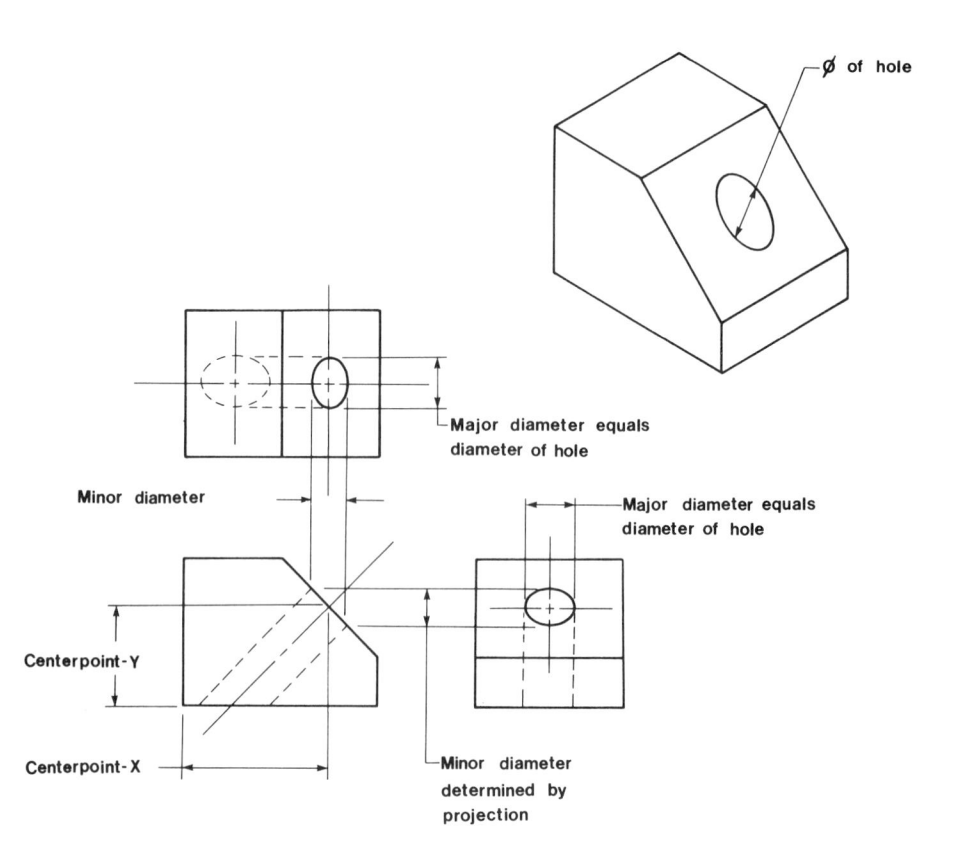

FIGURE 6-36 How to draw a hole that is perpendicular to a slanted surface.

Sec. 6-11 Holes   155

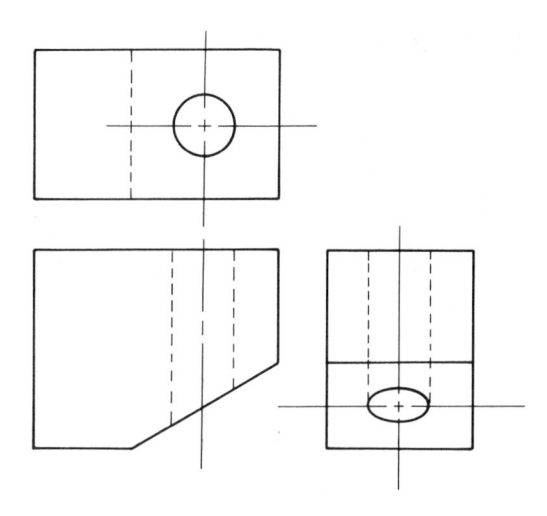

FIGURE 6-37 How to draw a hole that penetrates a slanted surface.

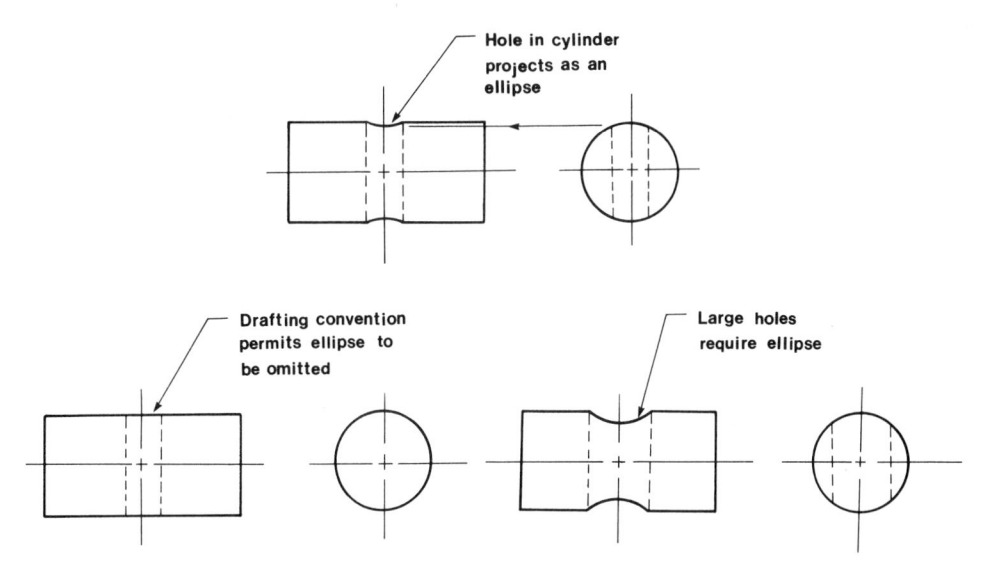

FIGURE 6-38 How to draw holes in cylindrical objects.

hole size from the front view into the side view using the dimensioning technique explained in Figure 6-7.

The ellipse in the top view has a major diameter equal to the diameter of the hole and a minor diameter equal to the foreshortened length of the hole projected from the front view into the top view.

Figure 6-37 shows an object which has a hole that penetrates a slanted surface. The top view is circular and the side view is elliptical. The major diameter, minor diameter, and centerpoint location in the side view are determined as explained above.

Holes in cylindrical-shaped surfaces will generate an elliptical shape in the front view as shown in Figure 6-38. These elliptical shapes are usually small, difficult to draw, and difficult to see on the final drawing. For this reason, drafting convention allows for these elliptical shapes to be omitted and replaced with straight lines as shown. Larger holes should use elliptical shapes. Whether or not an elliptical shape is required is up to the discretion of the draftsperson.

6-12 IRREGULAR SHAPES

Irregular shapes are curved shapes that do not have a constant radius. They are usually defined by a series of points referenced to an *XY* axis as shown in Figure 6-39. On-the-board technique requires that each point be plotted and then joined using an irregular (French) curve.

Computer graphic systems draw irregular lines by connecting a series of points using a *spline*. There are two types of spline constructions: open and closed. Figure 6-40 shows an example of each. The points that define a spline are inputted to the computer by coordinate values or by

Points	X	Y
1	0.0	1.25
2	.50	1.20
3	1.00	1.10
4	1.00	.92
5	2.00	.61
6	2.25	.50

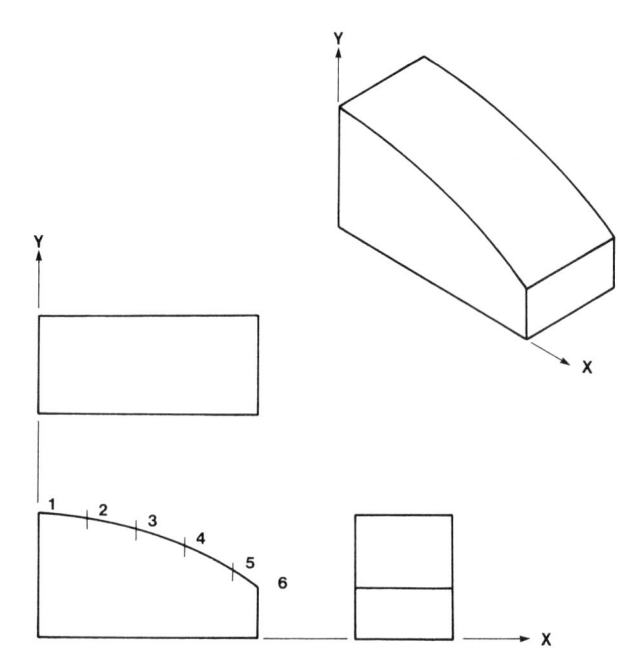

FIGURE 6-39 Object that contains an irregular surface.

FIGURE 6-40 Examples of open and closed splines.

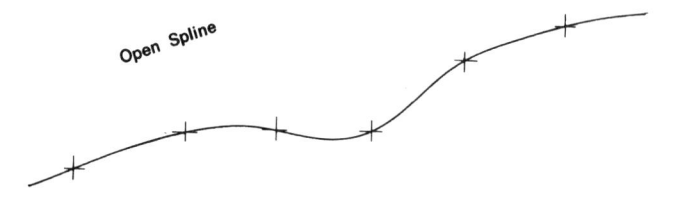

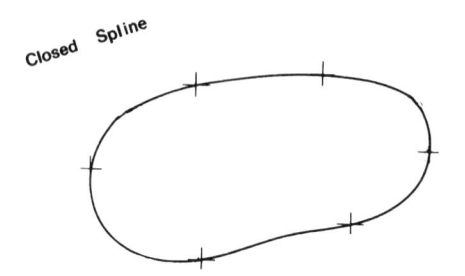

Sec. 6-12 Irregular Shapes

random locations using the computer cursor. Figure 6-41 shows an orthographic view problem that involves an irregular surface. The shape of the front and side views are known. It is also known that the forward edge of the top view will be an irregular shape, but is not defined. The specific points needed to define the edge shape must be derived from the given front and side views. Figure 6-41 shows the procedure. The procedure used in Figure 6-41 is as follows.

1. Draw the front and side views so that the lower left corner of the front view is on the origin.
2. Add points to the curved feature in the side view. The location of the points is arbitrary. The more points added, the more accurate the resulting projection.
3. Project the points into the front view.
4. Draw unlimited-length horizontal lines through the points added in the side view.
5. Draw unlimited-length vertical lines through all corners and feature intersections on the horizontal projection lines of step 4 with the slanted feature in the front view.
6. Use the dimensioning technique presented in Figure 6-7 or the projection technique of Figure 6-9, and transfer the feature distance from the Y axis to the X axis.
7. Use the dimensioning technique explained in Section 6-8 to transfer the curve points from the side view to the top view. Join the two points in the top view with the starting and end points of the feature using a spline. The resultant curve will be a top view of the feature represented by a slanted line in the front view and a curved line in the side view.
8. Trim all excess lines.

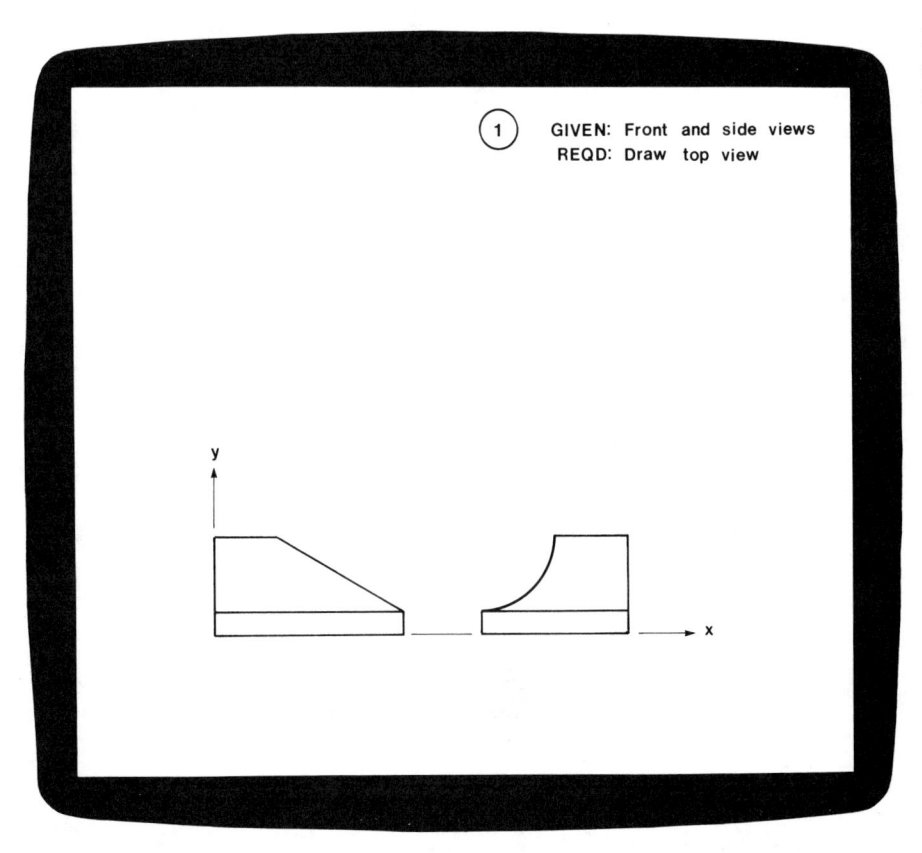

FIGURE 6-41 How to draw an irregular shape using projection.

FIGURE 6-41 (*cont.*)

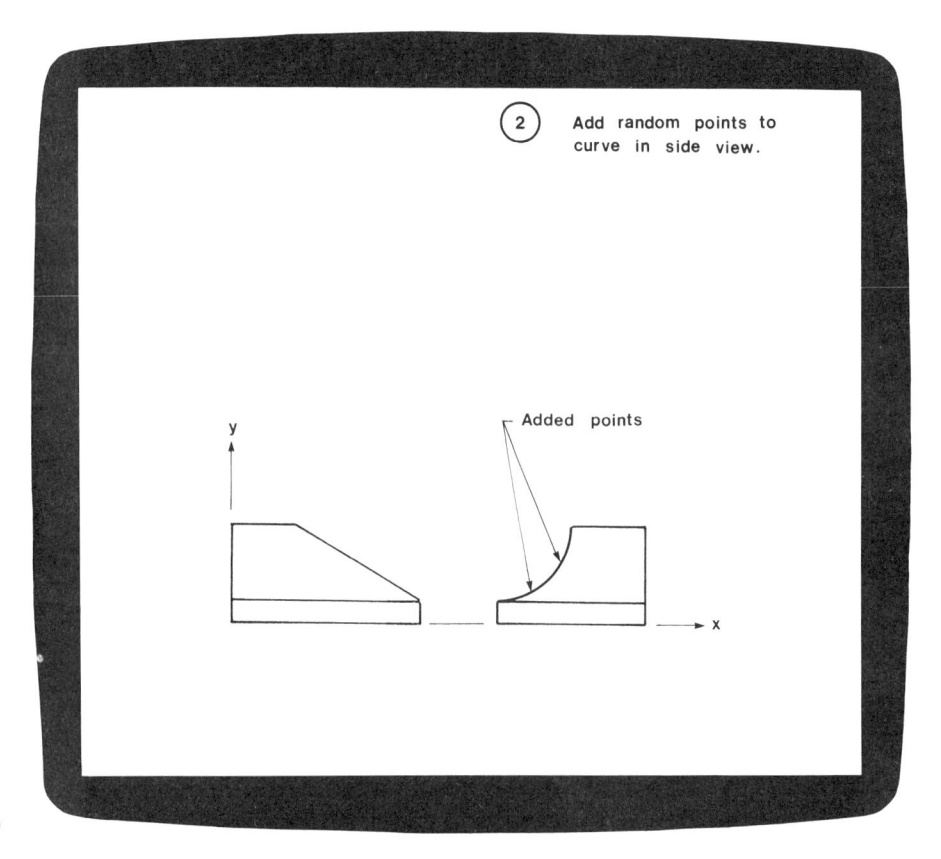

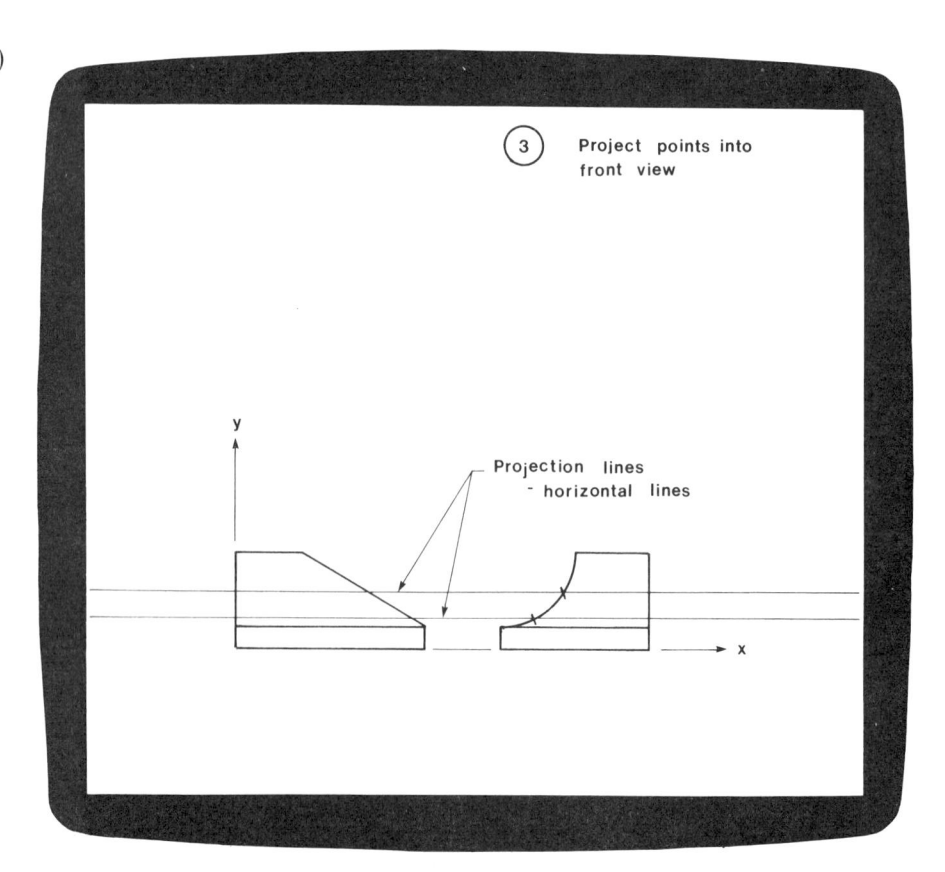

FIGURE 6-41 (*cont.*)

Sec. 6-12 Irregular Shapes

④ Add vertical projection lines

Project intersection points

FIGURE 6-41 (*cont.*)

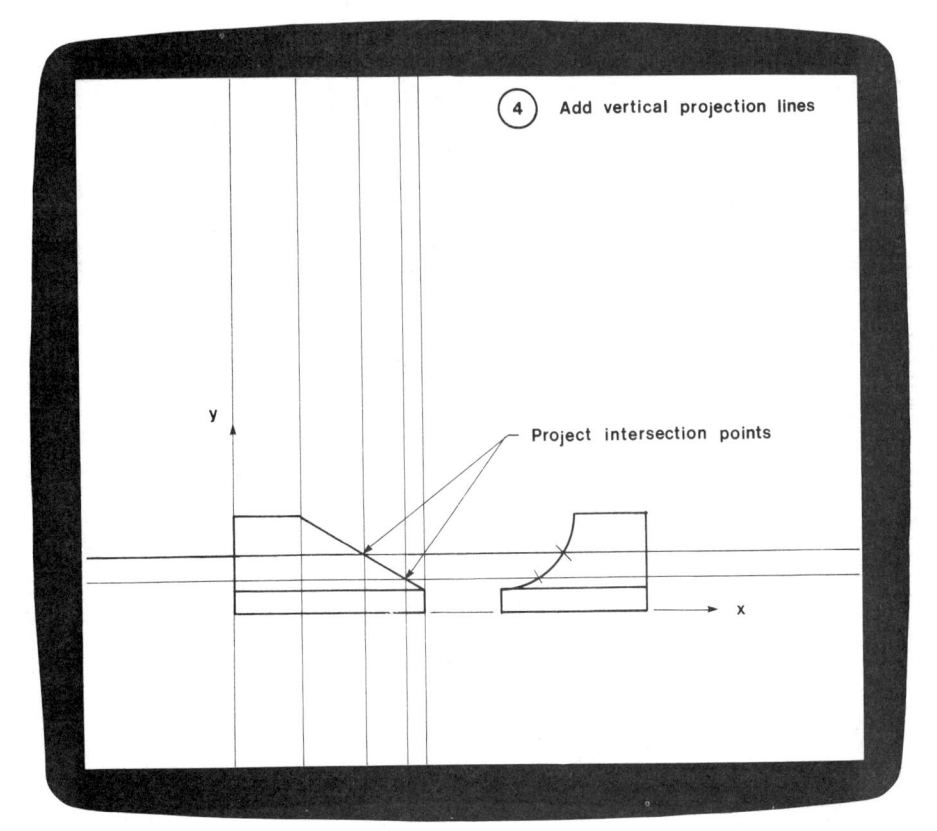

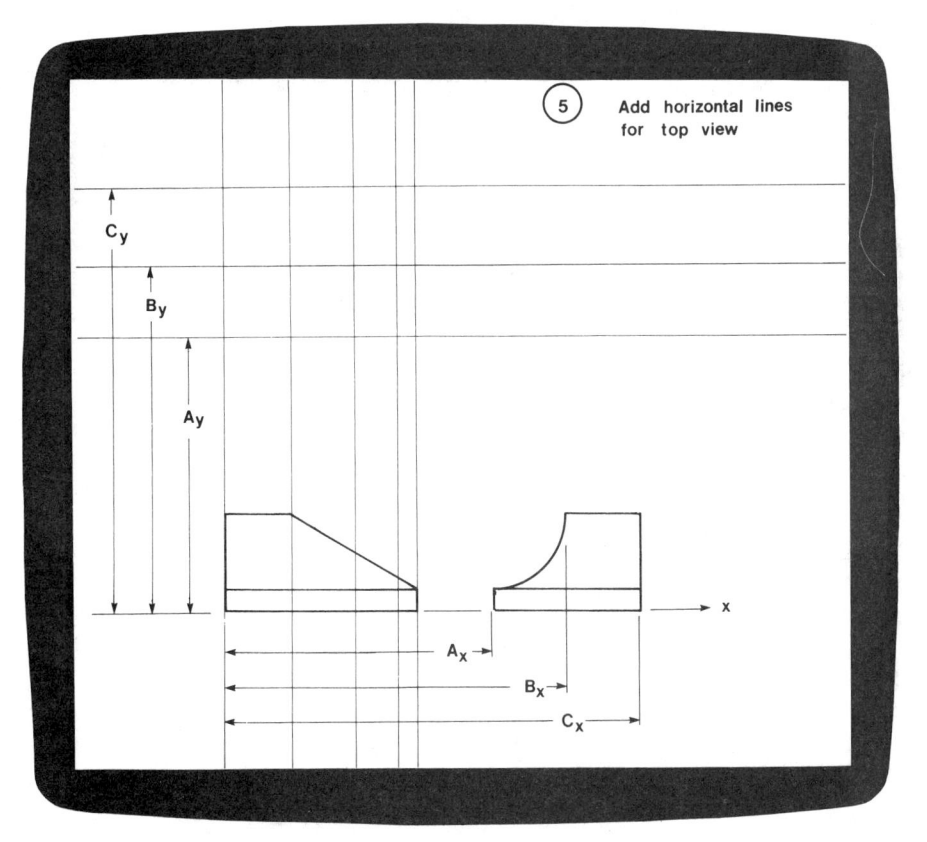

FIGURE 6-41 (*cont.*)

⑤ Add horizontal lines for top view

FIGURE 6-41 (*cont.*)

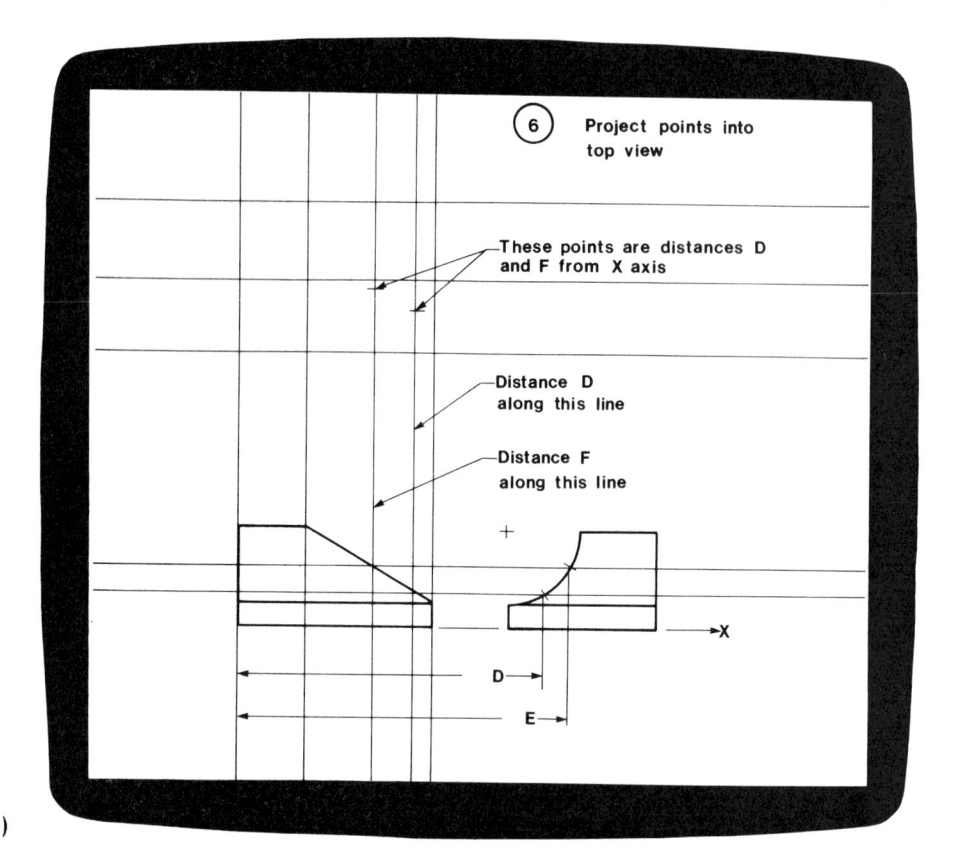

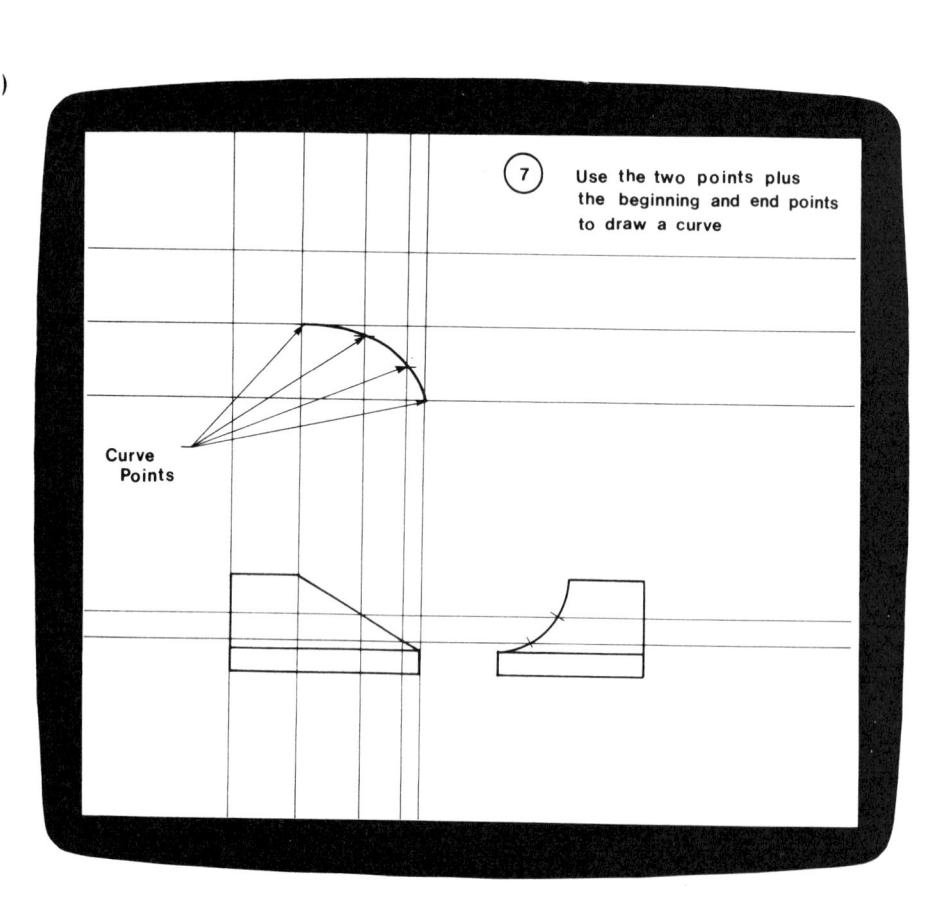

FIGURE 6-41 (*cont.*)

Sec. 6-13   Sheet Metal Objects

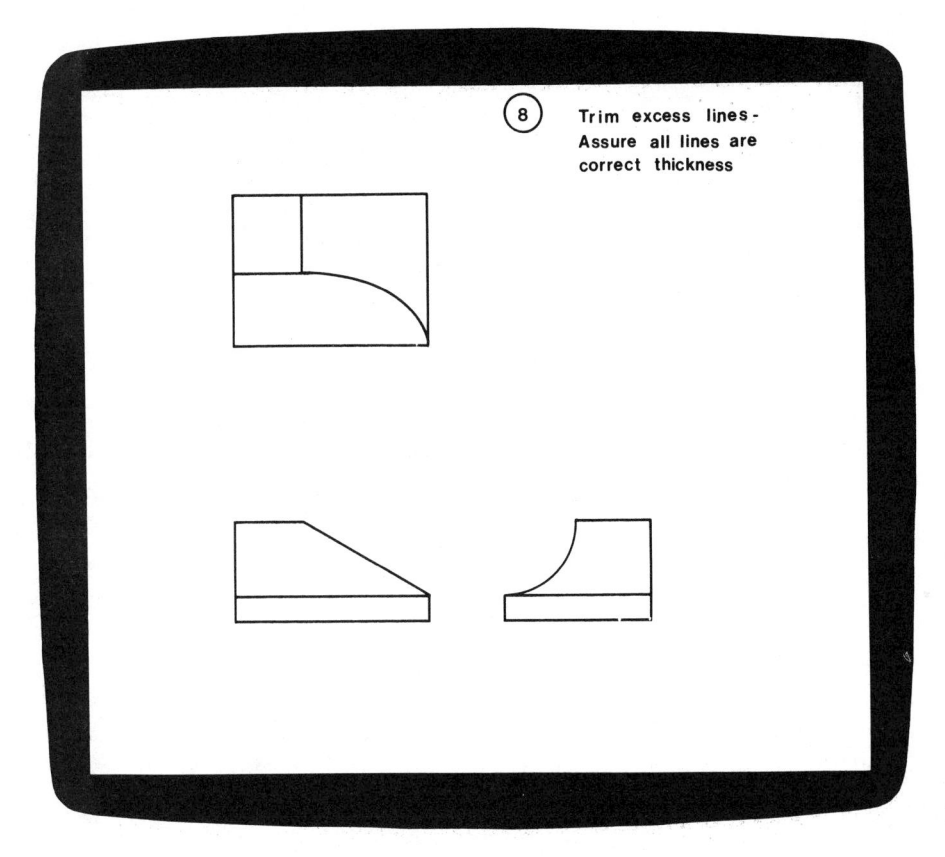

⑧ Trim excess lines - Assure all lines are correct thickness

FIGURE 6-41 (*cont.*)

6-13 SHEET METAL OBJECTS

Sheet metal objects are characterized by thin-walled features as shown in Figure 6-42. The bends in sheet metal objects are defined as an inside bend and an outside bend. The thickness of a sheet metal object is defined using a dimension or by specifying a gage. A listing of gage thickness is included Appendix B.

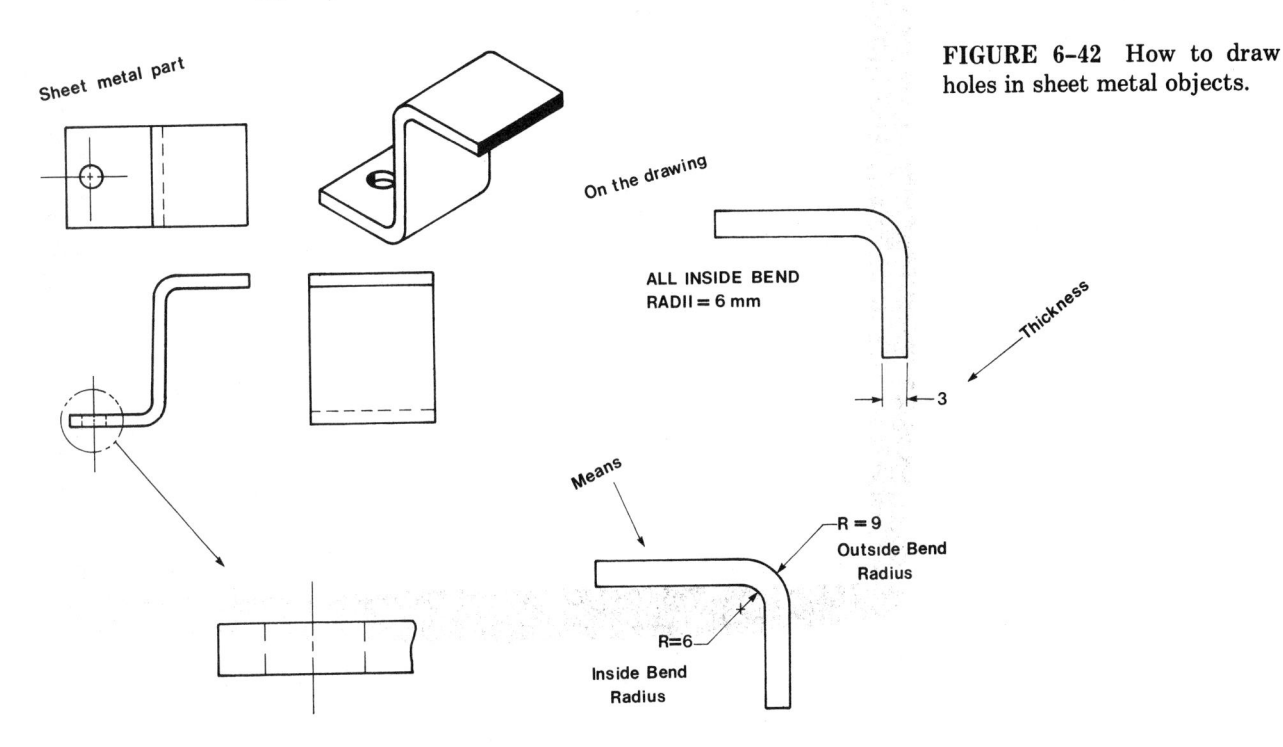

FIGURE 6-42 How to draw holes in sheet metal objects.

Sheet metal part

On the drawing

ALL INSIDE BEND RADII = 6 mm

Thickness

Means

R = 9 Outside Bend Radius

R = 6 Inside Bend Radius

FIGURE 6-43 How to draw orthographic views of very thin objects.

Usually, either the inside or outside bend radius is given for a sheet metal object, not both. The two bend radii are related to each other by the formula

inside bend radius + thickness = outside bend radius

This means that if the inside bend radius is 6 mm, as shown in Figure 6-42, and the material thickness is 3 mm, the outside bend radius equals 9 mm. It is important that correct values be used for both inside and outside bend radii when preparing orthographic views of sheet metal objects.

Holes in sheet metal objects are represented as shown in Figure 6-42. An enlarged detail may be used to help show holes clearly, but this is optional. If the sheet metal thickness is extremely small, it may be impossible to show any hidden lines. If so, only the hole centerline is drawn in the profile view, as shown in Figure 6-43. The top view of the hole is drawn as a circle, with centerlines.

6-14 CASTINGS

Objects produced by casting are characterized by rounded edges and surfaces which become tangent (blend together smoothly) to each other. The orthographic views of cast objects indicate points of tangency by using a *runout*. A runout is a short arc as shown in Figure 6-44. The many

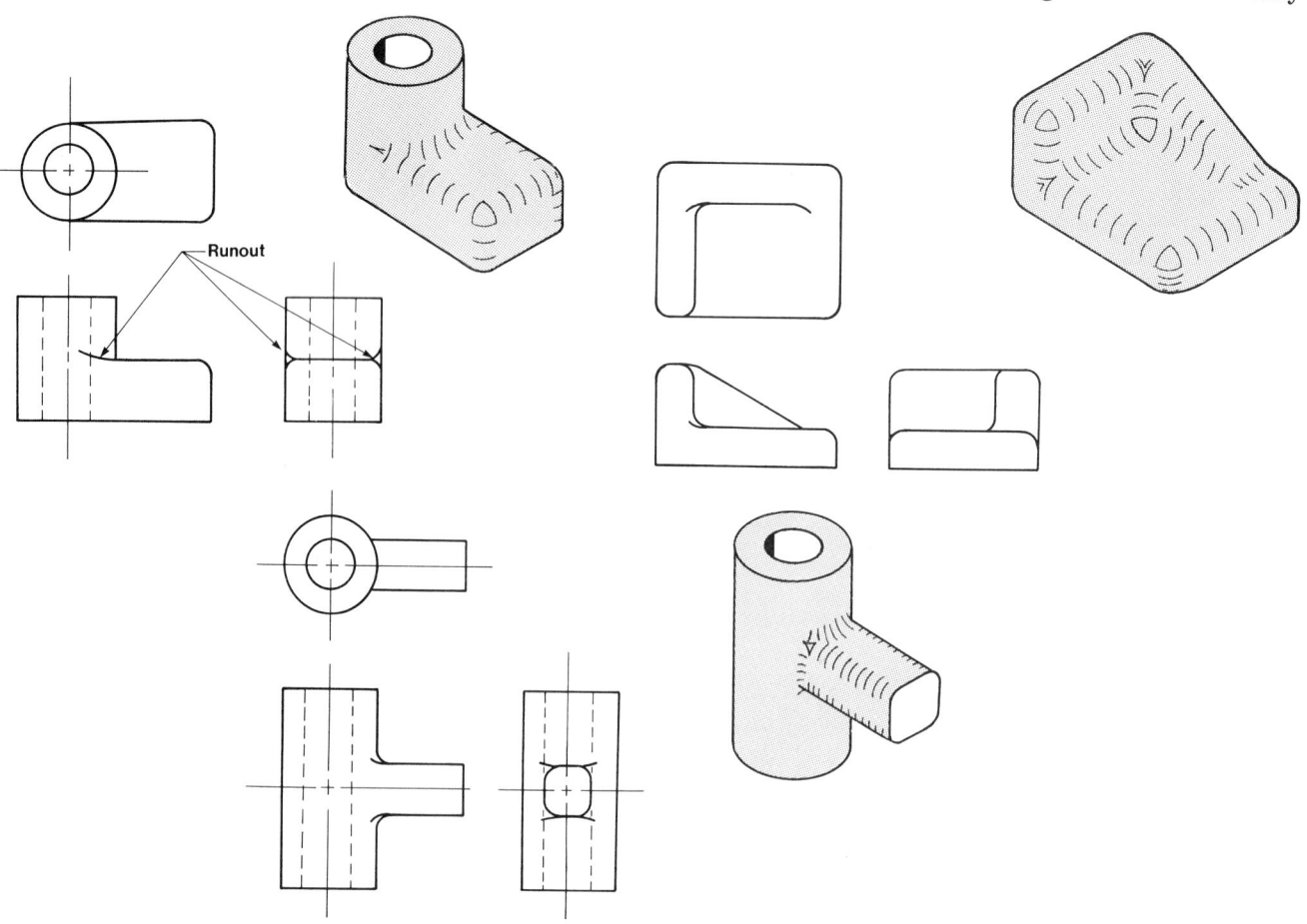

FIGURE 6-44 Examples of cast objects with runouts.

rounded edges follow the conventions outlined in Section 6-9. Several examples are shown in Figure 6-44.

A rounded surface on a casting that is convex is called a *round*, and one that is concave is called a *fillet* (Figure 6-45).

Cast surfaces are porous. This means that they are likely to crack if used as bearing surfaces. For example, as a screw is tightened against a cast surface, the bearing load is distributed unevenly (the load is pushing against only the high spots on the surface). Rather than machine the entire surfaces to produce a smooth surface preferred for bearing loads, cast objects are designed with bosses or are machined using spotfaces (Figure 6-46). A *boss* is a raised turret-like shape that allows just the top of the boss to be machined rather than the entire surface.

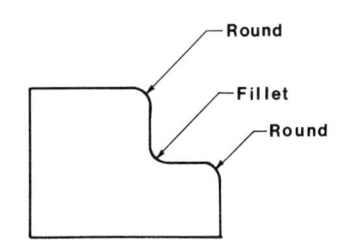

FIGURE 6-45 Definition of a fillet and a round.

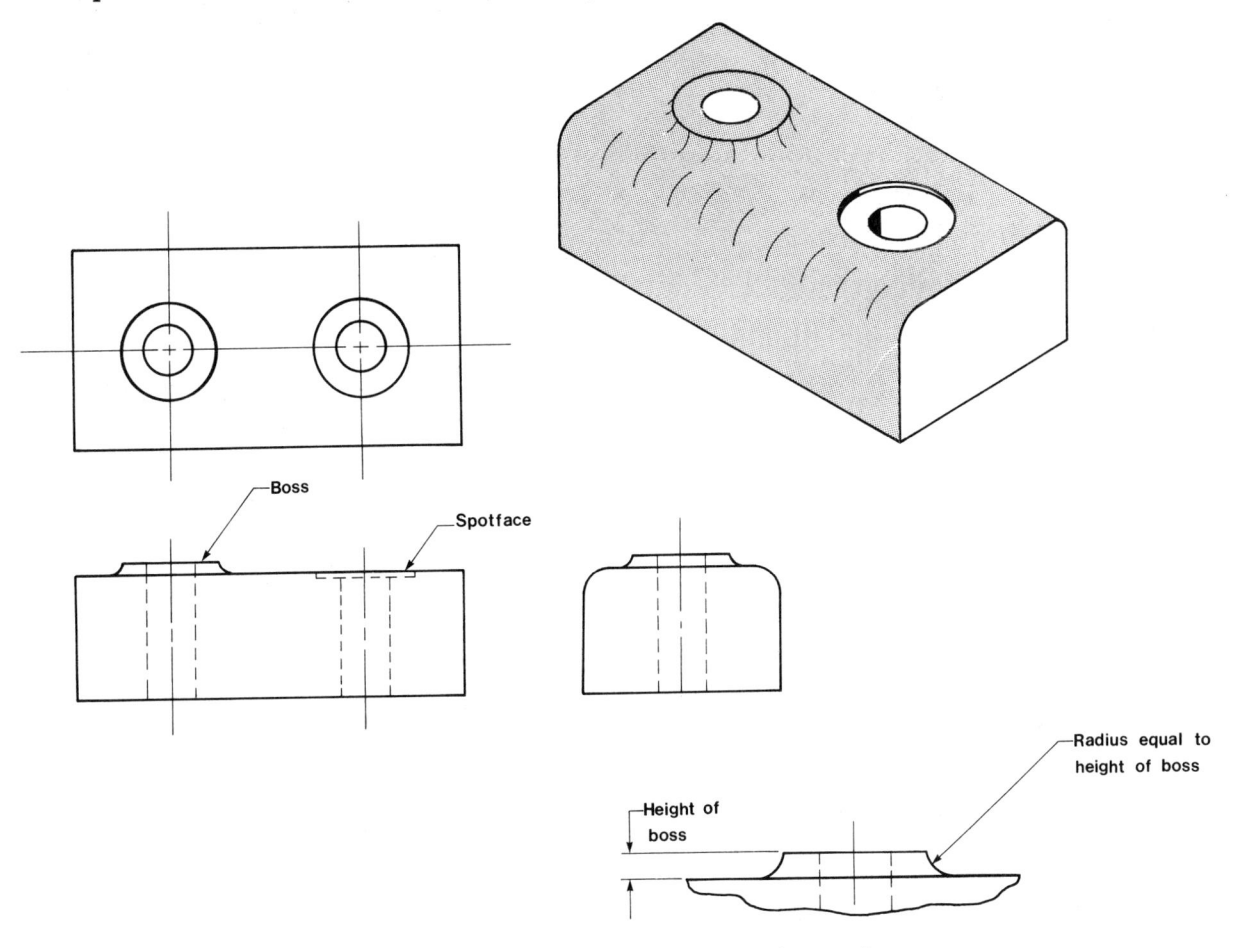

FIGURE 6-46 Definition of a boss and a spotface.

A *spotface* is a very shallow counterbore which also reduces the need for extensive machinery. Spotfacing is discussed in detail in Chapter 5.

6-15 THREE-DIMENSIONAL COORDINATE SYSTEMS AND ORTHOGRAPHIC VIEWS

Some large computer systems prepare orthographic views using a three-dimensional coordinate system as shown in Figure 6-47. The object is pictured as setting on a three-dimensional XYZ coordinate system. The

FIGURE 6-47 Three-dimensional axis system.

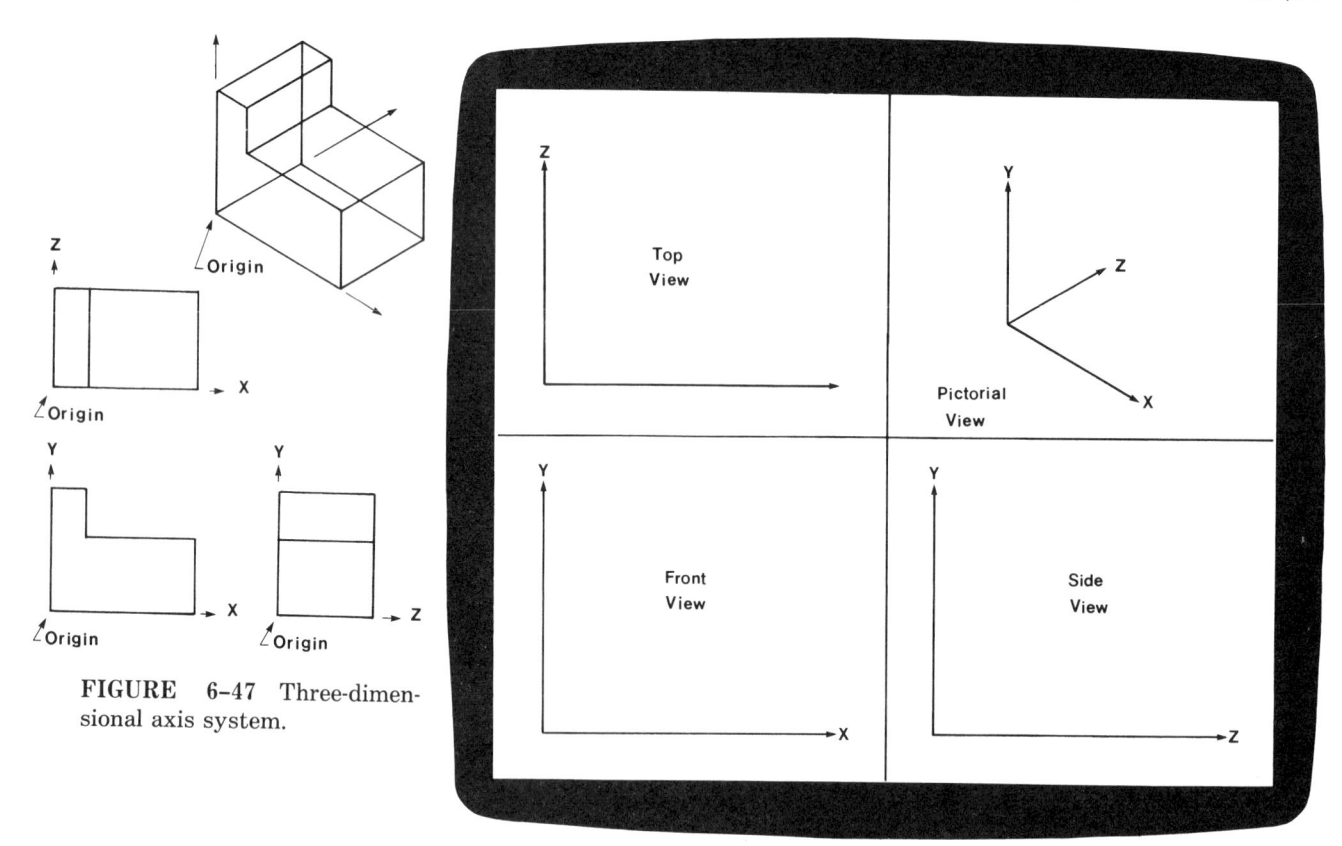

FIGURE 6-48 How to divide a computer screen into four areas for three orthographic views and a three-dimensional pictorial view.

resulting three orthographic views each have their own two-dimensional axis system. The front view uses the XY axis, the top, the XZ, and the side of the YZ. Dimensional values can be referenced directly to the appropriate size.

A three-dimensional coordinate system divides the computer screen into four areas as shown in Figure 6-48. Both the three orthographic views and the pictorial views can appear on the screen simultaneously (see front cover of this book). Some of the very advanced systems allow a design to work directly from the pictorial view using either a solid model

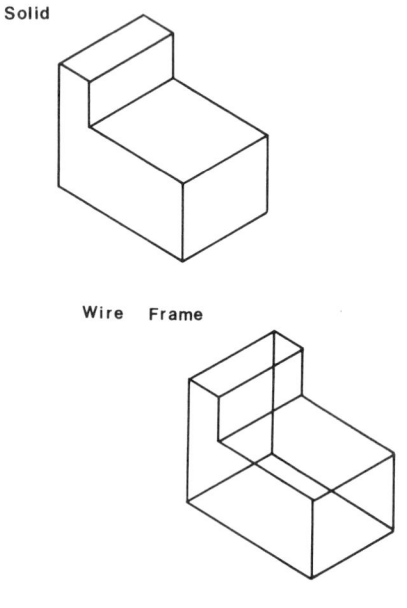

FIGURE 6-49 Examples of a solid model and a wire frame model.

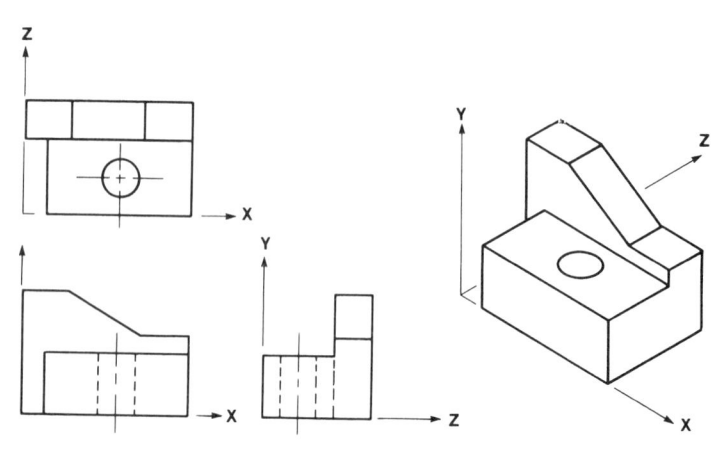

FIGURE 6-50 Three-dimensional axis system applied to a solid model and three orthographic views of the model.

Chap. 6   Problems

or wire frame model (Figure 6-49). Three-dimensional modeling allows the designer to "see" what is being designed. The orthographic views can then be drawn automatically from the pictorial model.

Three-dimensional coordinate systems are used extensively by computer numerically controlled (CNC) machines. It is important that the drafter and designer have a good visual understanding of how orthographic views are related to a three-dimensional system so that they can create drawings and objects which can be manufactured by CNC machines. Figure 6-50 shows an object and three orthographic views of that object. Note how the views align with either XY, XZ, or YZ coordinates.

PROBLEMS

Figures P6-1 through P6-43 are dimensioned pictorial drawings of objects. Draw three views (front, top, and right side) of each object as assigned. The units are noted for each problem.

P6-1	Metric	P6-16	Inches	P6-31	Metric
P6-2	Metric	P6-17	Metric	P6-32	Metric
P6-3	Inches	P6-18	Inches	P6-33	Metric
P6-4	Inches	P6-19	Metric	P6-34	Metric
P6-5	Metric	P6-20	Metric	P6-35	Metric
P6-6	Metric	P6-21	Metric	P6-36	Inches
P6-7	Metric	P6-22	Metric	P6-37	Inches
P6-8	Inches	P6-23	Metric	P6-38	Metric
P6-9	Metric	P6-24	Inches	P6-39	Metric
P6-10	Inches	P6-25	Metric	P6-40	Metric
P6-11	Metric	P6-26	Metric	P6-41	Metric
P6-12	Metric	P6-27	Metric	P6-42	Inches
P6-13	Metric	P6-28	Metric	P6-43	Inches
P6-14	Metric	P6-29	Inches		
P6-15	Metric	P6-30	Inches		

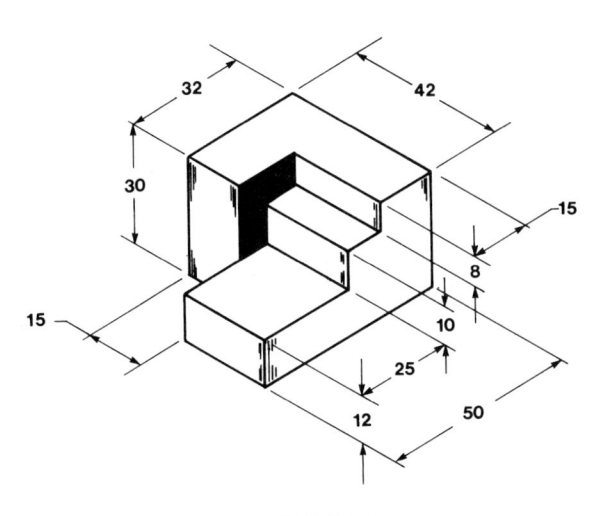

FIGURE P6-1

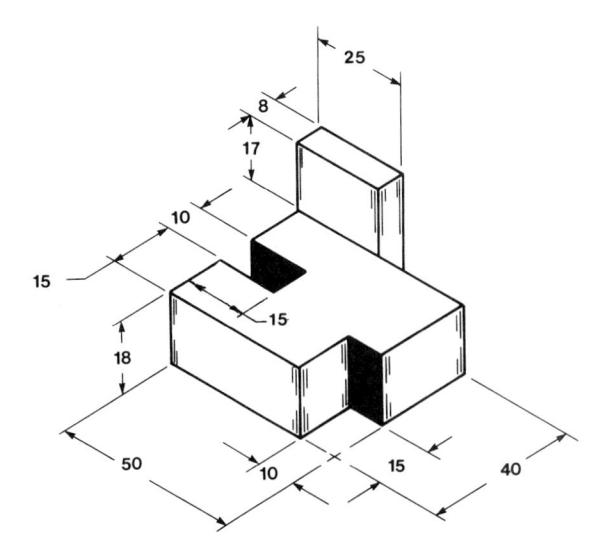

FIGURE P6-2

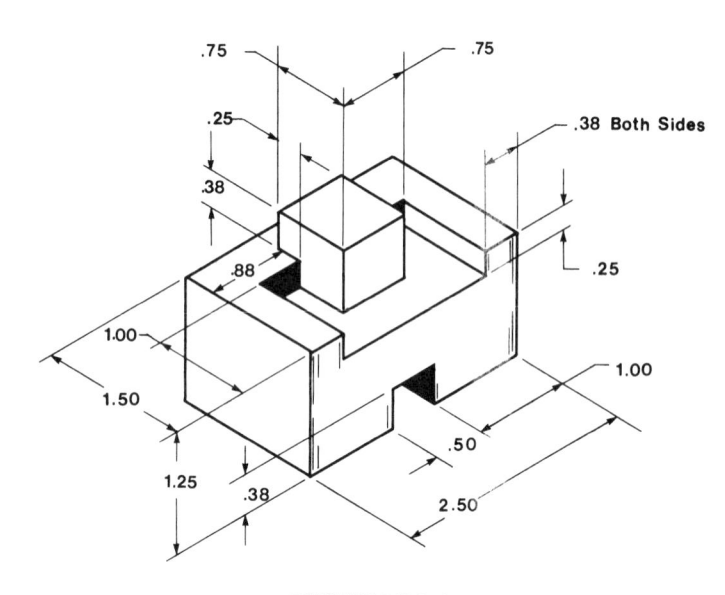

FIGURE P6-3

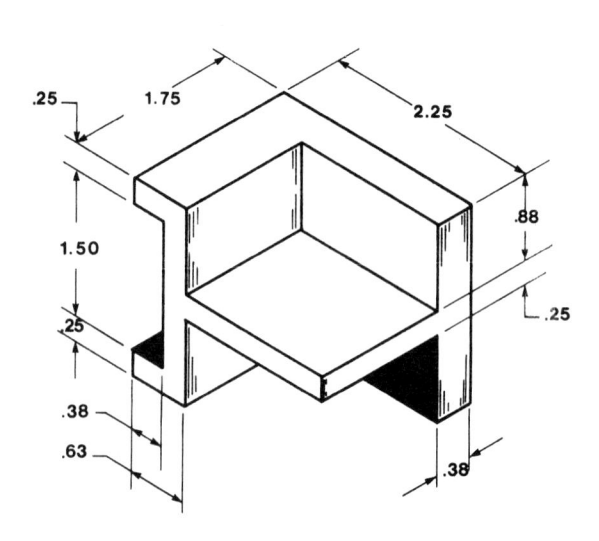

FIGURE P6-4

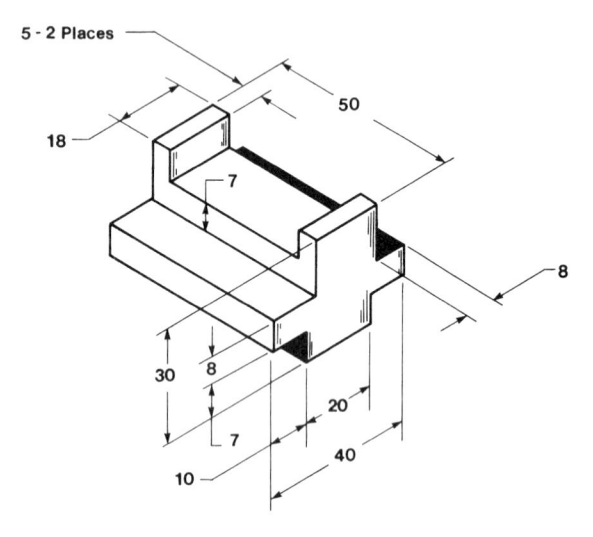

FIGURE P6-5

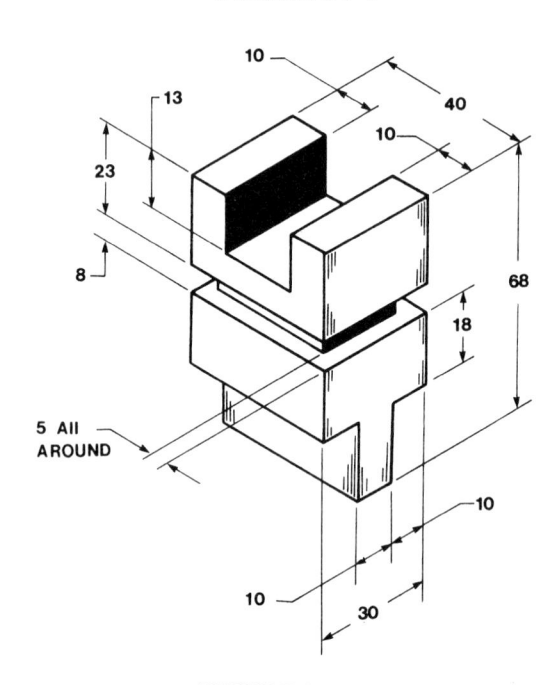

FIGURE P6-6

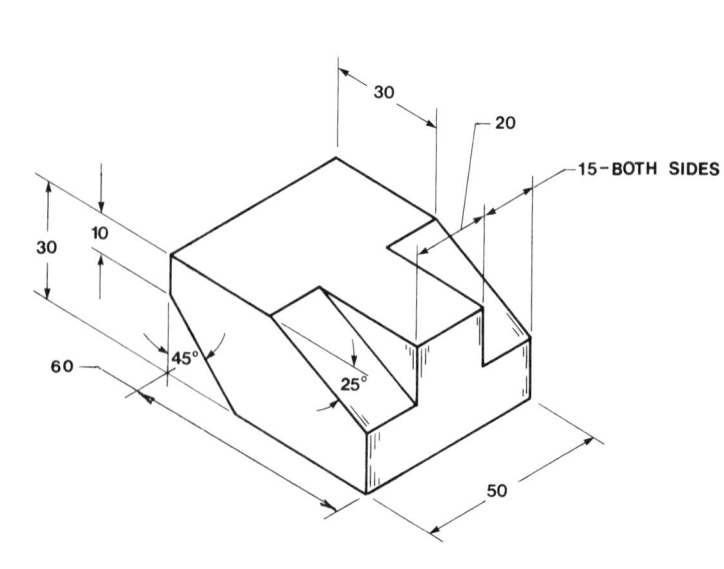

FIGURE P6-7

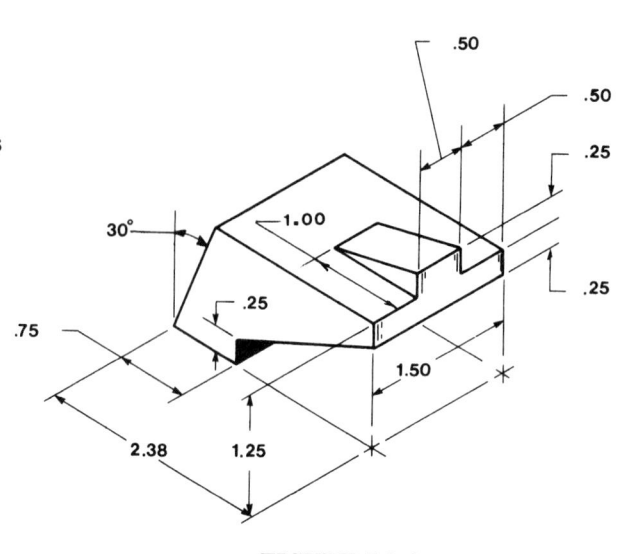

FIGURE P6-8

Chap. 6 Problems

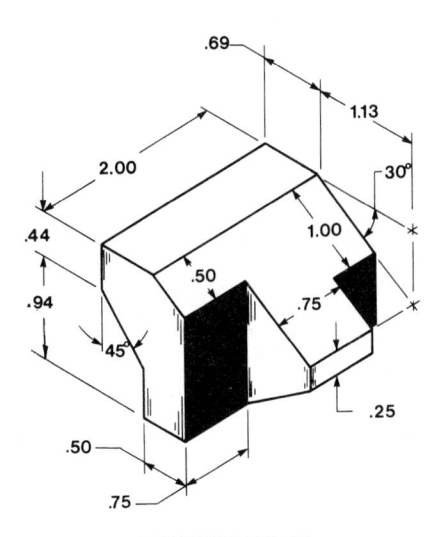

FIGURE P6-9

FIGURE P6-10

FIGURE P6-11

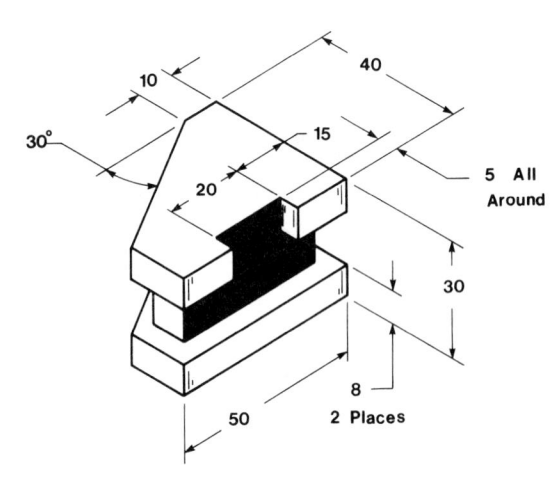

FIGURE P6-12

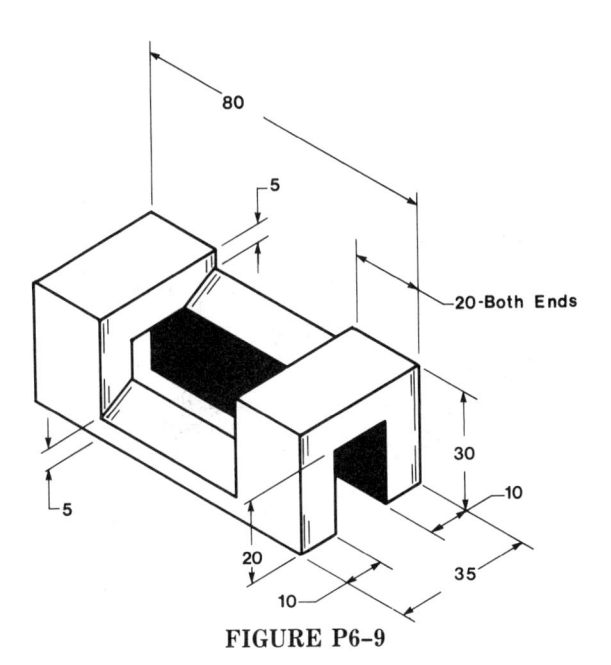

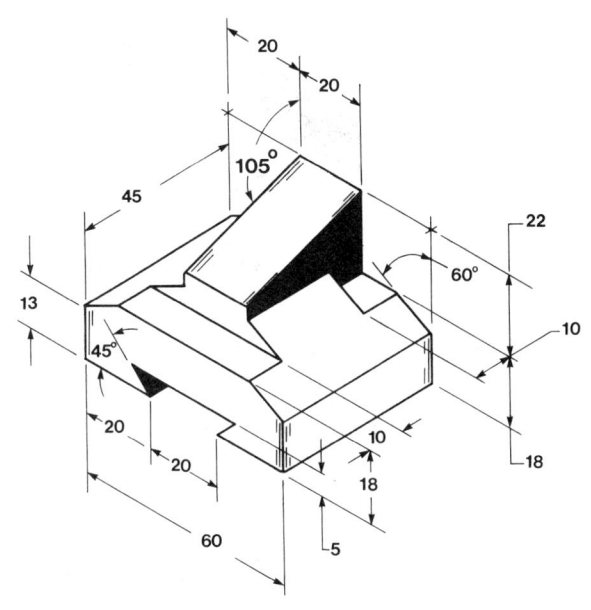

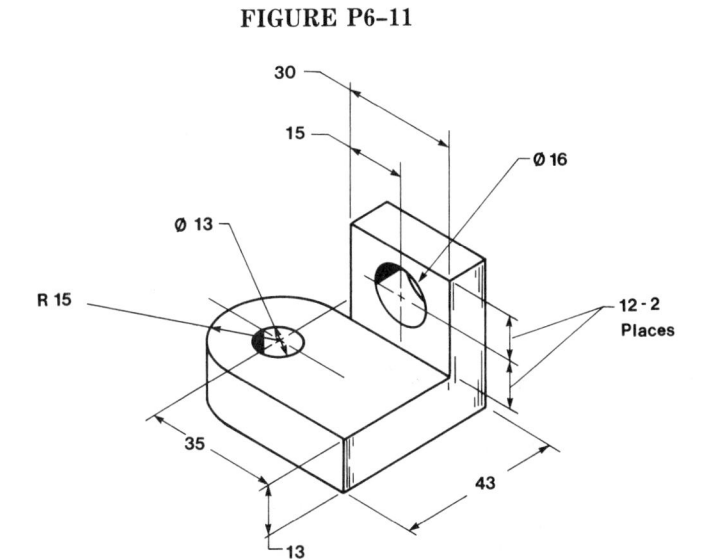

FIGURE P6-13

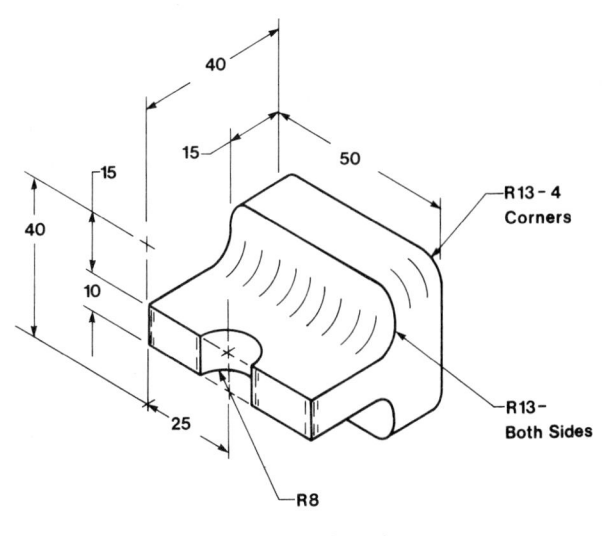

FIGURE P6-14

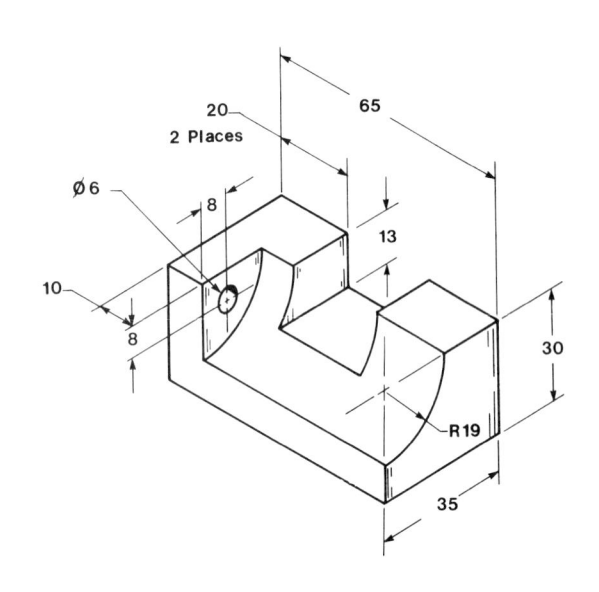

FIGURE P6-15

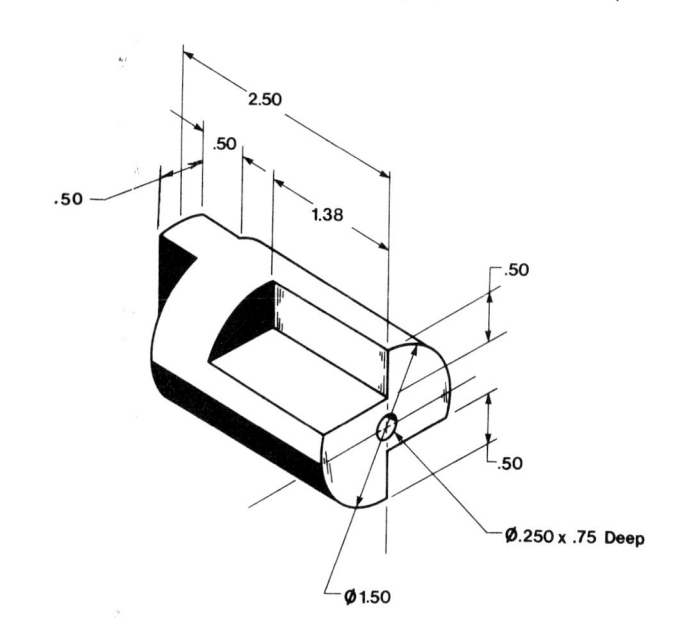

FIGURE P6-16

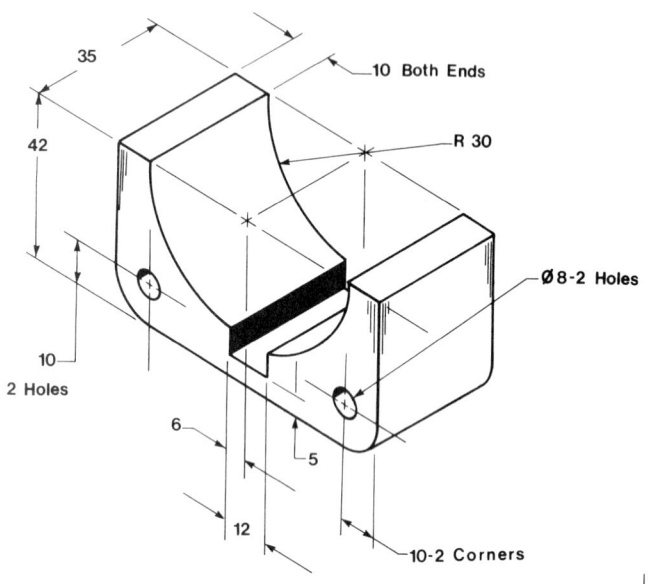

FIGURE P6-17

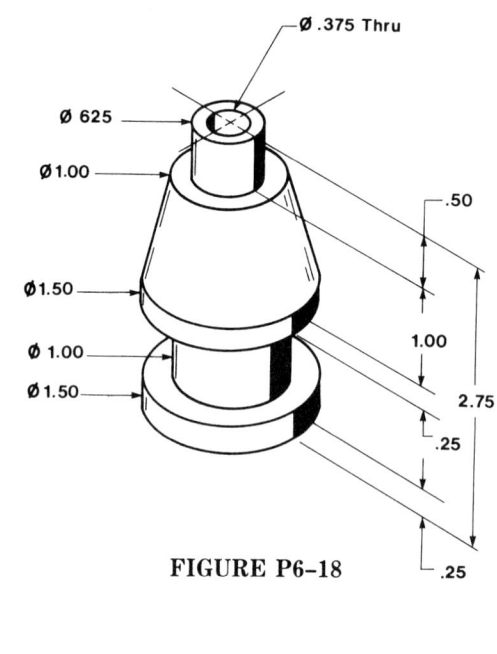

FIGURE P6-18

FIGURE P6-19

Note: Slot is 12 deep from centerline

Chap. 6 Problems

FIGURE P6-20

FIGURE P6-21

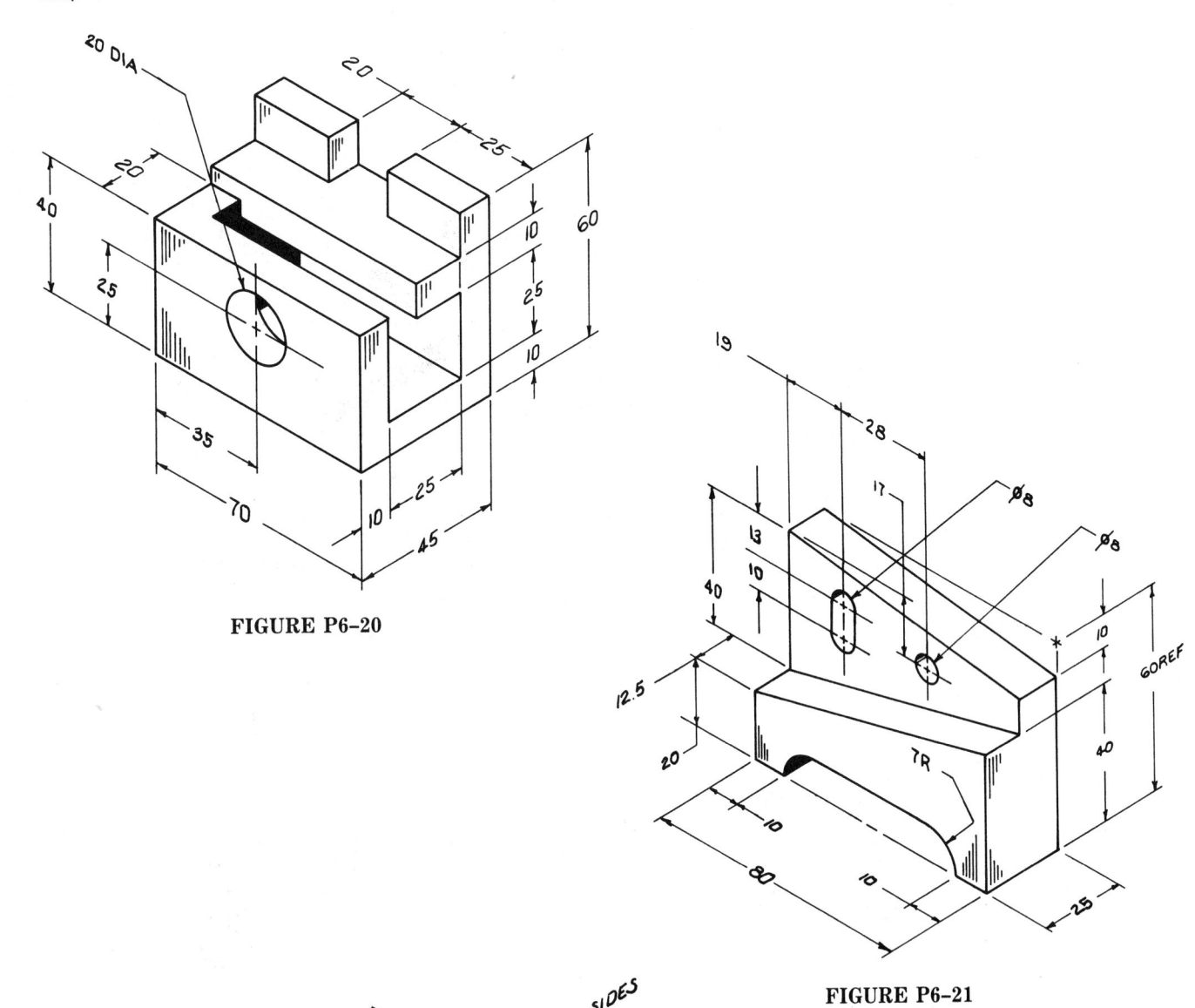

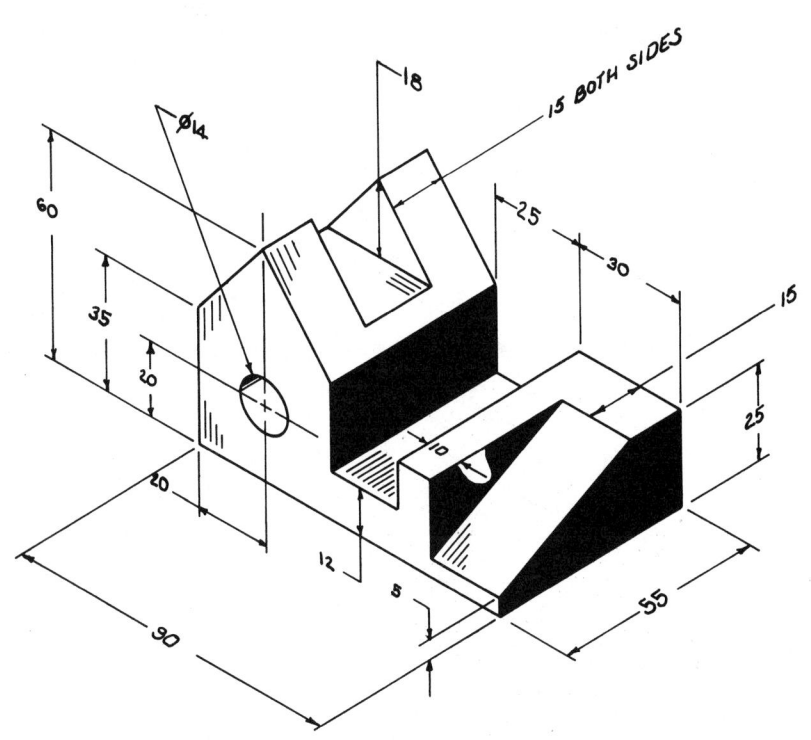

FIGURE P6-22

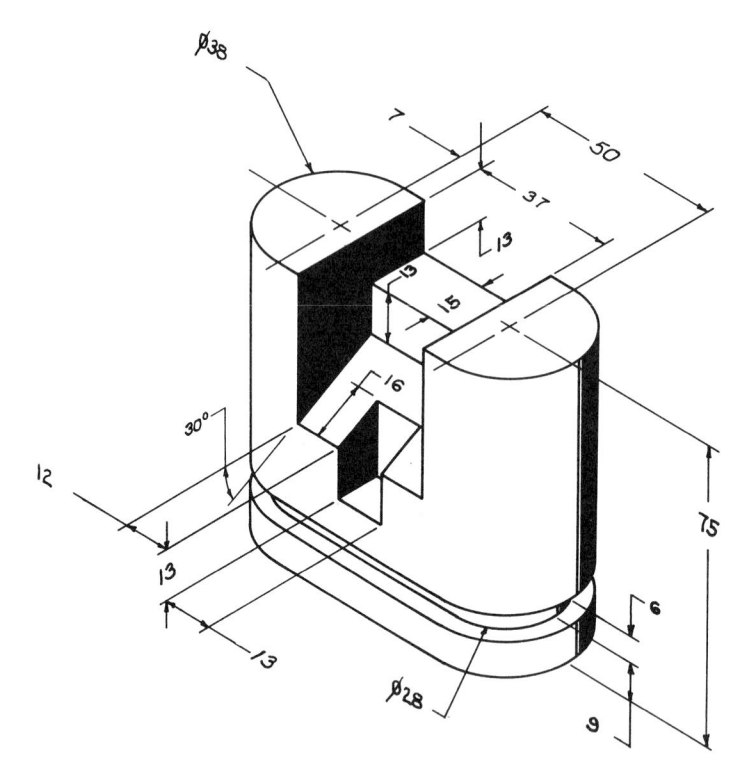

FIGURE P6–23

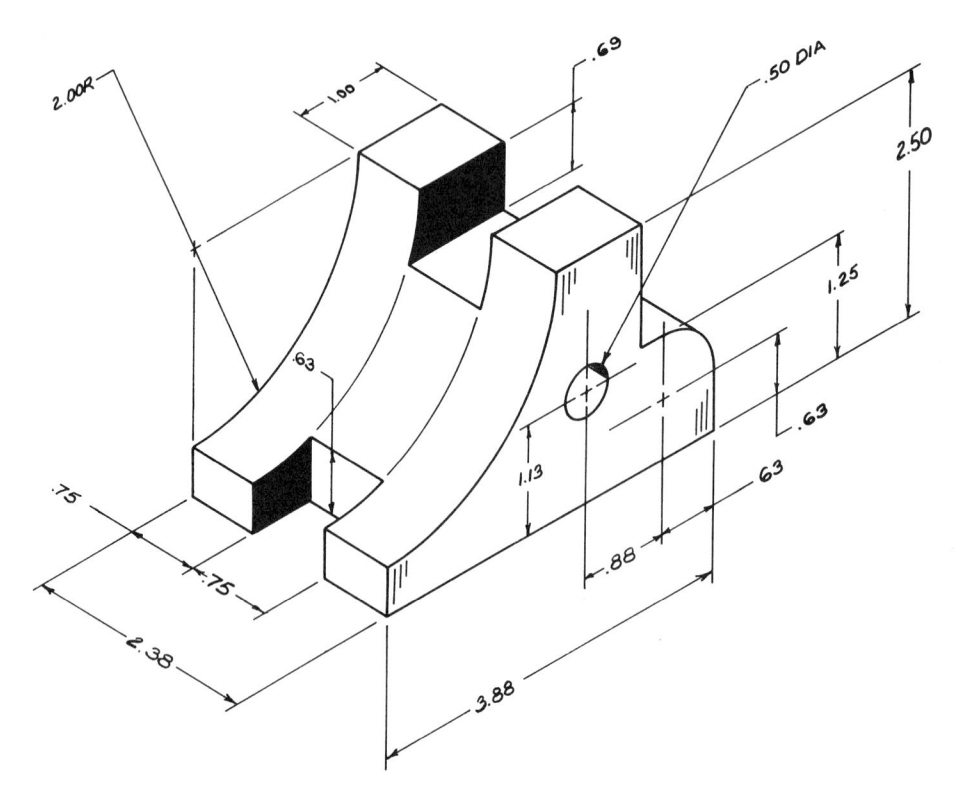

FIGURE P6–24

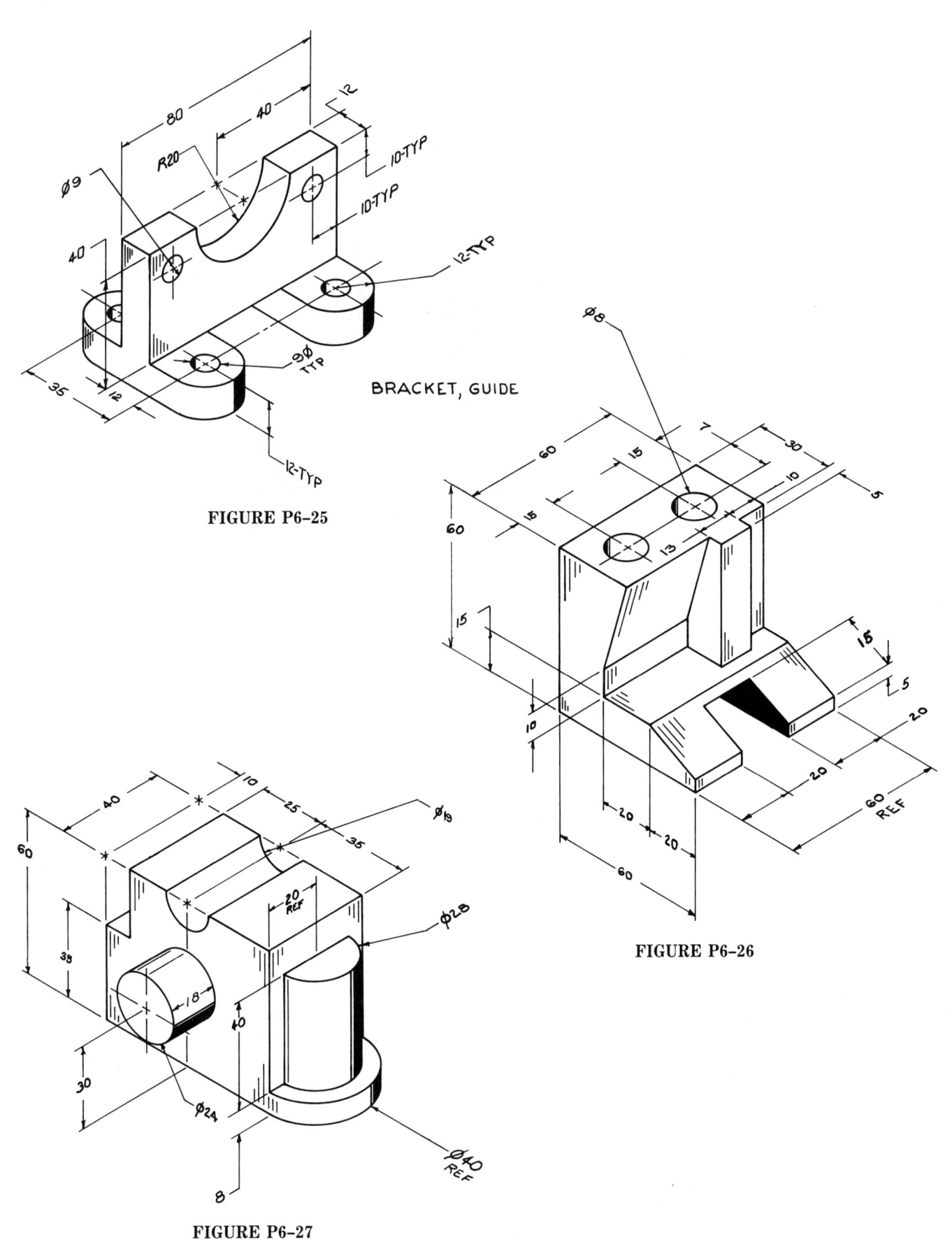

Chap. 6 Problems

FIGURE P6-25

FIGURE P6-26

FIGURE P6-27

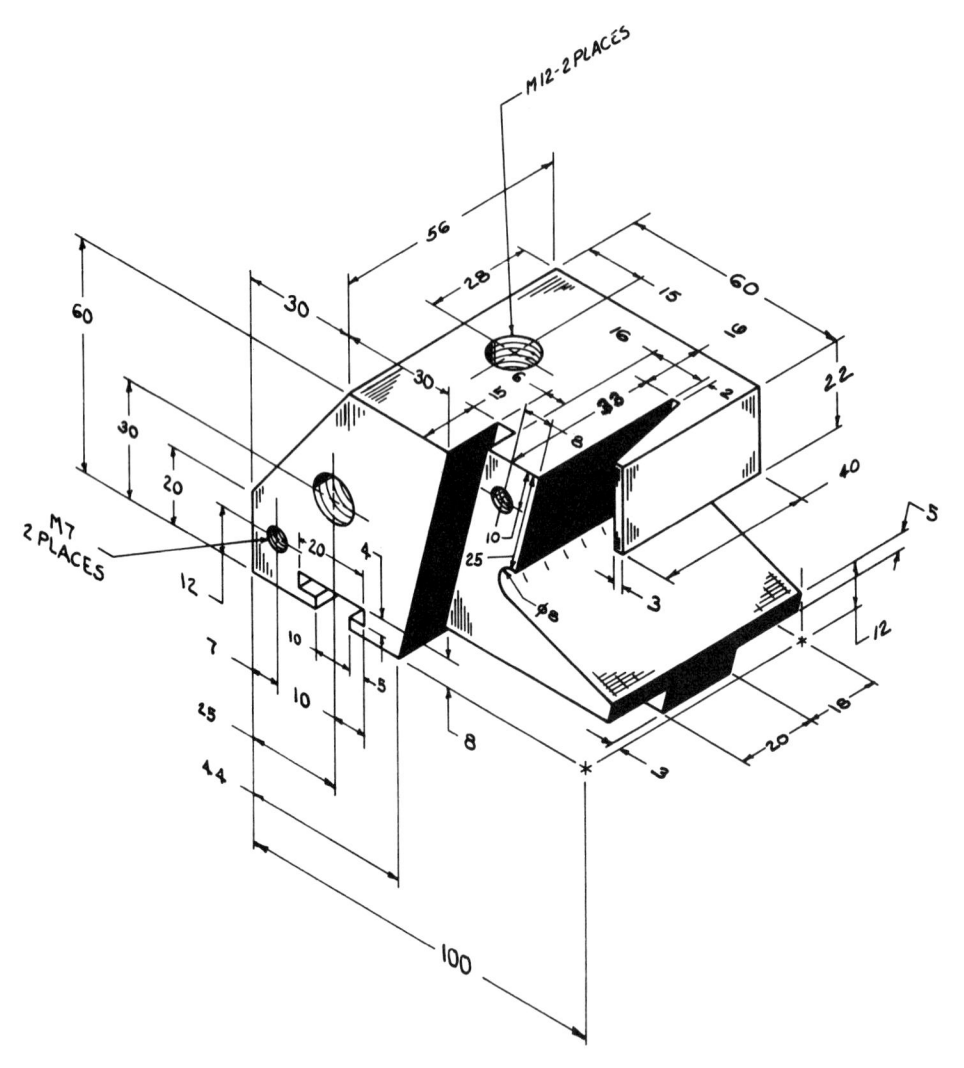

FIGURE P6-28

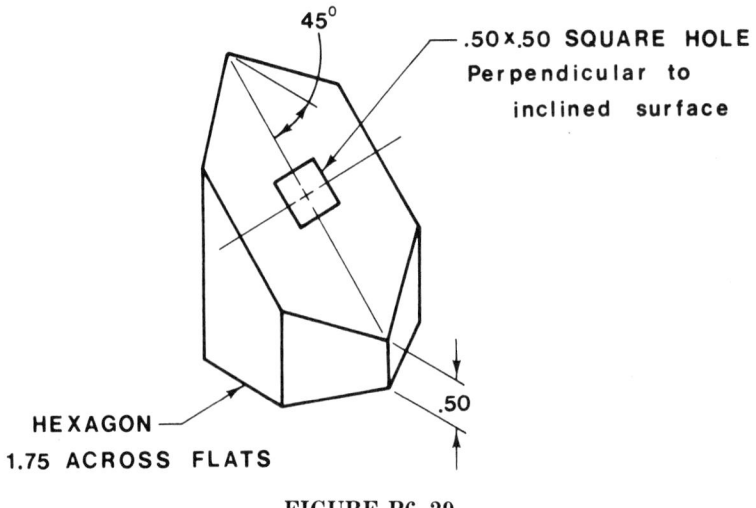

FIGURE P6-29

Chap. 6 Problems

FIGURE P6-30

FIGURE P6-31

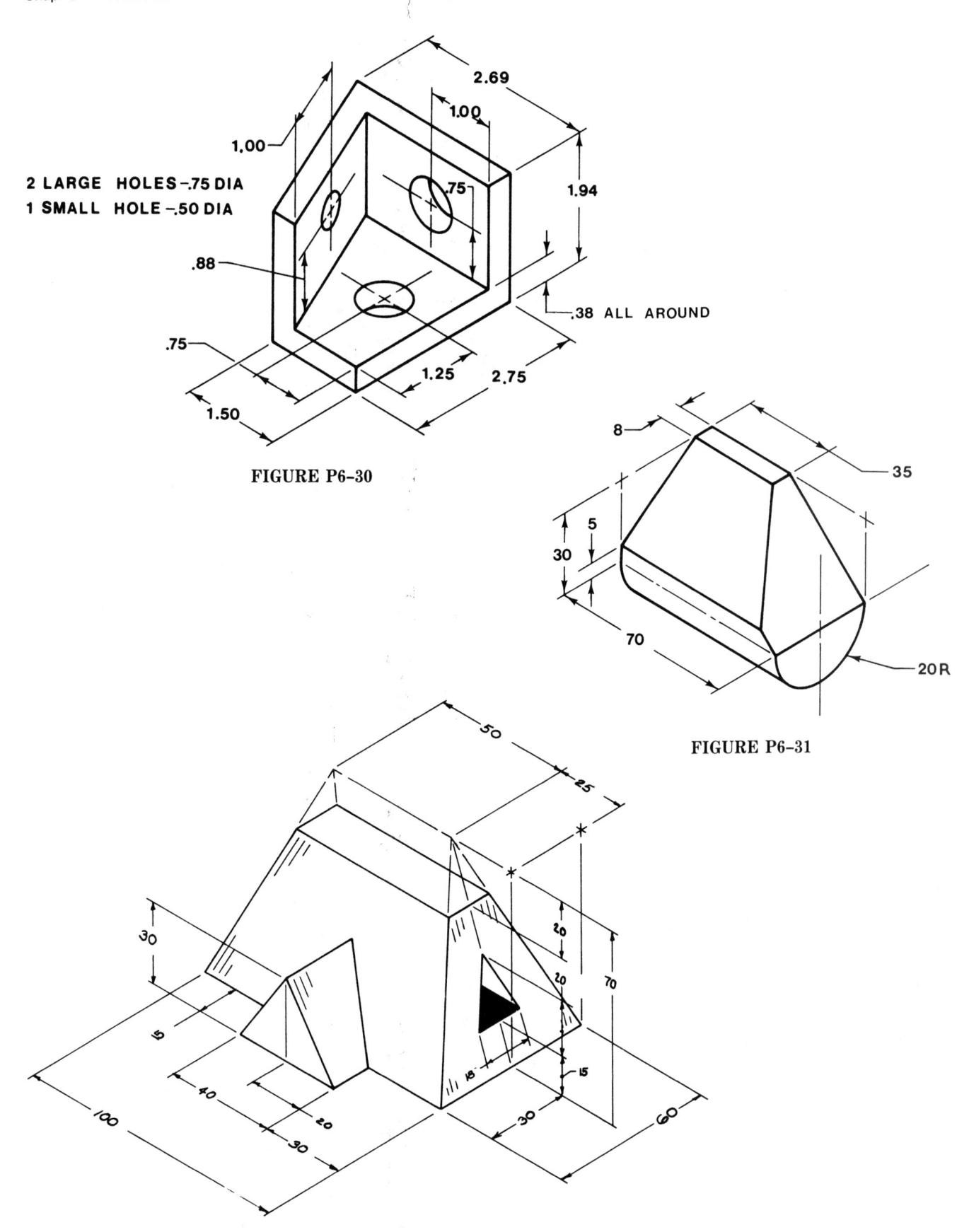

FIGURE P6-32

All dimensions are in millimeters.

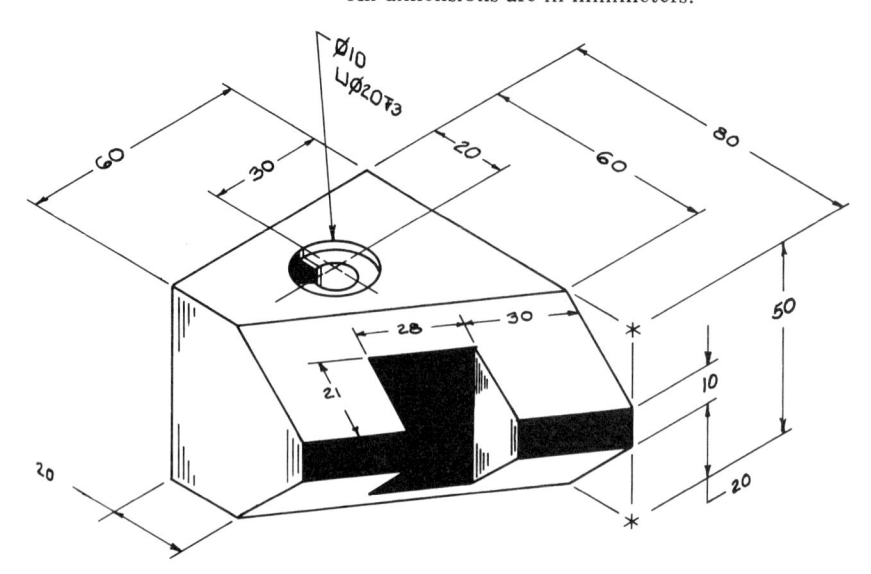

FIGURE P6-33

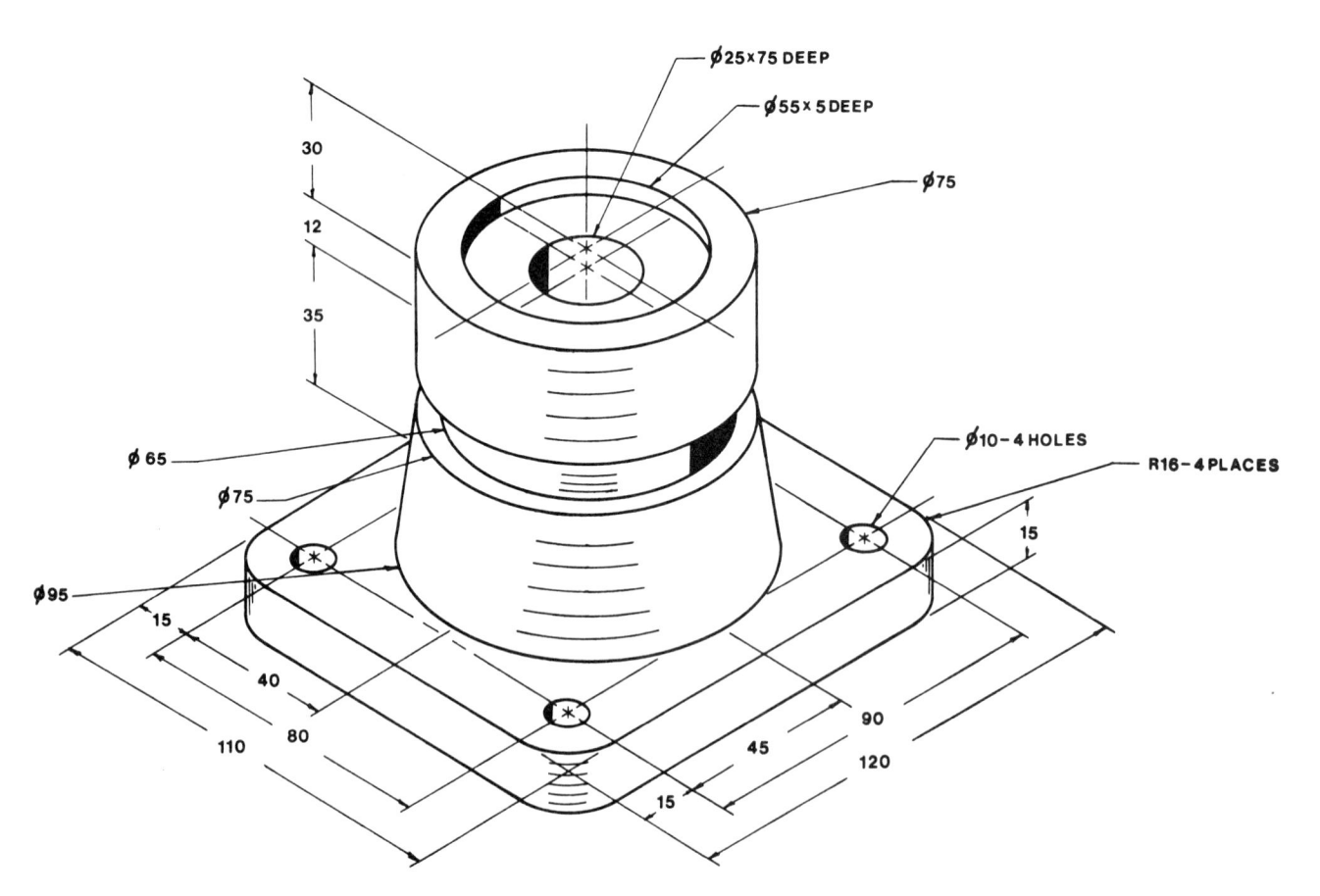

All dimensions are in millimeters.

FIGURE P6-34

Chap. 6 Problems

All dimensions are in millimeters.

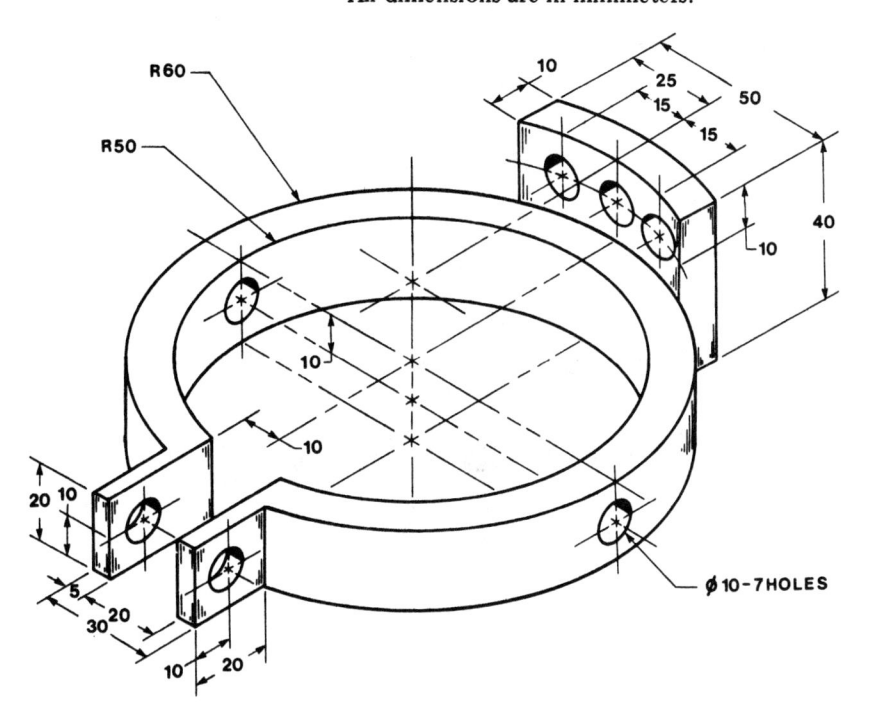

FIGURE P6-35

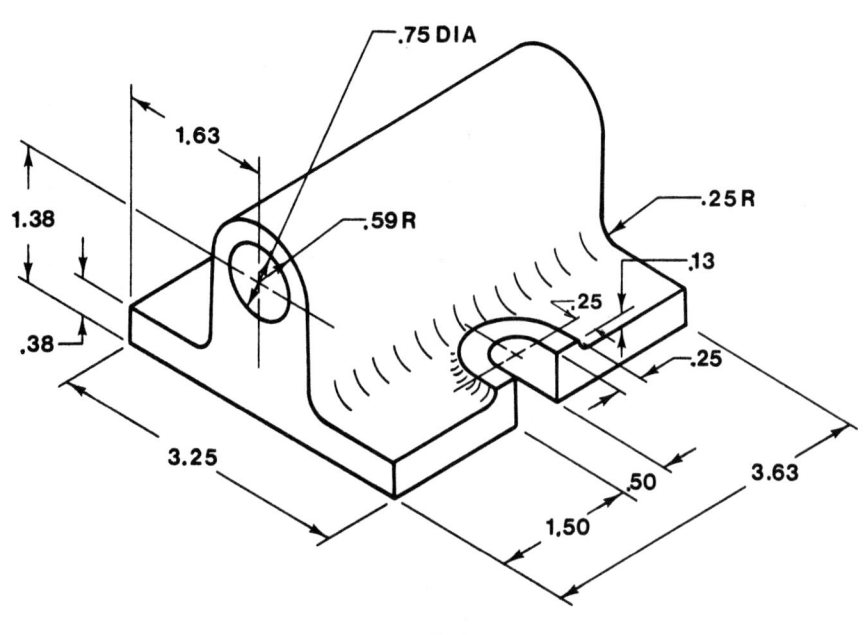

FIGURE P6-36

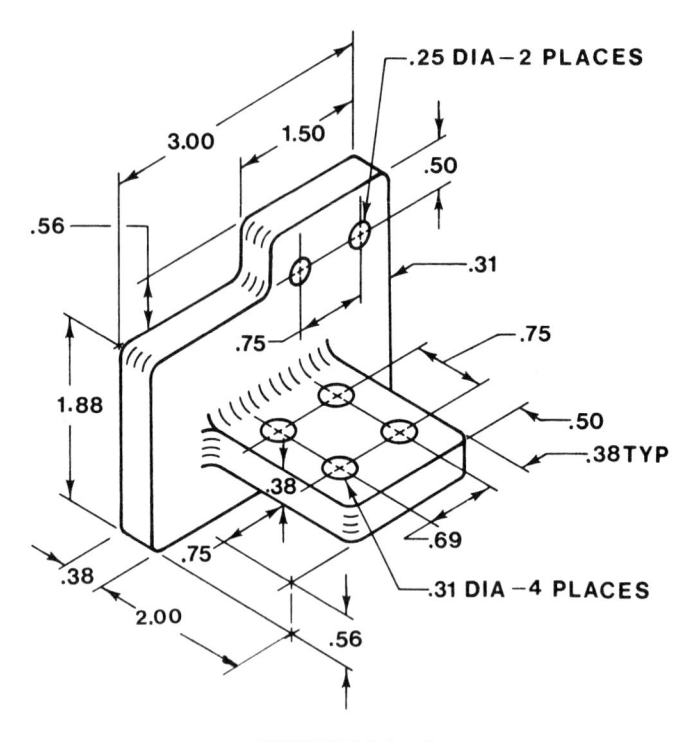

FIGURE P6-37

All dimensions are in millimeters.

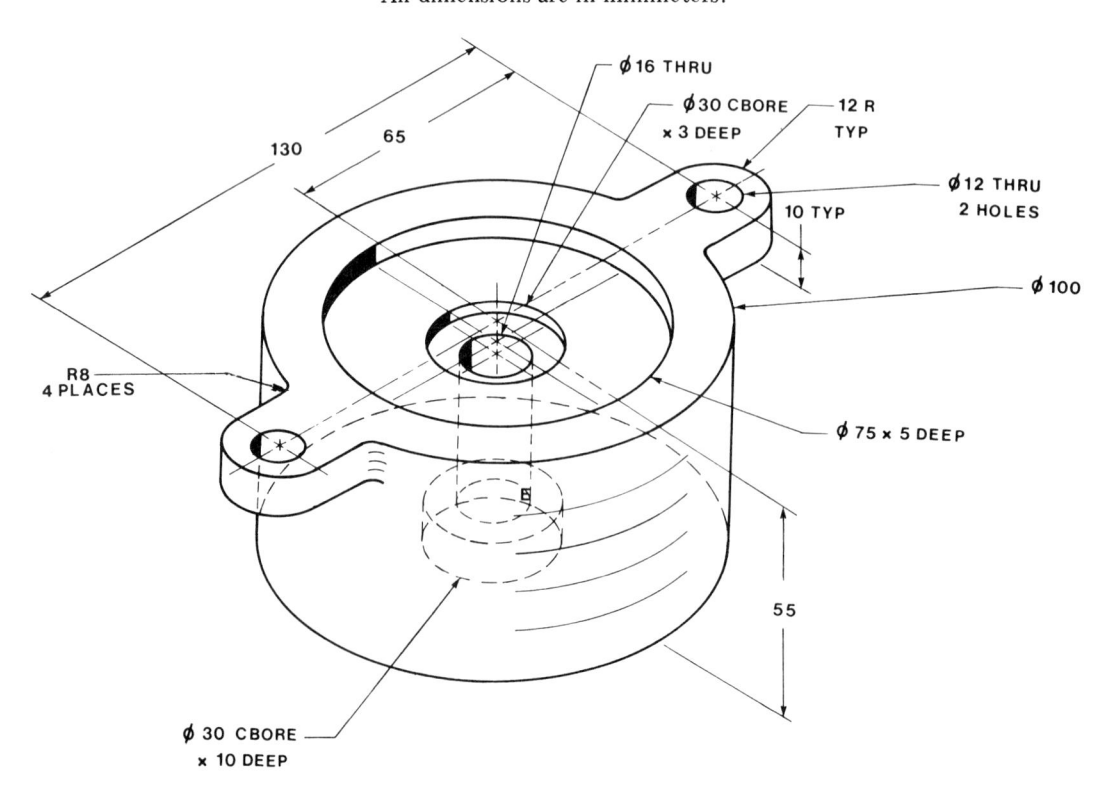

FIGURE P6-38

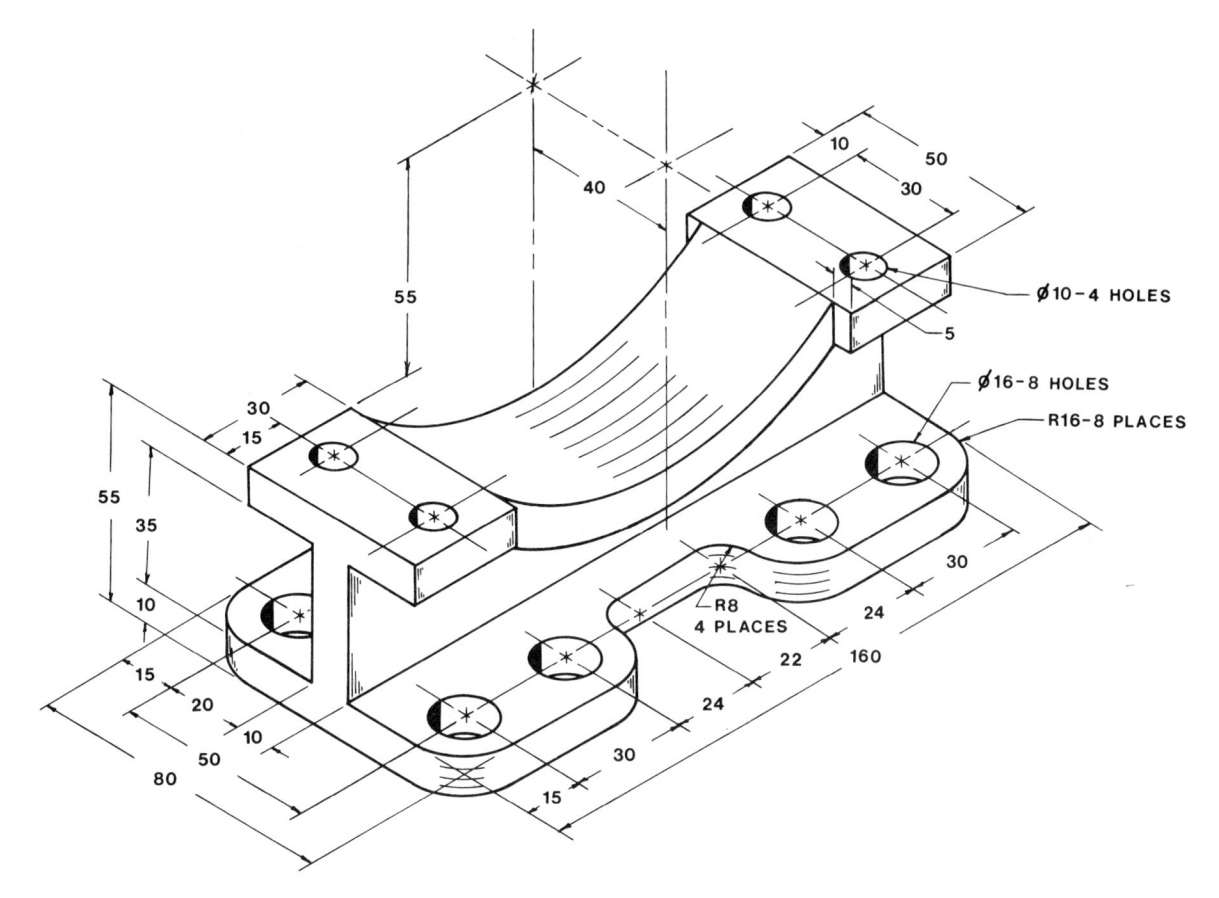

FIGURE P6-39

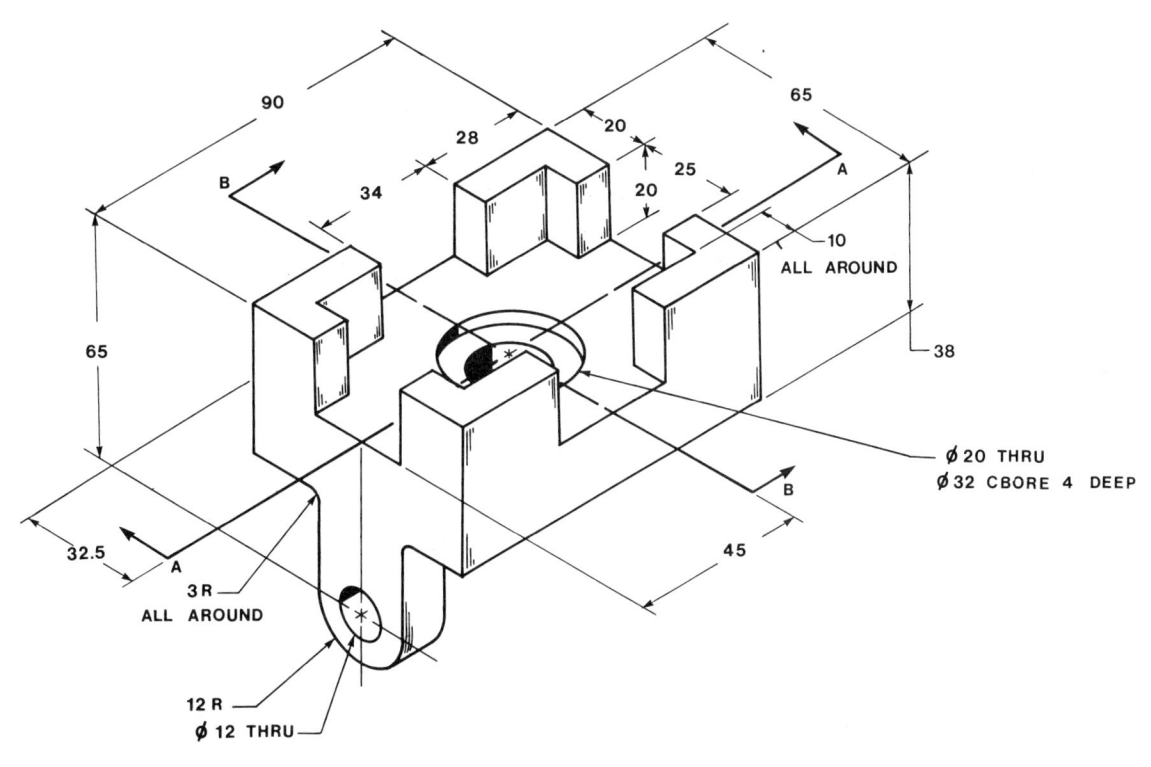

FIGURE P6-40

All dimensions are in millimeters.

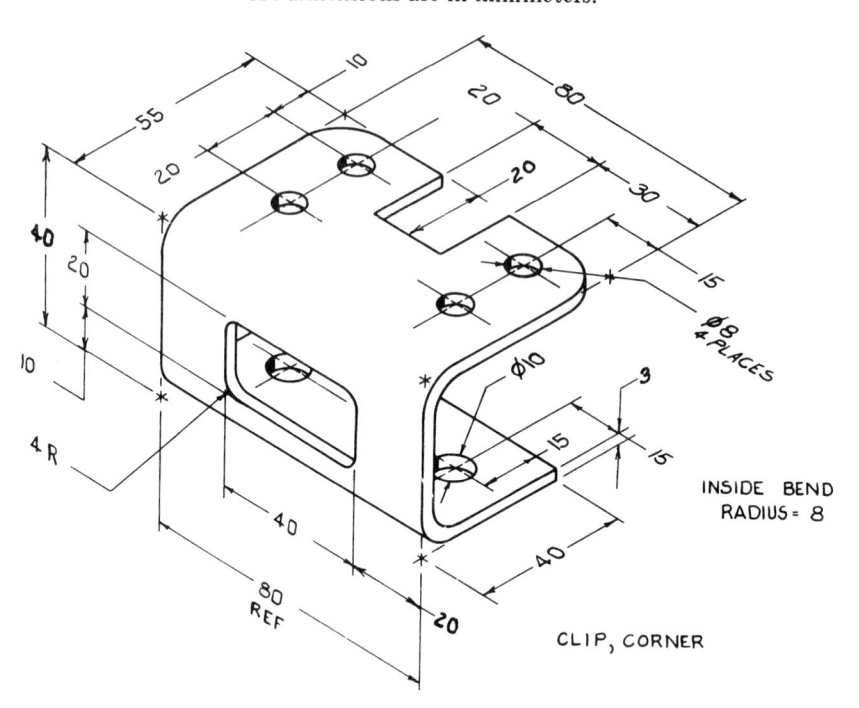

FIGURE P6-41

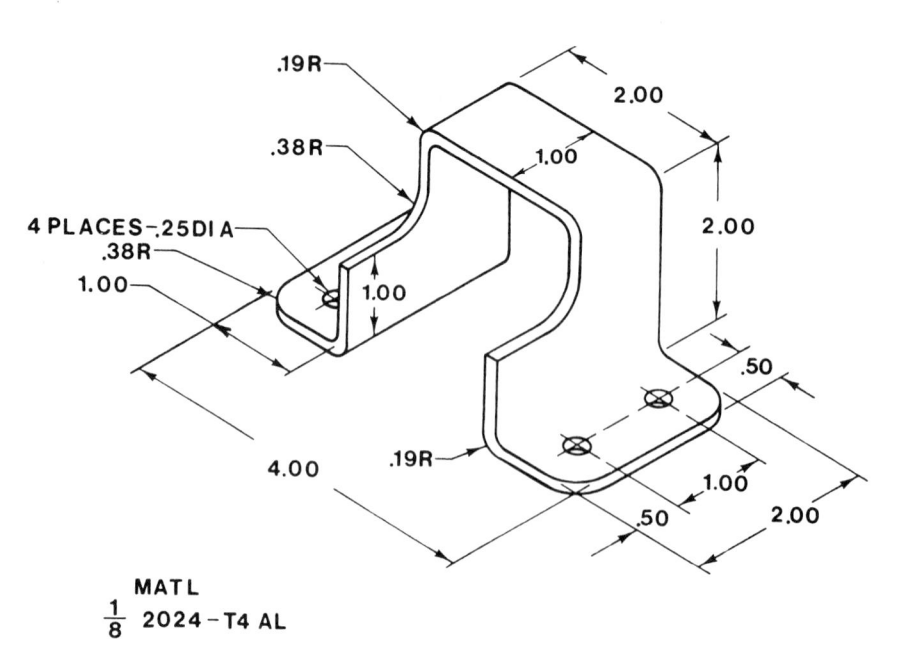

FIGURE P6-42

Chap. 6 Problems 179

FIGURE P6-43

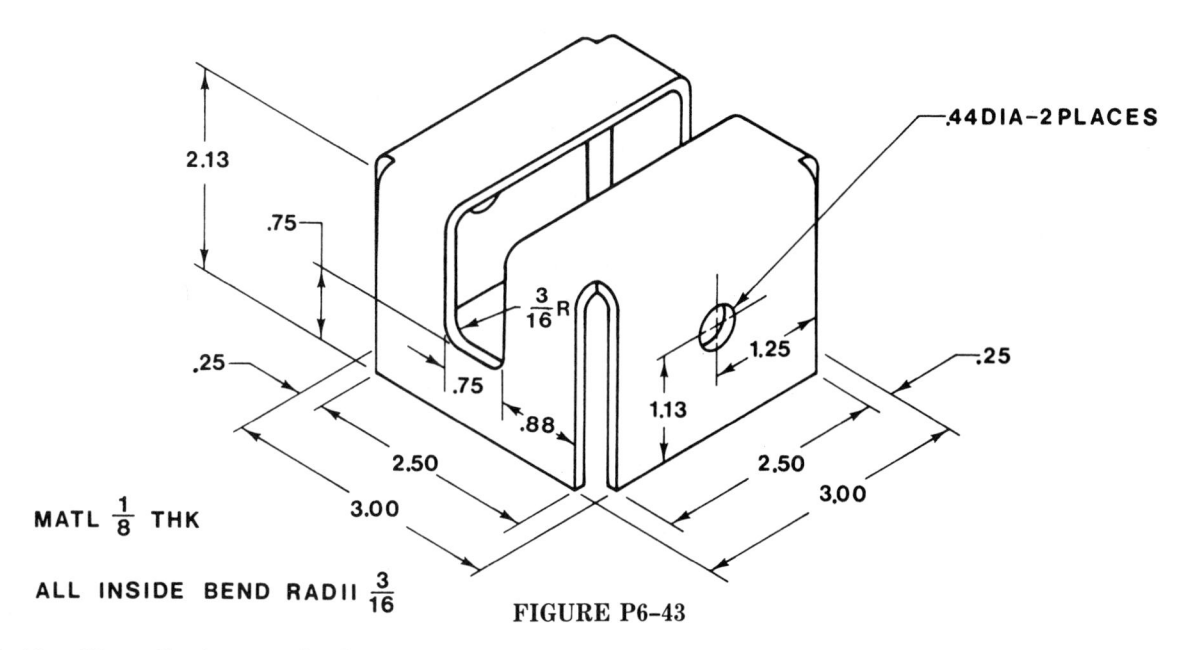

MATL 1/8 THK

ALL INSIDE BEND RADII 3/16

P6-44 Given the front and side views in Figure P6-44, redraw the given views and add the appropriate top view. Inches.

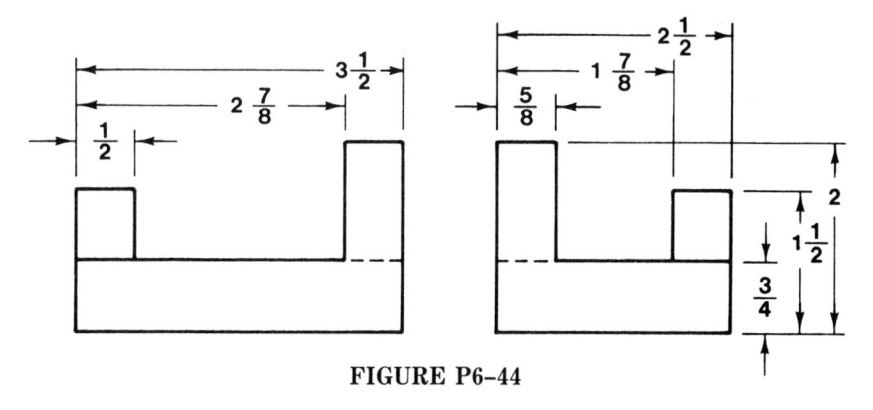

FIGURE P6-44

P6-45 Given the front and top views in Figure P6-45, redraw the given views and add the appropriate side view. Inches.

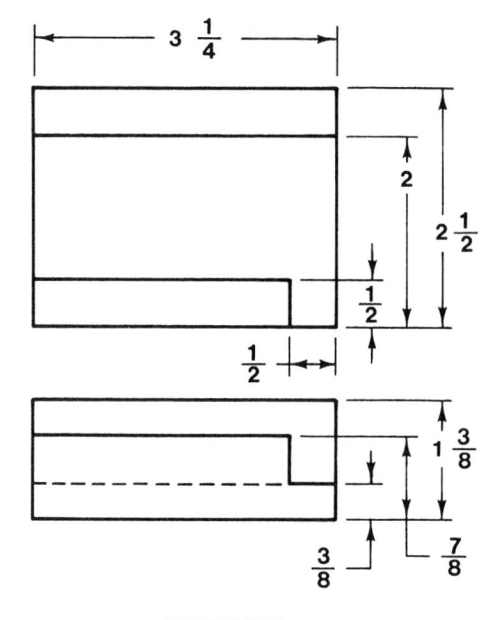

FIGURE P6-45

P6-46 Given the top and side views in Figure P6-46, redraw the given views and add the appropriate front view. Inches.

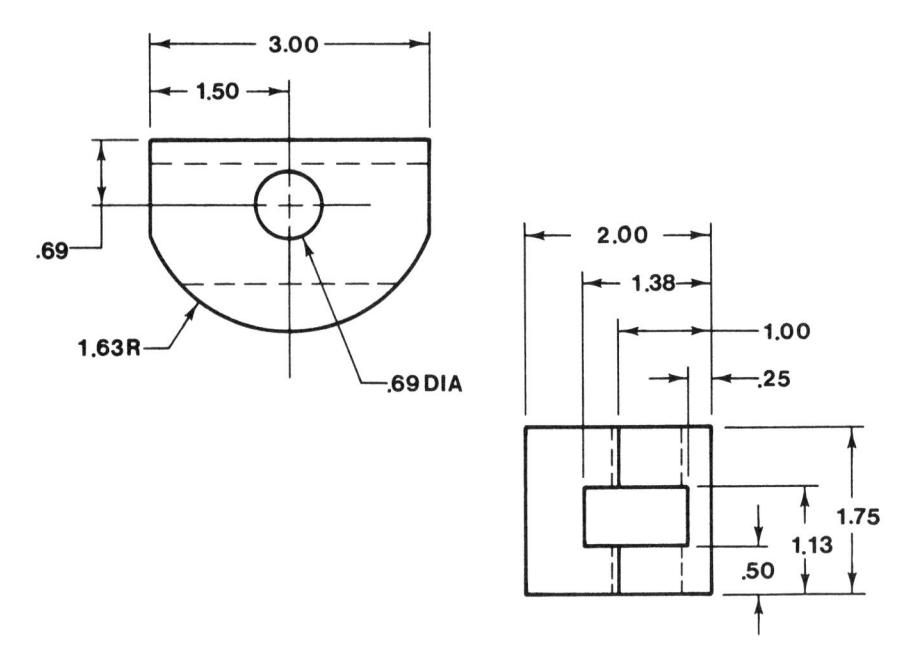

FIGURE P6-46

P6-47 Given the top and side views in Figure P6-47, redraw the given views and add the appropriate front view. Metric.

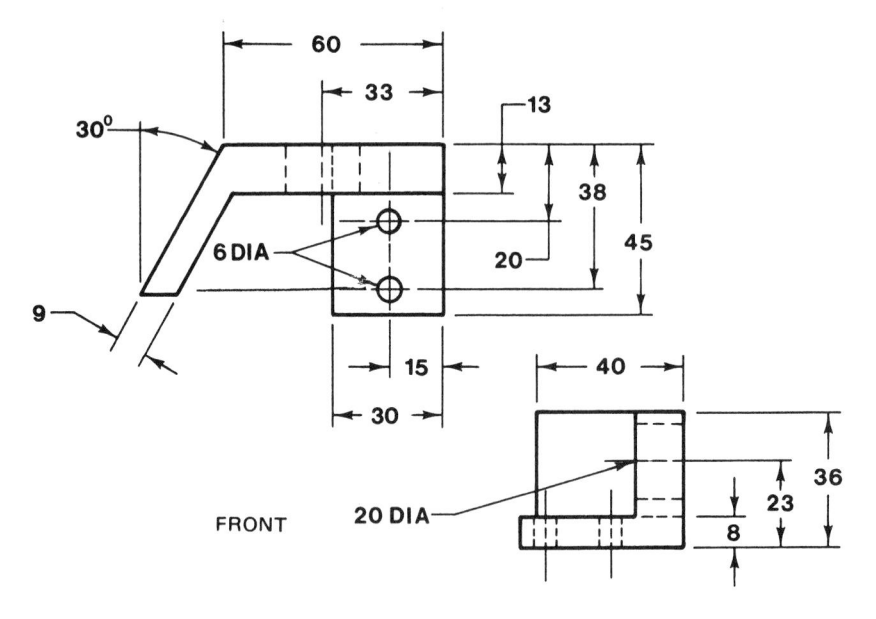

FIGURE P6-47

P6-48 Given the front and side views in Figure P6-48, redraw the given views and add the appropriate top view. Inches.

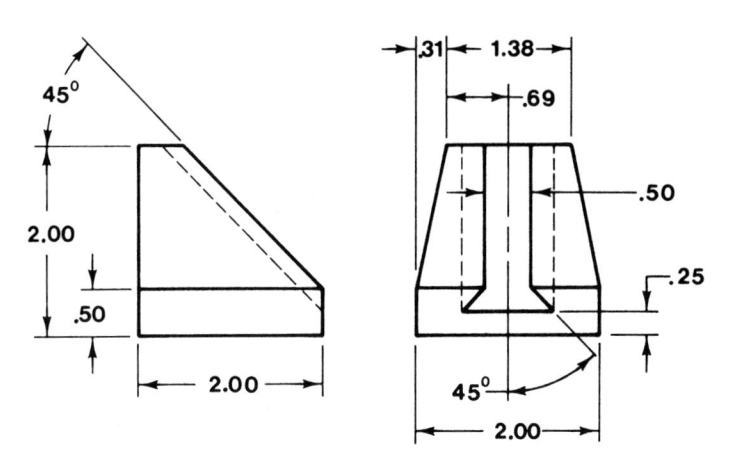

FIGURE P6-48

P6-49 Given the top and front views in Figure P6-49, redraw the given views and add the appropriate side view. Inches.

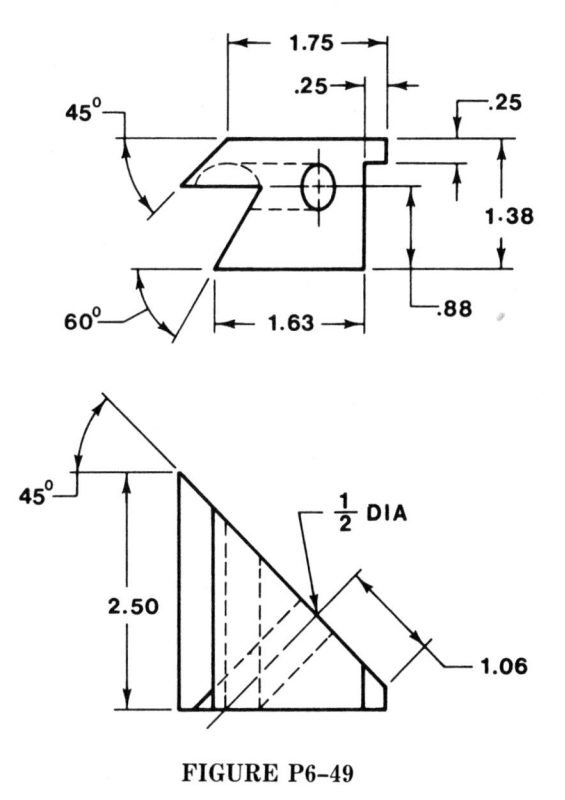

FIGURE P6-49

P6-50 Given the front and top views in Figure P6-50, redraw the given views and add the appropriate side view. Inches.

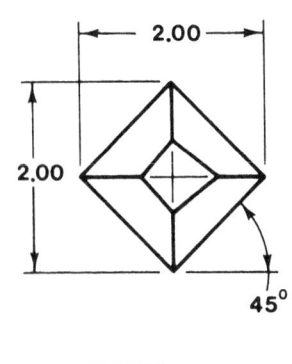

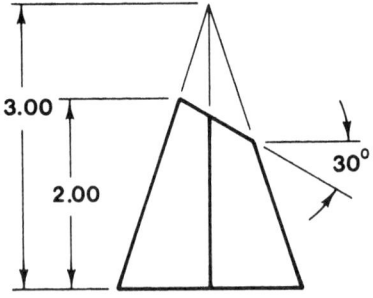

FIGURE P6-50

P6-51 Given the top and side views in Figure P6-51, redraw the given views and add the appropriate front view. Inches.

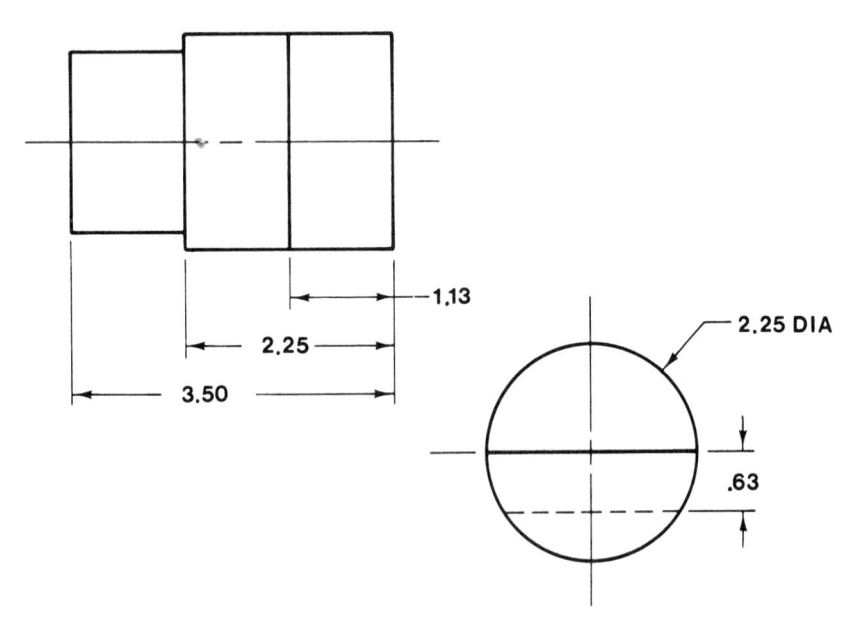

FIGURE P6-51

Chap. 6   Problems

P6-52   Given the front and side views in Figure P6-52, redraw the given views and add the appropriate top view. Inches.

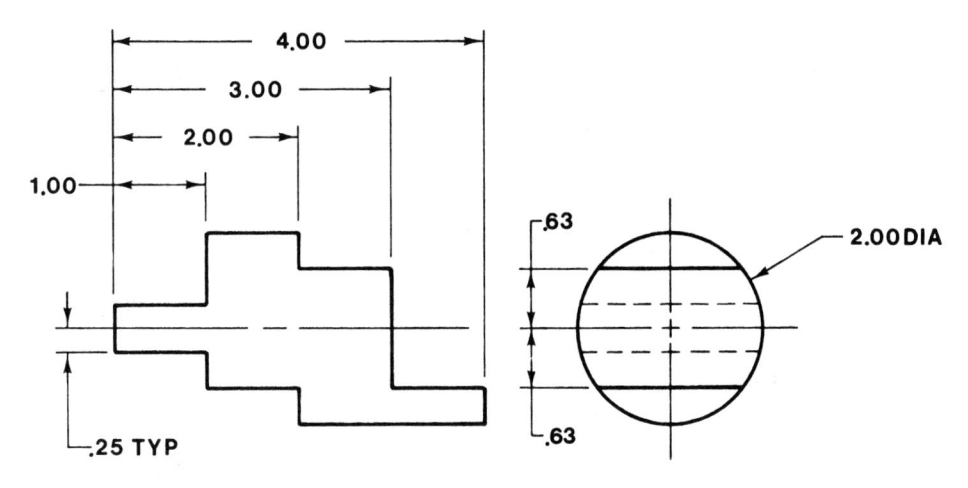

FIGURE P6-52

P6-53   Given the front and side views in Figure P6-53, redraw the given views and add the appropriate top view. Inches.

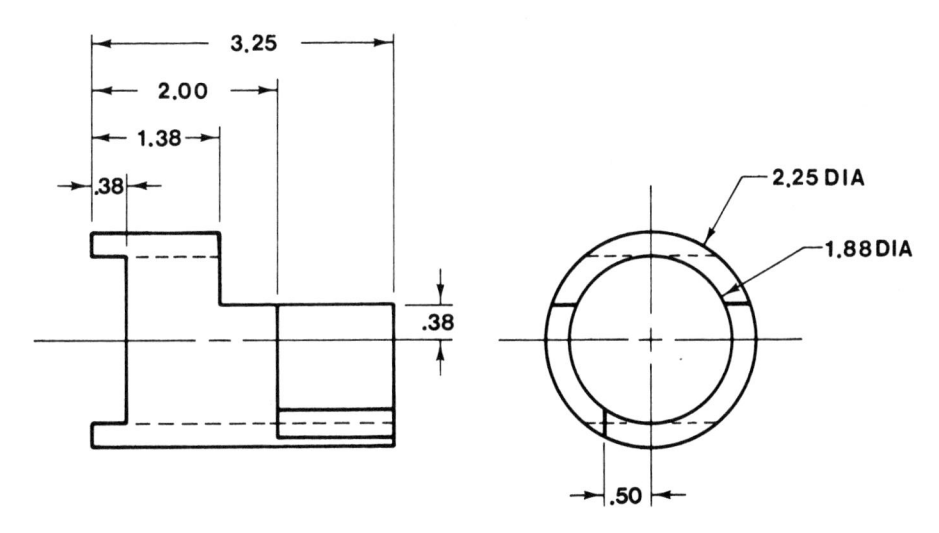

FIGURE P6-53

P6-54 Given the front and side views in Figure P6-54, redraw the given views and add the appropriate top view. Inches.

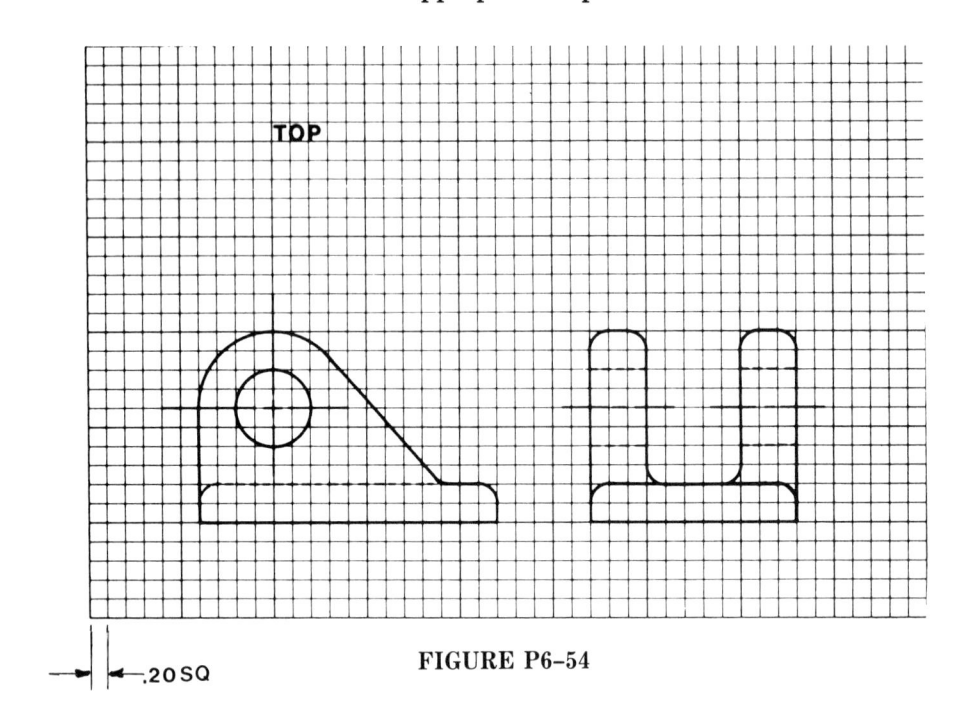

.20 SQ

FIGURE P6-54

7
SECTIONAL VIEWS

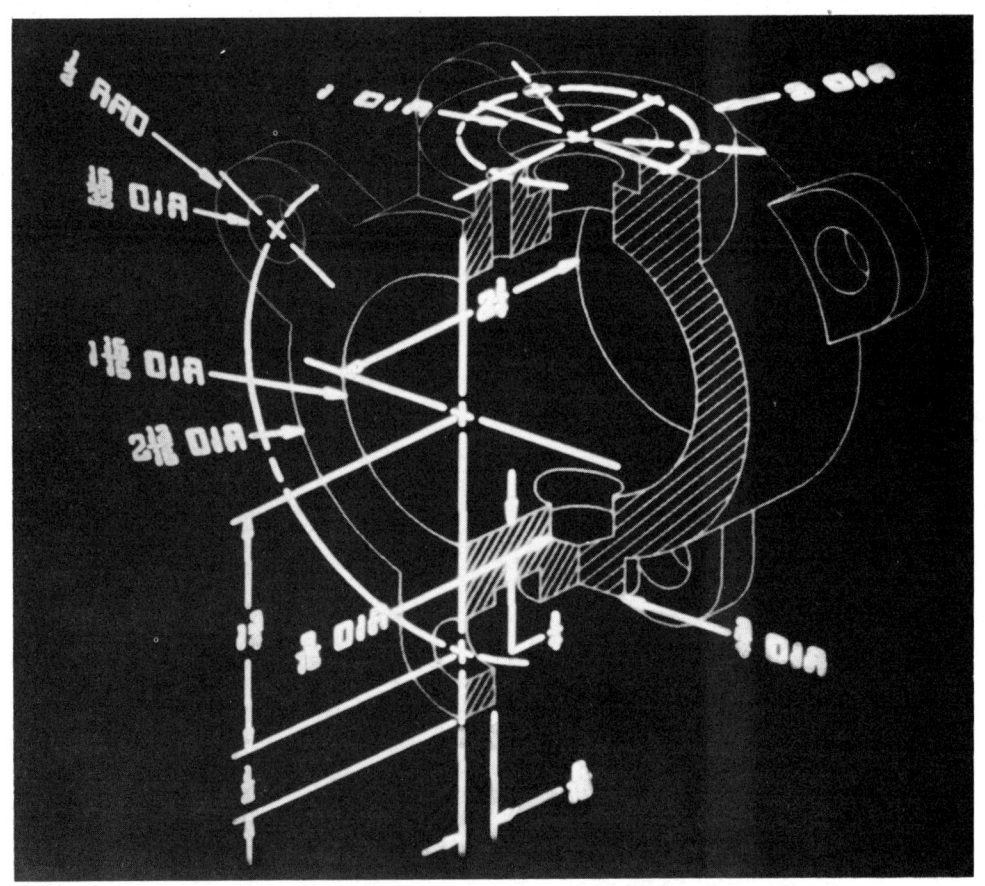

(Courtesy of McDonnell Douglas Manufacturing Industry Systems Company, St. Louis, Mo.)

7-1 INTRODUCTION

A *sectional view* is a special type of orthographic view that shows internal features of an object. Sectional views are used to help clarify drawings where the normal orthographic views are either too cluttered with lines or have too many overlapping lines to be easily understood.

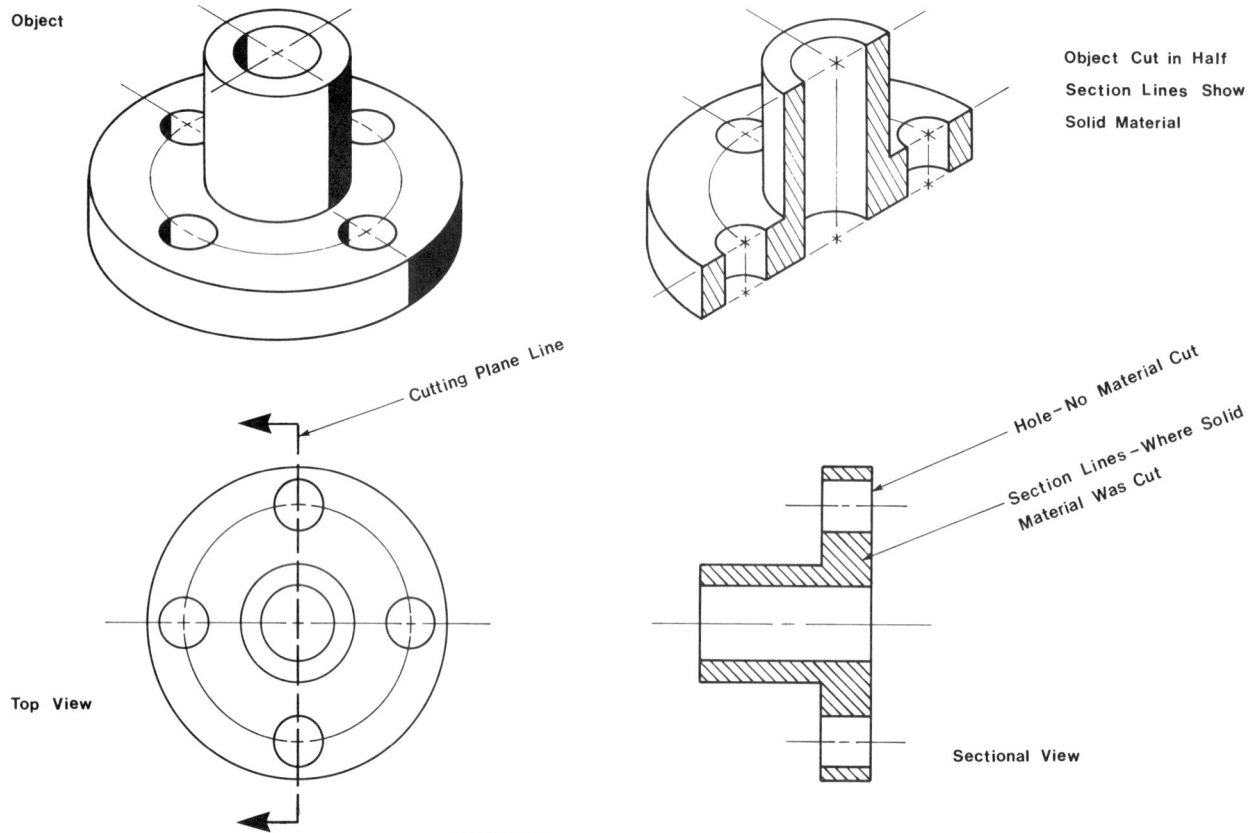

FIGURE 7-1 Sectional views.

Figure 7-1 shows the top and sectional views of an object. A cutting-plane line is used to define where, through the object, the sectional view is taken. Section lines show where the cutting-plane lines have passed through solid material.

7-2 SECTION LINES

Section lines show where solid material has been cut when taking a sectional view. Section lines are thin parallel lines, evenly spaced, and drawn at any angle, although most are drawn at 45° to the horizontal (Figure 7-2).

Sec. 7-2   Section Lines   187

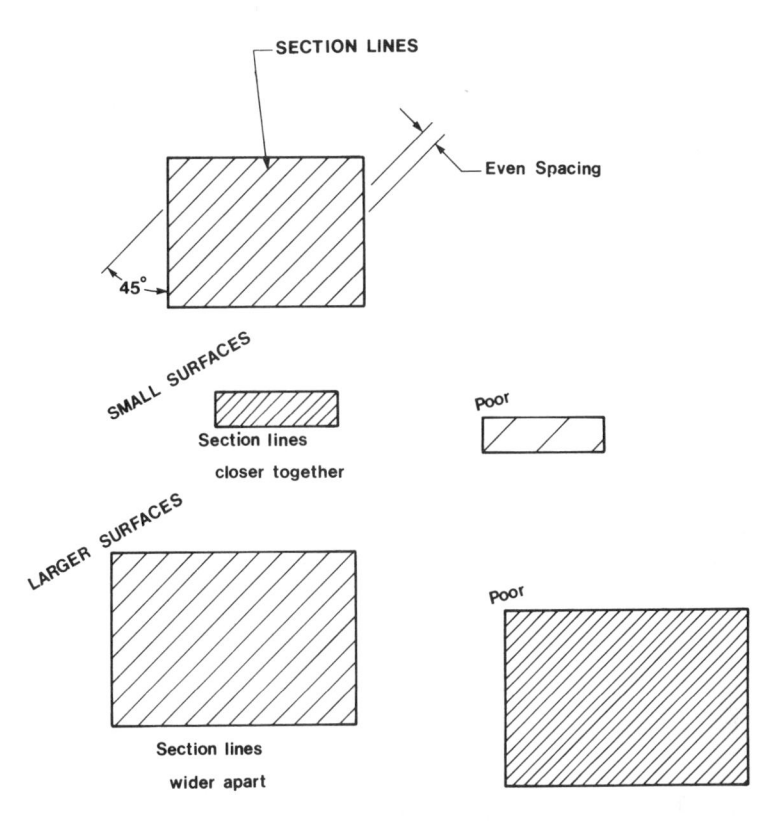

FIGURE 7-2 Sectional lines.

Section lines are spaced approximately 0.13 in. or 3.5 mm apart. Section-line spacing can be varied according to surface size. Smaller surfaces use closer spacing to help assure that the surface will be clearly seen (Figure 7-2), and larger surfaces use wider spacing to prevent dark, crowded-looking drawings. Some computer systems have only one spacing setting, meaning that all surfaces will have the same spacing distance.

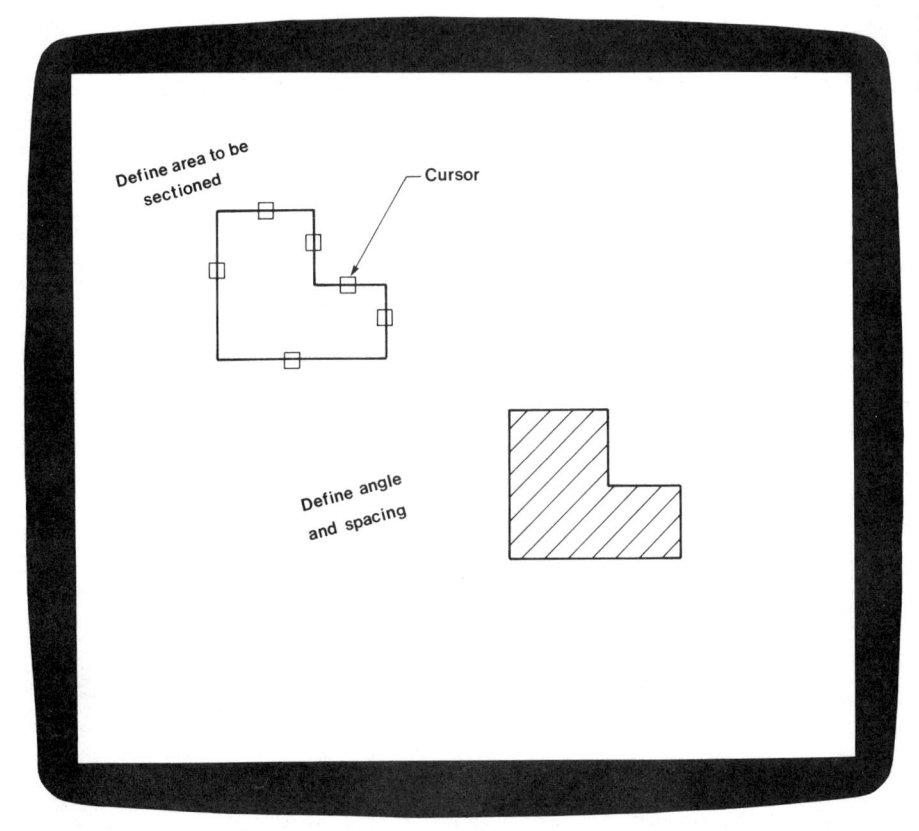

FIGURE 7-3(a) Area to be sectioned is defined using cursor location inputs.

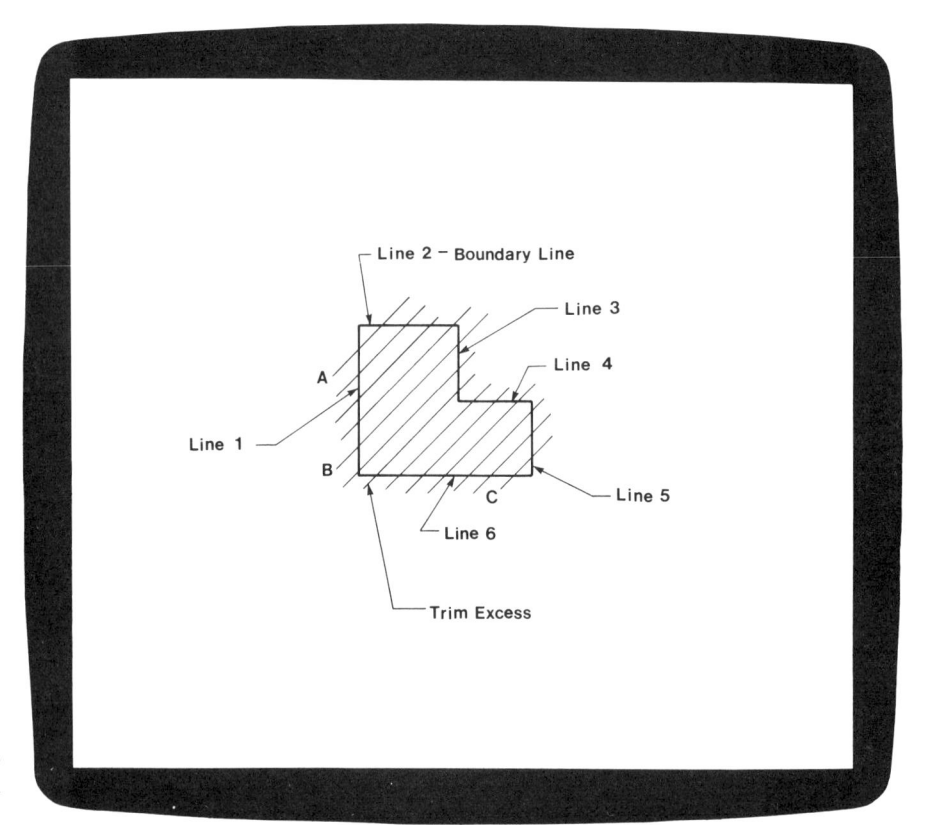

FIGURE 7-3(b) Section lines drawn as a series of parallel lines.

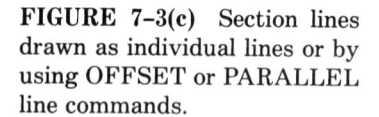

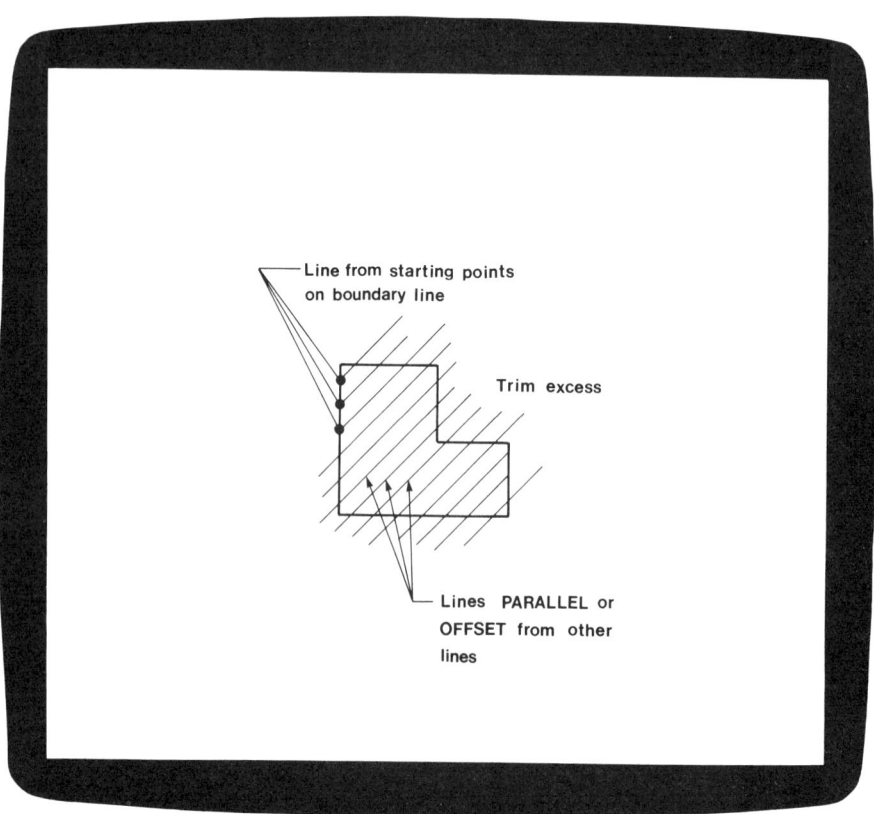

FIGURE 7-3(c) Section lines drawn as individual lines or by using OFFSET or PARALLEL line commands.

Sec. 7-2 Section Lines 189

Section lines are drawn using computer graphics systems in one of three ways, depending on the system. The most advanced systems draw section lines within a defined area as shown in Figure 7-3a. The cursor is used to define the lines that surround the area to be sectioned. Many of these systems then require a spacing and angle input.

Some systems add section lines by drawing a series of parallel lines between two boundary lines as shown in Figure 7-3B. Line A is drawn at a prescribed angle between lines 1 and 2. Excess is trimmed automatically or manually depending on the system.

Other lines are drawn parallel to the first. Boundary lines are varied as needed. For example, line B is between lines 1 and 3, line C between lines 6 and 5.

The third method for adding section lines using computer graphics systems is by drawing individual lines as shown in Figure 7-3c. Each line is drawn between points on the boundary and then trimmed as necessary. *Parallel* and *offset* commands can help simplify the procedure if available.

Section lines are never drawn parallel to any edge of the surface being sectioned. In Figure 7-4 a sectioned surface contains two edges 45° to the horizontal. It would be wrong to draw section lines at 45° for this surface. Some other angle should be used.

A common drawing error is to draw 45° section lines around a countersunk hole. The edges of a countersink are drawn at 45°, meaning that 45° section lines would be parallel to the edge of the countersink. An angle other than 45° should be used for the section lines.

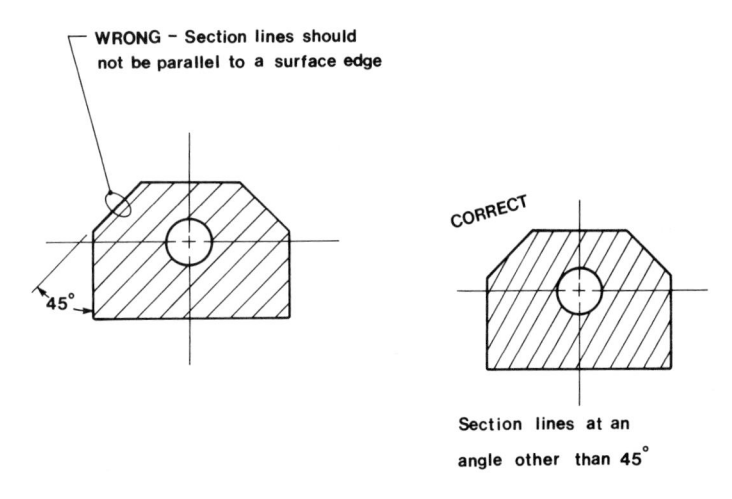

FIGURE 7-4 Do not draw section lines parallel to any object line in the view.

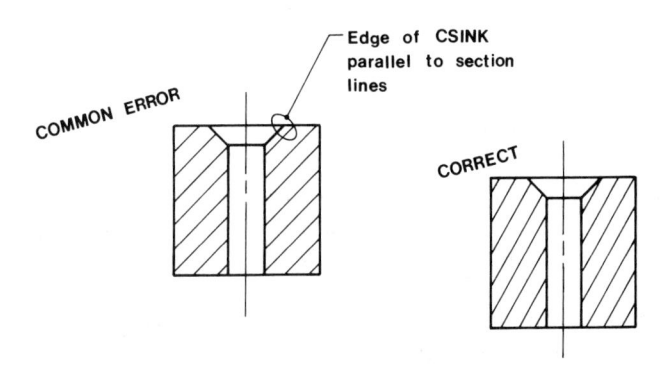

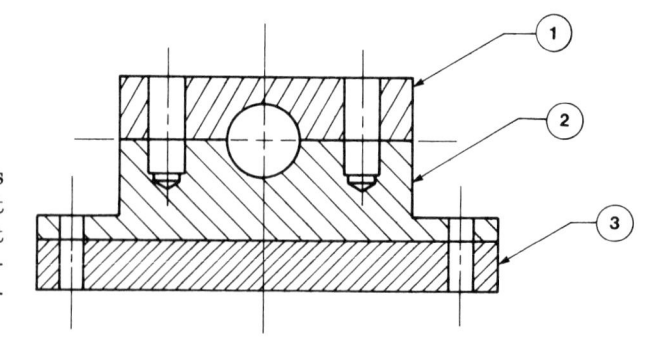

FIGURE 7-5 Sectional views that contain more than one part should contain sectional lines at different angle and spacing distance for each part to help assure clarity.

Standard Symbols for Section Lines

General Symbol

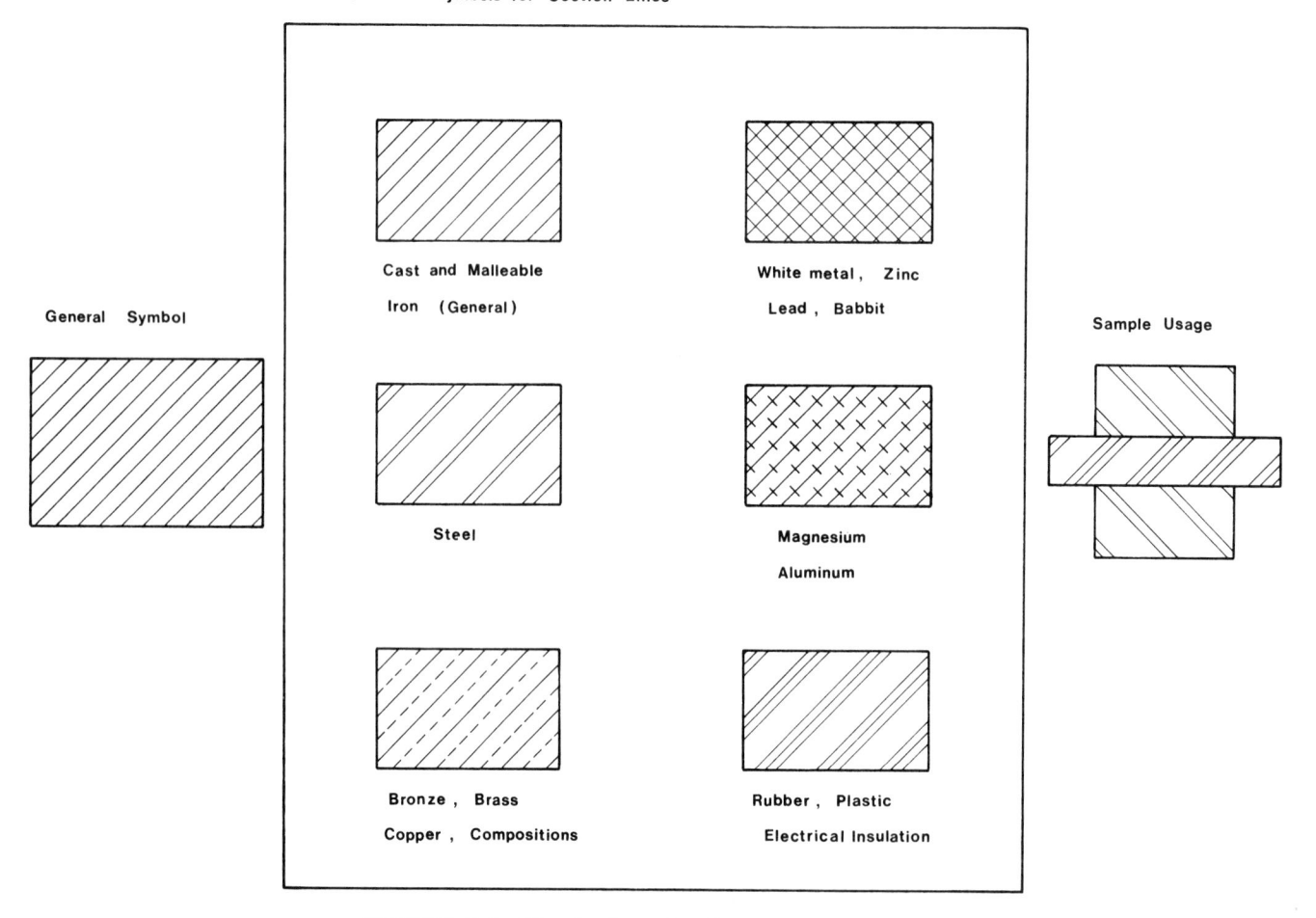

Cast and Malleable Iron (General)

White metal, Zinc Lead, Babbit

Steel

Magnesium Aluminum

Bronze, Brass Copper, Compositions

Rubber, Plastic Electrical Insulation

Sample Usage

FIGURE 7-6 Standard section lines symbols for designating material.

A sectional view may be taken through an assembly that contains more than one part (Figure 7-5). The angle and spacing of section lines are varied so that the cross section of each part is distinct.

Section lines may be used to designate an object's material by using the material symbols shown in Figure 7-6. The general symbol, evenly spaced, thin 45° lines, is used most often. It is acceptable for any material.

Cutting-plane lines are used to define where, through an object, a sectional view is taken (Figure 7-1).

7-3 CUTTING-PLANE LINES

Cutting-plane lines are drawn using either of two different patterns shown in Figure 7-7. Both types of cutting-plane lines are drawn using very thick lines. Cutting-plane lines are thicker than object lines.

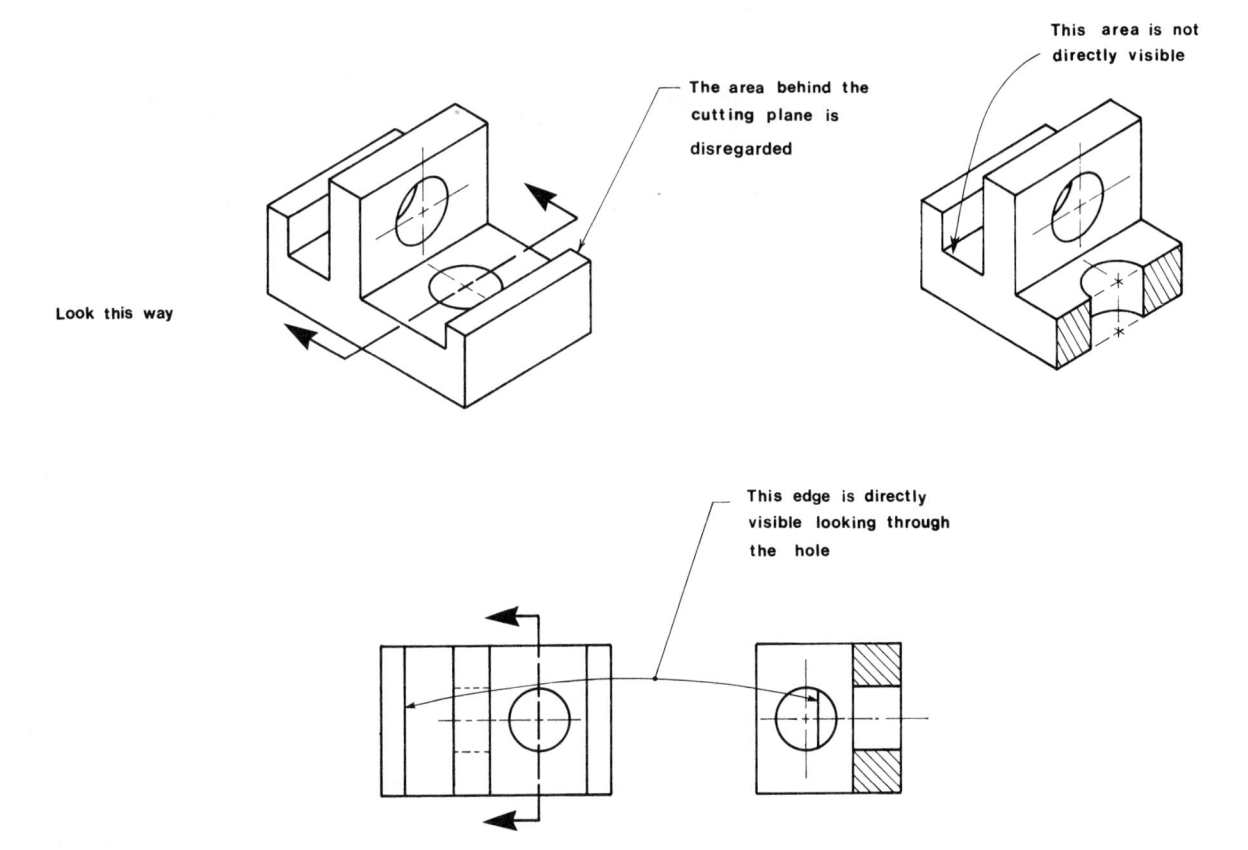

The arrowheads on cutting-plane lines indicate the direction of sight for the sectional view. The viewer should look at the object in the direction indicated by the arrowheads. Any surfaces that are *directly visible* in the direction indicated by the arrowheads are shown in the sectional view. Any surfaces not directly visible or located behind (away from the direction indicated by the arrowheads) are not shown in the sectional view. Hidden lines are not used in sectional views. Note in Figure 7-8 that a short section of one of the rear edges is directly visible through the hole, so is included in the sectional view.

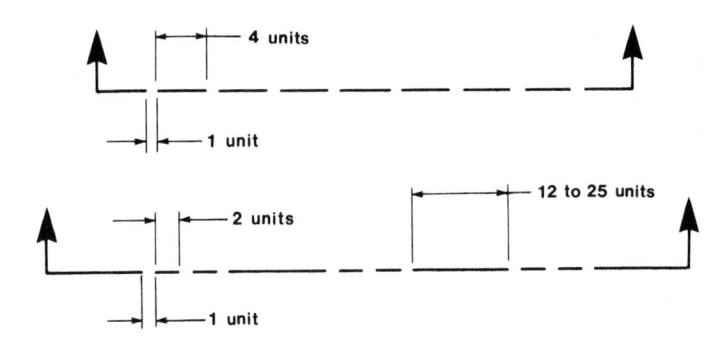

FIGURE 7-7 Patterns for cutting-plane lines.

FIGURE 7-8 Arrowheads on cutting-plane lines indicate the direction of sight for the sectional view.

Cutting-plane lines are added to a drawing one of four ways, depending on the system's capability (Figure 7-9). Some systems can draw cutting plane lines directly. Usually, the commands for cutting plane lines are contained within LINE or LINE FONT menus. Other systems require that a cutting plane be created from hidden and phantom line pat-

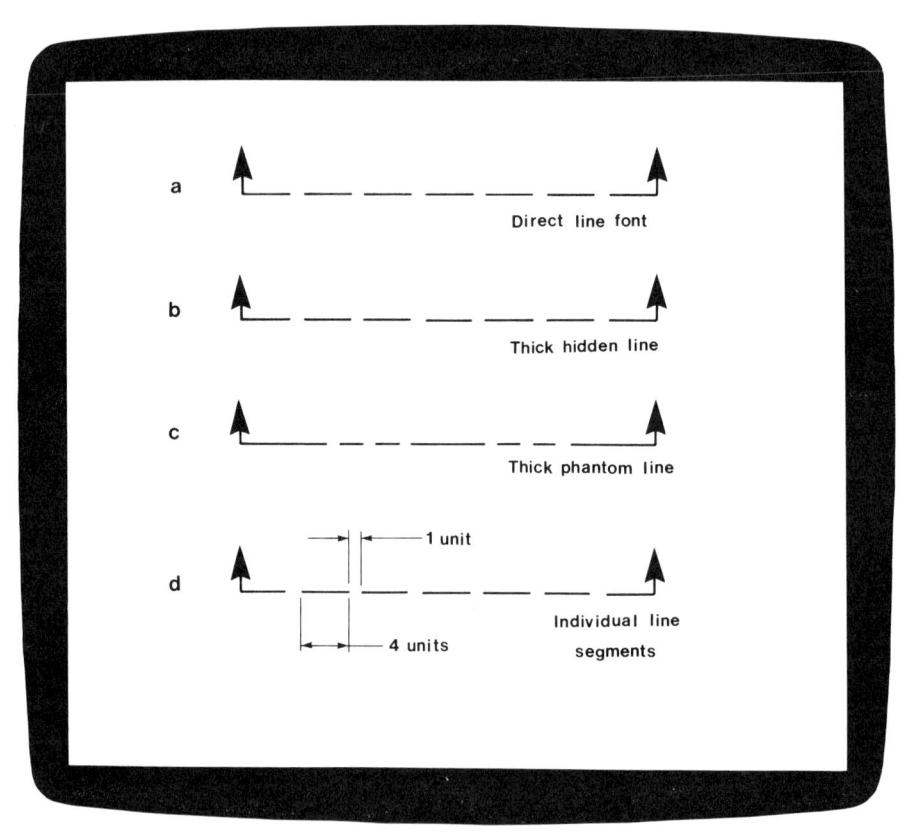

FIGURE 7-9 Cutting-plane line patterns.

FIGURE 7-10 Basic patterns for cutting-plane lines can be saved and used as needed.

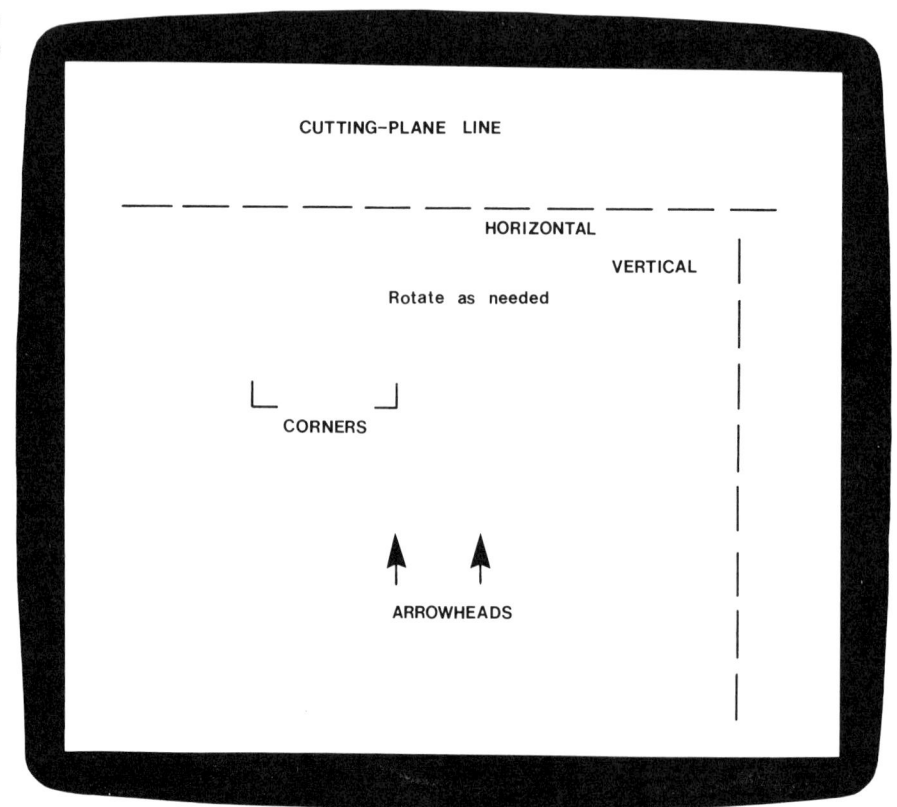

Sec. 7-3 Cutting-Plane Lines

terns (Figure 7-9, lines b and c, respectively). The lines are drawn thick or extra thick instead of the normal medium and thin configurations. Arrowheads are added at each end. The final method is to draw cutting plane lines as individual segments (Figure 7-9, line d).

Cutting-plane lines should be created and stored in memory if not available directly and called up as needed. Figure 7-10 illustrates a possible memory setup for cutting-plane lines.

Cutting-plane lines can change direction so that they pass through several features on a part. This is called an offset cutting-plane line. Each feature would then be included in the sectional view, as shown in Figures 7-11 and 7-12. There is no indication in the sectional view that the cutting plane has changed direction.

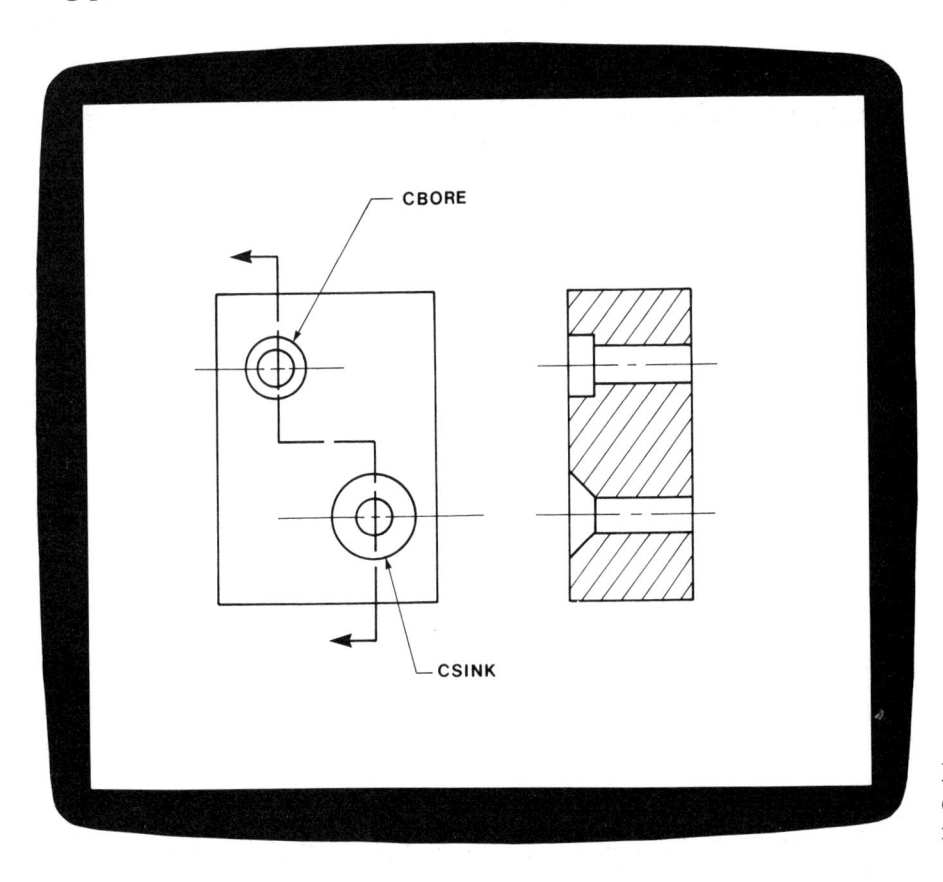

FIGURE 7-11 Example of an offset cutting-plane line and the resulting sectional view.

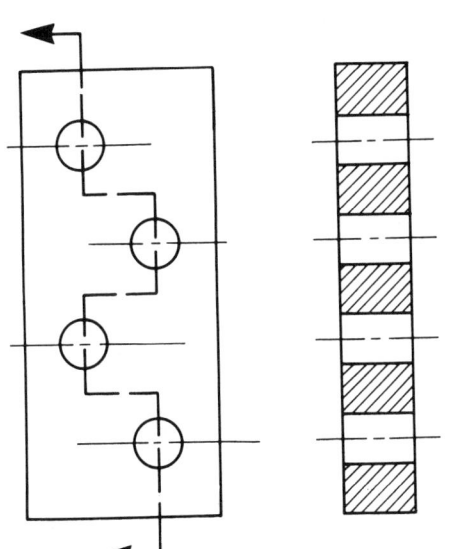

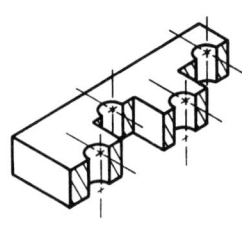

FIGURE 7-12 Example of an offset cutting-plane line and the resulting sectional view.

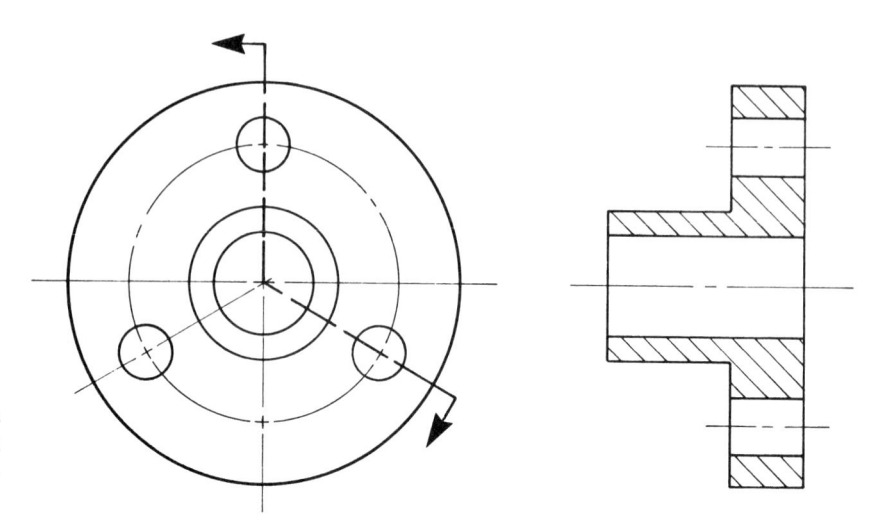

FIGURE 7-13 Example of a cutting-plane line drawn at an angle and the resulting sectional view.

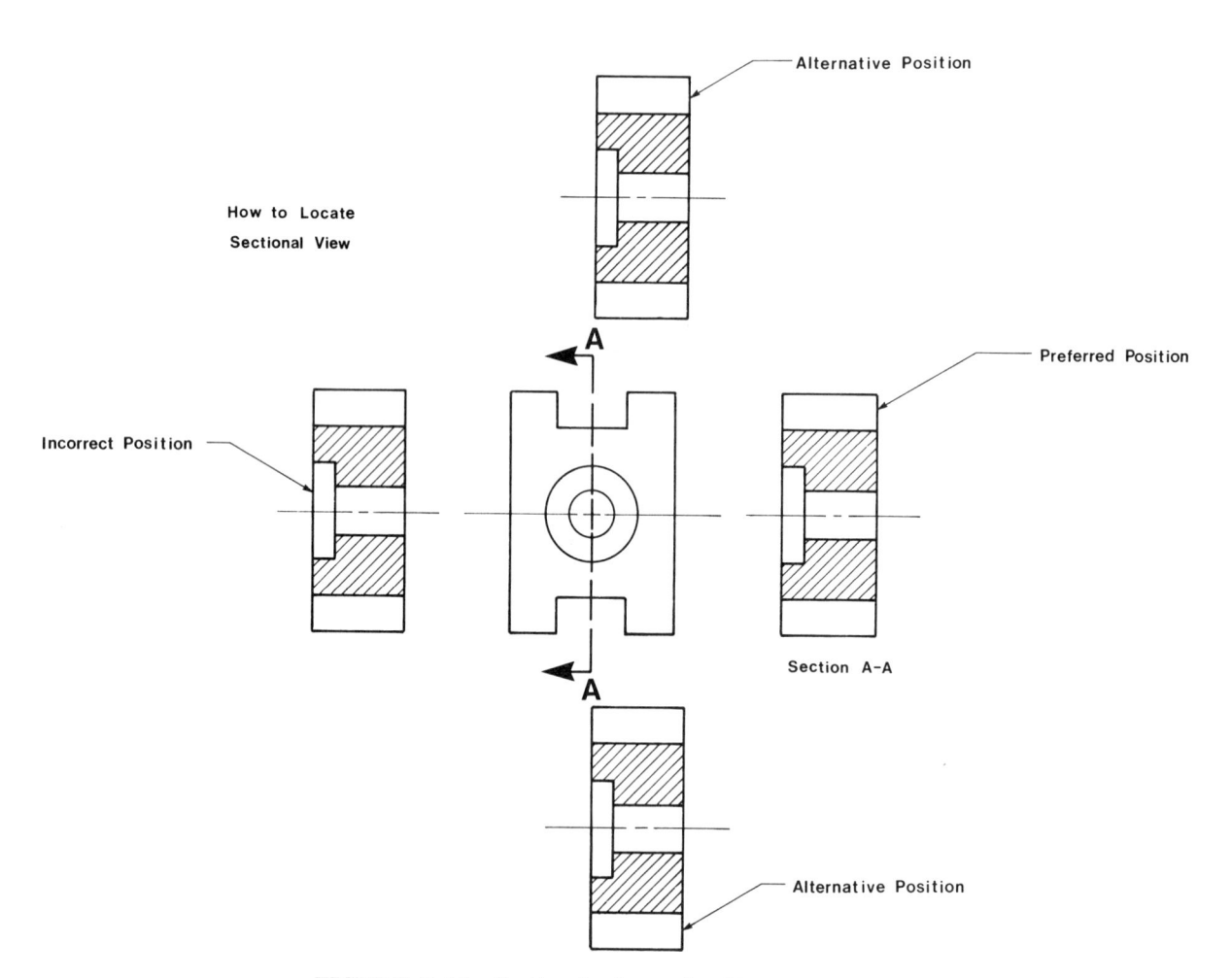

FIGURE 7-14 Sectional views should be located directly behind the direction indicated by the cutting-plane line.

Sec. 7-4 Multiple Sectional Views

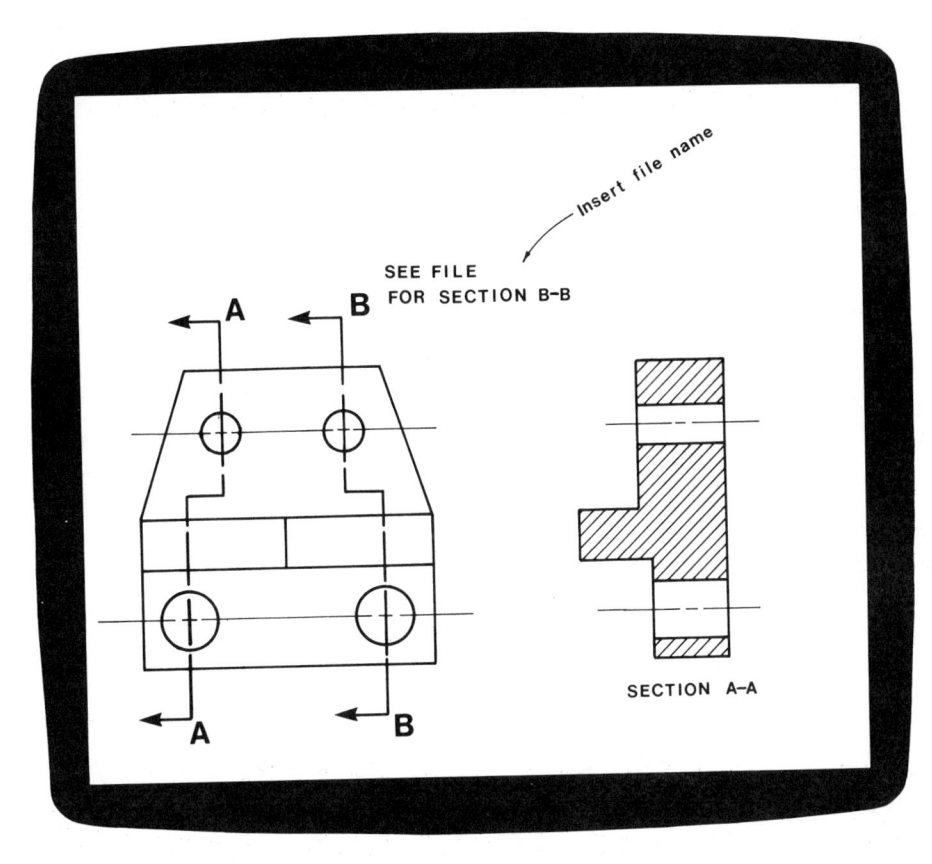

FIGURE 7-15 How to reference a sectional view that cannot be located behind the cutting-plane line.

Cutting-plane lines can also be drawn at an angle, as shown in Figure 7-13. However, the sectional view is not drawn exactly behind the cutting plane but is rotated as if the cutting-plane line were drawn straight through the object.

Sectional views should be located, if possible, directly behind the cutting-plane line, as shown in Figure 7-14. Sectional views may be located in line with the cutting plane line either above or below the object. Sectional views are *never* located in front of the cutting-plane line.

If there is insufficient space on the drawing to show a sectional view, it may be located in another drawing file and referenced to the cutting-plane line using a note as shown in Figure 7-15. The cutting-plane line is, in turn, referenced to the location of the sectional view. Use file names that clearly identify the sectional view.

7-4 MULTIPLE SECTIONAL VIEWS

Several sectional views may be taken through the same object, as shown in Figures 7-16 and 7-17. Each sectional view must be labeled using large bold letters. Identification letters for sectional views should be used in alphabetical order. The sectional views should be located as near as possible in alphabetical order on the drawing.

The letters I, O, and Q are not used to identify sectional views because their shape could be confused with feature shapes on the drawing. If there are more than 23 sectional views on a drawing, the lettering sequence starts with AA and continues through the alphabet using doubled letters.

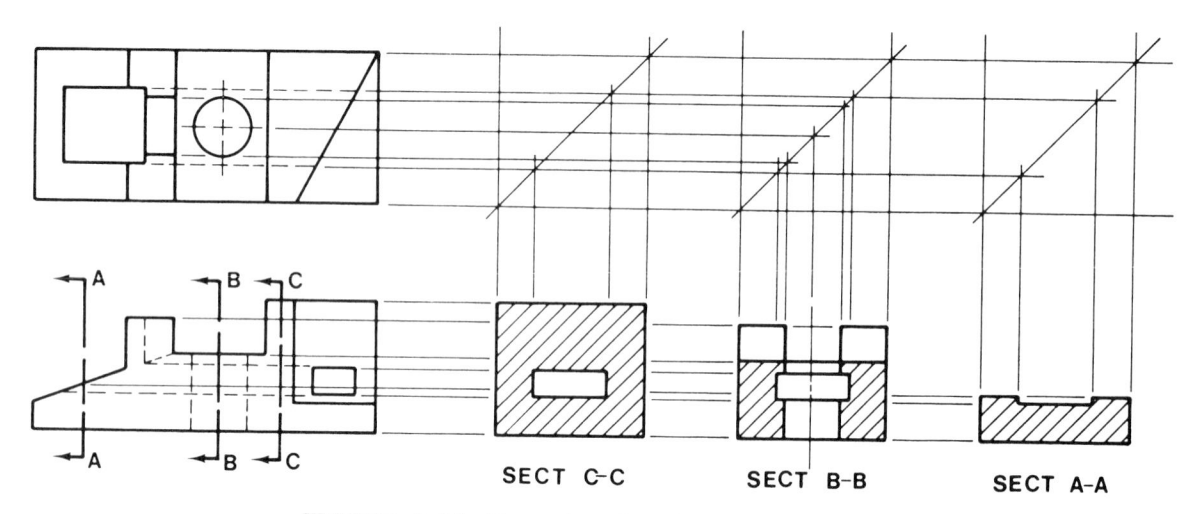

FIGURE 7-16 Example of multiple sectional views taken from a single front view.

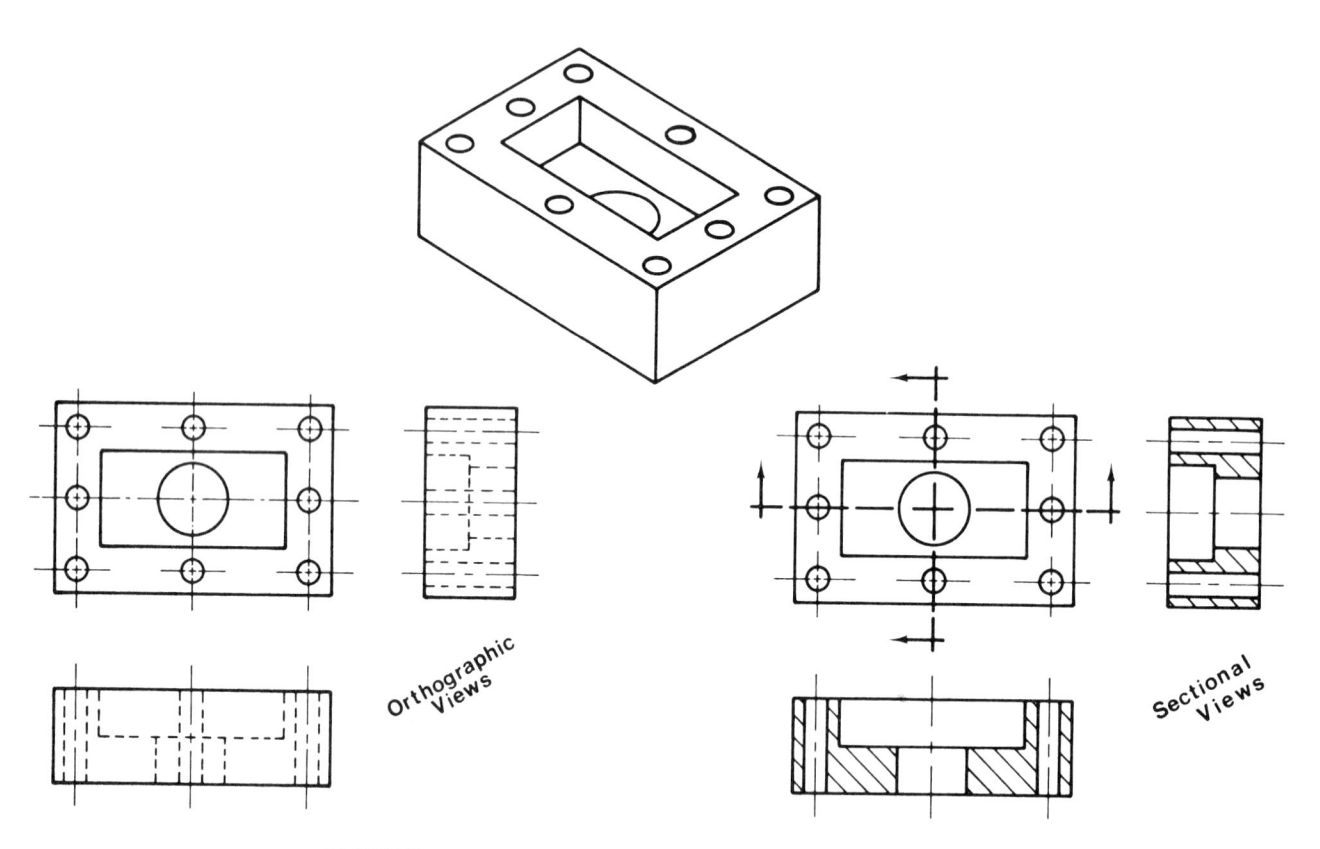

FIGURE 7-17 Example of two sectional views taken from a single front view.

7-5 BROKEN-OUT SECTIONAL VIEWS

Broken-out sectional views are sectioned views drawn directly on the orthographic views when only a small portion of the object needs a sectional view (Figure 7-18).

Sec. 7-7 Rotated Sectional Views

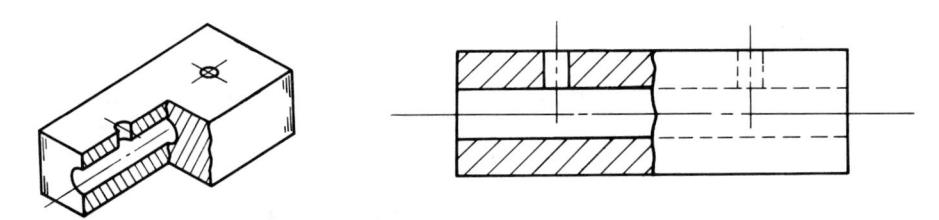

FIGURE 7-18 Example of a broken-out sectional view.

7-6 REVOLVED SECTIONAL VIEWS

Revolved sectional views are sectional views drawn directly on the orthographic views and rotated 90° to the plane of the paper (Figure 7-19). They are particularly useful in defining the shape of long features whose shape is constant.

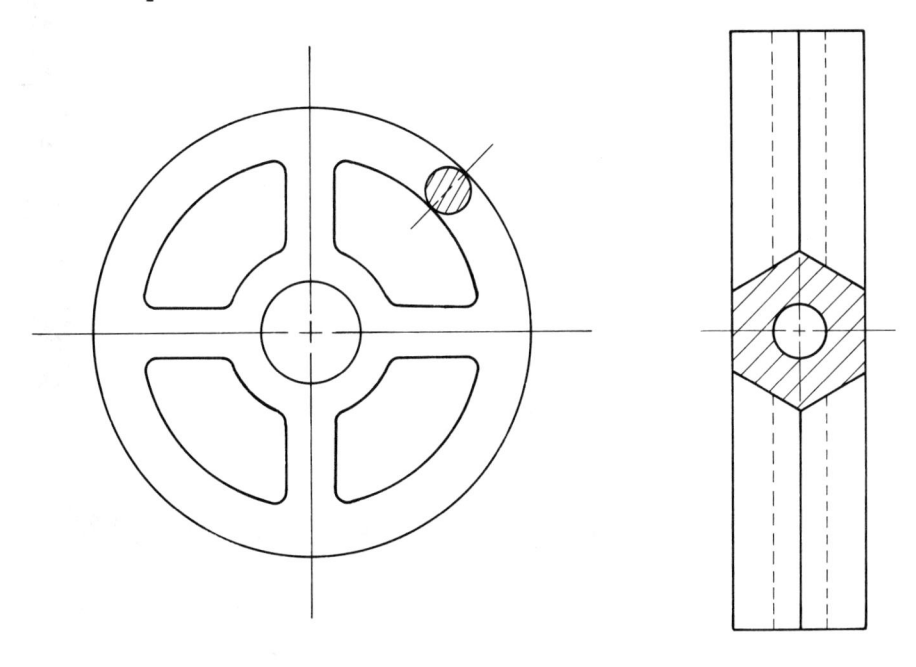

FIGURE 7-19 Examples of a revolved sectional view.

7-7 ROTATED SECTIONAL VIEWS

Sectional views may be rotated out of their normal projected positions as shown in Figure 7-20 provided that they are labeled with the angular value and direction of rotation.

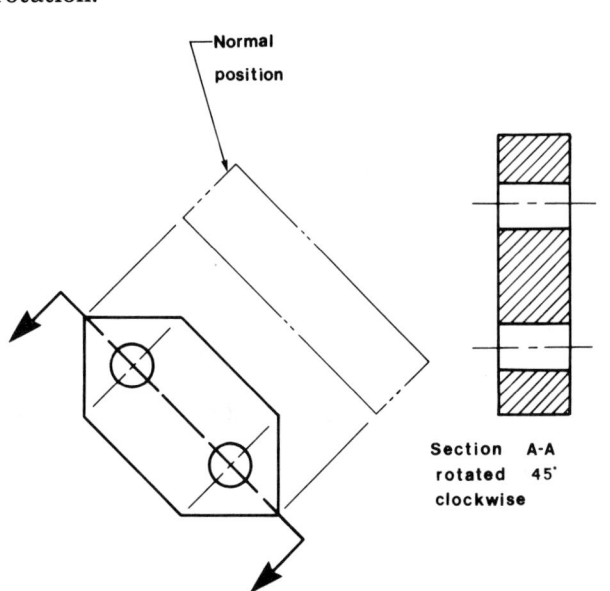

FIGURE 7-20 Example of a rotated sectional view.

Section A-A rotated 45° clockwise

7-8 REMOVED SECTIONAL VIEWS

Sectional views may be removed from their normal projection position as shown in Figure 7-21. Removed sectional views are similar to revolved sectional views but are detached from the orthographic views.

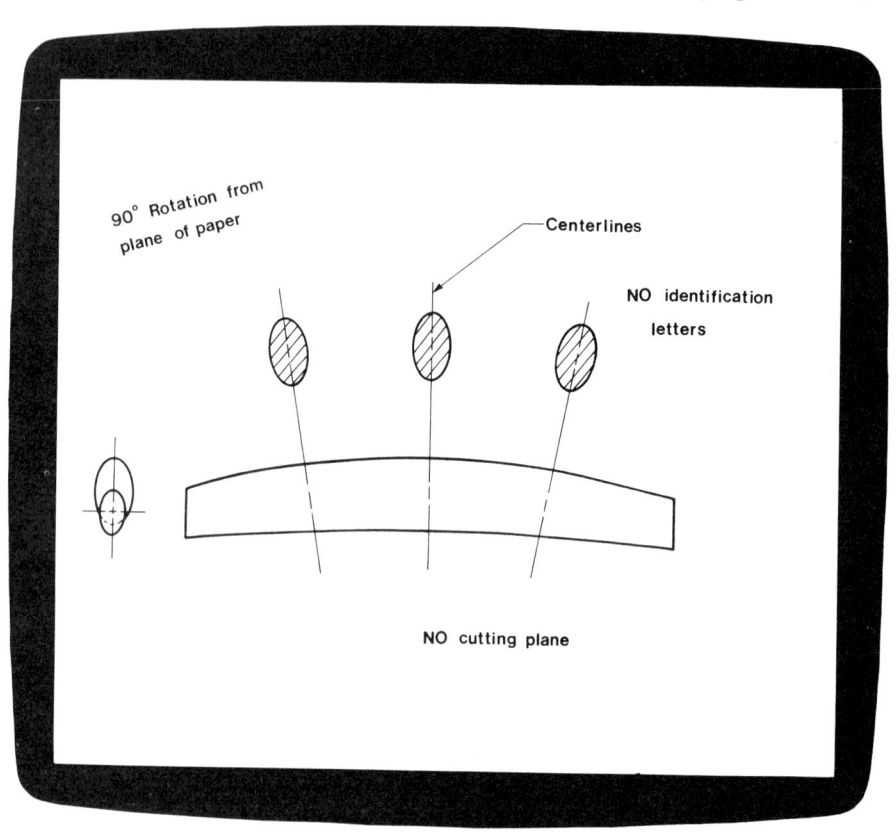

FIGURE 7-21 Examples of removed sectional views.

Removed sectional views do not need a cutting plane or identifying letters. The cutting-plane location is identified by a centerline. The removed sectional view is rotated about the centerline 90° to the plane of the paper.

7-9 HALF-SECTIONAL VIEWS

A half-sectional view is an orthographic view, half of which is a sectional view and half of which is a normal orthographic view. The two halves are separated by a centerline (Figure 7-22).

A full-sectional view is one that the cutting plane cuts completely across the object. In a half-sectional view, the cutting-plane line cuts only halfway across the object, as shown in Figure 7-22. Half-sectional cutting-plane lines use only one arrowhead and stop at the perpendicular centerline.

7-10 THIN SECTIONAL VIEWS

If possible, section lines should always be added to sectional views, but some objects are so thin that section lines cannot be added clearly. Sectional views of thin objects are drawn using thick black lines as shown in Figure 7-23.

Sec. 7-10 Thin Sectional Views

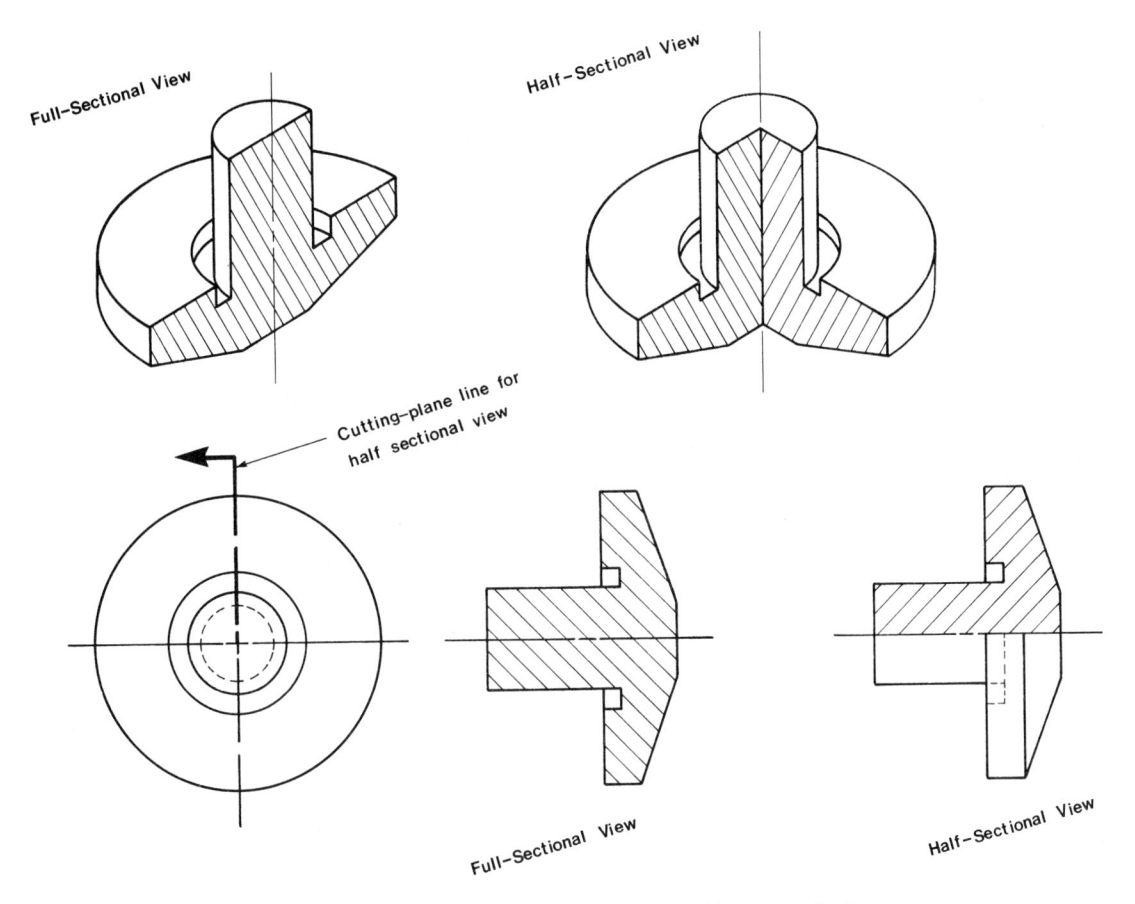

FIGURE 7-22 Examples of full- and half-sectional views.

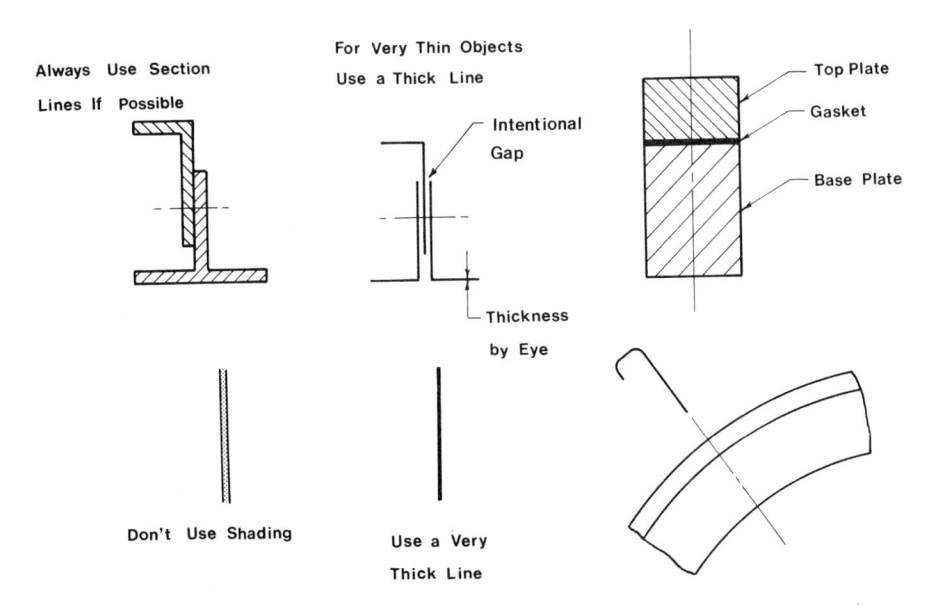

FIGURE 7-23 How to draw sectional views of very thin objects.

Any type of sectional view (revolved, removed, etc.) of a thin object may be drawn using a thick black line. Note that this type of line is not two object lines with shading in between, but is a single black line.

When two or more thin objects are drawn in sections using the thick-line technique, a small gap is always placed between the objects for clarity. The gap is small but should be wide enough so that each part can easily be distinguished from the others.

7-11 RIBS AND WEBS

Ribs and webs are drawn without section lines in sectional views, as shown in Figure 7-24. This is done to prevent confusion. If ribs and webs did use section lines, they could give a false impression of thickness, making the part appear stronger than it actually is.

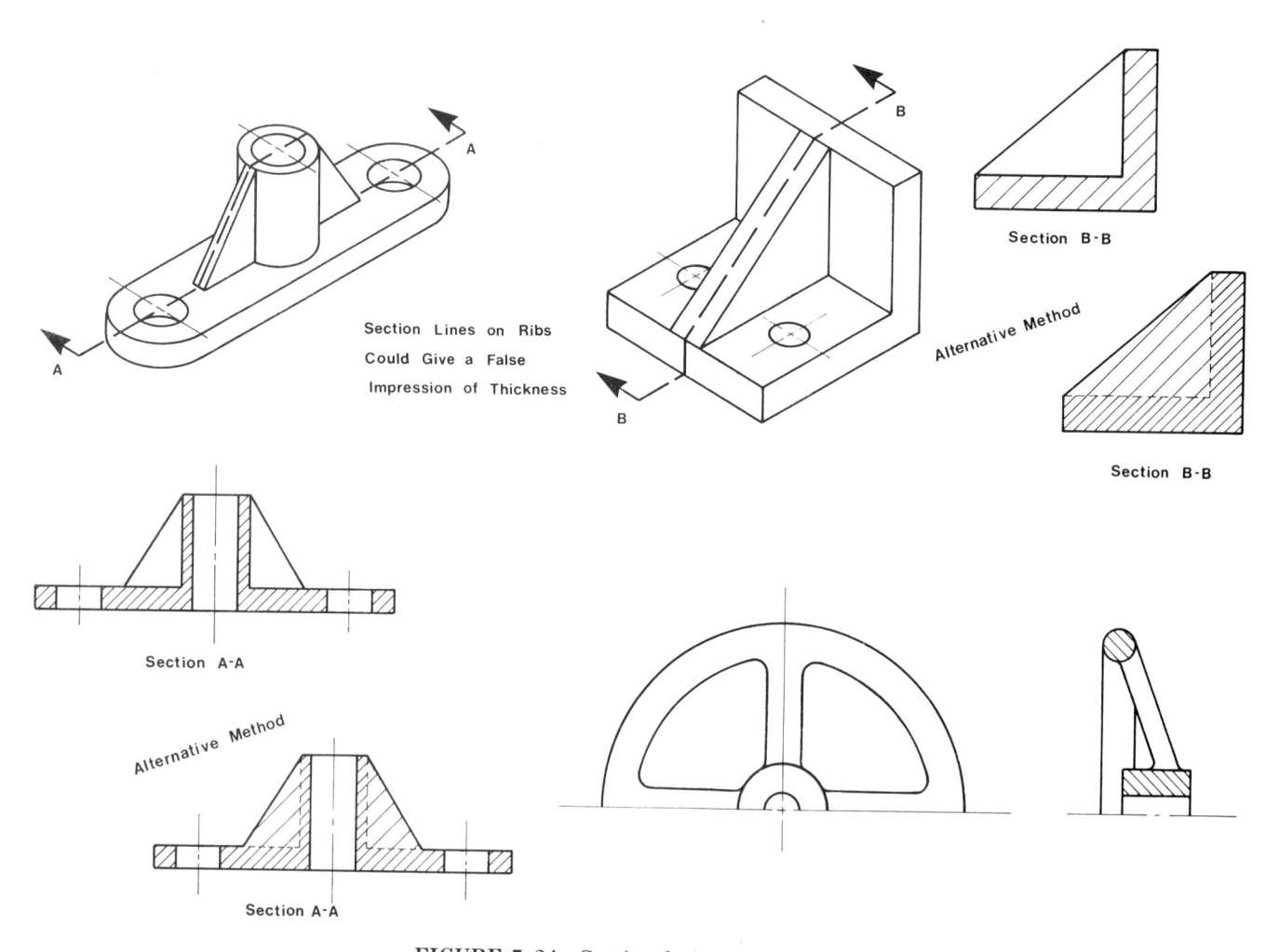

FIGURE 7-24 Sectional views of ribs and webs.

Figure 7-24 also shows an alternative method for drawing section lines on ribs and webs. The primary shape of the object is sectioned as before, but in the alternative method, every other section line is drawn across the rib and web section. Only the peripheral lines of the sectioned surface are drawn using object lines. Internal lines are drawn using hidden lines.

7-12 HOLES

A common mistake made when drawing sectional views of holes is the omission of the back edge of the hole. If a hole is cut in half in a sectional view, the back edges must be shown. Figure 7-25 shows a counterbored

Chap. 7 Problems   201

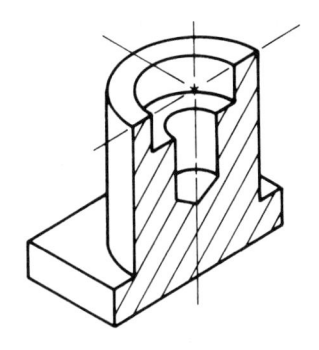

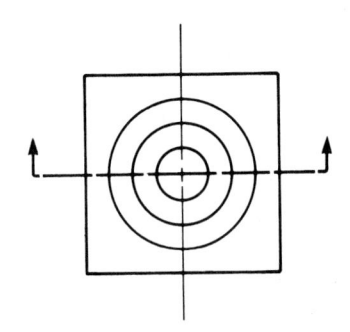

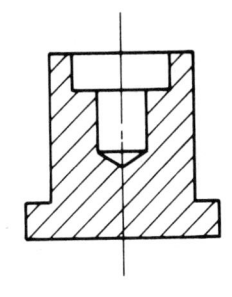

FIGURE 7-25 Sectional view of a drilled and counterbored hole.

hole, an isometric drawing, a regular orthographic view, and a sectional view. Note how lines that represent the back edges of the hole appear in the sectional view.

PROBLEMS

P7-1 Redraw the sectional view shown in Figure P7-1. Include the dimensions. Use the dimensional values given in the table.
  (a) Inches
  (b) Millimeters

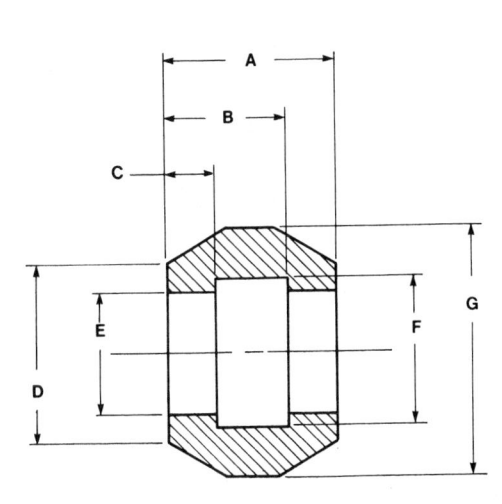

DIMENSIONS	INCHES	mm
A	.50	12
B	1.25	32
C	1.75	44
D	⌀1.75	44
E	⌀1.25	32
F	⌀1.50	38
G	⌀2.50	64

FIGURE P7-1

P7-2 Redraw the sectional view shown in Figure P7-2. Include the dimensions. Use the dimensional values given in the table.
  (a) Inches
  (b) Millimeters

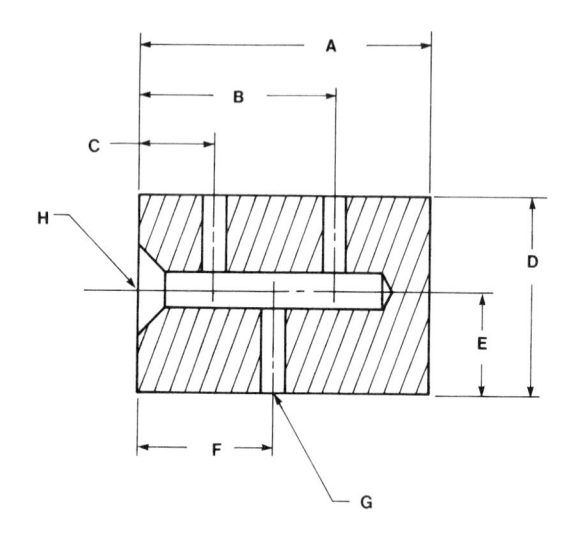

DIMENSIONS	INCHES	mm
A	3.00	72
B	2.00	48
C	.75	18
D	2.00	48
E	1.00	24
F	1.38	33
G	Ø.25	6
H	Ø.375 X 2.50 DEEP Ø.875 X 82° CSINK	Ø10 X 60 DEEP Ø24 X 82° CSINK

FIGURE P7-2

For Figures P7-3 through P7-5, redraw the given front view and redraw the given side view as a sectional view. The cutting-plane line should align with the vertical centerline in the front view. The dimensional units are as noted below.

P7-3 Inches
P7-4 Inches
P7-5 Millimeters

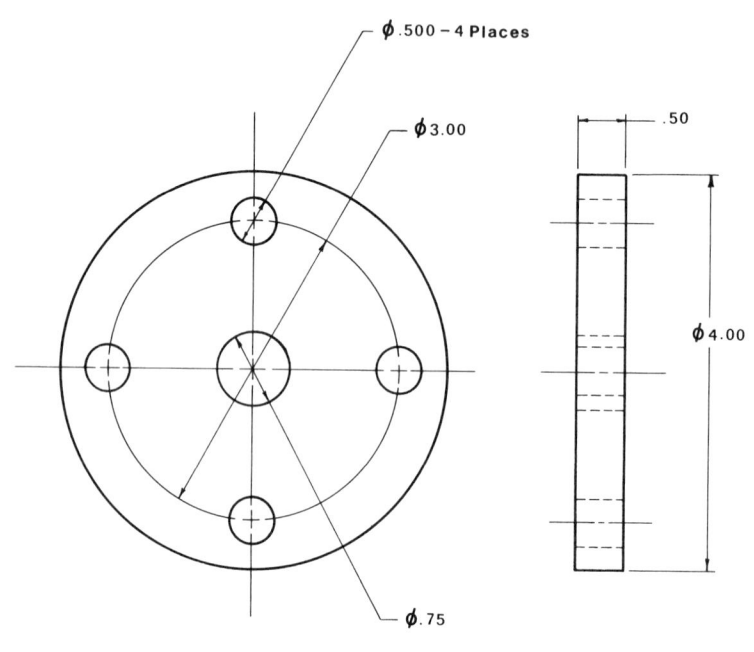

FIGURE P7-3

Chap. 7   Problems

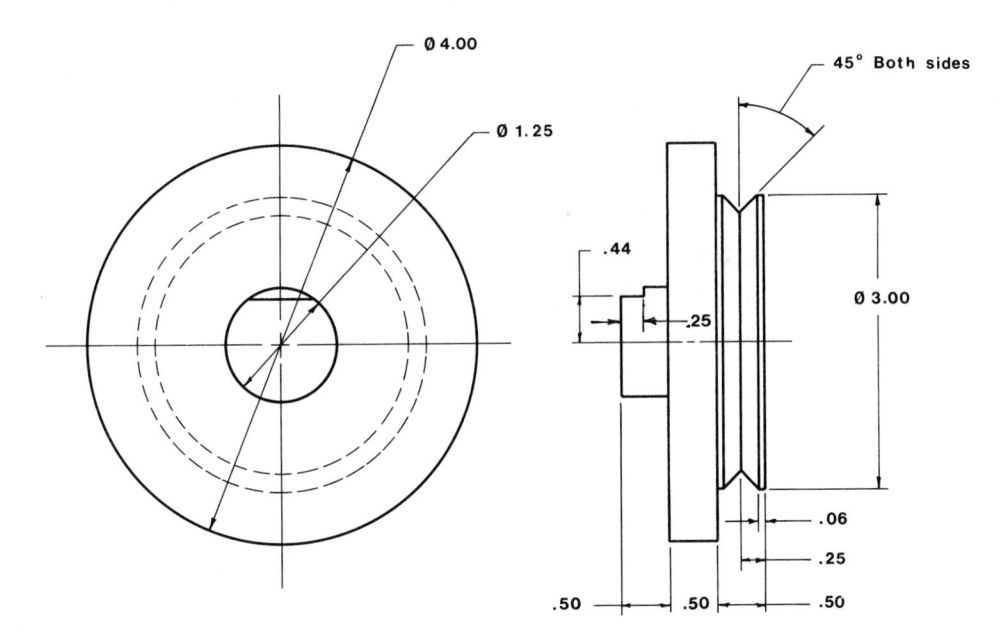

FIGURE P7-4

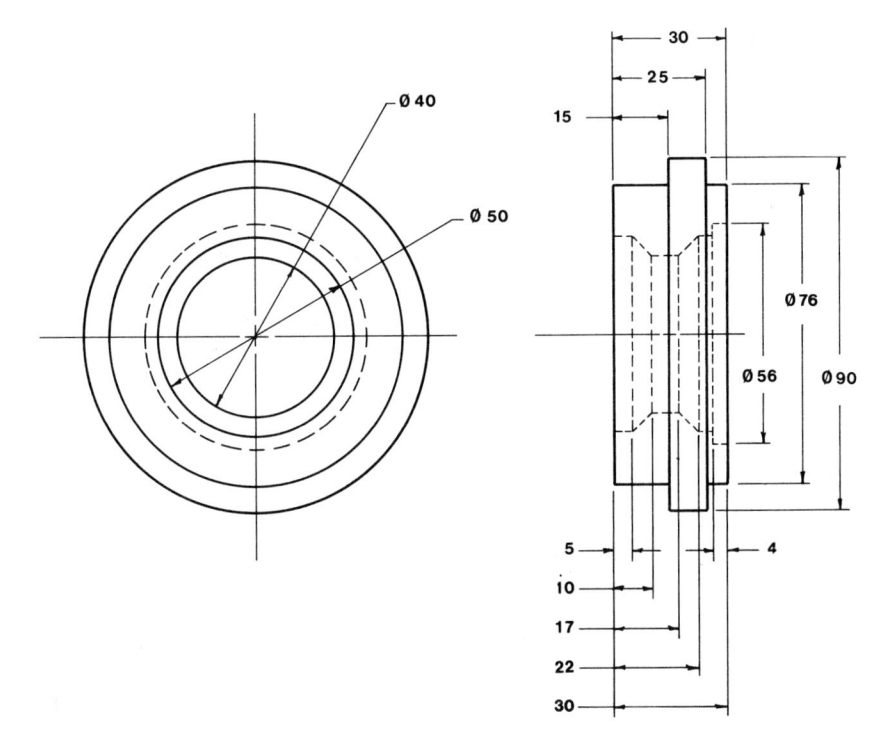

FIGURE P7-5

Draw a front and sectional view of the objects shown in Figures P7-6 through P7-10. Each object has been cut in half pictorially. Each object is symmetrical about the cutting plane. The dimensional units are as noted below.

P7-6 Millimeters
P7-7 Millimeters
P7-8 Inches
P7-9 Millimeters
P7-10 Inches

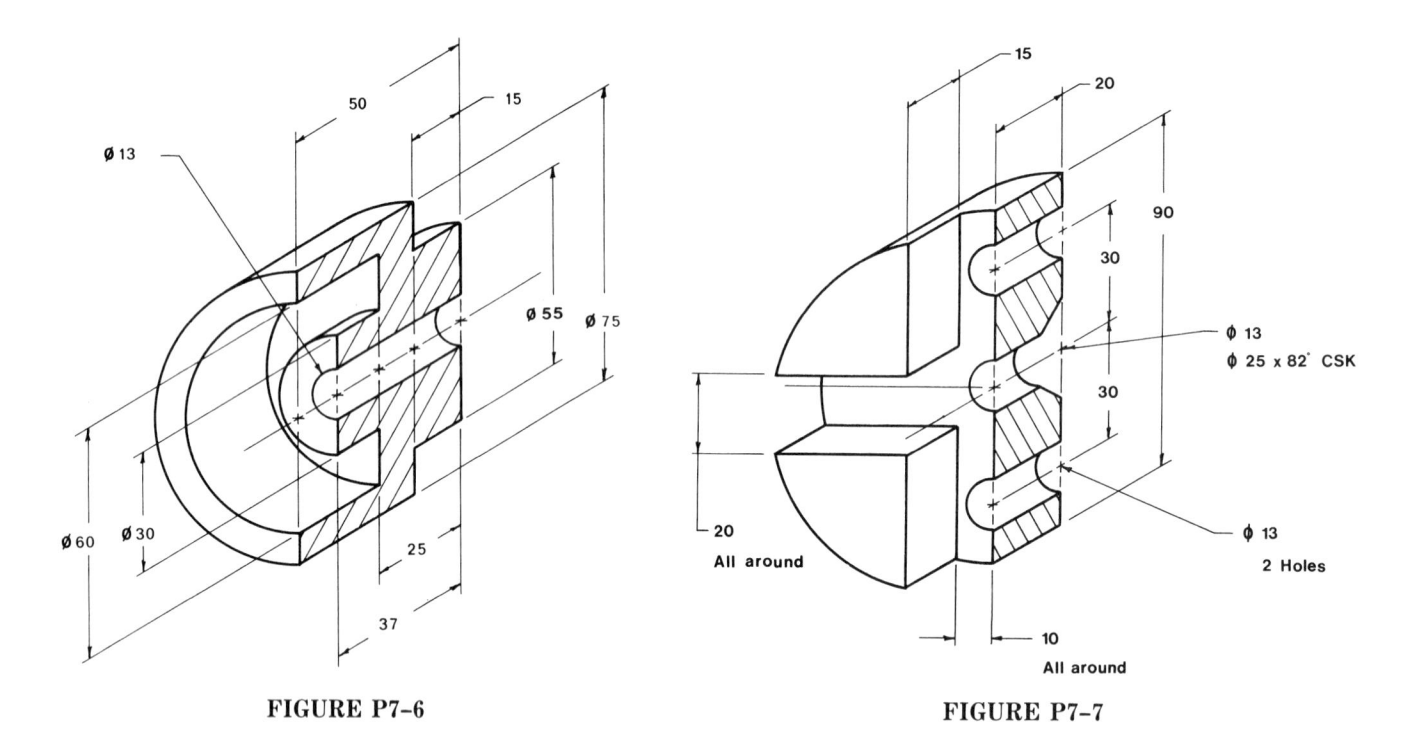

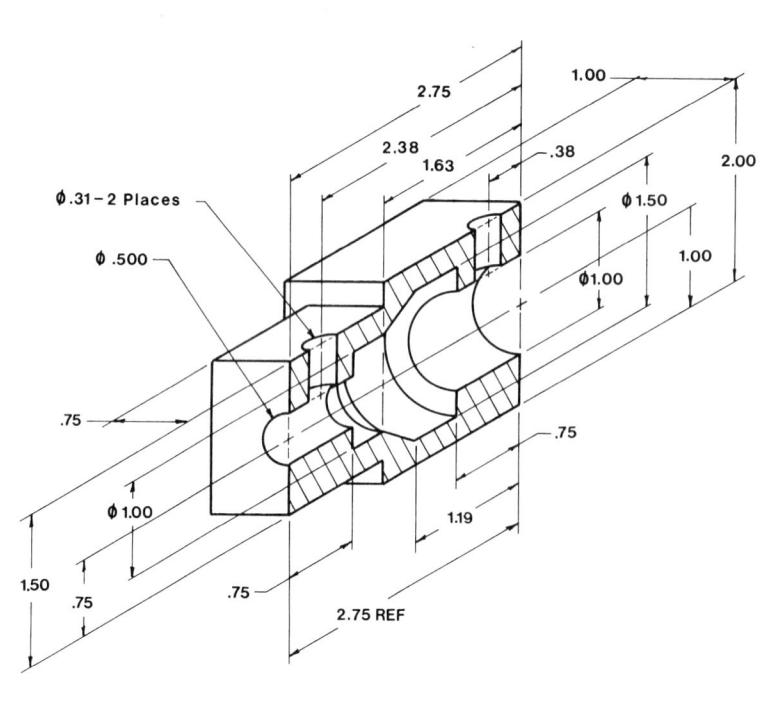

FIGURE P7-6

FIGURE P7-7

FIGURE P7-8

Chap. 7   Problems

FIGURE P7-9

FIGURE P7-10

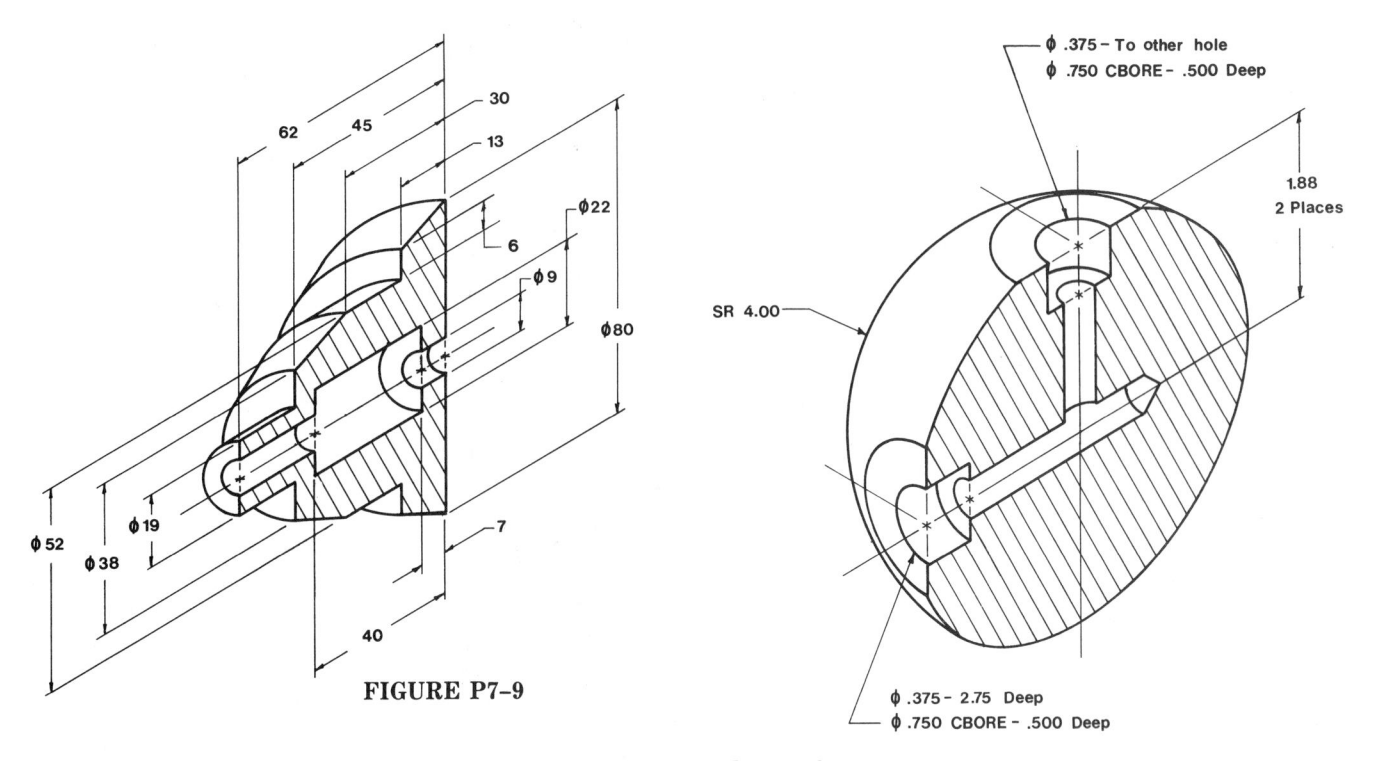

For Problems P7-11 through P7-16, draw at least one orthographic view and one sectional view of the objects shown in Figures P7-11 through P7-16. More views may be added if necessary. The dimensional units are as noted below.

P7-11	Millimeters	P7-14	Millimeters
P7-12	Inches	P7-15	Millimeters
P7-13	Millimeters	P7-16	Millimeters

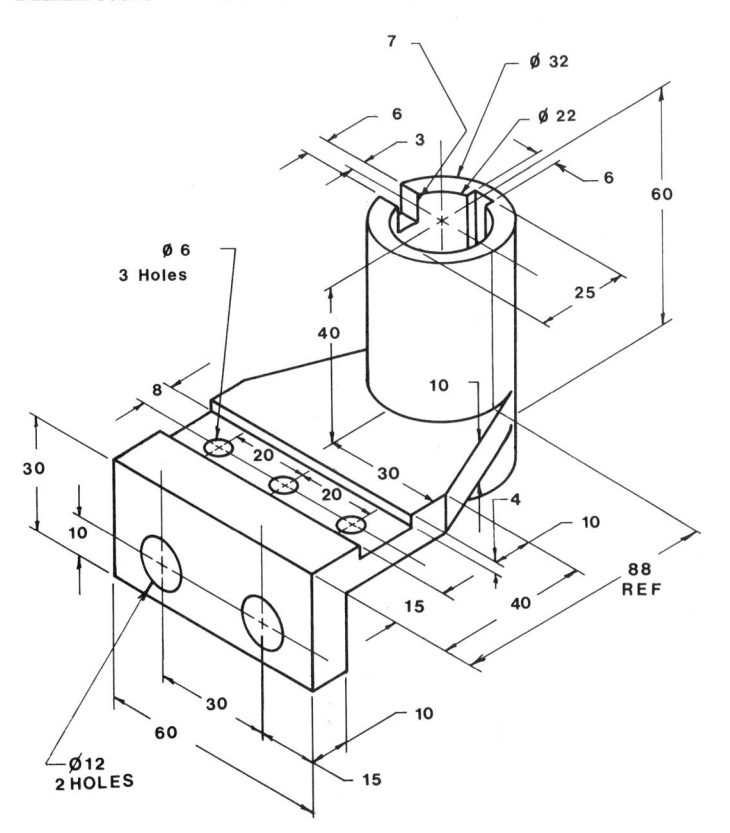

FIGURE P7-11

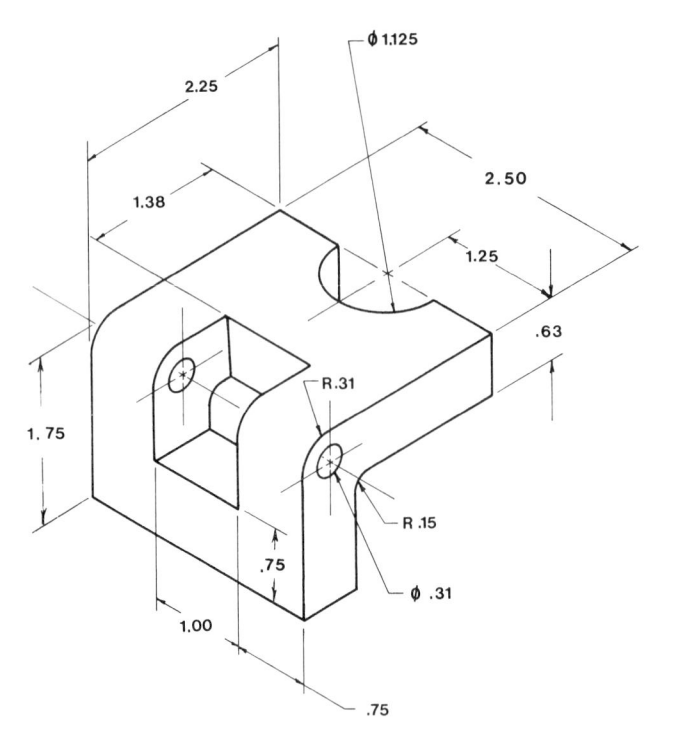

FIGURE P7-12

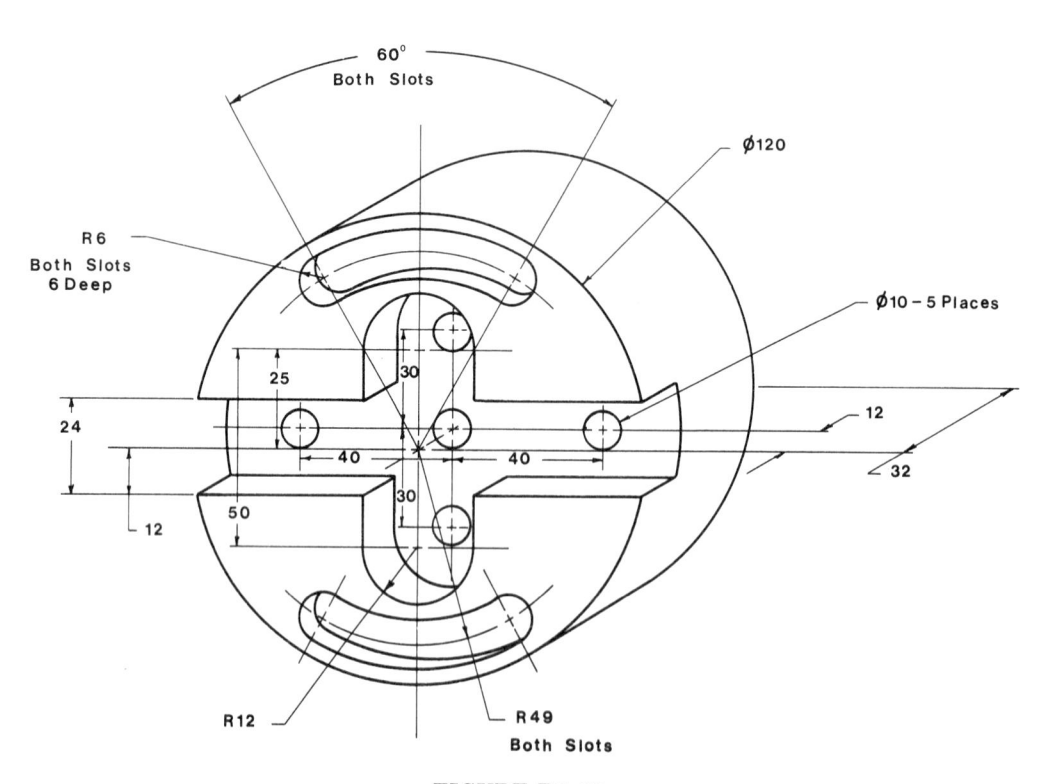

FIGURE P7-13

Chap. 7   Problems

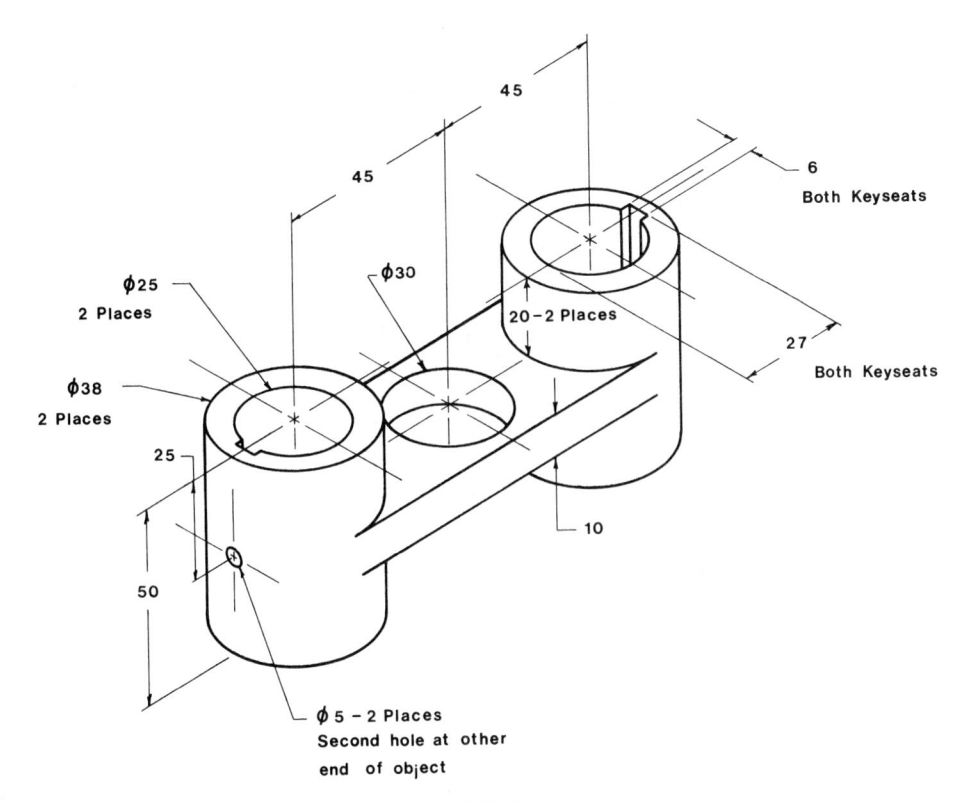

FIGURE P7-14

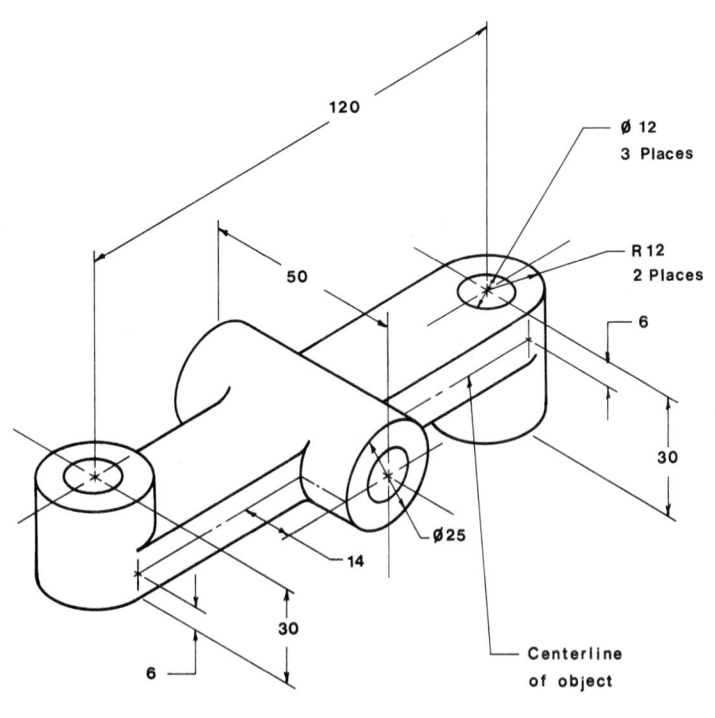

FIGURE P7-15

FIGURE P7-16

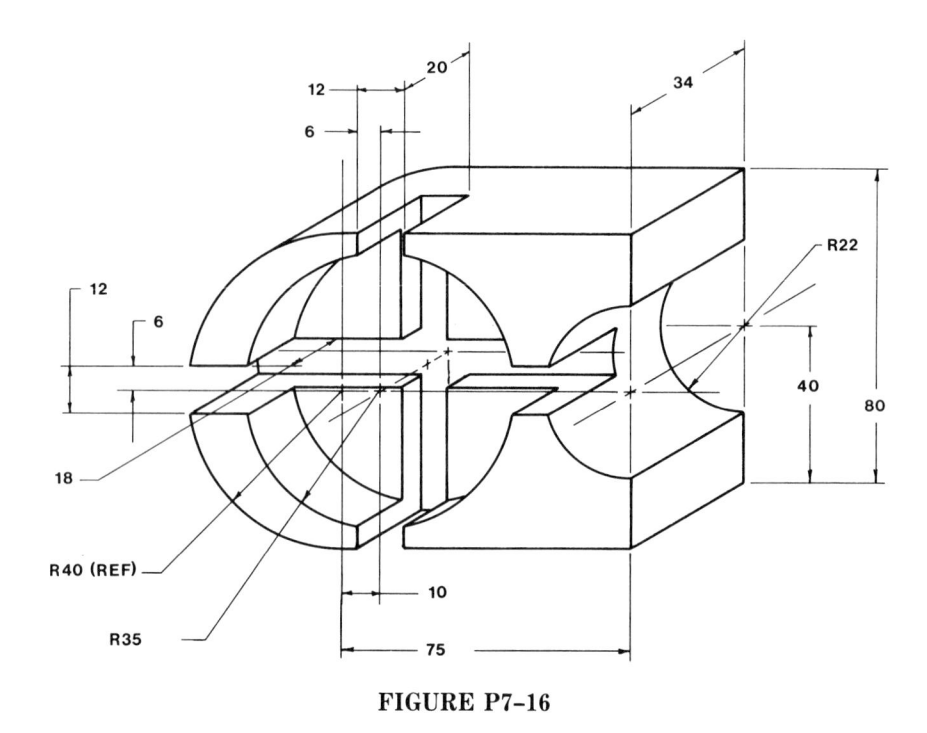

P7-17 Redraw the given front view in Figure P7-17 and add the three sectional views as indicated by the cutting plane lines. All dimensional values are in inches.

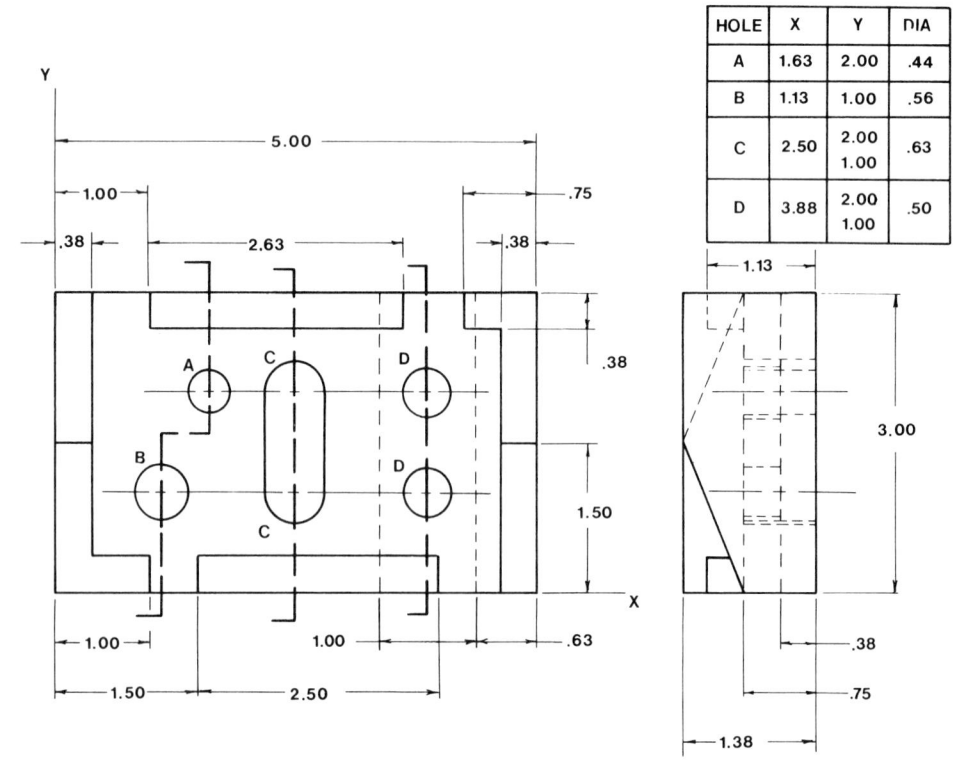

HOLE	X	Y	DIA
A	1.63	2.00	.44
B	1.13	1.00	.56
C	2.50	2.00 / 1.00	.63
D	3.88	2.00 / 1.00	.50

FIGURE P7-17

Chap. 7 Problems 209

P7-18 Redraw the given top view in Figure P7-18 and replace the given front view with a sectional view. All dimensional values are in inches.

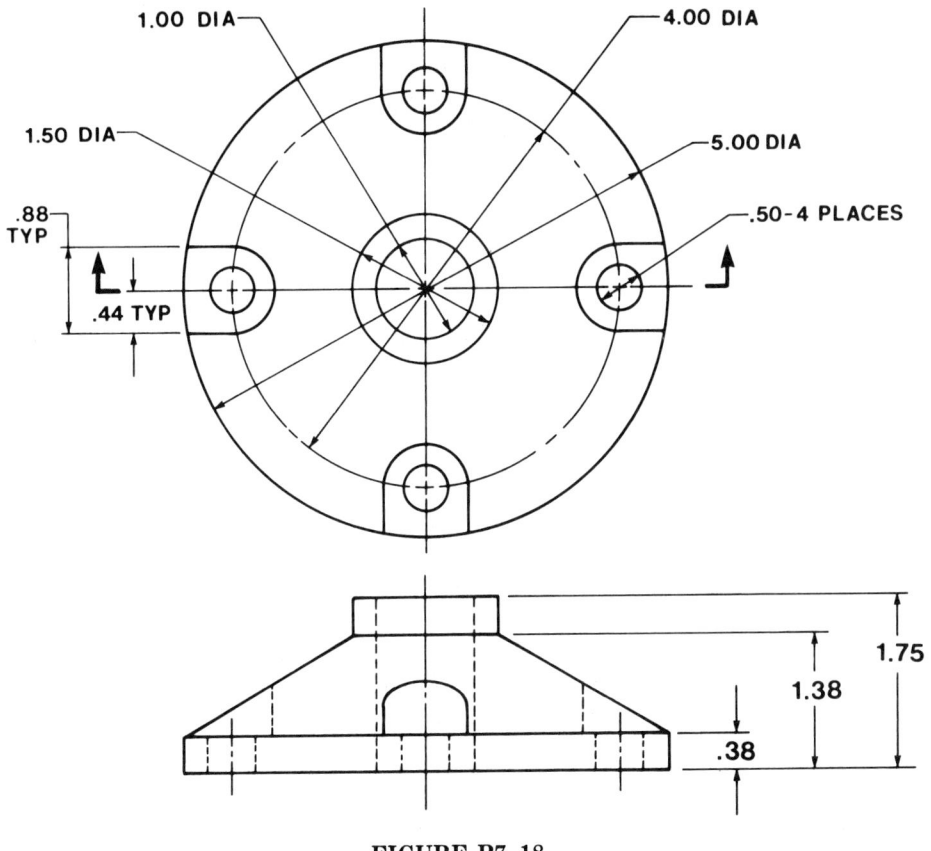

FIGURE P7-18

P7-19 Redraw the given front view in Figure P7-19 and replace the given side view with a sectional view. All dimensional values are in inches.

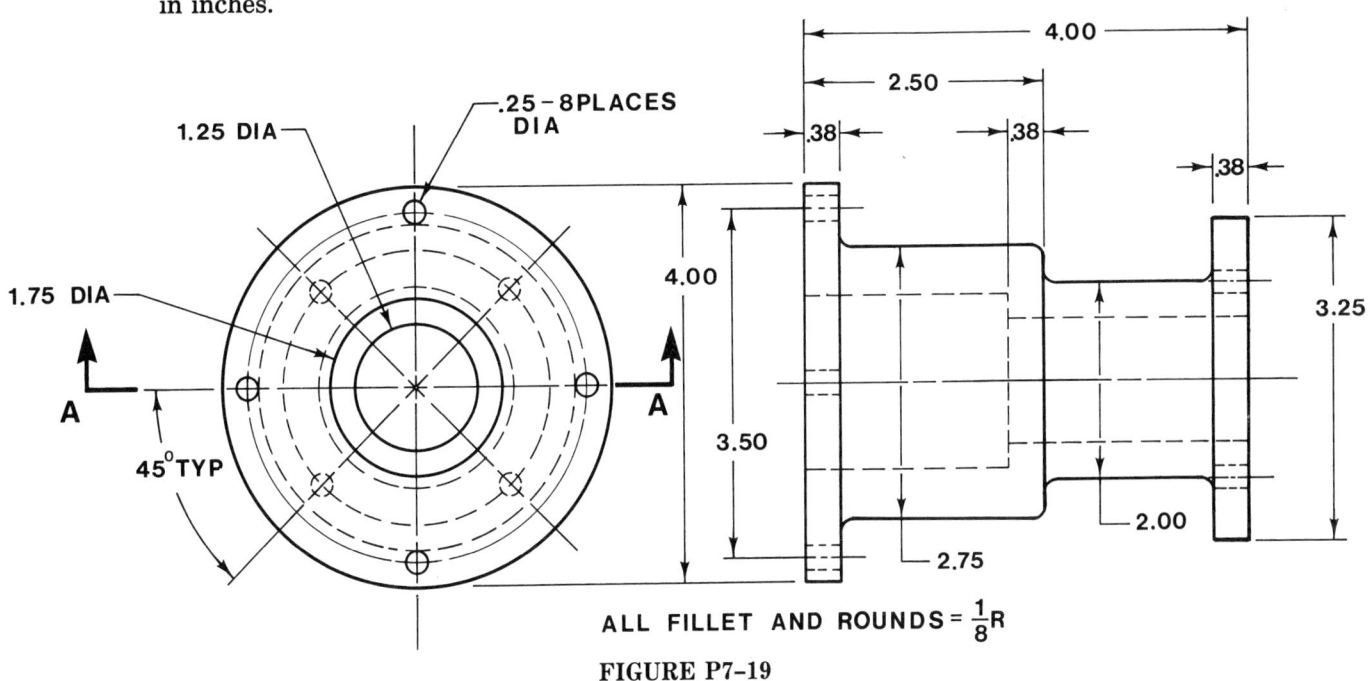

ALL FILLET AND ROUNDS = $\frac{1}{8}$R

FIGURE P7-19

P7-20 Redraw the half top view given in Figure P7-20 as a full (complete circle) view and replace the given front view with a sectional view. All dimensional values are in inches.

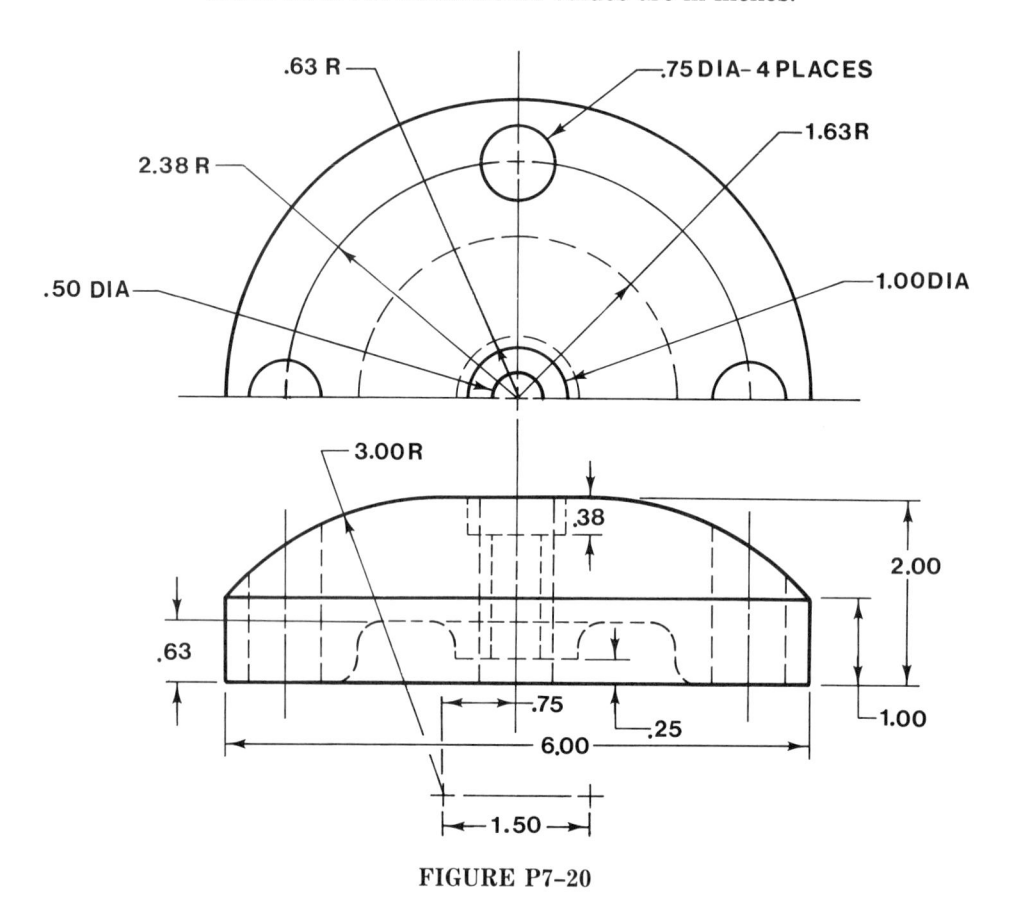

FIGURE P7-20

8
AUXILIARY VIEWS

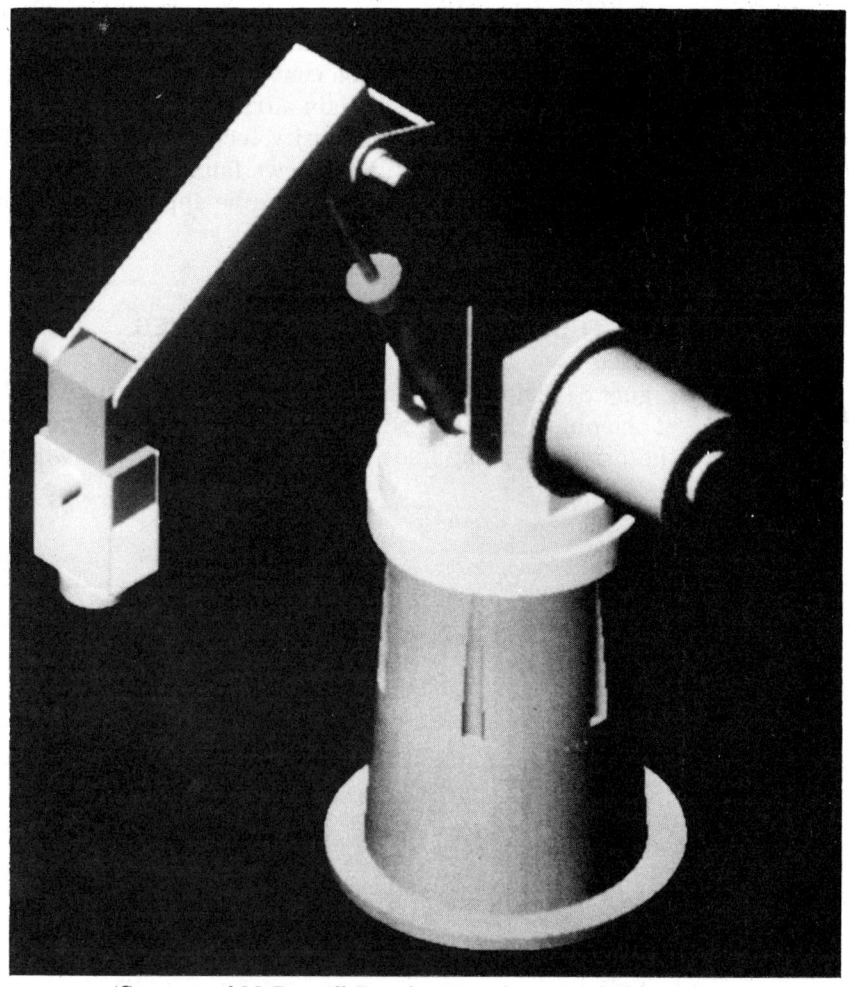

(Courtesy of McDonnell Douglas Manufacturing Industry Systems Company, St. Louis, Mo.)

8-1 INTRODUCTION

Auxiliary views are a special type of orthographic view. They are used in technical drawings to help clarify features that appear foreshortened in the conventional front, top, right side, left side, rear, and bottom views. Figure 8-1 shows front, top, side, and auxiliary views of an object. Surface A appears as an edge view in the front view, and foreshortened in the top and side views. Only the auxiliary view, taken at exactly 90° to surface A, shows the true shape of surface A.

Auxiliary views can be taken at any angle relative to another view as shown in Figure 8-2, but are most often taken at 90° to one of the object's surfaces. Views taken at angles other than 90° will project foreshortened distances. Auxiliary views show hidden edges and surfaces using hidden lines, and use the conventions outlined in Section 6-4.

In this chapter we explain auxiliary view drawing theory and show how it can be used to help clarify technical drawings. The chapter also explains secondary auxiliary views (auxiliary views of auxiliary views) and shows how auxiliary views can be applied using computer graphics systems.

8-2 TRUE-LENGTH LINES AND PLANES

Figure 8-3 shows an object containing surface 1-2-3-4. If the front view of the object is taken such that surface 1-2-3-4 appears at an angle to the principal plane lines, the top and side views will appear foreshort-

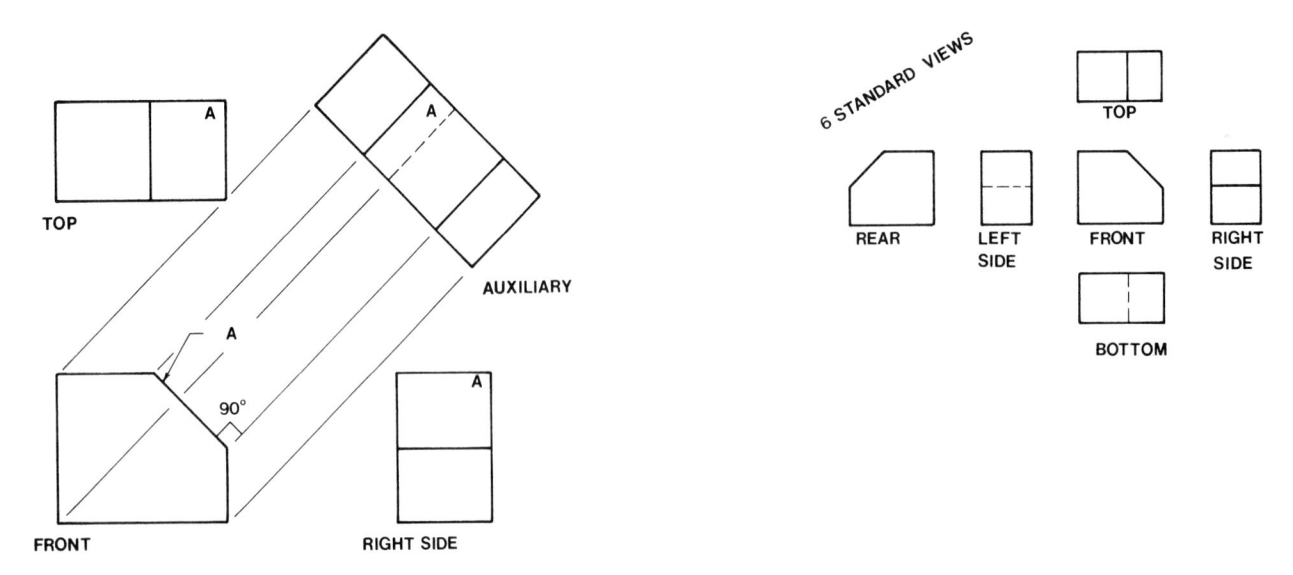

FIGURE 8-1 Auxiliary view.

Sec. 8-2   True-Length Lines and Planes   213

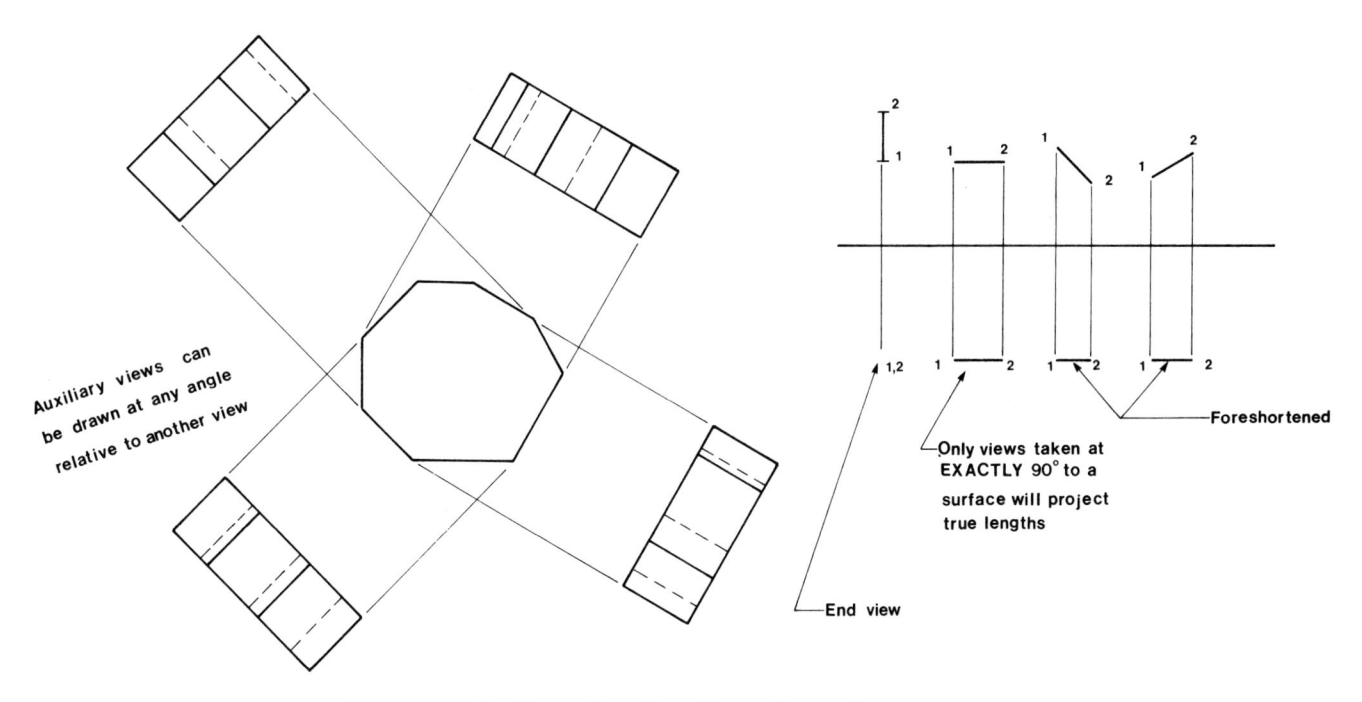

FIGURE 8-2 Examples of auxiliary views taken at various angles from another orthographic view.

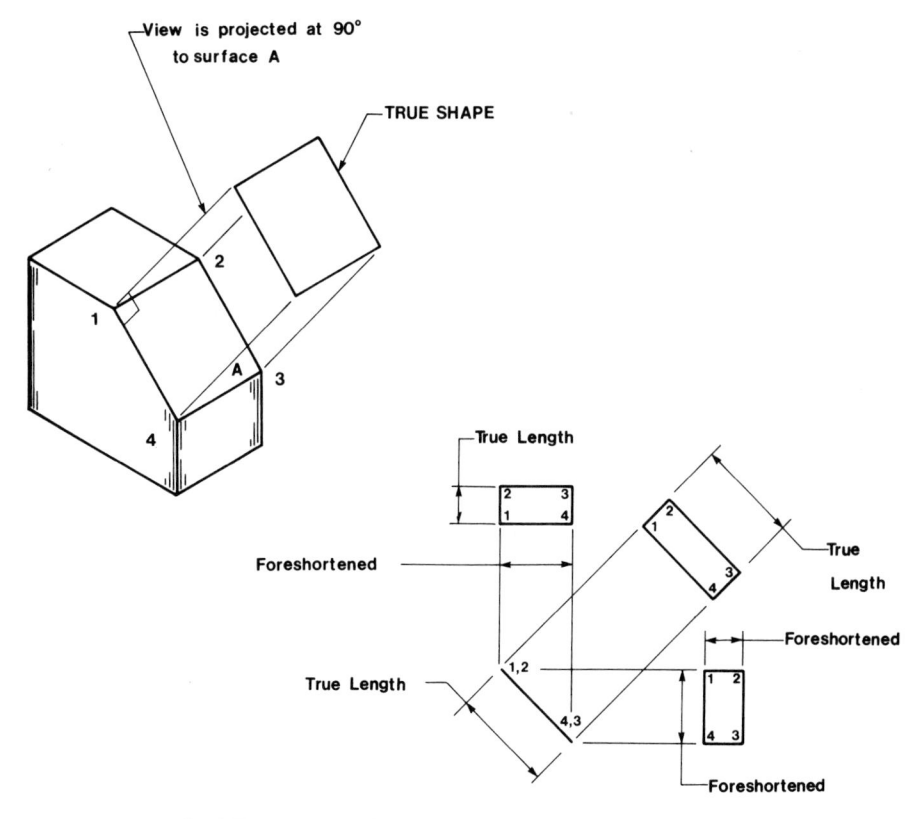

FIGURE 8-3 Auxiliary view taken at exactly 90° to a surface will show the true shape of the surface.

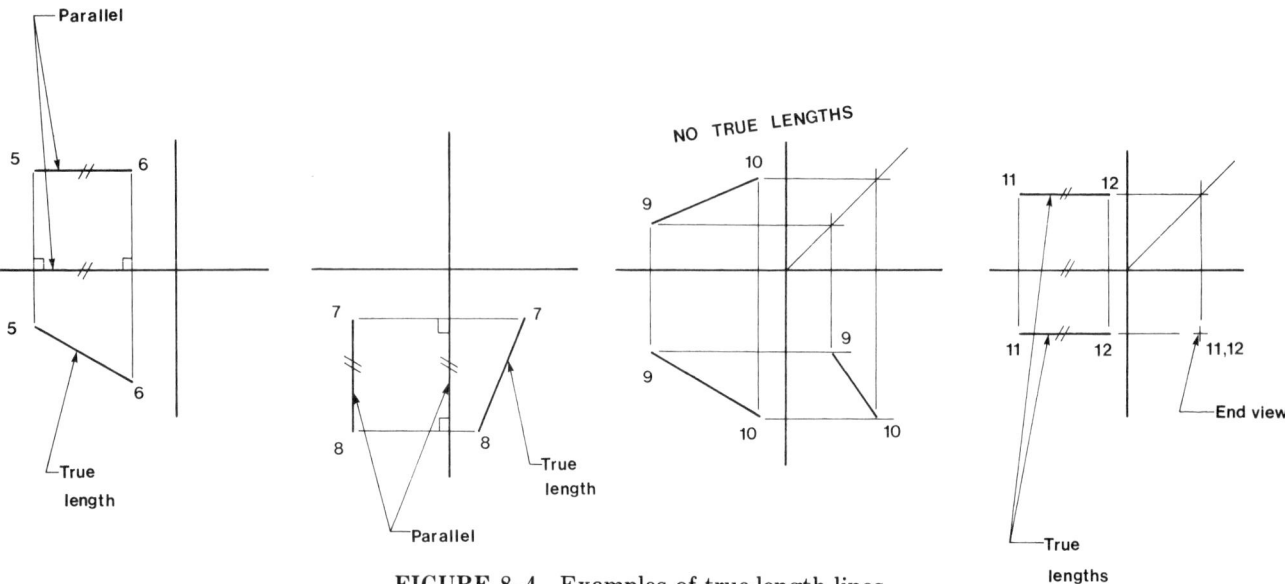

FIGURE 8-4 Examples of true-length lines.

ened, that is, shorter than the actual true length of the surface. Only an auxiliary view, taken at exactly 90° to surface 1-2-3-4, will show the true shape of the surface.

Figure 8-4 shows several examples of views that contain true-length lines. The top view of line 5-6 appears as a horizontal line. This means that it is parallel to the horizontal principal line. Therefore, the front view of the line, taken, by definition, at exactly 90° to the top view, is a true-length line. The front view of line 7-8 is parallel to the vertical principal line, so the side view, which is exactly 90° to the front view, is a true length line.

None of the views of line 9-10 is parallel to either principal plane line. Therefore, none of the given views — front, top, or side — is a true-length line. An auxiliary view would be necessary to define the line's true length.

Both the top and front views of line 11-12 are parallel to the horizontal principal plane line, so both are true-length lines. Note that in this arrangement, the side view is a point, or an end view of the line.

Figure 8-5 shows several examples of views that contain true-shaped planes. Plane 1-2-3-4 appears as a straight horizontal line in both the front and side views parallel to the horizontal principal plane line. The lines represent the end view of the plane. The top view is 90° to the front view, so projects as a true shape.

FIGURE 8-5 Examples of true-shaped planes.

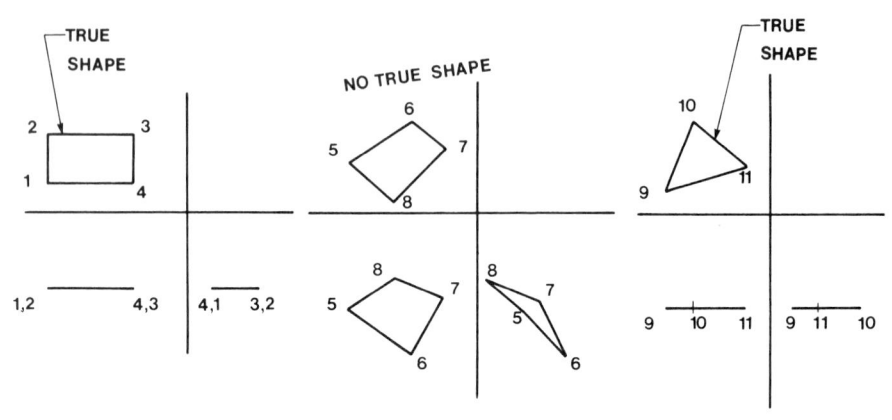

Sec. 8-3 Primary Auxiliary Views

Plane 5-6-7-8 has no edges parallel to either principal plane line. This means that none of the given views is a true shape. The front view of the triangular plane 9-10-11 is a straight horizontal line, making the top view true shaped.

8-3 PRIMARY AUXILIARY VIEWS

Figure 8-6 illustrates the procedure for drawing an auxiliary view. Two orthographic views are given, separated by the horizontal principal plane line. The distance between the two views is larger than normal to allow space for the auxiliary view.

Two construction lines are added in step 2: a line of sight and an auxiliary reference plane. The line of sight is drawn perpendicular to the

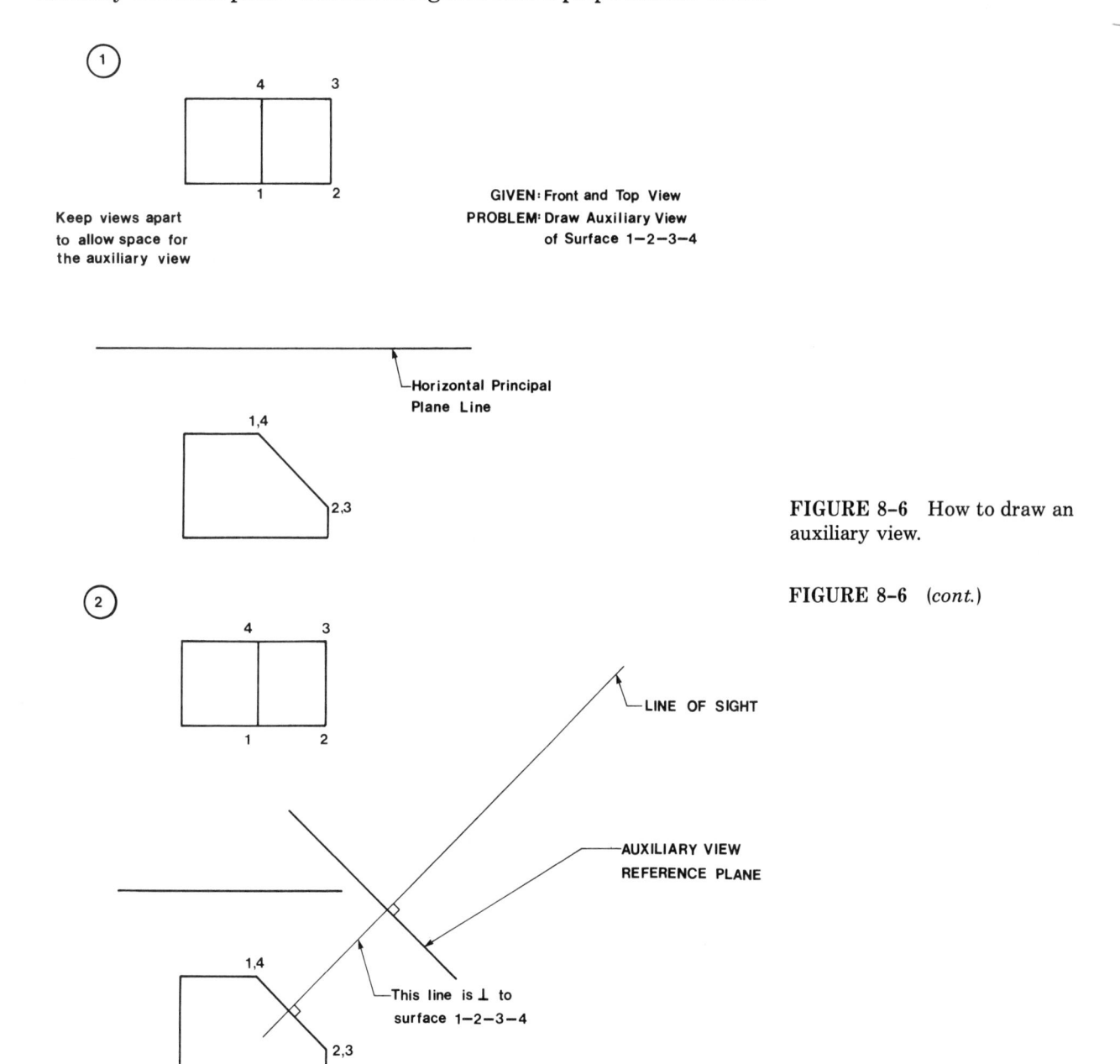

①
Keep views apart to allow space for the auxiliary view

GIVEN: Front and Top View
PROBLEM: Draw Auxiliary View of Surface 1-2-3-4

Horizontal Principal Plane Line

②
LINE OF SIGHT

AUXILIARY VIEW REFERENCE PLANE

This line is ⊥ to surface 1-2-3-4

FIGURE 8-6 How to draw an auxiliary view.

FIGURE 8-6 (cont.)

FIGURE 8-6 (cont.)

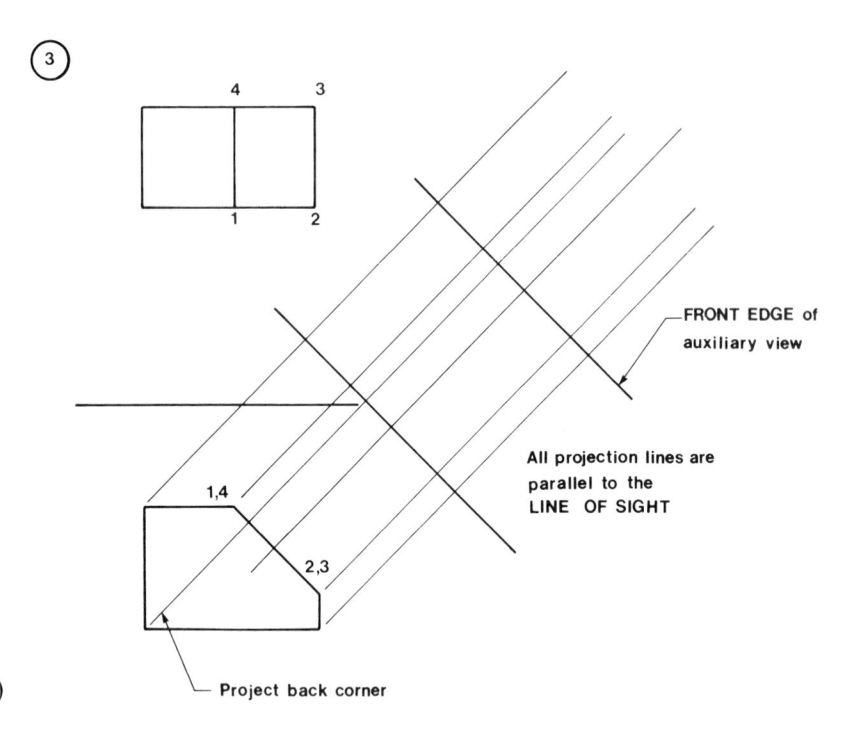

FIGURE 8-6 (cont.)

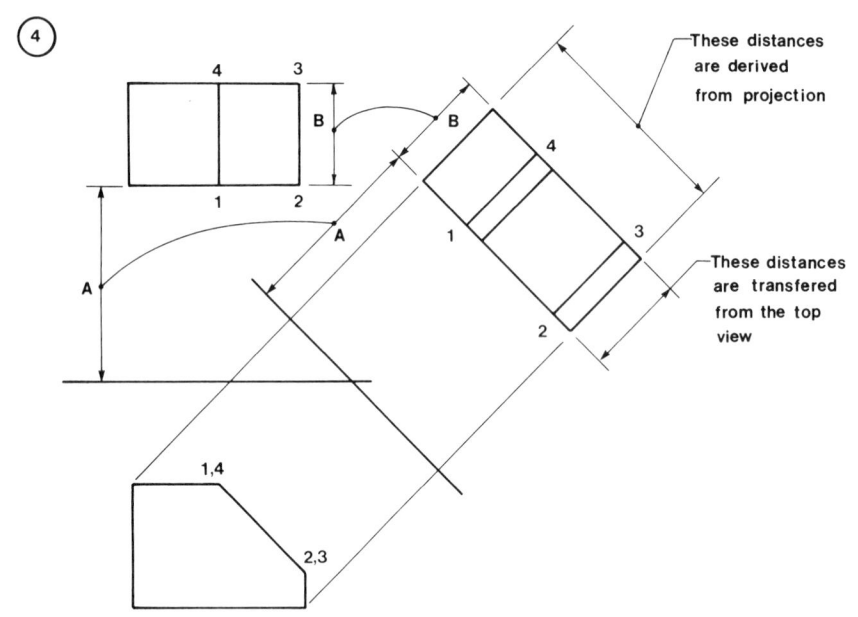

front view of surface 1-2-3-4. The auxiliary reference plane is in turn drawn perpendicular to the line of sight or parallel to surface 1-2-3-4. The location of the auxiliary reference plane is arbitrary but is usually placed so as to clear the top view or any other view on the drawing.

All edge lines are projected into the auxiliary view in step 3. All projection lines are parallel to the line of sight and perpendicular to the auxiliary reference plane. Note that the lower left corner of the front view is projected even though this line is not directly visible in the auxiliary view. It will appear as a hidden line in the auxiliary view.

Depth is added to the auxiliary view in step 4 by first measuring the distances from the horizontal principal plane line to the horizontal lines in the top view and then transferring these distances to the auxiliary view measuring from the auxiliary reference plane. Distance A is

Sec. 8-3   Primary Auxiliary Views   217

⑤

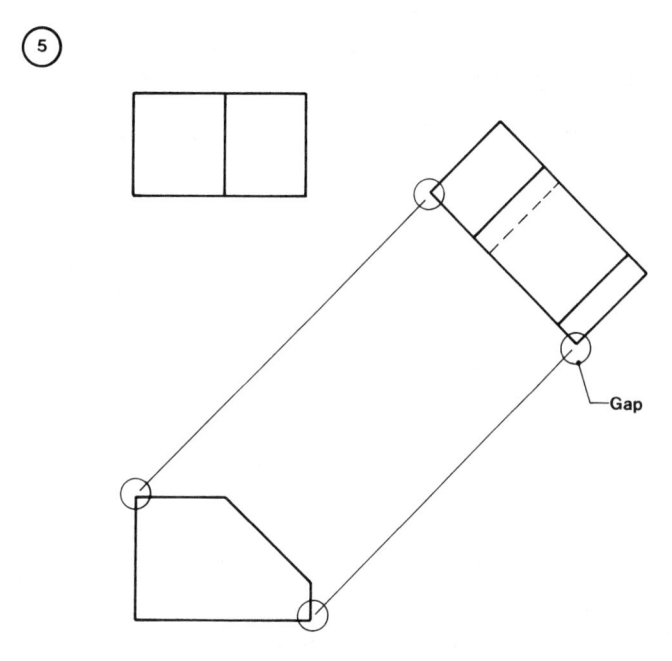

FIGURE 8-6 (cont.)

the distance from the front edge of the object to the horizontal principal plane line and the distance from the front edge of the object to the auxiliary reference line. Distance B is the distance to the back edge of the object in both views as measured from the two reference lines.

In step 5 the excess lines are erased and the object and hidden lines are drawn at their correct line thickness and pattern (line font). The two reference lines are also erased. It is a good practice to include part of the two projection lines which define the widest part of the auxiliary views. These lines help establish visually the relationship between the auxiliary view and the front view. The projection lines should be very thin and not touch either view as shown.

Auxiliary views can be created from any two orthographic views. In Figure 8-7 a front and right-side view are used to create the auxiliary

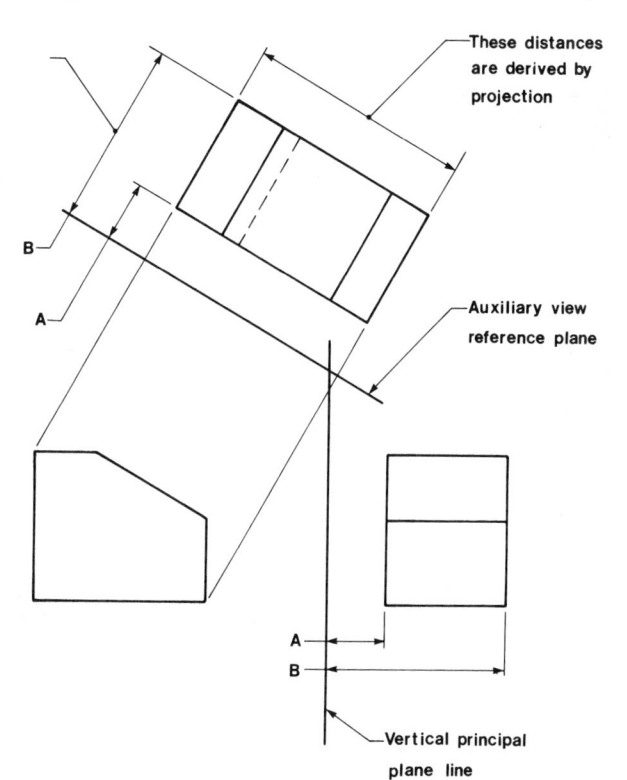

FIGURE 8-7 Auxiliary view created from a given front and right-side view.

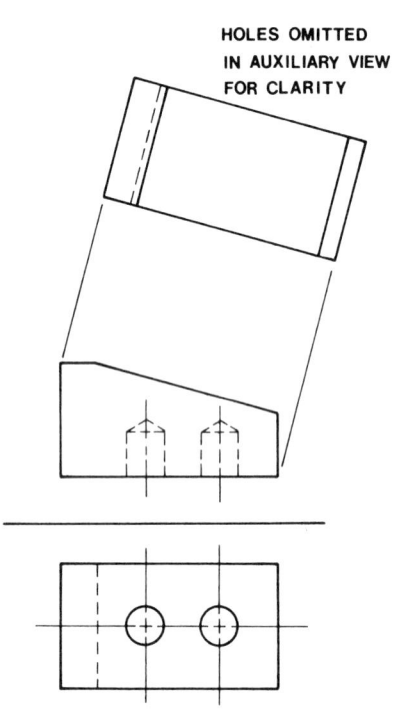

FIGURE 8-8 Auxiliary view created by projection from the top view.

FIGURE 8-9 How to create an auxiliary view using a computer graphics system.

view. The procedure is the same as presented for Figure 8-6 except that the depth distances A and B are measured from the vertical principal plane line and transferred to the auxiliary reference plane line as shown.

Figure 8-8 shows an auxiliary view taken from the top view. In this example, the holes were omitted in the top view for clarity. The angle of projection for the auxiliary view would cause the holes to appear as a series of elliptical shapes drawn using hidden lines. This would only add confusion to the drawing. If any feature of an object is omitted in an auxiliary view, it must be clearly noted next to the auxiliary view.

The procedure for drawing auxiliary views, presented in Figure 8-6, can be applied by computer graphic systems as Figure 8-9 illustrates. In step 1, the front and top views are located. In step 2, construction lines of unlimited length are drawn from each edge of the front view at an angle perpendicular to surface 1-2-3-4. The auxiliary reference line is added parallel to surface 1-2-3-4.

The depth measurements are added in step 3. The value of the depth distances are determined by measuring the distance from the horizontal reference line. This can be done by first having the computer dimension the distances from the horizontal principal plane line and then using these distances to draw the auxiliary view relative to the auxiliary plane reference line (step 3a).

Some computer systems can establish new coordinate systems for auxiliary views as shown in step 3b. Once established, measurements can be referenced directly to the new system using coordinate inputs, as with the basic X-Y system. Auxiliary axis systems are usually Y-Z axis sys-

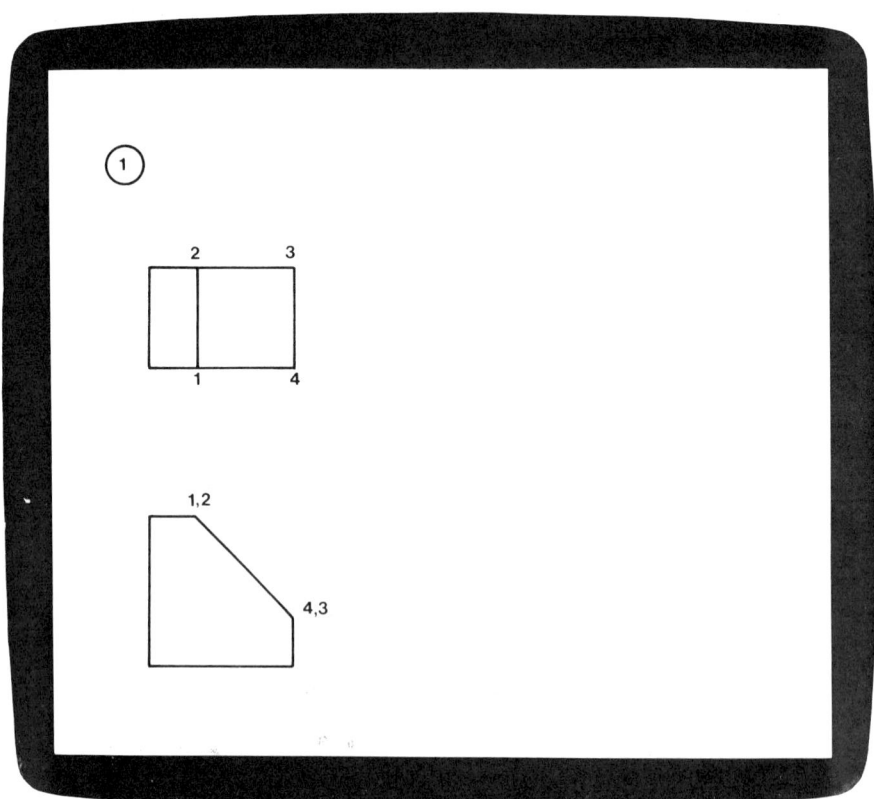

Sec. 8-3 Primary Auxiliary Views   219

FIGURE 8-9 (*cont.*)

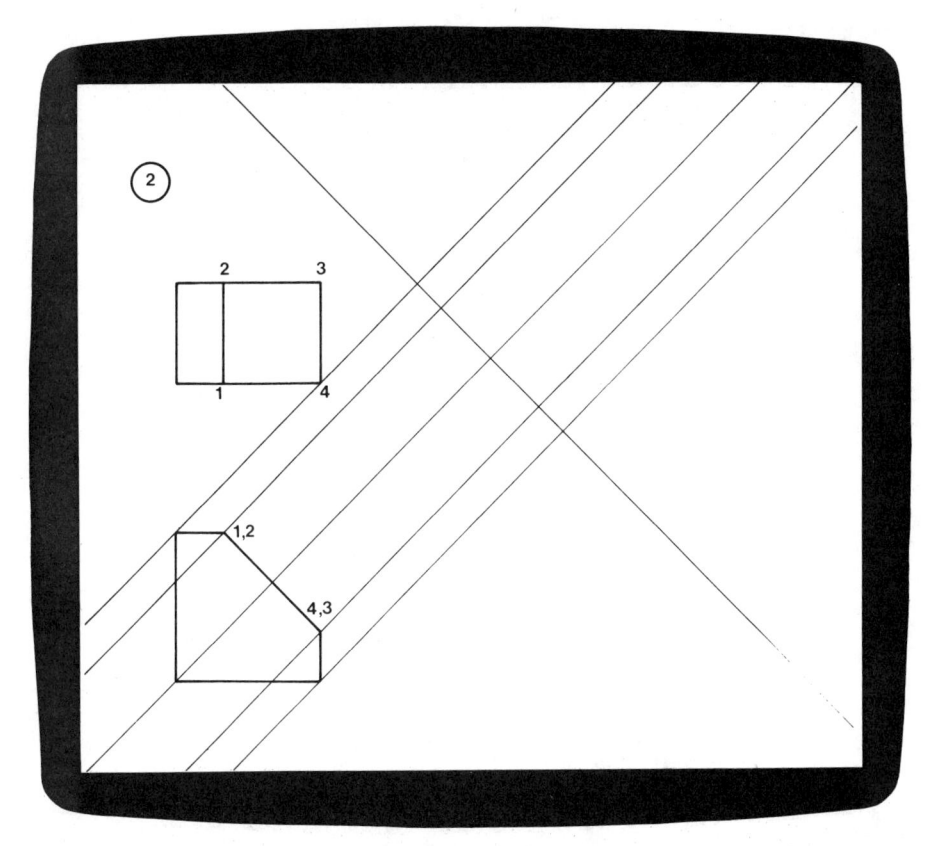

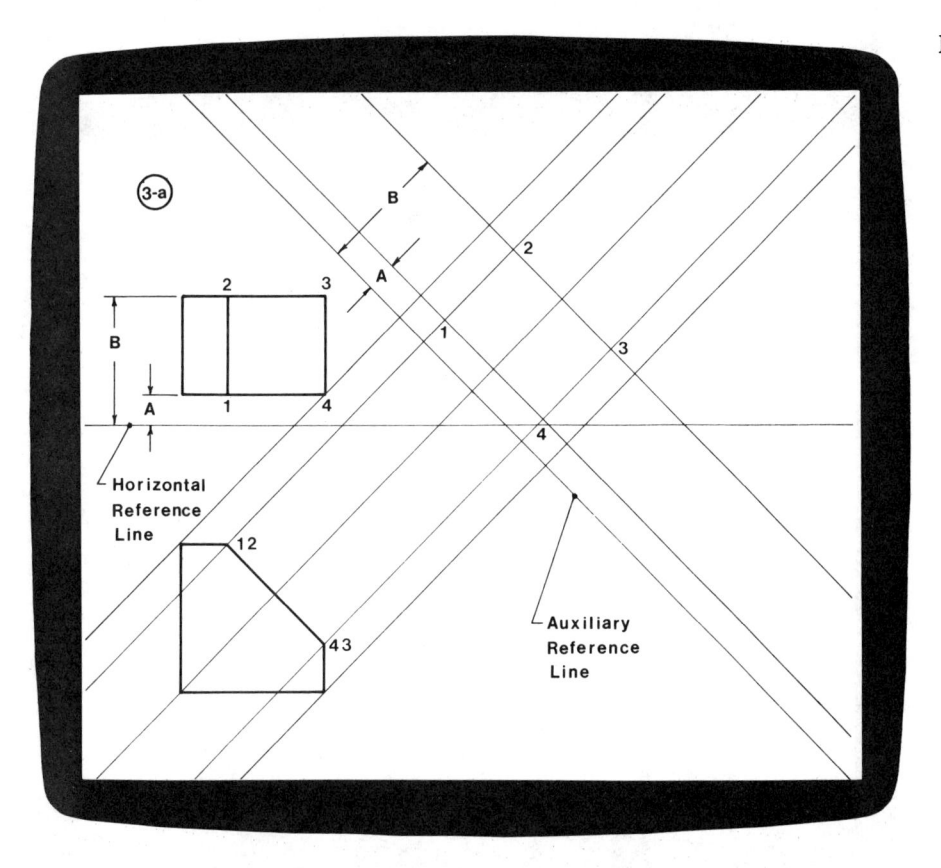

FIGURE 8-9 (*cont.*)

220　　　　　　　　　　　　　　　　　　　　　　　　　　Auxiliary Views　　Chap. 8

FIGURE 8-9 (*cont.*)

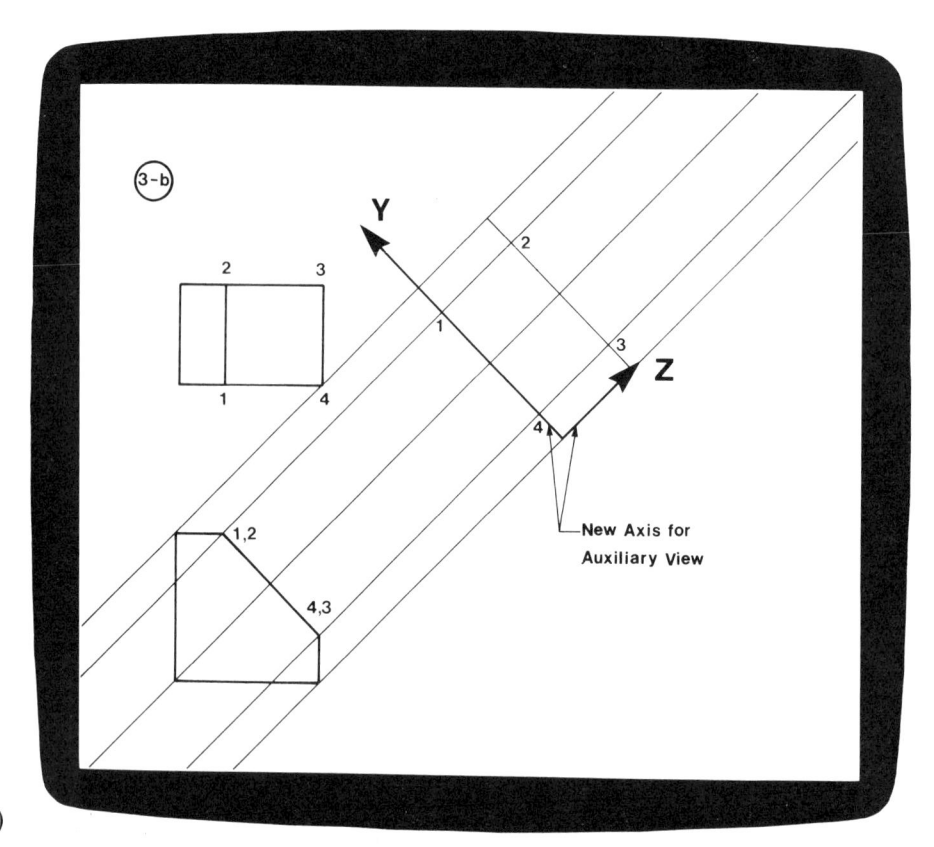

FIGURE 8-9 (*cont.*)

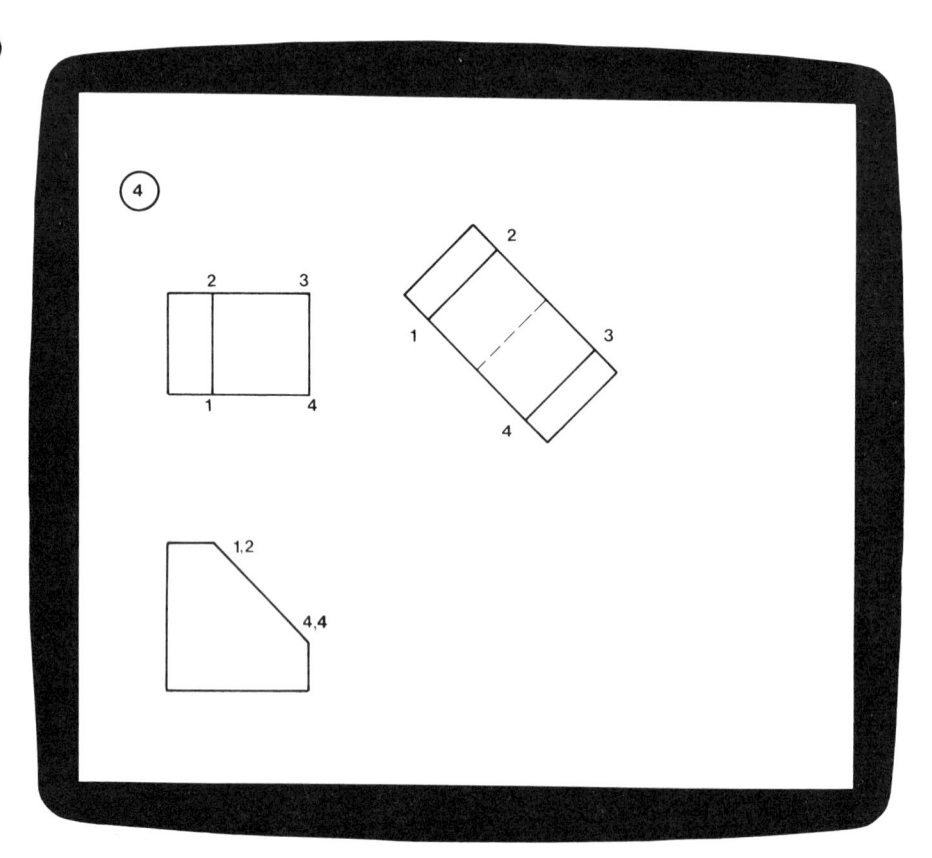

Sec. 8-3 Primary Auxiliary Views   221

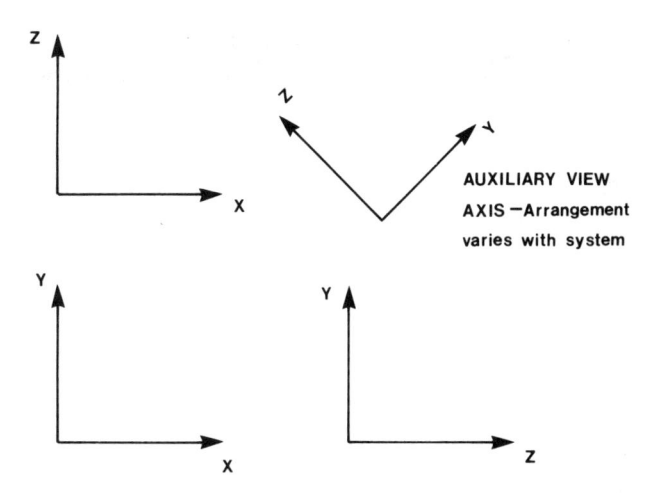

FIGURE 8-10 Auxiliary view reference system.

tems (Figure 8-10), meaning that an input of 1.5, 2 would indicate a Y value of 1.5 and a Z value of 2.

In step 4, the lines are trimmed and put in at their correct thickness and pattern.

A top or front view cannot simply be rotated into an auxiliary plane. The resultant view will be the same top or front view rotated and moved, but will not include the stretching and foreshortening necessary for a correct auxiliary view. Figure 8-11 shows a side view rotated and moved to the auxiliary view position and a true auxiliary view. Note the differences between the two views.

Auxiliary views can be created by rotating pictorial views assuming that the computer system has three-dimensional (3D) modeling capabilities. The object is rotated as a whole until the slanted surface is directly

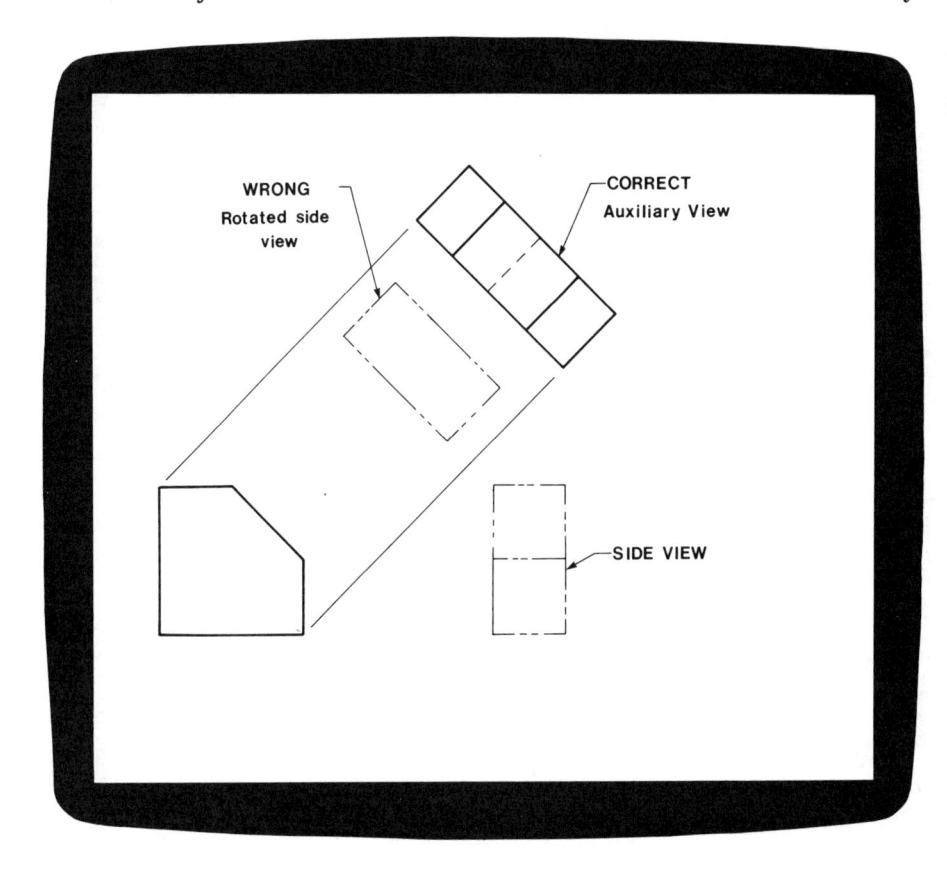

FIGURE 8-11 Auxiliary views are created by projection, not by rotating one of the other views.

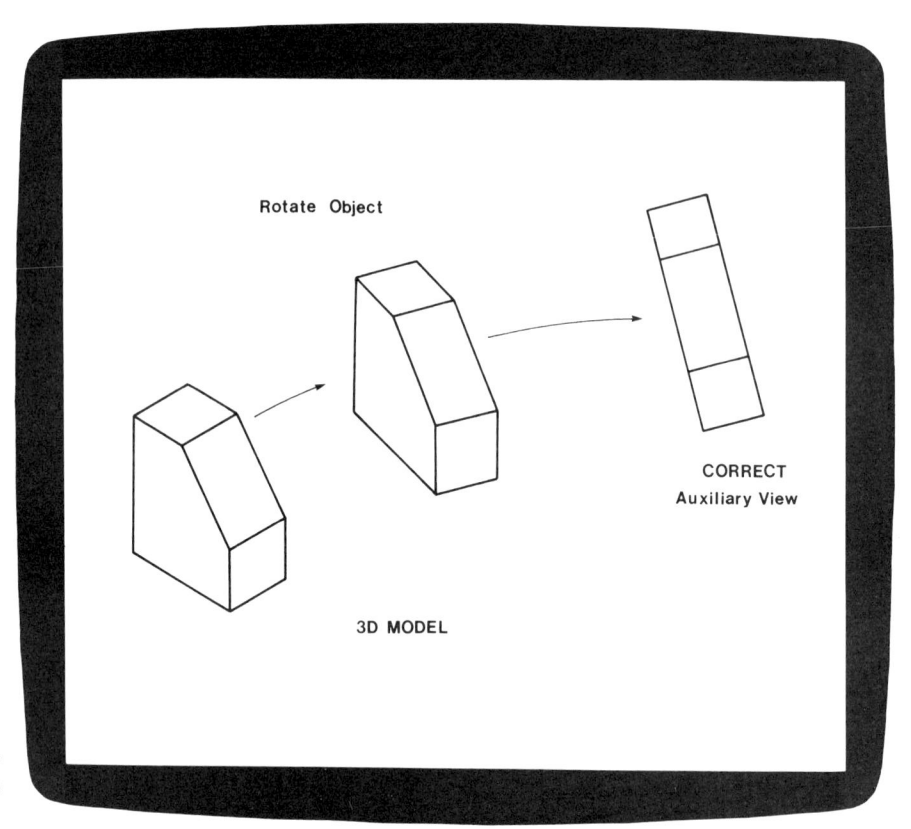

FIGURE 8-12 Three-dimensional models can be rotated to create auxiliary views.

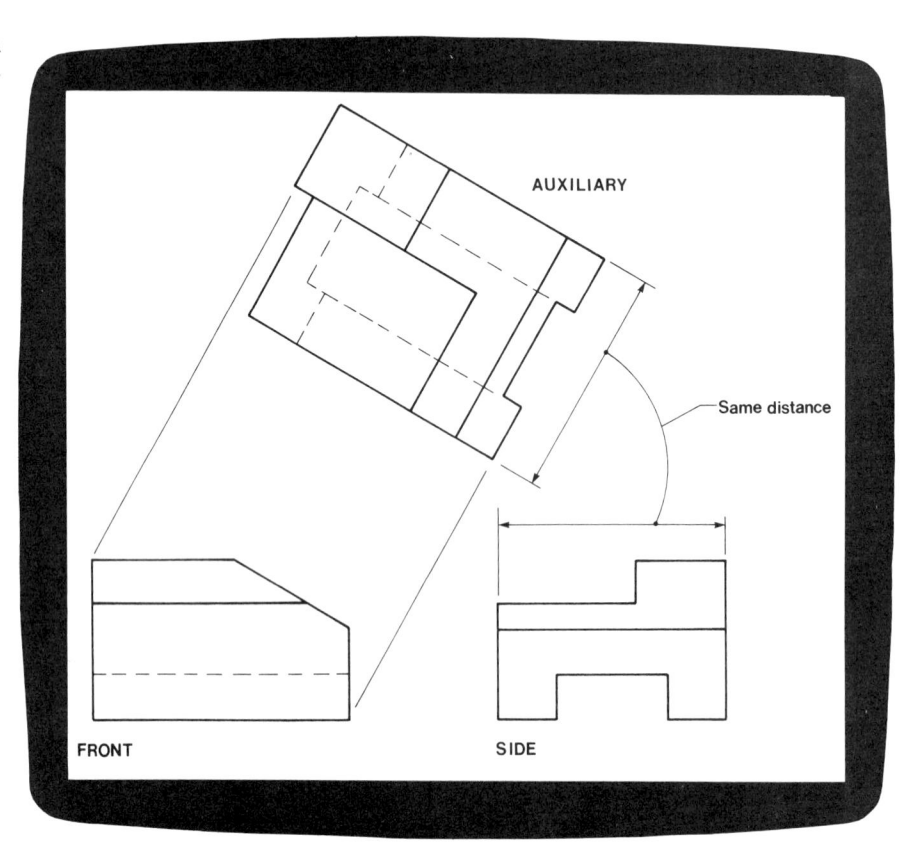

FIGURE 8-13 Example of a drawing that includes an auxiliary view.

Sec. 8-4 Partial Auxiliary Views 223

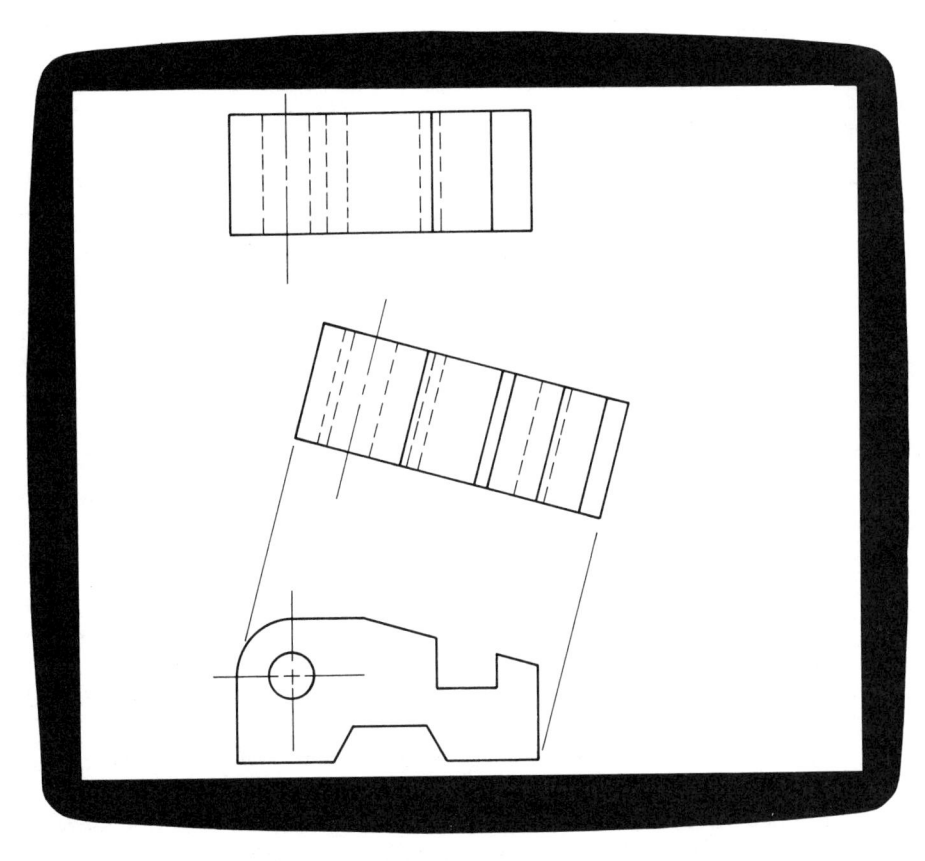

FIGURE 8-14 Example of a drawing that includes an auxiliary view.

parallel to the screen as shown in Figure 8-12. Rotating the three-dimensional picture of the object is like moving the viewing position to align directly over the slanted surface. The result will be a view taken at 90° to the surface, which is a correct auxiliary view. Figures 8-13 and 8-14 are examples of drawings that include auxiliary views.

8-4 PARTIAL AUXILIARY VIEWS

Partial auxiliary views are auxiliary views that show only part of an auxiliary view. For example, in Figure 8-15 an object is presented using a front and a bottom view as well as two partial auxiliary views. The two

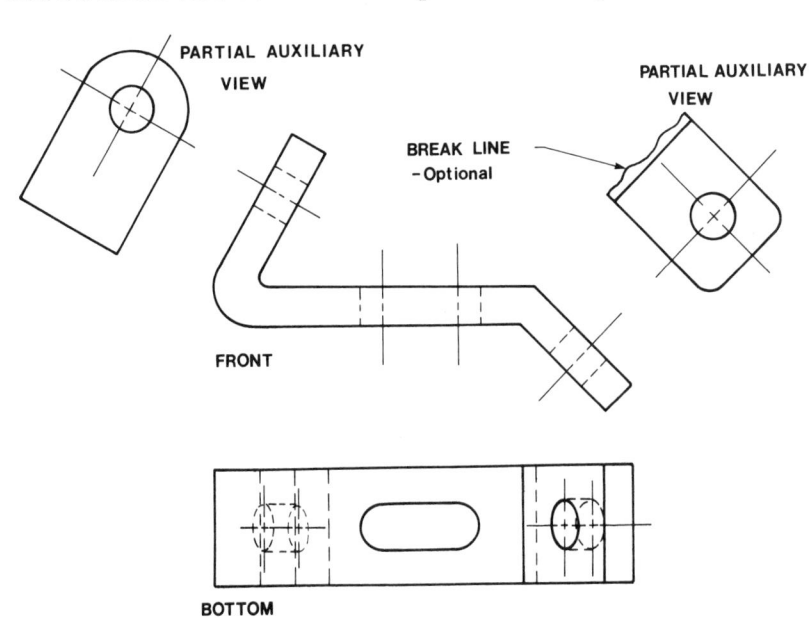

FIGURE 8-15 Examples of partial auxiliary views.

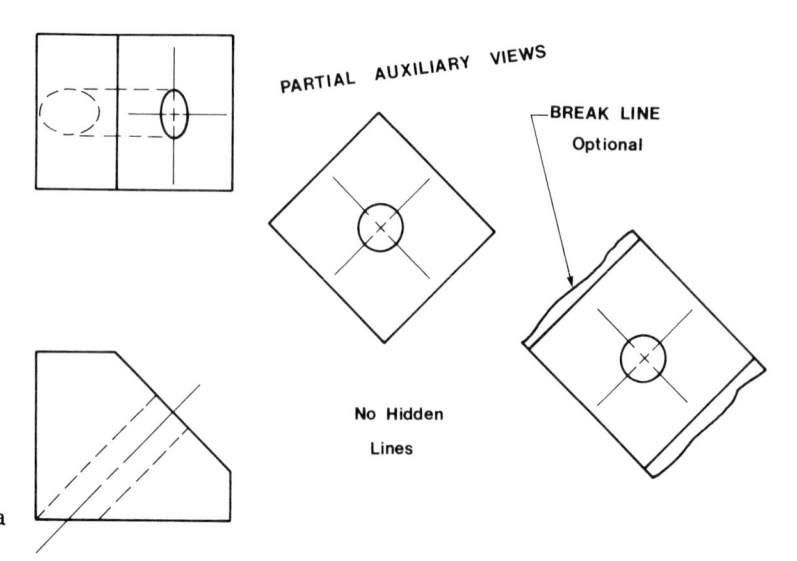

FIGURE 8-16 Example of a partial auxiliary view.

partial auxiliary views contain only one surface each. This combination of views serves to give a complete, true view of each of the slanted surfaces but avoids drawing the remainder of the object in a complete auxiliary view. Complete auxiliary views would show surfaces foreshortened and would not help overall to clarify the drawing.

Figure 8-16 shows another example of a partial auxiliary view. The view shows the true shape of the slanted surface. The hole in the surface appears as a circle. Partial auxiliary views may include only one surface or one surface plus a little of the surrounding surfaces, ending with break lines as shown. Hidden lines are omitted on partial auxiliary views.

8-5 AUXILIARY VIEWS OF ROUNDED SHAPES

Auxiliary views of rounded surfaces are sometimes confusing to draw because they contain no edges or corners for projection. Rounded surfaces can be projected by adding imaginary points and then projecting the points. The procedure is as follows.

1. Draw the necessary orthographic views. In the example shown in Figure 8-17, the front and side views are used to create the auxiliary view.

FIGURE 8-17 How to draw an auxiliary view of a rounded surface.

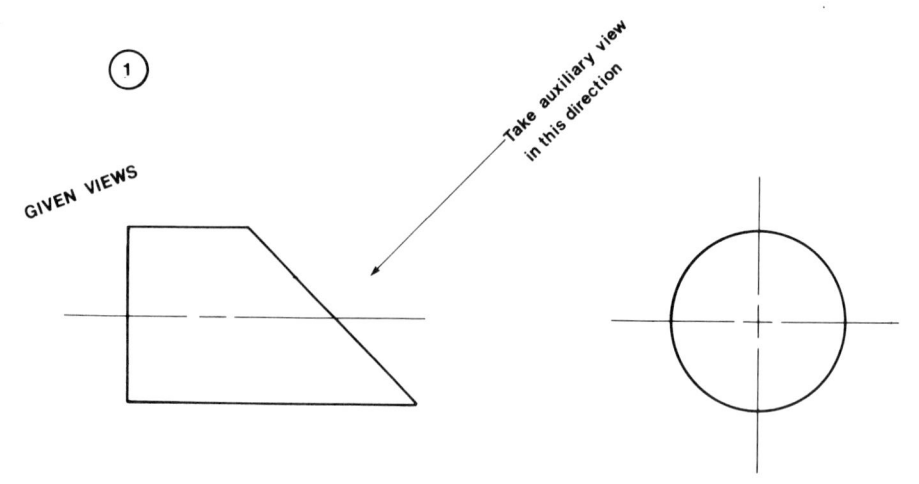

Sec. 8-5   Auxiliary Views of Rounded Shapes 225

2. Define the line of sight perpendicular to the slanted surface. Also define the vertical principal plane line and the auxiliary view reference plane.
3. Add points on the side view. In the example presented, 12 points were added 30° apart. Any number of points at any location on the periphery of the circle can be added. The more points added the more accurate the projected auxiliary view.

FIGURE 8-17 (cont.)

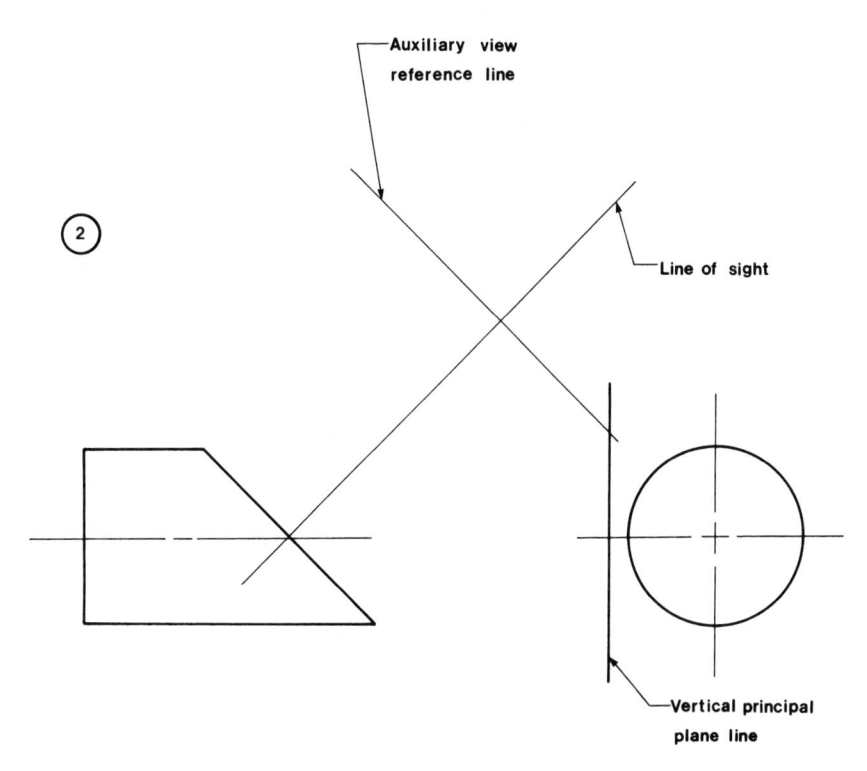

FIGURE 8-17 (cont.)

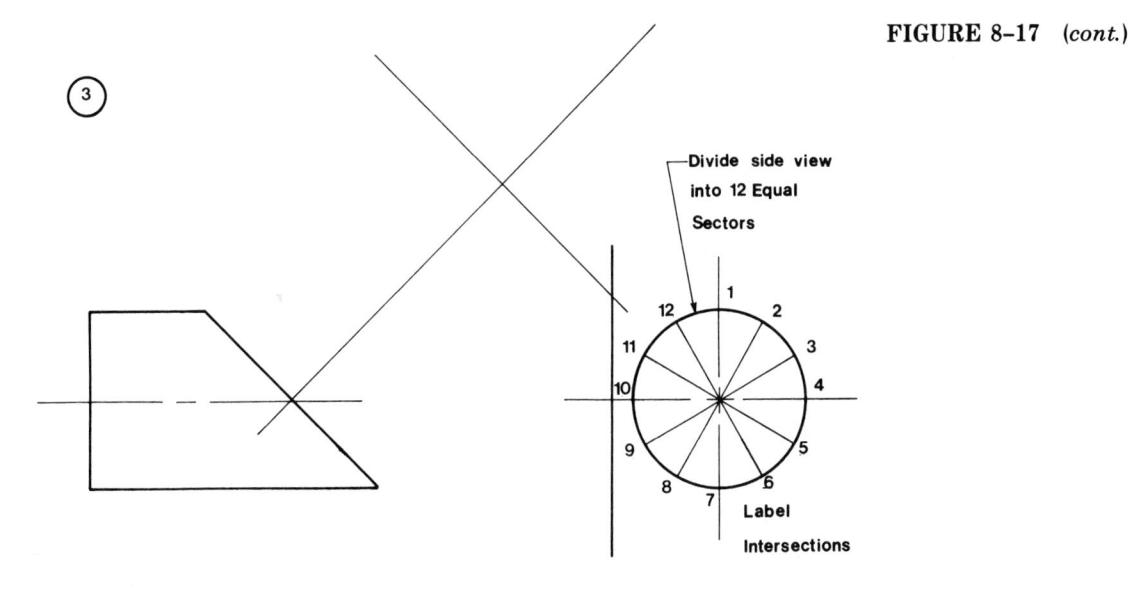

4. Project the points added in step 3 to the side view into the front view.

5. Project the points from the front view into the auxiliary view. This is done by drawing lines parallel to the line of sight through the intersections of the projection lines of step 4 with the front view of the slanted surface.

6. Define the width of the auxiliary view. This can be done using different techniques depending on the capabilities of the computer system. Step 6a uses the dimensioning function to define distances from the horizontal principal plane line. These distances are then transferred to the auxiliary view. Step 6b creates a new axis system Y-Z and then defines the width value

FIGURE 8-17 (*cont.*)

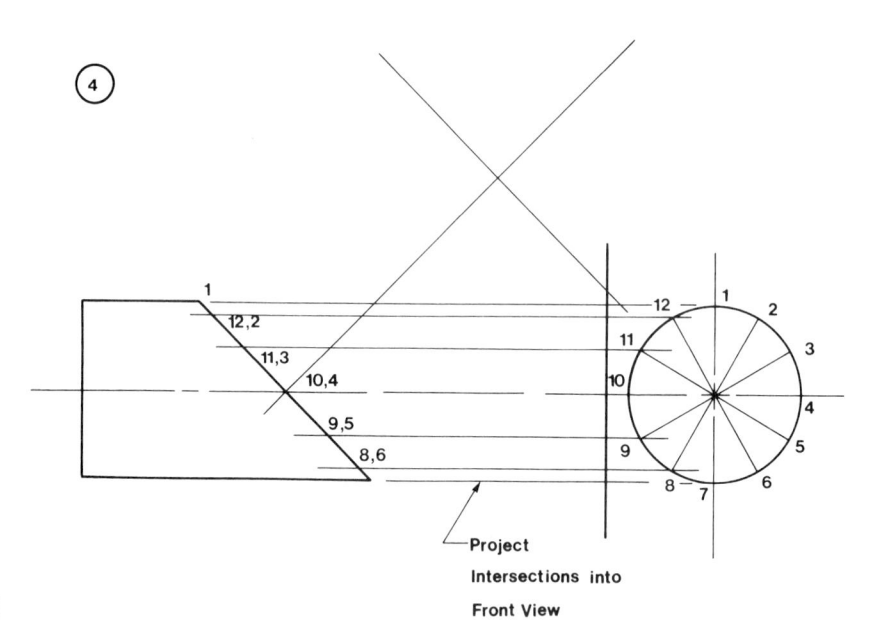

FIGURE 8-17 (*cont.*)

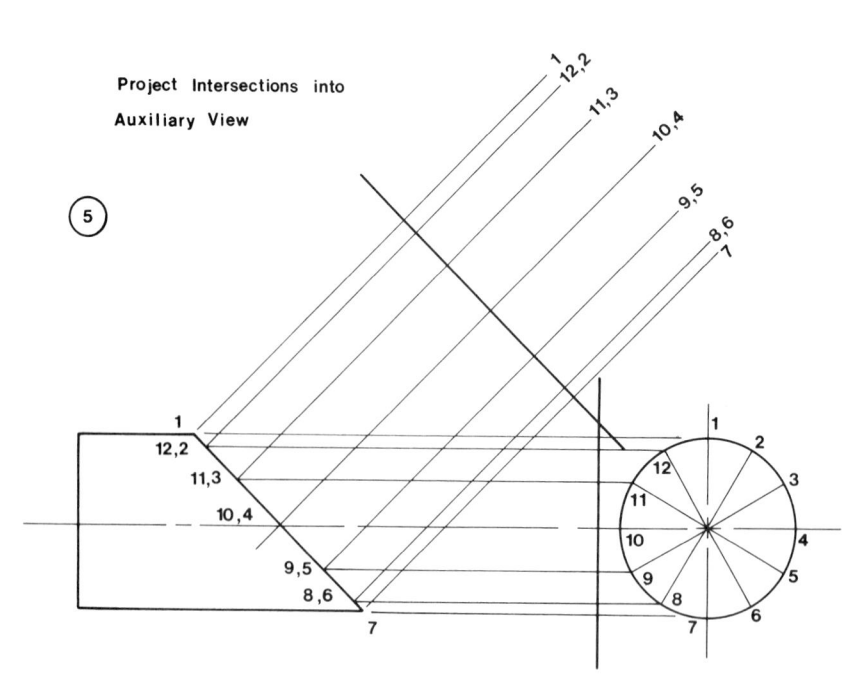

Sec. 8-5 Auxiliary Views of Rounded Shapes 227

relative to this new axis using coordinate values. Note that in step 6b the auxiliary view reference plane is drawn through the center of the surface (aligns with the centerline). Similarly, the horizontal principal plane line is drawn through the center of the top view. The distances are measured in the top view and transferred to the auxiliary view.

6a) Transfer Distances From Side View To Auxiliary View

6b) Transfer Distances Using the Centerline as Reference

FIGURE 8-17 (cont.)

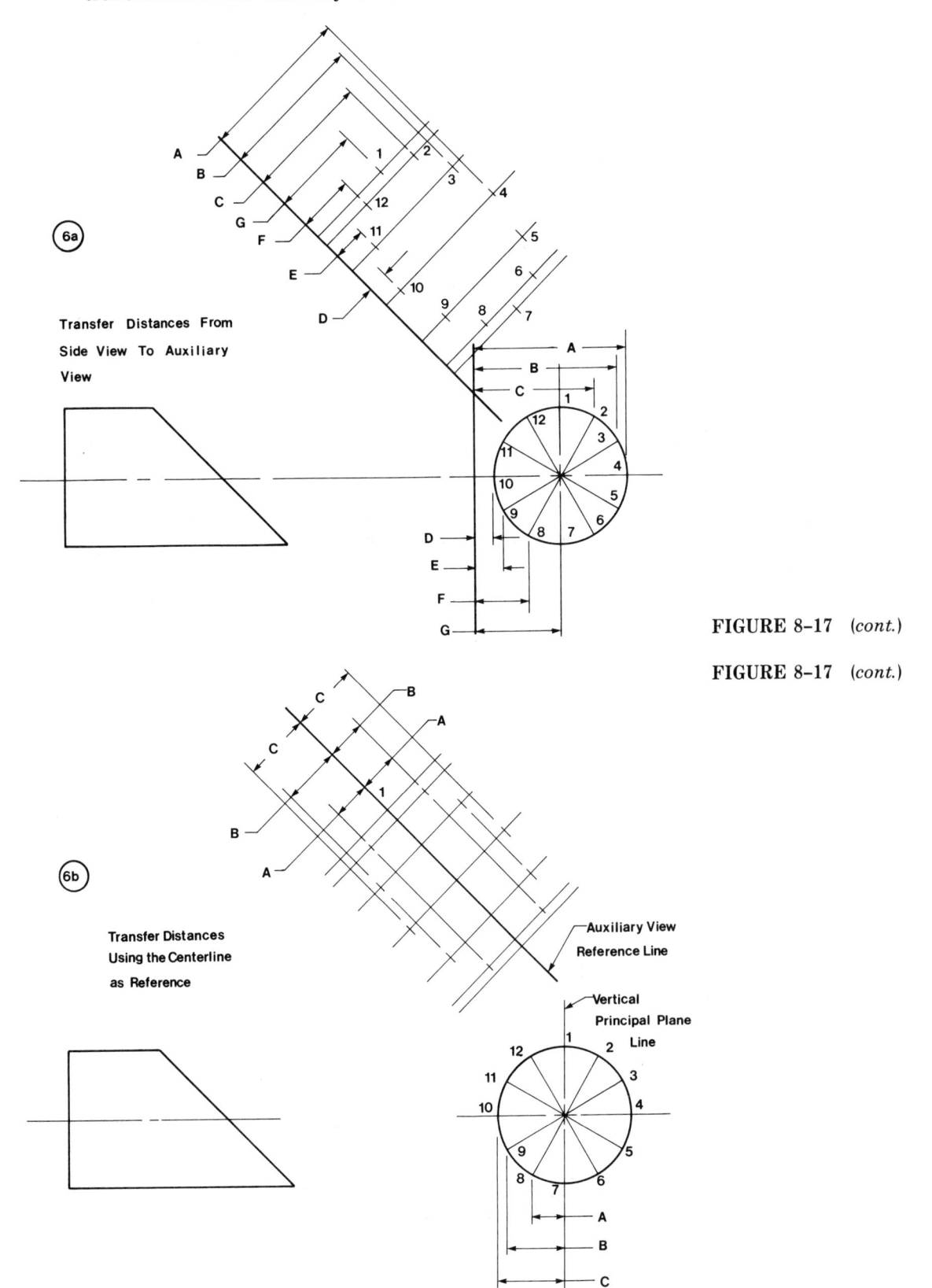

FIGURE 8-17 (cont.)

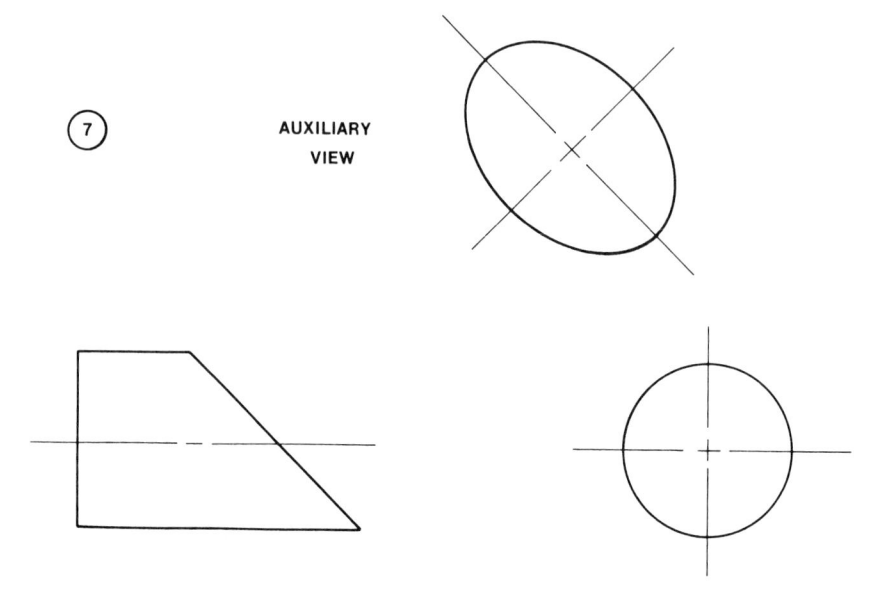

FIGURE 8-17 (cont.)

7. All lines are trimmed or erased as needed and all lines are drawn at their correct pattern.

Figure 8-18 shows an auxiliary view of a rounded surface derived from a front and a top view. The auxiliary view was derived using the procedure outline for Figure 8-17.

Figure 8-19 shows a comparison between a complete and partial auxiliary view of a rounded surface. Note that both examples — the external edge and the internal hole — are elliptical. In this example, the partial auxiliary view would be preferred, as the complete view presents all surfaces other than the slanted surface as foreshortened.

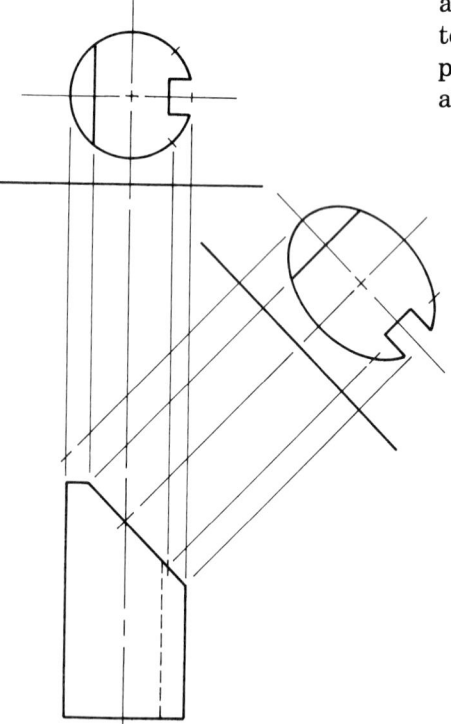

FIGURE 8-18 Auxiliary view projected from the top and front views.

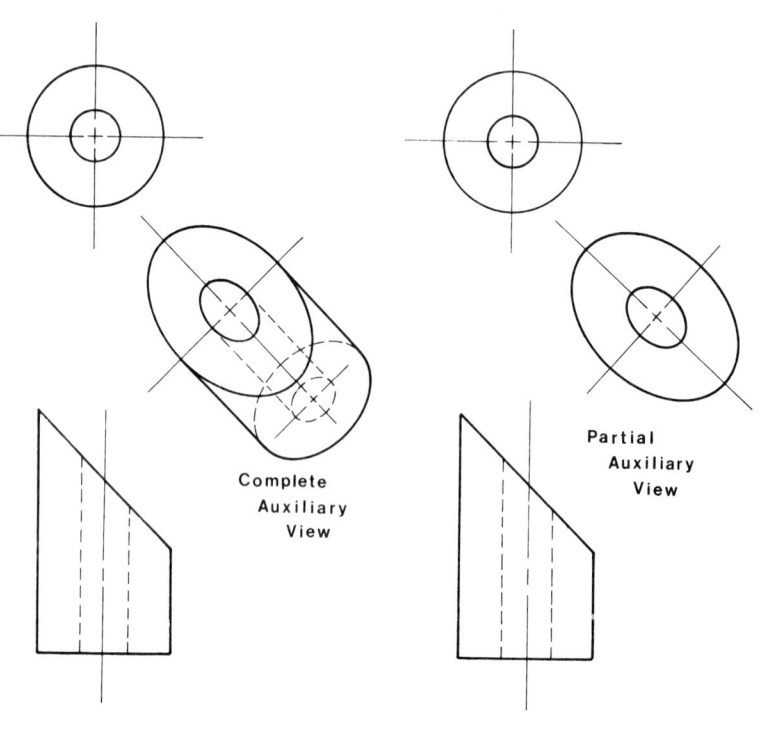

FIGURE 8-19 Comparison of complete and partial auxiliary views of a rounded surface.

8-6 AUXILIARY VIEW OF AN OBLIQUE SURFACE

The true shape of an oblique surface cannot be determined using a single auxiliary view; two auxiliary views are required. A secondary auxiliary view is taken at 90° to a primary view, which in turn is taken at 90° to an oblique surface.

Figure 8-20 shows three views of an object that contains an oblique surface 1-2-3-4. Figure 8-21 shows the procedure used to project the true shape of an oblique surface. The procedure is as follows.

1. Draw the front and top views plus the principal plane lines. Any two views can be used.
2. Establish the first auxiliary-view reference plane. This is done by finding an edge line of surface 1-2-3-4 that is parallel to one of the principal plane lines. In this example lines 2-3 and 1-4 in the top view are parallel to the horizontal principal plane line, so lines 2-3 and 1-4 in the front view are used to determine the line of sight for the first auxiliary view. The first auxiliary-view reference plane line is drawn perpendicular to the lines of sight as shown. The reference plane can be located anywhere along the line of sight.

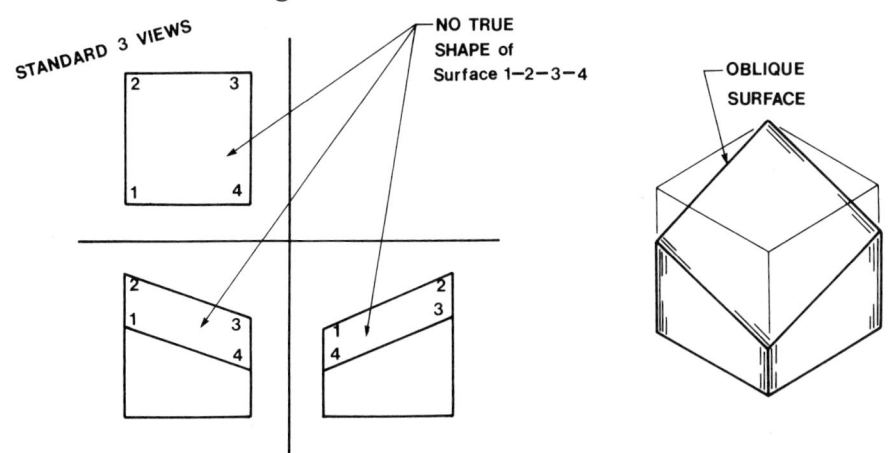

FIGURE 8-20 Object that contains an oblique surface.

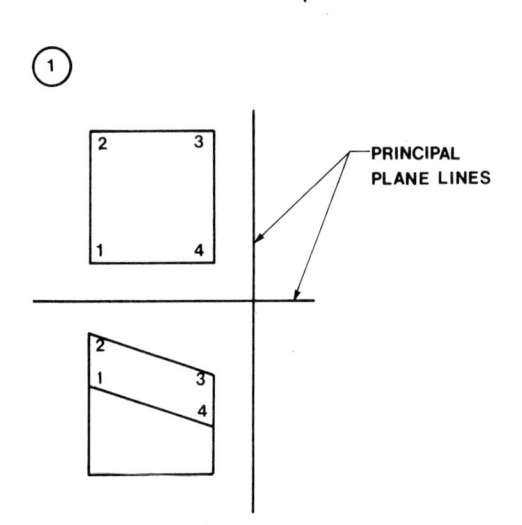

FIGURE 8-21 How to draw a secondary auxiliary view.

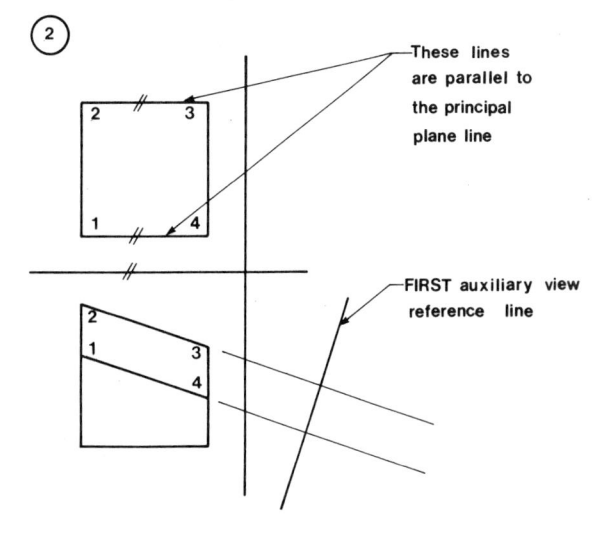

FIGURE 8-21 (cont.)

3. Draw the first auxiliary view of surface 1-2-3-4. The location of the first auxiliary view is found by measuring the distances between the horizontal view and points in the top view and then transferring these distances to the auxiliary view. The distances are laid out from the first auxiliary reference plane line and labeled as shown. The first auxiliary view of 1-2-3-4 shows an end view of 1-2-3-4 (a straight line).

4. Establish the second auxiliary-view reference plane line. This is done by drawing lines of sight perpendicular to the first auxiliary of surface 1-2-3-4. The second auxiliary-view reference plane line is then drawn perpendicular to these lines of sight parallel to the first auxiliary view.

5. Draw the second auxiliary view of surface 1-2-3-4. This is done by measuring the distances between the first auxiliary-view reference line to points on the surface in the front view and then

FIGURE 8-21 (cont.)

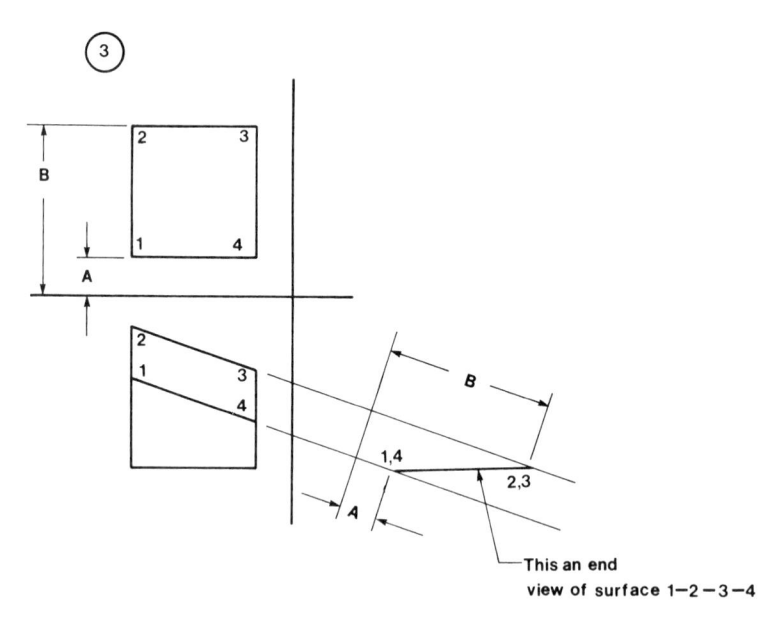

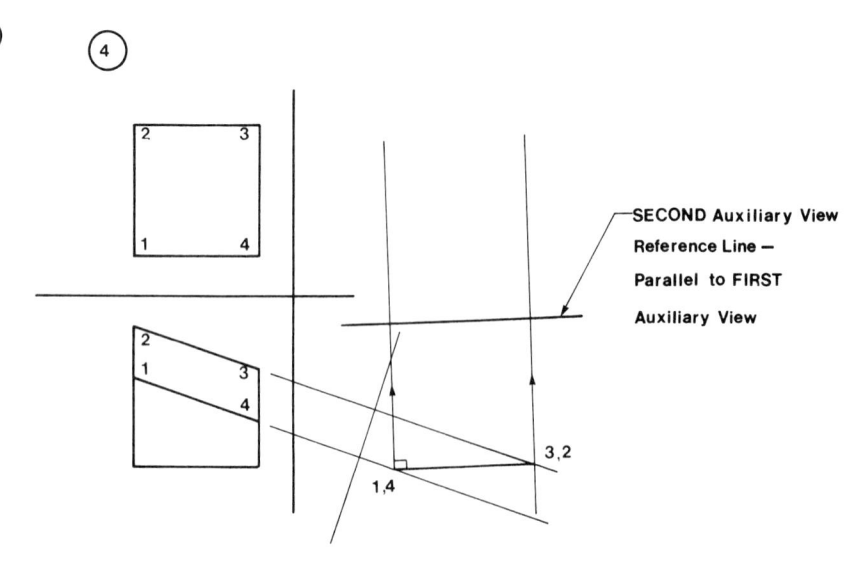

FIGURE 8-21 (cont.)

Sec. 8-6 Auxiliary View of an Oblique Surface   231

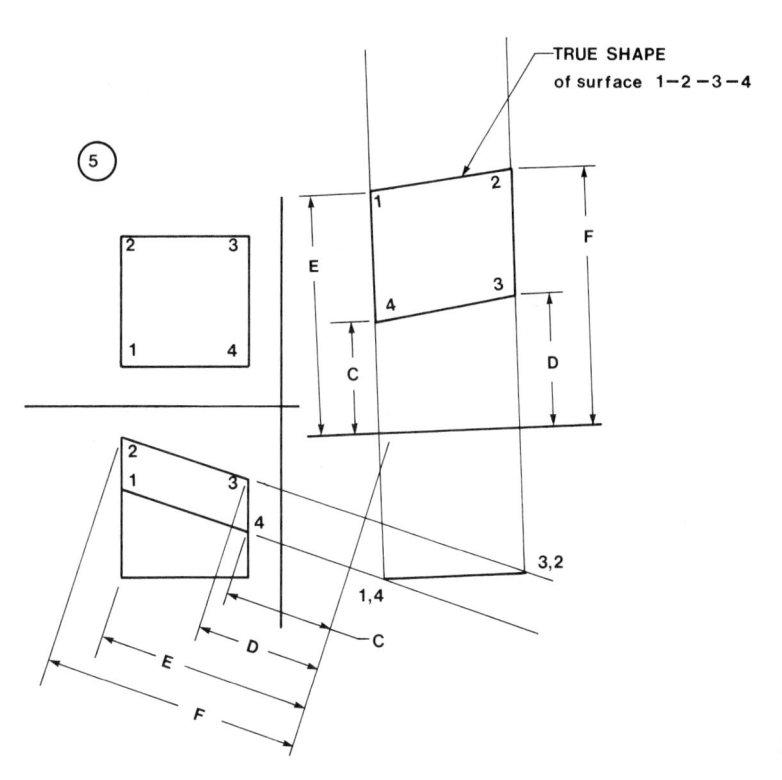

FIGURE 8-21 (*cont.*)

transferring these distances to the second auxiliary view. The distances are laid out from the second auxiliary-view reference plane line and labeled as shown. This secondary auxiliary view is the true shape of surface 1-2-3-4.

The procedure presented for surface 1-2-3-4 can be applied to the entire object (Figure 8-22).

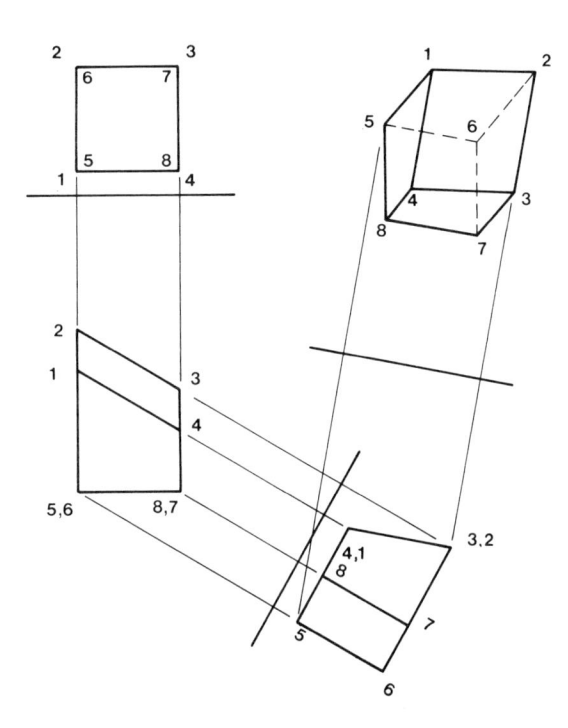

FIGURE 8-22 Secondary auxiliary view of the complete object presented in Figure 8-20.

Figure 8-23 shows a secondary auxiliary view of an oblique surface derived from a front and a side view. The procedure is similar to that presented for Figure 8-21. The procedure is as follows.

1. Draw the front and side views plus the principal plane lines.
2. Establish an edge view of the oblique surface. The lines of sight for the first auxiliary view are extensions of lines 1-2 and 4-3 because these lines are parallel to the vertical principal plane lines in the front view. The first auxiliary view location is found by measuring the distances from the vertical principal plane lines and points in the front view and transferring them to the first auxiliary view. The distances are laid out relative to the first auxiliary-view reference plane line. The first auxiliary view of plane 1-2-3-4 is an end view of the plane (a straight line).
3. Draw the second auxiliary view. Use the edge view to establish the lines of sight and measure the locating distances from the first auxiliary-view reference plane line to the side view. The distances are transferred and laid out relative to the second auxiliary view.

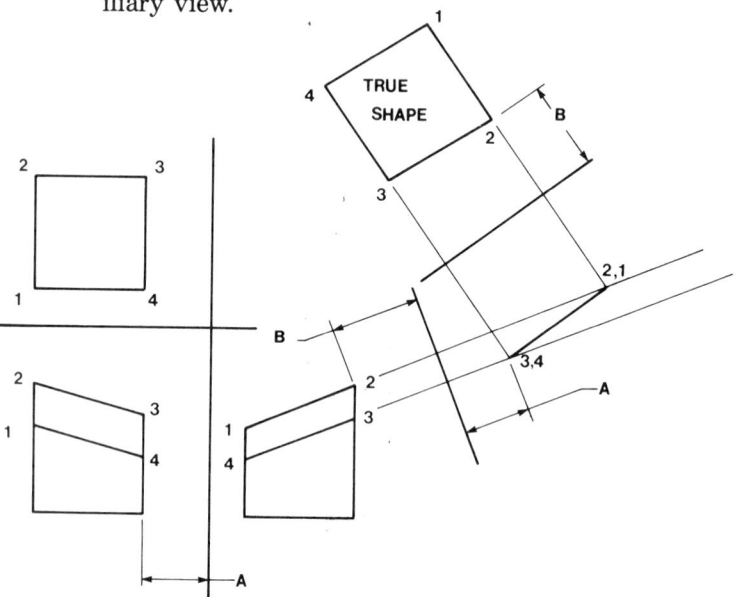

FIGURE 8-23 Example of an auxiliary view projected from a side view.

Figure 8-24 shows a plane that has no edge line parallel to either principal plane line. The true shape of the plane is found using the following procedure. Figure 8-24 illustrates the procedure.

1. Draw the front and top views plus the principal plane lines.
2. Draw a horizontal line from point 1 across the surface as shown. Label the intersection of the horizontal line and the edge of the plane x.

    This step amounts to defining a horizontal line within the plane whose front-view projection is of true length and can be used for line-of-sight direction for the first auxiliary view. This line of sight will ensure that the first auxiliary view will be an end view of the plane. A plane contains an infinite number of lines, so any line within the plane can be defined.
3. Project line 1-x into the front view. The location of point 1 is now in the front view. Point x is found by projecting a vertical line from point x, located on line 2-3, in the top view to the front

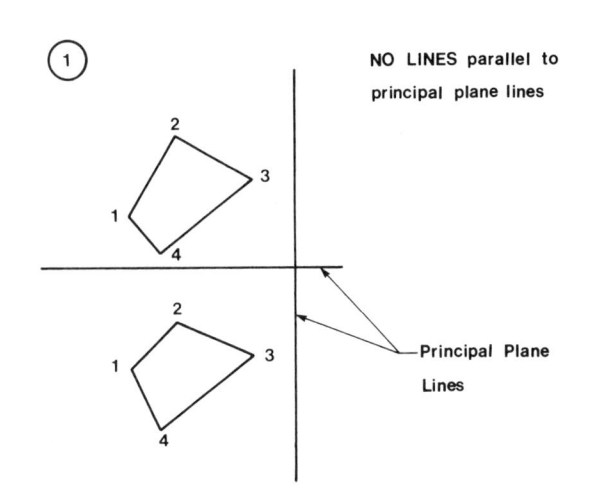

FIGURE 8-24 How to draw a secondary auxiliary view when there are no edge lines parallel to the principal plane lines.

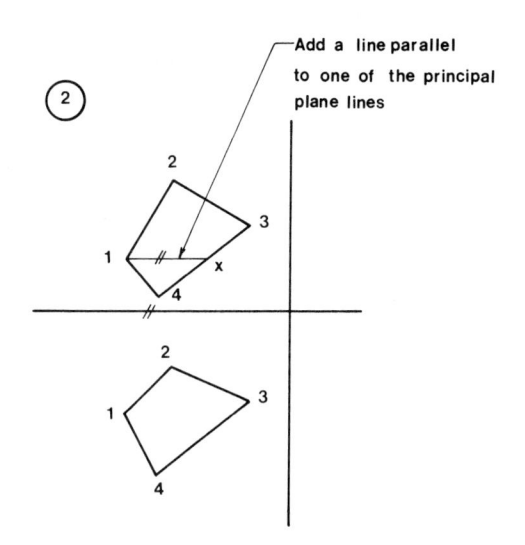

FIGURE 8-24 (cont.)

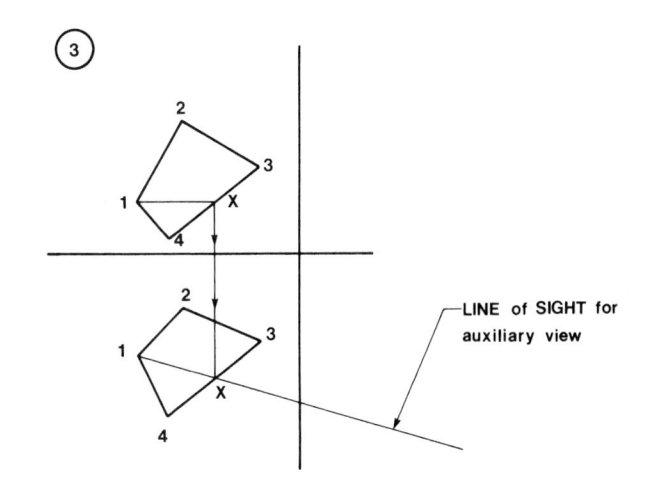

FIGURE 8-24 (cont.)

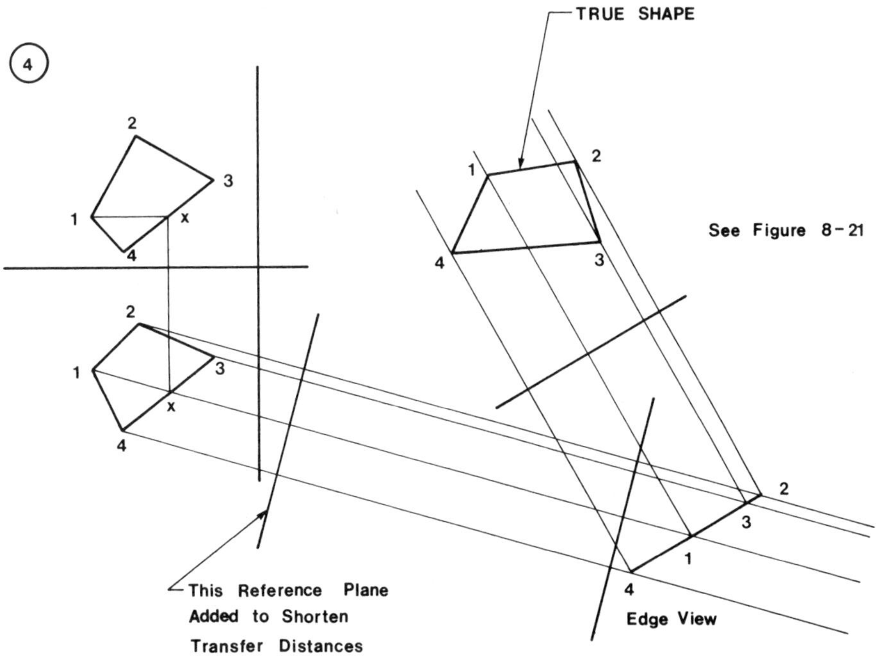

FIGURE 8-24 (cont.)

view of line 2-3. The intersection of the vertical projection line with line 2-3 in the front view locates point x in the front view.

4. Line 1-x in the front view is used as a line of sight for the auxiliary view. The procedure now follows that presented for the surface in Figure 8-21.

Secondary auxiliary views can be drawn using any two views, and neither of the views need have an edge line parallel to one of the principal plane lines. Figure 8-25 shows the procedure for a given front and top view, Figure 8-26 uses a front and top view but draws the line of sight from the top view, and Figure 8-27 uses a front and side view and draws the line of sight from the side view. If a top and a side view are given, it is best first to add the front view and then proceed with developing a line of sight.

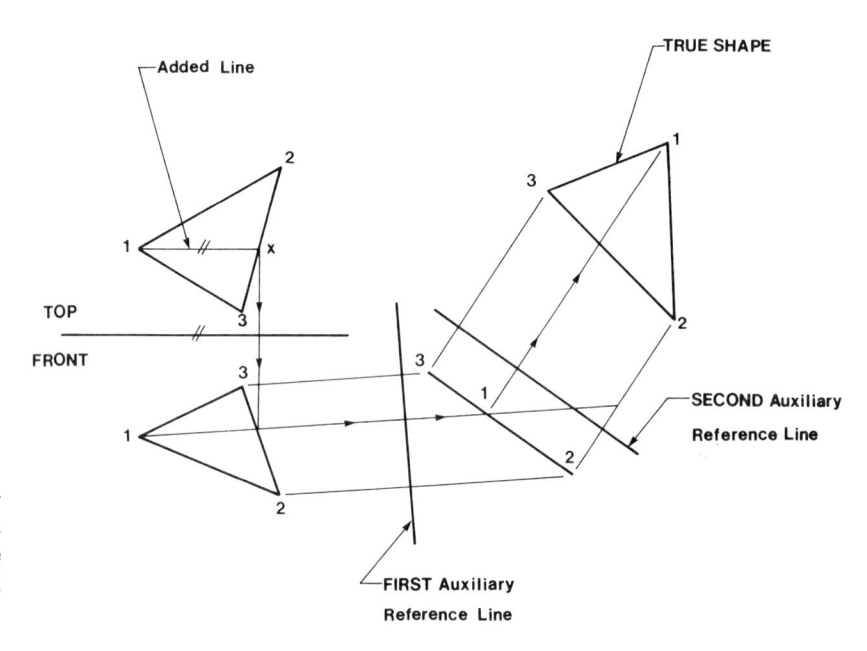

FIGURE 8-25 Secondary auxiliary view drawn from a given front and top view with no edge lines parallel to either principal plane line.

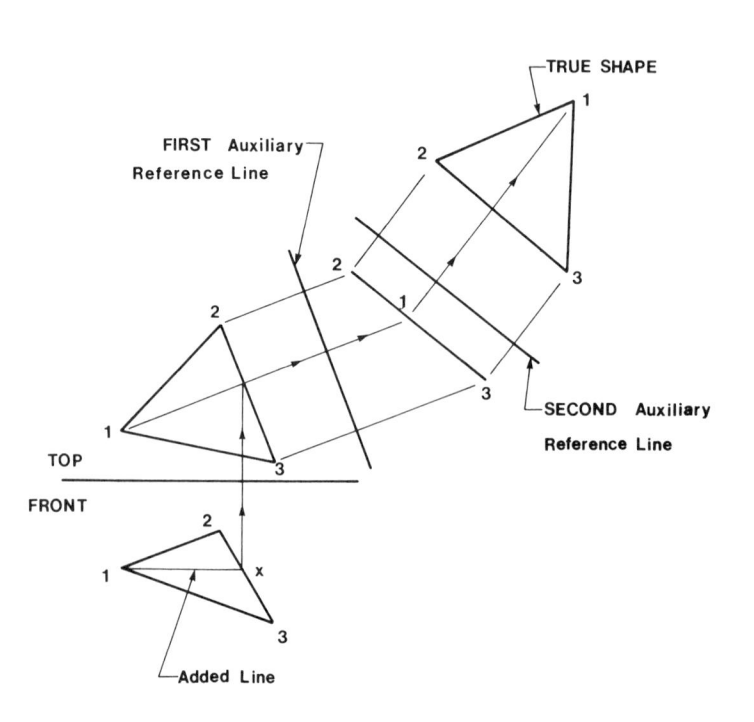

FIGURE 8-26 Secondary auxiliary view drawn from a given front and top view with no edge lines parallel to either principal plane line.

Sec. 8-6   Auxiliary View of an Oblique Surface   235

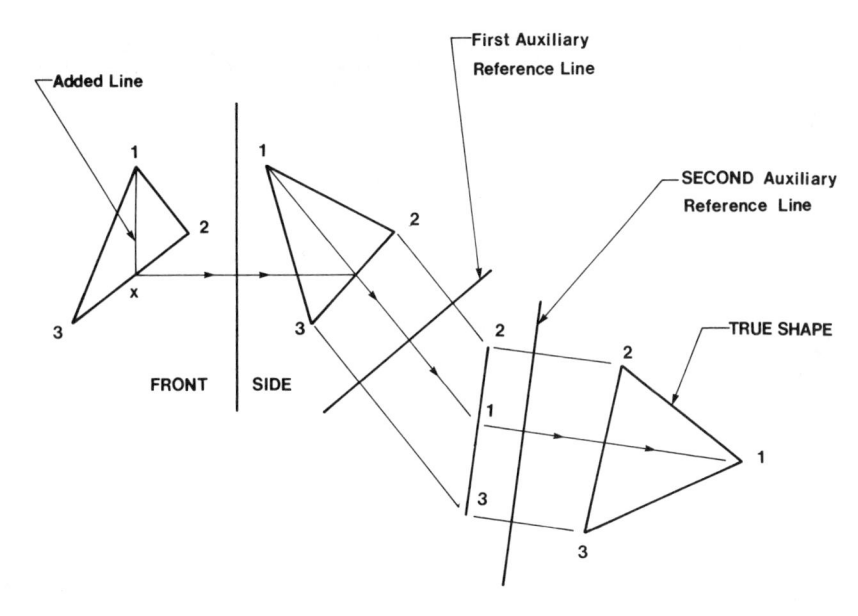

FIGURE 8-27 Secondary auxiliary view drawn from a given front and side view with no lines parallel to either principal plane line.

The procedure described for taking a secondary auxiliary view in Figure 8-21 can be applied using computer graphics systems. Figure 8-28 illustrates the procedure; the application is as follows.

1. Draw the front and top views plus a horizontal principal plane line as shown. Any two views can be used.

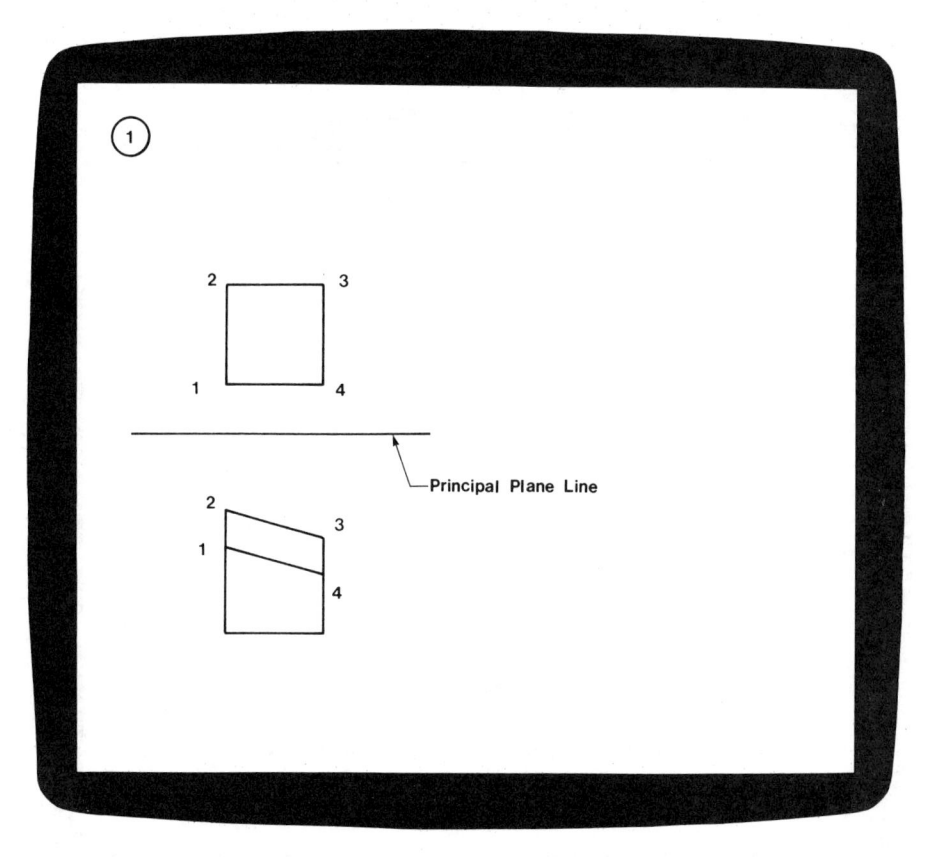

FIGURE 8-28 How to draw a secondary auxiliary view using a computer graphics system.

FIGURE 8-28 (cont.)

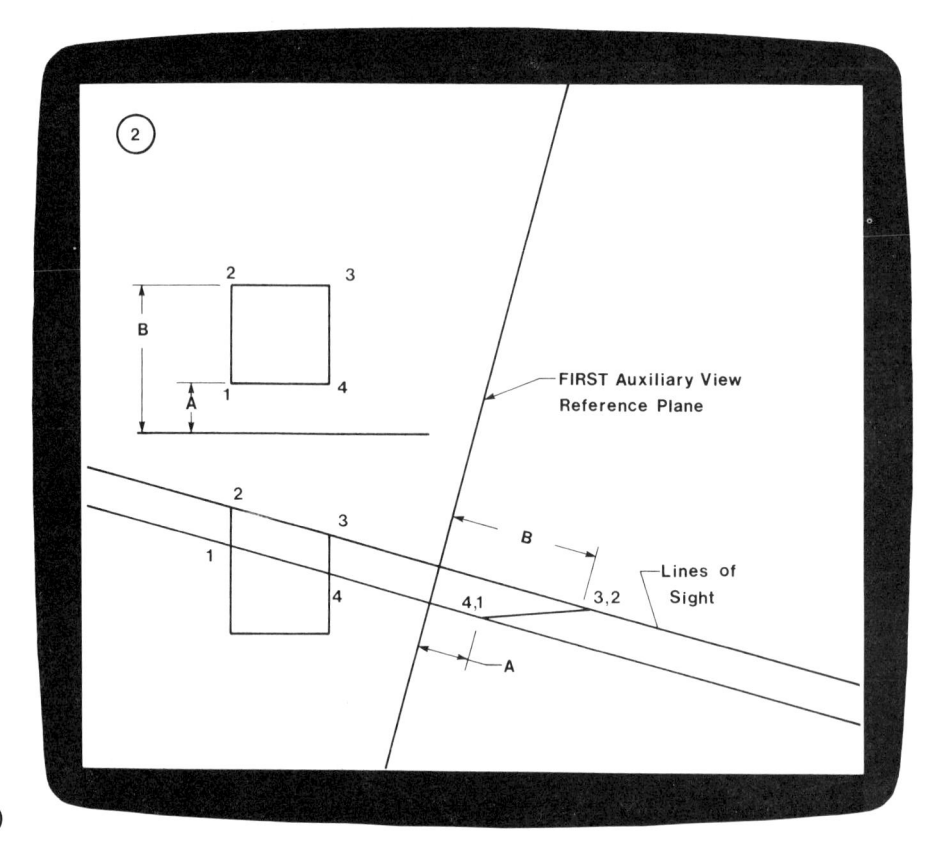

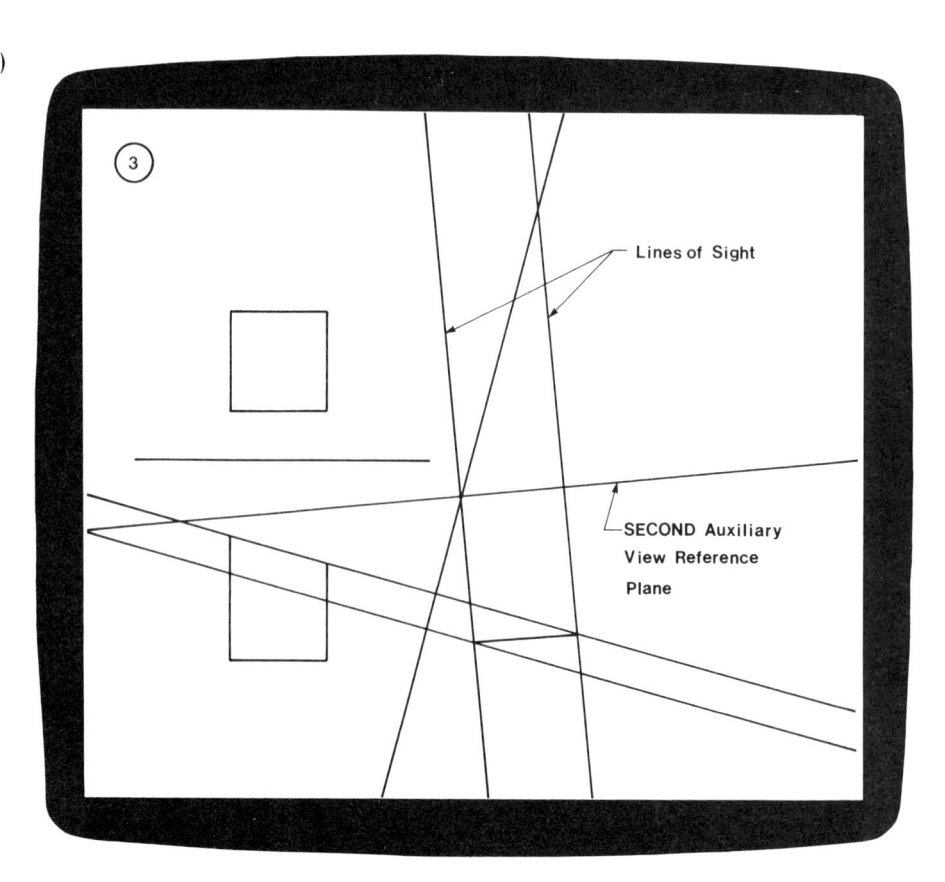

FIGURE 8-28 (cont.)

Chap. 8   Problems

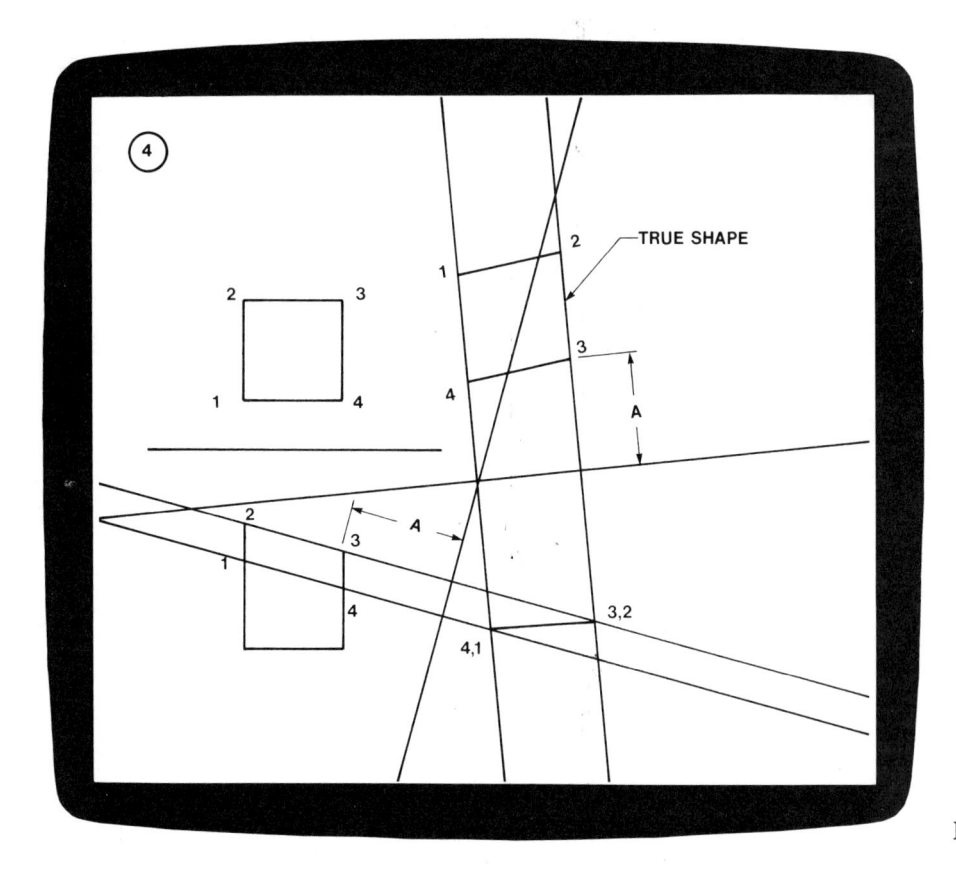

FIGURE 8-28 (cont.)

2. Project lines of sight from the front view. Lines 2-3 and 1-4 were chosen because their top views are parallel to the horizontal principal plane line. Establish the first auxiliary-view reference plane line. Transfer the distances from point 1-2-3-4 in the top view relative to the horizontal principal plane line to the auxiliary view. The resulting auxiliary view should be a straight line which is an end view of plane 1-2-3-4.

3. Project lines of sight perpendicular from the edge view of plane 1-2-3-4. Establish a second auxiliary view reference plane perpendicular to the lines of sight.

4. Transfer the distances from the points in the front view relative to the first auxiliary view reference line as shown. Trim all excess lines.

PROBLEMS

For Problems P8-1 through P8-6, draw two views (front, top, or side) of the objects shown in Figures P8-1 through P8-6. Also draw an auxiliary view of the slanted surface. The dimensional units are as noted below.

P8-1	Inches	P8-4	Millimeters
P8-2	Inches	P8-5	Millimeters
P8-3	Inches	P8-6	Millimeters

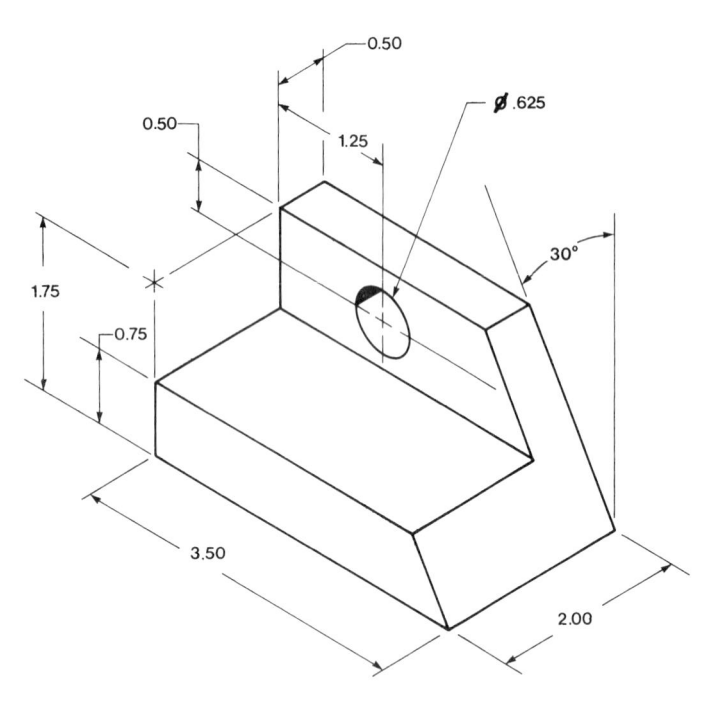

FIGURE P8-1

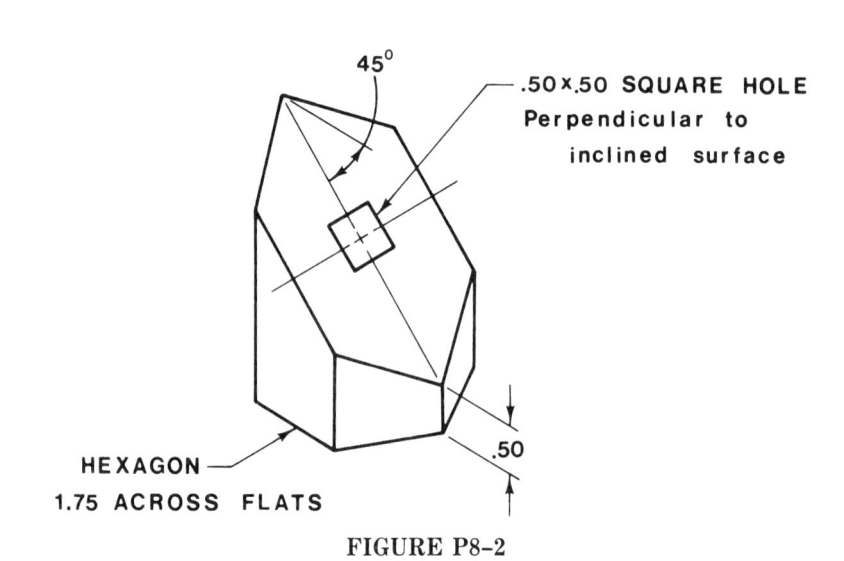

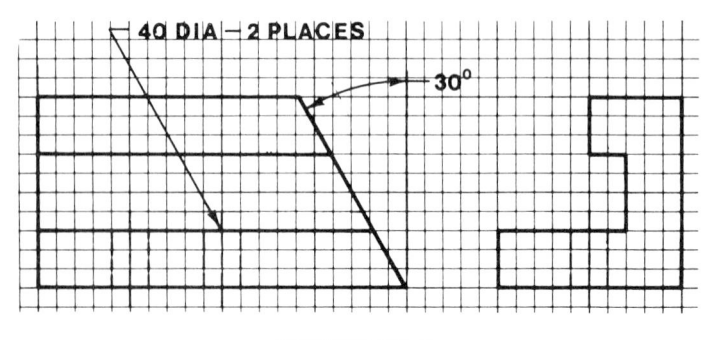

FIGURE P8-2

.50 × .50 SQUARE HOLE
Perpendicular to inclined surface

HEXAGON
1.75 ACROSS FLATS

FIGURE P8-3

40 DIA - 2 PLACES

Chap. 8　Problems

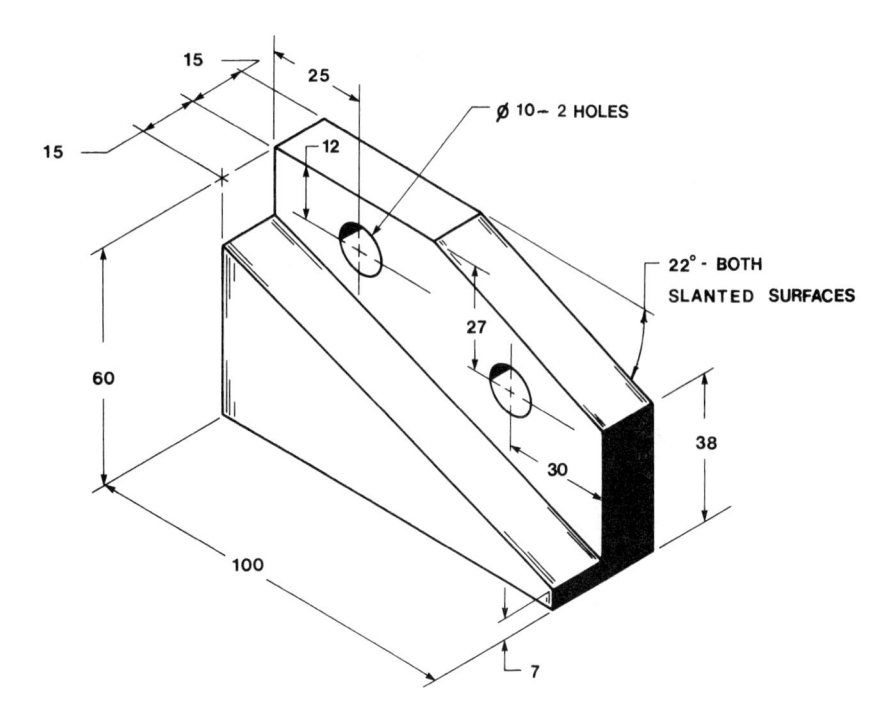

FIGURE P8-4

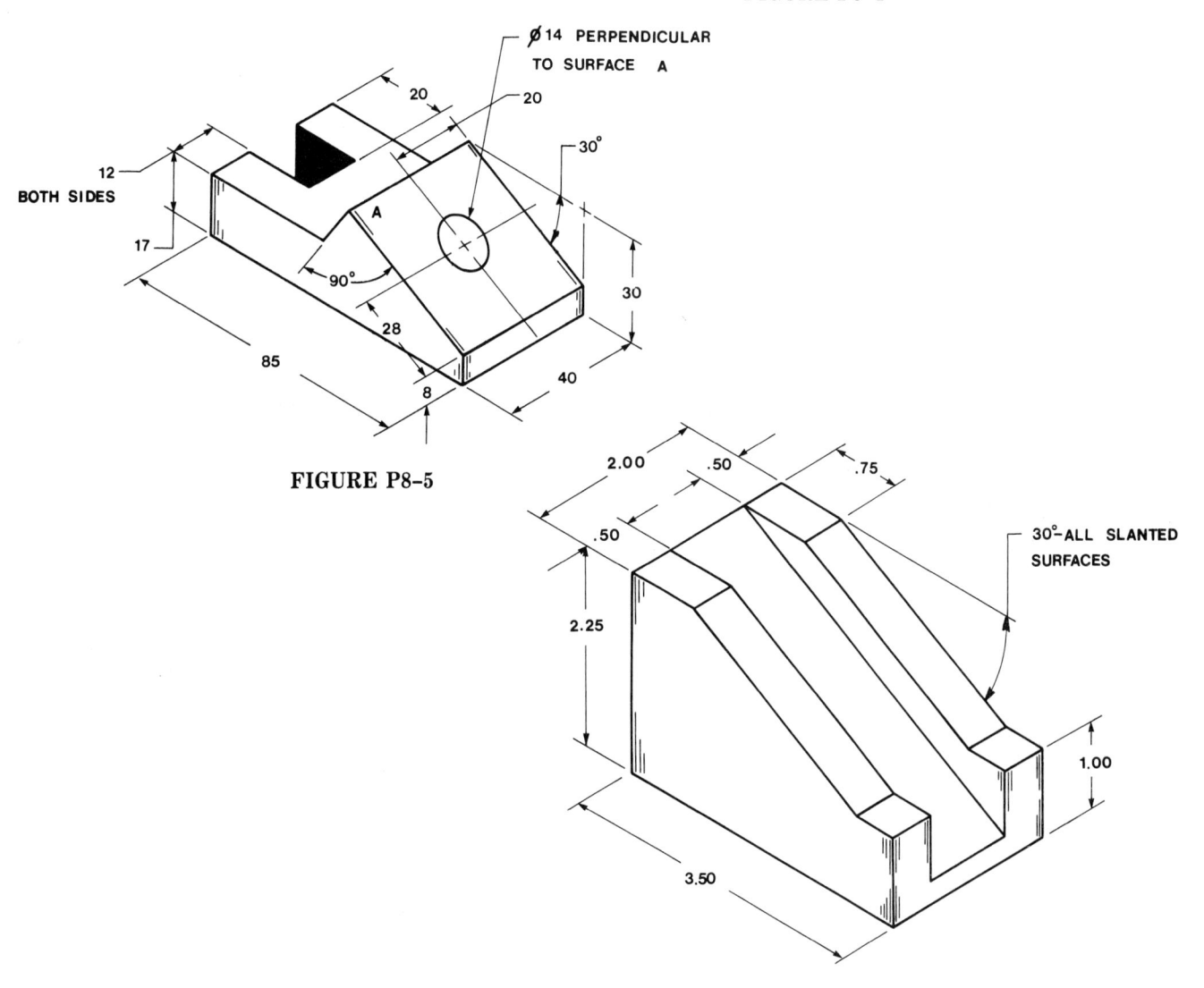

FIGURE P8-5

FIGURE P8-6

For Problems P8-7 through P8-12, draw at least one orthographic view of the objects shown in Figures P8-7 through P8-12 and add sufficient partial auxiliary views to show the true shape of all slanted surfaces. The dimensional units are as noted below.

P8-7 Millimeters   P8-10 Millimeters
P8-8 Millimeters   P8-11 Millimeters
P8-9 Inches   P8-12 Millimeters

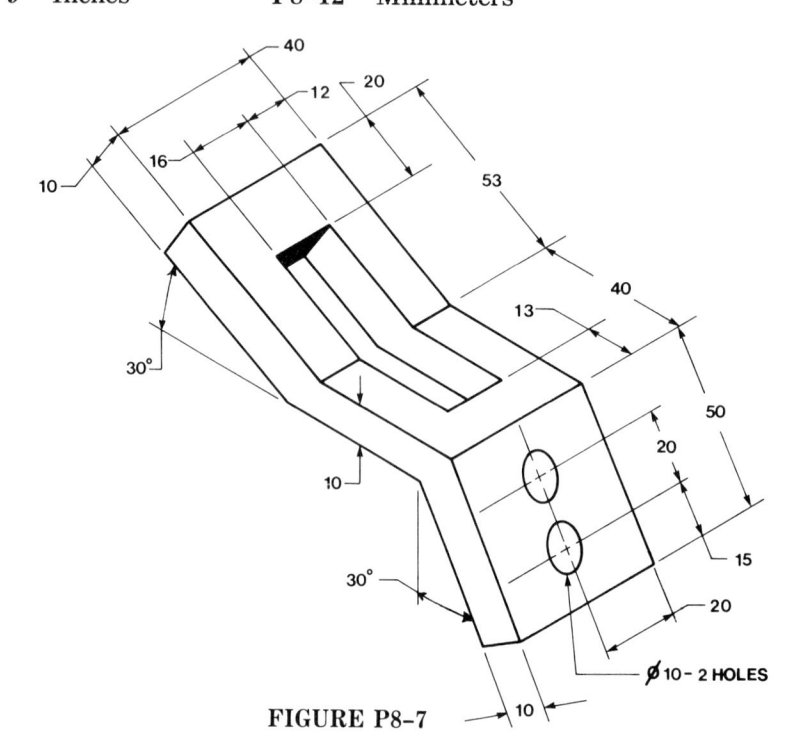

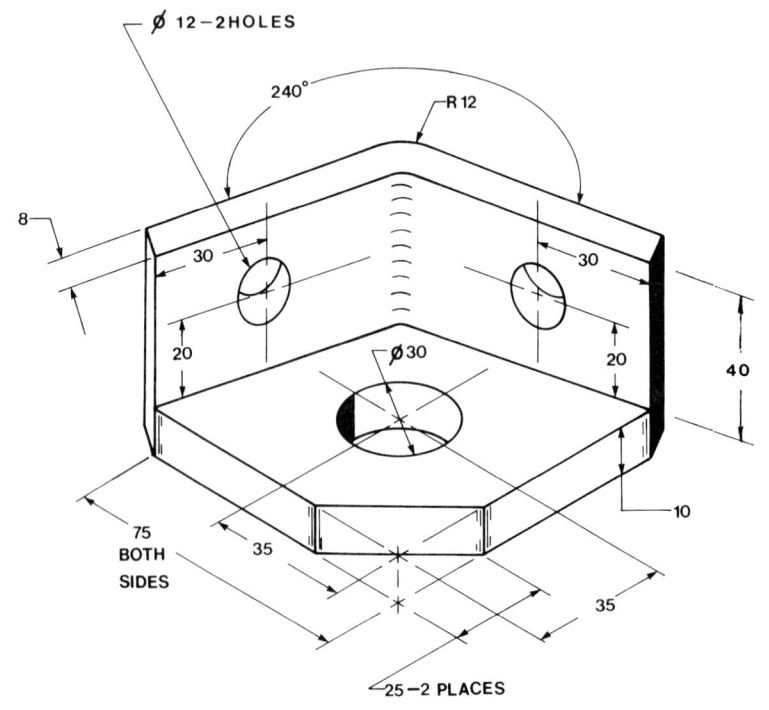

FIGURE P8-7

FIGURE P8-8

Chap. 8   Problems

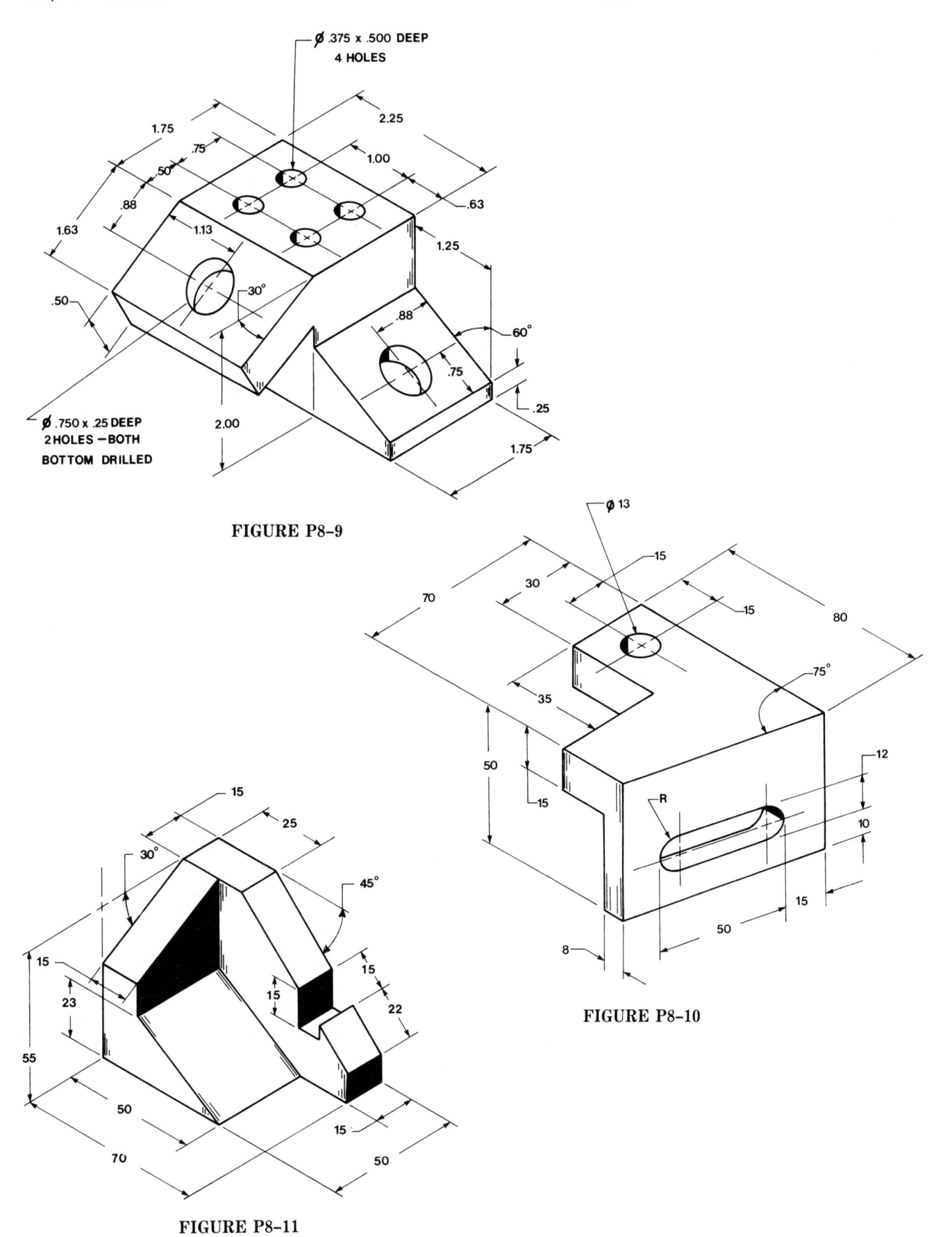

FIGURE P8-9

FIGURE P8-10

FIGURE P8-11

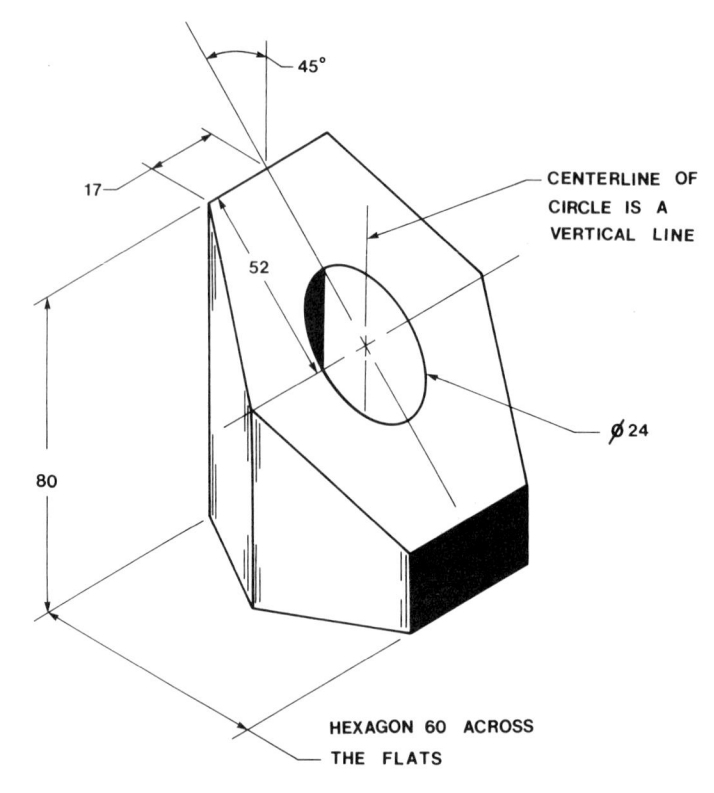

FIGURE P8-12

For Problems P8-13 through P8-18, draw two views (front, top, or side) of the objects shown in Figures P8-13 through P8-18. Also draw a complete or partial auxiliary view as assigned. The dimensional units are as noted below.

P8-13	Inches	P8-16	Millimeters
P8-14	Millimeters	P8-17	Millimeters
P8-15	Millimeters	P8-18	Inches

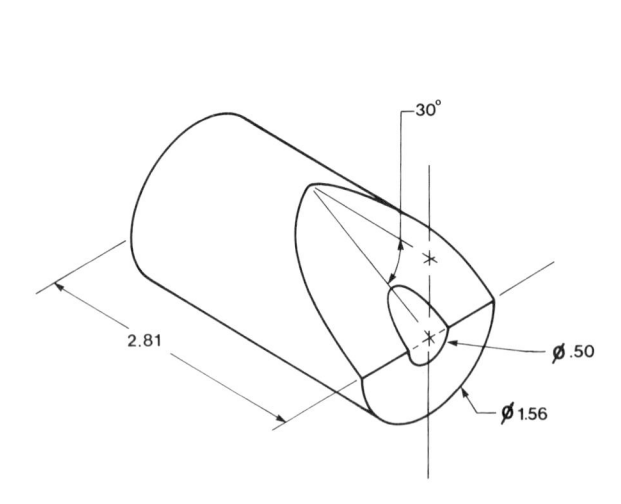

FIGURE P8-13

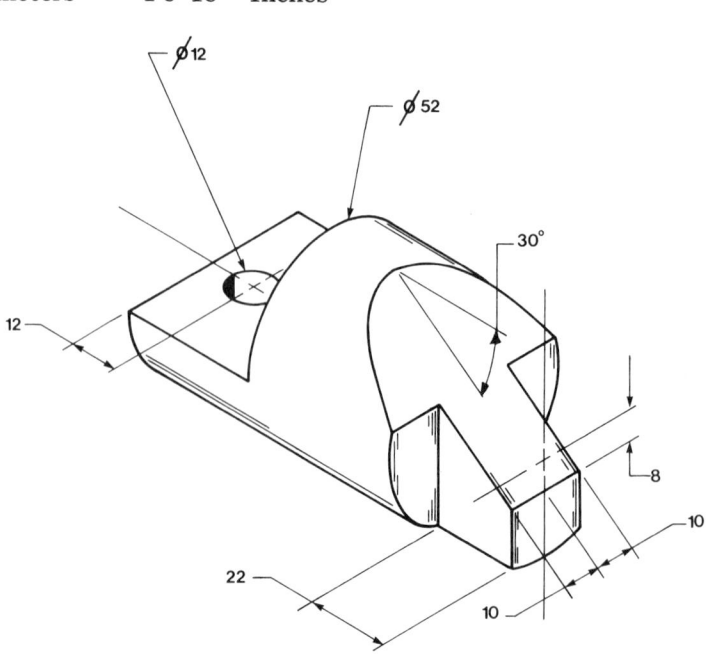

FIGURE P8-14

Chap. 8   Problems   243

FIGURE P8-15

Ø7 × 20 DEEP
9
12
30°
16
60
8
16
Ø58

FIGURE P8-16

30°
80
Ø50
Ø68

FIGURE P8-17

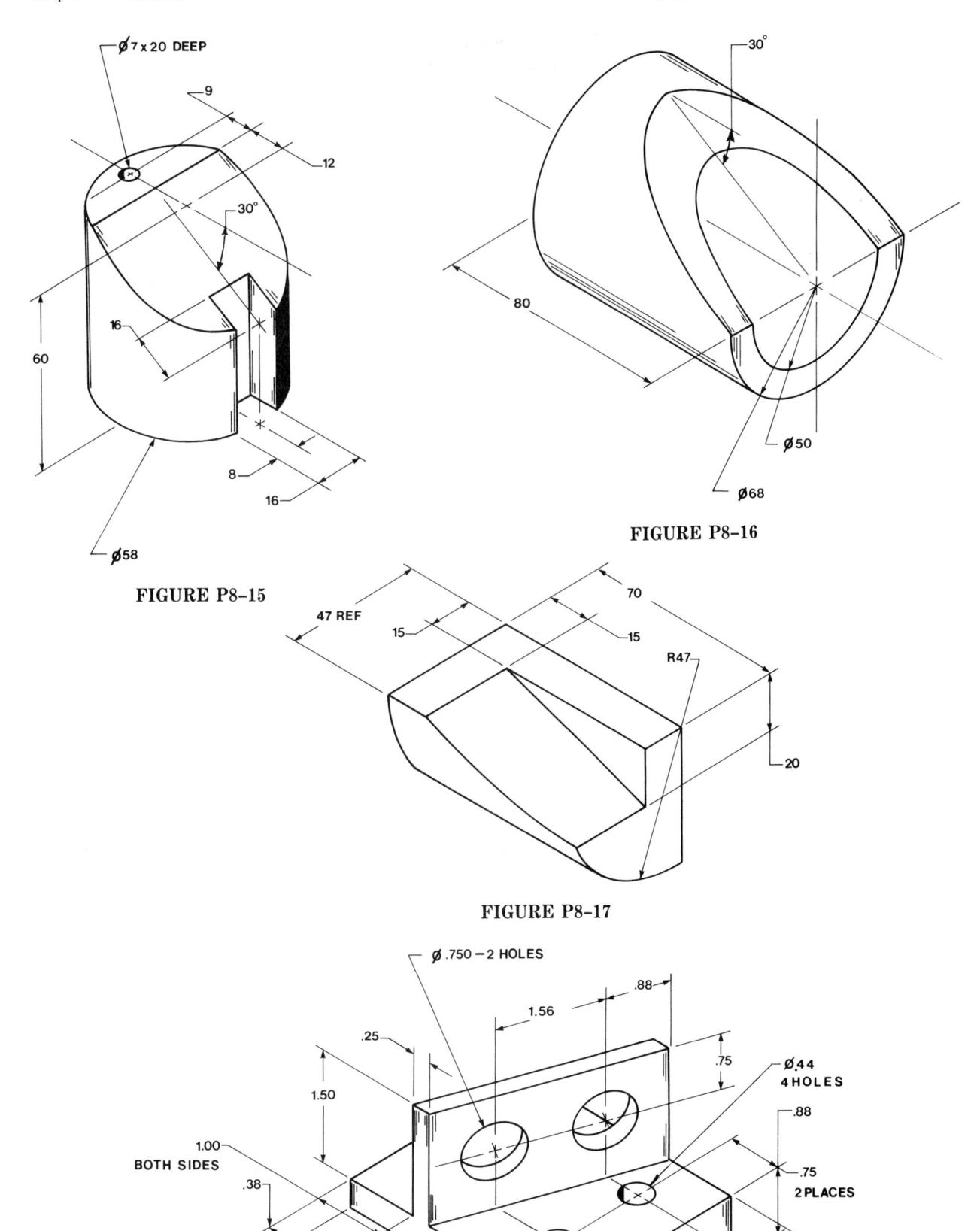

47 REF
15
70
15
R47
20

FIGURE P8-18

Ø.750 − 2 HOLES
.88
1.56
.25
.75
Ø.44 4 HOLES
1.50
.88
1.00 BOTH SIDES
.75 2 PLACES
.38
3.25
1.38
1.25 − 2 PLACES
.75 2 PLACES
2.75

P8-19 and P8-20 Draw sufficient views to define completely the objects shown in Figures P8-19 and P8-20. All dimensions are in millimeters.

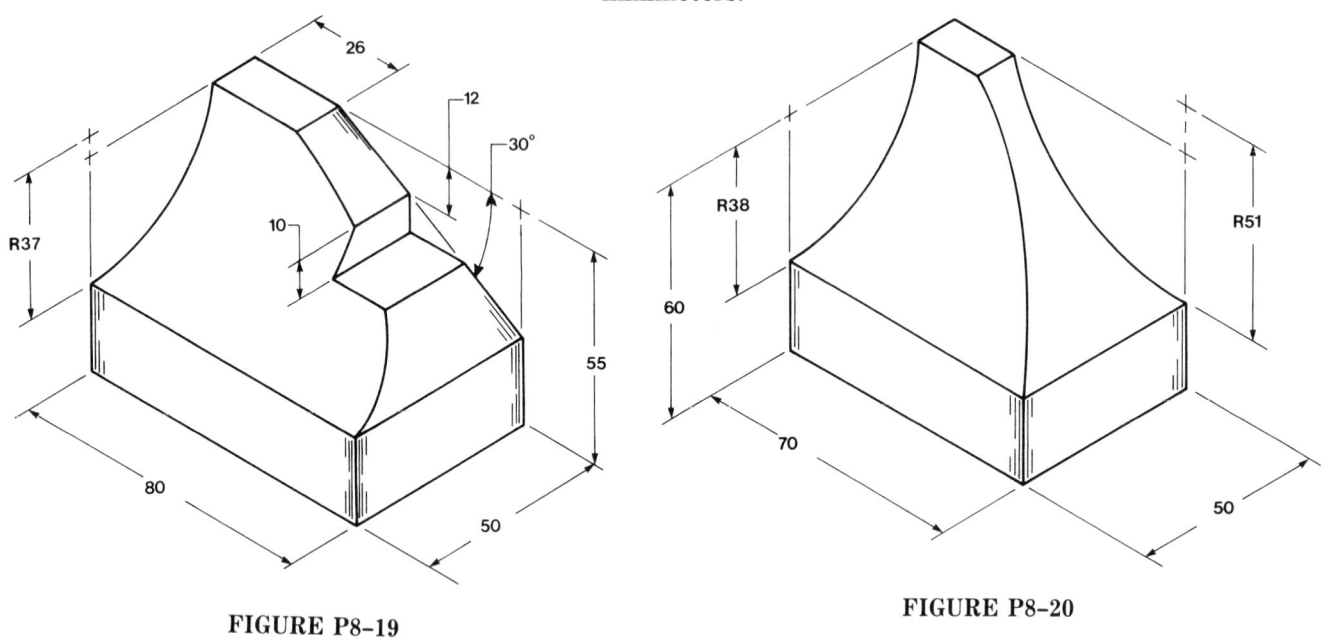

FIGURE P8-19

FIGURE P8-20

P8-21 and P8-22 Draw two views (front, top, or side) of the objects shown in Figures P8-21 and P8-22. Also draw a secondary auxiliary view of the oblique surface and label it TRUE SHAPE.

FIGURE P8-21

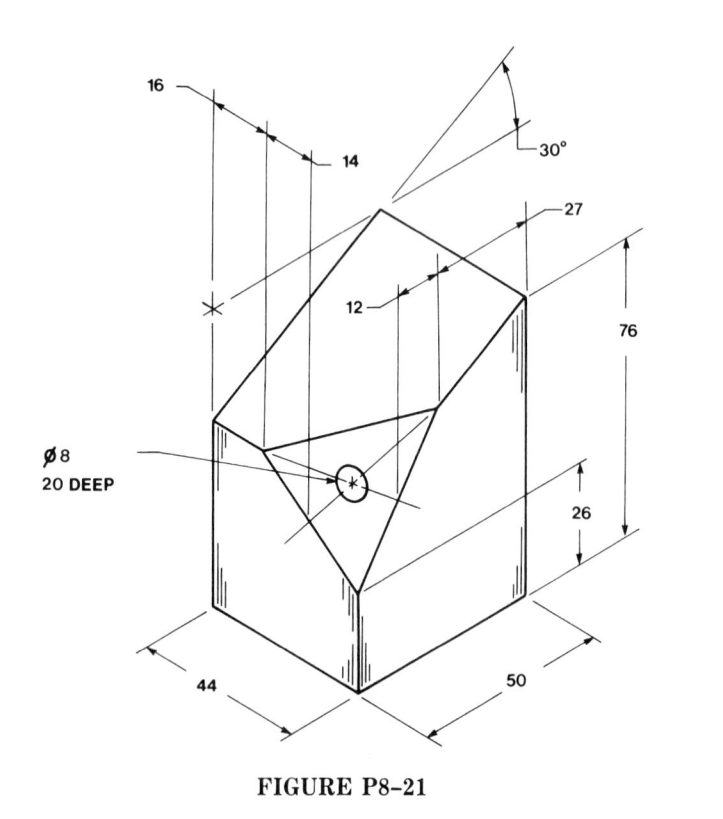

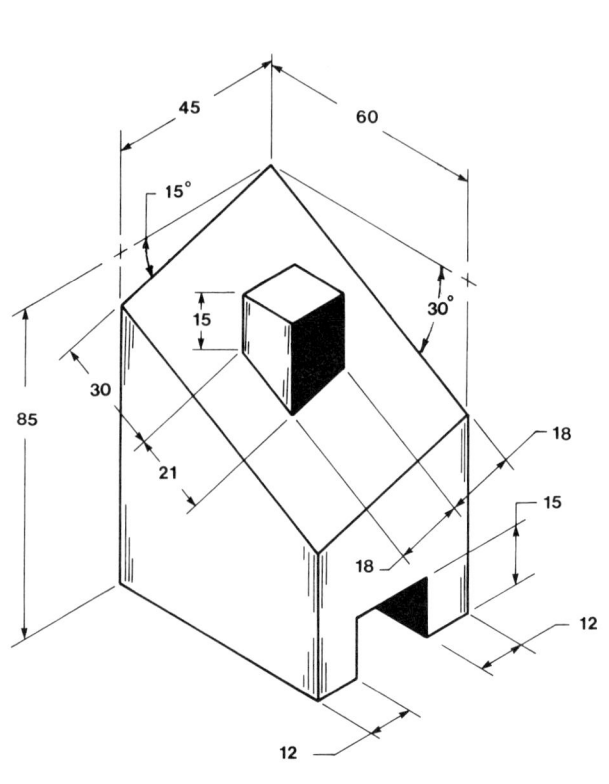

FIGURE P8-22

Chap. 8   Problems

P8-23 through P8-32 For Figures P8-23 through P8-32, redraw the given views of the planes and add sufficient auxiliary views to define the plane's true shape. The corner points of each view are defined relative to an *XY* axis using coordinate point values listed in the tables. Either inch or millimeter values can be used.

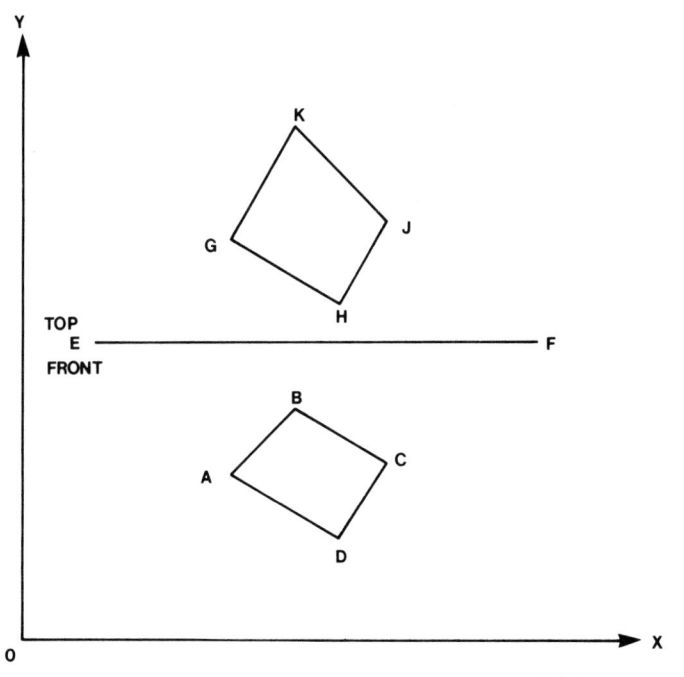

	X VALUES		Y VALUES	
POINTS	INCHES	mm	INCHES	mm
A	2.13	54	1.67	42
B	2.80	71	2.32	59
C	3.63	92	1.78	45
D	3.22	88	1.00	25
E	.74	19	3.00	75
F	5.28	134	3.00	75
G	2.13	54	4.00	100
H	3.22	88	3.37	86
J	3.63	92	4.20	107
K	2.80	71	5.16	131

FIGURE P8-23

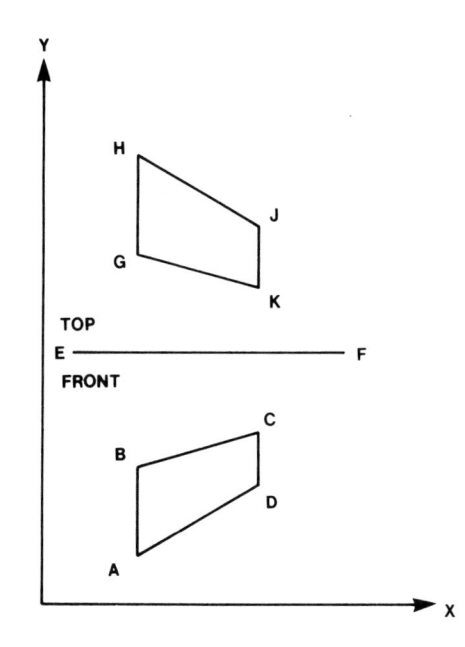

	X VALUES		Y VALUES	
POINT	IN.	mm	IN.	mm
A	.95	24	.48	12
B	.95	24	1.38	35
C	2.20	56	1.71	43
D	2.20	56	1.18	30
E	.25	6	2.50	64
F	3.13	80	2.50	64
G	.95	24	3.52	90
H	.95	24	4.50	114
J	2.20	56	3.79	96
K	2.20	56	3.17	81

FIGURE P8-24

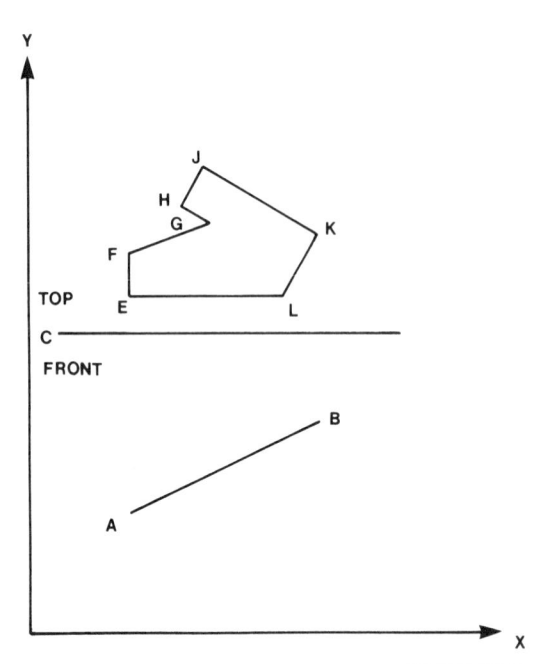

246   Auxiliary Views Chap. 8

FIGURE P8-25

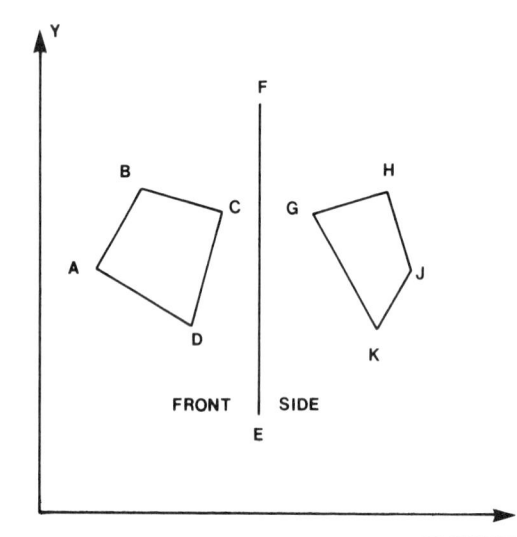

	X VALUES		Y VALUES	
POINT	IN.	mm	IN.	mm
A	1.00	25	1.21	31
B	3.00	75	2.11	54
C	.25	6	3.00	75
D	3.80	97	3.00	75
E	1.00	25	3.37	86
F	1.00	25	3.81	97
G	1.88	48	4.10	104
H	1.56	40	4.27	108
J	1.80	46	4.67	119
K	3.00	75	4.00	100
L	2.62	67	3.37	86

FIGURE P8-26

	X VALUES		Y VALUES	
POINT	IN.	mm	IN.	mm
A	.56	14	2.45	62
B	1.13	29	3.25	83
C	1.88	48	3.03	77
D	1.56	40	1.87	48
E	2.28	58	.90	23
F	2.28	58	4.10	104
G	2.83	72	3.03	77
H	3.60	91	3.25	83
J	3.84	98	2.45	62
K	3.51	89	1.87	47

FIGURE P8-27

	X VALUES		Y VALUES	
POINT	IN.	mm	IN.	mm
A	.75	19	.92	23
B	.75	19	2.51	64
C	1.48	38	2.23	57
D	1.67	42	1.45	37
E	2.48	63	.30	8
F	2.48	63	3.30	84
G	3.10	79	1.45	37
H	3.30	84	2.23	57
J	4.18	106	2.51	64
K	3.70	94	.92	23

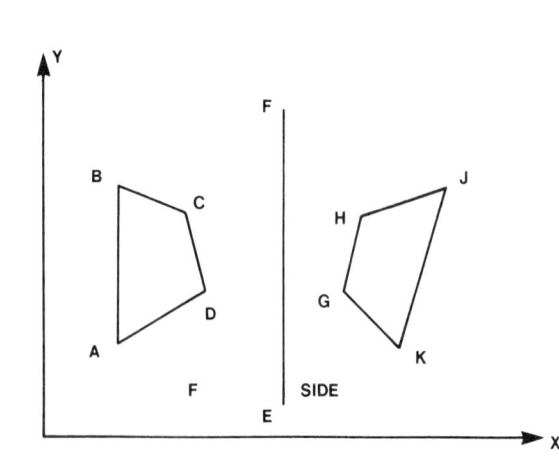

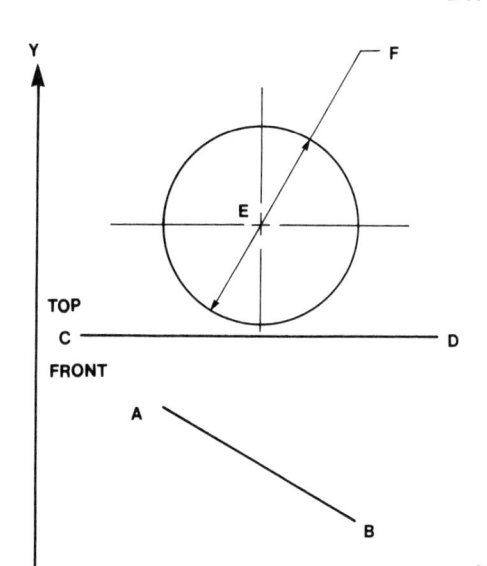

Chap. 8 Problems 247

FIGURE P8-28

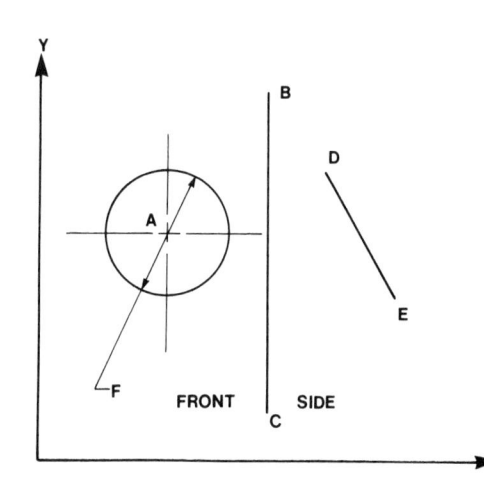

	X VALUE		Y VALUE	
POINT	IN.	mm	IN.	mm
A	1.30	33	1.66	42
B	3.30	84	.50	13
C	.25	6	2.35	60
D	4.13	105	2.35	60
E	2.30	58	3.47	88
F	⌀2.00	⌀50		

FIGURE P8-29

	X VALUE		Y VALUE	
POINT	IN.	mm	IN.	mm
A	1.32	34	2.30	58
B	2.35	60	3.68	93
C	2.35	60	.50	13
D	2.93	75	2.90	74
E	3.65	93	1.62	41
F	⌀1.25	⌀32		

FIGURE P8-30

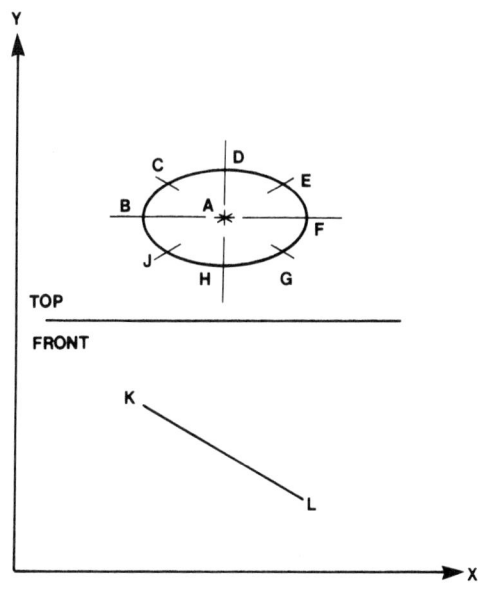

	X VALUES		Y VALUES	
POINTS	IN.	mm	IN.	mm
A	2.11	54	3.57	91
B	1.29	33	3.57	91
C	1.52	39	3.91	99
D	2.11	54	4.05	103
E	2.72	69	3.91	99
F	2.96	75	3.57	91
G	2.72	69	3.20	81
H	2.11	54	3.05	77
J	1.52	39	3.20	81
K	1.29	33	1.67	42
L	2.96	75	.73	19

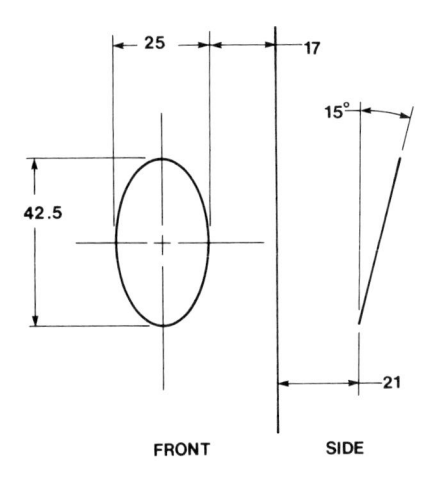

FIGURE P8-31

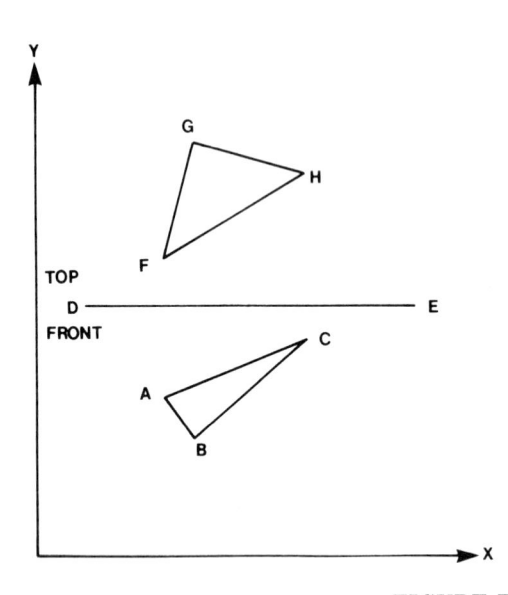

	X VALUES		Y VALUES	
POINT	IN.	MM	IN.	MM
A	1.25	32	1.58	40
B	1.62	41	1.18	30
C	2.80	72	2.15	55
D	.50	13	2.50	64
E	3.94	100	2.50	64
F	1.25	32	3.00	75
G	1.62	41	4.15	105
H	2.80	72	3.83	98

FIGURE P8-32

9
BASIC CONCEPTS OF TOLERANCES

IBM 5081 display. (Courtesy of International Business Machines Corporation.)

9-1 INTRODUCTION

In this chapter we introduce the basic concepts of tolerances. It includes tolerance nomenclature, drawing format requirements, and an explanation of how tolerances interact with design and manufacturing practices. Fits, allowances, surface finishes, and related inspection techniques are also covered.

Particular emphasis is placed on understanding what the numbers mean in a tolerance. We discuss how to evaluate tolerance limits and how to make judgments as to tolerance requirements for various design or manufacturing situations.

9-2 BILATERAL TOLERANCES

Bilateral tolerances are tolerances assigned using plus and minus values relative to a base dimension. In Figure 9-1 the base dimension 2.00 in. is assigned a bilateral tolerance of ±0.01 and the base dimension 1.00 in. is assigned a bilateral tolerance of ±0.01. No 0 is required to the left of the decimal point when stating an English unit.

The number of decimal points used to define a bilateral tolerance using English units must be matched by an equal number of decimal points in the base dimension. Figure 9-2 shows some examples. Metric

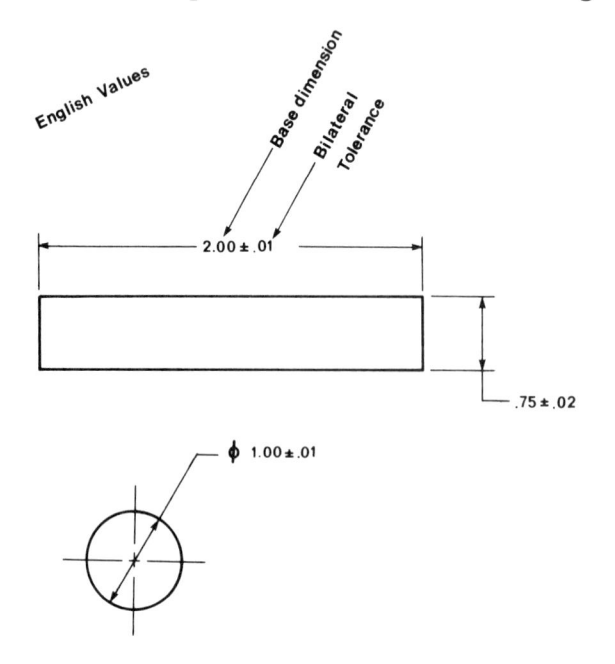

FIGURE 9-1 Examples of bilateral tolerances.

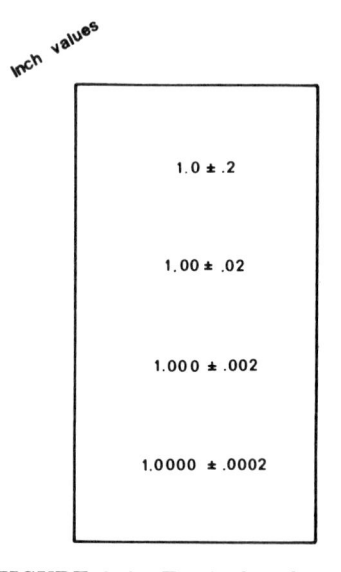

FIGURE 9-2 For inch values the number of decimal places in the tolerance must equal the number of decimal places in the base dimension.

Sec. 9-3   Unilateral Tolerances   251

dimensions may be listed as shown even if the tolerance values are not whole numbers. Figure 9-3 gives some examples. Note that a zero is required to the left of the decimal point when stating a metric tolerance.

Bilateral tolerances need not be of equal values relative to the base dimension, but neither value may be equal to zero. Figure 9-4 shows some examples.

9-3 UNILATERAL TOLERANCES

Unilateral tolerances are tolerances assigned using plus or minus values relative to a base dimension, with one of the tolerance values equal to zero. In Figure 9-5, the 1.75 dimension has a tolerance of plus 0.00 and minus 0.02. The 1.00 dimension has a tolerance of plus 0.02 and minus 0.00.

When inch values are used, the number of decimal points used to state the tolerance must be matched by an equal number of decimal points in the base dimension. No 0 is required to the left of the decimal point. Metric values may be stated using whole numbers and decimal tolerances. A 0 must be included to the left of the decimal point.

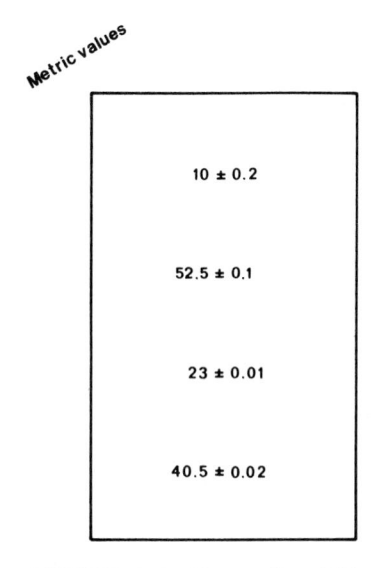

FIGURE 9-3 Examples of bilateral tolerances using metric values.

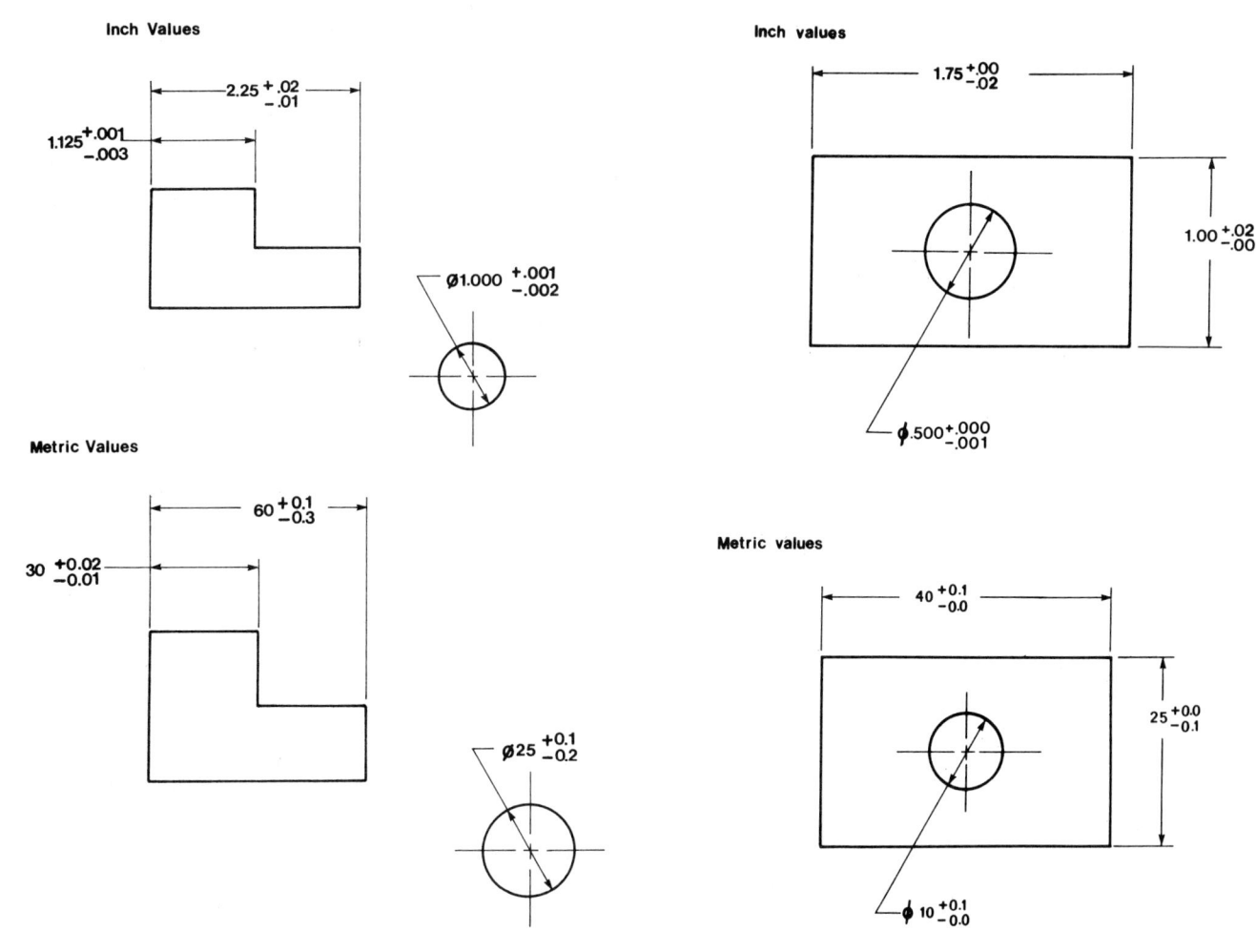

FIGURE 9-4 Examples of unequal bilateral tolerances.

FIGURE 9-5 Examples of unilateral tolerances.

9-4 LIMIT DIMENSIONS

Limit dimensions are dimensions that include tolerance values as part of the dimension values. The dimension contains two numbers: an upper and a lower limit. Figure 9-6 shows some examples of limit dimensions. No base dimensions are used with limit dimensions.

The larger numerical value dimension is always located above the smaller numerical value dimension. Both dimensions should contain the same number of decimal places whether done using inches or metric units.

9-5 ANGULAR TOLERANCES

Tolerances can be added to angular dimensions using either the bilateral, unilateral, or limiting method. Figure 9-7 shows examples of each. Either decimal degrees or degree, minute, second values may be used.

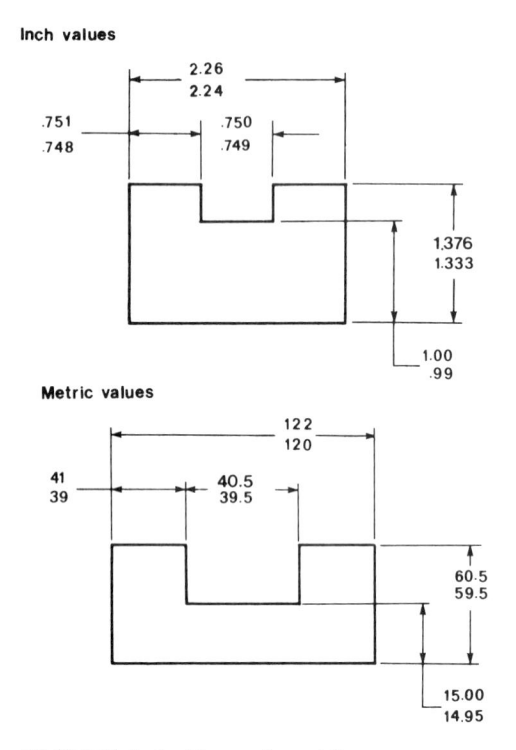

FIGURE 9-6 Examples of limit tolerances.

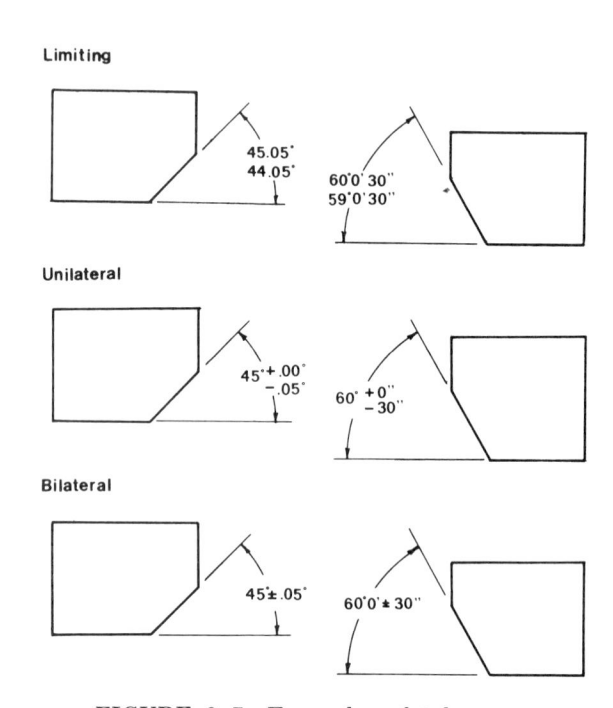

FIGURE 9-7 Examples of tolerances assigned to angular dimensions.

9-6 TOLERANCE ACCUMULATION

Tolerance accumulation is the buildup of successive tolerances along a series of features. In Figure 9-8 the four dimensions 10 ±0.01 could accumulate a total tolerance buildup of +0.04 (±0.01 for each dimension). The maximum total value could be as much as 40.04, the minimum total value, 39.96.

Tolerance buildup can be controlled by three different methods of dimensioning: chain dimensioning, baseline dimensioning, and direct dimensioning.

Chain dimensions can create tolerance buildup if not used carefully. Figure 9-9a shows an object that uses chain dimensioning to define the

Sec. 9-6   Tolerance Accumulation   253

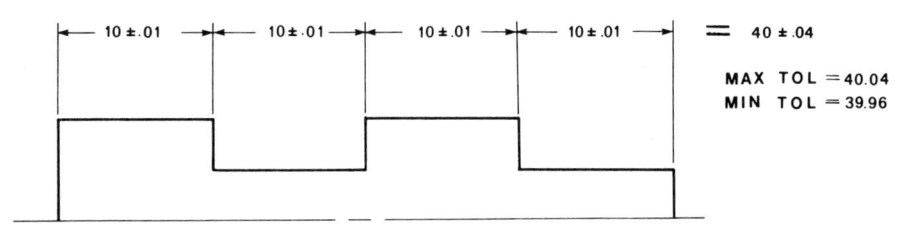

|← 10 ±.01 →|← 10 ±.01 →|← 10 ±.01 →|← 10 ±.01 →| = 40 ± .04

MAX TOL = 40.04
MIN TOL = 39.96

FIGURE 9-8 Tolerance build-up.

length and an overall dimension. This is called *double dimensioning* (see Section 5-20) and is a dimensional error. A worker could make each feature correctly at its upper limit of 1.26, for a total length of 3.78, and have the part rejected as too long based on the 3.75 ±0.01 overall dimension maximum limit of 3.76.

This situation is corrected by omitting one of the feature dimensions as shown in Figure 9-9b. Omitting the feature dimension avoids double dimensioning and prevents tolerance accumulation.

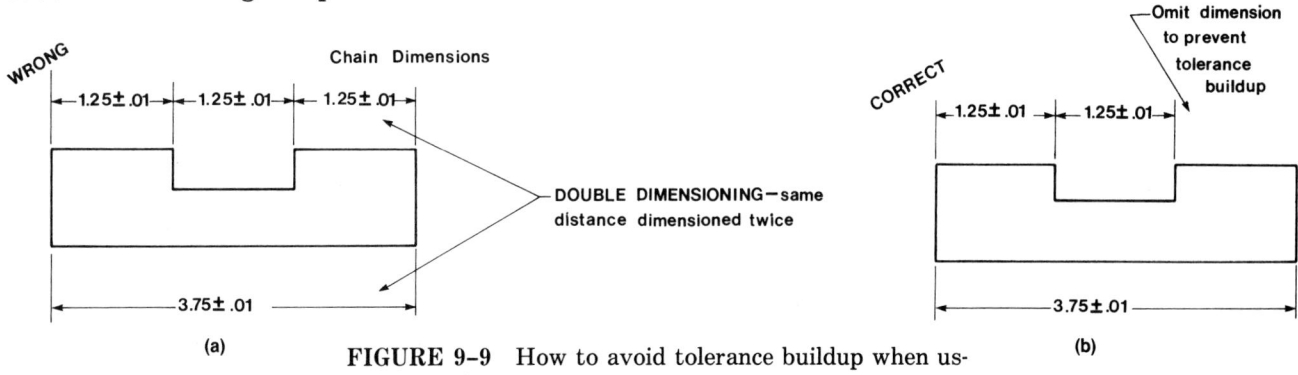

WRONG   Chain Dimensions
|←1.25±.01→|←1.25±.01→|←1.25±.01→|

DOUBLE DIMENSIONING—same distance dimensioned twice

|←————— 3.75±.01 —————→|

(a)

CORRECT
Omit dimension to prevent tolerance buildup
|←1.25±.01→|←1.25±.01→|

|←————— 3.75±.01 —————→|

(b)

FIGURE 9-9 How to avoid tolerance buildup when using chain dimensions.

Baseline dimensioning, as shown in Figure 9-10, prevents tolerance accumulation by referencing all dimensions to a baseline (also called a *datum line*). Baseline dimensioning (see Section 5-8) requires a larger area on the drawing to complete and must be redone if there is an error or if a feature is changed.

The *direct dimensioning* system is like a baseline system, except that it allows for specific dimensioning within the baseline dimensions. For example, the object shown in Figure 9-11 is dimensioned using the

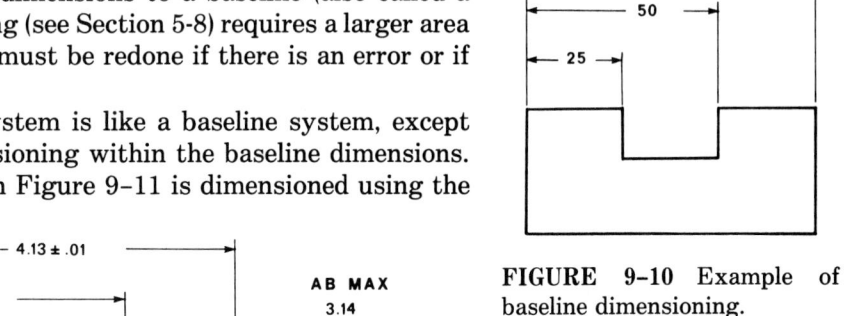

|←——————— 75 ———————→|
|←————— 50 —————→|
|←— 25 —→|

FIGURE 9-10 Example of baseline dimensioning.

|←——————— 4.13 ± .01 ———————→|
|←————— 3.13 ± .01 —————→|
|←——— 2.13±.01 ———→|
|← 1.13 ± .01 →|

A   B

|←——— 2.000±.001 ———→|
Direct dimension

AB MAX
3.14
1.12
2.02

AB MIN
3.12
1.14
1.98

FIGURE 9-11 Example of a direct dimensioning system.

baseline system with a direct dimension. Using the given baseline dimensions, the distance between points A and B could be as great as 2.02 or as small as 1.98, for a total of 0.04. The amount of variance can be decreased by adding a direct dimension as shown. The 2.000 ±0.001 direct dimension limits the variance between A and B to 0.002. Direct dimensioning is useful to help control tolerances between specific features and helps prevent tolerance accumulation.

9-7 TOLERANCE STUDIES

A tolerance study is a mathematical analysis of a group of tolerances to determine their maximum and minimum values. Designers do tolerance studies as a way of checking assigned tolerances to make sure that they match or fit as required.

Figure 9-12 shows two parts, A and B, with dimensions of 20 ± 0.1 and 30 ± 0.2, respectively. The maximum value of A and B combined is the addition of their two maximum values (20.1 + 30.2 = 50.3). The minimum value is the addition of the two minimum values (19.9 + 29.8 = 49.7). The total tolerance is the maximum value minus the minimum value (50.3 − 49.7 = 00.6).

Tolerance studies can be used to compare different dimensioning setups. Figure 9-13 shows an object dimensioned two different ways. If there were no tolerance, the three features of 1.00 length would be mathematically equal. How it was dimensioned would be irrelevant. However, there are always tolerances.

What is the length of feature B in Figure 9-13? The two different dimensioning setups use the same ± 0.01 tolerance on each dimensional value, but the resultant total tolerance values are different.

The maximum (MAX) value of feature B using method A is determined by subtracting the minimum values of features A (0.99) and C (0.99) from the maximum overall dimension (3.01). The result is that B MAX equals 1.03.

The minimum (MIN) value of feature B using method A is determined by subtracting the maximum values of A (1.01) and C (1.01) from the minimum overall dimension (2.99). The result is that B MIN equals 0.97.

Using method B, the maximum value of feature B is determined by subtracting the minimum value of the dimension from the baseline to the left edge of B (0.99) from the maximum value of the dimension from the baseline to the right edge of B (2.01). The result is that B MAX equals 1.02.

Using method B, the minimum value of feature B is determined by subtracting the maximum value of the dimension from the baseline to

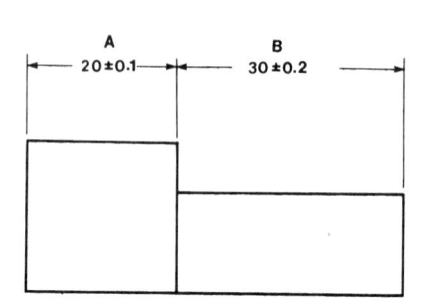

FIGURE 9-12 Example of a tolerance study.

Sec. 9-8 Sample Problem

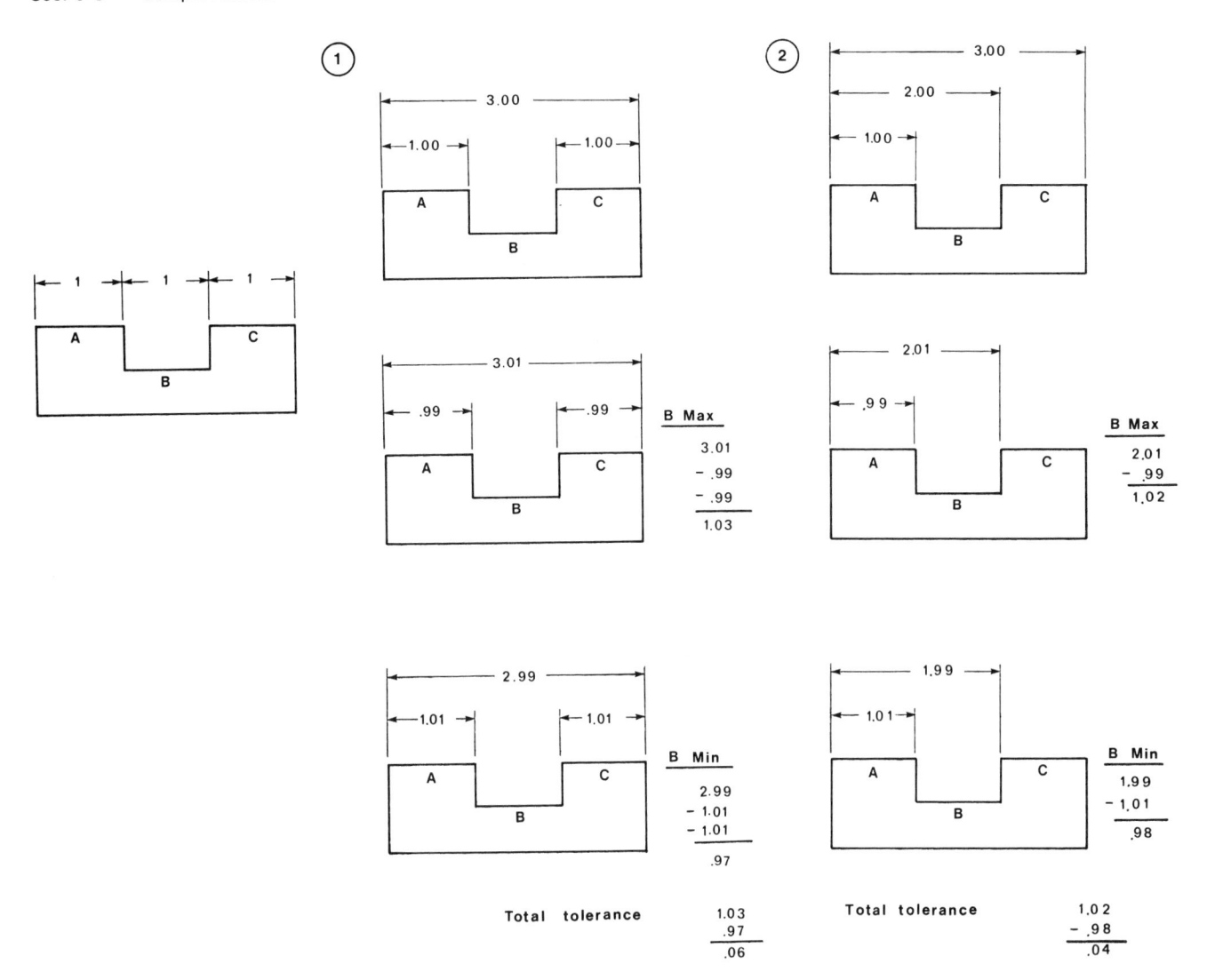

FIGURE 9-13 Comparison of two different dimensioning setups.

the left edge of B (1.01) from the minimum dimension from the baseline to the right edge of B (1.99). The result is that B MIN equals 0.98.

The total tolerance for each is found by subtracting the MIN value from the MAX value. For method A, the total tolerance is 0.06 and for method B, 0.04. Even though the dimensioned values all use the same ± 0.01 tolerance, the resulting tolerances differ by 0.02.

The choice of method A, method B, or some other method to dimension the object shown in Figure 9-13 depends on the function of surfaces A, B, and C. How much size variance is needed or permitted for each? The answer will vary according to the object's use. Shape alone is not enough to determine correct dimension locations and tolerances.

9-8 SAMPLE PROBLEM

Figure 9-14 presents a sample problem that shows how tolerance studies are used to choose tolerances and locate dimensions. The shapes involved are similar to the ones used in Figure 9-13. The problem is to dimension and tolerance parts 1 and 2 so that they always fit together and that the

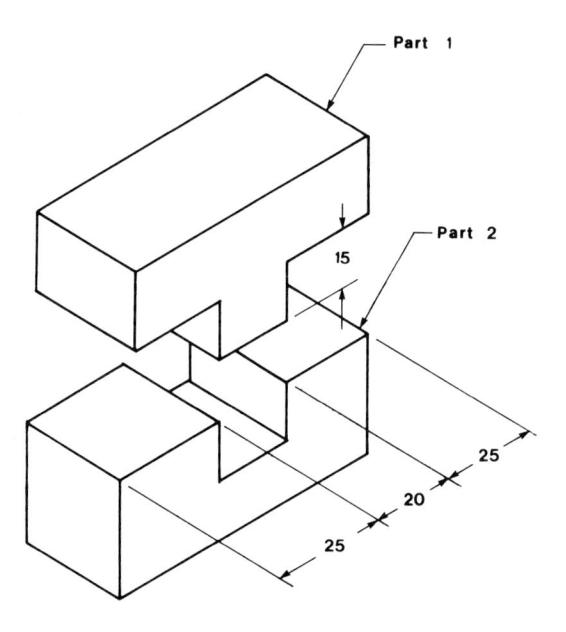

FIGURE 9-14(a) Sample tolerancing problem.

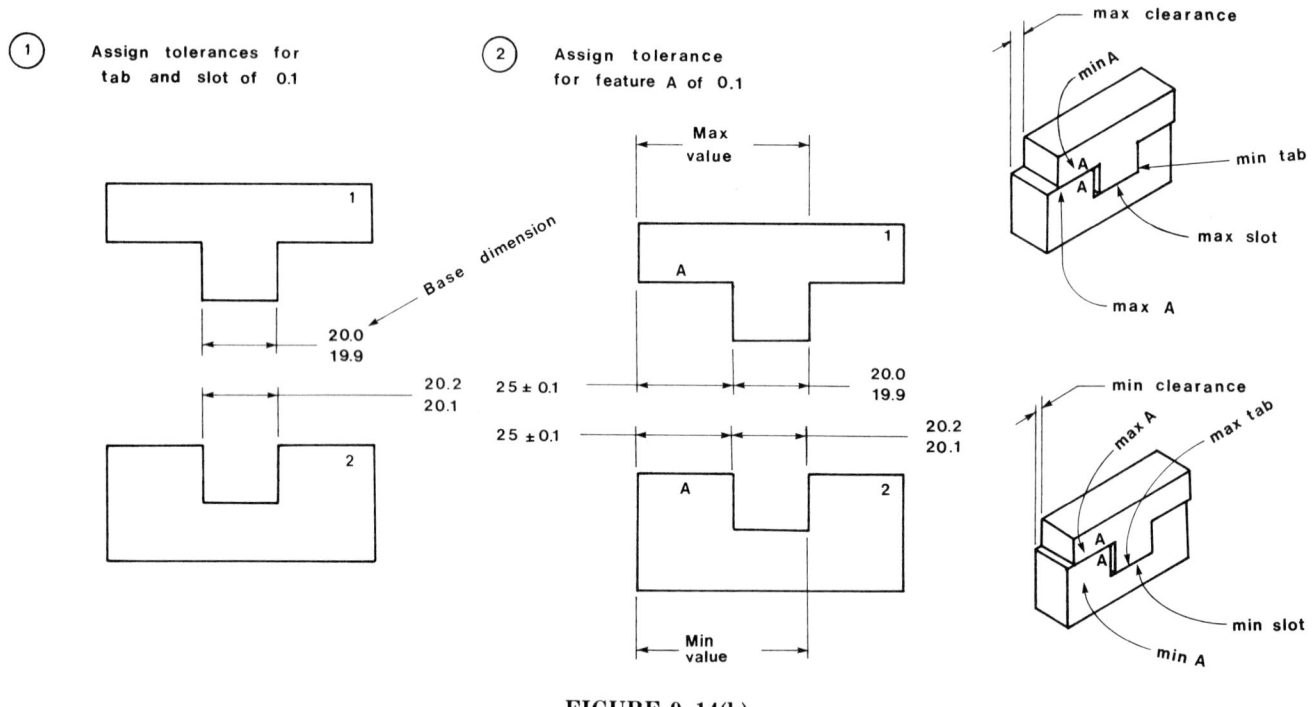

FIGURE 9-14(b)

ends never mismatch by more than a total of 0.8 mm maximum. A design sketch is shown in Figure 9-14a, which gives the nominal sizes (ideal dimensions if all features could be made perfectly).

The tab on part 1 must always fit into the slot of part 2, so we start by dimensioning these two features. There is no rule as to how to start choosing tolerances. We simply make a guess, work it through, then check

Sec. 9-8   Sample Problem

③ Assign tolerances to overall dimensions of ± 0.1

Check overall clearances

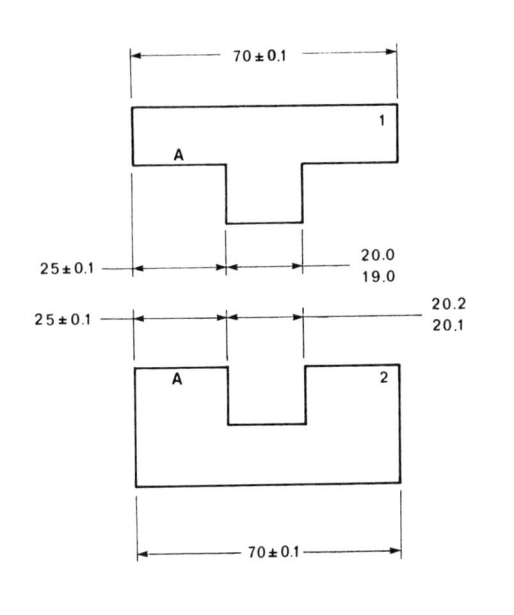

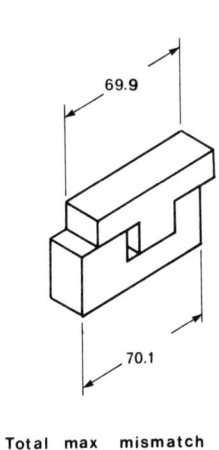

Total max mismatch
```
  0.5
+ 0.2
  0.7
```

FIGURE 9-14(b) (cont.)

and see if it is satisfactory. If not, we choose a new tolerance and try again.

For this example we assign a tolerance of 0.1 mm to the tab and 0.1 mm to the slot. Limit-type tolerances are used. The tab, starting with the given 20-mm nominal dimension, is dimensioned 20.0 and 19.9. Now that a maximum size of 20.0 is established, we allow a clearance of 0.1 mm, making the minimum slot size 20.0 + 0.1, or 20.1. The 20.1 is now used to tolerance the slot, resulting in a slot dimension of 20.2 and 20.1.

A tolerance study yields the values

```
max:    20.2        slot    max
      - 19.9        tab     min
        0.3 mm

min:    20.1        slot    min
      - 20.0        tab     max
        0.1 mm
```

minimum clearance = 0.1 mm
maximum clearance = 0.3 mm

We next dimension and tolerance feature A. We could assign the same tolerances that we did for the tab and slot, but these tolerances are fairly tight. They are acceptable for interfacing parts, but excessive for features that just touch each other.

Here we assign a bilateral tolerance of ± 0.1, or twice as large as that assigned the tab and slot. This results in a total tolerance for each of 0.2. Note that the two features are independent of each other, but are related to each other through the slot and tab interface.

We now do a tolerance study which includes both the slot and tab dimension and the proposed 25 ± 0.1 dimensions.

max:		20.2	slot	max
	+	25.1	A	max
		45.3		
		19.9	tab	min
	+	24.9	A	min
		44.8		
		45.3		
	−	44.8	maximum clearance	
		0.5		
min:		20.1	slot	min
	+	24.9	A	min
		45.0		
		20.0	tab	max
	+	25.1	tab	max
		45.1		
		45.1		
	−	45.0	minimum clearance	
		0.1		

This means that the maximum mismatch between the ends of parts 1 and 2 is 0.5 mm. The problem statement permits a maximum mismatch of 0.8, so the assigned tolerances are within the designated design limits. If a 0.5-mm mismatch is considered too exact, we can go back and reassign tolerances to get closer to the 0.8 value.

We now assign tolerances to the overall dimensions and check their effects on the match between the two parts. In the maximum condition, we add the maximum clearance of 0.5 to the additional tolerance of ±0.1 assigned to the overall dimensions. The result is a total maximum mismatch of 0.7 mm (Figure 9-14b).

The 0.7-mm mismatch is within the prescribed 0.8-mm limit, so the assigned tolerances are acceptable. The depth and width dimensions would be assigned and studied in a similar manner.

9-9 LIMITS AND FITS

Assigning tolerances to matching parts is done so frequently that a standardized system of limits and fits has been established. English units (inches) use the practices outlined in ANSI B4.1, and metric units (millimeters) use the practices presented by the International Standards Organization (ISO) and reiterated in ANSI B4.2. We discuss both systems in this section.

Some important terms used with limits and fits are as follows.

Basic Size The ideal size of a feature. All tolerances are calculated from and assigned to a basic size (Figure 9-15).

Fit A general term used to describe how matching parts fit together.

Clearance Fit Tolerances that always allow a space (clearance) between matching parts (Figure 9-16).

Sec. 9-9   Limits and Fits   259

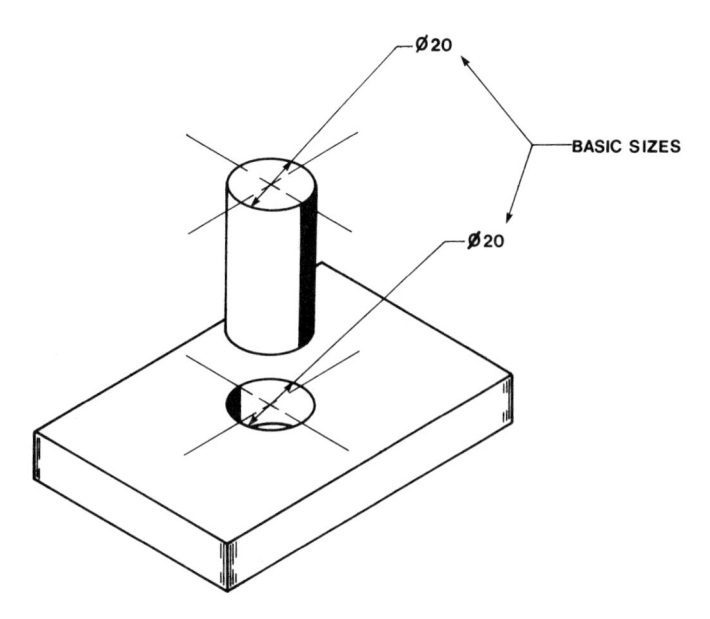

FIGURE 9-15   Basic sizes.

FIGURE 9-16   Clearance.

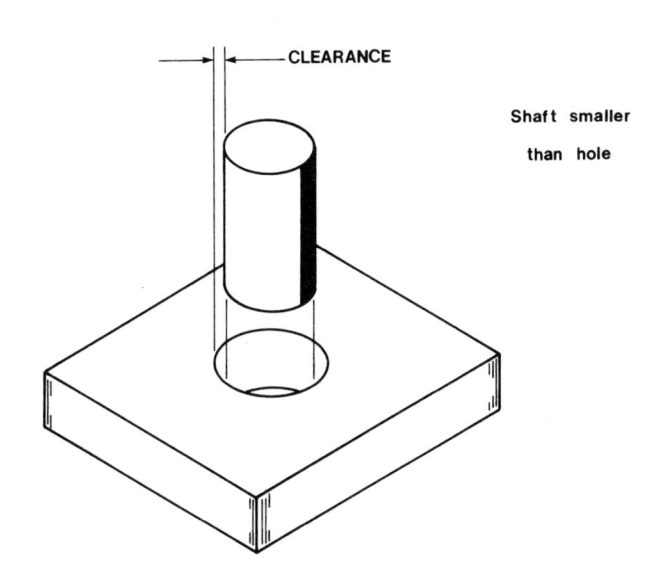

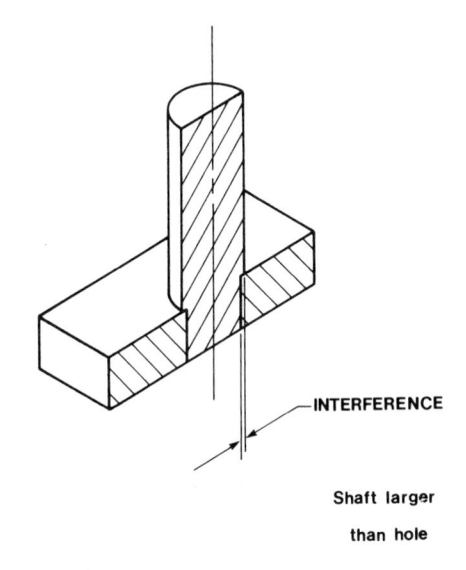

FIGURE 9-17   Interference.

Interference Fit   Tolerances that permit either clearance or interference. Usually, a slight amount of clearance or interference between parts (Figure 9-17).

There are five specific categories of fits for matching parts dimensioned using inches. The categories are listed in Figure 9-18a. Each of these groups is in turn made up of subgroups or classes. Each class has an assigned number which references a table of tolerance values.

The choice of class of fit depends on the design criteria of the particular situation. Each class of fit has a general design usage or set of manufacturing requirements.

Inches Only

Type	Class	Description
RC	RC1–RC9	Running or sliding
LC	LC1–LC11	Locational Clearance
LT	LT1–LT6	Transition Clearance
LN	LN1–LN3	Locational Interference
FN	FN1–FN5	Force or shrink

(a)

Metric Only

Hole Basis Symbol	Shaft Basis Symbol	Description
H11/c11	C11/h11	Loose Running Fit
H9/d9	D9/h9	Free Running Fit
H8/f7	F8/h7	Close Running Fit
H7/g6	G7/h6	Sliding Fit
H7/h6	H7/h6	Locational Clearance
H7/k6	K7/h6	Locational Transition
H7/n6	N7/h6	Locational Transition
H7/p6	P7/h6	Locational Interference
H7/s6	S7/h6	Medium Drive Fit
H7/u6	U7/h6	Force Fit

(b)

FIGURE 9-18 Class-of-fit designations for both (a) English and (b) metric values.

RC1 Close Sliding Fit Accurate location, no perceptible play.

RC2 Sliding Fits Accurate location, parts move easily, but not intended for free running.

RC3 Precision Running Fits Slow speeds, light loads, precise free running.

RC4 Close Running Fits Accurate free running, medium speeds, medium loads, minimum play.

RC5&6 Medium Running Fits Fast speeds, heavy loads.

RC7 Free Running Fits Less accurate and/or large temperature variations.

RC8&9 Loose Running Fits Large tolerances required.

LC1 thru LC 11 Locational Clearance Fits Parts stationary, freely assembled and disassembled. LC1 is snug, LC 11 is loose.

LT1 thru 6 Location Transition Fits Accurate location, either small clearance or interference is acceptable.

LN Locational Interference Fits Very accurate location, rigid alignment, light bore pressure.

FN2 Medium Drive Fits Medium assembly pressure, most steels, high-grade cast iron.

FN3 Heavy Drive Fits Heavy assembly pressure, medium steel parts, not for cast irons.

FN4 and 5 Force Fits Heavy assembly pressure.

The ISO symbols and descriptions for fits are shown in Figure 9-18b. Each category has general design usage or manufacturing requirements.

H11/c11, C11/h11 Loose Running Fit For wide commercial tolerances or allowances on external members.

H9/d9, D9/h9 Free Running Fit Not for use where accuracy is essential, but good for large temperature variations, high running speeds, or heavy journal pressures.

H8F7, F8h7 Close Running Fit For running on accurate machines and for accurate location at moderate speeds and journal pressures.

H7/g6, G7/h6 Sliding Fit Not intended to run freely, but to move and turn freely and locate accurately.

H7/h6, H7/h6 Locational Clearance Fit Provides snug fit for locating stationary parts; but can be freely assembled and disassembled.

H7/kg, K7/h6 Locational Transition Fit For accurate location, a compromise between clearance and interference.

H7/n6, N7/h6 Locational Transition Fit For more accurate location, where greater interference is permissible.

H7/p6, P7/h6 Locational Interference Fit For parts requiring rigidity and alignment with prime accuracy of location but without special bare pressure requirements.

H7/s6, S7/h6 Medium Drive Fit For ordinary steel parts or shrink fits on light sections, the tightest fit usable with cast iron.

H7/u6, U7/h6 Force Fit Suitable for parts that can be highly stressed or for shrink fits where the heavy pressing forces required are impractical.

9-10 BASIC HOLE AND BASIC SHAFT SYSTEMS

When determining limit and fit tolerance, either the hole or the shaft is assumed to be nominal and is used as the basis for all other calculations. If the hole is considered nominal, it is called the *basic hole system*. If the shaft is used, it is called the *basic shaft system*.

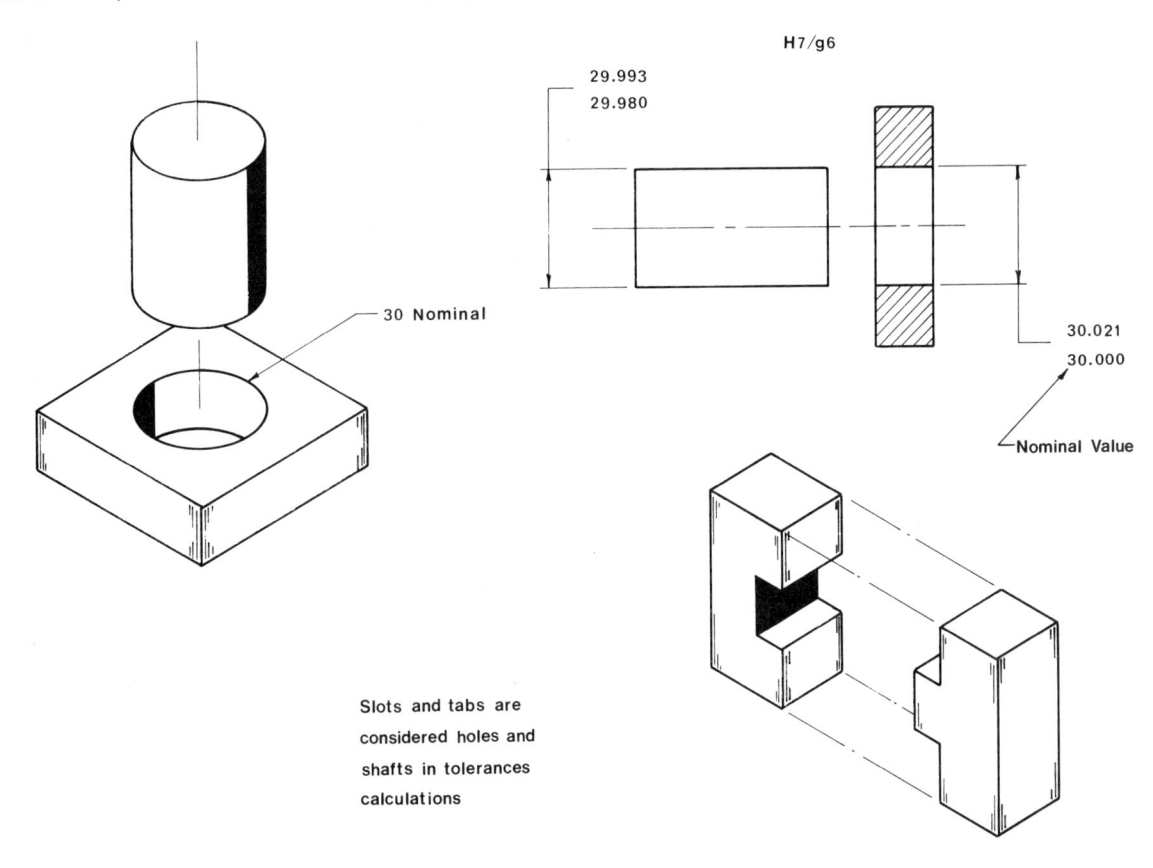

Slots and tabs are considered holes and shafts in tolerances calculations

FIGURE 9-19 Basic hole system.

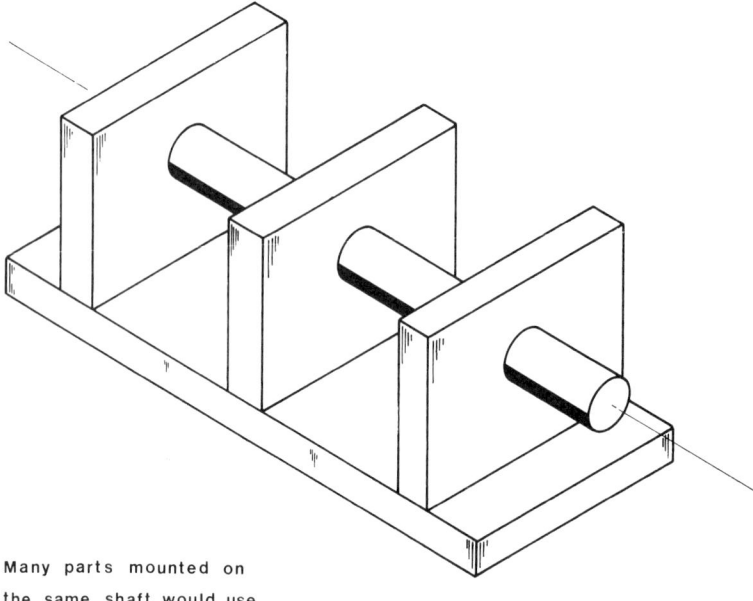

FIGURE 9-20 Basic shaft system.

Many parts mounted on the same shaft would use the basic shaft system

The terms hole and shaft, as used when referring to fit tolerance calculations, are really general terms for any matching paralleled edges. Slots and tabs, keys and keyway tolerances are also determined using the basic hole and basic shaft systems. However, because the majority of matching parallel edges are hole and shaft combinations, the systems use their names.

The basic hole system is the more frequently used of the two systems because each drill bit produces only one fixed-sized hole. Holes that are not equivalent to drill bit sizes require at least two machine operations: an initial drilling, then an enlargement. Shafts are made in one setup, usually on a lathe, and size variations are easier to make (Figure 9-19, p. 261). Therefore, it is easier to match a shaft to a hole than a hole to a shaft.

The tables in Appendix D for fit tolerances are, except where identified, set up for the basic hole system. Sections 9-12 and 9-13 explain how to use the tables to determine fit tolerances.

The basic shaft system is used when one shaft is mounted through several holes. In this situation, it is easier to match several holes to one shaft (Figure 9-20).

9-11 TOLERANCE SYMBOLS

The ISO has set up a standardized system of symbols which combines international tolerance grades (ITs), a tolerance position letter, and the basic feature size to completely define the desired tolerances of a feature (Figure 9-21). The first number in the symbol is featured basic size: 60 mm for the shaft feature, 30 mm for the hole. The capital H after the 30-mm basic hole size signifying the tolerances are determined using the basic hole system. The lowercase f after the 60-mm basic shaft size defines the fundamental deviation.

Figure 9-22 shows pictorial representations of the tolerance position lettering system. Part (a) shows the basic hole system and part (b) shows the basic shaft system.

Sec. 9-11   Tolerance Symbols   263

60 f 7
- Base Size
- Tolerance Position Letter
- IT Grade

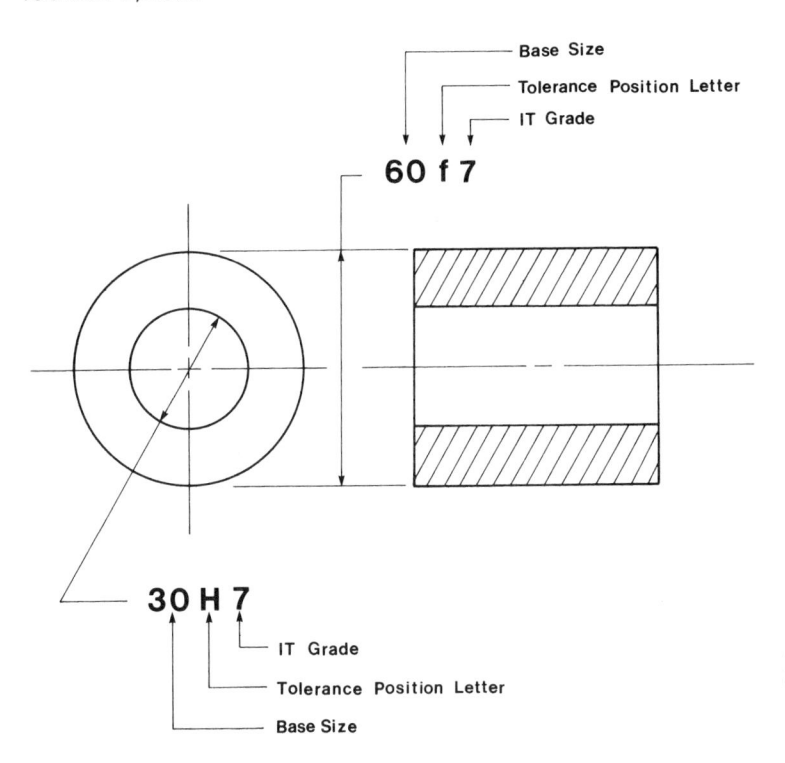

30 H 7
- IT Grade
- Tolerance Position Letter
- Base Size

FIGURE 9-21 Tolerance symbols using international tolerance grades.

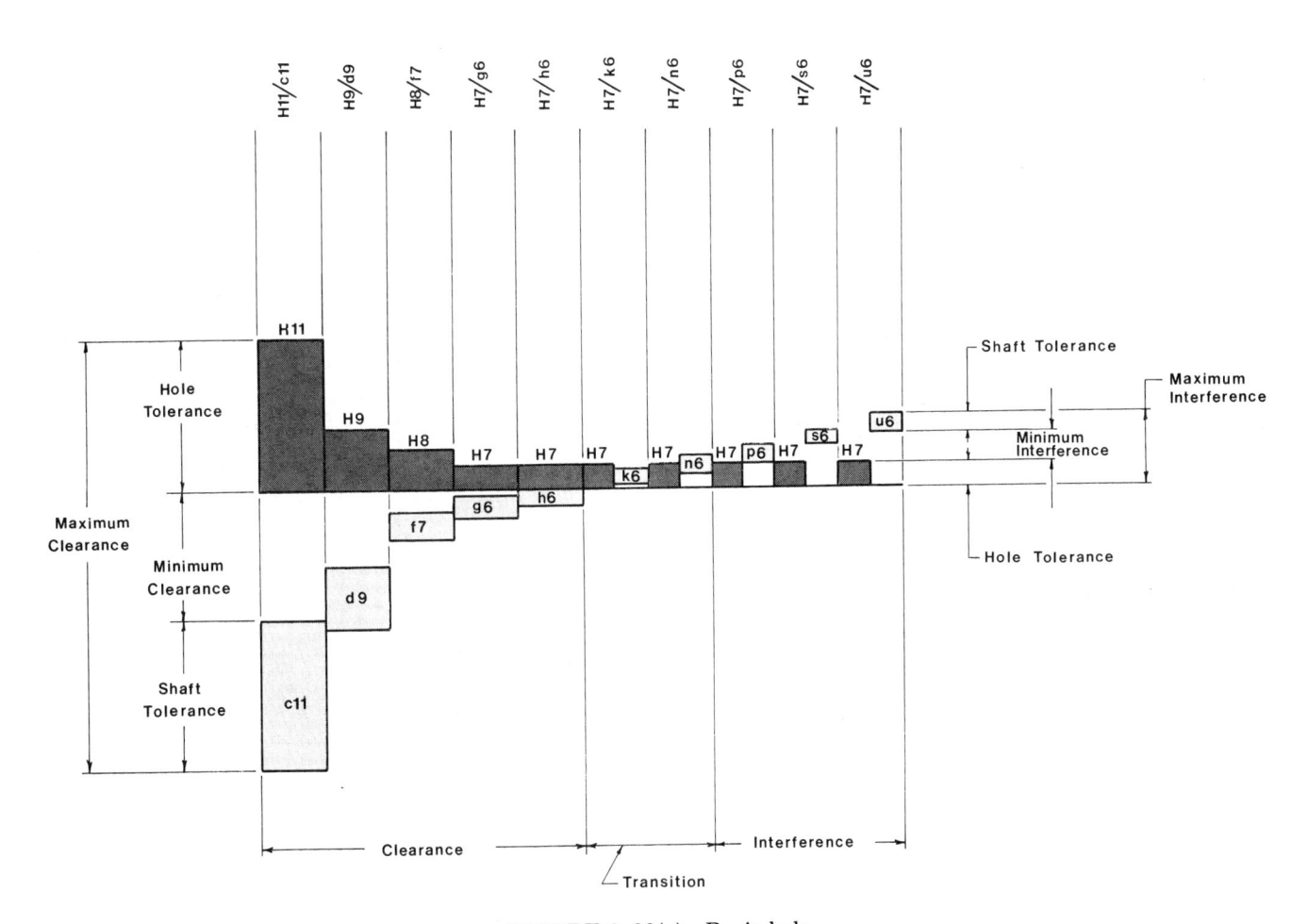

FIGURE 9-22(a) Basic hole.

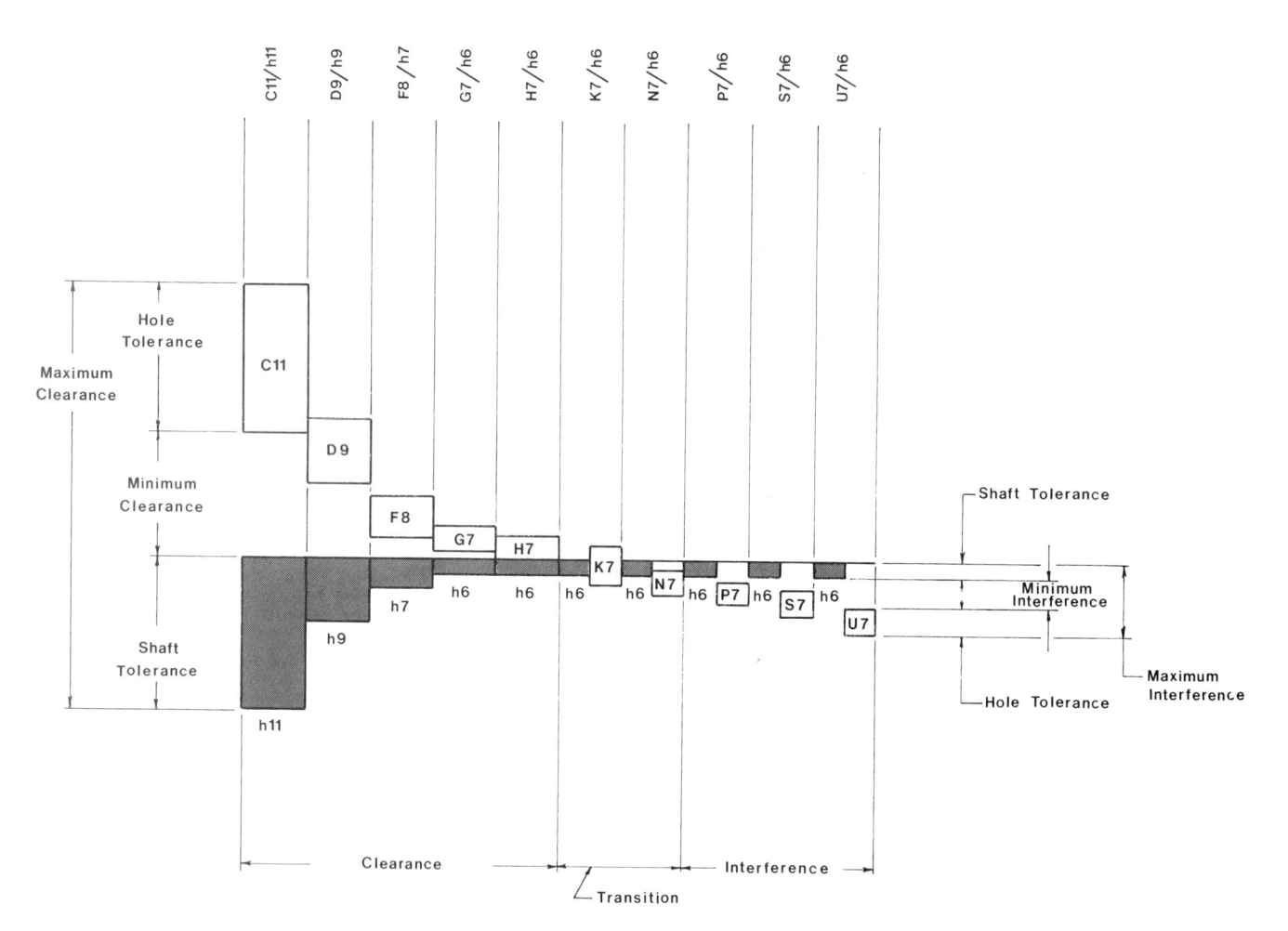

FIGURE 9-22(b) Basic shaft systems.

Over		IT01	IT0	IT1	IT2	IT3	IT4	IT5	IT6	IT7	IT8	IT9	IT10	IT11	IT12	IT13	IT14	IT15	IT16
0	3	0.0003	0.0005	0.0008	0.0012	0.002	0.003	0.004	0.006	0.010	0.014	0.025	0.040	0.060	0.100	0.140	0.250	0.400	0.600
3	6	0.0004	0.0006	0.001	0.0015	0.0025	0.004	0.005	0.008	0.012	0.018	0.030	0.048	0.075	0.120	0.180	0.300	0.480	0.750
6	10	0.0004	0.0006	0.001	0.0015	0.0025	0.004	0.006	0.009	0.015	0.022	0.036	0.058	0.090	0.150	0.220	0.360	0.580	0.900
10	18	0.0005	0.0008	0.0012	0.002	0.003	0.005	0.008	0.011	0.018	0.027	0.043	0.070	0.110	0.180	0.270	0.430	0.700	1.100
18	30	0.0006	0.001	0.0015	0.0025	0.004	0.006	0.009	0.013	0.021	0.033	0.052	0.084	0.130	0.210	0.330	0.520	0.840	1.300
30	50	0.0006	0.001	0.0015	0.0025	0.004	0.007	0.011	0.016	0.025	0.039	0.062	0.100	0.160	0.250	0.390	0.620	1.000	1.600
50	80	0.0008	0.0012	0.002	0.003	0.005	0.008	0.013	0.019	0.030	0.046	0.074	0.120	0.190	0.300	0.460	0.740	1.200	1.900
80	120	0.001	0.0015	0.0025	0.004	0.006	0.010	0.015	0.022	0.035	0.054	0.087	0.140	0.220	0.350	0.540	0.870	1.400	2.200
120	180	0.0012	0.002	0.0035	0.005	0.008	0.012	0.018	0.025	0.040	0.063	0.100	0.160	0.250	0.400	0.630	1.000	1.600	2.500
180	250	0.002	0.003	0.0045	0.007	0.010	0.014	0.020	0.029	0.046	0.072	0.115	0.185	0.290	0.460	0.720	1.150	1.850	2.900
250	315	0.0025	0.004	0.006	0.008	0.012	0.016	0.023	0.032	0.052	0.081	0.130	0.210	0.320	0.520	0.810	1.300	2.100	3.200
315	400	0.003	0.005	0.007	0.009	0.013	0.018	0.025	0.036	0.057	0.089	0.140	0.230	0.360	0.570	0.890	1.400	2.300	3.600
400	500	0.004	0.006	0.008	0.010	0.015	0.020	0.027	0.040	0.063	0.097	0.155	0.250	0.400	0.630	0.970	1.550	2.500	4.000
500	630	0.0045	0.006	0.009	0.011	0.016	0.022	0.030	0.044	0.070	0.110	0.175	0.280	0.440	0.700	1.100	1.750	2.800	4.400
630	800	0.005	0.007	0.010	0.013	0.018	0.025	0.035	0.050	0.080	0.125	0.200	0.320	0.500	0.800	1.250	2.000	3.200	5.000
800	1000	0.0055	0.008	0.011	0.015	0.021	0.029	0.040	0.056	0.090	0.140	0.230	0.360	0.560	0.900	1.400	2.300	3.600	5.600
1000	1250	0.0065	0.009	0.013	0.018	0.024	0.034	0.046	0.066	0.105	0.165	0.260	0.420	0.660	1.050	1.650	2.600	4.200	6.600
1250	1600	0.008	0.011	0.015	0.021	0.029	0.040	0.054	0.078	0.125	0.195	0.310	0.500	0.780	1.250	1.950	3.100	5.000	7.800
1600	2000	0.009	0.013	0.018	0.025	0.035	0.048	0.065	0.092	0.150	0.230	0.370	0.600	0.920	1.500	2.300	3.700	6.000	9.200
2000	2500	0.011	0.015	0.022	0.030	0.041	0.057	0.077	0.110	0.175	0.280	0.440	0.700	1.100	1.750	2.800	4.400	7.000	11.000
2500	3150	0.013	0.018	0.026	0.036	0.050	0.069	0.093	0.135	0.210	0.330	0.540	0.860	1.350	2.100	3.300	5.400	8.600	13.500

FIGURE 9-23 Values for standard international tolerance grades.

Sec. 9-12   Fit Tolerances in Inches   265

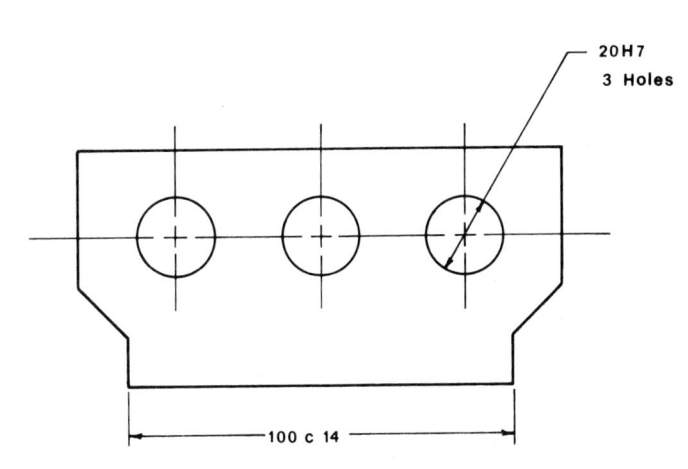

FIGURE 9-24 Examples of how tolerance symbols are used on a drawing.

Figure 9-22 also shows the relative range of each category. For example, the H11 designation has a very large tolerance range, the H7 a much smaller range.

The number following the letter specifies the international tolerance grade. IT grades are shown in Figure 9-23 and are defined by the ISO. In the example shown in Figure 9-21, the number 7 on a base size of 60 mm means a permitted tolerance range of 0.030 mm. Figure 9-24 is an example of how tolerance symbols might be used on a drawing.

9-12 FIT TOLERANCES IN INCHES

Assume that we want to assign fit tolerances to the hole and shaft combination shown in Figure 9-25. The nominal size for each is 0.5 in. nominal, and we want to specify a locational clearance fit. The fit can be fairly loose.

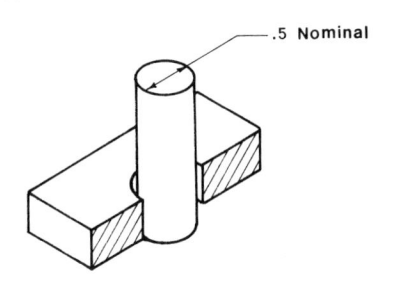

From table in appendix

Nominal Size Range (in.)	Limits of clearance	Class LC 8 Standard limits	
		Hole H10	Shaft d9
.40–.71	2.0 6.4	+2.8 −0	−2.0 −3.6

Values are in thousandths of an inch

CL Max = .0020
CL Min = .0064

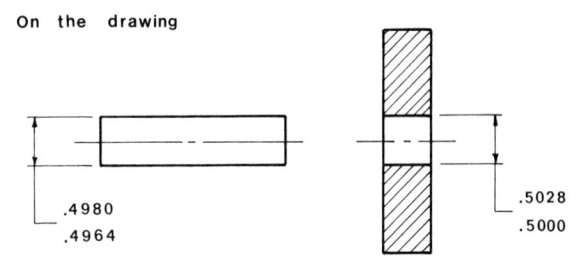

General clearance formulas

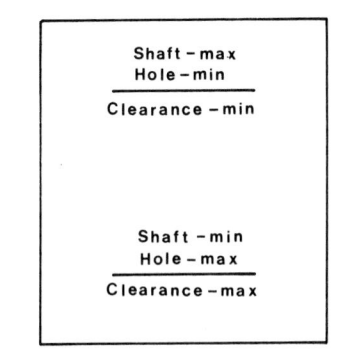

Shaft − max
Hole − min
―――――――
Clearance − min

Shaft − min
Hole − max
―――――――
Clearance − max

FIGURE 9-25 How to use fit tables to tolerance clearance fits.

First we study the table of locational clearance fits in Appendix D (Table D-6). We see that the table is based on the basic hole system (all holes have a lower value of 0). LCI ranges, for $\frac{1}{2}$-in. values, permit a clearance limit of 0.0007 in., which is a very tight tolerance. We are allowed to be fairly loose, so we continue to study various LC categories until we find one acceptable. Assume that we choose LC8.

The hole is toleranced at +2.8 and 0. For a basic $\frac{1}{2}$-in. hole, this means that the tolerance limits are

$$\begin{array}{ll}
0.5000 & \text{nominal} \\
+0.0 & \\
\hline
0.5000 & \text{lower limit — hole}
\end{array}$$

$$\begin{array}{ll}
0.5000 & \text{nominal} \\
+0.0028 & \\
\hline
0.5028 & \text{upper limit — hole}
\end{array}$$

The shaft is toleranced as −2.0 and −3.6. With the basic $\frac{1}{2}$-in. hole dimension the shaft tolerance limits are

$$\begin{array}{ll}
0.5000 & \\
-0.0020 & \\
\hline
0.4980 & \text{upper limit — shaft}
\end{array}$$

$$\begin{array}{ll}
0.5000 & \\
-0.0036 & \\
\hline
0.4964 & \text{lower limit — shaft}
\end{array}$$

The limits-of-clearance numbers 2.0 and 6.4 represent the smallest and largest amounts of clearance between the hole and shaft and are derived as follows.

$$\begin{array}{ll}
-0 & \text{smallest hole} \\
-2.0 & \text{largest shaft} \\
\hline
2.0 & \text{smallest amount of clearance}
\end{array}$$

$$\begin{array}{ll}
+2.8 & \text{largest hole} \\
-3.6 & \text{smallest shaft} \\
\hline
6.4 & \text{largest amount of clearance}
\end{array}$$

Assume now that we are working with another hole–shaft matchup and that the nominal size is $\frac{1}{2}$ in. This time we will tolerance for an FN 2 force fit.

We start by studying the force fit table in Appendix D (Table D-9), specifically the values listed for $\frac{1}{2}$ in. and FN2. The final tolerance values are calculated as follows: For the hole,

$$\begin{array}{ll}
0.5000 & \text{nominal} \\
+\ 0.0 & \\
\hline
0.5000 & \text{lower limit — hole}
\end{array}$$

$$\begin{array}{ll}
0.5000 & \text{nominal} \\
+\ 0.0007 & \\
\hline
0.5007 & \text{upper limit — hole}
\end{array}$$

For the shaft,

$$\begin{array}{ll}
0.5000 & \\
+\ 0.0012 & \\
\hline
0.5012 & \text{lower limit — shaft}
\end{array}$$

Sec. 9-13   Fit Tolerances in Millimeters   267

$$\begin{array}{r}0.5000\\+\ 0.0016\\\hline 0.5016\end{array}\ \text{upper limit} - \text{shaft}$$

Figure 9-26 shows how these values are added to a drawing. The classification FN2 does not appear on the drawing, only the calculated tolerance values.

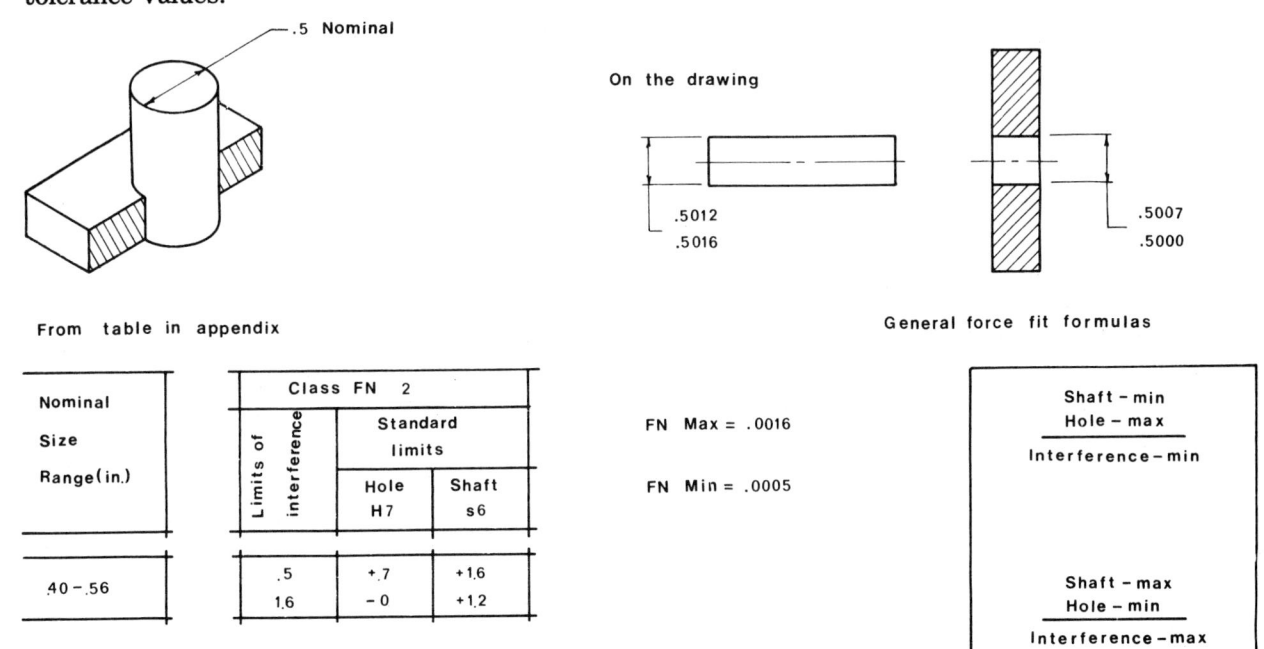

FIGURE 9-26   How to use fit tables to tolerance interference fits.

The fit tables in Appendix D for inch values are calculated for the basic hole system only. Section 9-14 explains how to convert these values for use in the basic shaft system.

9-13 FIT TOLERANCES IN MILLIMETERS

Assume that we have been asked to assign tolerances to shaft-hole combinations which has a 10-mm nominal size and is to fit using a sliding-clearance fit (Figure 9-27). Values for fits using metric units can be looked up directly in the table for clearance fits in Appendix D. No further calculations are necessary as with tables for inch values. The tolerance values are:

Upper limit — hole: 10.015
Lower limit — hole: 10.000
Upper limit — shaft: 9.995
Lower limit — shaft: 9.986

FIGURE 9-27   Clearance fits for metric units.

Decimal		
0.010	2.00	8.50
0.012	2.20	9.00
0.016	2.40	9.50
0.020	2.60	10.00
0.025	2.80	10.50
0.032	3.00	11.00
0.040	3.20	11.50
0.05	3.40	12.00
0.06	3.60	12.50
0.08	3.80	13.00
0.10	4.00	13.50
0.12	4.20	14.00
0.16	4.40	14.50
0.20	4.60	15.00
0.24	4.80	15.50
0.30	5.00	16.00
0.40	5.20	16.50
0.50	5.40	17.00
0.60	5.60	17.50
0.80	5.80	18.00
1.00	6.00	18.50
1.20	6.50	19.00
1.40	7.00	19.50
1.60	7.50	20.00
1.80	8.00	---

Fractional							
1/64	0.015625	5/32	0.15625	7/16	0.4375	3/4	0.7500
1/32	0.03125	3/16	0.1875	1/2	0.5000	7/8	0.8750
1/16	0.0625	1/4	0.2500	9/16	0.5625	1	1.0000
3/32	0.09375	5/16	0.3125	5/8	0.6250	1 1/4	1.2500
1/8	0.1250	3/8	0.3750	11/16	0.6875	1 1/2	1.5000

Fractional							
1 3/4	3 1/4	4 3/4	6 1/2	9 1/2	12 1/2	15 1/2	18 1/2
2	3 1/2	5	7	10	13	16	19
2 1/4	3 3/4	5 1/4	7 1/2	10 1/2	13 1/2	16 1/2	19 1/2
2 1/2	4	5 1/2	8	11	14	17	20
2 3/4	4 1/4	5 3/4	8 1/2	11 1/2	14 1/2	17 1/2	
3	4 1/2	6	9	12	15	18	

Basic Size		Basic Size	
first	second	first	second
1		25	
	1.1		28
1.2		30	
	1.4		35
1.6		40	
	1.8		45
2		50	
	2.2		55
2.5		60	
	2.8		70
3		80	
	3.5		90
4		100	
	4.5		110
5		120	
	5.5		140
6		160	
	7		180
8		200	
	9		220
10		250	
	11		280
12		300	
	14		350
16		400	
	18		450
20		500	
	22		550

FIGURE 9-28 Preferred sizes for decimal, fractional, and metric values.

Note that only a few values are listed under BASIC SIZE for all the fit tables using metric values. For example, there are no 3.7 or 32-mm values listed. This is because those values listed are preferred values and should, as often as possible, be used for design purposes. Figure 9-28 lists the preferred sizes together with some second-choice values.

Designers should always try to use preferred values. Stock sizes, manufacturing tools, inspection devices, and much design information has been designed and calculated to match preferred values. Other values can be used but require adjustment to both equipment and calculations so, if possible, should be avoided.

9-14 BASIC SHAFT SYSTEM SAMPLE PROBLEMS

Fit tolerances for the basic shaft system using inch values are determined using the same tables as those used for the basic hole system, with some adjustments. If we are asked to determine the tolerance values for a shaft and hole which is $\frac{1}{2}$ in. nominal and uses a LC7 clearance fit, we would look up the values in Table D-6.

For example, for an LC8 clearance fit (Figure 9-25) we find the following values for the basic hole system:

	Hole	Shaft
	+2.8	−2.0
	−0	−3.6

Sec. 9-15 Surface Finish 269

These values are converted to the basic shaft system by changing the SHAFT-MAX value to 0. This requires the given shaft value to be increased by 0.002 (values given are in thousandths of an inch). All other values are also increased by 0.002 to maintain the LC8 tolerance ranges. The resulting values for the basic shaft system are:

Hole	Shaft
+4.8	−0
+2.0	−1.6

Basic shaft system values for millimeter values can be found directly using the basic shaft system tables in Appendix D. The procedure is the same as described for the basic hole system example in Section 9-13.

9-15 SURFACE FINISH

Another important consideration when calculating tolerance values is surface finish. *Surface finish* refers to quality of a finished surface, how smooth or rough the surface is.

Figure 9-29 shows a photograph of a metal block whose top surface contains four different surface finishes. The left side is a ^{8} finish, the center two types are ^{16}s, and the right is a ^{32}. All are considered fairly smooth surfaces. Note the difference in the appearance of the four different finishes.

Rough surfaces are faster and easier to manufacture than smoother surfaces but are unacceptable for bearing or fast-moving matching surfaces. The designer should always try to use as rough a surface (largest possible tolerance range) as possible that will still satisfy the design requirements.

Surface finishes are measured using either microinches (μin.) or micrometers (μm). A microinch equals 0.000 001 in. A micrometer equals 0.000 001 m. 1 in. = 0.0254 m.

Roughness, as used for surface finishes, refers to the irregularities in the surface texture which usually results from the production process.

FIGURE 9-29 Comparison of various finishes.

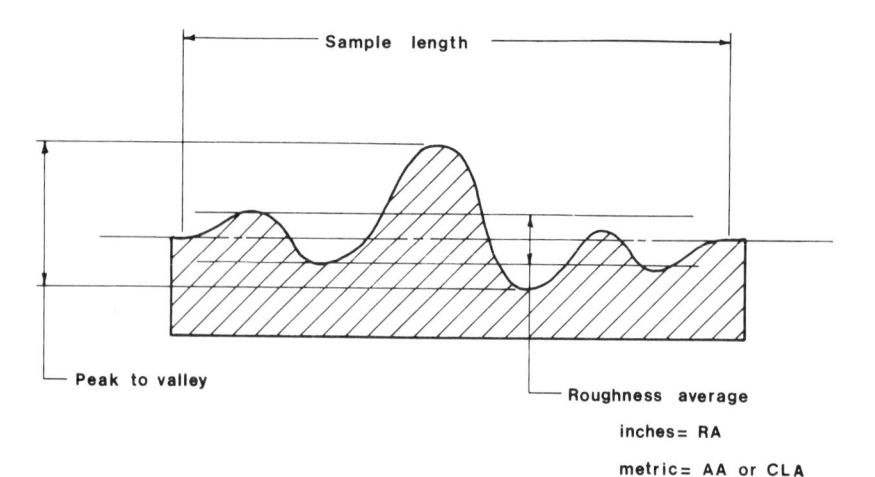

FIGURE 9-30 Surface finish notations.

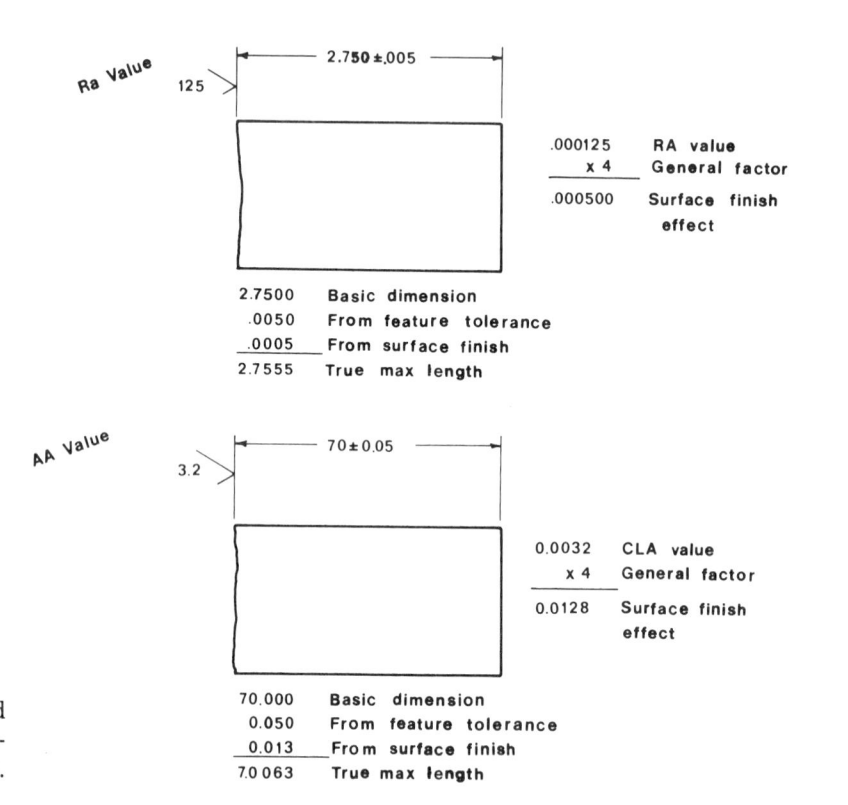

FIGURE 9-31 How to add surface finish values to dimension and tolerance calculations.

Roughness is measured by taking an average of the absolute values of a measured profile height deviation over a defined sample length. The roughness average is abbreviated as *RA* for inch values and AA (arithemic average) for metric values; the term CLA (centerline average) is also used (Figure 9-30).

The highest points on a surface are called *peaks*, the lowest *valleys*. Typically, the maximum peak-to-valley heights (R_{max}) are at least three times the roughness average.

The effect of surface finish on feature tolerances are approximated by multiplying the *RA* value by 4 and adding it to the specified feature tolerance. For example, in Figure 9-31 the 2.750 length has a tolerance

Sec. 9-16   Surface Finish Symbols

of +0.005 and an end surface finish $RA = 125$ in. If 125 in. is multiplied by 4, the resultant value is 0.0005 in.

$$\begin{array}{r} 0.000125 \;\; RA \\ \times 4 \\ \hline 0.000500 \;\; \text{surface finish factor} \end{array}$$

The value 0.0005 in. must be added to the other tolerance values to find the true maximum feature length.

It is important to consider the effects of surface finish when designing parts that require close fits, carry heavy loads, or slide rapidly over one another.

9-16 SURFACE FINISH SYMBOLS

The basic symbol for specifying surface finishes on a drawing is shown in Figure 9-32. There are many variations of the basic symbol.

Note in the figure the symbol variations for removing material and for not removing material. The basic symbol permits either consideration as long as the final surface finish requirements are met. The material removal symbol mandates some sort of machining process and prohibits using stock or cast surfaces even if they meet specifications. Conversely, the symbol preventing material removal prohibits any machining process and requires stock or cast surfaces to be used.

R_a values are specified on drawings using numerical values as shown in Figure 9-33. Surface finish symbols may be added to the drawing along

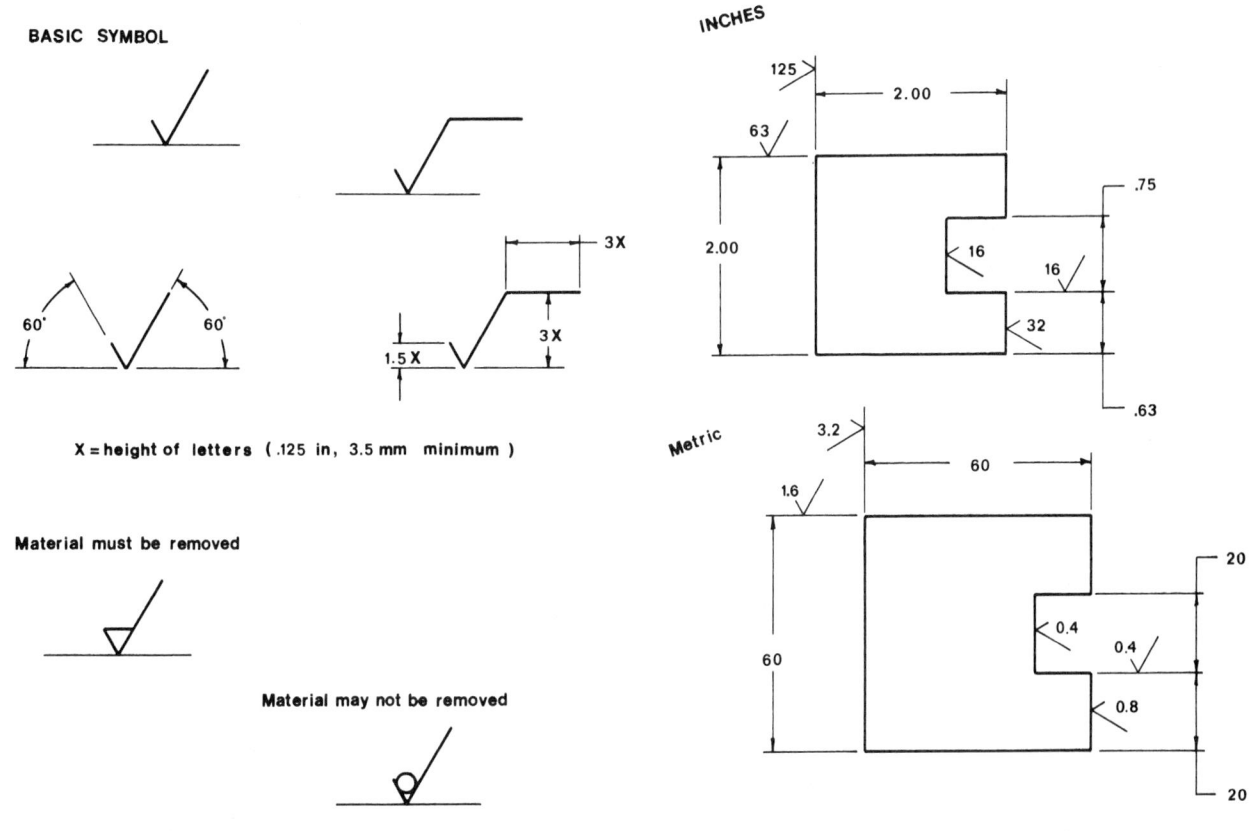

FIGURE 9-32   Symbols for surface finishes.

FIGURE 9-33   How to apply surface finish symbols to a drawing.

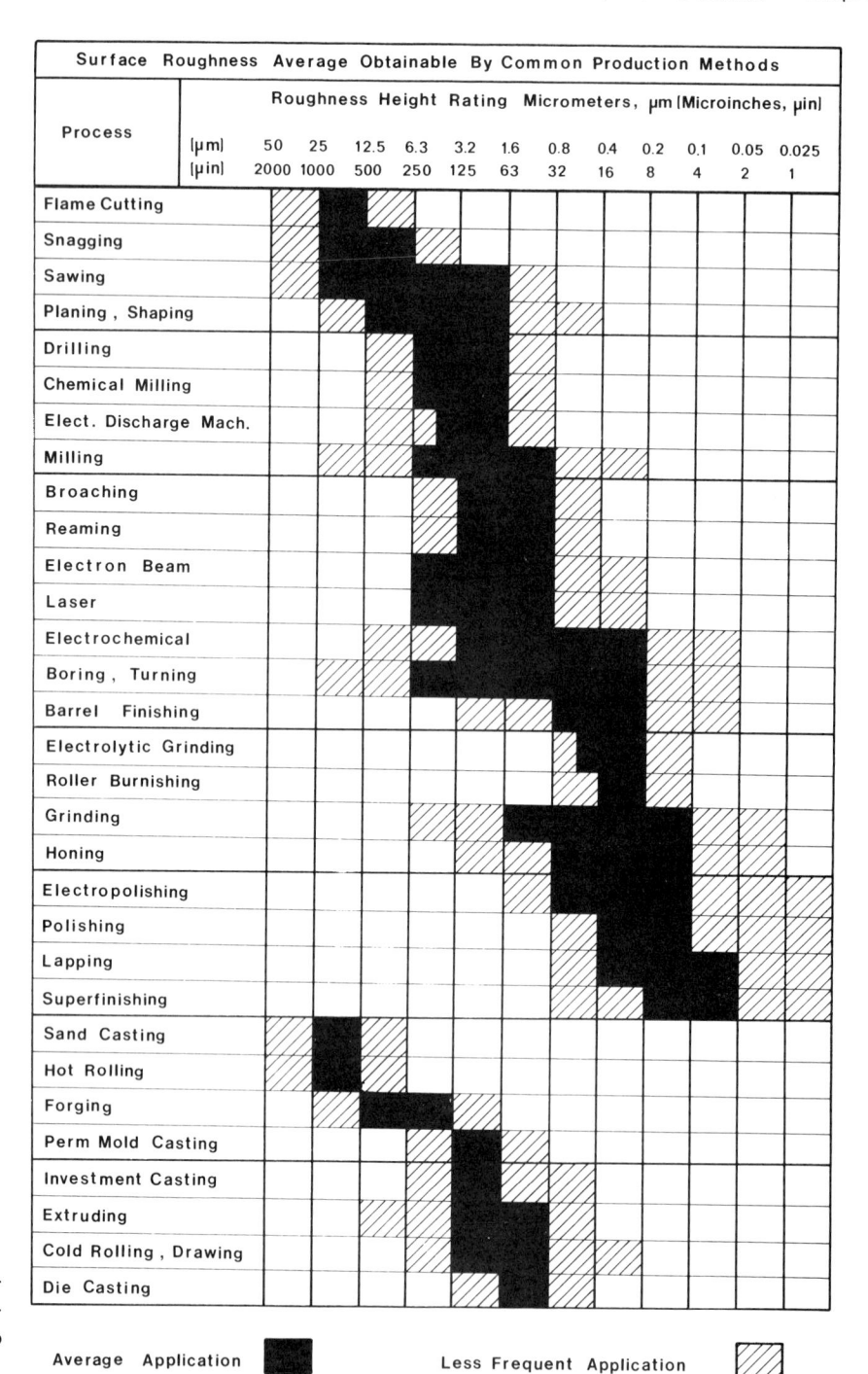

FIGURE 9-34 Preferred surface finish values and the manufacturing processes used to create them.

extension lines or directly to a profile view of the applicable surface. Symbols are not placed on dimension lines. Figure 9-34 lists the preferred R_a values and the manufacturing processes used to obtain the values.

The *lay* of a surface finish refers to the direction of the predominant surface pattern and serves to control the direction of machining for the object. Figure 9-35 shows a part where the machining marks are visible. These machine marks establish the lay of the surface finish. Figure 9-36 shows the surface lay symbols and shows how the lay symbols are added to the basic surface finish symbol.

Sec. 9-16   Surface Finish Symbols   273

FIGURE 9-35   Machine marks establish the lay of a surface finish.

Designers sometimes prefer to specify a range of R_a values. This permits greater flexibility in manufacturing. Surface finish ranges are included on a drawing by specifying the maximum and minimum R_a values as shown in Figure 9-37.

Inches

Symbol	Meaning
=	Parallel
⊥	Perpendicular
X	Angular
M	Multidirectional
C	Circular
R	Radial
P	Nondirectional

Metric

Inches

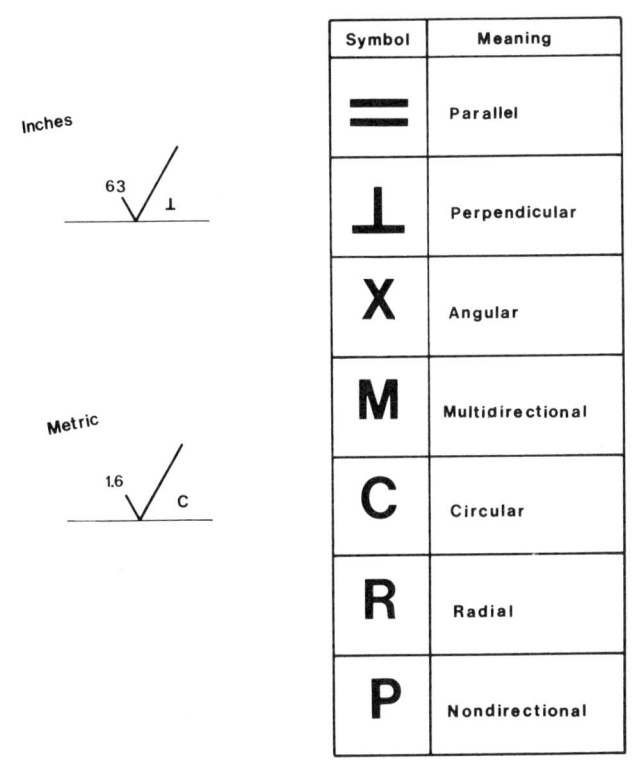

Metric

FIGURE 9-36   Lay symbols for surface finishes.

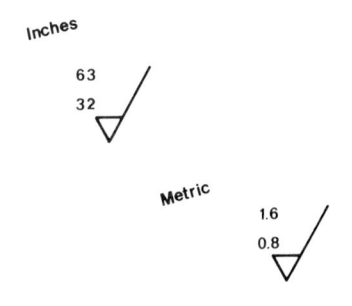

FIGURE 9-37   Drawing notations that specify a range for surface finish.

9-17 INSPECTION OF TOLERANCED DIMENSIONS

The inspection of finished parts is as important as their design and manufacture. Parts are inspected to verify that they are within the tolerances specified by the designer and in many cases, to determine how much the machinist will be paid. Many workers are paid "piecemeal," that is, by the number of parts they make which meet the specified dimensions and tolerances.

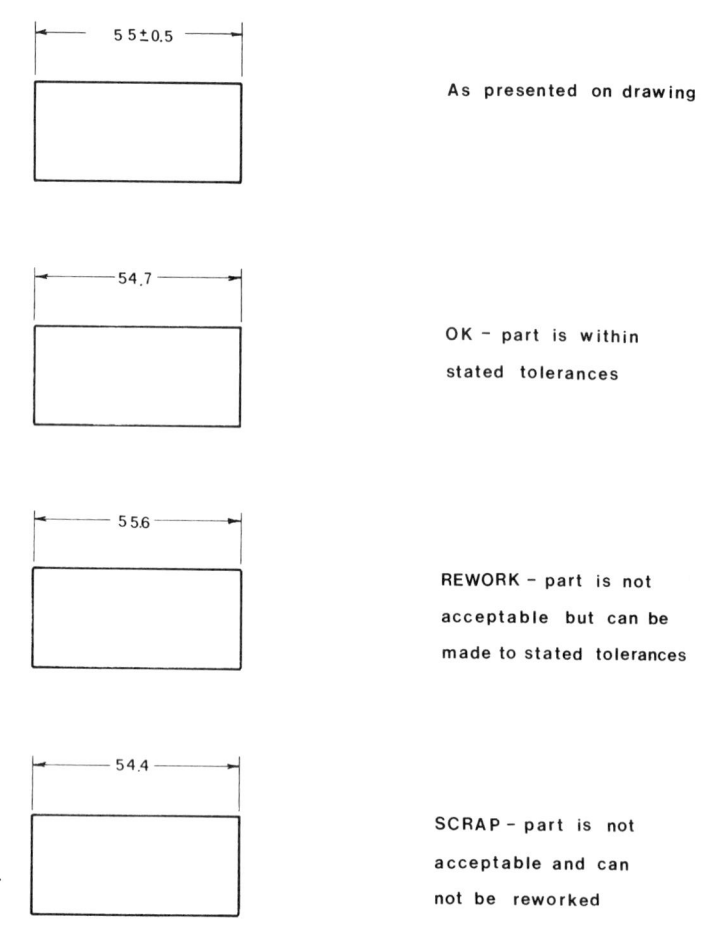

FIGURE 9-38 Inspection classifications.

55±0.5 — As presented on drawing

54.7 — OK - part is within stated tolerances

55.6 — REWORK - part is not acceptable but can be made to stated tolerances

54.4 — SCRAP - part is not acceptable and can not be reworked

There are three general categories for inspected parts: OK, rework, and scrap (Figure 9-38). The OK category means that the part is acceptable. It meets the dimensions and tolerances specified on the drawing. The *rework* category means that the part does not meet the drawing specifications, but can be remachined to bring it within the specified tolerances. The *scrap* category means that the part is not within the drawing specifications and further, cannot be reworked to meet the specifications. The part must be thrown away.

9-18 DUAL DIMENSIONING

Dual dimensioning is using both millimeters and inch values on the same drawing to define the same distances. Dual dimensioning is helpful when a company is in transition and is converting from U.S. Customary units

Sec. 9-18 Dual Dimensioning 275

to SI metric or when vendors or customers use different measuring systems.

There are two ways to dual-dimension a drawing: the position method and the bracket method. Figure 9-39 shows the position method, Figure 9-40, the bracket method.

The *position method* locates dimensions, expressed in inches and millimeters, in approximately the same position on the drawing. Metric units are always placed above or to the left of the inch units. The two values are separated by a horizontal line or aligned and separated by a long slash line.

The *bracket method* is primarily an inch system with the metric equivalent of each inch value added to the drawing enclosed in brackets just to the right or underneath the inch value. It is useful when redoing an existing inch-unit drawing to include metric units. The metric values are simply added to the existing drawing.

It should be noted that the latest edition of ANSI Y14.5M-1982, "Dimensioning and Tolerancing," no longer features dual dimensioning. Reference to dual dimensioning is limited to one paragraph at the very end of the standard. The standard includes only metric units.

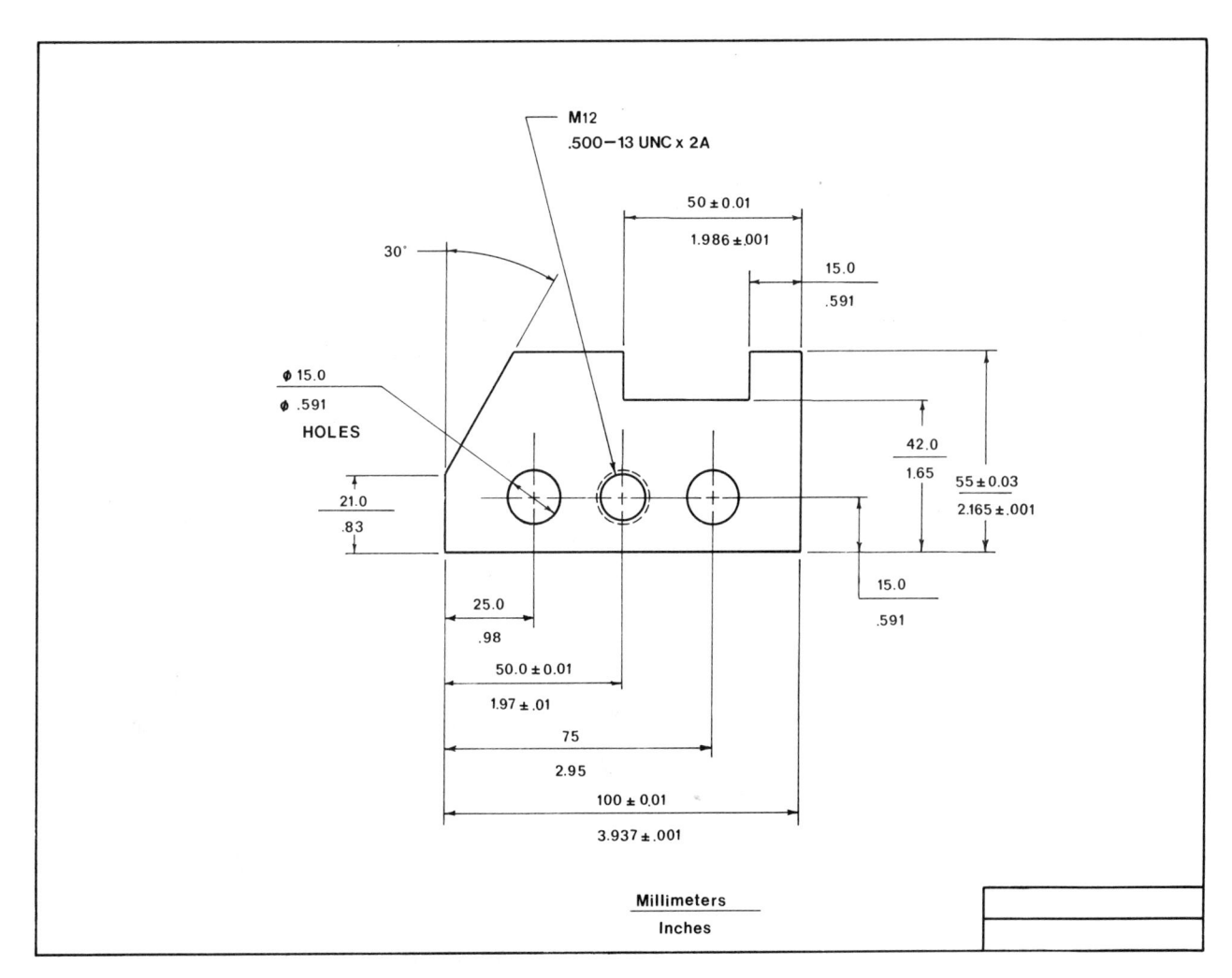

FIGURE 9-39 Position method of dual dimensioning.

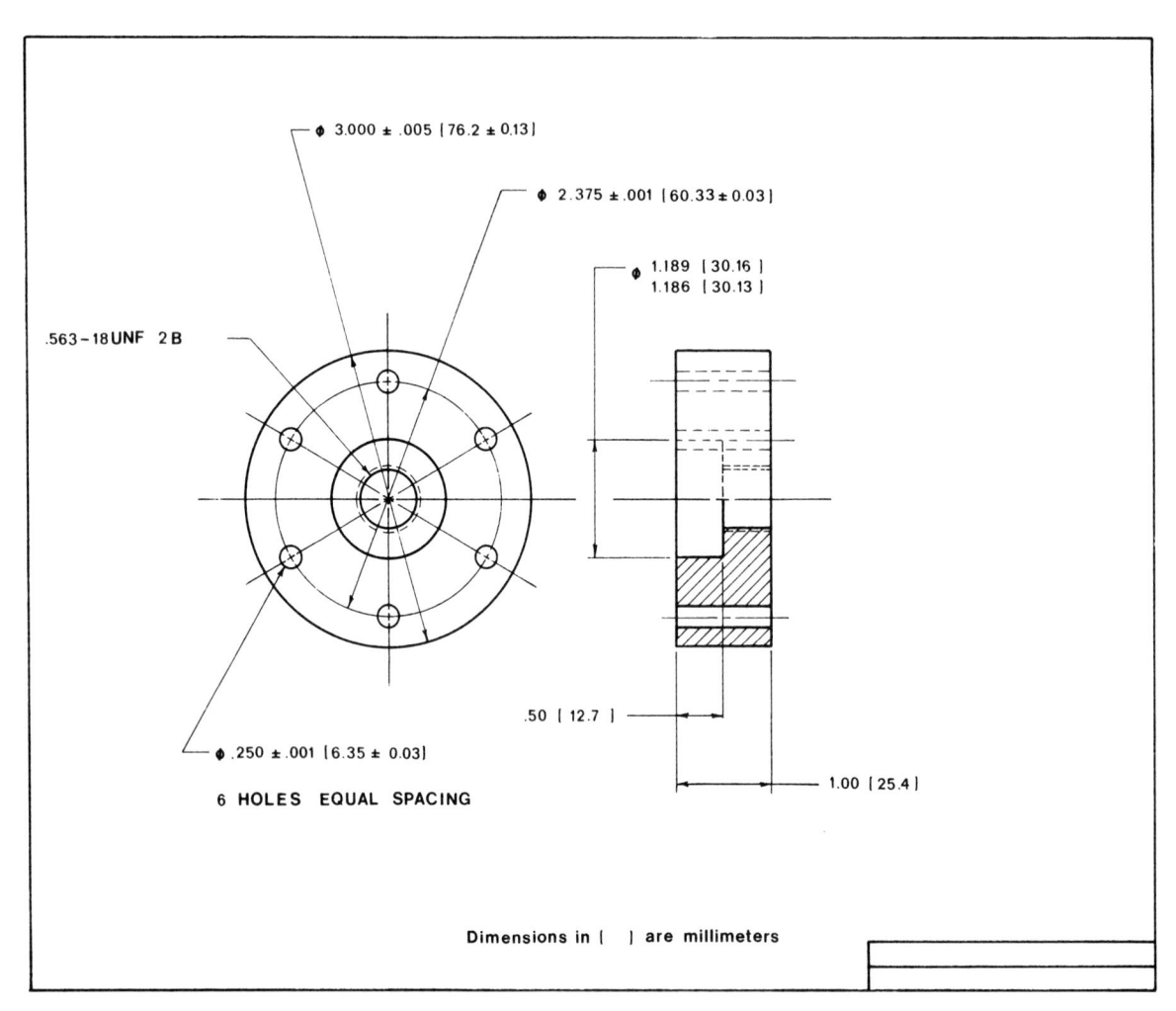

FIGURE 9-40 Bracket method of dual dimensioning.

PROBLEMS

P9-1 Redraw Figure P9-1 using the dimensions and tolerances listed below. Add the dimensions and tolerances in the appropriate places. All values are in millimeters.

1. 37.5 ± 0.01
2. 10.05
   10.00
3. 5 + 0.01
       − 0
4. 45 ± 0.01° − 2 ANGLES
5. 40 ± 0.1
6. 22 ± 0.05
7. 12 ± 0.1
8. 25 ± 0.02
9. 50 ± 0.02
10. 75 ± 0.02

Chap. 9 Problems

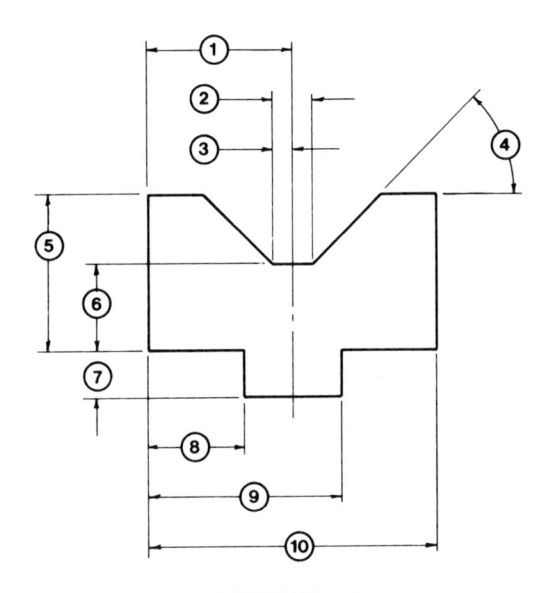

FIGURE P9-1

P9-2 Redraw Figure P9-2 using the dimensions and tolerances listed below. Add the dimensions and tolerances in the appropriate places. All values are in millimeters.

1. 17 ± 0.05
2. 6 × 20 ± 0.01
   (= 100 ± 0.1)
3. 150 ± 0.3
4. 16.02
   15.99
5. 7 + 0
   − 0.01
6. 14.01
   13.98
7. 19 ± 0.1
8. 38 ± 0.1
9. 6 × 12 ± 0.01
10. MATL = 12 GA − SAE 1020 ST

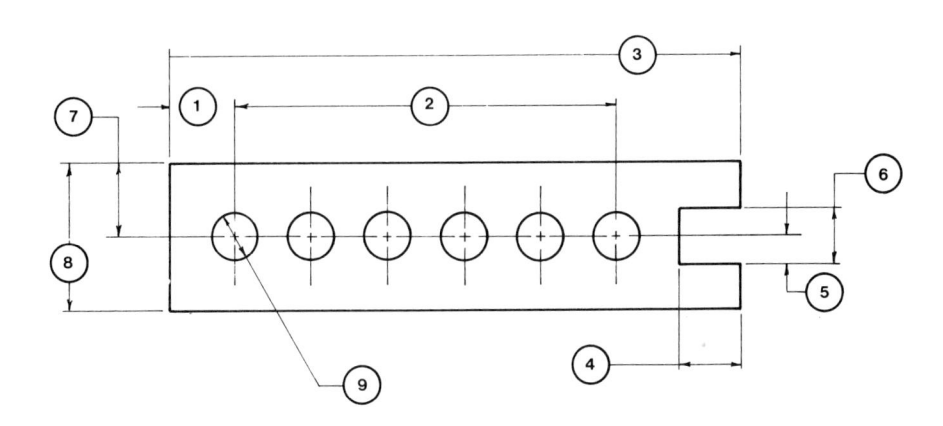

FIGURE P9-2

278 Basic Concepts of Tolerances   Chap. 9

P9-3 Redraw Figure P9-3 using the following dimensions and tolerances. Include the dimensions and tolerances on the final drawing.

1. 7.25 ± 0.05
2. 3.63 ± 0.03
3. 1.750 ± 0.005
4. 0.875 ± 0.002
5. 0.50 ± 0.01
6. 0.25 ± 0.01
7. 1.13 ± 0.01
8. 0.63
   0.61
9. 0.63
   0.61
10. 1.13 ± 0.01
11. 0.500 ± 0.010
    − 2 SLOTS
12. 0.252 − 4 HOLES
    0.248
13. 3.25 ± 0.05
14. 2.500 ± 0.003
15. 2.000 ± 0.003
16. 1.125 ± 0.060
17. 1.250 ± 0.005
18. 3.000 ± 0.005
19. 4.750 ± 0.005
20. 7.25 ± 0.05 REF
21. 0.500 × 1.250 − 3 SLOTS
22. 0.25 ± − 4 HOLES
23. 0.25 ± − 4 HOLES

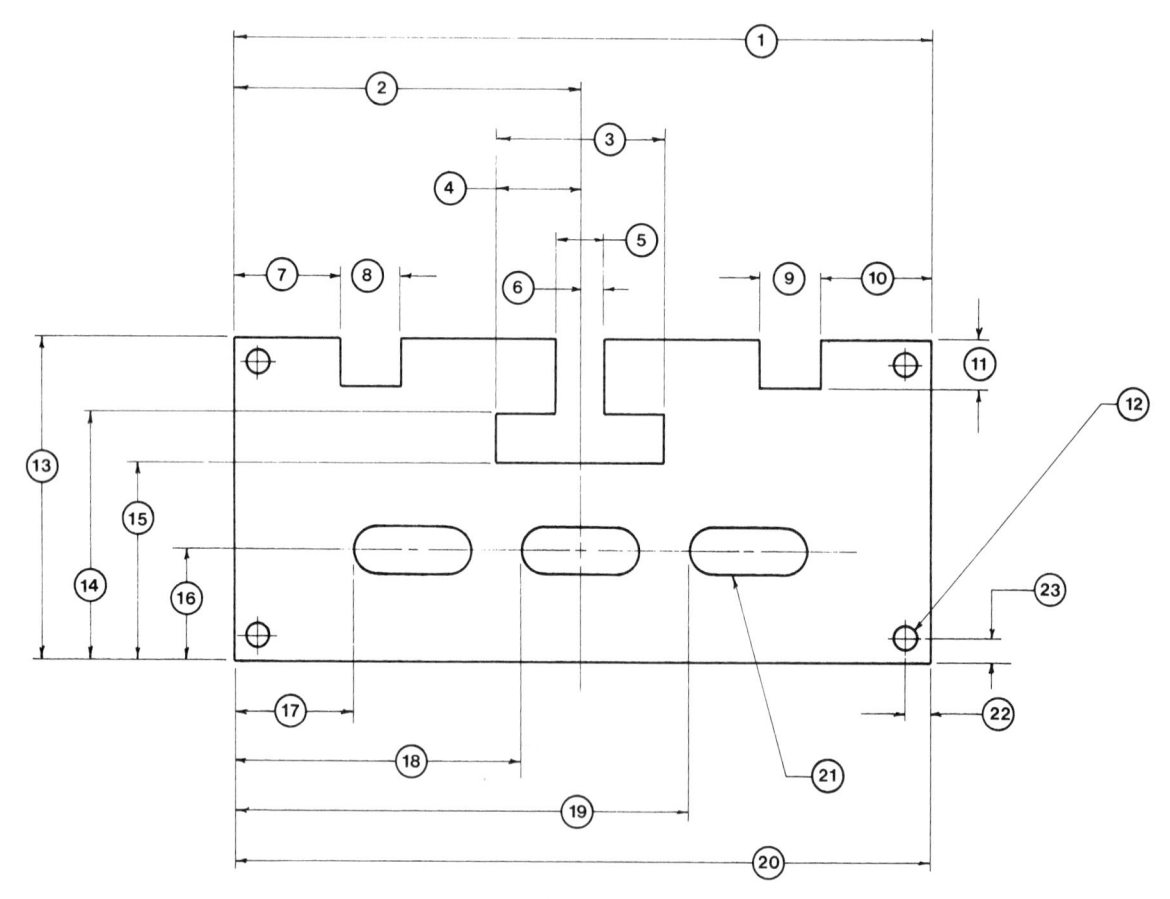

FIGURE P9-3

P9-4 Redraw Figure P9-4 using the dimensions, tolerances, and surface finishes listed below. Add the dimensions and tolerances in the appropriate places. All values are in inches.

1. 2.000 ± 0.001
2. 2.000 + 0.002
         − 0
8. 32
9. 32
10. 125

Chap. 9   Problems

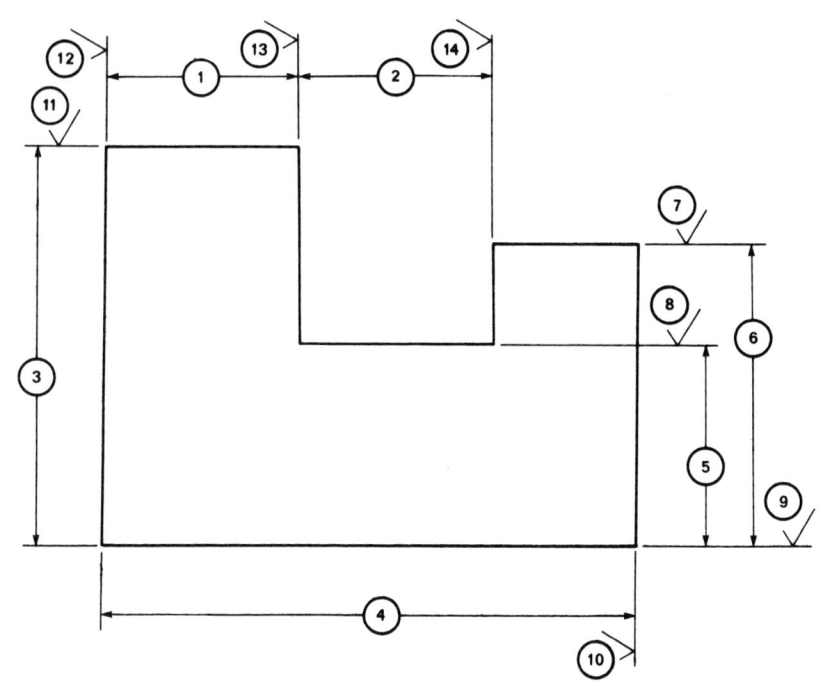

3. 4.000 ± 0.002
4. 5.500 + 0
          − 0.001
5. 2.002
   1.999
6. 3.000 ± 0.003
7. 64

11. 64
12. 32
13. 32
14. 32

FIGURE P9-4

P9-5 Figure P9-5 shows the same shape dimensioned two different ways. One is called Part 101, the other Part 102. Compare the effects on feature size of the various dimensioning techniques. Present answers in a neat list with each value labeled. All values are in inches.

1. Part 101   Part 102
   A max   A max
   A min   A min
2. Part 101   Part 102
   B max   B max
   B min   B min
3. Part 101   Part 102
   C max   C max
   C min   C min
4. Part 101   Part 102
   A + B max   A + B max
   A + B min   A + B min
5. Part 101   Part 102
   A + B + C max   A + B + C max
   A + B + C min   A + B + C min

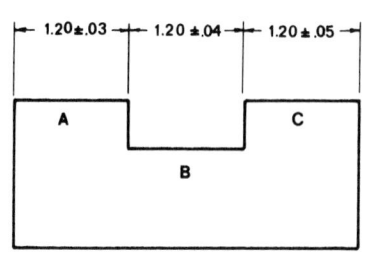

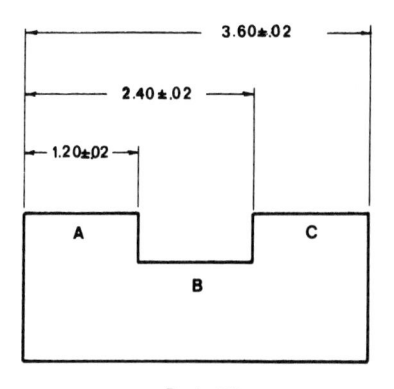

FIGURE P9-5

P9-6 Figure P9-6 shows the same shape dimensioned two different ways. One is called Part 101, the other Part 102. Compare the effects on feature size of the various dimensioning techniques. Present answers in a neat list with each value labeled. All values are in millimeters.

1. Part 101   Part 102
    A max   A max
    A min   A min
2. Part 101   Part 102
    B max   B max
    B min   B min
3. Part 101   Part 102
    C max   C max
    C min   C min
4. Part 101   Part 102
    A + B max   A + B max
    A + B min   A + B min
5. Part 101   Part 102
    A + B + C max   A + B + C max
    A + B + C min   A + B + C min
6. Part 101   Part 102
    D max   D max
    D min   D min
7. Part 101   Part 102
    A + B + C + D max   A + B + C + D max
    A + B + C + D min   A + B + C + D min

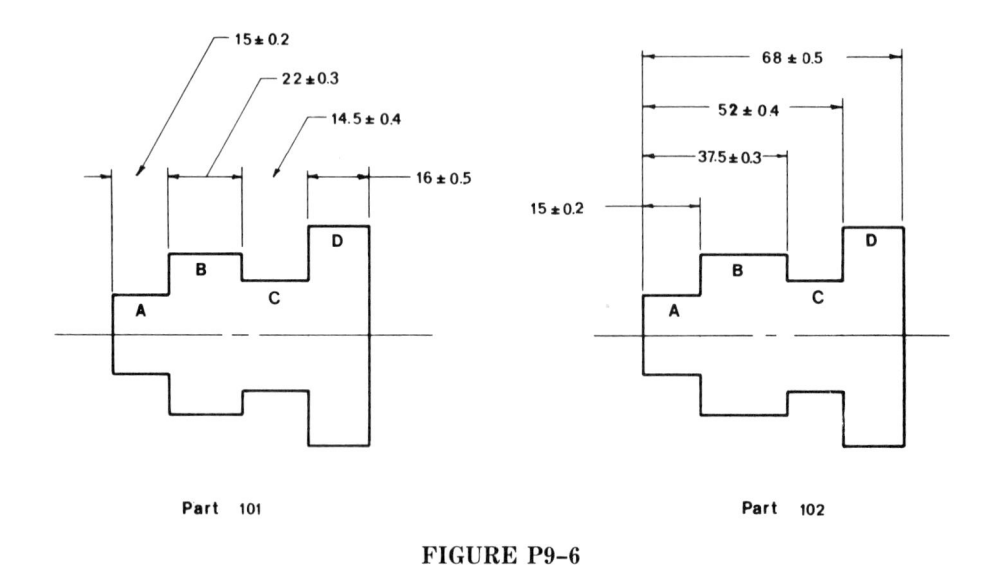

Part 101

Part 102

FIGURE P9-6

P9-7 Prepare drawings of Parts 43-1 and 43-2 as shown in Figure P9-7, including dimensions and tolerances. Choose dimensions and tolerances that assure a maximum mismatch between surfaces A and B of 0.05 in., and a total height tolerance of 2.25 ± 0.06. All sizes given are nominal.

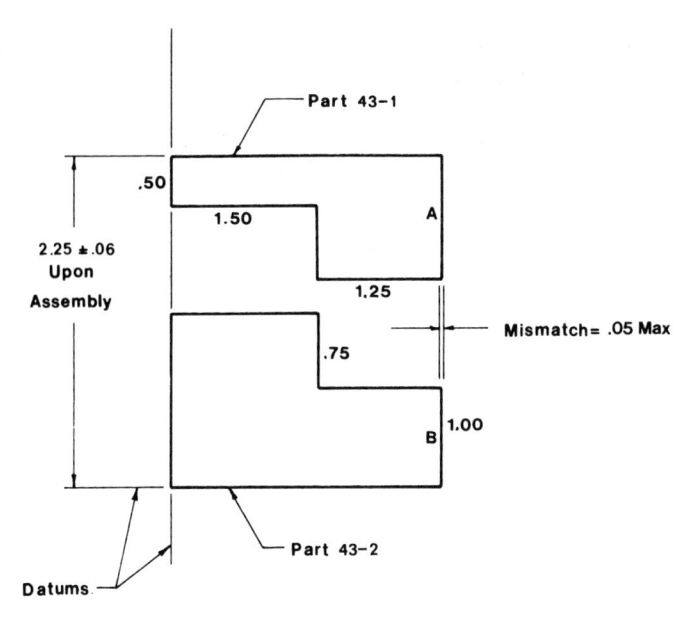

FIGURE P9-7

P9-8 Prepare drawings of Parts 725-01 and 725-02 as shown in Figure P9-8, including dimensions and tolerances. Choose dimensions and tolerances that assure a maximum mismatch between surfaces A and B of 0.1 mm, and a total weight of 60 ± 0.4. All sizes given are nominal.

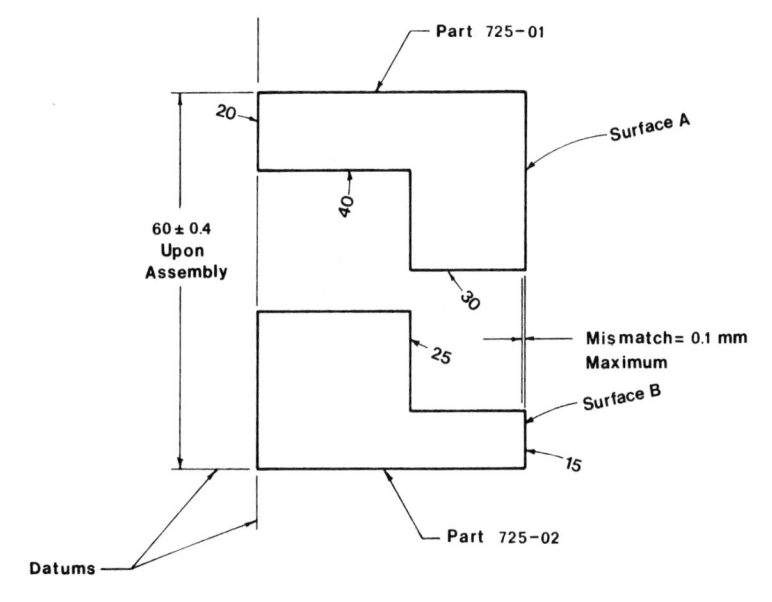

FIGURE P9-8

P9-9 Prepare a drawing of Part 507S103, shown in Figure P9-9. Include dimensions and tolerances which enable the part to fit over the given plug gage. The dimensions given for the plug gage are "as measured" and have no tolerance variance. A maximum mismatch of 0.5 mm is permitted between the ends of the plug gage and Part 507S103. The plug gage must fit in either possible orientation.

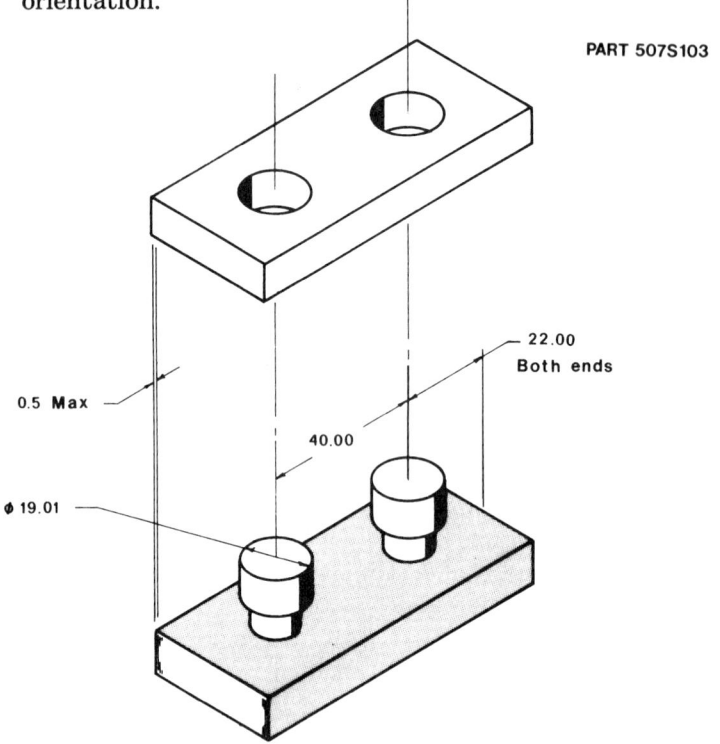

FIGURE P9-9

P9-10 Prepare drawings of Parts 4A and 4B as shown in Figure P9-10. Part 4A must always fit into Part 4B. The minimum permissible clearance is 0.3 mm between the shaft of Part 4A and the hole of Part 4B. The maximum mismatch between the outside surfaces is 0.5 mm. The shaft should never extend completely through the hole.

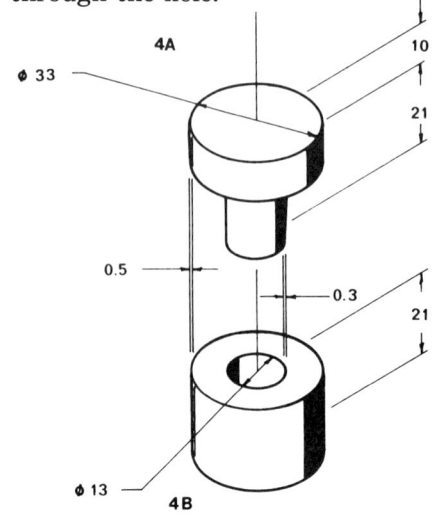

FIGURE P9-10

P9-11 Redraw the charts shown in Figure P9-11 and add the appropriate values for hole, shaft, clearance, and interference maximums and minimums. Determine the value from the nominal sizes listed below. Use the basic hole system. All values are in inches.

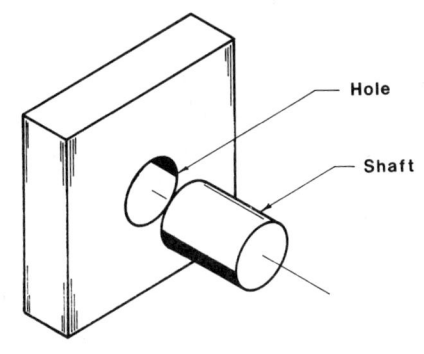

A. 0.50 − RC6
B. 1.00 − RC6
C. 0.375 − RC6
D. 0.625 − RC6
E. 1.25 − RC6

F. 0.05 − FN2
G. 1.00 − FN2
H. 0.375 − FN2
I. 0.625 − FN2
J. 1.25 − FN2

FIGURE P9-11

P9-12 Redraw the charts shown in Figure P9-11 and add the appropriate values for hole, shaft, clearance, and interference maximums and minimums. Determine value from the nominal sizes listed below. Use the basic hole system. All values are in millimeters.

A. 20 mm − H8/f7 F. 20 − N7/h6
B. 26 mm − H8/f7 G. 40 − N7/h6
C. 10 mm − H8/f7 H. 10 − N7/h6
D. 27 mm − H8/f7 I. 27 − N7/h6
E. 23 mm − H8/f7 J. 55 − N7/h6

P9-13 Redraw the charts shown in Figure P9-11 and add the appropriate values for hole, shaft, clearance, and interference maximum and minimums. Determine values from the nominal sizes listed below. Use the basic shaft system.

A. 1.00 in. − RC2 F. 1.50 in. − LN2
B. 20 mm − H11/c11 G. 50 mm − K7/h6
C. 0.44 in. − RC8 H. 0.25 in. − LN3
D. 10 mm − H7/g6 I. 5 mm − P7/h6
E. 30 mm − H7/h6 J. 12 mm − U7/h6

P9-14 Calculate the maximum and minimum values for the total height of Parts P1, P2, P3, and P4 as shown in Figure P9-14. Prepare a table as shown and list the appropriate values. Four sets of parts labeled condition A, B, C, and D are to be considered. The values for the detail drawing are as follows:

Condition A
(inches)

1. 1.00 ± 0.0
2. 0.52
   0.49
3. 1.25 ± 0.02
4. 1.00 + 0.03
        − 0.00
5. 0.50 ± 0.03
6. 1.25 + 0.04
        − 0.00

Condition B
(inches)

1. 1.000 ± 0.050
2. 0.525
   0.485
3. 1.250 ± 0.025
4. 1.000 ± 0.035
        − 0.007
5. 0.500 + 0.036
6. 1.250 + 0.046
        − 0.000

Condition C
(metric)

1. 25 ± 0.1
2. 12.4
   11.7
3. 30 ± 0.2
4. 25 + 0.3
      − 0.1
5. 25 ± 0.3
6. 32 + 0.2
      − 0

Condition D
(metric)

1. 25.0 ± 0.04
2. 12.43
   11.72
3. 30 ± 0.25
4. 25.0 + 0.32
        − 0.09
5. 25 ± 0.35
6. 32.0 + 0.25
        − 0

Chap. 9 Problems 285

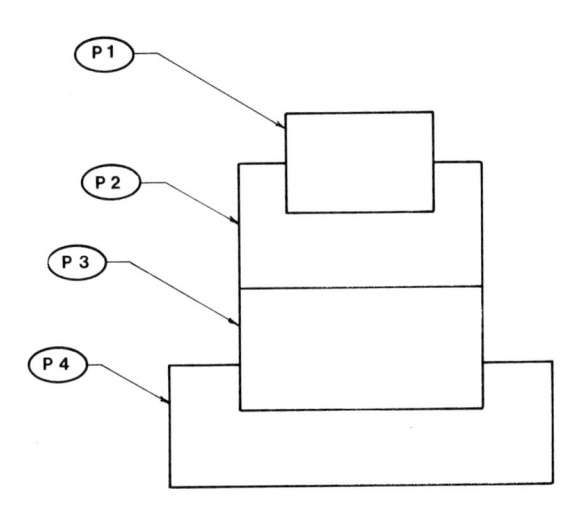

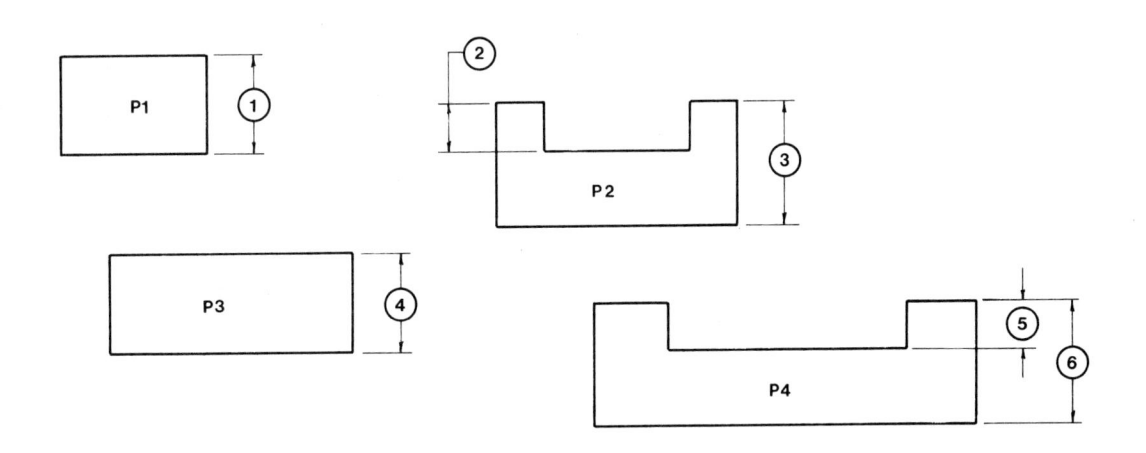

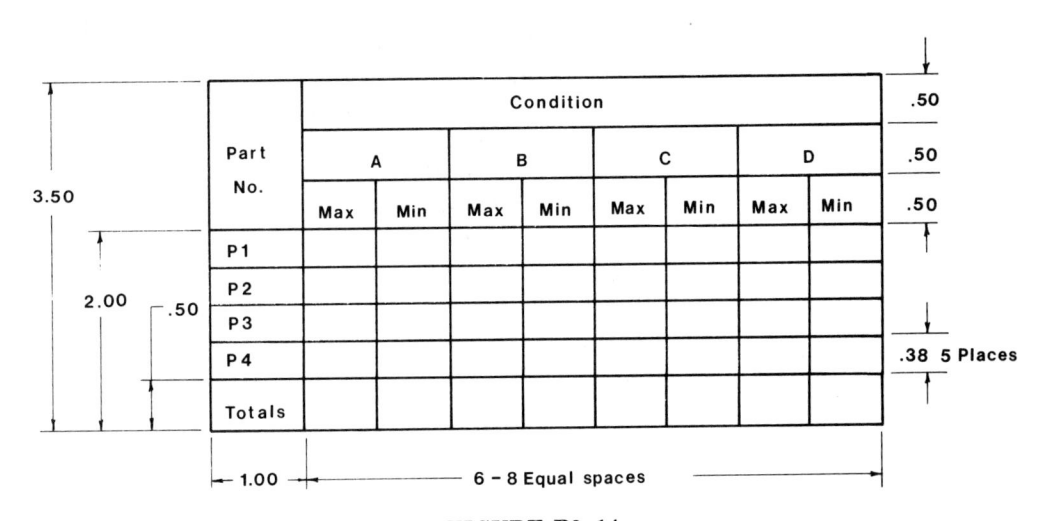

FIGURE P9-14

P9-15 Calculate the maximum and minimum values for the features specified in Figure P9-15. Present your answers in a neat list with each value labeled. Figures A and D use inch values, figures B and C, millimeters.

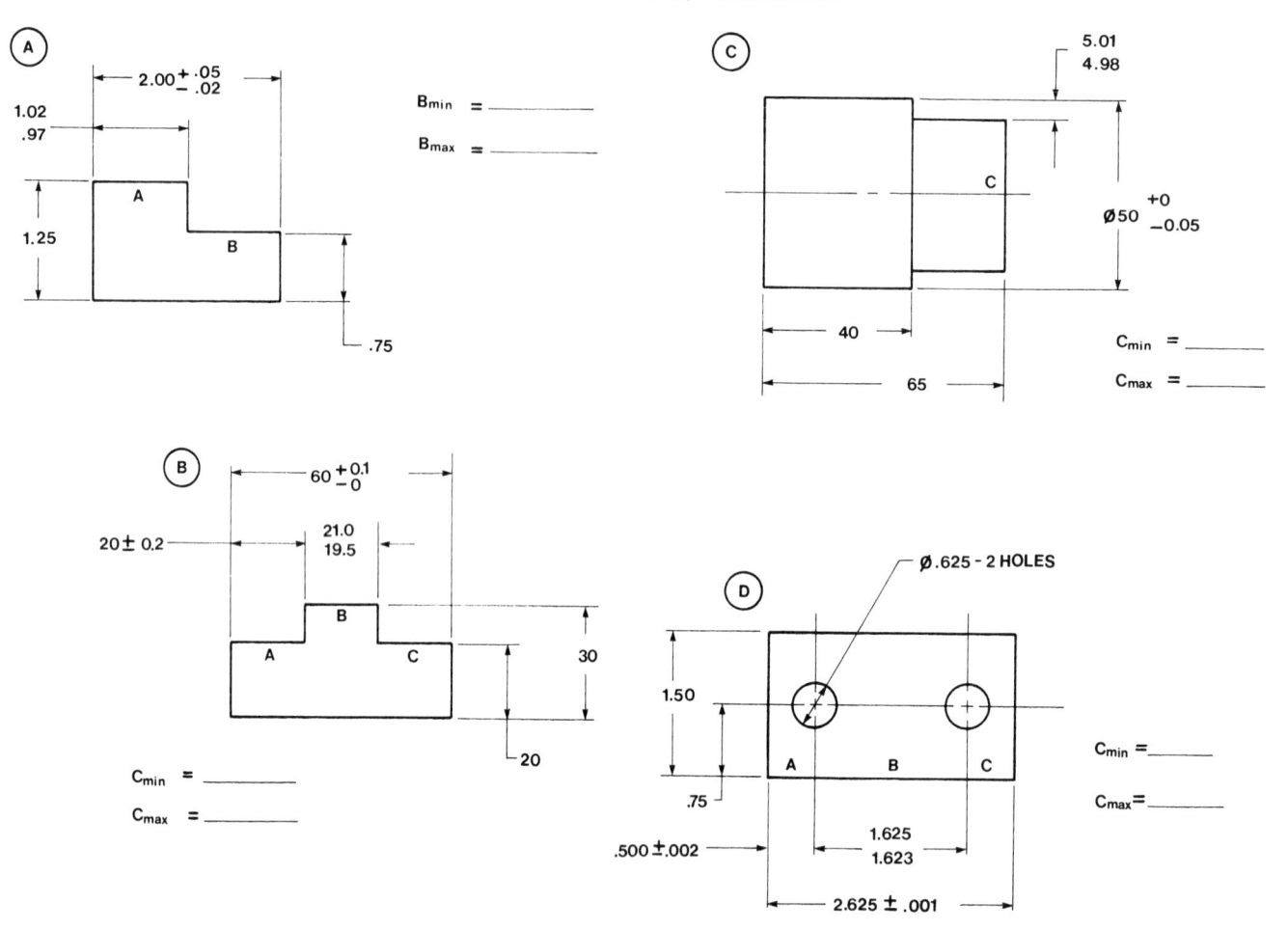

B_{min} = _____

B_{max} = _____

C_{min} = _____

C_{max} = _____

C_{min} = _____

C_{max} = _____

C_{min} = _____

C_{max} = _____

FIGURE P9-15

P9-16 Prepare an inspection report as shown in Figure P9-16a. Complete the inspection report for the drawing shown in Figure P9-16b. The "as measured" values are noted below. Under the RESULTS heading, list whether each as-measured value is OK (within tolerance), REWORK (over tolerance), or SCRAP (under tolerance). Unless otherwise specified, all dimensions have a tolerance of ±0.02 mm.

1. 25.1
2. 20.03
3. 49.8
4. 20.00
5. 38.025
6. 20.005
7. 52.97

Chap. 9 Problems   287

[Figure P9-16: (a) Inspection Report form with columns BASE DIMENSION, TOLERANCES (MAX, MIN), AS MEASURED, RESULTS; rows numbered 1–10. Dimensions: 1.00 – 3 PLACES, .50 – 10 PLACES. (b) Plate 72–732–A drawing with numbered dimensions: ① 25, ② Ø 20.05/20, ③ 50, ④ 20±0.01, ⑤ 38±0.02, ⑥ 20±0.01, ⑦ 53.]

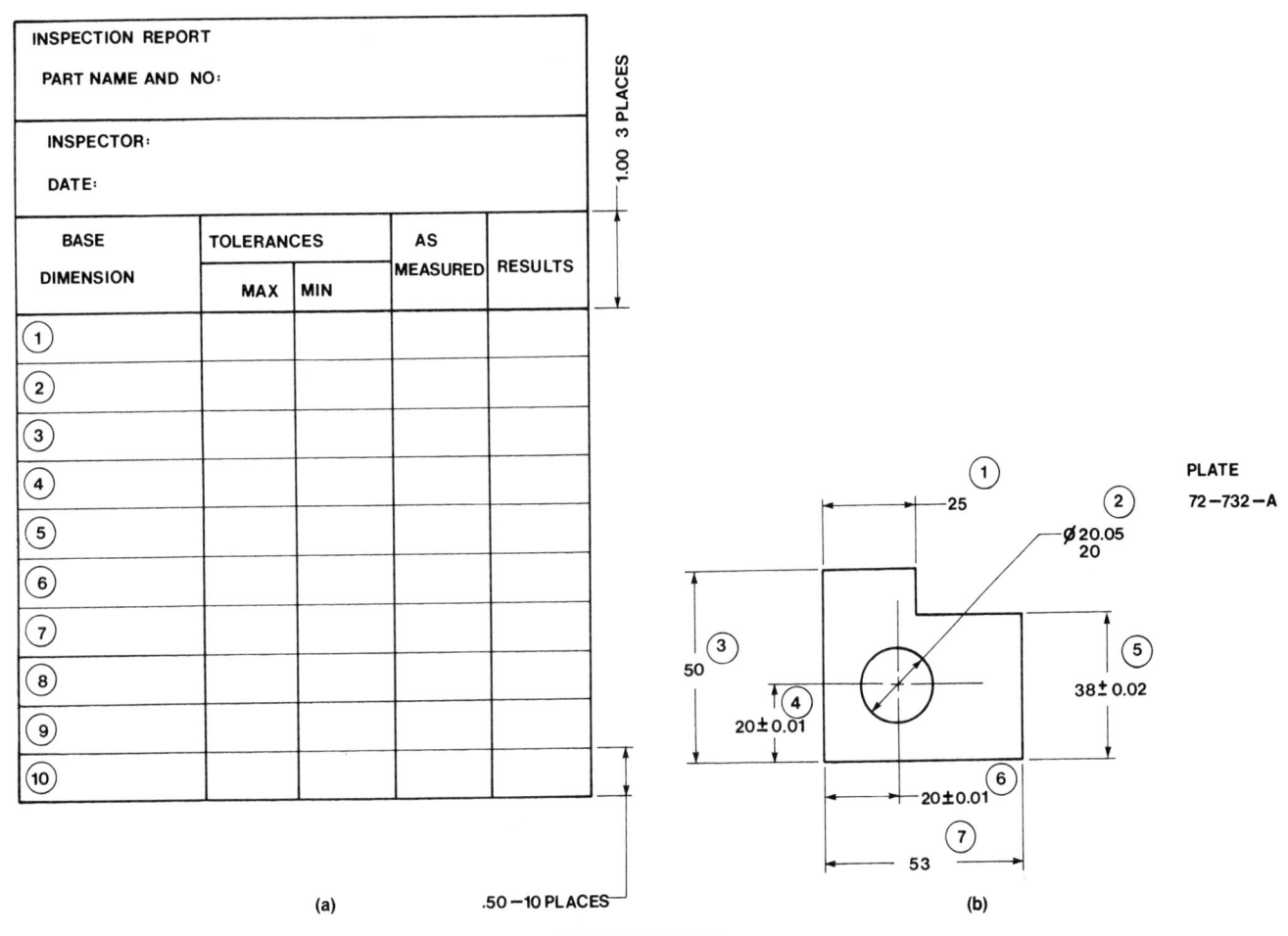

FIGURE P9-16

P9-17   Prepare an inspection report as shown in Figure P9-16a. Complete the inspection report for the drawing shown in Figure P9-17. The "as measured" values are noted below. Under the RESULTS heading, list within each as-measured value is OK (within tolerance), REWORK (over tolerance), or SCRAP (under tolerance). Unless otherwise specified, all dimensions have a tolerance of ± 0.01 in.

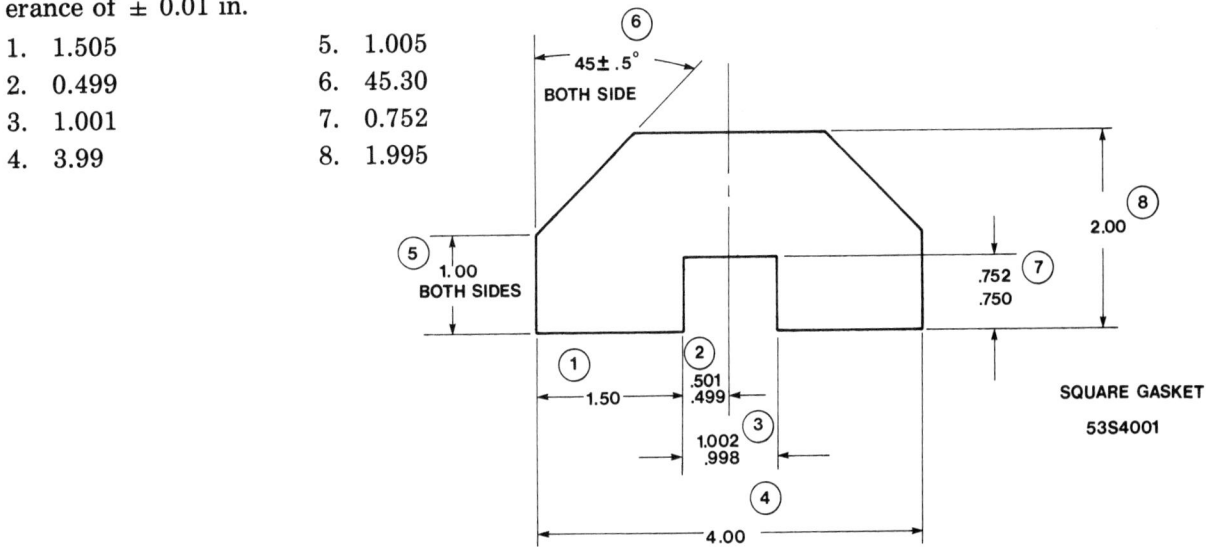

   1. 1.505   5. 1.005
   2. 0.499   6. 45.30
   3. 1.001   7. 0.752
   4. 3.99   8. 1.995

[Figure P9-17: Square Gasket 53S4001 drawing with numbered dimensions: ① 1.50, ② .501/.499, ③ 1.002/.998, ④ 4.00, ⑤ 1.00 BOTH SIDES, ⑥ 45±.5° BOTH SIDE, ⑦ .752/.750, ⑧ 2.00.]

FIGURE P9-17

P9-18 Prepare an inspection report as shown in Figure P9-16a. Complete the inspection report for the drawing shown in Figure P9-18. The "as measured" values are noted below. Under the RESULTS heading, list whether each as-measured value is OK (within tolerance), REWORK (over tolerance), or SCRAP (under tolerance). Unless otherwise specified, all dimensions have a tolerance of ±0.03 mm.

1. 49.97
2. 10.04
3. 30.025
4. 40.06
5. 19.99
6. 9.96
7. 10.02
8. 9.995

FIGURE P9-18

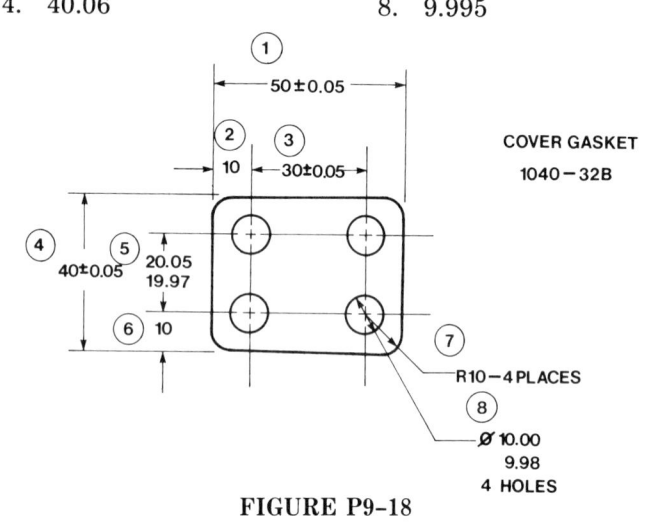

P9-19 Prepare drawings of each of the two parts shown in Figure P9-19. All values noted below are in millimeters. Assign tolerances as needed to achieve the final condition values.

A. 100
B. 30
C. 100
D. 10
E. 15
F. 20

Final condition

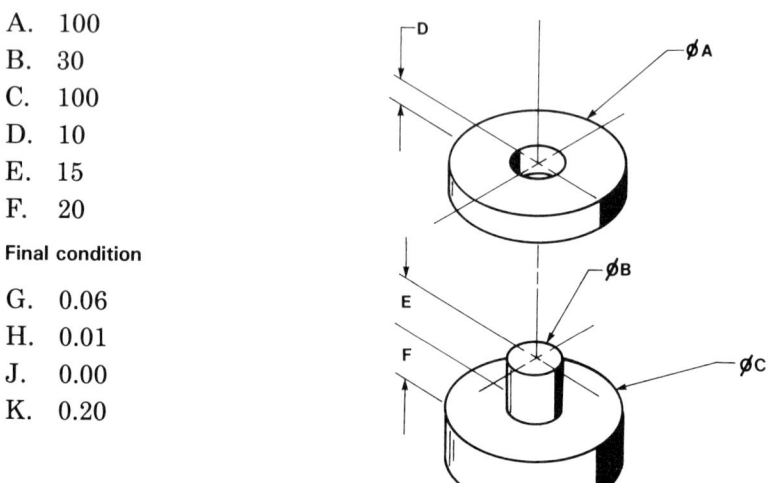

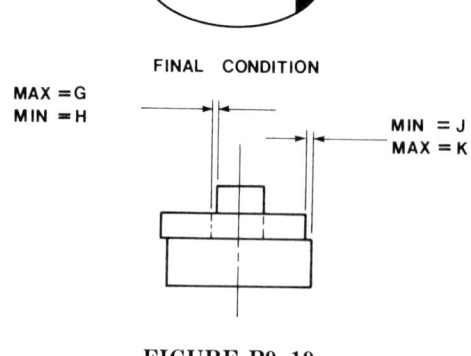

G. 0.06
H. 0.01
J. 0.00
K. 0.20

FIGURE P9-19

P9-20 Prepare drawings of each of the two parts shown in Figure P9-19. All values noted below are in inches. Assign tolerances as needed to achieve the final condition values.

- A. 2.00
- B. 0.75
- C. 2.00
- D. 0.38
- E. 0.50 km
- F. 0.63

Final condition

- G. 0.020
- H. 0.006
- J. 0.000
- K. 0.050

10
THREADS AND FASTENERS

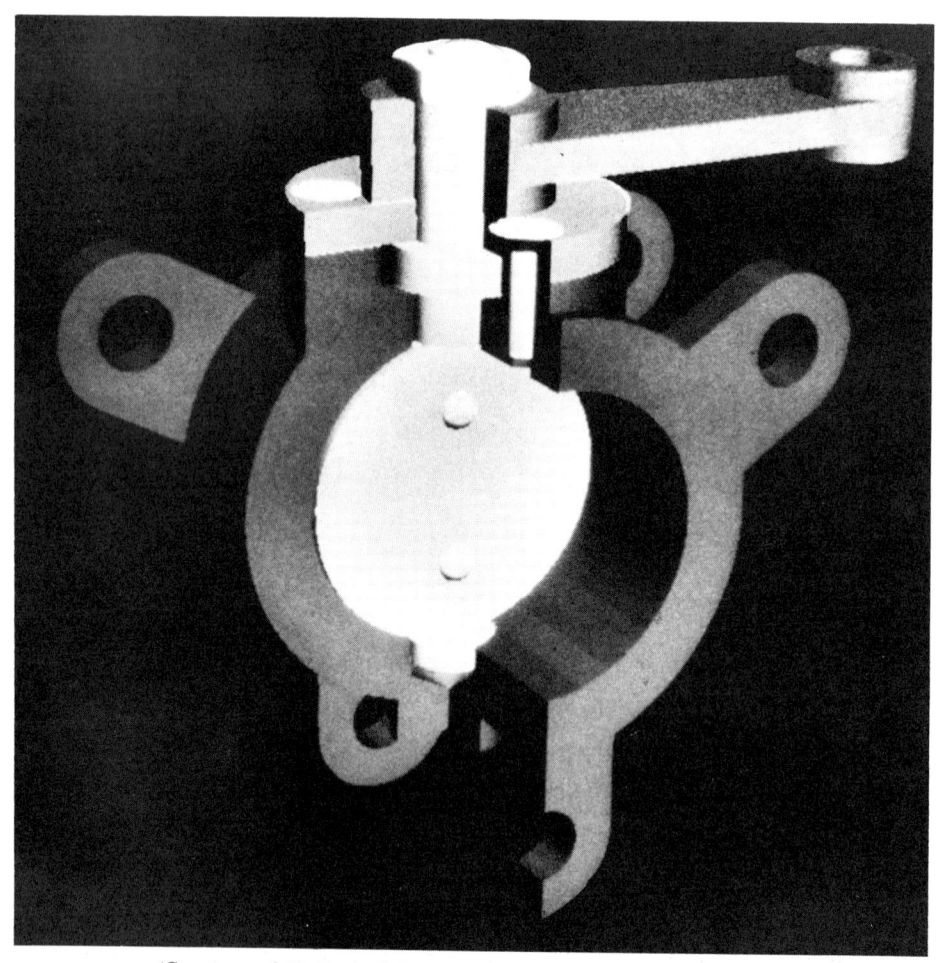

(Courtesy of McDonnell Douglas Manufacturing Industry Systems Company, St. Louis, Mo.)

10-1 INTRODUCTION

In this chapter we explain how to draw and prepare drawing callouts for threads and fasteners. Some basic design guidelines for fastener usage are included, as well as drawing and callout information for washers, keys, and rivets.

We also offer suggestions for building a computer file of thread and fastener shapes. Once completed, the file can be used to supply thread shapes quickly for detail and assembly drawings.

10-2 TERMS AND DEFINITIONS

Figure 10-1 illustrates several terms and definitions associated with both internal and external threads. The peak of a thread is called the *crest* and the lowest point is called the *root*. The distance across the thread, as measured from root to root, is called the *minor diameter*. The distance across the thread, as measured from crest to crest, is called the *major diameter*. Threads are specified by their major diameters.

Threads cut from cylindrically shaped stock are called *external threads*. Examples of external threads are found on bolts and screws. Threads cut into a part are called *internal threads*. Examples of internal threads are found in nuts and threaded holes.

Threads cut to American Standard specifications are defined using a major diameter and a pitch. The pitch of a thread is the distance between the thread's crests defined in terms of a unit inch. For example, a

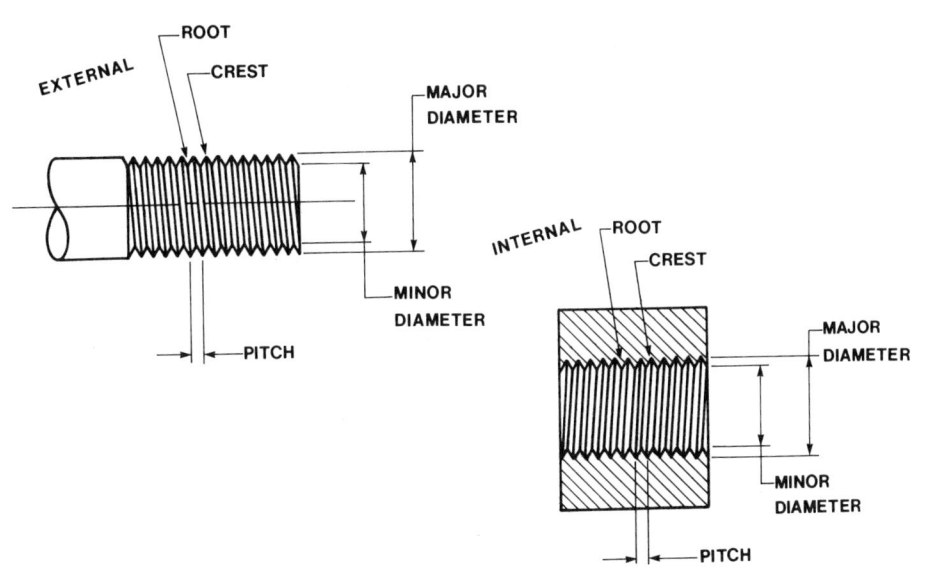

FIGURE 10-1 Thread terminology.

AMERICAN STANDARD THREADS

PITCH = number of threads/inch

METRIC THREADS

PITCH = number of threads/mm

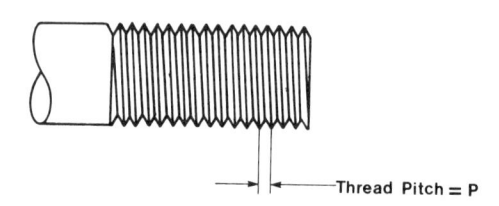

Thread Pitch = P

FIGURE 10-2 Example of a thread callout using American Standard notations.

EXAMPLE

PITCH LENGTH for .250−20 UNC Thread
20 Threads per inch
$\frac{1}{20}$ = .05 inch

0.250-20UNC thread callout means that the major diameter of the thread is 0.250 in. with 20 threads per inch (Figure 10-2).

Coarse metric threads are specified using only a major diameter. All other types of metric threads are specified using a major diameter and a pitch. For example, an M10 thread means a coarse metric thread with a major diameter of 10 mm; a 10 × 1.25 thread means a fine thread with a major diameter of 10 mm and a pitch of 1.25 (Figure 10-3).

Both American Standard and Metric threads are standardized. Tables of standard sizes are included in Appendix A.

FIGURE 10-3 Examples of metric thread callouts and a listing of Standard Metric Thread sizes.

STANDARD METRIC THREADS

DIA	COARSE THD PITCH	FINE THD PITCH	DIA	COARSE THD PITCH	FINE THD PITCH
1.6	0.35		12	1.75	1.25
2	0.4		16	2	1.5
2.5	0.45		20	2.5	1.5
3	0.5		24	3	2
4	0.7		30	3.5	2
5	0.8		36	4	3
6	1		42	4.5	3
8	1.25	1	48	5	3
10	1.5	1.25			

SAMPLE THREADS

COARSE
M 10

FINE
M 10 x 1.25

Sec. 10-2 Terms and Definitions

There are four general types of American Standard threads: Unified National Coarse (UNC), Unified National Fine (UNF), Unified National Extra Fine (UNEF), and Unified National (UN). All series use the same standardized major diameters but have different pitches. A 0.250-diameter thread has 20 threads per inch in UNC, 28 in UNF, and 32 in UNEF.

Unified National Threads (UN) are called *constant-pitch* threads. All threads in a given series have the same pitch regardless of diameter. For example, all UN-12 threads have 12 threads per inch.

The class of fit defines the quality of the thread, that is, the manufacturing tolerances. Class ratings are 1, 2, 3, and 4, with 1 being the least accurate and 4 being the most accurate. Most threads are manufactured to class 2 specifications. A class 3 thread is used on a micrometer.

Threads are specified on a drawing using callouts as shown in Figure 10-4. The callout specifies the major diameter, the threads per inch, the type of thread, the class of fit, and whether the thread is internal or external (A means external, B internal). Length and depth requirements are added as needed.

Example 1 of Figure 10-4 is a typical example of drawing callout for a threaded hole. The hole passes completely through the part, so no depth specification is needed. Example 2 shows a threaded hole with a depth callout, and example 3 shows an external thread with a length requirement. Drawing callouts are sometimes shortened by omitting the class of fit and internal/external portions. This is acceptable because the picture portion of the drawing will define whether the thread is internal or external, and almost all threads are class 2. If no class of fit is specified, it is assumed that the thread is a class 2.

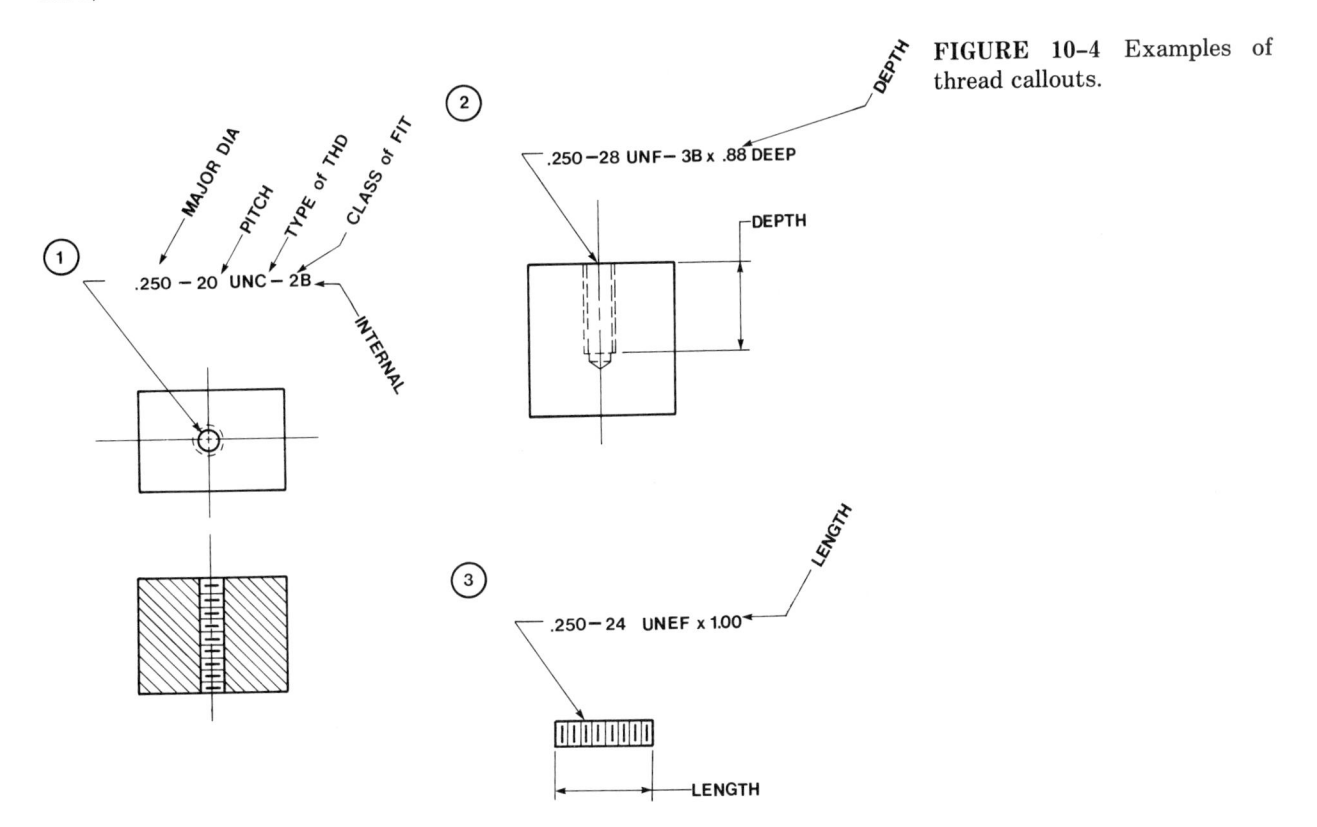

FIGURE 10-4 Examples of thread callouts.

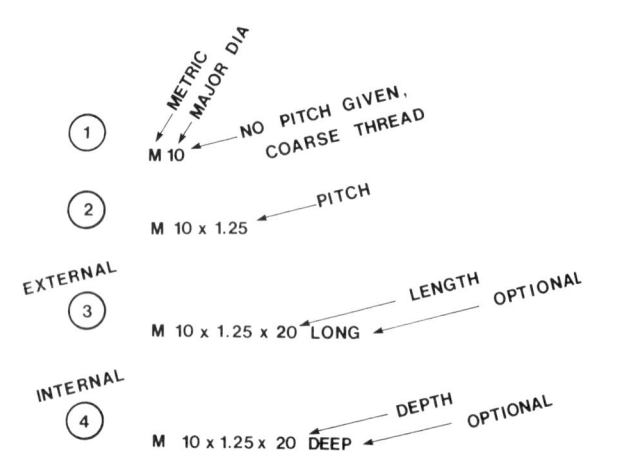

FIGURE 10-5 Examples of metric thread drawing callouts.

① M 10 ← METRIC MAJOR DIA, NO PITCH GIVEN, COARSE THREAD

② M 10 x 1.25 ← PITCH

EXTERNAL ③ M 10 x 1.25 x 20 LONG ← LENGTH OPTIONAL

INTERNAL ④ M 10 x 1.25 x 20 DEEP ← DEPTH OPTIONAL

Figure 10-5 shows some sample drawing callouts for metric threads. If a hole passes completely through a part, a thread depth callout is not required.

10-3 THREAD DEPTHS AND LENGTHS

Thread depth values define the length of the threaded portion of a hole, *not* the total length of the hole. A threaded hole is produced by first drilling a pilot hole using a twist drill and then tapping the hole (cutting the threads into the pilot hole). The tapping bit (tool used to cut the threads) is not advanced to the very bottom of the pilot hole, as "bottoming out" the tapping bit could cause damage to the bit. A short portion of the pilot hole always extends beyond the threaded portion of the hole. On drawings this is represented as shown in Figure 10-6.

The pilot hole extends approximately 2P (2 times the pitch) beyond the bottom of the thread. In addition, a conical point is drawn 30° to the direction of the threads. The conical point represents the shape cut by a twist drill.

A list of standard twist drill sizes is included in Appendix E. The pilot drill diameter is slightly less than the minor diameter of the thread. For drawing purposes, they are approximated.

Figure 10-7 shows how the length of an external thread is defined. External threads are usually finished with a chamfer (see Section 5-10). The chamfer is drawn but not defined unless a very specific chamfer is needed. The chamfered portion is included as part of the thread length.

There are two ways to define the length of threads which do not run the entire length of a shaft: options 1 and 2 in Figure 10-7. Option

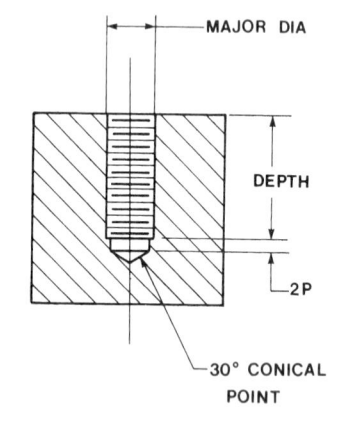

FIGURE 10-6 Threaded hole with a pilot hole that extends beyond the threaded portion of the hole.

FIGURE 10-7 How to define the length of an external thread.

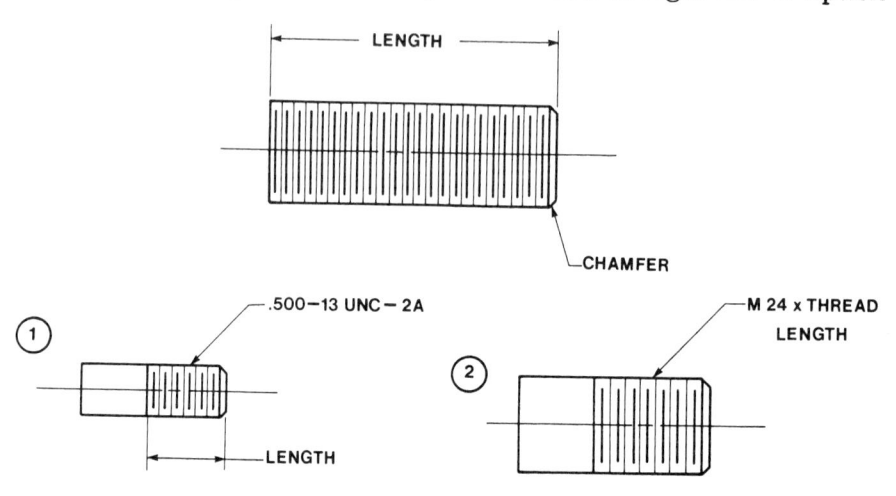

Sec. 10-3 Thread Depths and Lengths

1 uses a length dimension plus a drawing callout. Option 2 uses only a drawing callout.

There are three ways to represent threads on technical drawings: the detailed, schematic, and simplified representations. Figures 10-1 and 10-2 use the detailed representation. It is an accurate picture of a thread but very difficult and time-consuming to draw. It is rarely used on technical drawings except for special situations, such as sales presentations where many nontechnical people are present.

Figure 10-8 shows how to prepare a schematic thread representation. The representation applies for both American Standard and metric threads. The procedure is as follows:

1. Establish a reference point for the thread by drawing a centerline and an end construction line perpendicular to the centerline.

2. Draw the major diameter and the thread length. The major diameter is always equal to the thread size specification. A 0.500-13UNC thread is drawn as a 0.500 distance even though in actual manufacturing practice the thread is slightly smaller than 0.500.

3. Thin lines, evenly spaced, are added as shown. Ideally, the spacing of these lines would be equal to the pitch of the thread, but this is usually not possible, particularly for smaller threads. Any even spacing is acceptable. (0.125 for American Standard and 4 mm for metric is a good approximation.) Make the spacing larger for large pitches and smaller for small pitches. If two different-sized threads are used on the same drawing, make the spacing different for the two threads.

4. Add heavy, shorter lines midway between the lines added in step 3. The length of these lines is arbitrary, but all lines should be of equal length. (About $2P$ less than the major diameter is a good rule of thumb.) There should be a visual contrast between the thickness of the lines of steps 3 and 4 unless it is not within the system's capability.

5. Trim all excess lines and add the appropriate drawing callout.

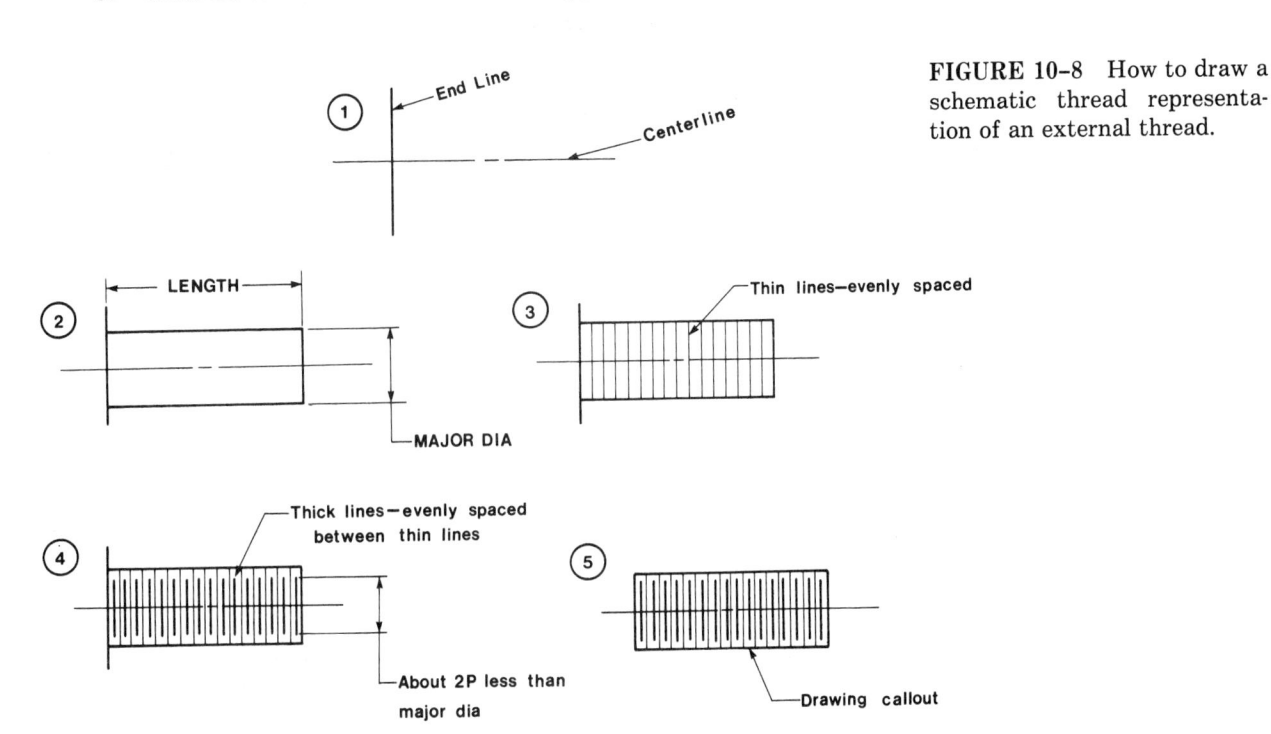

FIGURE 10-8 How to draw a schematic thread representation of an external thread.

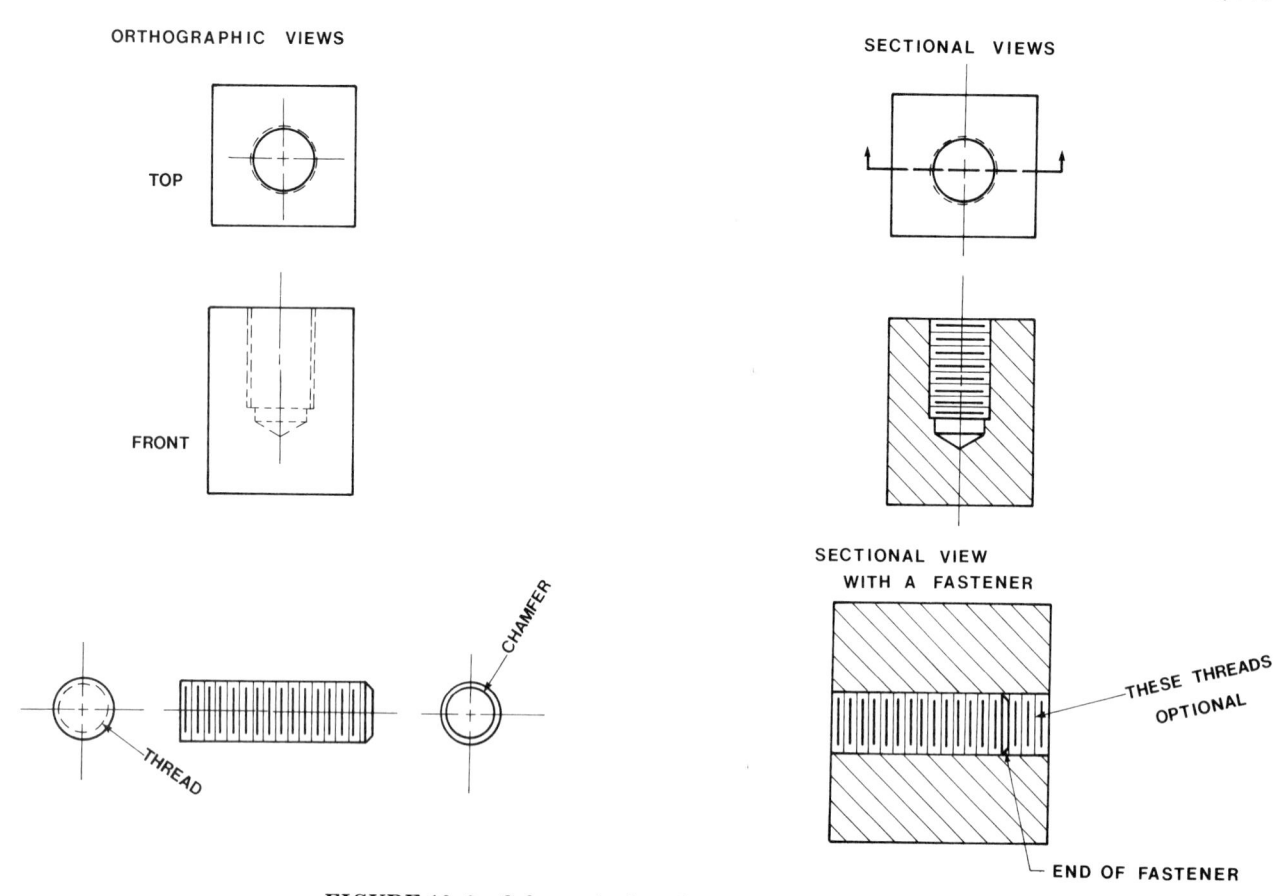

FIGURE 10-9 Schematic thread representation of an internal thread.

Figure 10-9 shows the schematic thread representation for internal and external threads using orthographic and sectional views. Top and front views are also shown. The top views are drawn using two concentric circles of almost the same diameter. It is acceptable to exaggerate the distance between the circles for drawing clarity.

Figure 10-10 shows how to draw the simplified representation. The procedure is as follows:

1. Establish a reference point for the thread by drawing a centerline and an end construction line perpendicular to the centerline. Their intersection will be the reference point.

FIGURE 10-10 How to draw a simplified representation of an external thread.

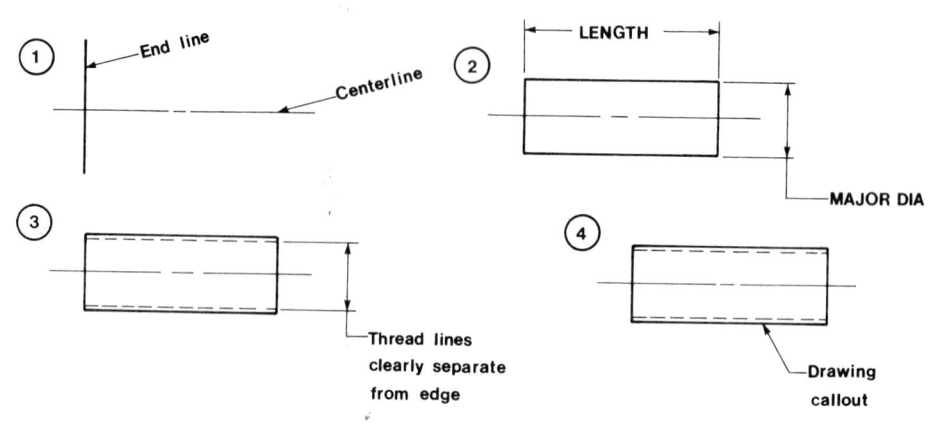

Sec. 10-4 Screws and Bolts

2. Draw the major diameter and the thread length. The major diameter is always equal to the thread size specification.
3. Add thin hidden lines as shown. The hidden lines are drawn at any small distance from the edge of the thread which allows a clear distinction between the edge line and the hidden line.
4. Trim all excess lines and add the appropriate drawing callout.

Figure 10-11 shows the simplified thread representation for internal and external threads using orthographic and sectional views. Top and front views are also shown. The top views are drawn using two concentric circles of almost the same diameter. It is acceptable to exaggerate the distance between the circles for drawing clarity.

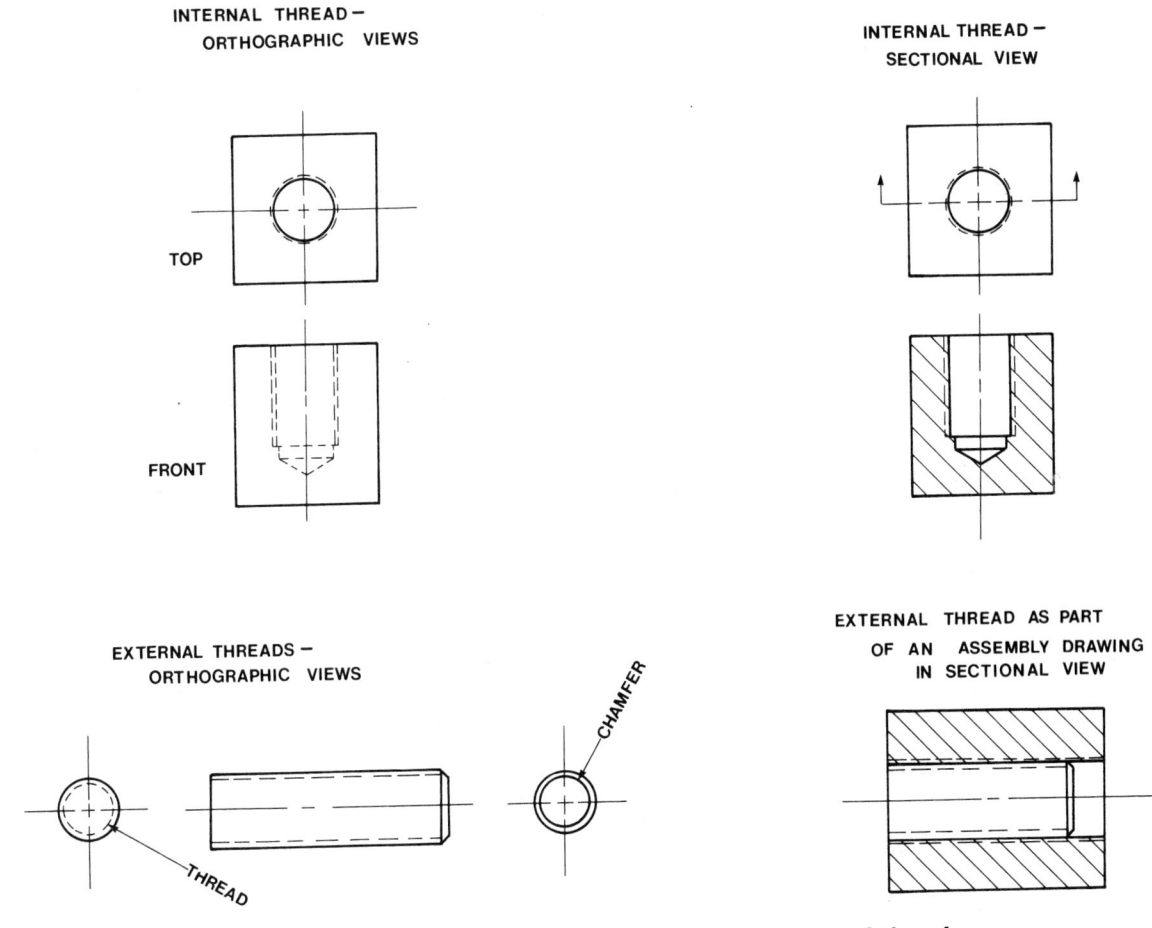

FIGURE 10-11 Simplified representation of an internal thread.

10-4 SCREWS AND BOLTS

A *screw* is a mechanical fastener that screws into a threaded hole. It does not require a nut. A *bolt* is a mechanical fastener that passes through a part or parts and is connected to a nut.

Both screws and bolts are manufactured with different head configurations. Figure 10-12 shows six different head styles. Note that in the top views, no hidden lines are used.

HEXAGON **SQUARE** **FLAT** **FILLISTER** **SOCKET** **ROUND**

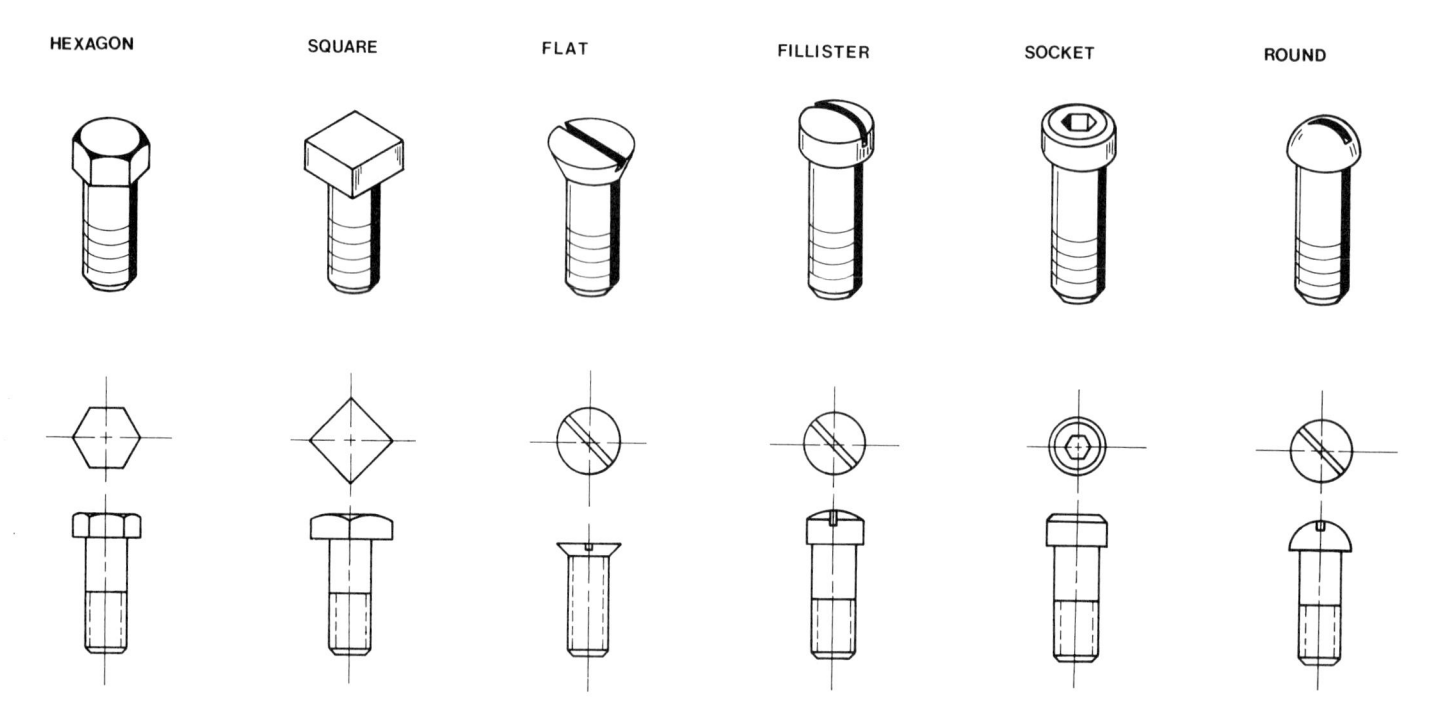

FIGURE 10-12 Six different head configurations for screws and bolts.

Figure 10-13 shows how to draw a square-head fastener. The procedure is as follows:

1. Establish centerlines for the top and front views. The vertical centerline should be aligned between the top and front view.
2. Draw a circle about the centerlines of the top view. As a rule of thumb, the circle's diameter equals 1.50D, where D equals the value of the major diameter. Draw a construction line parallel to the line drawn in step 1 that defines the bottom of the head. This new line should be 0.67D from the bottom line. Draw lines representing the major diameter, length, and chamfer, if required.
3. Circumscribe a square about the circle in the top view. Draw projection lines from the top view into the front view from the corners of the square as shown. These lines will define the edges of the head in the front view.
4. Draw arcs of radius D as shown. Use heavy lines for the arcs.
5. Trim all excess lines and bring the remaining lines to their correct thickness. Add the appropriate thread representation. Figure 10-13 also gives two examples of two head sizes that can be calculated using the proportions stated in the examples relative to the major diameter D. A 0.500-13UNC thread has a major diameter of 0.500 in. The head height is equal to 0.67D or 0.67(0.500) or 0.34. The circle diameter for the top view is equal to 1.50D or 1.50(0.500) or 0.75 in. An M16 thread has a major diameter of 16 mm. The head height is 0.67D or 0.67(16) or 11 mm (rounded off). The circle diameter is 1.50D or 1.50(16) or 26 mm.

Sec. 10-4 Screws and Bolts   299

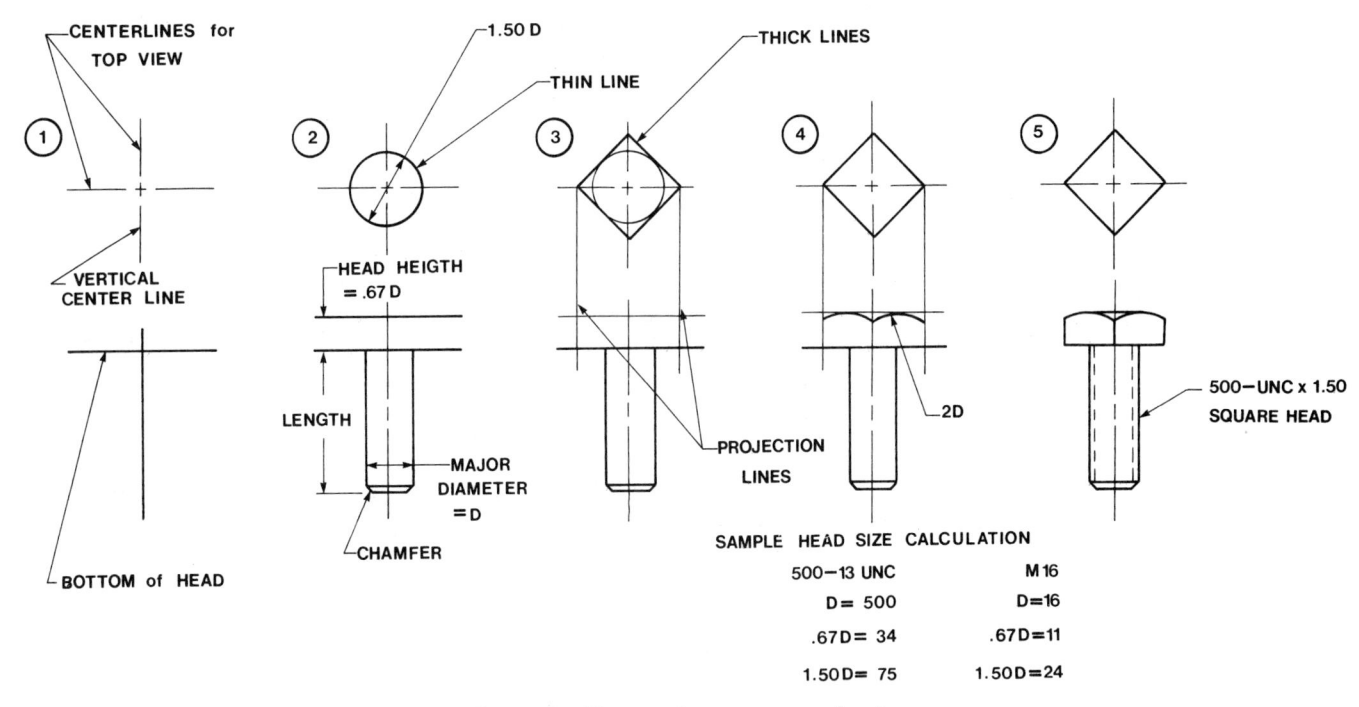

FIGURE 10-13 How to draw a square head.

Figure 10-14 shows how to draw a hexagon head. The procedure is as follows:

1. Establish centerlines for the top and front views. The vertical centerlines should be aligned between the front and top views.

2. Draw a circle about the centerline in the top view. The circle's diameter equals 1.50D, where D equals the value of the major diameter. Draw a construction line parallel to the line drawn in step 1 that defines the bottom of the head. This new line should be 0.67D from the bottom line. Draw lines representing the major diameter, length, and chamfer, if required. See Figure 10-13 for an interpretation of head-size formulas.

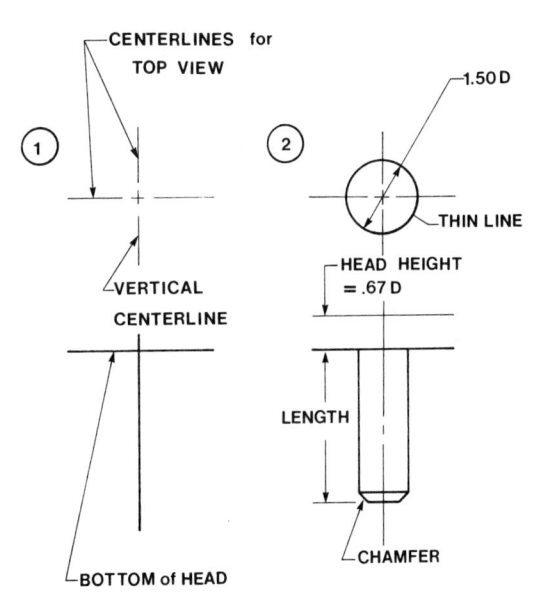

FIGURE 10-14 How to draw a hexagon head.

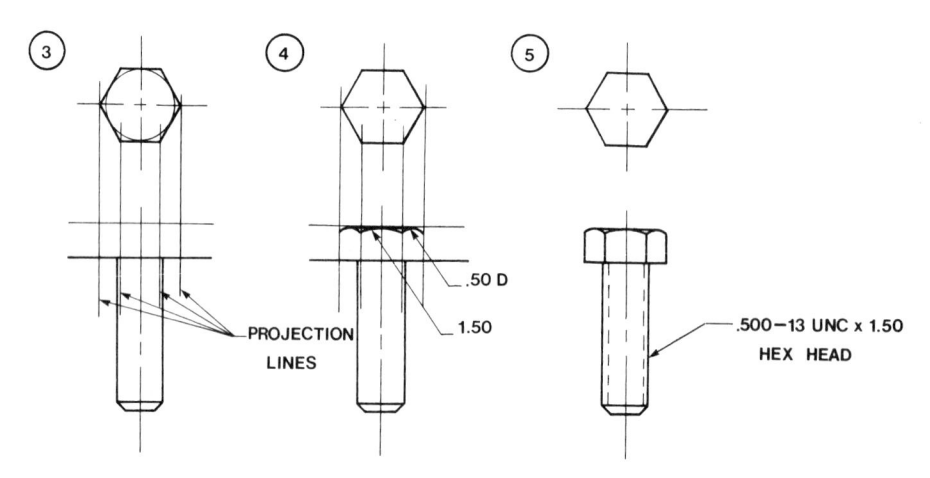

FIGURE 10-14 *(cont.)*

3. Circumscribe a hexagon around the circle in the top view. (See Section 4-10 for this construction.) Project lines from the corners of the hexagon into the front view as shown.
4. Draw three arcs, one of radius D between the middle to projection lines as shown, and two, one on each side, of radius $0.25D$, as shown.
5. Trim all excess lines and add the appropriate thread representation. Bring all lines to their correct thickness.

Square and hexagon heads are always oriented as shown in Figures 10-13 and 10-14. This is done to ensure clarity and to prevent confusion as to the type of head required. For example, a hex head oriented 90° to that shown in Figure 10-14 would look similar to a square head in the front view, causing possible confusion.

Fastener lengths are always measured from under the head to the end of the threaded shaft, including any chamfers. The head height is not included as part of the length definition. The only exception to this is a flat-head fastener. Flat-head fasteners *do* include the head height as part of the length definition (Figure 10-15).

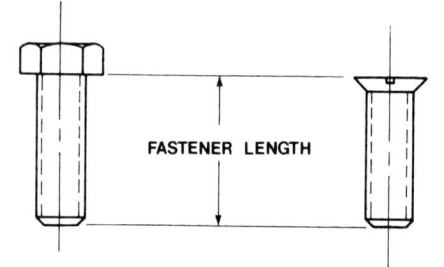

FIGURE 10-15 Fastener length designations do not include the head height, except for flat head fasteners.

10-5 NUTS

There are many different types of nuts, but square and hex nuts are the most common. The drawing callout for a nut is similar to a thread callout for a fastener but without any length or depth specification. Figure

FIGURE 10-16 Samples of square and hexagon nuts with appropriate drawing callouts.

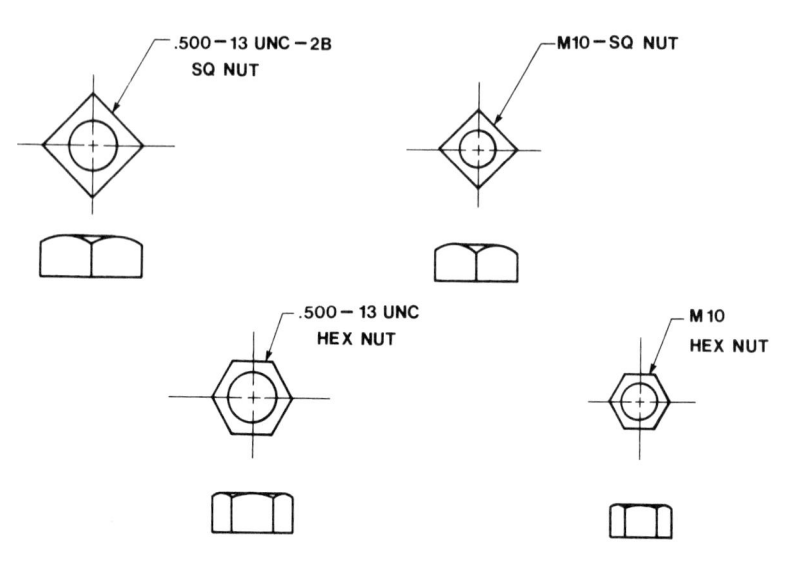

Sec. 10-6　Assembled Fasteners　　　301

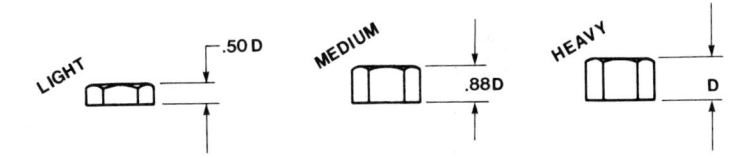

FIGURE 10-17 Light, medium, and heavy head sizes.

10-16 shows four examples of nut-drawing callouts. The hidden lines representing threads in the nut are sometimes omitted for clarity.

Figure 10-17 shows the relationship between three different head heights: light, medium, and heavy. Each height is defined in terms of D, the major diameter of the thread.

10-6　ASSEMBLED FASTENERS

Figure 10-18 shows a nut assembled to a bolt. Note that there are no hidden lines in any of the views. The bottom view shows two concentric circles, which represent the major diameter and chamfered portion of the bolt.

Figure 10-19 shows a screw assembled into a part. Illustration 1 shows a sectional view of a hex-head screw using the schematic representation. Note that the threaded hole extends beyond the bottom of the screw a distance equal to approximately $2P$, where P equals the thread's pitch. The threaded portion of the hole is made longer than the screw so that the screw will not bottom out—in other words, hit the end of the hole. The untapped portion of the pilot hole, and the conical point created by the twist drill, are also shown.

No threads are shown beyond the bottom of the screw in the threaded hole. This serves to help clarify the end of the screw. It is acceptable to draw threads completely to the bottom of the hole if desired.

Illustration 2 of Figure 10-19 shows a sectional view of a screw using the simplified representation. The threaded hole extends beyond the bottom of the screw, and the untapped portion of the pilot hole is shown as well as the conical point created by the twist drill.

Illustration 3 shows an orthographic view of a screw assembled into a part. Both the threads on the screw and those in the threaded hole are shown. Again, the untapped portion of the pilot hole and the conical portion of the hole are also drawn.

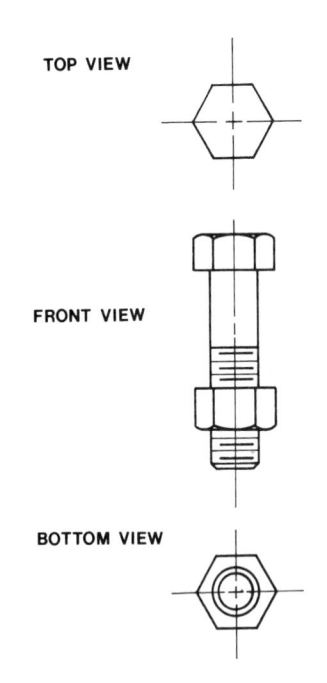

FIGURE 10-18 Drawing of a nut assembled to a bolt.

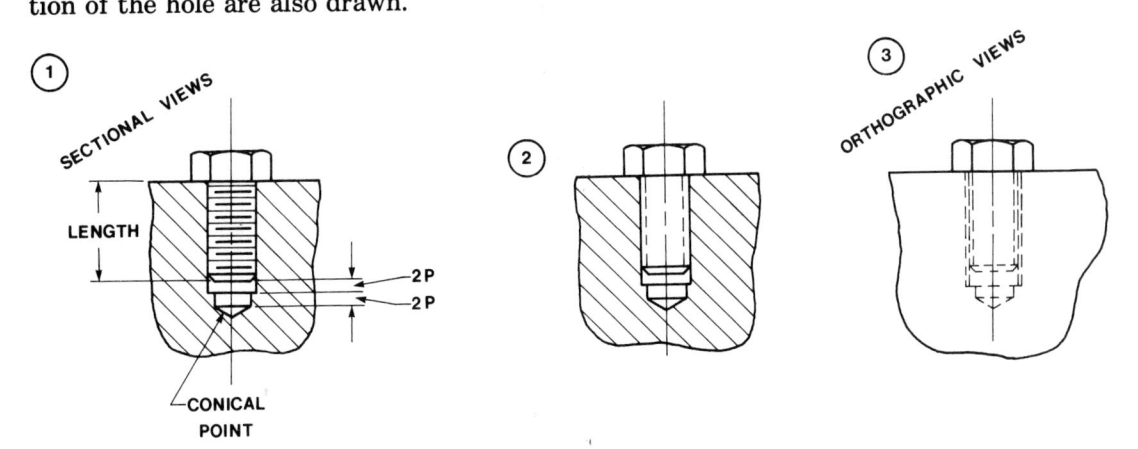

FIGURE 10-19 Example of a screw assembled into a part.

10-7 DESIGN GUIDELINES

There are several guidelines for choosing and locating fasteners. They are general "rules of thumb" which help the designer. Nothing can replace a thorough analysis of the design, but these guidelines represent good starting places for most designs.

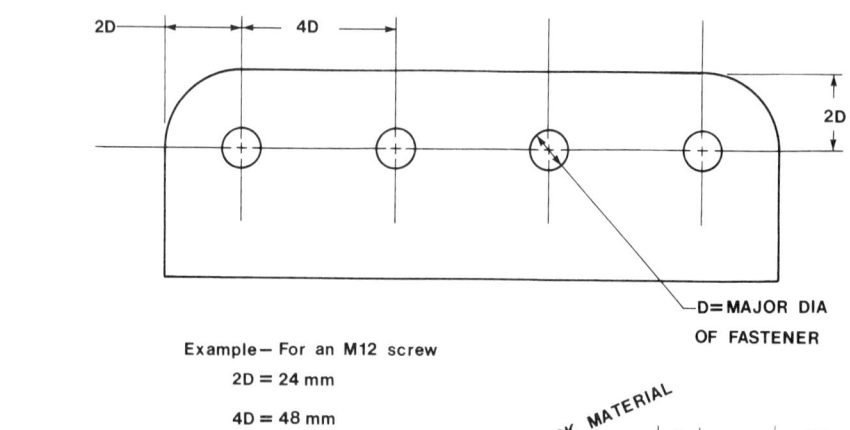

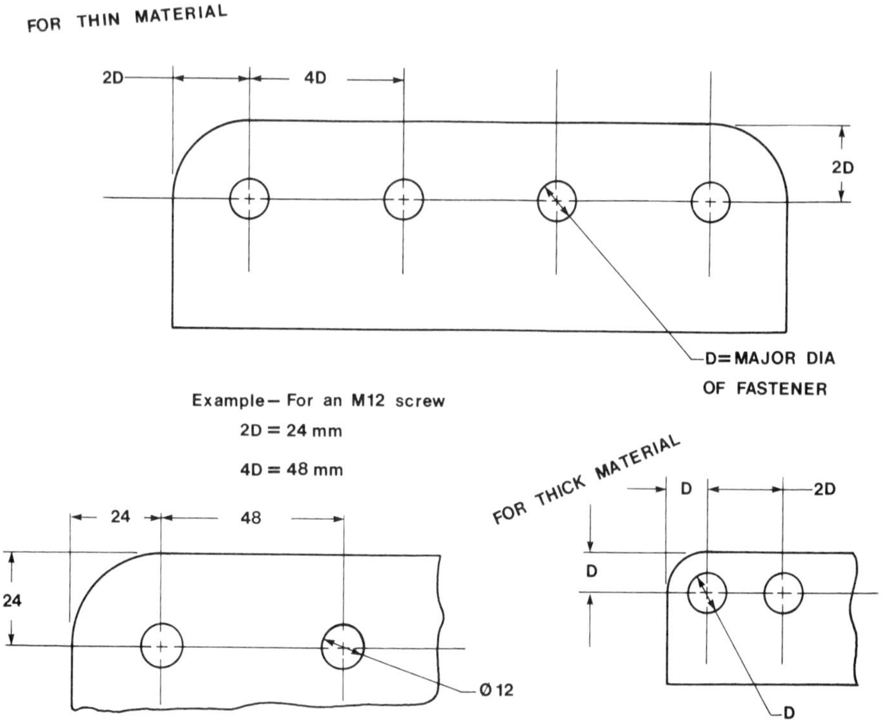

FIGURE 10-20 Design guidelines for locating fasteners in thin parts.

FIGURE 10-21 Comparison of UNC, UNF, and UNEF threads.

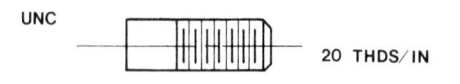

Locate fasteners in thin material no closer than 2D from the edge of a part (Figure 10-20). This means that the centerpoint of the hole through which the fastener assembles should not be closer than two times the diameter of the hole from the edge of the part. If the fastener were an M12, the minimum distance from the hole centerpoint to the edge of the part is 2D or 2(12) or 24 mm.

The centerpoints for a row of fasteners should be located at least 4D apart (Figure 10-20). If an M12 fastener were called for, the distance between fasteners should be no less than 4D or 4(12) or 48 mm. These distances may be reduced in thicker materials, as shown in Figure 10-20. Always allow tool clearance for all fasteners.

The more threads per inch, the stronger the joint between the fastener and the part. Think of threads as fingers. The more fingers used to grasp a part, the stronger the grip. If, for example, a 0.250-diameter fastener is required, a UNEF thread has 32 threads per inch, while a UNC has only 20 (Figure 10-21). The UNEF has 12 more threads per inch and forms a stronger joint.

However, it is not always advisable to use a fastener with more threads. Fasteners with more threads are slightly more expensive and are more susceptible to corrosion. Always start with UNC threads and go to UNF or UNEF threads as necessary.

Use standard-sized threads and fasteners. It is possible to manufacture many different-sized threads, but using only standard sizes helps assure cost efficiency. The tools (taps and dies) for making standard threads are more readily available.

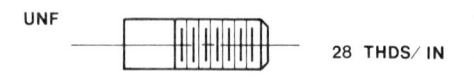

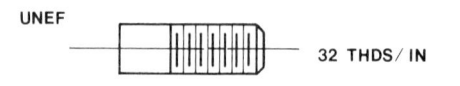

Sec. 10-7 Design Guidelines   303

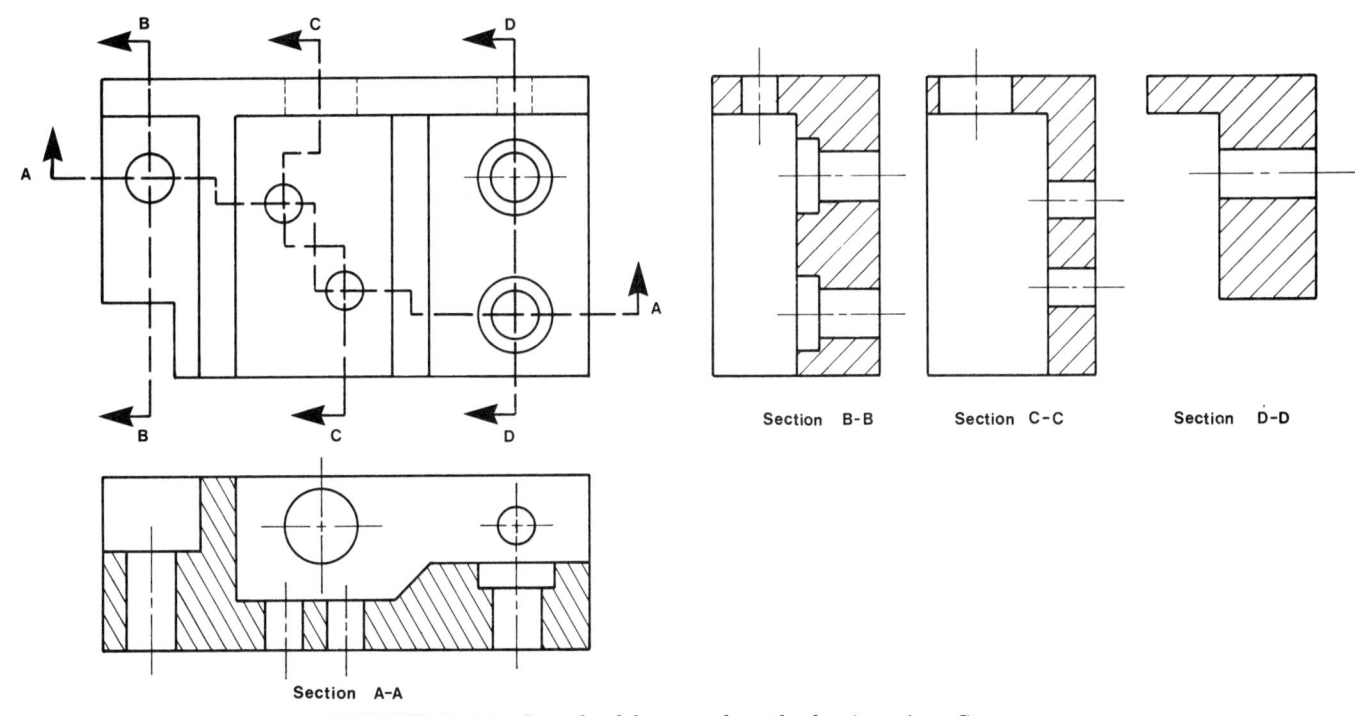

FIGURE 10-22 Standard fastener lengths for American Standard and metric sizes.

Fasteners are also produced in standardized length increments. Figure 10-22 shows partial tables of standard fastener lengths for both American Standard and metric sizes. Whenever possible, these standard lengths should be utilized.

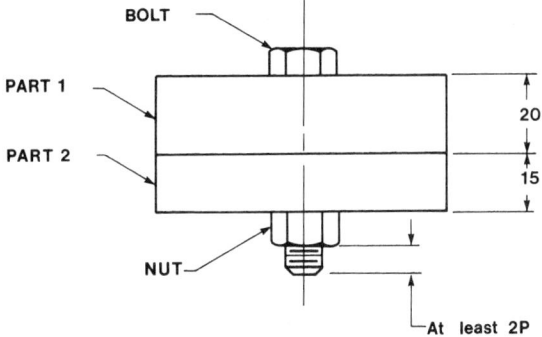

FIGURE 10-23 How to choose a thread length.

Figure 10-23 shows a sample design problem which requires the designer to define a fastener length. The bolt must pass through parts 1 and 2. In addition, the bolt length must accept a nut and allow at least two threads to protrude beyond the nut to ensure a good interface between the bolt and the nut. Adding the heights of parts 1 and 2, nut height, and thread protrusion requirements yields 48.0 mm. The nearest length value available to 48.0 mm is 50 mm, so a M10 × 50/long hex head bolt would be specified on the drawing.

Figure 10-24 shows a design problem which requires the designer to match a fastener length to a hole depth. An M10 × 30 long hex head screw is specified. The hole must be deep enough to accommodate the screw plus at least two additional threads, or 2P. This is a total length of 33 mm, so the hole depth must be at least 33 mm. The pilot hole depth would be at least 2P beyond the threads, or 36 mm plus the conical point.

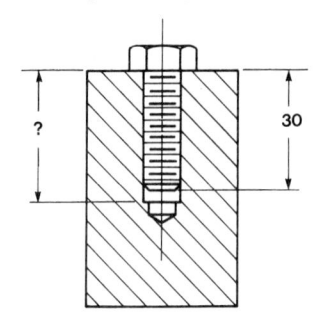

The last thread on a partially threaded shaft or a threaded hole is incomplete. This is another reason why for internal threads, good design

FIGURE 10-24 How to choose a hole depth for a given fastener.

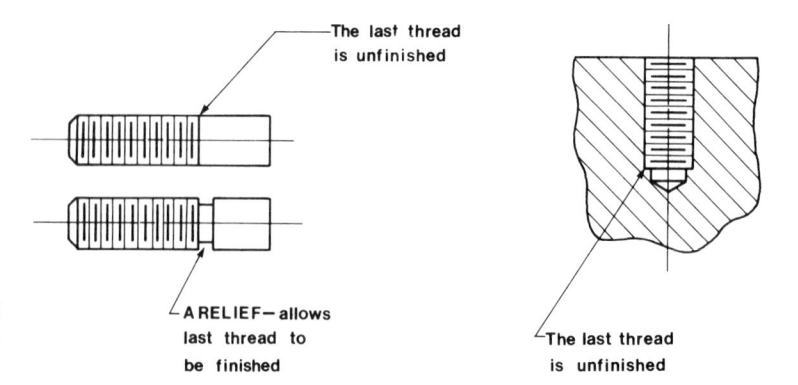

FIGURE 10-25 Last thread on a partially threaded shaft or a threaded hole is incomplete.

practice calls for two threads beyond the end of the fastener. The last thread is incomplete and cannot be considered usable. The second additional thread allows for tolerance variations.

External threads which are not cut the entire length of a shaft, as shown in Figure 10-25, are also incomplete and not usable. If the entire external thread must be used, a relief is cut into the shaft just beyond the required usable thread length. A relief is an undercut cut into the shaft that allows the thread-cutting tool to pass completely through the last thread, producing a "full thread."

10-8 WASHERS

Washers are used to help distribute fastener loads more evenly onto the surface of a part and to help provide correct spacing between parts. Washers are defined by their inside diameter, outside diameter, and thickness (Figure 10-26).

There are many different types of washers, including, among others, American National type A or B plain, helical spring, and external

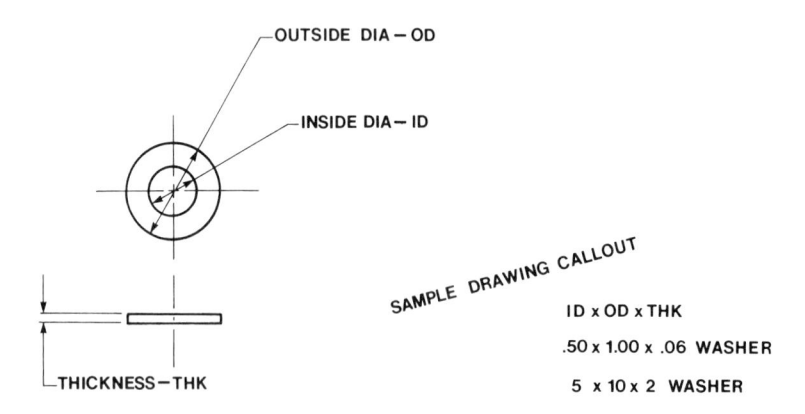

FIGURE 10-26 Washer terminology.

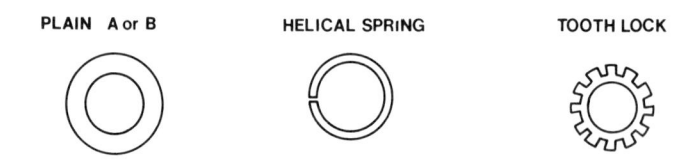

FIGURE 10-27 Examples of different types of washers.

Sec. 10-9 Setscrews and Studs 305

NOMINAL INSIDE DIAMETER	OUTSIDE DIAMETER	THICKNESS
.164	438	.049
.188	.562	.049
.250	.625	.065
.312	.875	.083
.375	1.000	.083
.438	1.250	083
.500	1.062	.095
.562	1.156	.095
.625	1.312	.095
.750	1.469	.134
.875	1.750	.134
1.000	2.000	.134

Nominal sizes are intended for use with comparable nominal screw or bolt diameters

FIGURE 10-28 Some standard washer sizes.

tooth lock washers (Figure 10-27). Figure 10-28 shows a partial list of standard washer sizes. As with fasteners and thread sizes, standard washer sizes should be used whenever possible.

10-9 SETSCREWS AND STUDS

Setscrews are threaded fasteners generally used to attach two rotating parts, such as a pulley and a shaft, as shown in Figure 10-29. There are four basic types of headless setscrews: slotted, hexagon socket, fluted socket, and square head (Figure 10-30).

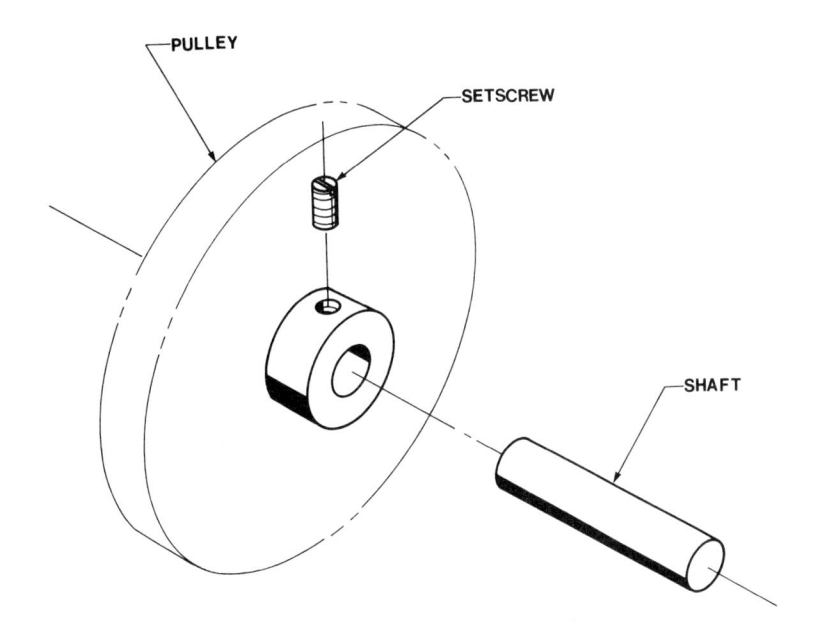

FIGURE 10-29 Example of a setscrew usage.

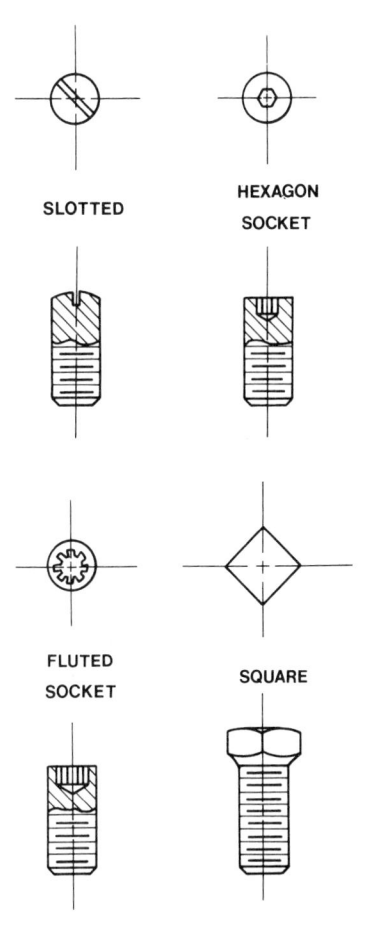

FIGURE 10-30 Four basic types of setscrews.

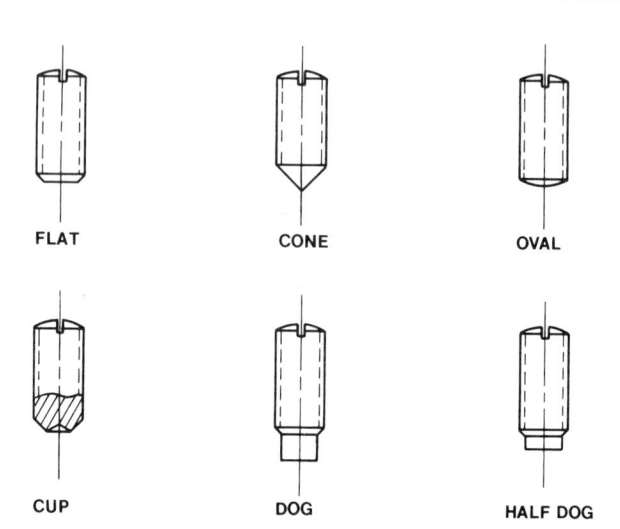

FIGURE 10-31 Six possible point configurations for setscrews.

FLAT   CONE   OVAL
CUP   DOG   HALF DOG

Setscrews also come with one of six possible point configurations: flat, cone, oval, cup, dog, and half dog (Figure 10-31). Any possible combination of head type and point configuration is available.

Figure 10-32 is a partial list of standard setscrew sizes. The choice of head type and point configuration depends on how the setscrew is used. In general, square heads can withstand the greatest tightening loads, followed by splined sockets, hex sockets, and slotted heads. Point configurations are chosen to match opposing features. Dogs fit into holes, and flats, cones, and ovals into dimples. Setscrews may also be pressed directly against the rounded surfaces of shafts.

Studs are shafts which are partially threaded (Figure 10-33). Studs can also be made so that the unthreaded end can be forced into a part (see Section 9-9 for a further explanation) with the threaded end protruding for assembly into another part or into a nut. Studs can also be screwed into a part, allowing the unthreaded end to be used for aligning other parts.

INCHES

DIAMETER	LENGTHS										
	3	4	5	6	8	10	12	16	20	21
M 3	•	•	•	•	•	•	•			
M 4		•	•	•	•	•	•	•		
M 5			•	•	•	•	•	•	•	
M 6				•	•	•	•	•	•	•
M 8					•	•	•	•	•	•
M 10						•	•	•	•	•
M 12							•	•	•	•
M 16								•	•	•
M 20									•	•
M 24										•

ADDITIONAL SIZES AVAILABLE

INCHES

DIAMETER	LENGTHS									
	.250	.313	.375	438	.500	.563	.625	.750	.875	1.000
5 (.125)	•	•	•	•	•	•	•	•	•	•
6 (.138)	•	•	•	•	•	•	•	•	•	•
8 (.164)	•	•	•	•	•	•	•	•	•	•
10 (.190)	•	•	•	•	•	•	•	•	•	•
12 (.216)	•	•	•	•	•	•	•	•	•	•
.250	•	•	•	•	•	•	•	•	•	•
.313	•	•	•	•	•	•	•	•	•	•
.375	•	•	•	•	•	•	•	•	•	•
.438	•	•	•	•	•	•	•	•	•	•
.500	•	•	•	•	•	•	•	•	•	•
.563			•	•	•	•	•	•	•	•
.625				•	•	•	•	•	•	•
.750					•	•	•	•	•	•

ADDITIONAL SIZES AVAILABLE

FIGURE 10-32 Some standard setscrew sizes.

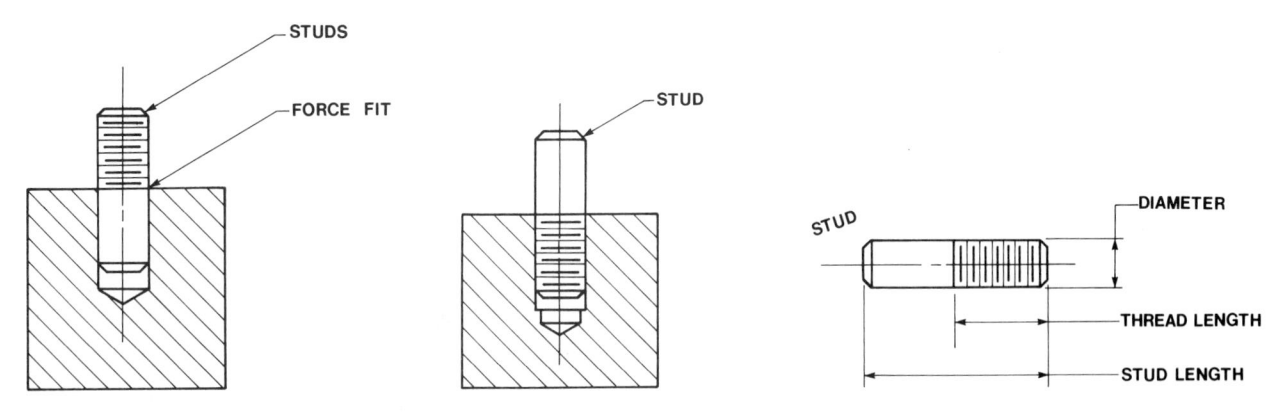

FIGURE 10-33 Stud terminology.

Studs are dimensioned as shown in Figure 10-33. The thread length may be defined as shown or as part of the drawing callout. Only standard thread sizes should be specified.

10-10 KEYS

Keys are small parts used to transfer motion between two rotating parts. In Figure 10-34 a square key is used between a shaft and a gear. The power from the rotating shaft is transferred through the key to the gear. There are four different types of keys: square, gib, Pratt and Whitney, and Woodruff (Figure 10-35).

Square keys are pieces of square stock cut to specified lengths. They are defined using a drawing callout that includes the length of one side of the square and the total key length. For example, 0.25 SQ × 1.00 LONG.

Gib, Pratt and Whitney, and Woodruff keys are manufactured to a predefined set of standard sizes. Gib keys are tapered and forced between the shaft and the matching part, forming a fit that transfers the rotary motion while maintaining the lateral position of the shaft. Pratt and Whitney keys fit into a rounded slot which prevents lateral movement. Woodruff keys are crescent shaped, which allows the shaft to pivot within the matching part and still transfer the rotary motion.

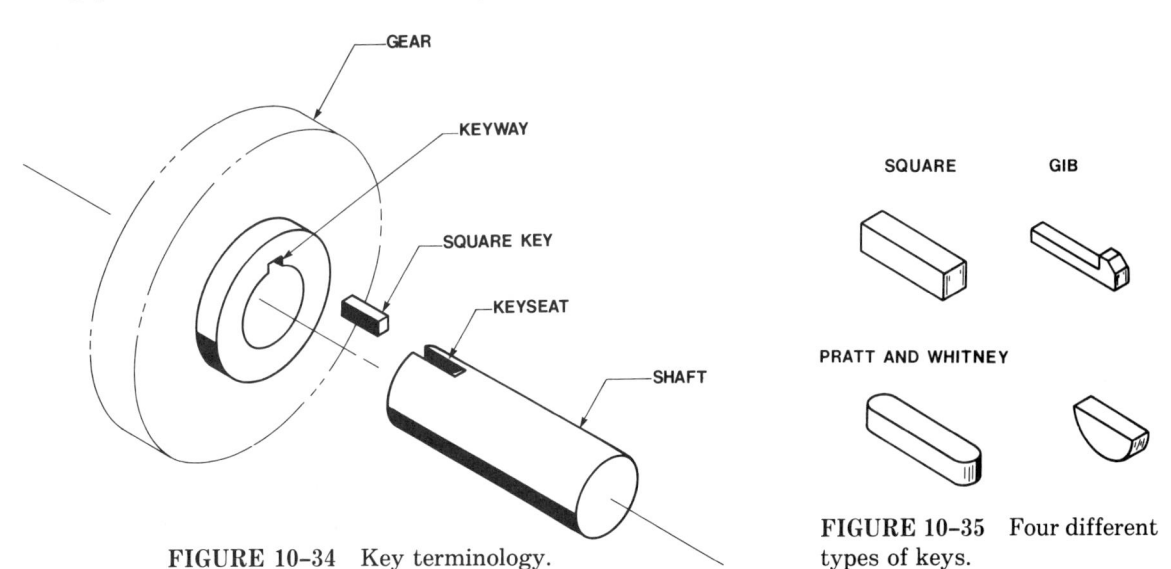

FIGURE 10-34 Key terminology.

FIGURE 10-35 Four different types of keys.

10-11 RIVETS

There are two general categories of rivets: small and large. *Small rivets* are used for joining sheet metal parts such as are used in aircraft. *Large rivets* are used in construction work, such as bridges and buildings.

There are five different head styles available on small rivets: flat, countersunk, button, pan, and truss (Figure 10-36). Rivet sizes are standardized. Tables of rivet sizes are available from rivet manufacturers.

There are six different head styles available on large rivets: button, high button, cone, flat, round, and pan. Figure 10-37 shows examples of each head style and gives the head-size proportion in terms of the rivet's diameter.

Small rivets are usually used in large groups or rows. An aircraft, for example, uses thousands of rivets. Figure 10-38 shows a row of rivets that joins two pieces of sheet metal to form a lap joint. The rivets are indicated on the drawing by short perpendicular centerpoint lines in the front view and a longer centerline in the side view. This type of rivet representation saves drawing time.

Rivet drawing callouts give the rivet's diameter, length, and head type, as shown in Figure 10-38. Rivet patterns are dimensioned using the hole pattern techniques explained in Section 5-8.

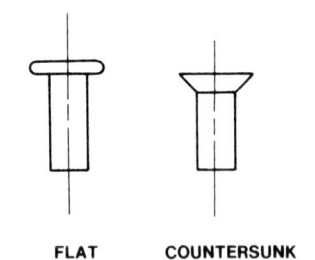

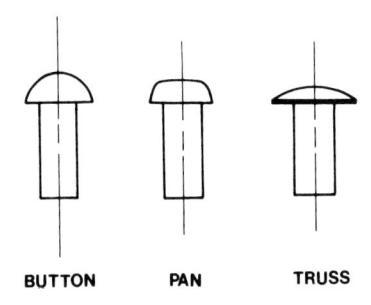

FIGURE 10-36 Head types for small rivets.

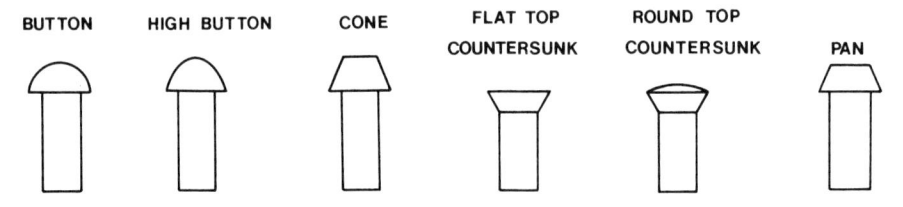

FIGURE 10-37 Head types for large rivets.

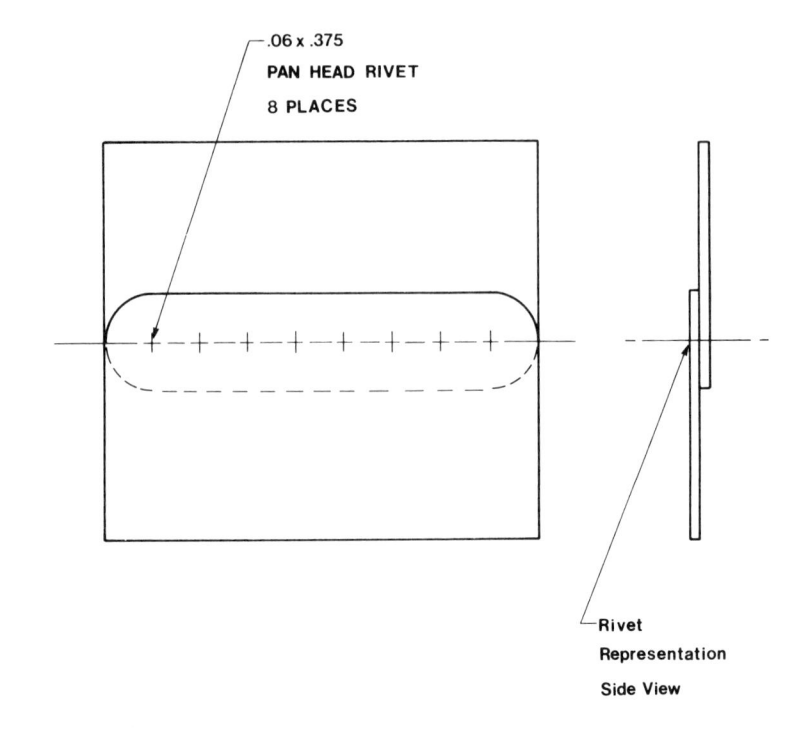

FIGURE 10-38 How to represent a row of rivets on a drawing.

10-12 SPRINGS

There are two general types of springs: *tension* and *compression*. They are shown on a drawing using one of two representations: detailed or schematic. Figure 10-39 shows a detailed representation of a spring. This representation is time consuming to draw, so is rarely used.

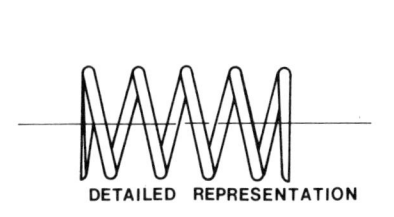

FIGURE 10-39 Detailed representation of a spring.

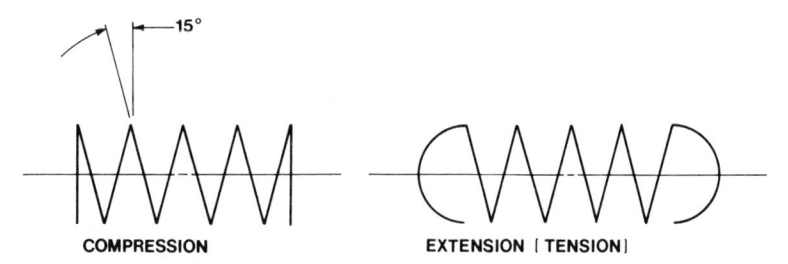

FIGURE 10-40 Schematic representation of a compression and a tension spring.

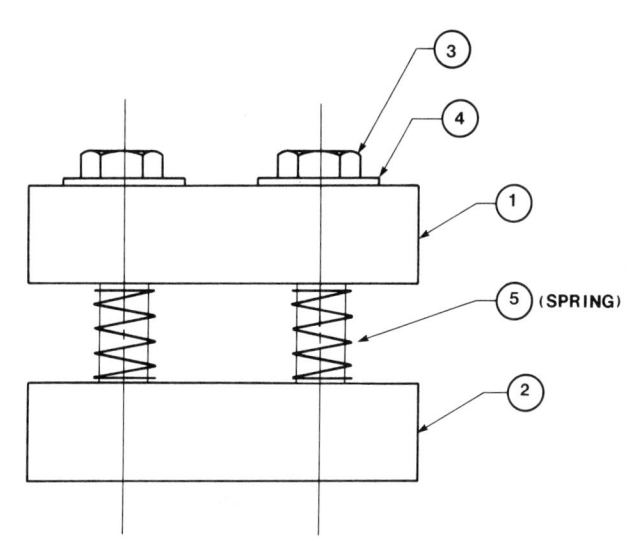

FIGURE 10-41 Example of compression springs drawn using the schematic representation in an assembly drawing.

Figure 10-40 shows a schematic representation of both tension and compression springs. Ideally, the distance between the slanted lines in the representation would be equal to the distance between the coils of the spring, but this is usually not possible, particularly for small, tight springs. The slanted lines are drawn at any angle, although 15° is most often used. Figure 10-41 shows an example of how a schematic spring representation would appear in an assembly drawing.

10-13 BUILDING A REFERENCE LIBRARY

One big advantage that computer drafting systems have over conventional drafting techniques and practices is their ability to remember and redraw the same shape over and over again. Any shape stored in the computer memory can be called up and redrawn in seconds. These shapes

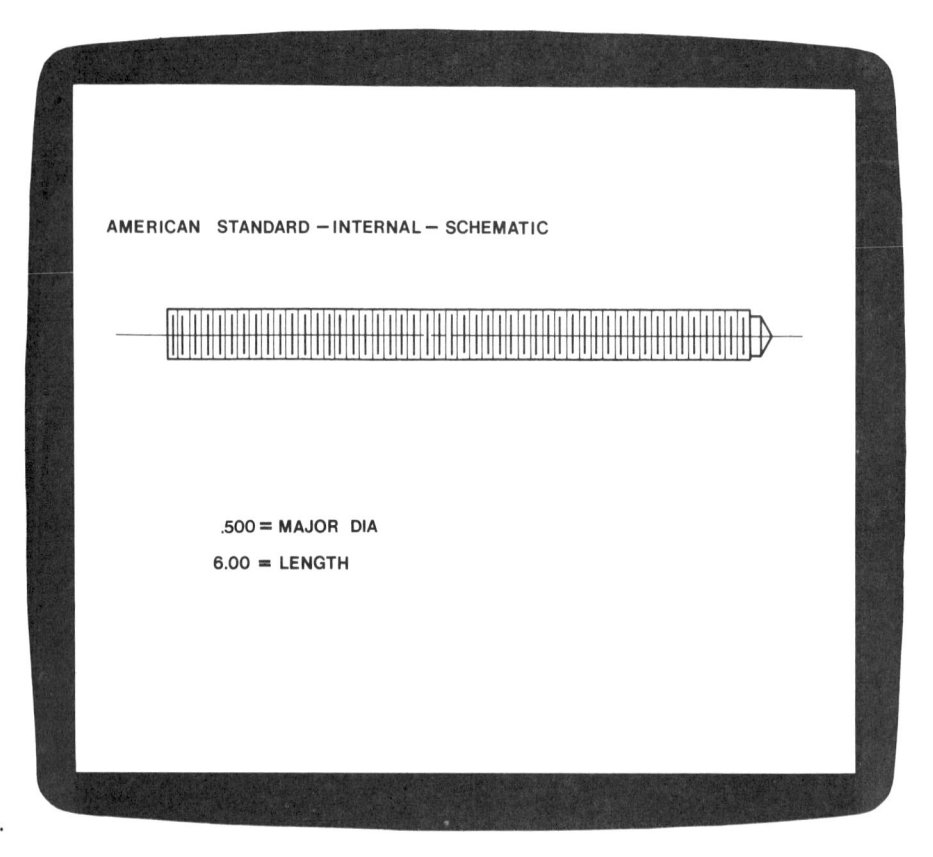

FIGURE 10-42 Internal thread.

can also be easily enlarged or reduced in scale as needed, as well as rotated to any desired orientation. Thread and fastener shapes are really composites of several simple shapes which can easily be stored in a computer's memory. In this section we outline one possible way to create a thread and fastener shape library for computers.

Figure 10-42 shows an internal thread using the schematic representation. The thread was drawn using a major diameter equal to 0.500 and thread lines located 0.125 in. apart. The thread length was drawn at 6.00 in., as this distance is longer than the depth of most threaded holes. The thread can be shortened to fit design requirements. It is easier to trim a longer thread than to add threads to a shorter one.

Figure 10-43 shows a sample problem that involves using a thread shape stored in memory. The drawing calls for a 0.375-16UNC × 1.50 LONG internal thread. The thread is oriented 90° to the shape in memory. The procedure is as follows:

1. Establish the correct diameter. This can be done by reducing the scale of the filed drawing. Call the drawing out of memory and display it on the screen. The file drawing has a major diameter of 0.500 and the required diameter is 0.375. Divide 0.375 by 0.500 to get the new scale. In this example, the scale factor is 0.75. Reduce the drawing by a factor of 0.75 to produce the 0.375-diameter thread required on the drawing. If a 1.000-diameter thread was required, the scale factor would have to be 2.00.

Sec. 10-13   Building a Reference Library   311

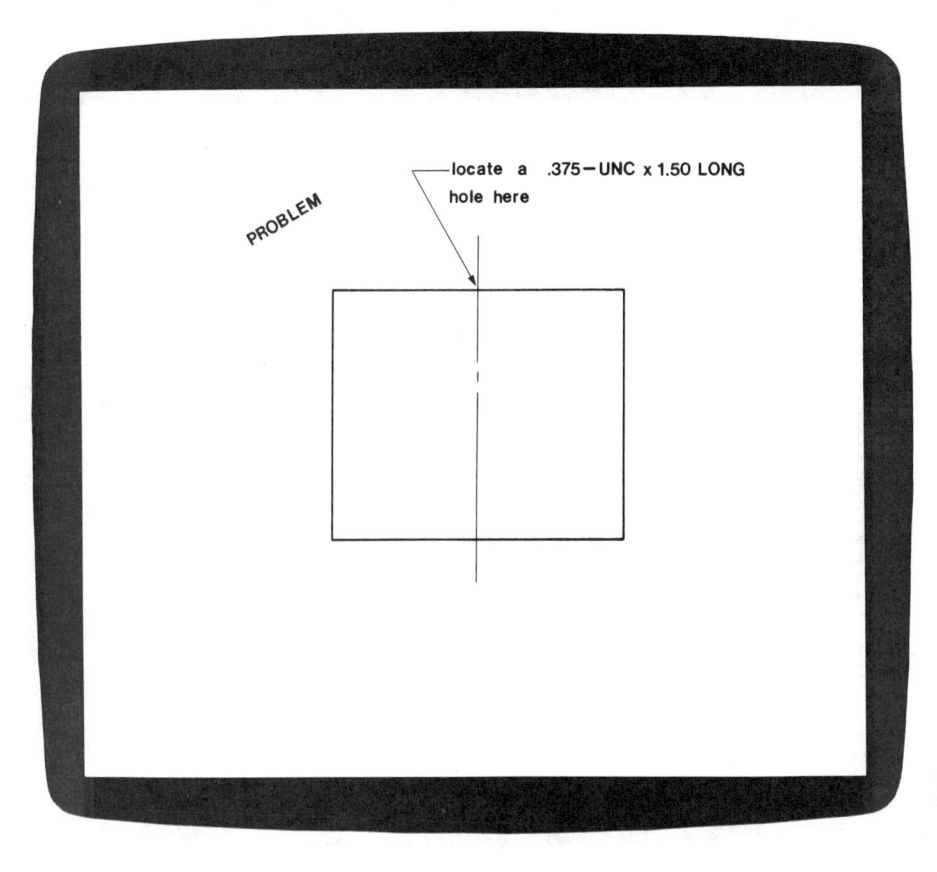

FIGURE 10-43 Sample problem that involves using a thread shape stored in memory.

2. Establish the required length. This is done by trimming the excess thread length. The original drawing is 6.00 long, so trim 4.50 off to get the desired 1.50 length. Note that the original thread drawing shown in Figure 10-42 has a thin solid construc-

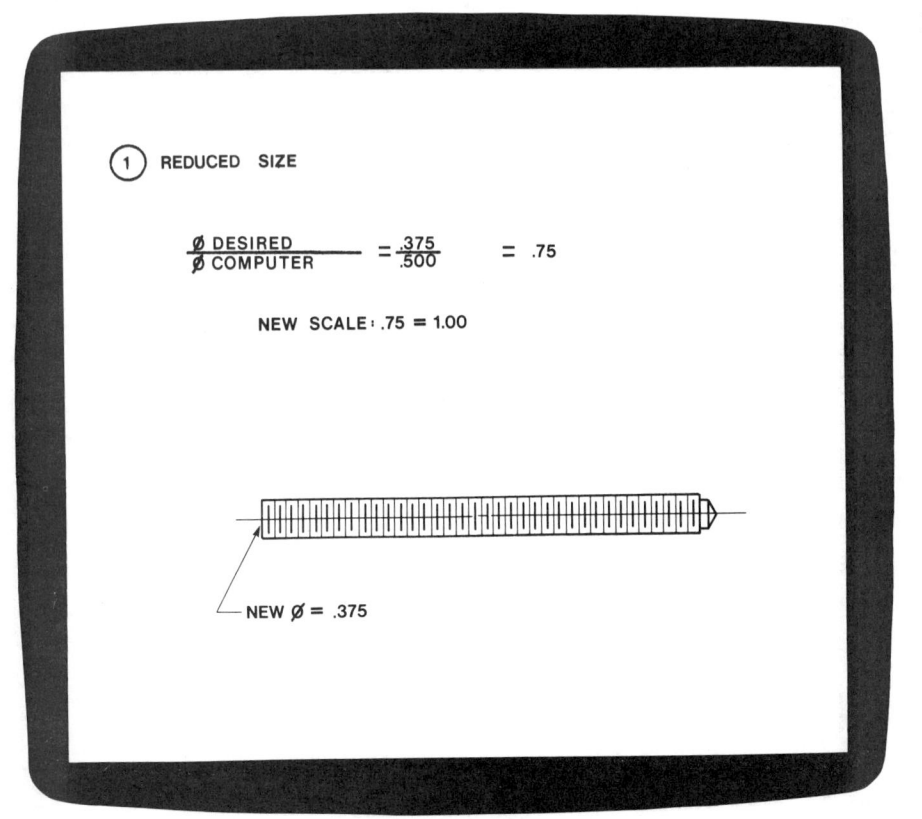

FIGURE 10-43 (cont.)

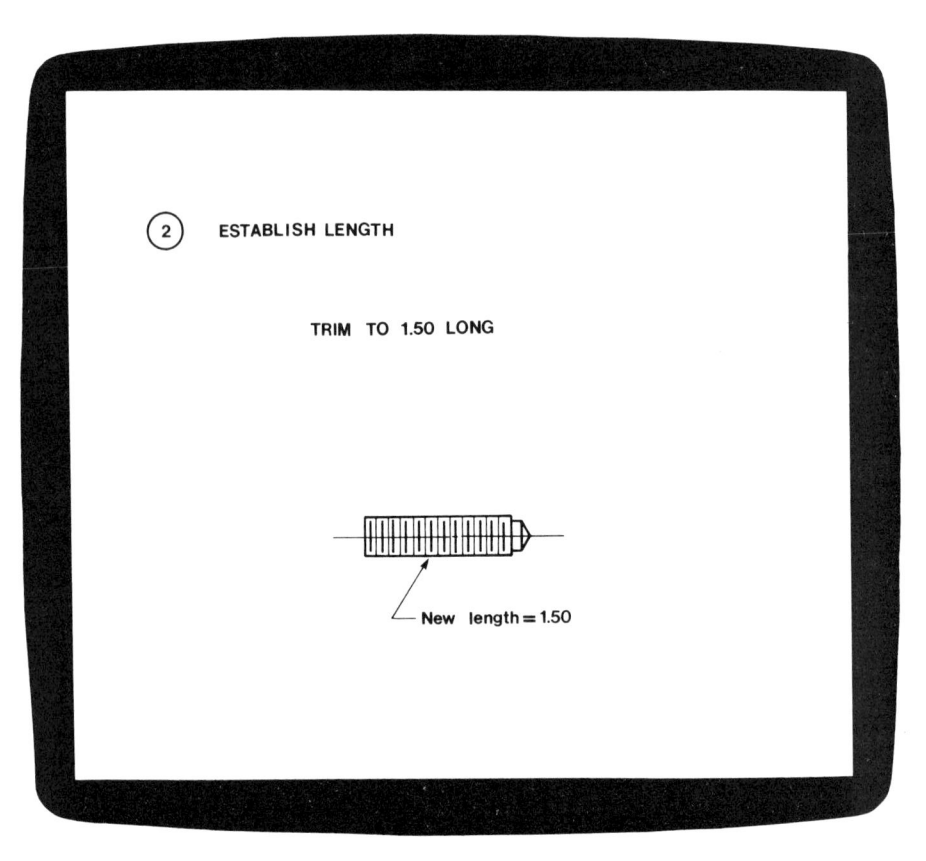

FIGURE 10-43 (cont.)

tion instead of a centerline. This line can be trimmed and then converted to the centerline configuration, assuring proper spacing on the new thread. This is called *changing line font*.

3. Rotate the thread 90° clockwise and position it within the new drawing.

FIGURE 10-43 (cont.)

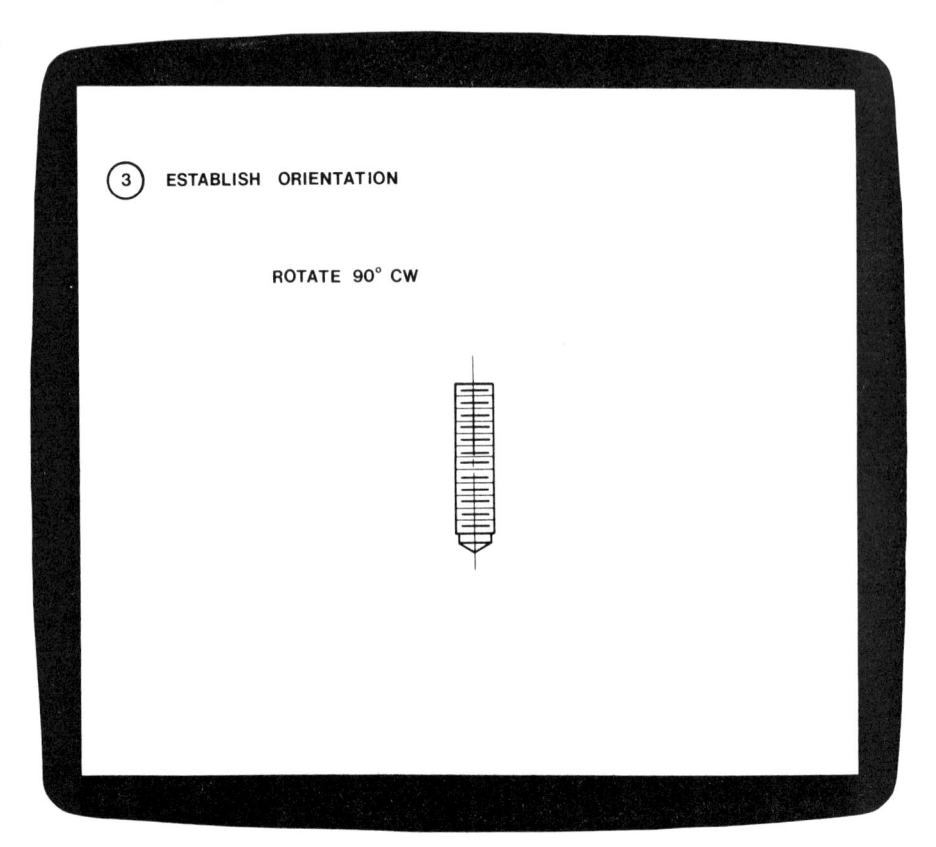

Sec. 10-13 Building a Reference Library 313

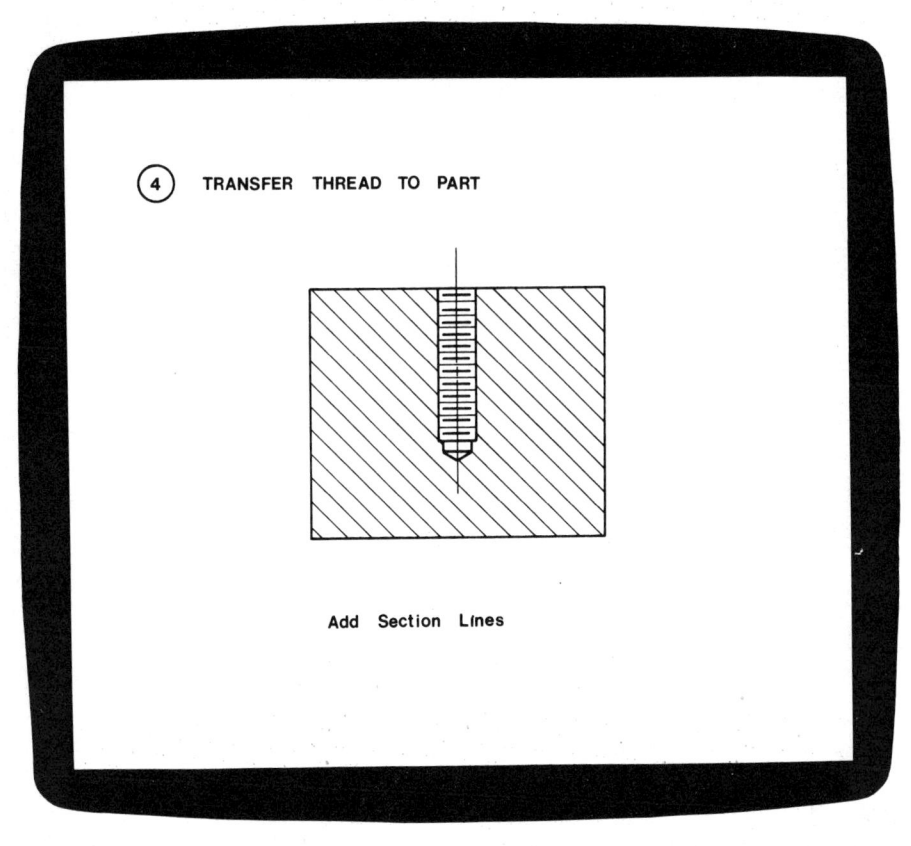

[Figure: Screen showing "④ TRANSFER THREAD TO PART" with a sectioned square containing an internal thread representation, labeled "Add Section Lines"]

FIGURE 10-43 (*cont.*)

4. Redraw the thread on the new drawing, making it a permanent part of that drawing.

Other thread and fastener shapes can be drawn and manipulated in a similar manner. Samples of different thread representations are shown in Figures 10-44 to 10-58.

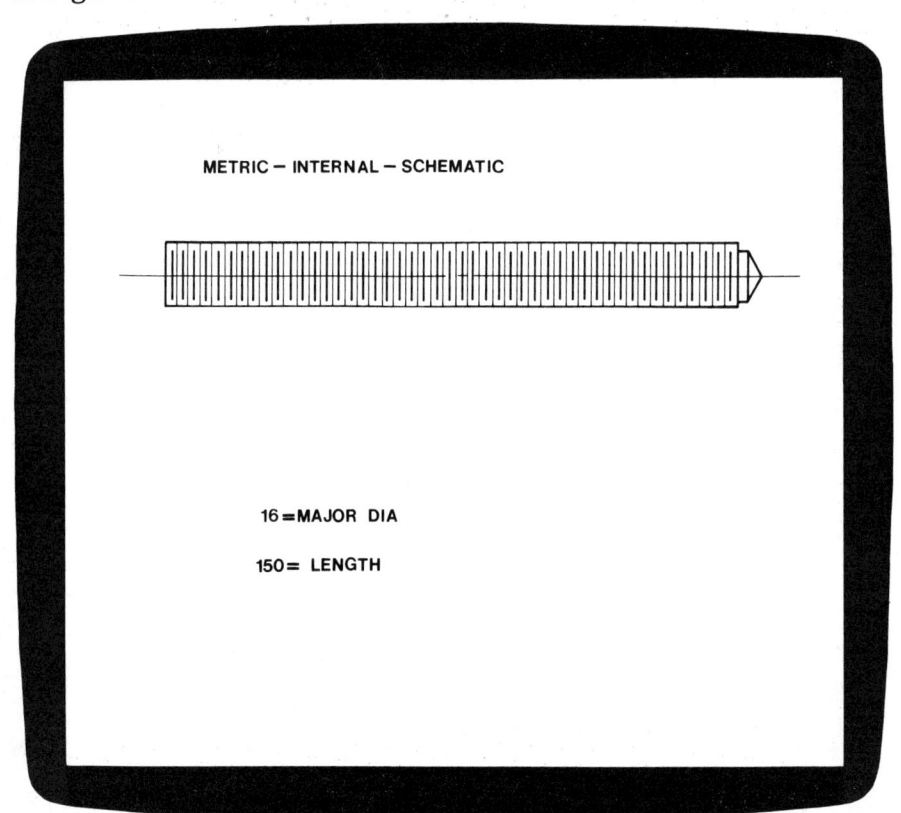

FIGURE 10-44

[Figure: Screen showing "METRIC – INTERNAL – SCHEMATIC" with a schematic thread representation, labeled "16 = MAJOR DIA" and "150 = LENGTH"]

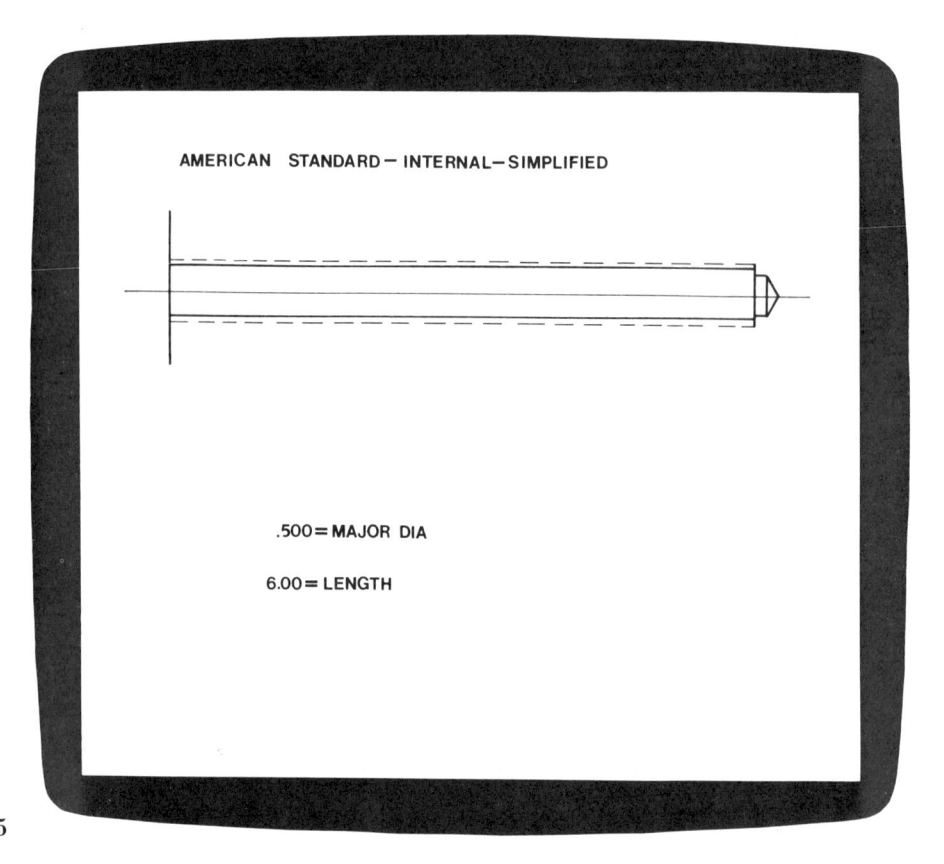

FIGURE 10–45

AMERICAN STANDARD – INTERNAL – SIMPLIFIED

.500 = MAJOR DIA

6.00 = LENGTH

FIGURE 10–46

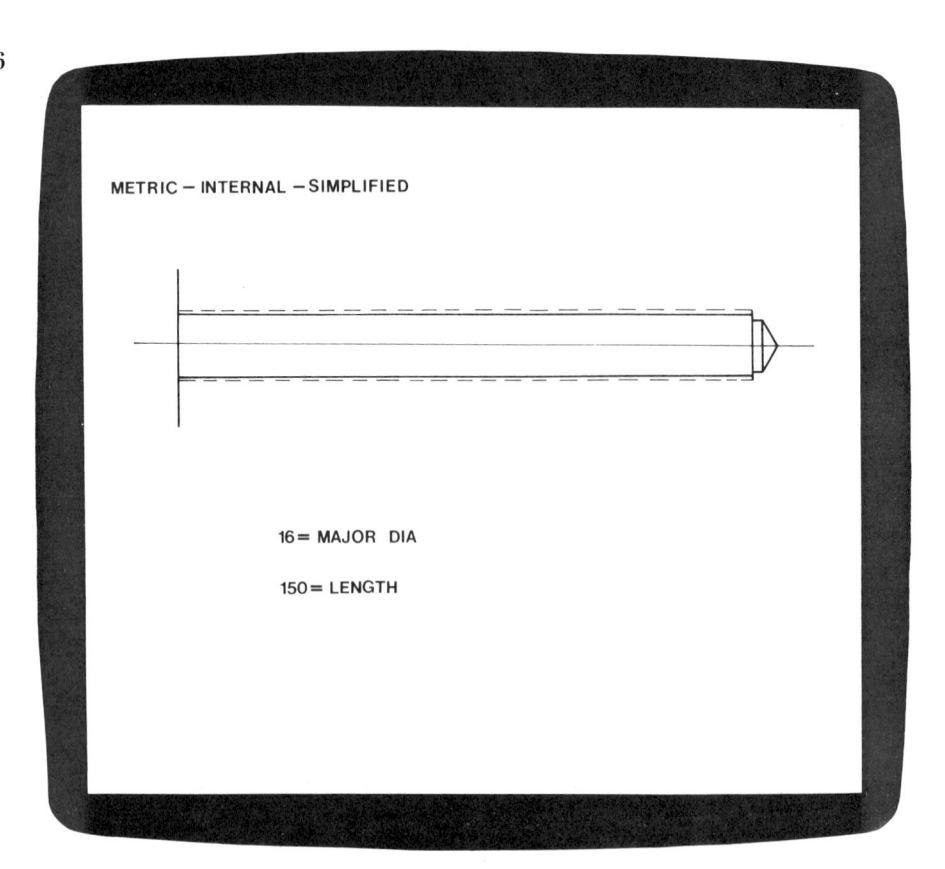

METRIC – INTERNAL – SIMPLIFIED

16 = MAJOR DIA

150 = LENGTH

Sec. 10-13 Building a Reference Library   315

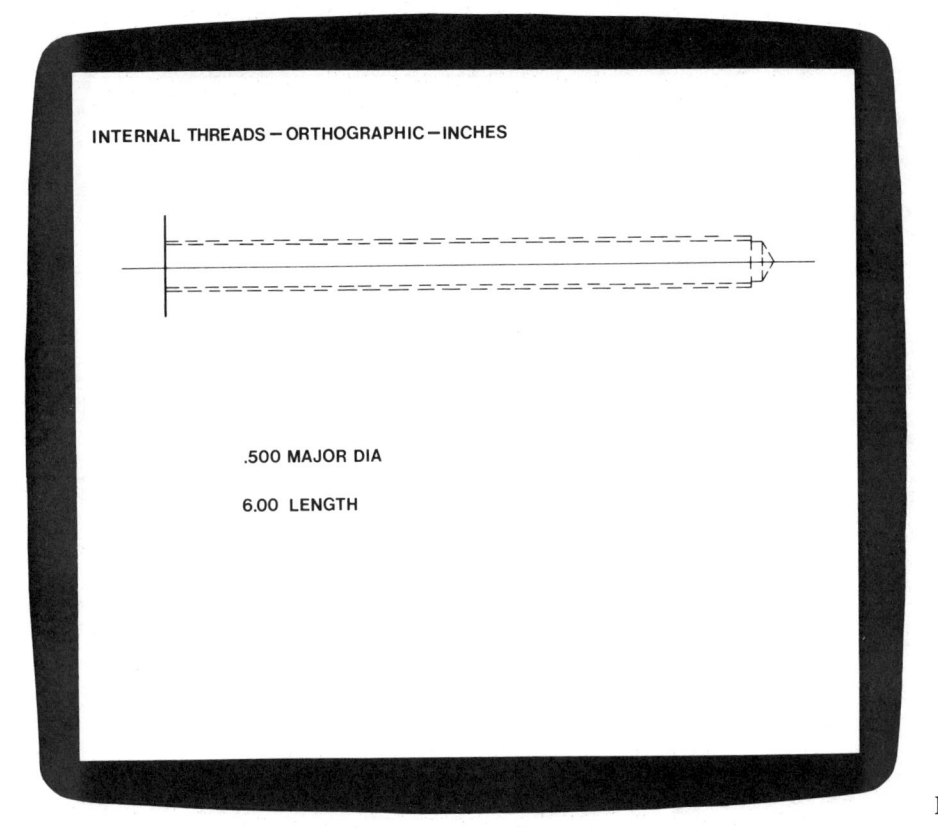

INTERNAL THREADS — ORTHOGRAPHIC — INCHES

.500 MAJOR DIA

6.00 LENGTH

FIGURE 10-47

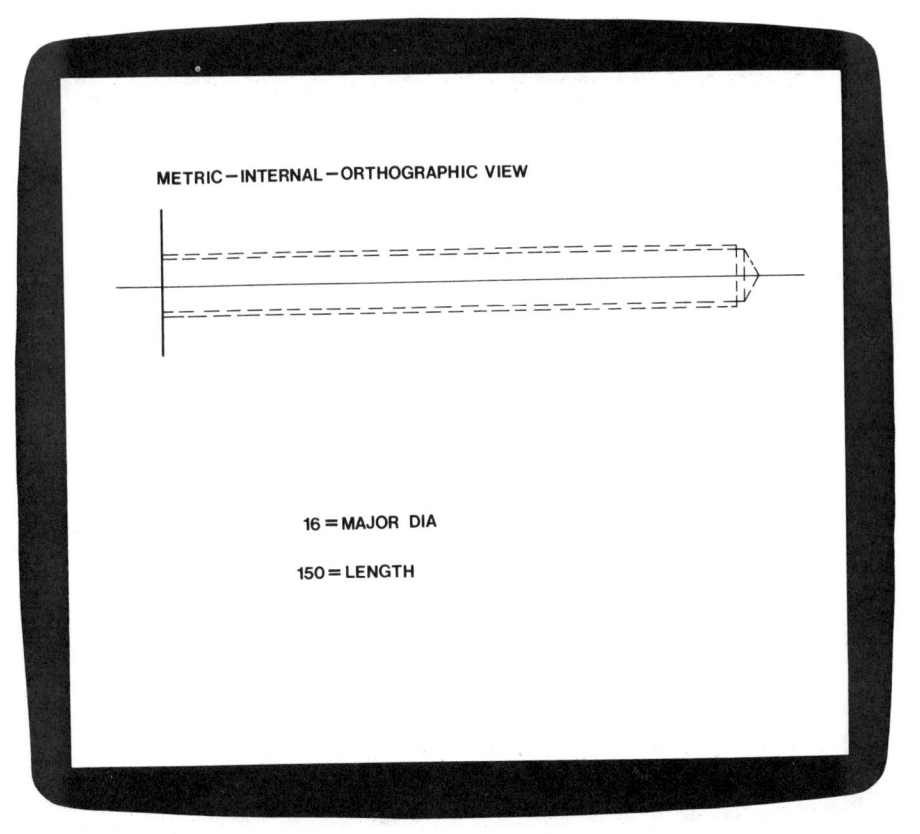

FIGURE 10-48

METRIC — INTERNAL — ORTHOGRAPHIC VIEW

16 = MAJOR DIA

150 = LENGTH

316 Threads and Fasteners Chap. 10

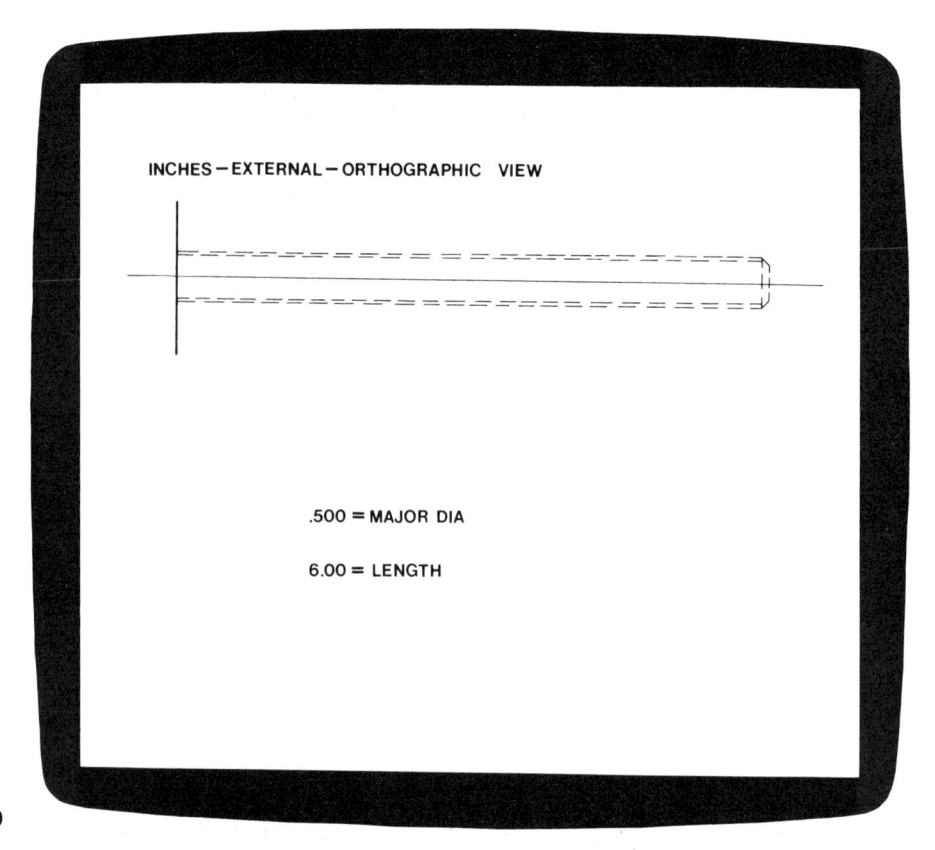

INCHES – EXTERNAL – ORTHOGRAPHIC VIEW

.500 = MAJOR DIA

6.00 = LENGTH

FIGURE 10-49

FIGURE 10-50

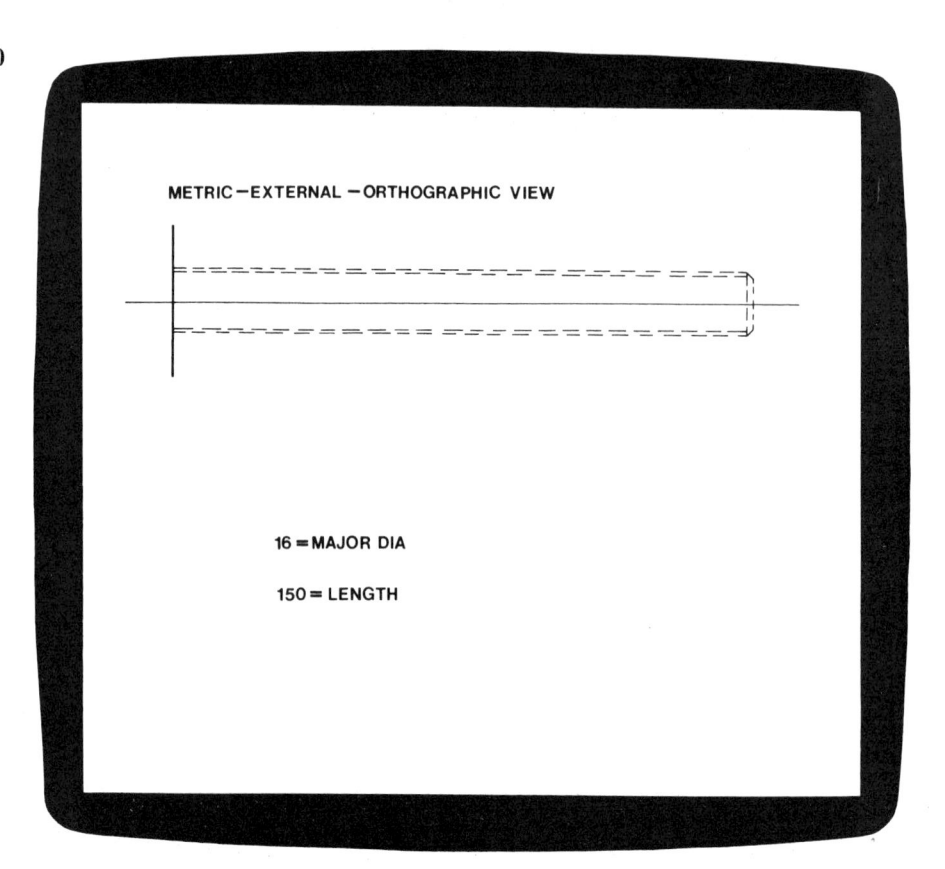

METRIC – EXTERNAL – ORTHOGRAPHIC VIEW

16 = MAJOR DIA

150 = LENGTH

Sec. 10-13   Building a Reference Library

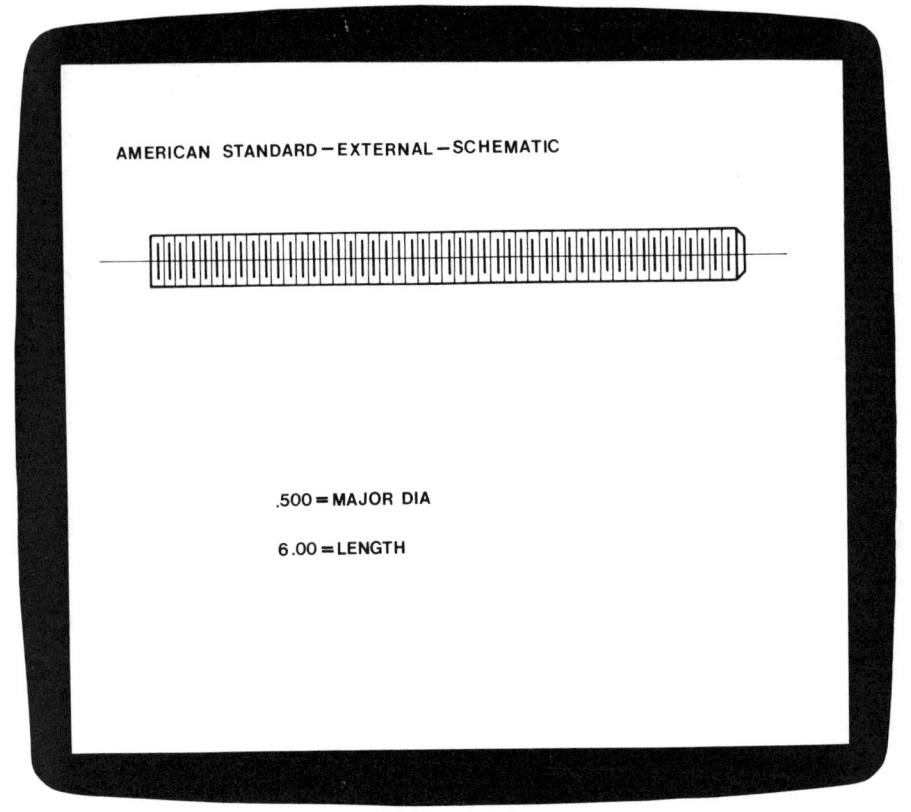

AMERICAN STANDARD – EXTERNAL – SCHEMATIC

.500 = MAJOR DIA

6.00 = LENGTH

FIGURE 10–51

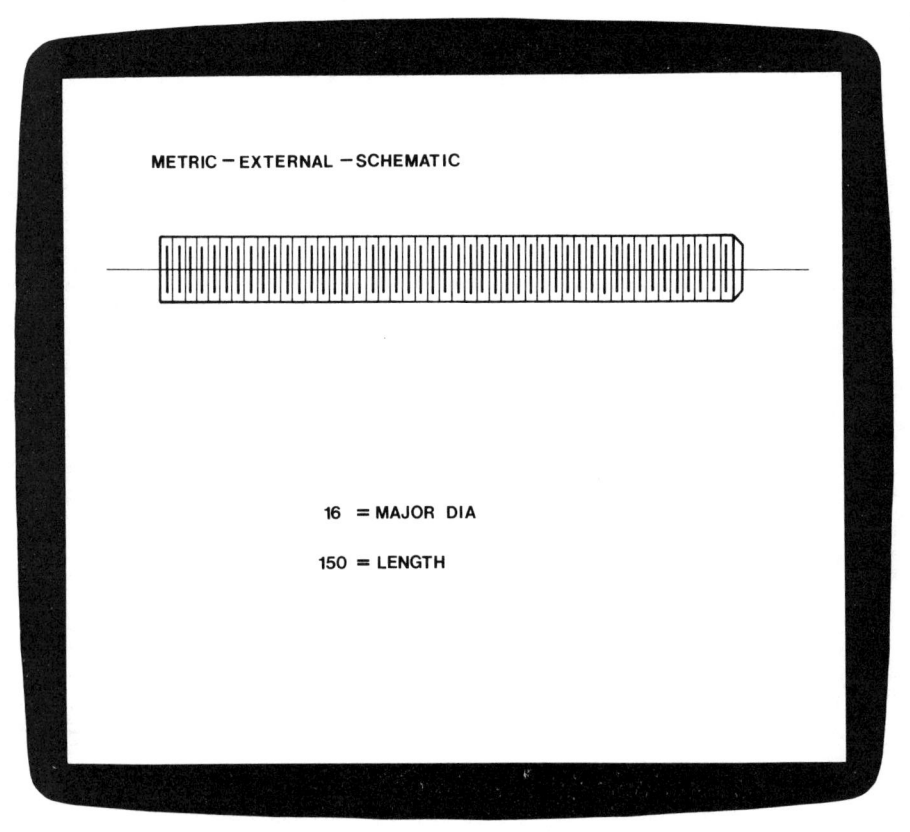

FIGURE 10–52

METRIC – EXTERNAL – SCHEMATIC

16 = MAJOR DIA

150 = LENGTH

AMERICAN STANDARD – EXTERNAL – SIMPLIFIED

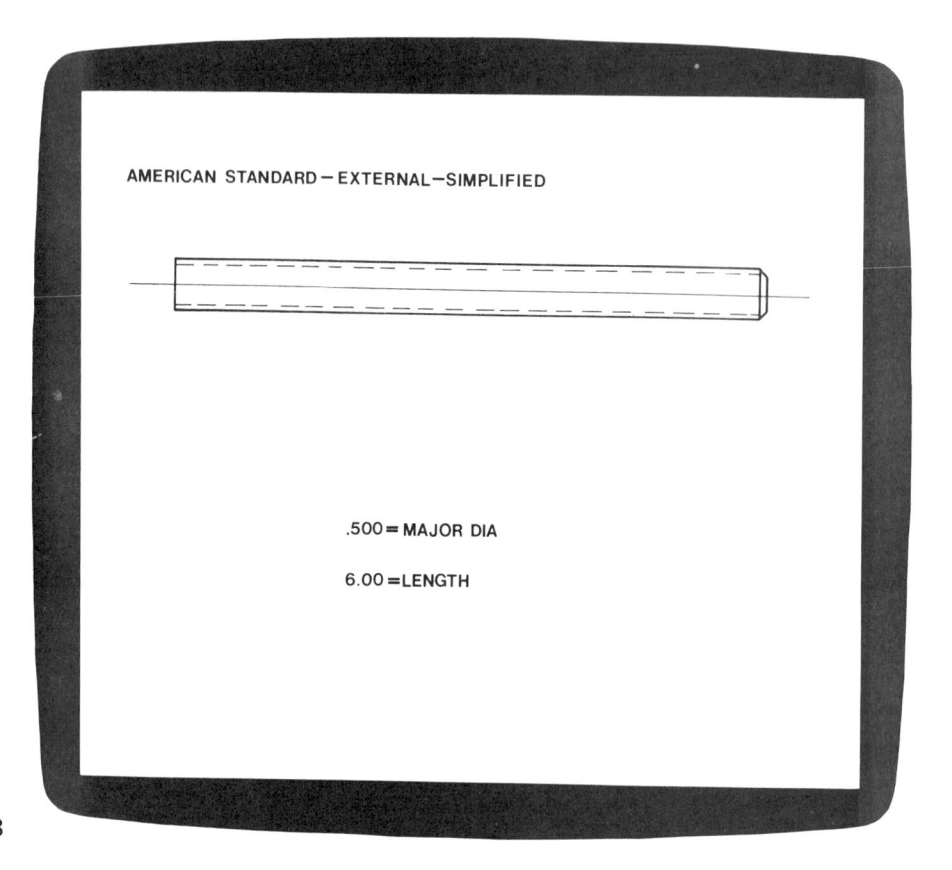

.500 = MAJOR DIA

6.00 = LENGTH

FIGURE 10-53

FIGURE 10-54

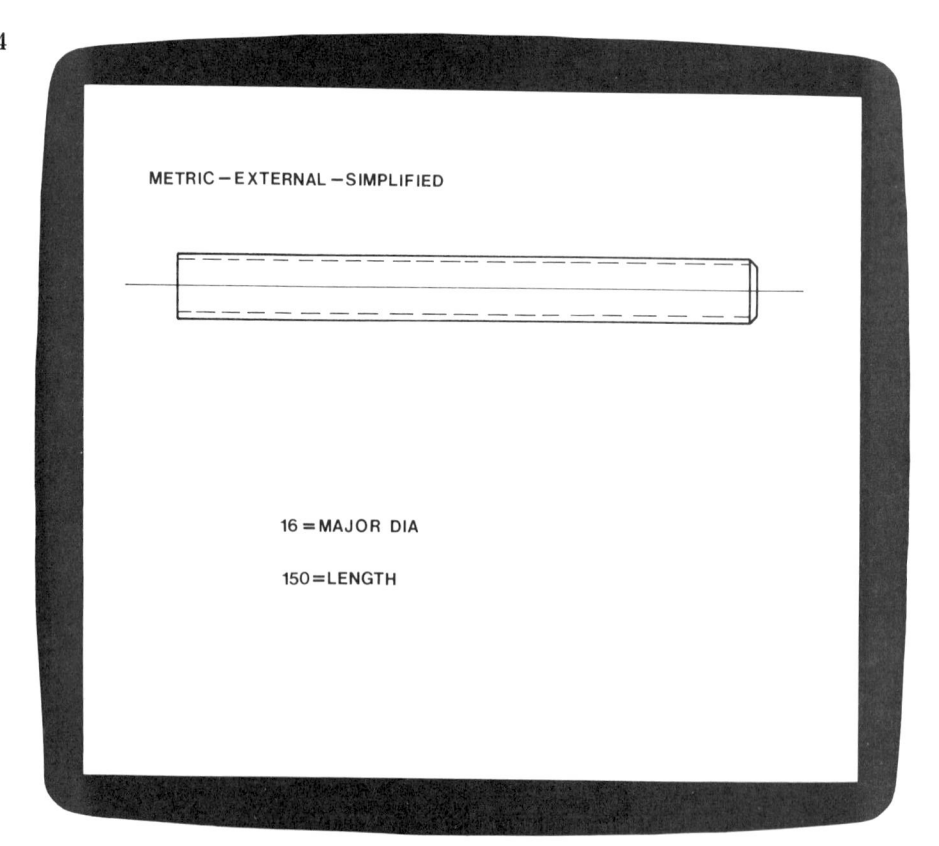

METRIC – EXTERNAL – SIMPLIFIED

16 = MAJOR DIA

150 = LENGTH

Sec. 10-13   Building a Reference Library

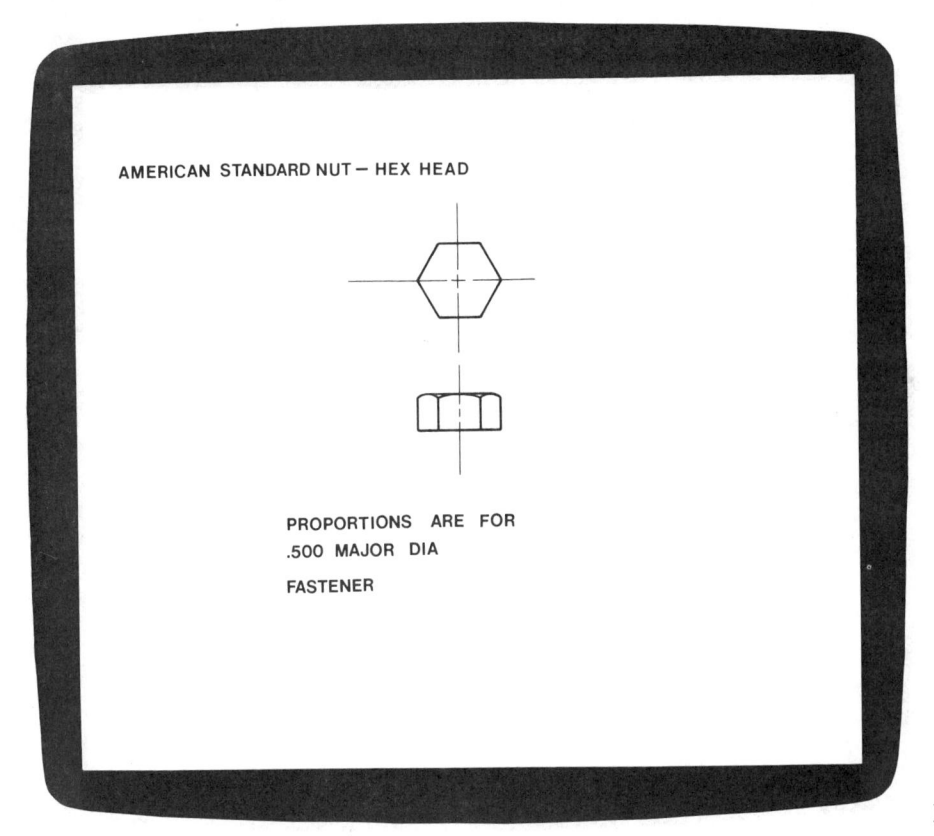

AMERICAN STANDARD NUT — HEX HEAD

PROPORTIONS ARE FOR
.500 MAJOR DIA
FASTENER

FIGURE 10-55

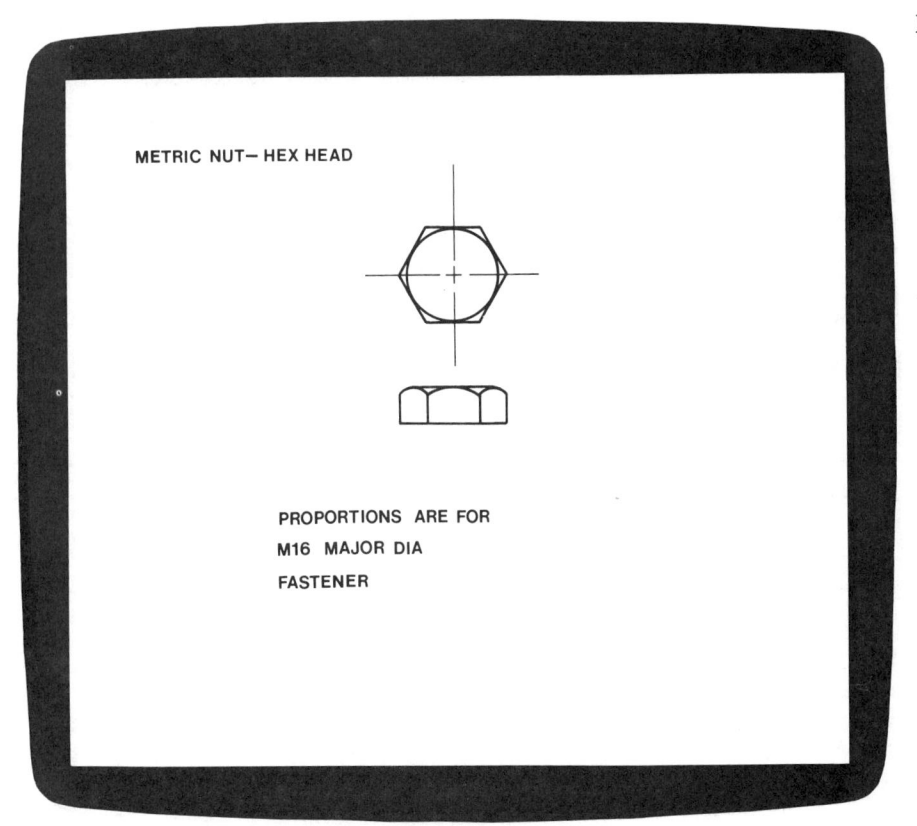

FIGURE 10-56

METRIC NUT — HEX HEAD

PROPORTIONS ARE FOR
M16 MAJOR DIA
FASTENER

320   Threads and Fasteners   Chap. 10

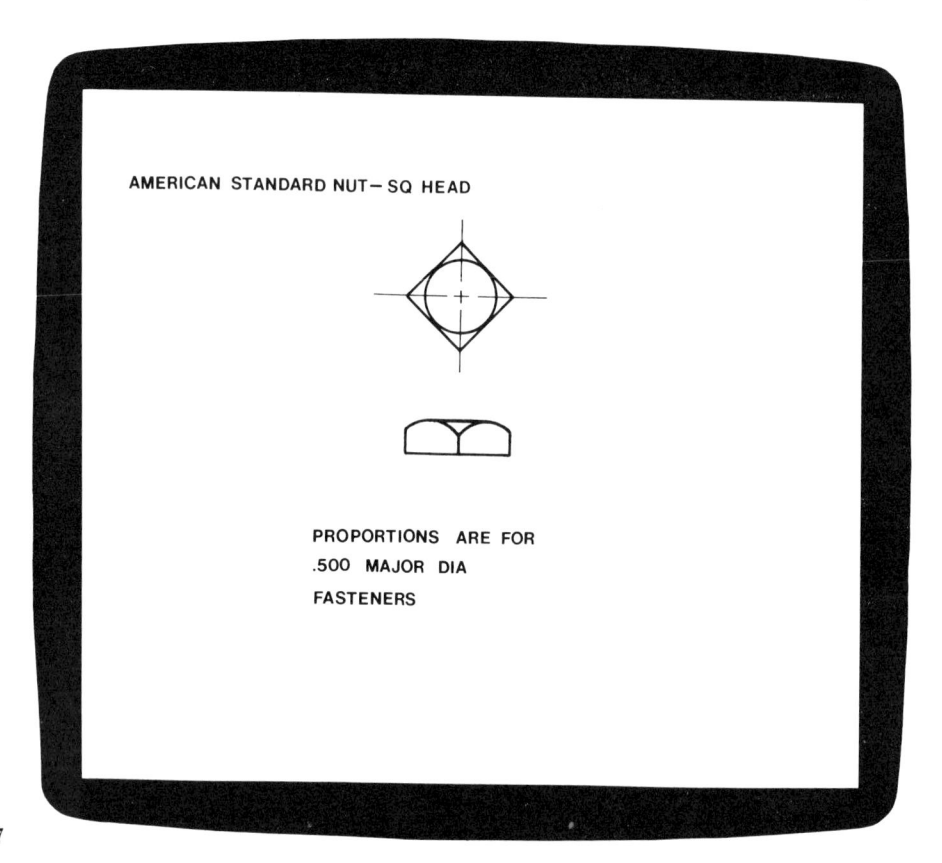

FIGURE 10-57

AMERICAN STANDARD NUT — SQ HEAD

PROPORTIONS ARE FOR
.500 MAJOR DIA
FASTENERS

FIGURE 10-58

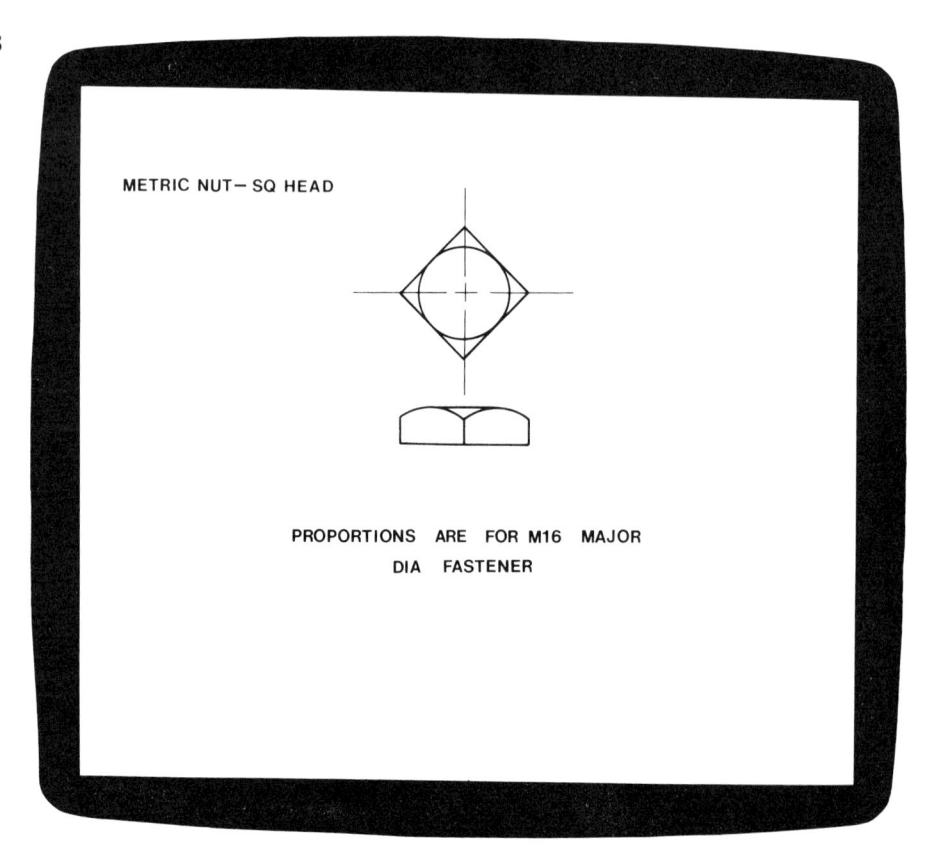

METRIC NUT — SQ HEAD

PROPORTIONS ARE FOR M16 MAJOR
DIA FASTENER

PROBLEMS

P10-1   Draw the following fasteners. All fasteners have 45° chamfers of length equal to one pitch of the stated thread.

   (a) 0.250 − 20 UNC × 1.50 LONG
       HEX HEAD SCREW
   (b) 0.500 − 13 UNC × 3.00 LONG
       SQ. HEAD BOLT
   (c) 6 (0.138) − 32 UNC × 0.75 LONG
       SLOTTED SET SCREW − FLAT POINT
   (d) 0.375 − 28 UNEF × 2.00 LONG
       SQ. HEAD SCREW
   (e) 10 (0.194) − 32 UNF × 1.00 LONG
       HEX HEAD SCREW

P10-2   Draw the following fasteners. All fasteners have 45° chamfers of length equal to one pitch of the stated thread.

   (a) M16 × 30
       HEX HEAD SCREW
   (b) M12 × 1.25 × 20
       SQ. HEAD BOLT
       10 THREAD LENGTH
   (c) M4 SLOTTED SET SCREW
       FLAT POINT
   (d) M24 × 50
       SQ. HEAD SCREW
   (e) M10 × 1.25 × 25
       HEX HEAD SCREW

P10-3 Draw a front and top orthographic view of Parts 1 and 2 as shown in Figure P10-3 joined by the following fasteners. Locate a washer under the head and under the nut in each assembly. Each assembly contains two screws, two nuts, and four washers. Use the inch values given in the table.

(a) 0.500 − 13 UNC × 1.75 HEX HEAD BOLT
0.50 THREAD LENGTH
0.63 × 1.13 × 0.06 WASHER
ϕ0.56 HOLES IN PARTS 1 and 2

(b) 0.250 − 28 UNF × 1.50 HEX HEAD BOLT
0.50 THREAD LENGTH
0.31 × 0.75 × 0.06 WASHER
ϕ0.31 HOLES IN PARTS 1 and 2

(c) 0.375 − 16 UNC × 2.00 SQ. HEAD BOLT
0.50 THREAD LENGTH
0.63 × 1.25 × 0.13 WASHER
ϕ0.56 HOLES IN PARTS 1 and 2

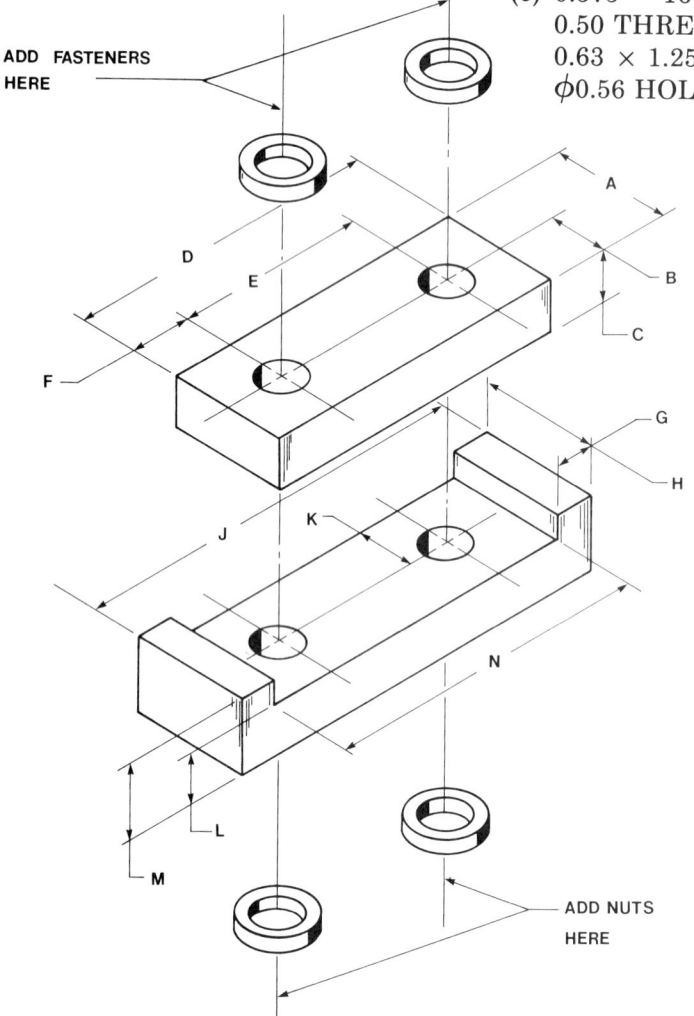

DIMENSION	INCHES	mm
A	1.25	32
B	.63	16
C	.50	13
D	3.25	82
E	2.00	50
F	.63	16
G	.38	10
H	1.25	32
J	4.13	106
K	.63	16
L	.50	13
M	.75	10
N	3.38	86

FIGURE P10-3

P10-4 Draw a front and top orthographic view of Parts 1 and 2 as shown in Figure P10-3 joined by the following fasteners. Locate a washer under the head and under the nut in each assembly. Each assembly contains two screws, two nuts, and four washers. Use the millimeter values given in the table.

(a) M16 × 40 HEX HEAD BOLT
10 THREAD LENGTH
20 × 30 × 4 WASHER
ϕ18 HOLES IN PARTS 1 and 2

(b) M8 × 40 HEX HEAD BOLT
10 THREAD LENGTH
12 × 24 × 3 WASHER
ϕ12 HOLES IN PARTS 1 and 2

(c) M12 × 1.25 × 40 SQ. HEAD BOLT
10 THREAD LENGTH
12 × 24 × 3 WASHER
ϕ12 HOLES IN PARTS 1 and 2

P10-5 (a) Draw a front and top view of the assembly shown in Figure P10-5. Use the inch values listed in the table. Part 221 is a flat plate with two holes positioned to match the larger holes of Parts 220. The two holes in Part 221 are 2.25 in. apart.

(1) Assemble two 0.750 − 16 UNF × 2.00 SQ. HEAD BOLTS and appropriate NUTS in the two larger holes. Also include two 0.875 × 1.50 × 0.13 washers, one under the head and one under the nut.

(2) Assemble two 0.250 − 28 UNF × 1.00 HEX HEAD BOLTS and appropriate NUTS in the smaller holes. No washers are required.

(b) Draw a front and top view of the assembly shown in Figure P10-5. Use the millimeter values listed in the table. Part 221 is a flat plate with two holes positioned to match the larger holes of Parts 220. The two holes in Part 221 are 58 mm apart.

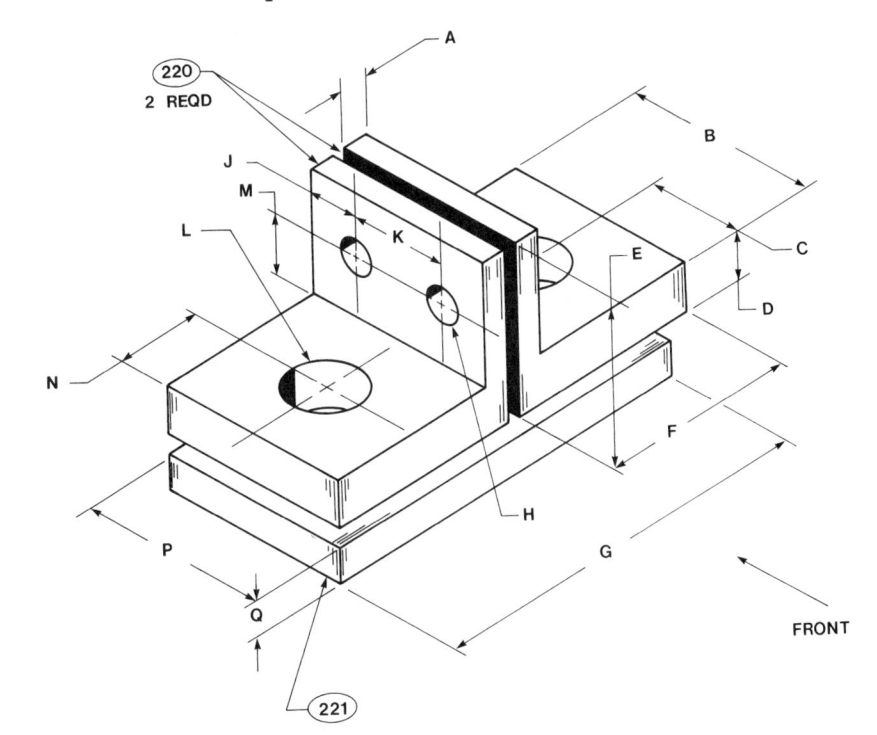

DIMENSION	INCHES	mm
A	.25	6
B	2.00	50
C	1.00	25
D	.50	13
E	1.75	45
F	2.00	50
G	4.00	100
H	⌀.438	⌀11
J	.50	12.5
K	1.00	25
L	⌀.781	⌀19
M	.63	16
N	.88	22
P	2.00	50
Q	.25	6

FIGURE P10-5

(1) Assemble two 16 × 1.5 × 40 SQ. HEAD BOLTS and appropriate NUTS in the two larger holes. Also include two 24 × 36 × 2 washers, one under the head and one under the nut.

(2) Assemble two 12 × 1.25 × 18 HEX HEAD BOLTS and appropriate NUTS in the smaller holes. No washers are required.

P10-6 (a) Draw a front and top view of the assembly shown in Figure P10-6. Use the inch values from the table.

(1) Add a 0.625 − 11 UNC × 2.50 HEX HEAD BOLT with an appropriate NUT so that it passes through both Parts 12 and 13. Assume that there is ϕ0.66 hole in Part 13 which aligns with the hole in Part 12.

(2) Add two 0.250 − 20 UNC × 0.50 SET SCREWS to Part 12 as indicated.

(b) Draw a front and top view of the assembly shown in Figure P10-6. Use the millimeter values from the table.

(1) Add a M16 × 60 HEX HEAD BOLT with an appropriate NUT so that it passes through both Parts 12 and 13. Assume that there is ϕ17 hole in Part 13 which aligns with the hole in Part 12.

(2) Add two M6 × 14 SET SCREWS to Part 12 as indicated.

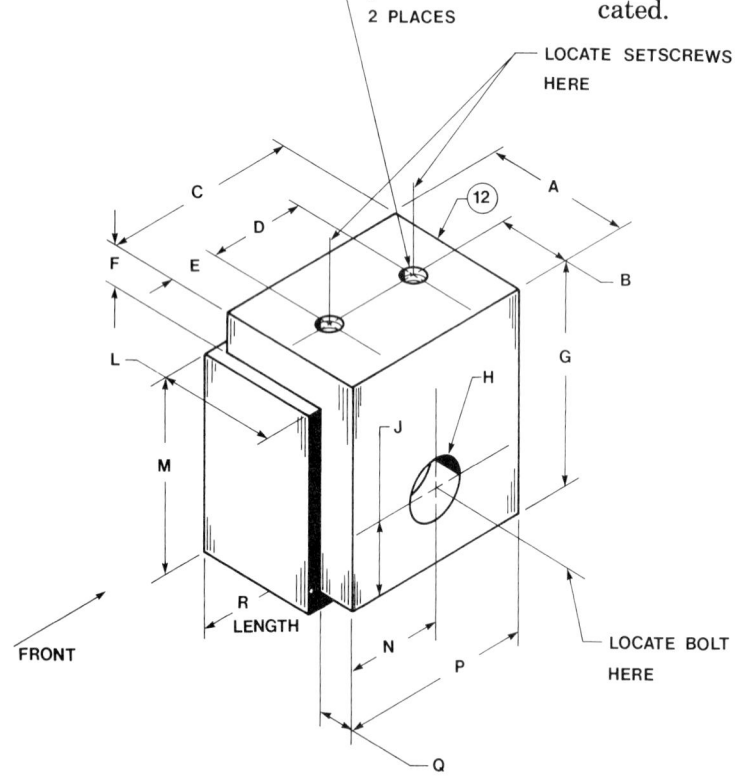

DIMENSION	INCHES	mm
A	1.50	38
B	.75	16
C	2.00	50
D	1.00	25
E	.50	12.5
F	.38	9
G	2.25	57
H	⌀.66	⌀17
J	.75	19
K	.250-20 UNC	M6
L	1.25	32
M	2.00	50
N	1.00	25
P	2.00	50
Q	.38	9
R	2.00	50

FIGURE P10-6

P10-7 Use the format shown in Figure P10-7 and add the following fasteners.

(a) Use the inch dimensions and draw a front and a top orthographic view. Add and label the following fasteners.

Chap. 10   Problems

   (1) 0.375 − 24 UNF × 1.00
       HEX HEAD SCREW
   (2) 0.500 − 13 UNC × 1.00
       SQ. HEAD SCREW
   (3) 0.190 − 24 UNC × 0.75 SLOTTED SETSCREW
       FLAT POINT
   (4) 0.500 − 20 UNF × 1.00
       FLAT HEAD SCREW

(b) Use the inch dimensions and draw a front sectional view and a top orthographic view. Add and label the following fasteners. Use the schematic thread representation.
   (1) 0.250 − 20 UNC × 1.00
       HEX HEAD SCREW
   (2) 0.375 − 16 UNC × 1.00
       SQ. HEAD SCREW
       Add a 0.41 × 0.75 × 0.06
       WASHER under the screw head
   (3) 0.138 − 32 UNC × 0.75
       HEXAGON SOCKET SETSCREW
       OVAL POINT
   (4) 0.500 − 13 UNC × 1.00
       FLAT HEAD SCREW

(c) Use the metric dimensions and draw a front and a top view. Add and label the following fasteners.
   (1) M12 × 25 HEX HEAD SCREW
   (2) M16 × 1.5 × 2.5 SQ. HEAD SCREW
   (3) M4 × 20 FLAT POINT
   (4) M10 × 1.25 × 25 FLAT HEAD SCREW

(d) Use the metric dimensions and draw a front sectional view and a top orthographic view. Add the label the following fasteners. Use the schematic representation.
   (1) M8 × 25 HEX HEAD SCREW
   (2) M12 × 1.25 × 10 SQ. HEAD SCREW
       Add a 14 × 24 × 3 WASHER under the screw head
   (3) M6 HEXAGON SOCKET SETSCREW OVAL POINT
   (4) M6 × 25 FLAT HEAD SCREW

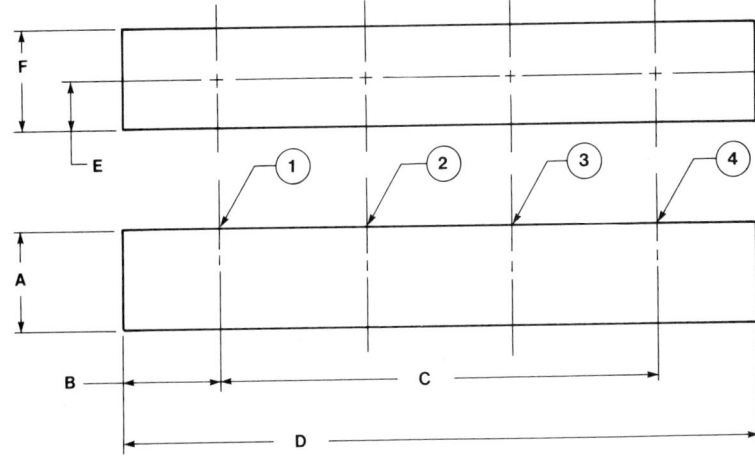

DIMENSION	INCHES	mm
A	1.00	25
B	1.00	25
C	3 X 1.00	3 X 40
D	6.5	170
E	.50	13
F	1.00	26

FIGURE P10-7

P10-8 Redraw the orthographic view given in Figure P10-8 as a sectional view. Add the following bolt, appropriate nut, and washer. Use the schematic thread representation.

(a) Use the inch dimensions and add:
0.375 − 16 UNC × 2.50 HEX HEAD BOLT with a 0.75 thread length and a 0.50 × 1.00 × 0.06 WASHER

(b) Use the millimeter dimensions and add:
M10 × 70 HEX HEAD BOLT with a 20 thread length and a 12 × 24 × 4 WASHER

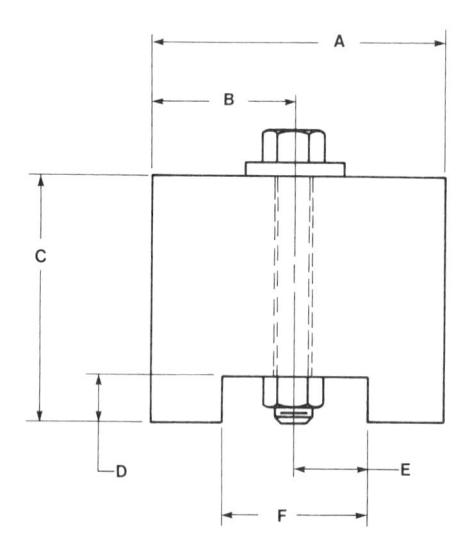

DIMENSION	INCHES	mm
A	3.00	76
B	1.50	38
C	2.50	64
D	.50	13
E	.75	19
F	1.50	38

FIGURE P10-8

P10-9 Redraw the orthographic view given in Figure P10-9 as a sectional view. Add the following screws, washers, and nuts. Use the schematic thread representations.

(a) Use the inch dimensions and add:
(1) 0.250 − 20 UNC × 1.00 FLAT HEAD SCREW through the M hole and into the S hole.
(2) 0.164 − 32 UNF × 1.00 HEX HEAD SCREW through the N hole and into the R hole. Locate a 0.250 × 0.500 × 0.13 WASHER under the screw head.
(3) 0.375 − 14 UNC × 1.00 SQ. HEAD SCREW with appropriate NUT through the P and Q holes. Locate one 0.41 × 0.75 × 0.06 WASHER under the screw head and another under the NUT.

(b) Use the millimeter dimensions and add:
(1) M6 × 25 FLAT HEAD SCREW through the M hole and into the S hole.
(2) M4 × 25 HEX HEAD SCREW through the N hole and into the R hole. Locate a 6 × 12 × 3 WASHER under the screw head.
(3) M10 × 1.25 × 35 SQ. HEAD SCREW with appropriate NUT through the P and Q holes. Locate one 12 × 24 × 5 WASHER under the screw head and another under the NUT.

P10-10 Draw a front and top orthographic view of the object shown in Figure P10-10.

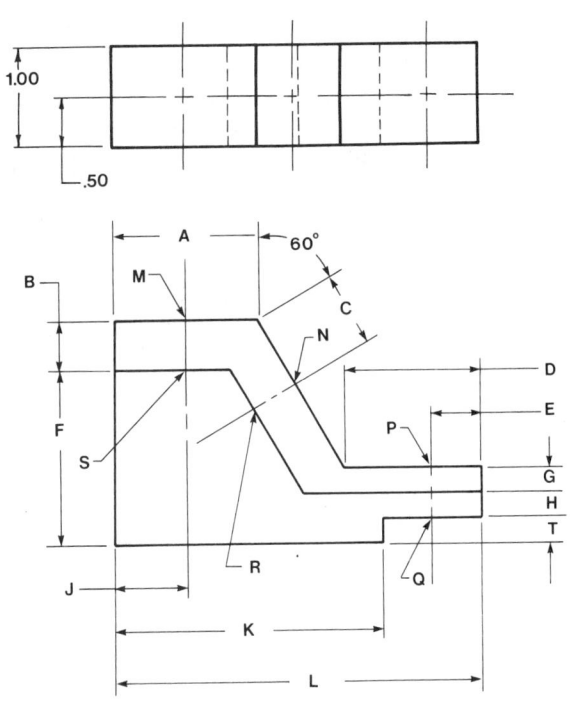

Chap. 10   Problems

DIMENSION	INCHES	mm
A	1.50	38
B	.50	13
C	.75	19
D	1.38	35
E	.50	13
F	1.75	44
G	.25	6
H	.25	6
J	.75	19
K	2.75	70
L	3.75	96
M	⌀.31	⌀8
N	⌀.25	⌀6
P	⌀.41	⌀12
Q	⌀.41	⌀12
R	.164-32 UNF X .50 DEEP	M4 X 14 DEEP
S	.250-20 UNC X 1.63 DEEP	M6 X 14 DEEP
T	.25	6

FIGURE P10-9

(a) Use the inch dimensions listed in the table and add the following fasteners.
   (1) 0.190 − 32 UNF × .50 HEX HEAD SCREW
   (2) 0.164 − 36 UNF × .50 SLOTTED SETSCREW, FLAT POINT − 2 REQD.

(b) Use the millimeter dimensions listed in the table and add the following fasteners.
   (1) M8 × 10 HEX HEAD SCREW
   (2) M6 × 10 SLOTTED SETSCREW, FLAT POINT − 2 REQD.

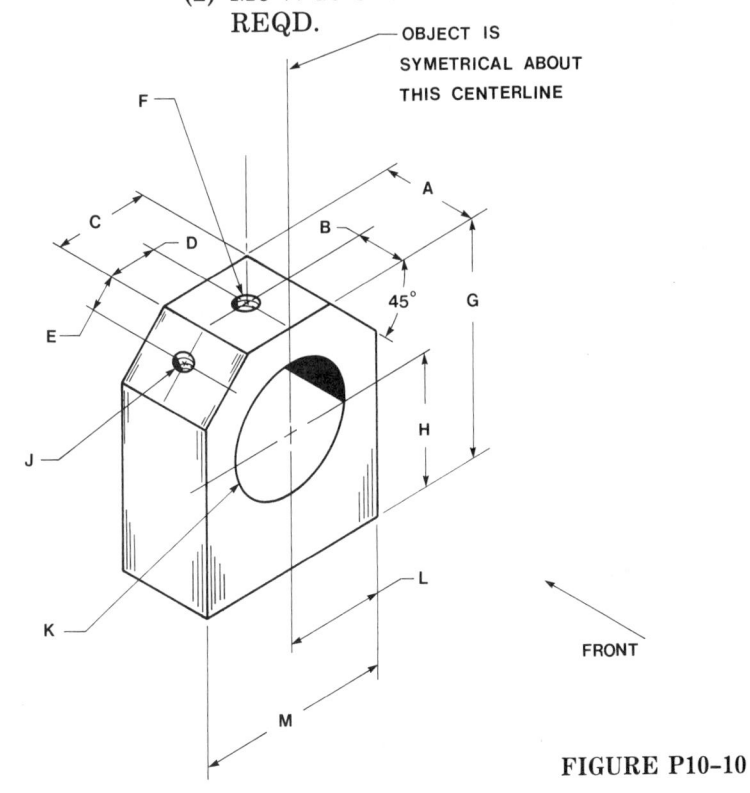

DIMENSION	INCHES	mm
A	1.00	26
B	.50	13
C	1.00	26
D	.50	13
E	.38	10
F	.190-32 UNF	M8 X 1
G	2.38	60
H	1.38	34
J	.164-36 UNF	M6
K	⌀1.25	⌀30
L	1.00	26
M	2.00	52

FIGURE P10-10

P10-11 Draw a front and top orthographic view of both objects shown in Figure P10-11 as explained below. The given hole diameters are nominal sizes. Choose appropriate fasteners and, when required, nuts. Holes that are not threaded are clearance holes and should be sized accordingly. The completed solution should include three drawings: a front and top view of Part 23 with dimensions, a front and top view of Part 24 with dimensions, and a front view of Parts 23 and 24 assembled together with appropriate fasteners in place. The assembled view need not be dimensioned, nor contain any hidden lines, but should include a drawing callout for each fastener. Use *only* standard thread sizes and lengths. All threads are coarse.

(a) Use the inch dimensions given in the table and the following fasteners.

(1) ϕ0.375, HEX HEAD, NUT

(2) ϕ0.438, HEX HEAD, Tapped Hole in Part 24, 0.75 DEEP

(3) ϕ0.375, FLAT HEAD, NUT

(b) Use the millimeter dimensions given in the table and add the following fasteners.

(1) ϕ10, HEX HEAD, NUT

(2) ϕ12, HEX HEAD, Tapped Hole in Part 24, 18 DEEP

(3) ϕ10, FLAT HEAD, NUT

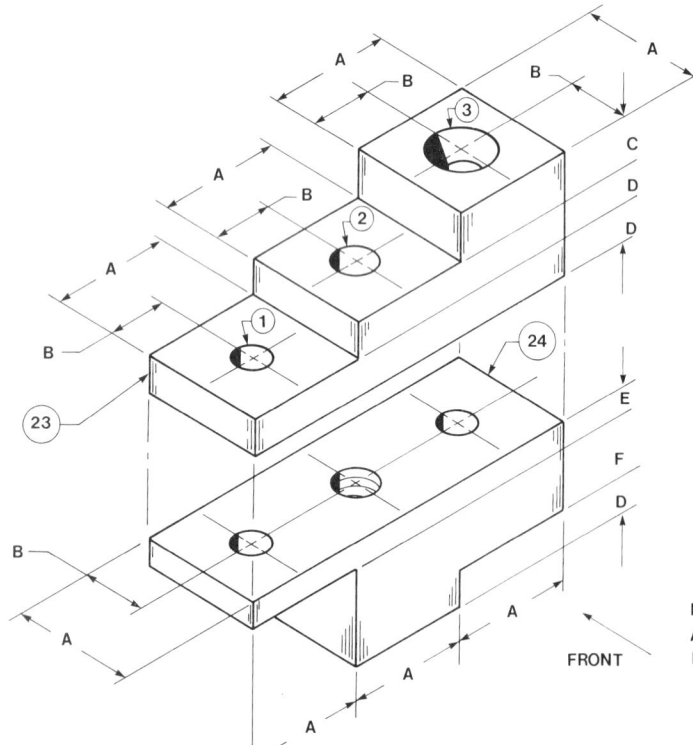

DIMENSION	INCHES	mm
A	1.25	32
B	.63	16
C	.50	13
D	.38	10
E	.25	7
F	.63	16

NOTE: HOLES IN PART 24 ALIGN WITH THOSE IN PART 23.

FIGURE P10-11

Chap. 10 Problems 329

P10-12 Based on the sizes given in Figure P10-12, choose fasteners for locations W, X, Y, and Z that will hold Parts 1, 2, 3, and 4 together as shown. All fasteners should have hex heads, use coarse threads, and have appropriate nuts. The fastener's head should be located on an entirely flat surface. Use the schematic thread representation. Redraw the given sectional view using the dimensions listed in the table and add appropriate fasteners. Identify each fastener with a drawing callout.

(a) Use inch dimensions.
(b) Use millimeter dimensions.

(W) (X) (Y) (Z) INDICATES FASTENER LOCATIONS

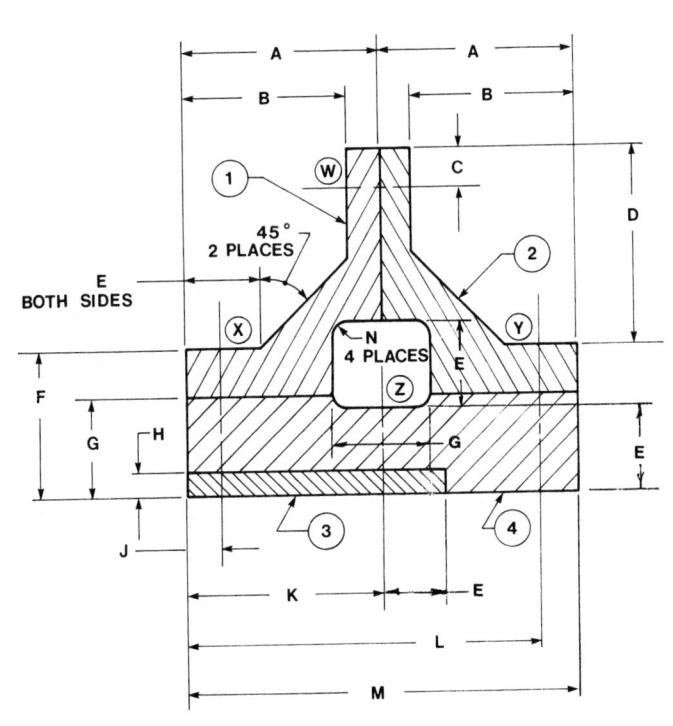

DIMENSION	INCHES	mm
A	1.00	50
B	1.63	41
C	.38	10
D	2.00	50
E	.75	19
F	1.50	38
G	1.00	25
H	.25	6
J	.38	10
K	2.00	50
L	3.63	92
M	4.00	100
N	R.13	3

FIGURE P10-12

11 PRODUCTION DRAWINGS

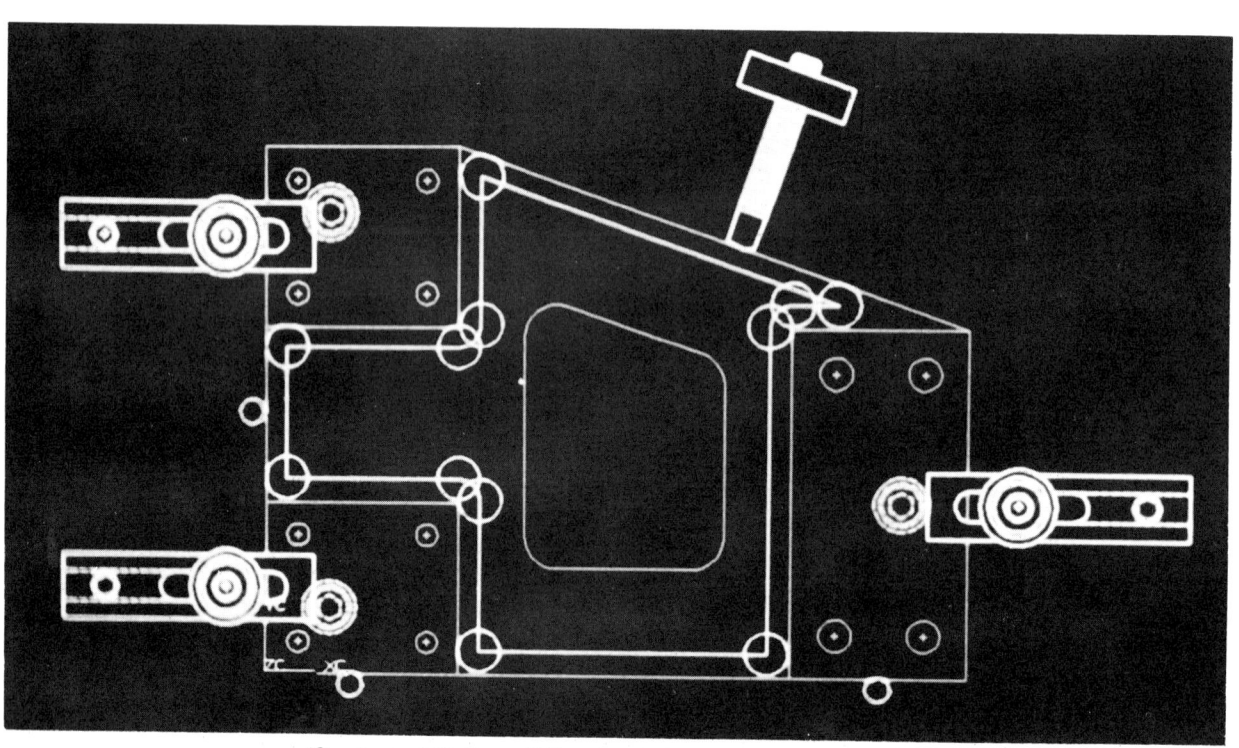

(Courtesy of McDonnell Douglas Manufacturing Industry Systems Company, St. Louis, Mo.)

11-1 INTRODUCTION

Production drawings are drawings used to manufacture objects. There are two broad categories of working drawings: assembly drawings and detail drawings. In this chapter we explain both types of drawings and define their relationship. Included in the discussion are detailed explanations of parts lists, drawings title blocks, and how drawings are revised.

11-2 ASSEMBLY DRAWING

An *assembly drawing* is a drawing that shows how objects are combined to create a final assembly. All information needed to assemble the objects must be included. The information may include specific assembly dimensions, torque requirements for bolts, finishing instructions (painting, for example), and any other appropriate company or customer specification. Figure 11-1 shows an assembly drawing of a simplified pressure vessel.

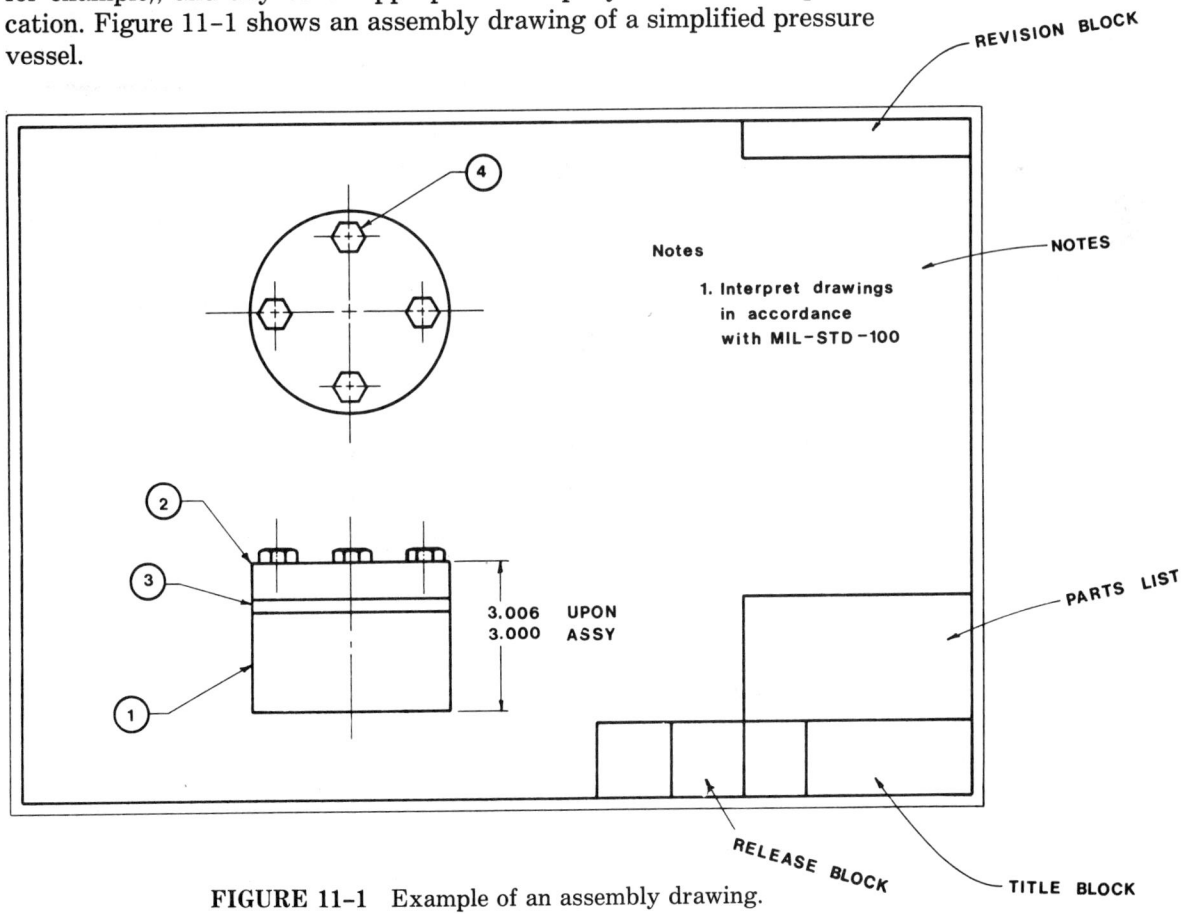

FIGURE 11-1 Example of an assembly drawing.

331

Assembly drawings do *not* contain hidden lines. If needed, sectional views may be added, but the intent of an assembly drawing is to give an overview of how parts are assembled. Specific information about an individual part is found on detail drawings.

Each part of an assembly is identified by a circled number (some companies use an ellipse) called a *bubble*. Bubbled numbers are assigned on each assembly drawing independently of numbers used on other assembly drawings. It is possible for a part that is used on several different assemblies to have a different bubble number on each assembly drawing. Bubbled numbers serve only to cross-reference parts within a single assembly drawing.

Generally, the larger, more important parts are given the lower numbers. In Figure 11-1, the large BASE CYLINDER is assigned number 1, the COVER PLATE number 2, and so on. Fasteners are usually assigned the highest numbers. Note that the fasteners in Figure 1-1 are assigned the number 4.

The same part, used more than once on the same assembly, need be identified by number only once if its other positions are obvious. In Fig-

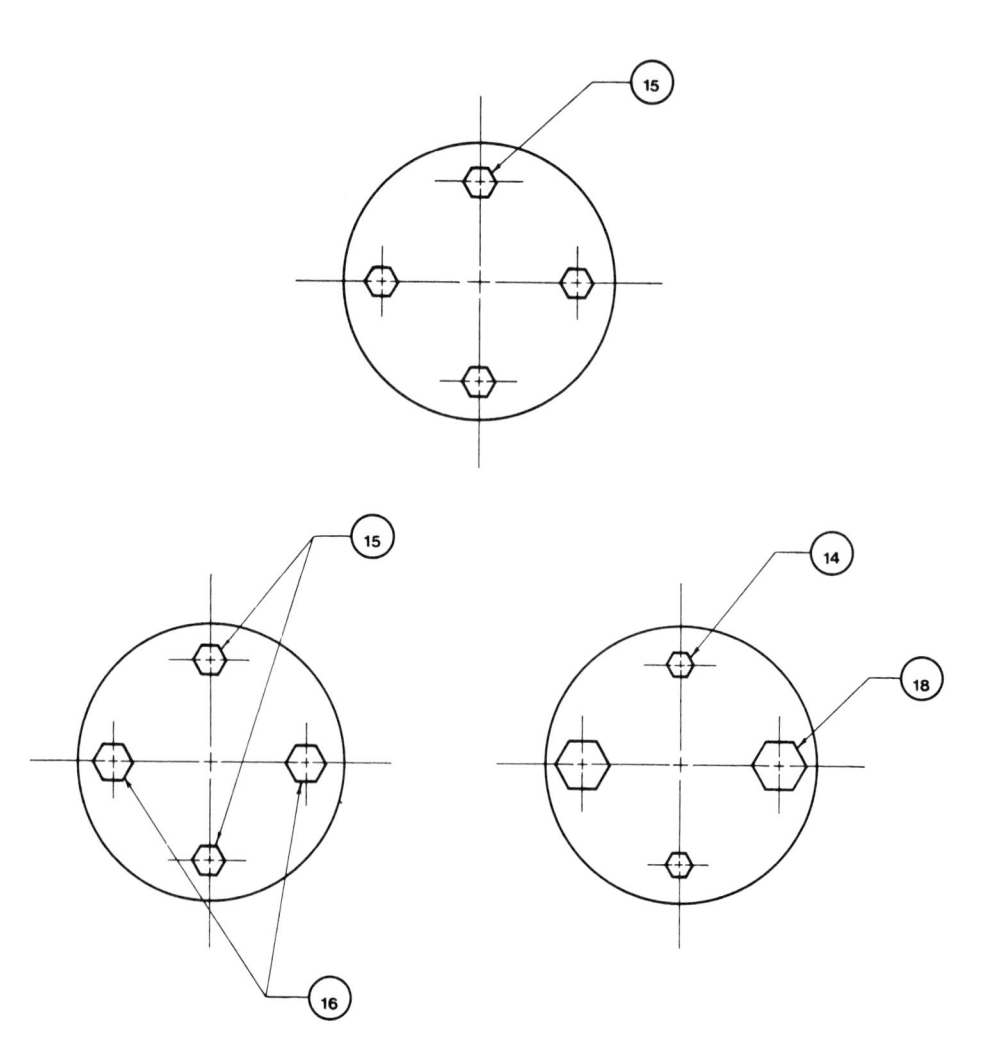

FIGURE 11-2 How to use leader lines with item numbers.

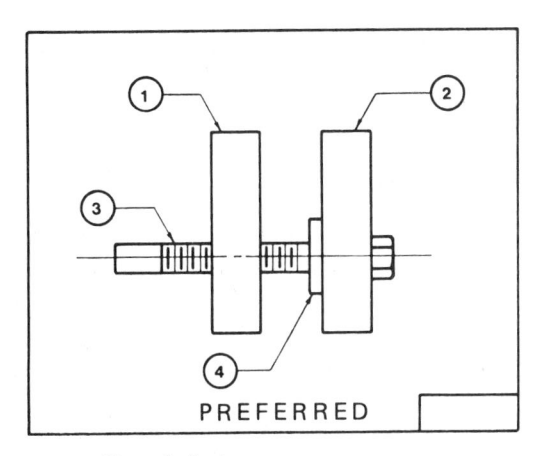

Sec. 11-2   Assembly Drawing   333

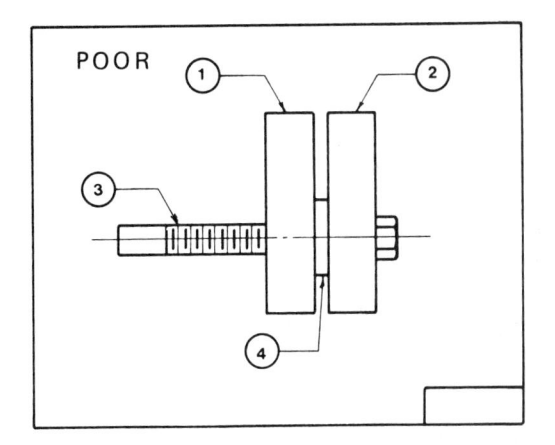

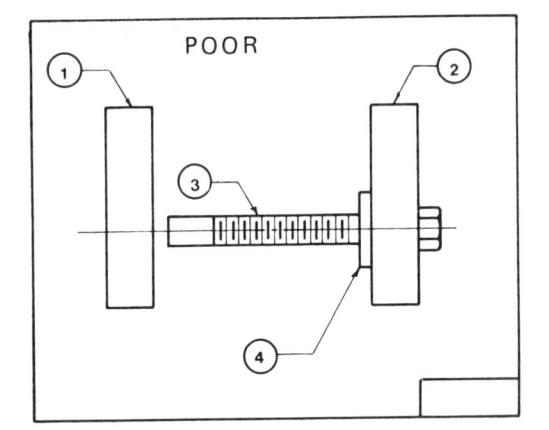

FIGURE 11-3   How to position parts in an assembly drawing.

ure 11-1, only one type of fastener is used, so only one identifying number is needed.

In Figure 11-2, it is not obvious in the lower left figure which fasteners are used in which locations, so multiple numbers and multiple leaders from a single number are used. Either method is acceptable.

Parts must be shown in their assembled position. Assemblies with moving parts should be shown in a natural or neutral position. For example, the clamp assembly shown in Figure 11-3 shows the clamp jaws at about the halfway-open point. This position is preferred to the fully open or closed position. Simply aligning the parts along a common centerline is unacceptable.

Assembly drawings are referred to as "top" drawings because they are the first drawing, in a group of drawings, that should completely define the assembly. Each part in the assembly has an individual drawing called a detail drawing. Specific information about individual parts is included on the detail drawings, not on the assembly drawing.

Specific areas on the field of an assembly drawing are designated for specific usage. For example, a title block is always located in the lower right-hand corner of the drawing. Parts lists, revision blocks, and notes

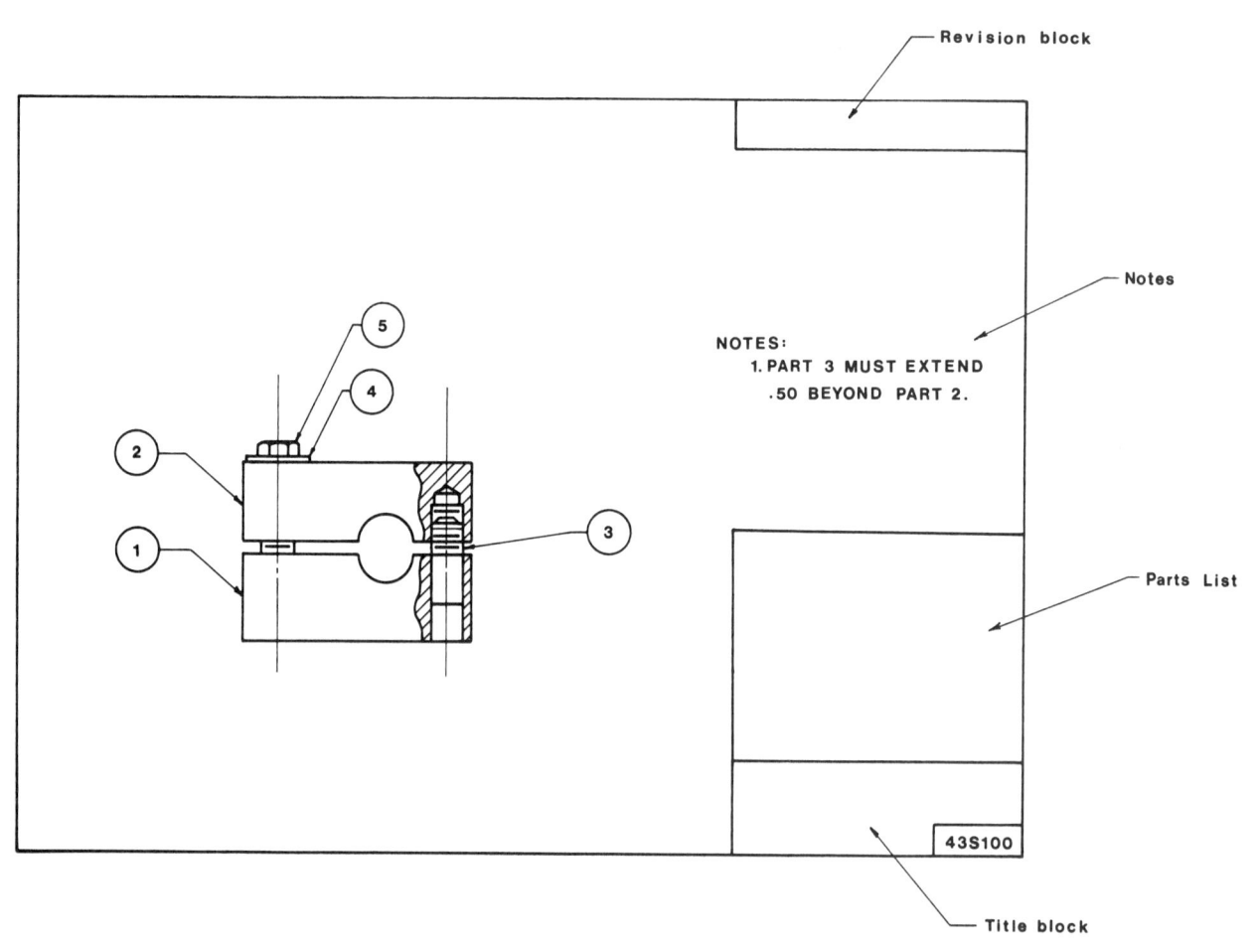

FIGURE 11-4 Specific areas on an assembly drawing are designated for specific usage.

are located as shown in Figure 11-4. Each of these areas is discussed in separate sections within this chapter.

11-3 DETAIL DRAWINGS

Detail drawings are drawings of individual parts and should include all information necessary to manufacture the part. The part must be correctly dimensioned and toleranced using accepted drawing formats. The material required and any specific manufacturing instructions must be clearly defined (Figures 11-5 and 11-6).

Companies use a variety of systems to number and title detail drawings. Numbers for drawings are usually kept in a log book. A new drawing would be assigned the next available number. This type of system prevents duplication of numbers. Drawing numbers should not be confused with assembly drawing bubble numbers. Drawing numbers are often coded so that they can be more easily categorized and referenced. For example, a drawing number such as 502PV88A could be the number 2 part of assembly 500. PV could mean a pressure vessel, 88 the year the design was created, and A the paper size (an A size equals $8\frac{1}{2} \times 11$ drawing size).

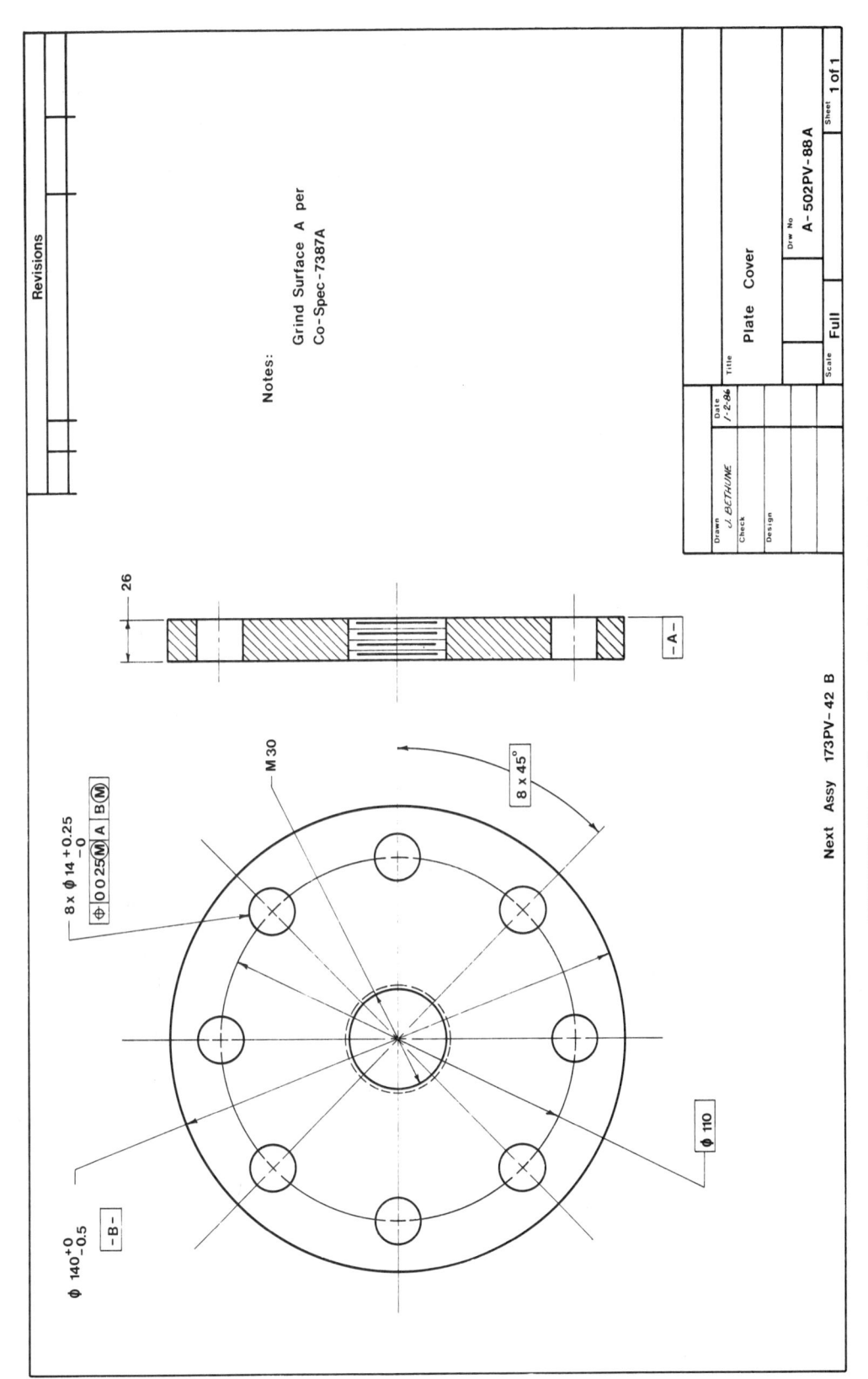

FIGURE 11-5 Example of a detailed drawing.

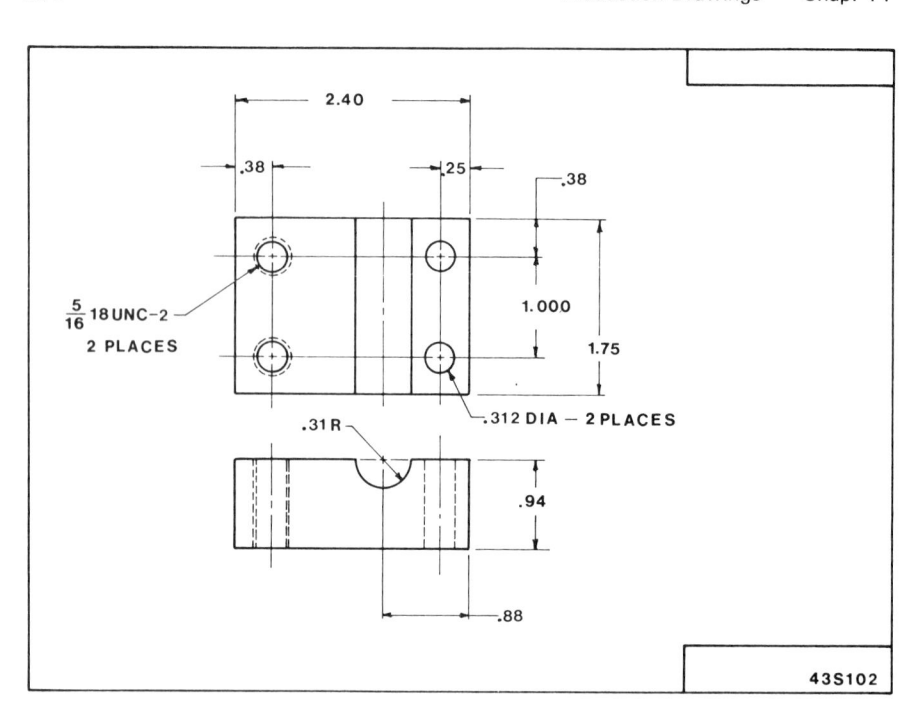

FIGURE 11-6 Example of a detailed drawing.

11-4 DRAWING TITLE ASSIGNMENT

Choosing a drawing title is an important part of creating an accurate drawing. The title should clearly, and as completely as possible, describe the object.

Drawing titles are arranged in a specific order: *noun* or *noun phrase*, followed by *modifiers* or *modifying phrases*. For example, in Figure 11-7, the drawing title is shown as SHAFT, HIGH SPEED—30 MM, LOWER. SHAFT is the noun, and HIGH SPEED is a modifying phrase. When speaking, the object would be referred to as a high-speed shaft, but when used as a drawing title, the noun must come first.

The modifiers are listed so that each further defines the exact function, shape, or location of the noun. In Figure 11-7 the modifier HIGH SPEED helps define the type of shaft. The assembly may contain several types of shafts. The size modifier 30 mm distinguishes the particular shaft from other high-speed shafts, and the modifier LOWER distinguishes the shaft from other 30-mm high-speed shafts.

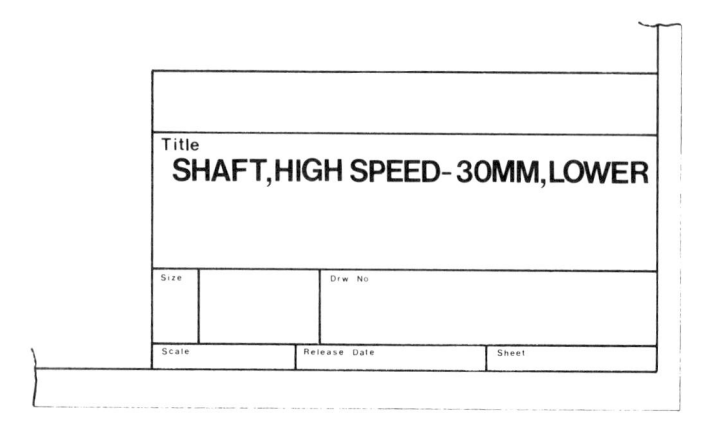

FIGURE 11-7 Sample drawing titles.

A noun phrase such as GEAR BOX is not broken down to BOX, GEAR. The phrase GEAR BOX is thought of as a single noun.

Abbreviations are not acceptable in drawing titles, with three exceptions: assembly may be written ASSY, subassembly SUBASSY, and installation INSTL. All other words must be written out using correct, complete spellings. The latest unabridged edition of *Webster's International Dictionary* is considered the final authority for all spellings and definitions.

Drawing titles should be kept as simple as possible. Assemblies with few parts can often use one- or two-word titles.

11-5 TITLE BLOCKS

Title blocks list information for identifying and processing drawings. The size and format for title blocks varies greatly from company to company. In this section we discuss title blocks as recommended for use by the

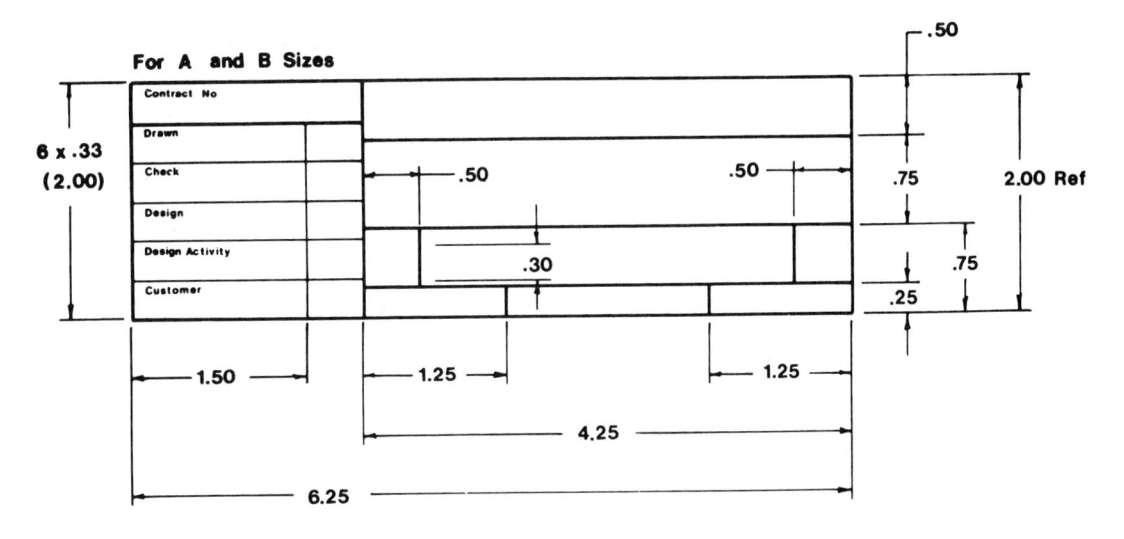

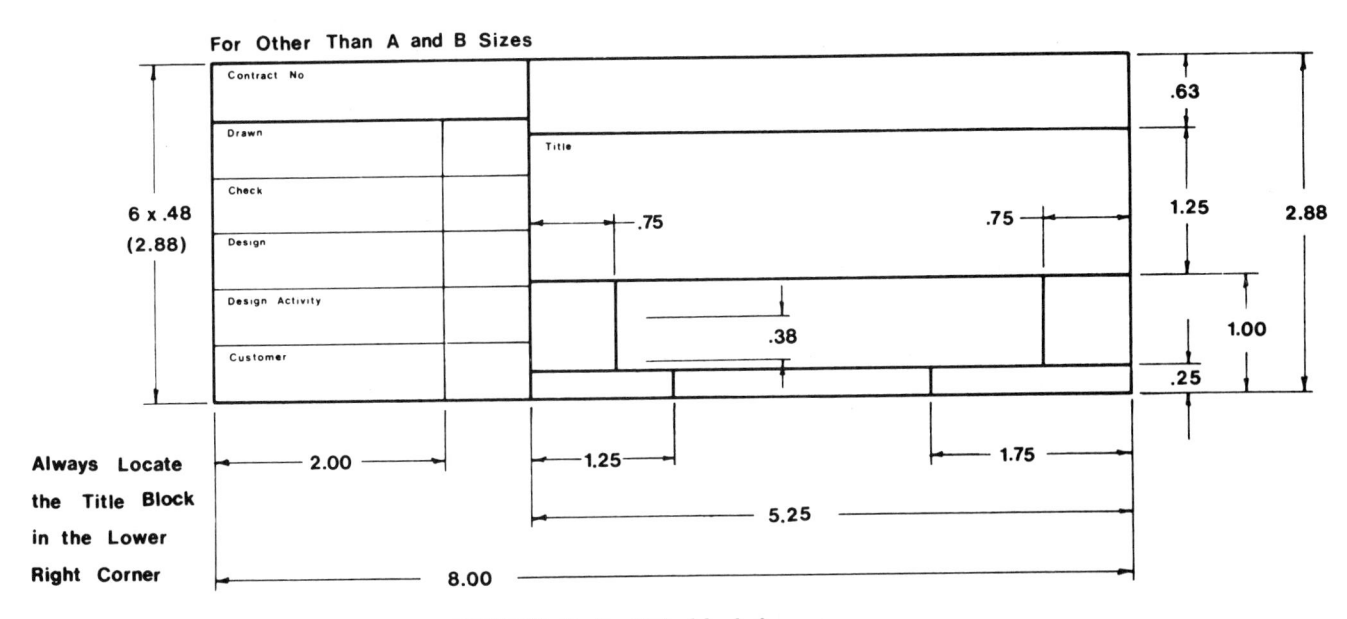

FIGURE 11-8 Title block formats.

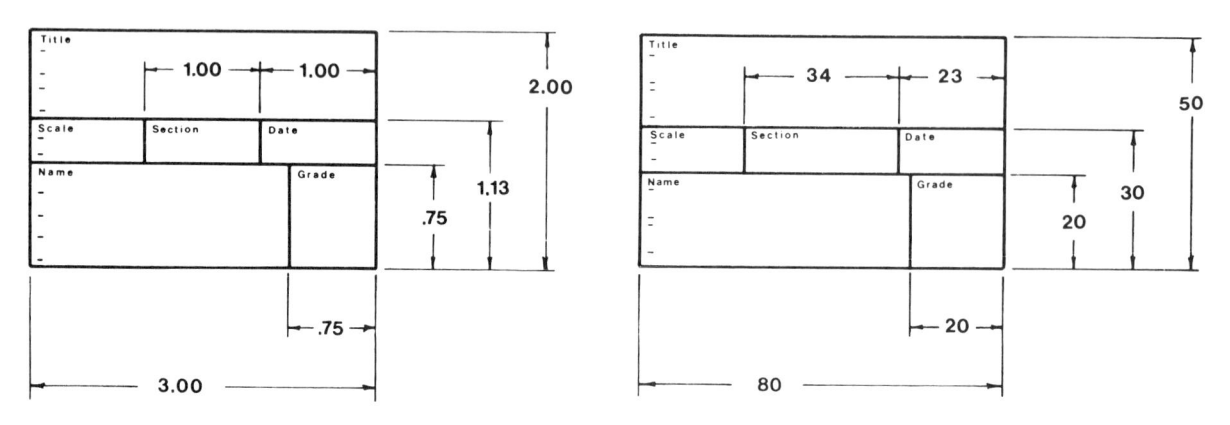

FIGURE 11-9 Simplified title block formats.

Department of Defense and Commerce in DOD-STD-100 by the American National Standards Institute in ANSI Y14.1.

Figure 11-8 (see p. 337) shows two title blocks, one for smaller drawings, the other for larger drawings. They are identical except for size.

When a drawing is complete, the drafter initials the block marked DRAWN and adds the date (see the title block in Figure 11-6). The drawing would then proceed through a checking and release procedure until it is "released." Once released, a drawing can be used for manufacturing.

Figure 11-9 shows two simplified title blocks. Computer graphics systems reference drawings by file names. Whenever possible, file names and drawing titles should be the same.

A title block format can be stored in the computer's memory and called up as needed. The two title blocks defined in Figure 11-9 should be sufficient for most small assembly and detail drawing.

11-6 PARTS LISTS (BILLS OF MATERIALS)

Parts lists are listings of all parts used to build assemblies. They are also called *bills of materials*. Included on the list are *item numbers* (bubbled assembly drawing numbers), *part* or *identification numbers,* the quantity of each part, and the material specifications. Figure 11-10 shows two

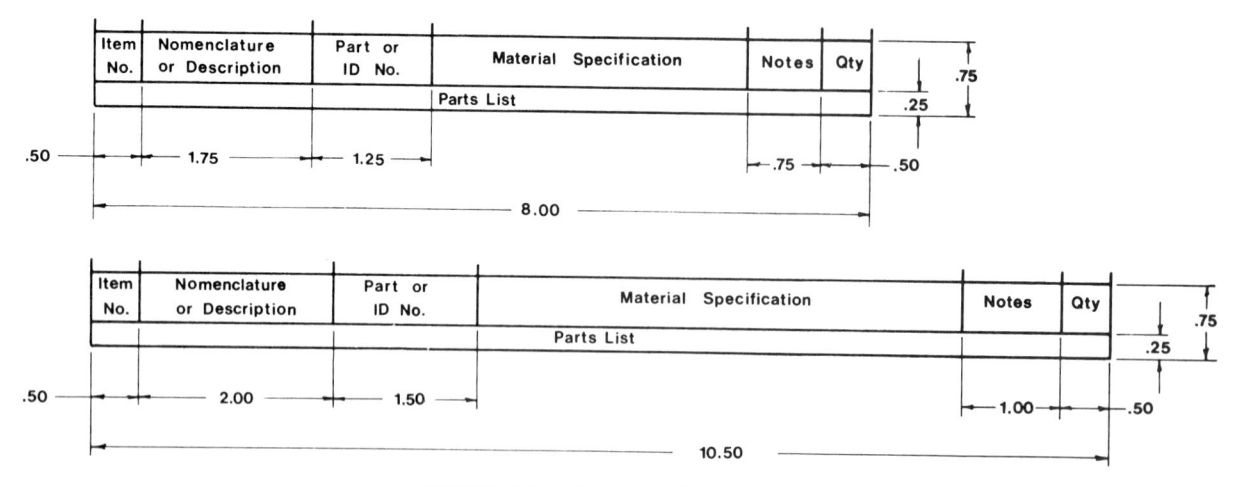

FIGURE 11-10 Parts list format.

Sec. 11-6   Parts Lists (Bills of Materials)   339

parts lists formats. As with title blocks, parts lists formats vary greatly from company to company and the ones presented in Figure 11-10 represent only two possible formats.

Parts lists can be located on assembly drawings just above the title block, along the right edge of the drawing, or within separate files within the assembly drawing file. Some companies prepare parts lists on separate sheets of paper and consider them as separate drawings. Item numbers are listed from the bottom of the drawing up (Figure 11-11).

Standard parts such as screws and washers are not assigned part numbers but are listed by name and specification. The screw in Figure 11-12 is listed by name and by specification callout 0.31 − 18 UNC × 1.38 HEX HEAD. This is sufficient information to define the part. No detail drawing is needed for the part, so no drawing number is assigned.

A *standard part* is a part that is purchased from a vendor and used, without modification, in an assembly. Screws, washers, nuts, and other types of fasteners are the most common type of standard parts. Other standard parts are gears, ball bearings, and specific subassemblies.

Item No	Nomenclature or Description	Part or ID No	Material/Specification	Note	Qty
5	.250-20UNC x 1.50 Long Hex Head		SAE 1020 Steel		8
4	.38 x .76 x .06 Washer		SAE 1020 Steel		8
3	Bracket	56574	SAE 1020 Steel	⚠1	2
2	Holder	56573	SAE 1020 Steel		1
1	Base	56572	SAE 1020 Steel		1

FIGURE 11-11   Sample parts list.

NO	DESCRIPTION	MATL	PART NUMBER	QTY
5	SCREW	ST	.31-18 UNC x 1.38 HEX HEAD	2
4	WASHER	ST	.375 x .875 x .083	2
3	GUIDE PIN	SAE 1020	43S103	2
2	TOP CLAMP	SAE 1020	43S102	1
1	BASE CLAMP	SAE 1020	43S101	1

FIGURE 11-12   Sample parts list.

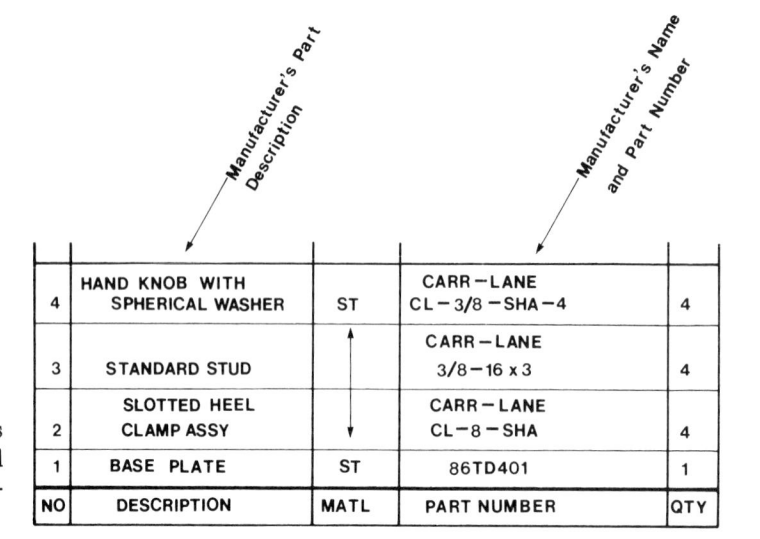

FIGURE 11-13 Sample parts list that includes standard parts listed by their manufacturers' part numbers.

NO	DESCRIPTION	MATL	PART NUMBER	QTY
4	HAND KNOB WITH SPHERICAL WASHER	ST	CARR-LANE CL-3/8-SHA-4	4
3	STANDARD STUD	↑	CARR-LANE 3/8-16 x 3	4
2	SLOTTED HEEL CLAMP ASSY	↓	CARR-LANE CL-8-SHA	4
1	BASE PLATE	ST	86TD401	1

Arrows point to "Manufacturer's Part Description" and "Manufacturer's Name and Part Number".

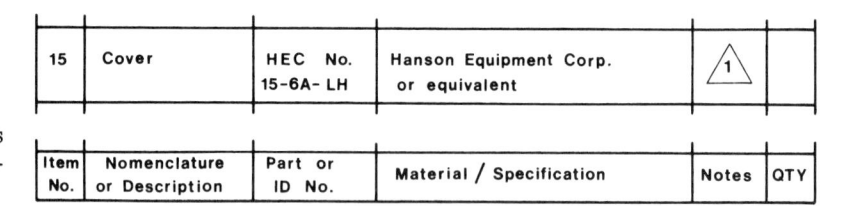

FIGURE 11-14 The words "or equivalent" eliminate single-source vendors.

Notes
1. Purchase from Hanson Equipment Corp. Danvers, MA 01923 or equivalent

Item No.	Nomenclature or Description	Part or ID No.	Material / Specification	Notes	QTY
15	Cover	HEC No. 15-6A-LH	Hanson Equipment Corp. or equivalent	△1	

Standard parts are specified in a parts list by their manufacturer's part number (Figure 11-13).

Companies and government agencies are reluctant to limit purchased standard parts to one vendor, called a "single source." If only the Hanson Equipment Corp. part number shown in Figure 11-14 were listed, then only that specific gear could be used. Hanson Equipment Corp. would be a single-source vendor. The note "or equivalent" is added to the specification column to allow substitution and thereby eliminate a single-source vendor.

11-7 DRAWING REVISIONS

Drawings used in industry are constantly being changed. Products are improved or corrected and drawings must be changed to reflect and document these changes.

Drawing changes are listed in the *revision block*. Revision blocks are located in the upper right-hand corner of the drawing as shown in Figure 11-15 or in a separate file within the assembly drawing file. Figure 11-15 also shows a general format for revision blocks.

Figure 11-16 shows a sample drawing with a revision incorporated. Revisions are listed and identified by letter. Each revision is briefly de-

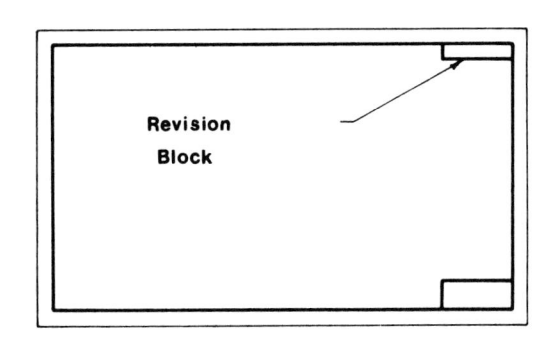

Sec. 11-7 Drawing Revisions 341

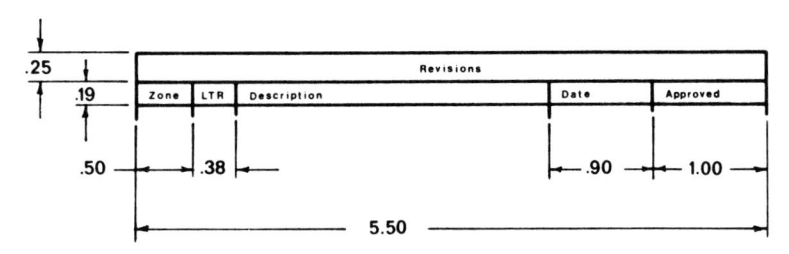

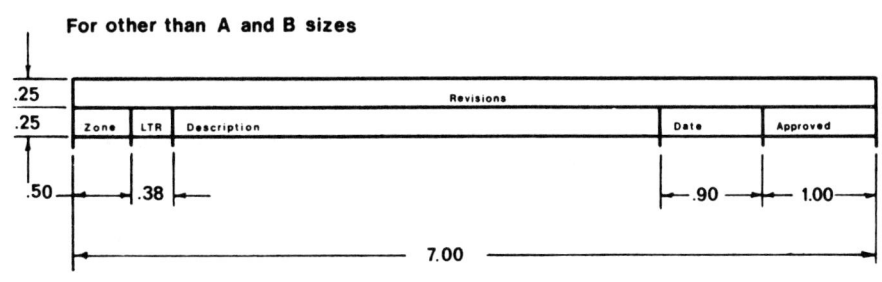

FIGURE 11-15 Formats for revision blocks.

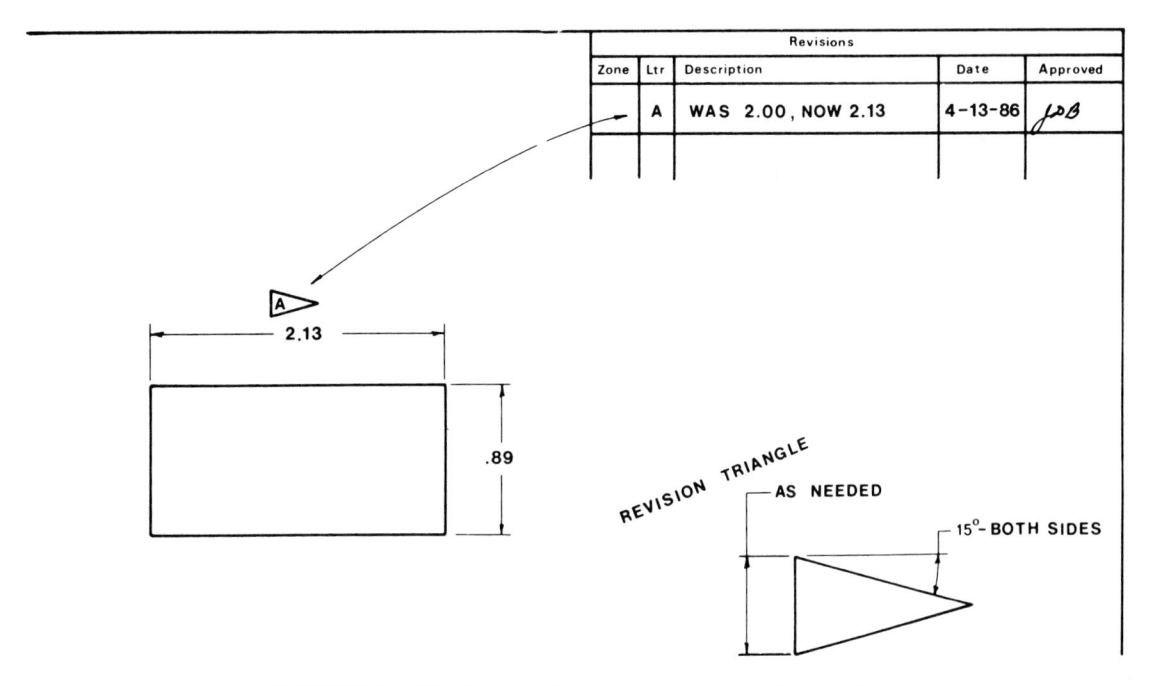

FIGURE 11-16 Sample drawing with a revision block.

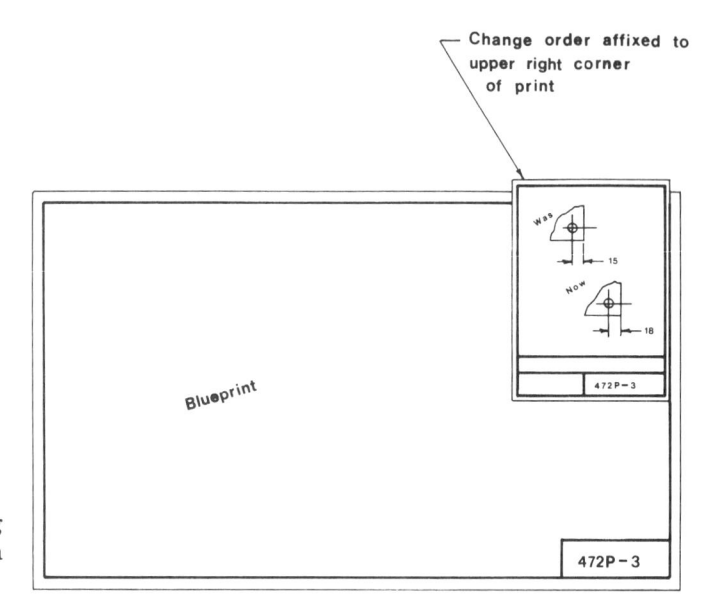

FIGURE 11-17 Engineering change order affixed to a drawing.

scribed in the DESCRIPTION column. It is important that revision descriptions be as accurate as possible. They are often used to trace drawing requirements for parts produced before the changes were incorporated.

Revisions are incorporated on a drawing by first adding the information to the revision block using the next available letter. The information is then added to the field of the drawing in the appropriate place. For example, revision A shown in Figure 11-16 changed a dimension from 2.00 to 2.13. The change is clearly listed in the revision block and has been incorporated onto the field of the drawing. The letter A, inside a triangle, is added next to the revised dimension. Anyone reading the drawing will know that this dimension has been changed and can reference the specific change in the revision block.

After changes have been incorporated in a drawing, it is considered a new drawing and must go through the company's release procedure. Companies often require a revision letter suffixed to the end of the original drawing number. This helps prevent confusion as to which drawing is most current.

Changes can quickly be added to a drawing by using a change order. These are called engineering change orders (ECDs), change orders (COs), engineering orders (EDs), and by other names, depending on the company's preference. Change orders are handled separately from drawing revisions and are processed more quickly than drawing revisions.

The change order shown in Figure 11-17 changes the 15-mm hole to an 18-mm hole. The change order is affixed to the main drawing or added to the drawing reference file and at a later date will be incorporated onto the field of the drawing. Always check a drawing for revisions and change orders before matching it with production parts.

11-8 DRAWING ZONES

Drawings are divided into zones identified by a letter and a number. Letters define the vertical distances, numbers the horizontal distances (Figure 11-18). A specific zone is located by projecting horizontal lines from

Sec. 11-8   Drawings Zones   343

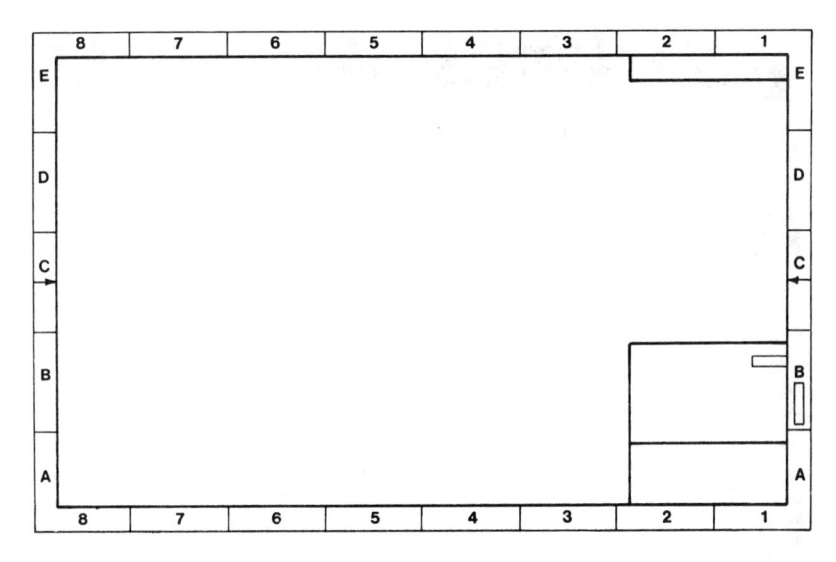

FIGURE 11-18 Drawing zones used to reference areas of a drawing.

the appropriate letter and vertical lines from the number. The intersection of the projected lines outlines the zone.

Computer graphic systems can isolate parts of a drawing using ZOOM and PAN capabilities. Figure 11-19 shows the effects of these functions. Figure 11-19a shows a part in original scale. *Zoom* allows the user to close in on the drawing and in effect make it appear larger. In Figure 11-19b zoom is applied to the lower right corner of the object. The result is an enlargement of the hole and chamfered corner. The remainder of the drawing is now so large that it exceeds the screen capacity

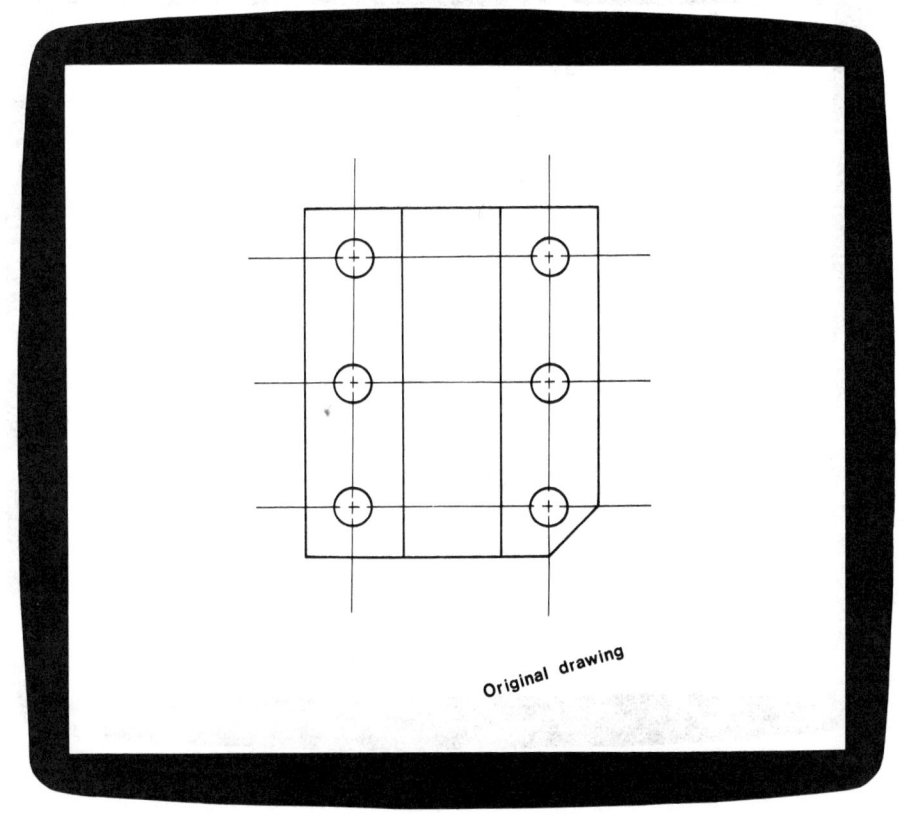

FIGURE 11-19(a) Sample part drawing.

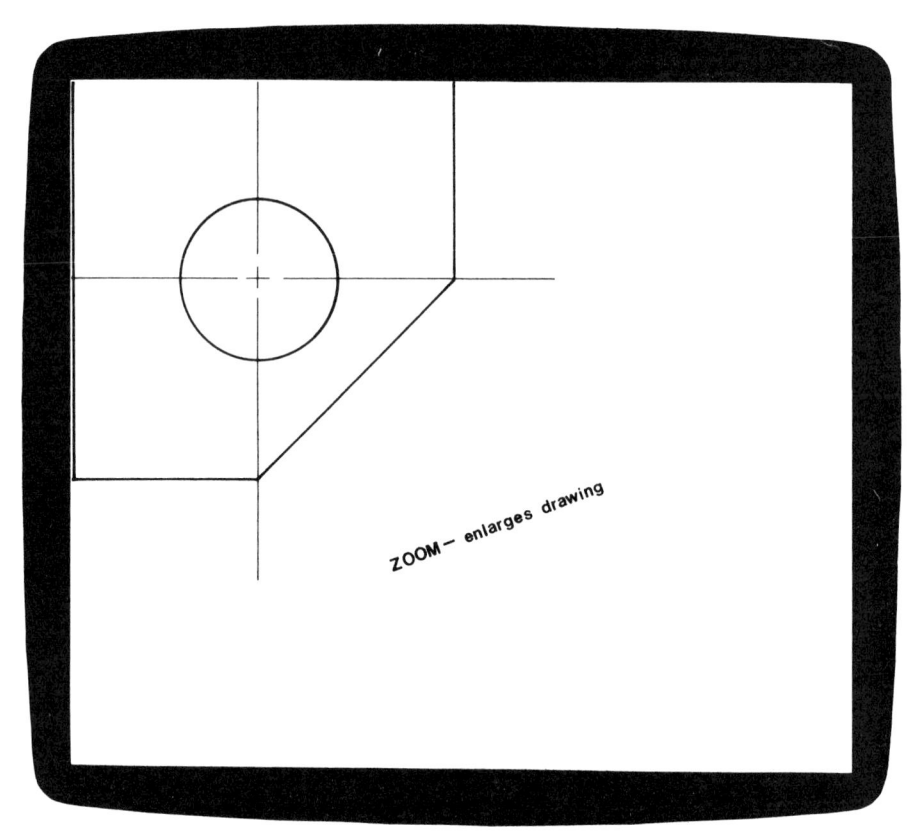

FIGURE 11-19(b) Zoom function applied to the original drawing.

FIGURE 11-19(c) Pan function applied to the original drawing.

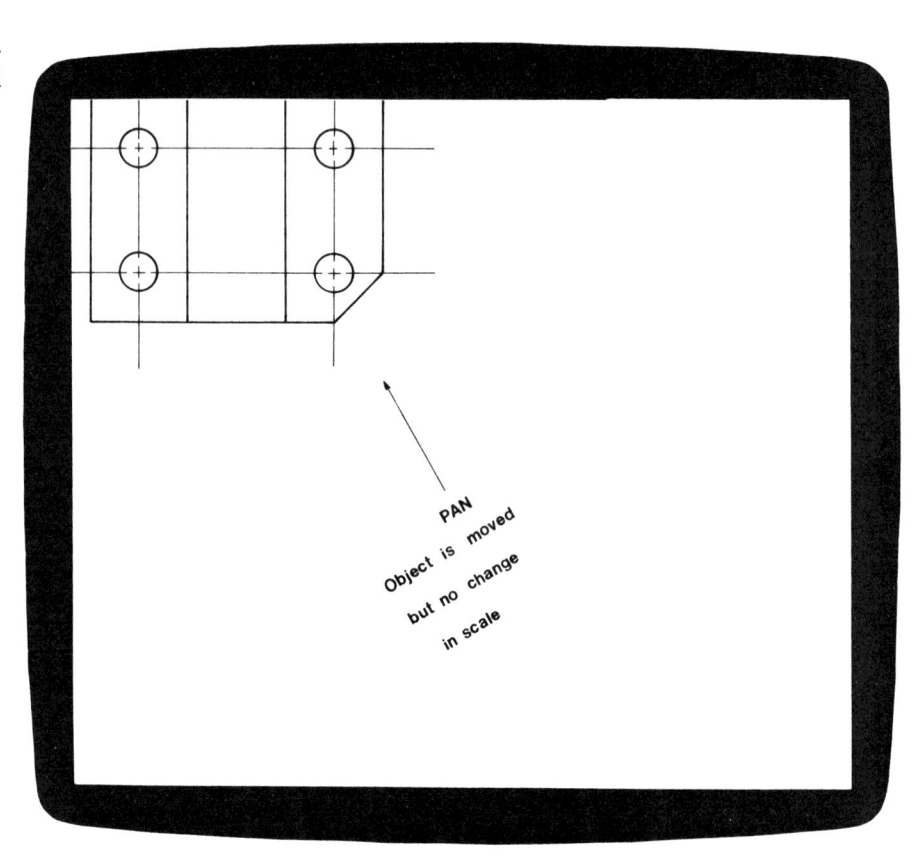

and is not visible. Some systems identify the area to be zoomed by light pen or cursor; others only zoom to the center of the drawing and must use the pan feature to move the desired area within the screen's visual capabilities.

Pan moves the drawing but does not change its scale. In Figure 11-19c the object is panned, moving the chamfered corner to the top left corner of the drawing. Pan is controlled by a light pen, joystick, or cursor, depending on the system.

11-9 DRAWING NOTES

Drawing notes are pieces of information relative to the drawing which are not part of the visual presentation. Drawing notes are located along the right-hand side of the drawing between the title and revision blocks as shown in Figure 11-20 or in a separate file within the assembly drawing file.

The numbers for notes that apply to specific parts are enclosed in triangles as shown in Figure 11-20. The triangles and numbers are then located on the field of drawing next to the appropriate part. For example, the torque instruction of note 3 applied to part number 3 is placed next to the number 1 callout to call attention to the fact that a note applies to this part. Note 4 lists two vendors who supply part 3, so 4 is placed in the parts list next to part 3.

Companies vary as to how they list and reference drawing notes. The preceding represents a general approach.

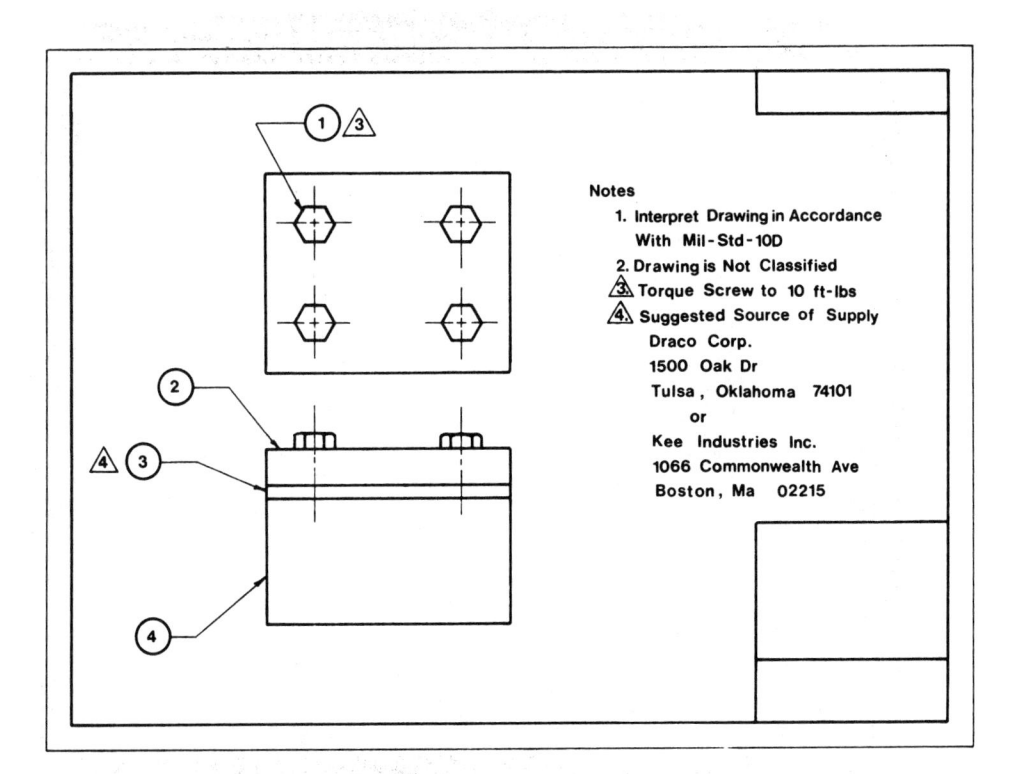

FIGURE 11-20 Drawing notes.

11-10 PRINTERS AND PLOTTERS

Hard copies of drawings (blueprints) are created by computer graphic systems using printers and plotters. Larger drawings are prepared on plotters and smaller drawings on printers. There are two general types of plotters: flatbed and drum. Figure 11-21 shows a drum plotter.

A *flatbed plotter* has two movable crossbars which pass over a fixed sheet of drawing paper. Ink pens are controlled by the movable crossbars. Flatbed plotters are very accurate and are well suited for large drawings. Their biggest drawback is their size. They are very large and require a large operating area.

Drum plotters move pens laterally back and forth across a rotating drum. They also produce accurate drawings and require much less space than do flatbed plotters. The disadvantage of drum plotters is the way they move the drawing paper. Because the paper is moved rapidly, it must be securely and accurately aligned before drawings are produced. Any slippage will affect drawing accuracy.

There are two general types of printers: impact and nonimpact. *Impact printers* strike against an ink ribbon, producing a mark on the paper. Daisywheel printers are impact printers. Impact printers produce high-quality letters and are used most often in business applications.

Nonimpact printers spray ink onto a drawing using either an ink-jet or dot-matrix setup. Ink-jet printers are the more common type of printer used in conjunction with computer graphics systems and technical drawing work.

The ink pens and jets used in computer graphic systems are very sensitive and must be cleaned regularly. If not cleaned properly and regularly, they will not produce the accuracy and quality desired. Think of cleaning pens and jets as being equivalent to sharpening your pencil.

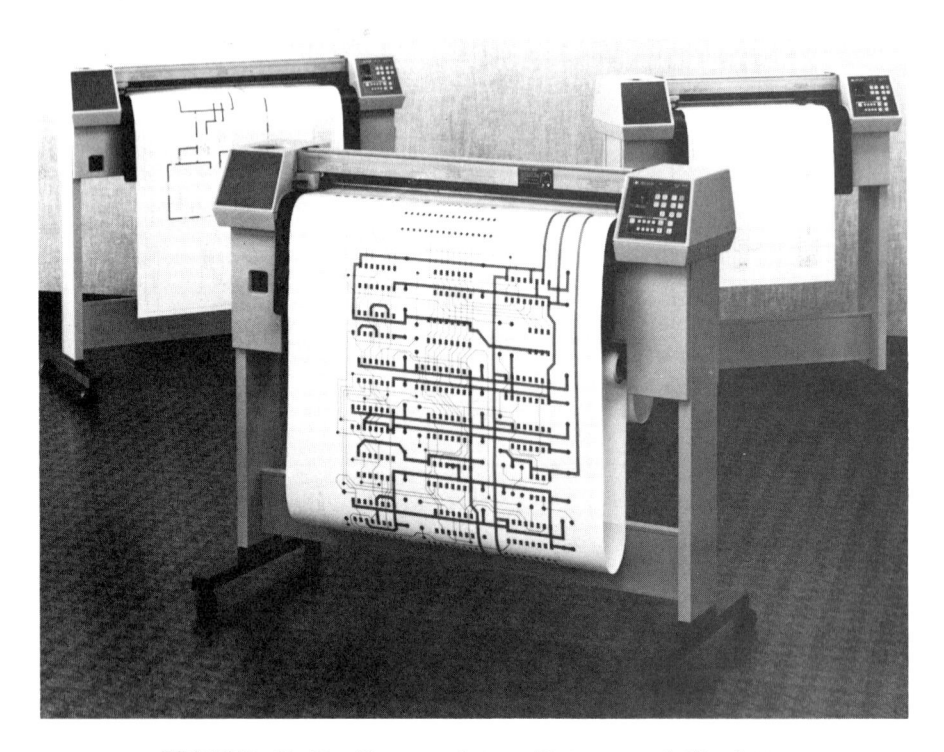

FIGURE 11-21 Drum printer. (Courtesy of Hewlett-Packard, Palo Alto, Calif.)

PROBLEMS

For Problems P11-1 through P11-6, prepare an assembly drawing, a parts list, and an appropriate detail drawing for the assemblies shown in Figures P11-1 through P11-6. The units for the dimensions given are as noted below.

- P11-1 Millimeters
- P11-2 Millimeters
- P11-3 Millimeters
- P11-4 Inches
- P11-5 Millimeters
- P11-6 Inches

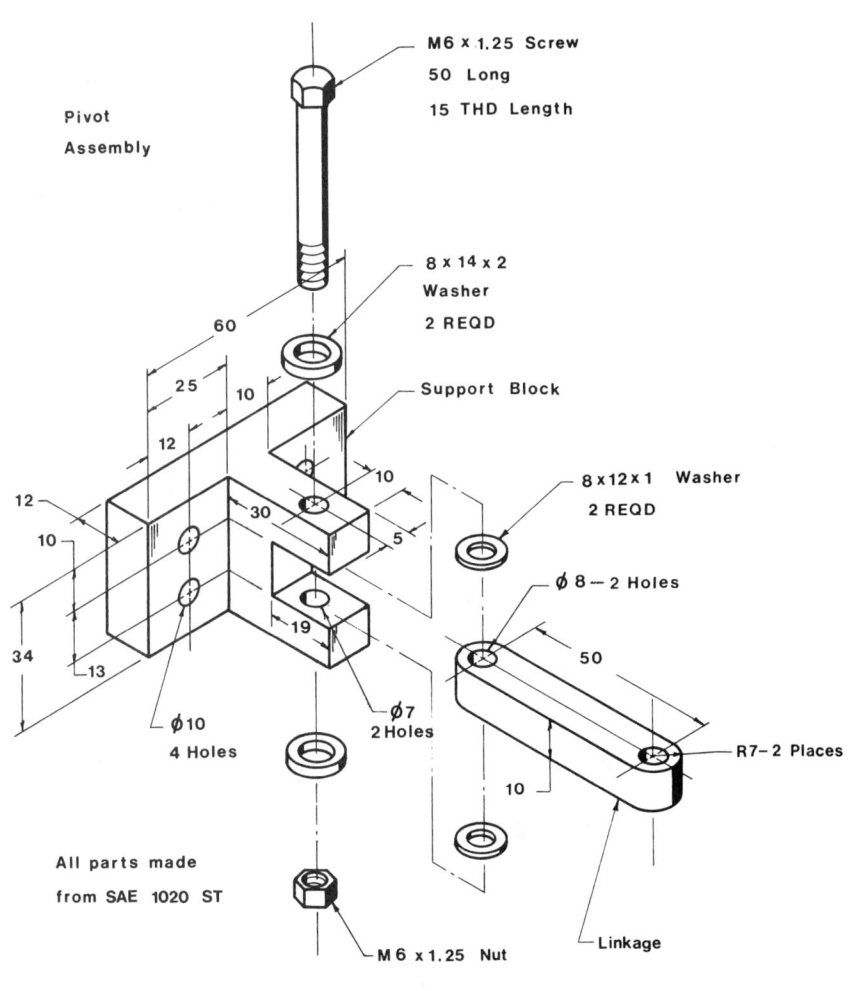

FIGURE P11-1

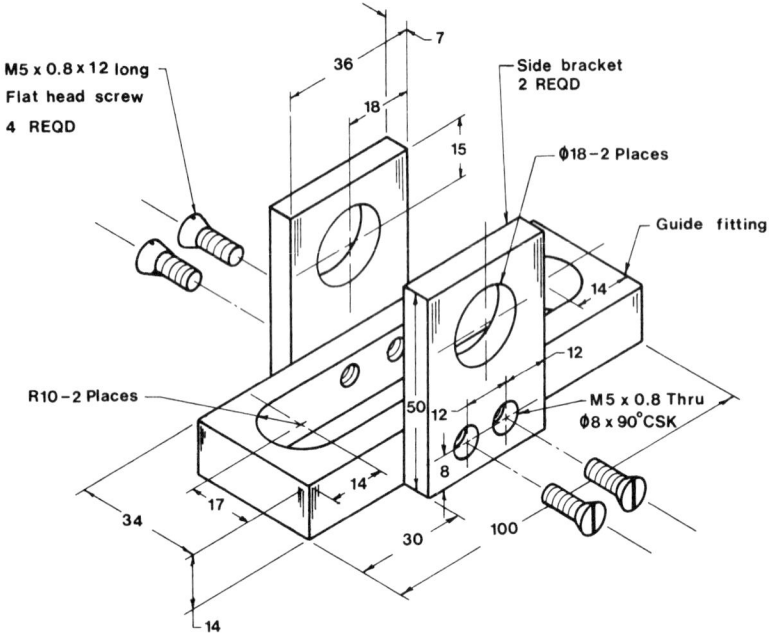

FIGURE P11-2

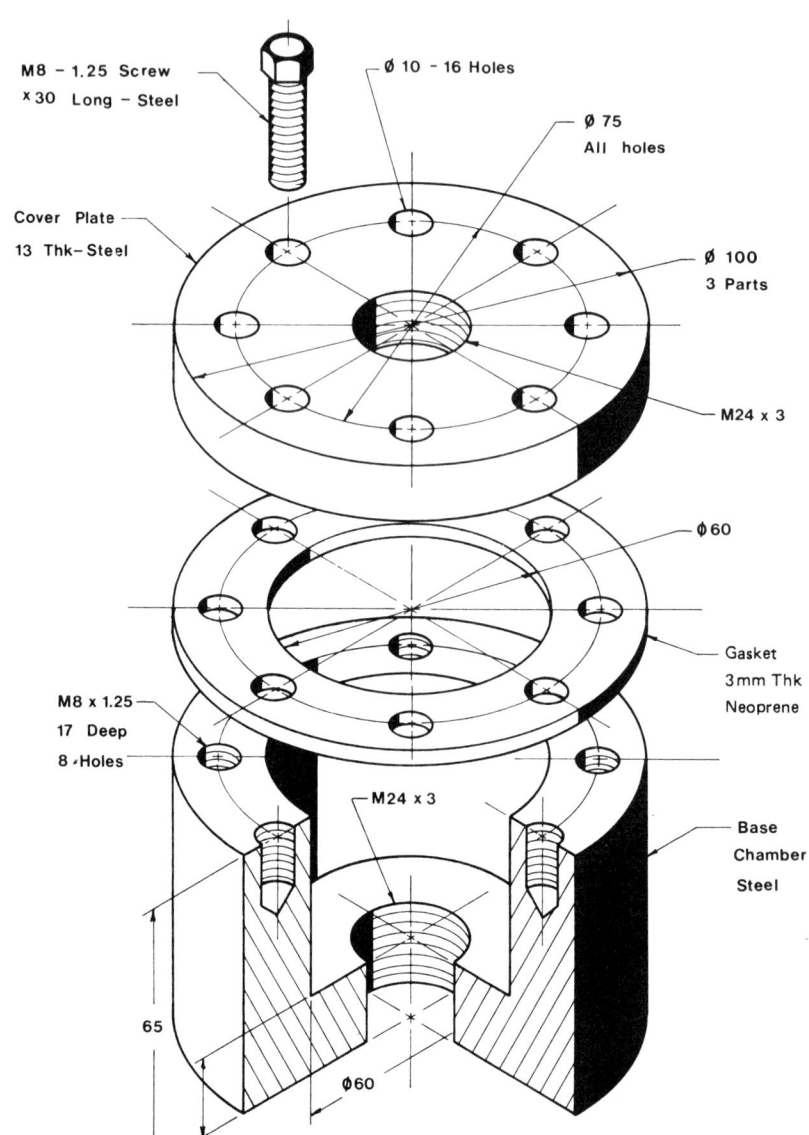

FIGURE P11-3

Chap. 11 Problems

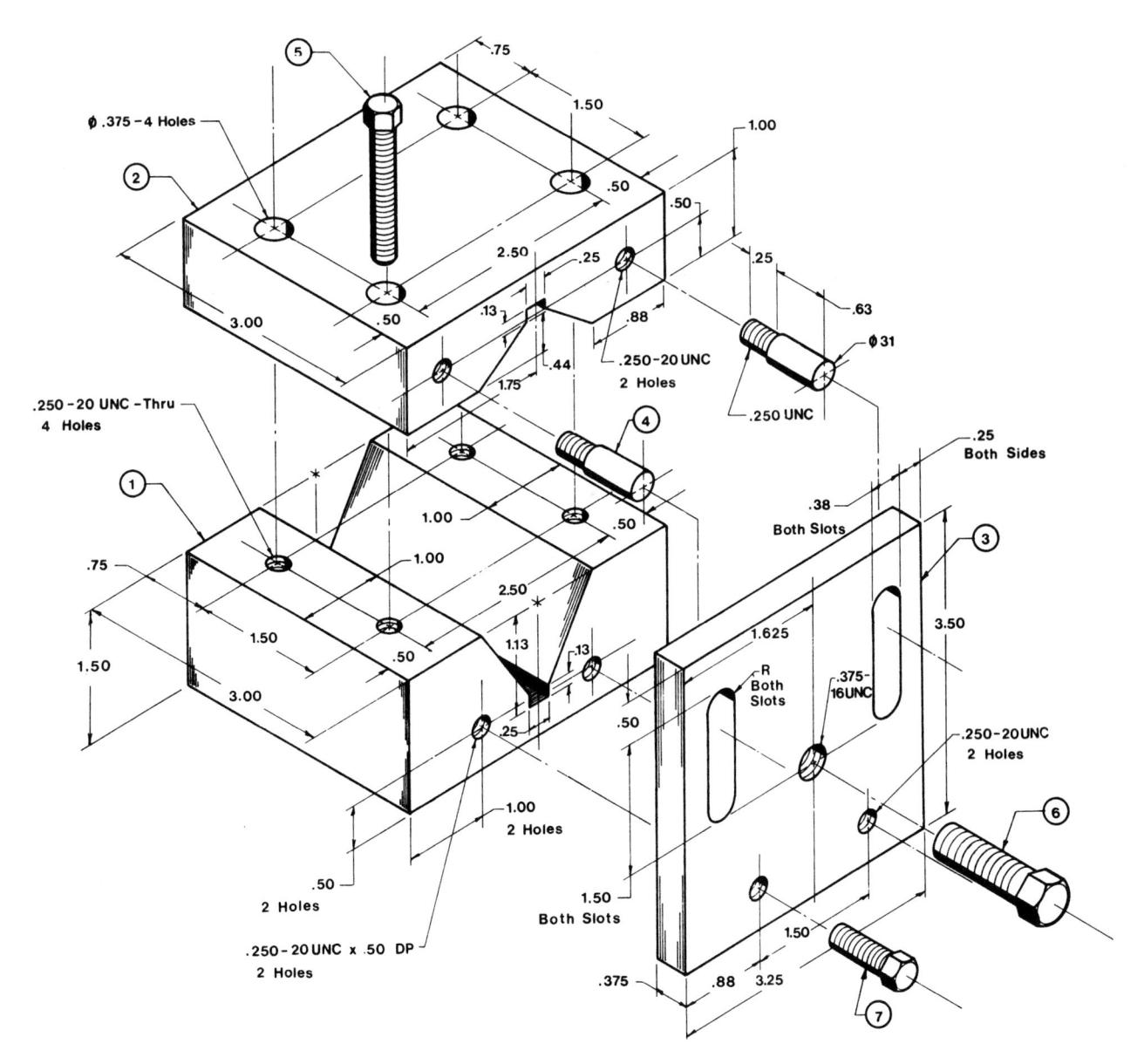

FIGURE P11-4

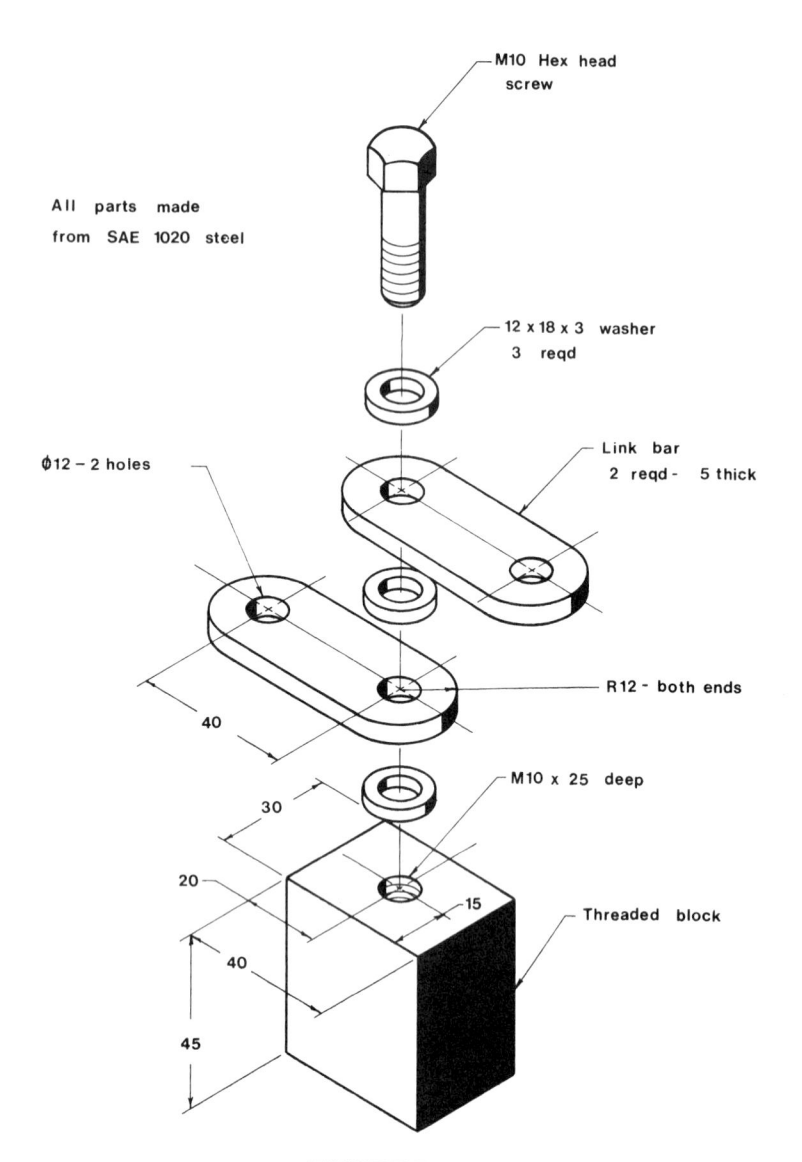

FIGURE P11-5

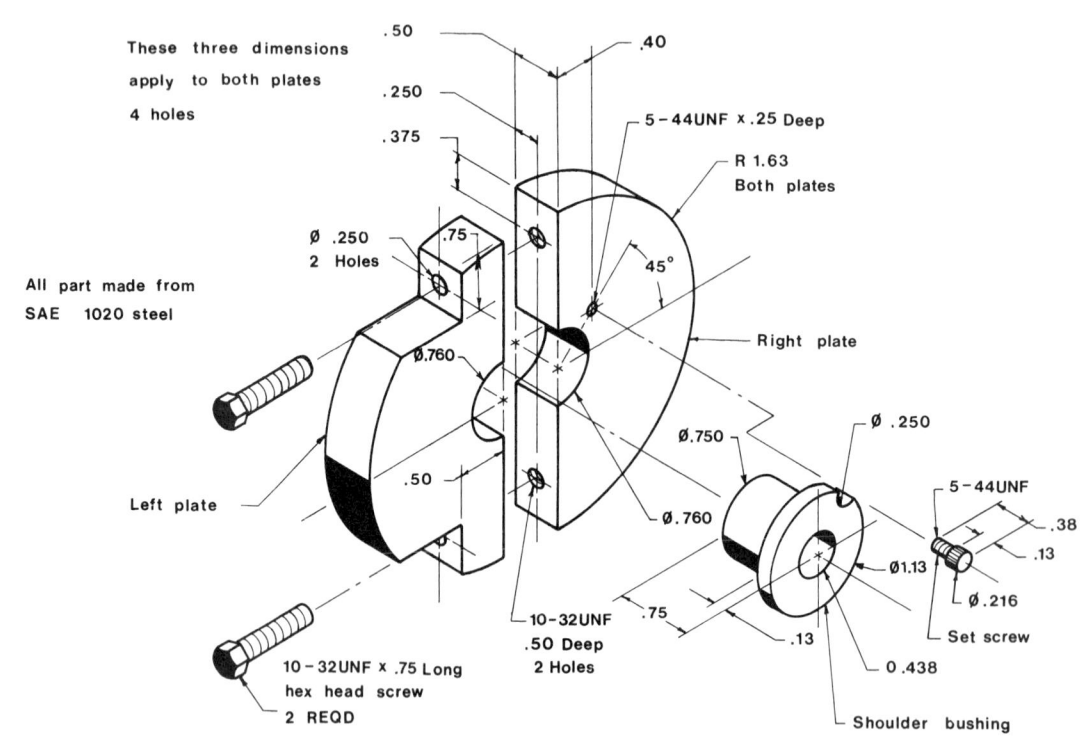

FIGURE P11-6

12
THREE-DIMENSIONAL DRAWINGS: PICTORIALS

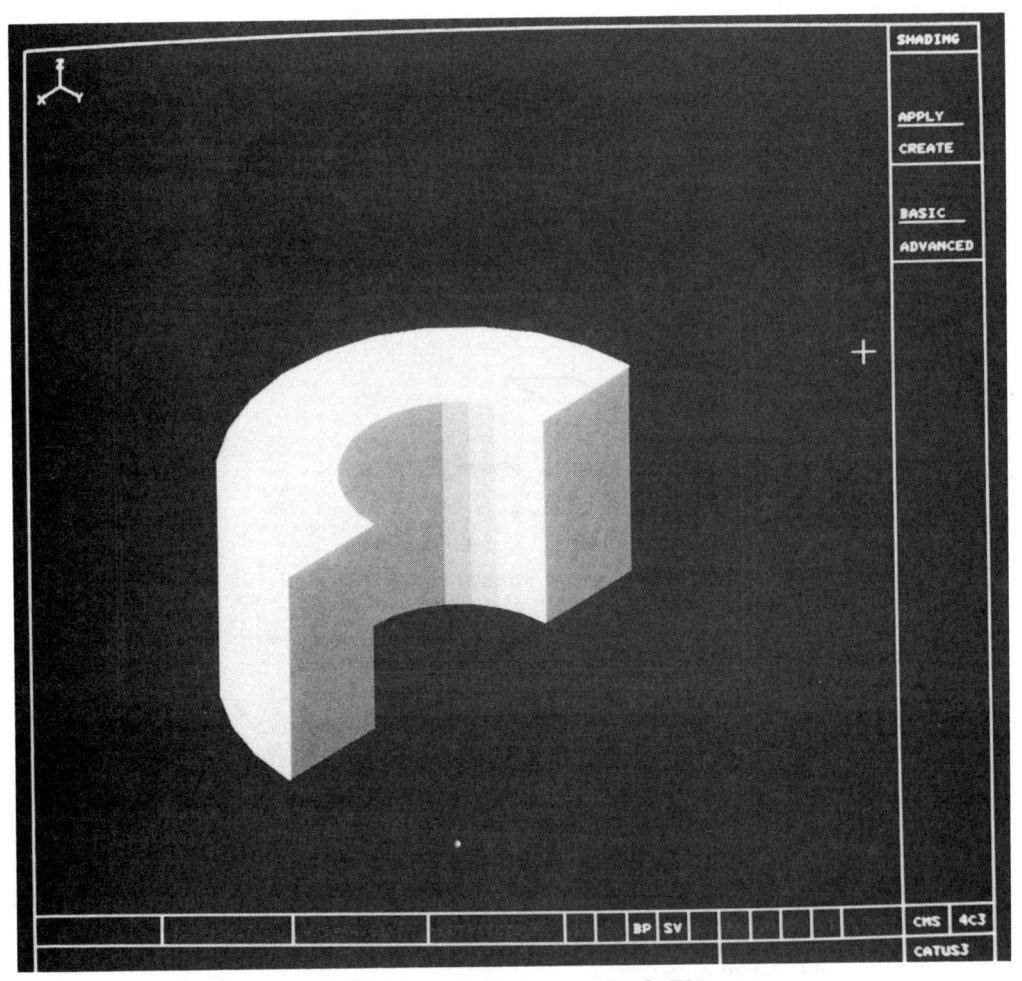

Half hollow cylinder drawn using CATIA.

12-1 INTRODUCTION

In this chapter we explain how to draw three-dimensional or pictorial drawings. Included is an explanation of several different three-dimensional axis systems, how to locate points and lines within a three-dimensional axis system, and how to draw three-dimensional geometric shapes.

We also explain how to create three-dimensional drawings by adding and subtracting solids and by trimming existing shapes to create new more complex ones. The chapter also includes instructions for creating three-dimensional drawings from given orthographic views.

12-2 THREE-DIMENSIONAL AXIS SYSTEMS

There are two basic types of three-dimensional axis systems; axonometric and perspective (Figure 12-1). *Axonometric axis systems* have parallel receding lines. Note how, in Figure 12-1, the rectangular prism la-

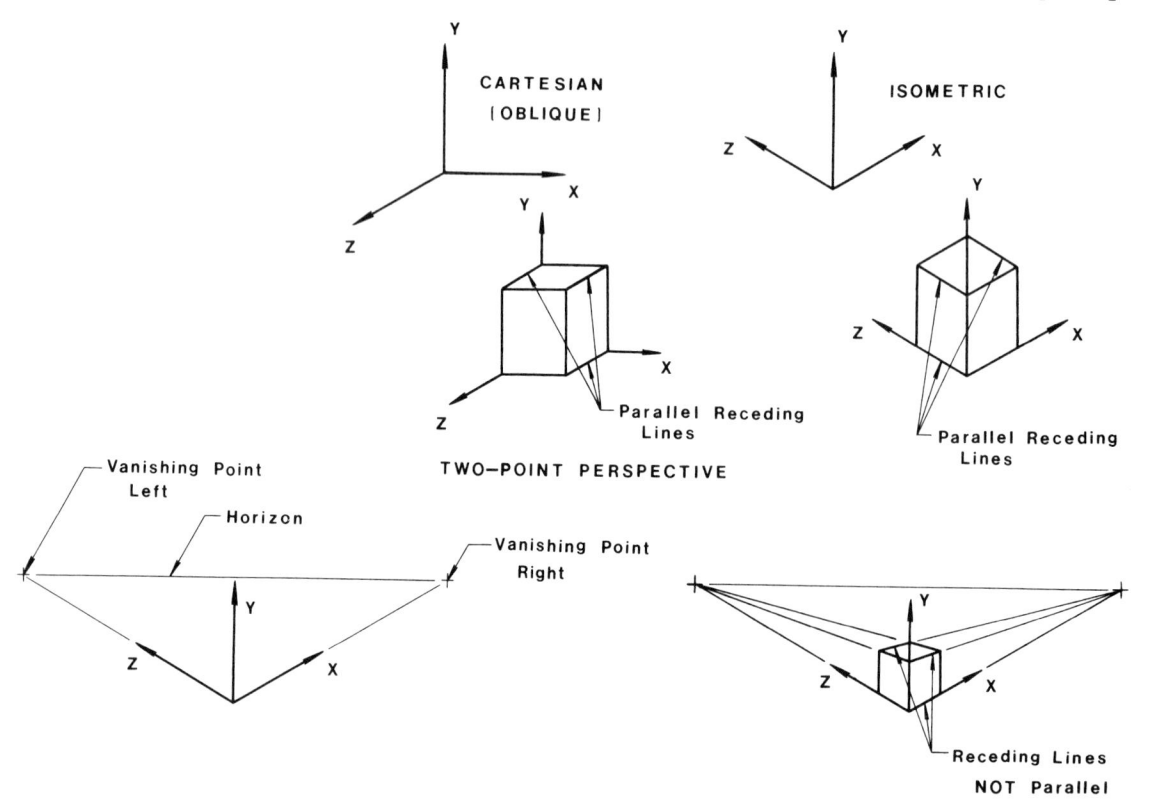

FIGURE 12-1 Examples of different types of three dimensional drawings.

Sec. 12-2 Three-Dimensional Axis Systems

beled "isometric" is created by three sets of three parallel lines: three vertical lines, three lines slanted 30° to the right, and three lines slanted 30° to the left. The 30° lines are receding lines and are parallel.

Perspective drawings have receding lines that converge to one or two vanishing points depending on the type of perspective drawing. Note how the rectangular prism labeled Two-Point Perspective has three vertical lines, three lines that if continued would converge on a vanishing point to the right, and three lines that if continued would converge on a vanishing point to the left. The lines drawn to the vanishing points are receding lines and are not parallel.

Most computer graphic systems draw three-dimensional drawings referenced to either an isometric or a cartesian axis system. Both are axonometric systems. The parallel receding lines are easier to control and allow for easier dimensional transfers both to and from orthographic views.

Figure 12-2 shows a three-dimensional cartesian coordinate system. *Cartesian* is the mathematical name for an axis system that is defined by three perpendicular planes that intersect along lines parallel to the intersection of the other two planes. A three-dimensional cartesian axis is represented as shown.

Pictorial drawings drawn on this type of axis are also called *oblique drawings*. An oblique axis contains a vertical line, a horizontal line, and a receding line drawn at any acute angle, usually 30° (Figure 12-3). The

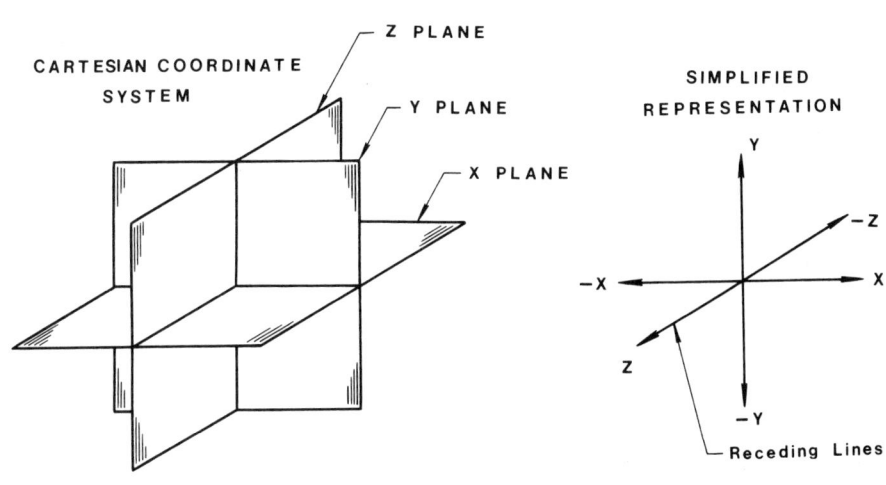

FIGURE 12-2 Cartesian coordinate system.

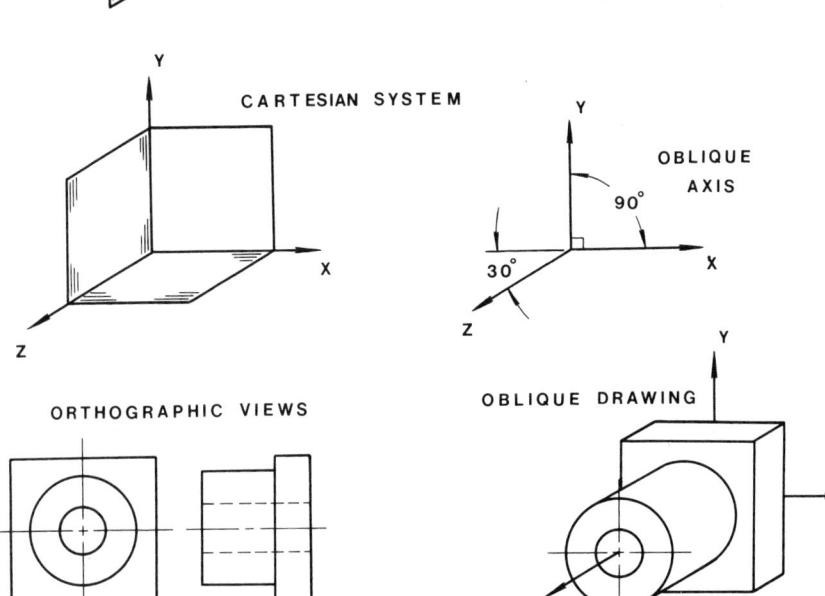

FIGURE 12-3 Oblique drawing based on a Cartesian coordinate system.

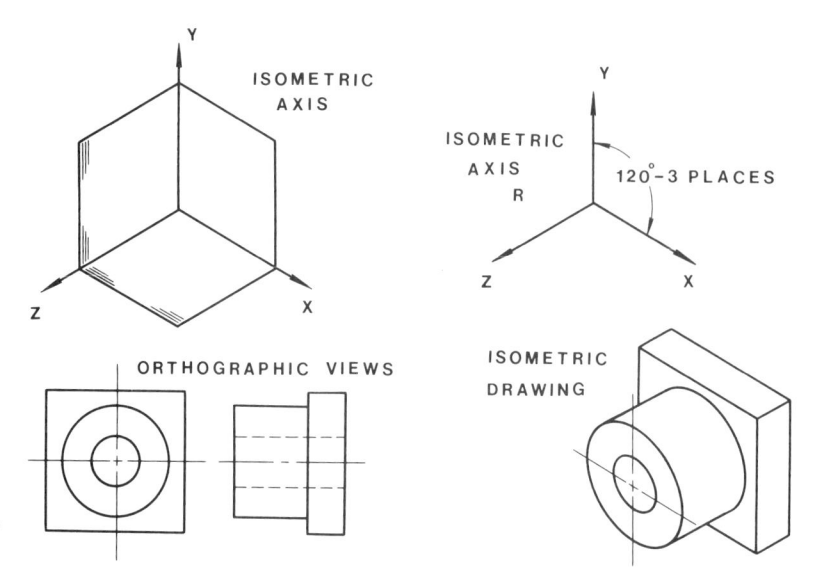

FIGURE 12-4 Isometric axis system.

perpendicular axis lines make it easier to transfer orthographic views to three-dimensional views. Note how the circular shapes in the front orthographic view remain circular (a curve of constant radius) when drawn on an oblique axis (see Section 12-14).

Isometric drawings tend to give a more visually pleasing picture than do obliques, and so are more popular, although slightly more difficult to draw. Figure 12-4 shows an isometric axis system and a representation of the system. The three reference planes are drawn as shown: one vertical, one at 30° to the right, and one 30° to the left. Although not drawn at 90° to each other, an isometric axis represents three planes at 90° to each other. The 30° receding lines are used to create a more realistic visual picture, that is, to make the drawing look more like the real object.

Compare the oblique and isometric drawings of the object shown in Figures 12-3 and 12-4. The oblique drawing has an elongated appearance, whereas the isometric seems more visually correct. The isometric drawing has some distortion toward the back of the drawing, but it is far less noticeable than the elongation in the oblique axis.

12-3 THREE-DIMENSIONAL COORDINATE VALUES

Three-dimensional coordinate values are expressed in the form X, Y, Z. Figure 12-5a shows a point A whose coordinate value is 6, 5, 3. This means that $X = 6$, $Y = 5$, and $Z = 3$. The point is located by counting

FIGURE 12-5 How to locate a point A (6,5,3) on a Cartesian axis and an isometric axis.

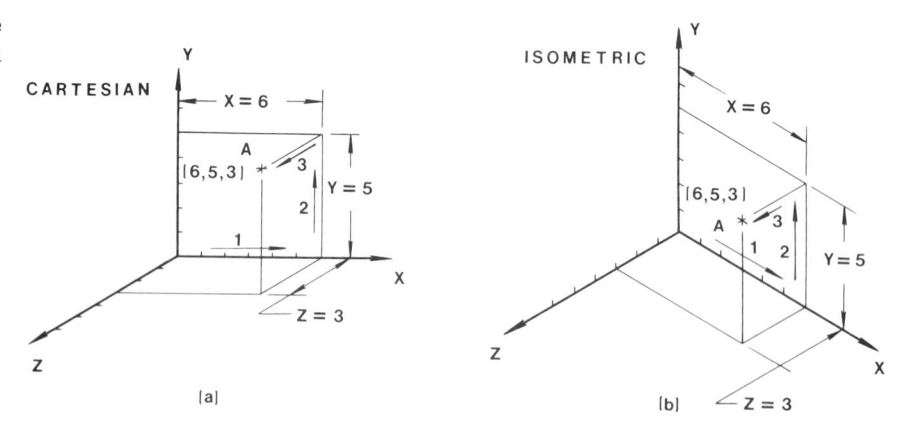

Sec. 12-4 Axis Orientation

out 6 units along the X axis, then 5 along the Y axis, and 3 along the Z axis. Figure 12-5b shows another point A with the same coordinate values located relative to an XYZ isometric axis. The locating procedure is the same as described above.

XYZ values may be positive or negative. Figure 12-6 shows how to locate two points with coordinates of $(-6, 7, -4)$ and $(8, -4, 7)$. Negative X values are to the left of the origin, negative Y values are below the origin, and negative Z values are behind (into the paper) the origin. Computer graphic systems use different directions for positive and negative values, so always check the axis system reference labels before preparing a drawing.

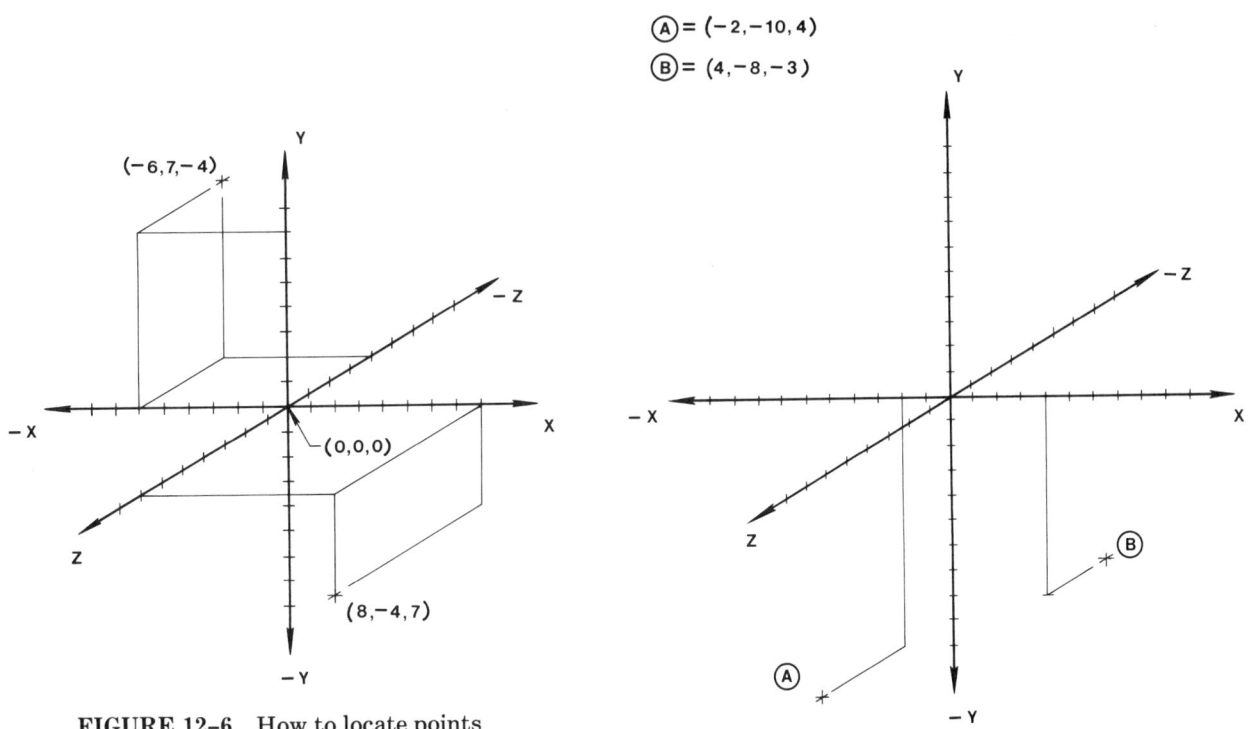

FIGURE 12-6 How to locate points on a Cartesian axis.

FIGURE 12-7 How to determine the coordinates for given points.

Figure 12-7 shows two points and asks for the coordinate values. The procedure is the reverse of that used to locate points in Figure 12-5. First determine the Z value, then the Y value, and finally the X value, as shown. State the values in the form X, Y, Z.

12-4 AXIS ORIENTATION

Three-dimensional axis systems may be turned or rotated to different positions, thereby generating different views of an object. In Figure 12-8 an object is drawn using six different isometric axis orientations and six different cartesian axis orientations. Usually, orientation is chosen so as to expose the most features. Example 1, in the isometric examples, clearly shows both the slot and the hole. Example 4 is a poor orientation as it shows only the edge of the slot and does not show the slot's depth.

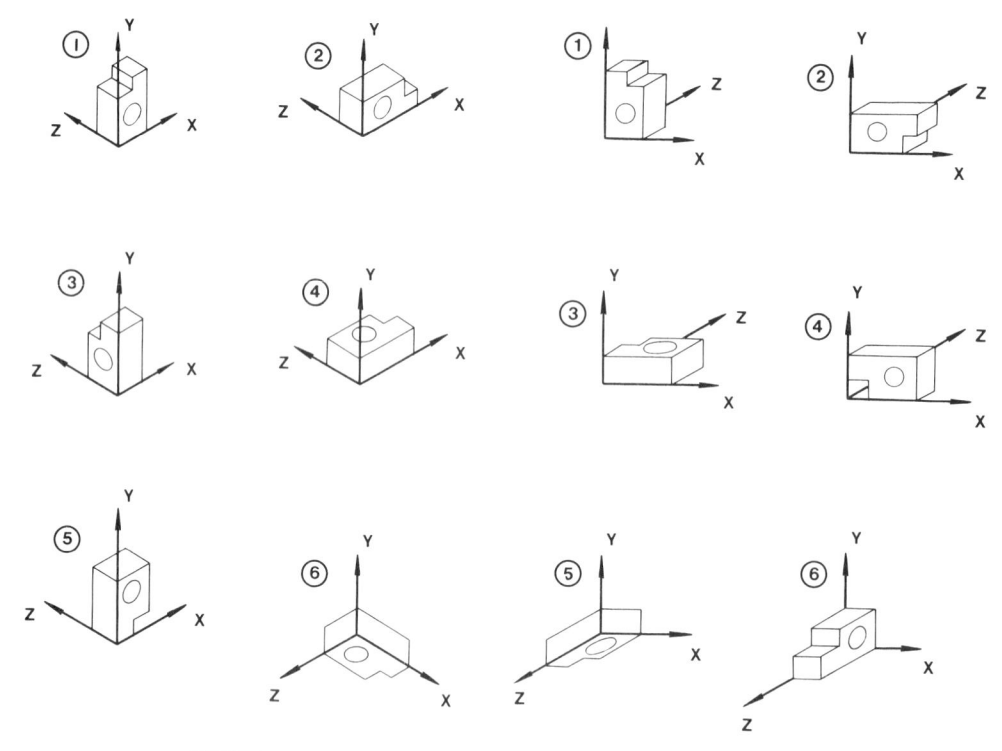

FIGURE 12-8 Examples of different orientations using both Cartesian and isometric axes.

More complex objects sometimes require multiple three-dimensional views for clear definition. Larger computer graphic systems allow the drafter to turn and rotate an object, exposing different sides of the object as needed. This in turn gives greater visualization and understanding of the object (Figure 12-9).

FIGURE 12-9 Some larger systems have the ability to rotate an object to different orientations.

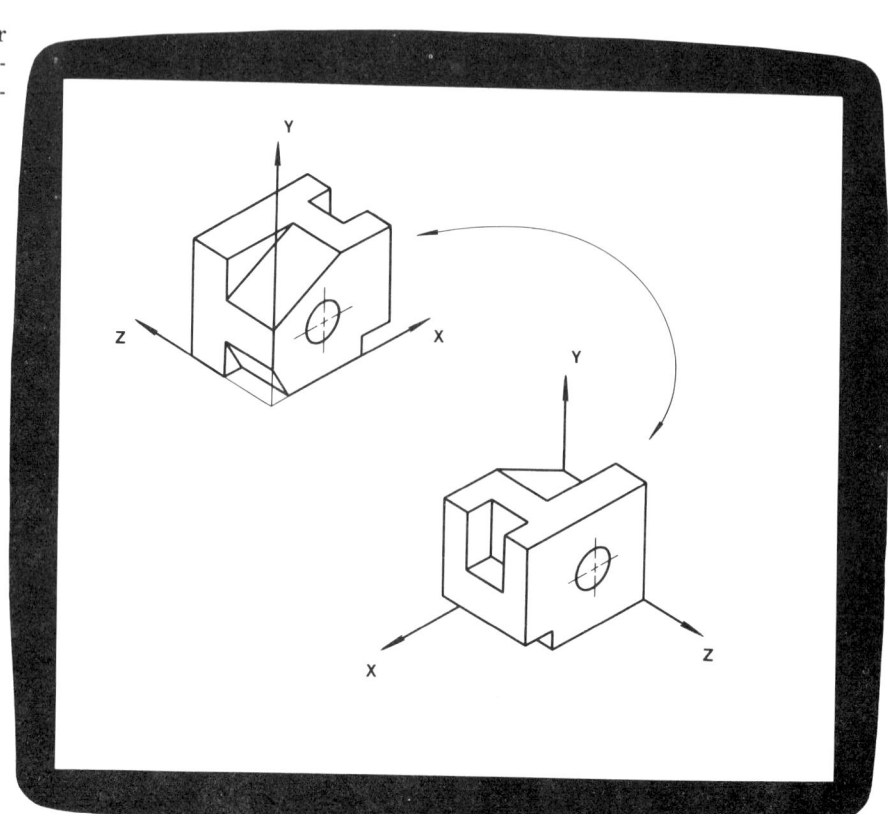

12-5 RIGHT RECTANGULAR PRISMS

Figure 12-10 shows several three-dimensional geometric shapes. (Two-dimensional geometric shapes are covered in Chapter 4.) Three-dimensional geometric shapes are the bases for three-dimensional drawings.

Each geometric shape requires specific information for accurate size definition and positional location and orientation. For example, the rectangular prism shown in Figure 12-11a has edge lengths of 4, 4, and 2, as shown. The prism's location is defined by assigning one of the corners as a vertex and then defining the location of the prism's vertex as a location relative to the screen axis. The vertex for the prism shown is $x, y, z = 0, 0, 0$, the same as the vertex of the screen axis.

Figure 12-11b uses a corner vertex location of 3, 4, 2.5, and size values of 5, 2, −3.5. Both locational and size references are required to draw a rectangular prism.

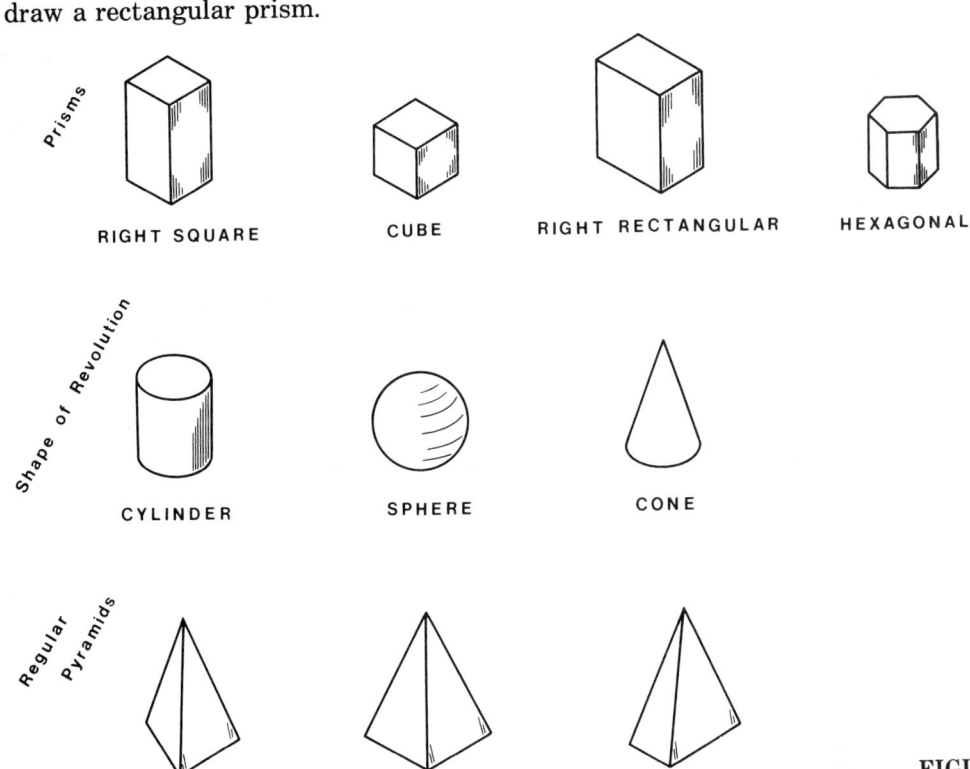

FIGURE 12-10 Some three dimensional geometric shapes.

FIGURE 12-11 How to locate and define the size of rectangular prisms.

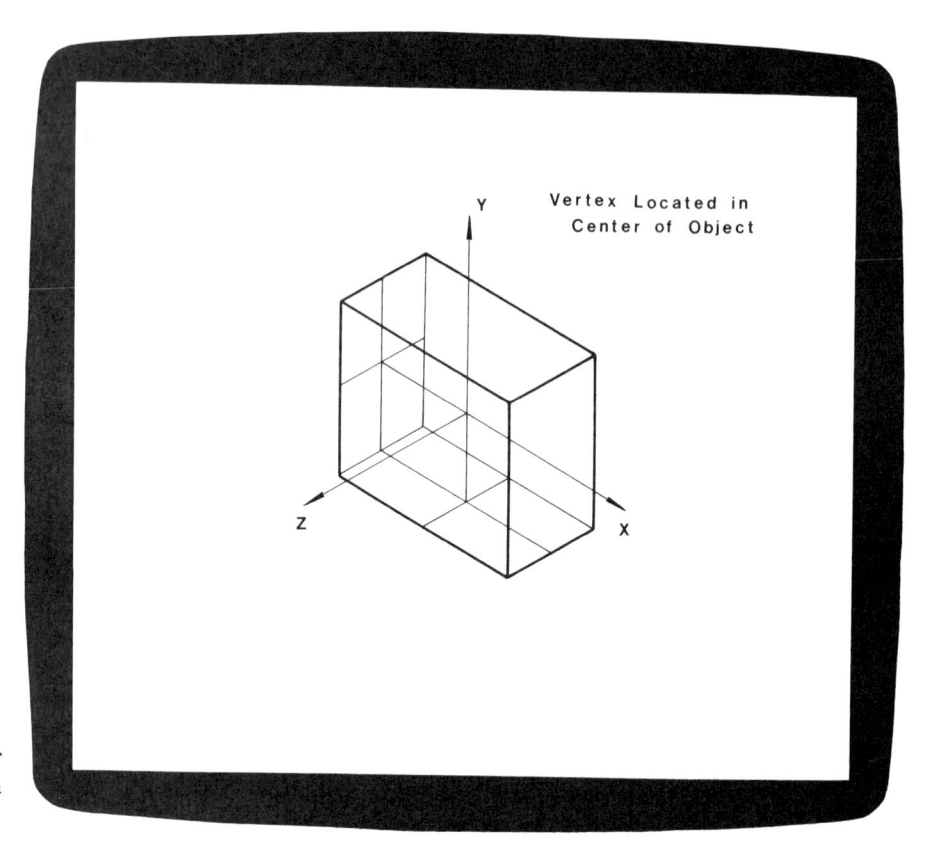

FIGURE 12-12 Rectangular prism with the vertex located in the center of the object.

The locational vertex of a prism need not be on one of the corners. It could be located at the center of the prism as shown in Figure 12-12. Center vertex location is helpful when working with centerlines between interfacing parts.

12-6 CYLINDERS

Figure 12-13 shows how to locate and define a cylinder using two different methods. The first method references the cylinder to an axis of revolution, the second to a single vertex point. In addition to an axis of revolution, cylinder definition requires a diameter or radius, and a length or height.

FIGURE 12-13 A cylinder is defined using an axis of rotation or a vertex.

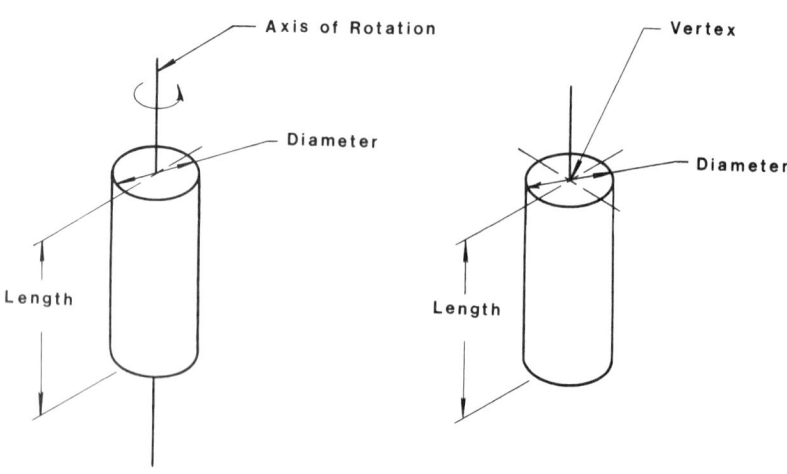

Sec. 12-6 Cylinders

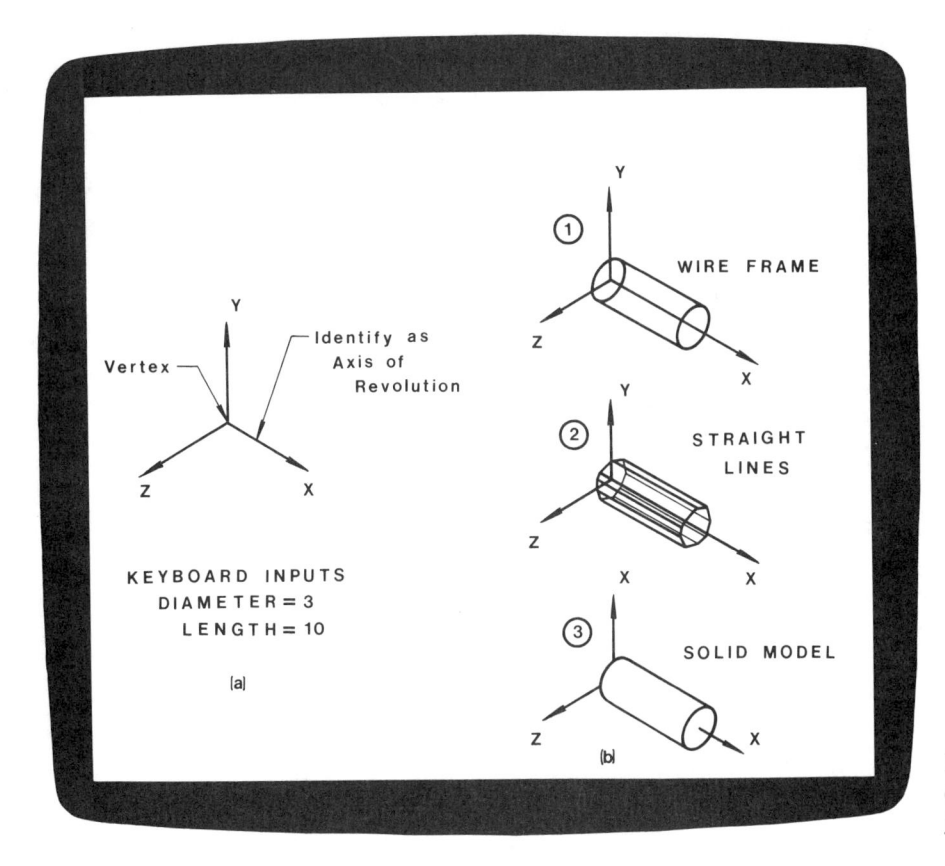

FIGURE 12-14 Examples of different ways to draw solid objects.

Figure 12-14a shows a sample problem that requires us to draw a cylinder of diameter 3, a height of 10, and an orientation along the horizontal axis. The procedure is as follows:

1. Use the *X* axis as the axis of revolution. The problem requires horizontal orientation, so the horizontal *X* axis can be used. The axis of revolution must be an existing line and is identified using the cursor (see Figure 12-14).
2. The diameter size 3, and the length 10, are inputted via the keyboard.
3. The finished cylinder should appear on the screen. Figure 12-14b shows three possible finished outputs. Cylinder 1 shows a wire frame model; that is, the cylinder appears to be made of individual lines (wires) and allows the viewer to look through and into the object. Cylinder 2 is a composite of many straight-line segments. The circular-shaped top and bottom of the cylinder are actually made from a series of straight lines. The edges on the top and bottom surfaces are joined by lines. Cylinder 3 is a solid-model pictorial of the cylinder. The end surfaces are circular, and lines not directly visible are not shown.

Figure 12-15 shows a cylinder of diameter 2 and length 9 created using a vertex point of 5, 0, 4. A vertical construction line of infinite length was drawn through the vertex point and used as an axis of rotation. The diameter and length values were inputted via the keyboard. The vertical construction line was erased after the cylinder was completed.

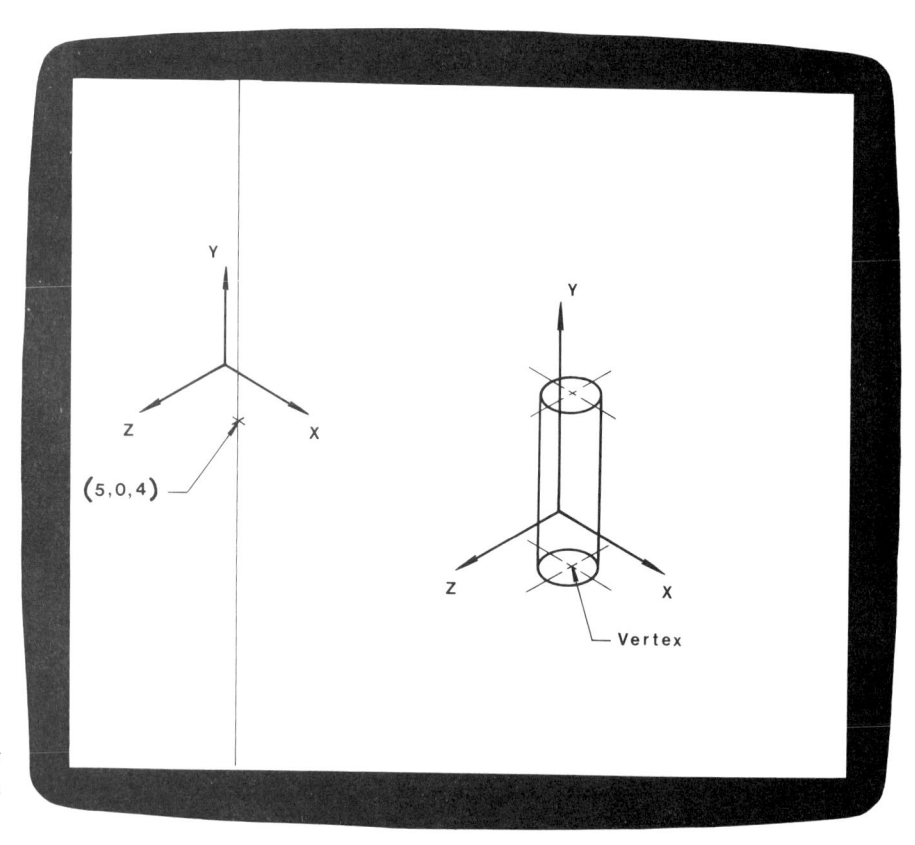

FIGURE 12-15 How to draw a cylinder through a given vertex.

12-7 GENERAL PRISMS

Figure 12-16 shows some general prism shapes. Prisms are defined first by a locating vertex point and a finite base plane, that is, a plane defined by enclosed lines. The base plane may be of any shape: triangular, square, rectangular, hexagonal, and so on. Lines are extended from the plane to define the length of the prism. All prisms shown in Figure 12-16 are right prisms; that is, the length lines are at 90° to the end planes. The locating vertex point may be anywhere on or within the prism, but is normally one of the corner points of the base plane, or a point within the base plane.

FIGURE 12-16 Examples of solid prisms.

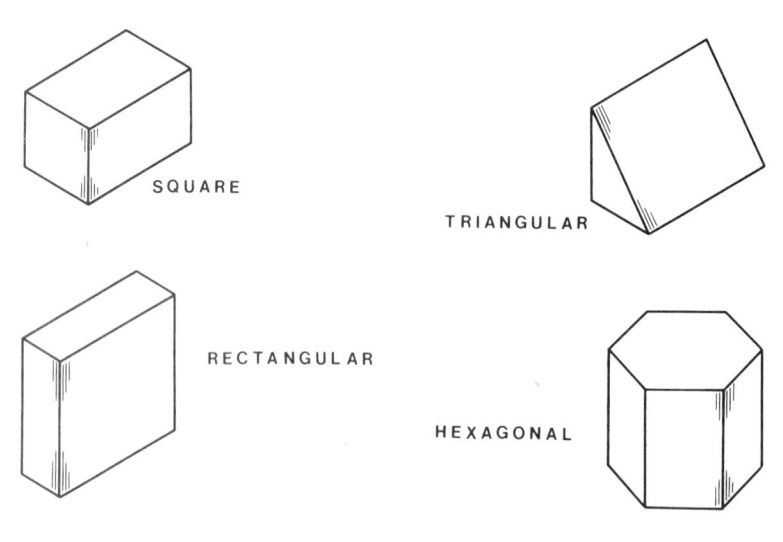

Sec. 12-8　Pyramids

Figure 12-17 shows an oblique prism. The length lines of an oblique prism are not at 90° to the base plane. In the example shown, the length lines are at a 15° angle to the square base plane.

12-8 PYRAMIDS

Figure 12-18 shows how to draw a right square pyramid. Pyramids are defined by the shape of their base planes. A base plane is a finite plane made from interconnected lines. Any shaped plane may be used. Each corner of the base plane is joined to a common apex point using straight lines. The apex point is located by defining it as a coordinate point. For example, in Figure 12-19 a rectangular pyramid was drawn about the vertical Y axis. The apex point was defined using the coordinates 0, 8, 0 and corners on the base were joined to the apex.

Pyramids may be located using the apex as a vertex point, by defining a vertex point within the base plane, or by using any point within the pyramid. The choice of vertex point depends on the system's capabilities and how the pyramid is located relative to the screen axis.

Figure 12-20 shows an offset pyramid. The apex of an offset pyramid is not located directly over the center of the base plane.

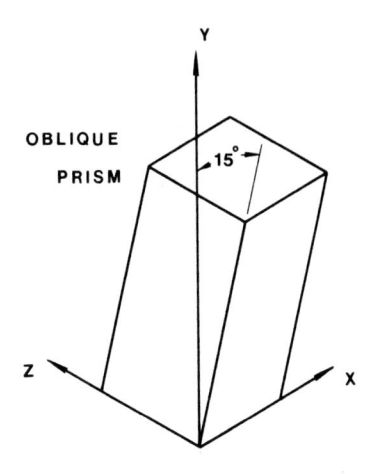

FIGURE 12-17 Oblique prism.

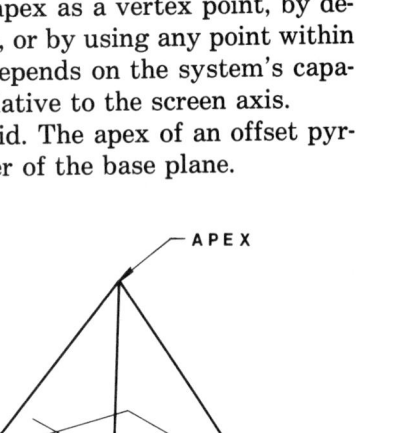

FIGURE 12-18 Right square pyramid.

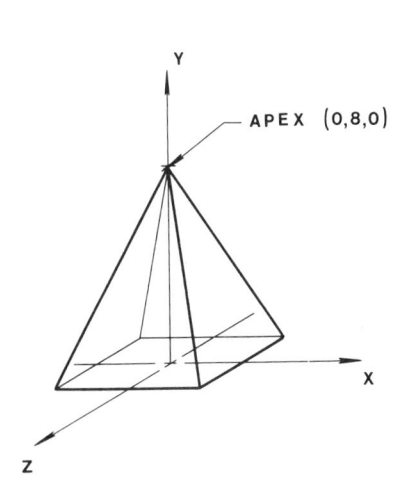

FIGURE 12-19 Right square prism located about an XYZ axis.

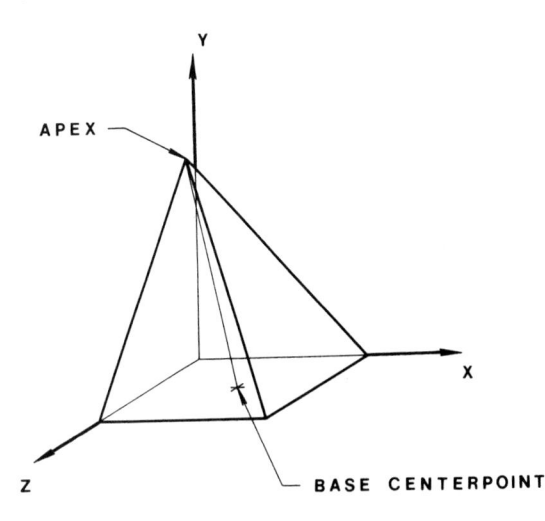

FIGURE 12-20 Offset pyramid.

Figure 12-21 shows how to create a square right pyramid without using a coordinate value for the apex. The procedure is as follows:

1. Draw the square base. Define each corner of the square. In this example, a vertex point of 4, 0, −3 was used to locate one of the corner points.
2. Draw lines across the square from corner to corner as shown. The intersection of these lines defines the centerpoint of the square base.
3. Draw a vertical line (a line perpendicular to the base plane) from the centerpoint of the base of length equal to the required height of the pyramid. In this example, a height of 12 was required.
4. Define the end of the vertical line as the apex.
5. Connect the corners of the base plane to the apex.
6. Erase all excess lines.

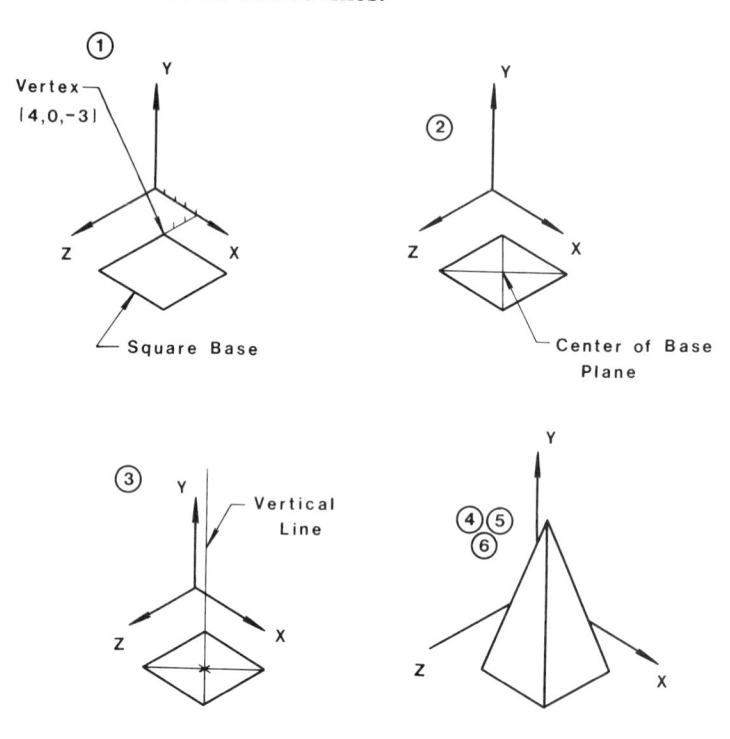

FIGURE 12-21 How to draw a right square pyramid at a specified location.

Figure 12-22 shows two truncated pyramids. A *truncated pyramid* is a pyramid with its top cut off. A truncated pyramid is defined by a base plane and an apex height as with regular pyramids, but in addition requires definition of the height and angle of the truncation. The pyramid

FIGURE 12-22 Examples of truncated pyramids.

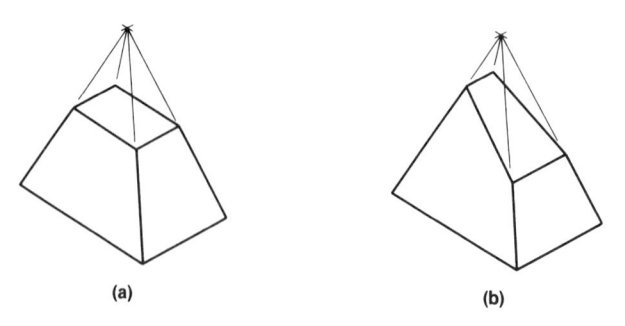

(a)   (b)

Sec. 12-9   Cones   363

in Figure 12-22a has been truncated by a plane parallel to the base plane. This type of truncation may be defined using a truncation height or by defining the size of the truncation plane. The truncated pyramid in Figure 12-22b has a slanted truncation plane. This type of truncation is generally achieved by first drawing a regular pyramid and then modifying it by slicing off the top as needed. Modification of geometric shapes is described in Section 12-12.

12-9 CONES

Figure 12-23 shows a regular cone, an oblique cone, and a truncated cone. The locating vertex of a cone is almost always the centerpoint of the circular base plane. Once the vertex is established, the diameter of the circular base plane and the cone height are inputted. A right cone has its axis of revolution perpendicular to the base plane; an oblique cone has its axis of revolution at an angle other than 90°.

Figure 12-24 shows two examples of truncated cones. The cone in part (a) is truncated by a plane parallel to the base plane. This type of truncation is generally created by first locating the vertex, and drawing the circular base plane and the height as if it were a regular cone. The truncation plane is defined by giving either a diameter or a truncation height.

Cones with regular truncations are generally created by first drawing a regular cone and then modifying it by slicing off the top as shown in Figure 12-24b. Modifications of geometric shapes are described in Section 12-12.

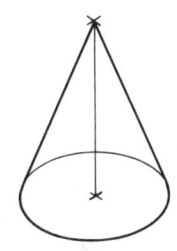

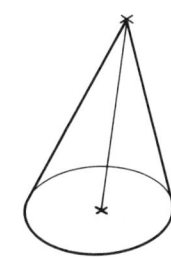

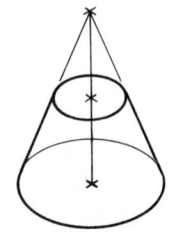

FIGURE 12-23 Cones.

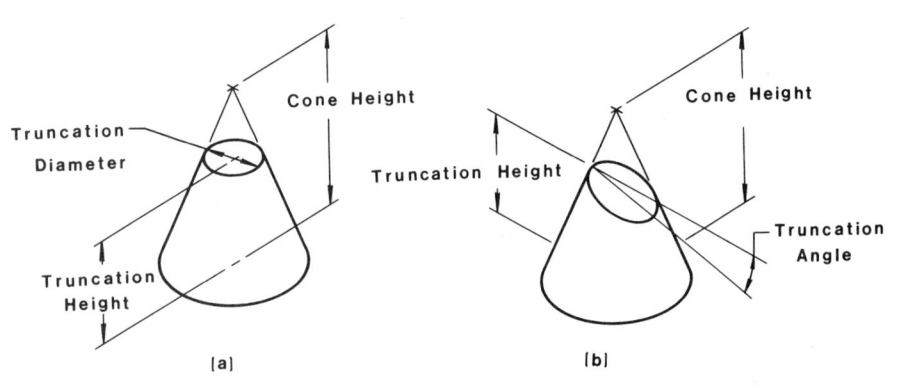

FIGURE 12-24 Examples of truncated cones.

12-10 SPHERES

Figure 12-25 shows two spheres. Spheres are drawn by first locating the vertex point. The centerpoint of the sphere is almost always the vertex point. Once located, the sphere diameter or radius is inputted, usually via the keyboard.

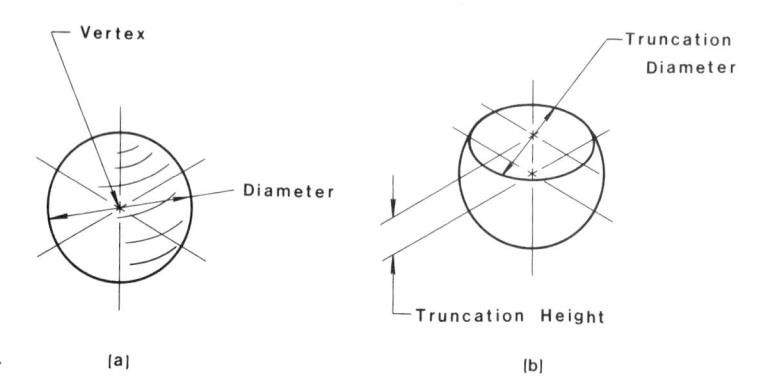

FIGURE 12-25 Spheres.

Spheres may be truncated as shown in Figure 12-25b. The truncation shown uses a plane parallel to a plane through the centerpoint and perpendicular to the vertical axis. The truncation is defined by a distance from the center vertex or by a diameter. If an angular truncation is required, the sphere must be modified as described in Section 12-12.

12-11 COMBINING GEOMETRIC SHAPES

Geometric shapes may be combined to form more complex shapes. Figure 12-26 shows a right square prism intersection by a cylinder. The system used to create the picture was an IBM 5085 using CATIA.

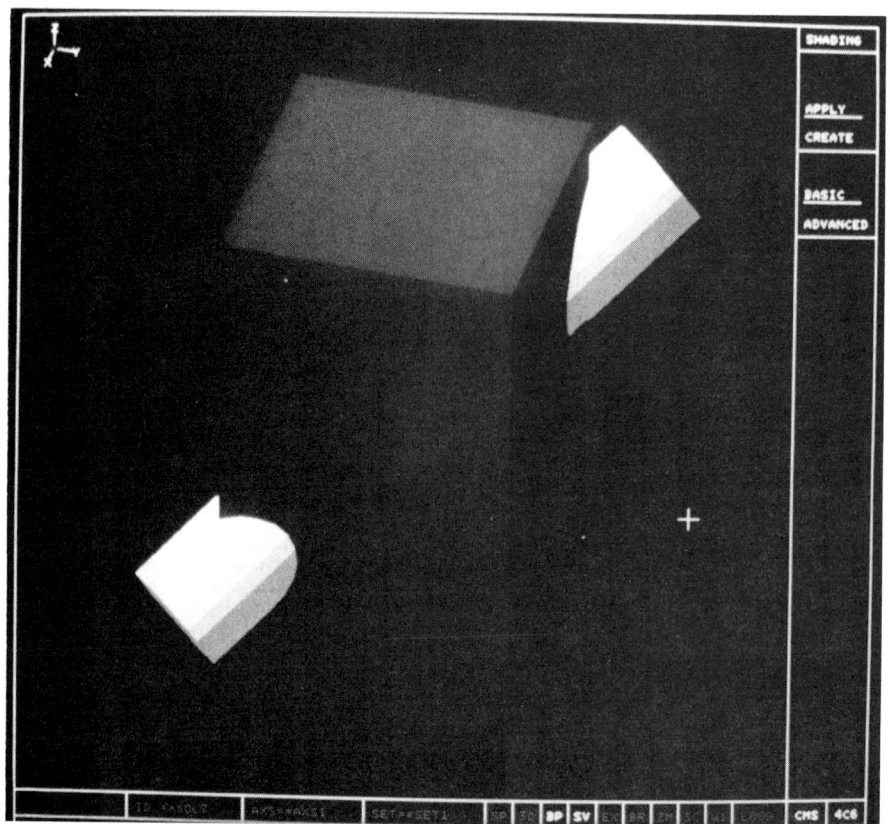

FIGURE 12-26 Two solid objects may be joined or subtracted.

Figure 12-27 shows two variations of a cylinder intersecting a right rectangular prism. They serve to illustrate the concepts of adding and subtracting solids. Figure 12-27b has the cylinder added to the prism. This is called joining solids. To the computer, the two are now one entity. Figure 12-27c has had the cylinder subtracted from the prism. The result is a hole or negative cylinder.

A Cylinder and a Prism Drawn Separately

(a)

Added Together (Joined)

(b)

Cylinder Subtracted from Prism

(c)

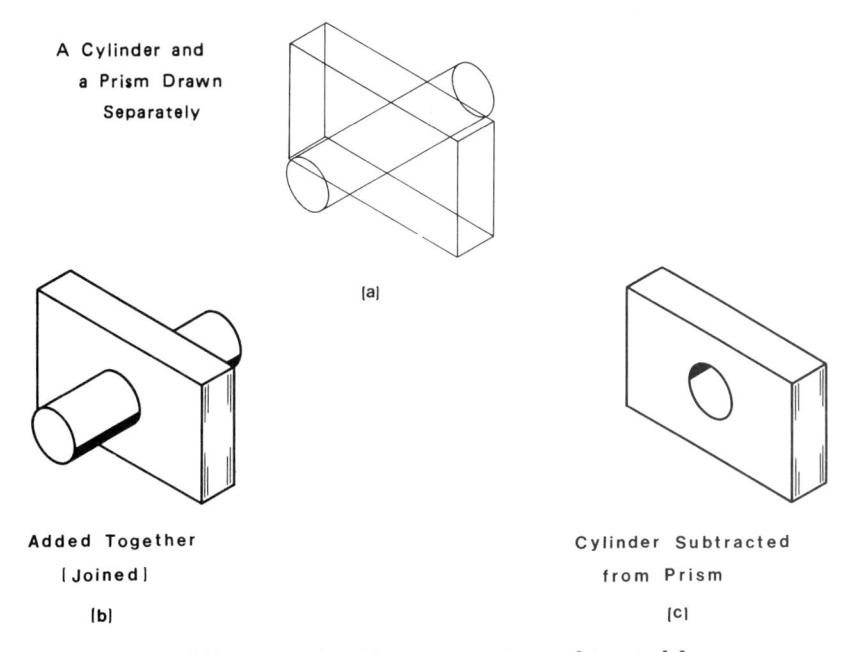

FIGURE 12-27 Smaller square prism subtracted from a larger rectangular prism.

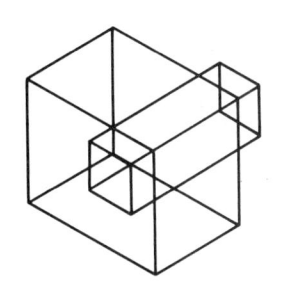

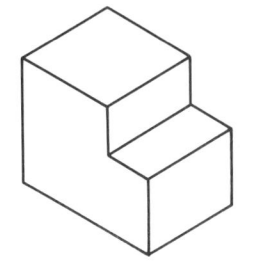

FIGURE 12-28 How to change the shape of a solid.

Figure 12-28 shows a rectangular prism that has a square prism subtracted from the corner as shown.

12-12 MODIFYING THREE-DIMENSIONAL GEOMETRIC SHAPES

Drawing objects in three dimensions is a very similar process to manufacturing the objects. The craftsman starts with a piece of stock, generally a block or rounded piece of material, and cuts away what is not needed. To draw an object in three dimensions, the drafter starts with a geometric shape and slices away what is not needed. For example, to

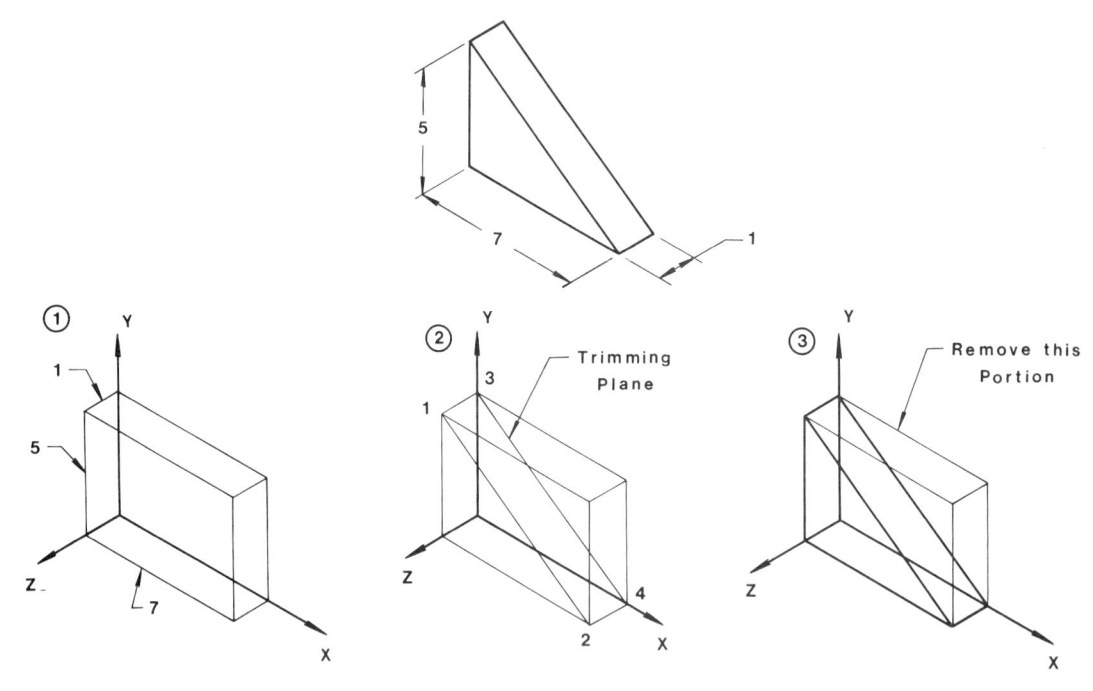

FIGURE 12-29 Smaller cylinder subtracted from a larger one.

draw the wedge-shaped object shown in Figure 12-29, start with a right rectangular prism and slice away the top half, leaving the desired shape. The procedure is as follows:

1. Draw a right rectangular prism as shown. The dimensions used in this example were 7, 5, 1.

2. Define a plane that cuts through the object and that can be used to separate the unneeded portion of the object from the part to be saved. This process is similar to line trimming when working with two-dimensional drawings, as described throughout the book. Construction lines were used to establish borders or end points so that lines drawn to one side of the construction lines could be trimmed or erased. After the trimming was complete, the construction lines were also erased. Trimming in three dimensions requires surfaces to be trimmed and therefore requires a plane to establish the trimming boundary. In the example shown in Figure 12-29, lines 1-2 and 3-4 are drawn across the corners. A trimming plan 1-3-4-2 is defined. Trimming planes are defined in different ways depending on the system. Some systems require line input, others use points. The planes may be infinite or finite. The plane shown in Figure 12-29 is finite.

3. Trim away the top portion of the prism, leaving the desired wedge shape. The trimming plane could be erased, although in this example the trimming plane is also the top surface of the wedge, so is not erased.

Figure 12-30 shows a large cylinder that has a smaller cylinder removed from its center. A vertical plane aligned with the Y axis was defined as a trimming plane and the front half of the object was removed. The trimming plane was then erased.

Sec. 12-12 Modifying Three-Dimensional Geometric Shapes   367

Figure 12-31 shows an object that is a composite of geometric shapes and the trimming plane technique. First a rectangular prism was drawn. Then a cylinder and a square prism were removed to produce the hole and square cutout. Finally, a trimming plane was established using the four points 1, 2, 3, 4. The corner above the trimming plane was removed and the trimming plane was erased.

Figure 12-32 shows another object made using both the solid remove and trimming techniques. First a rectangular prism was drawn, then a square prism was subtracted. Finally, a trimming prism was created using points 1, 2, 3, 4, and the corner to the right of the trimming plane was removed. The trimming plane was erased.

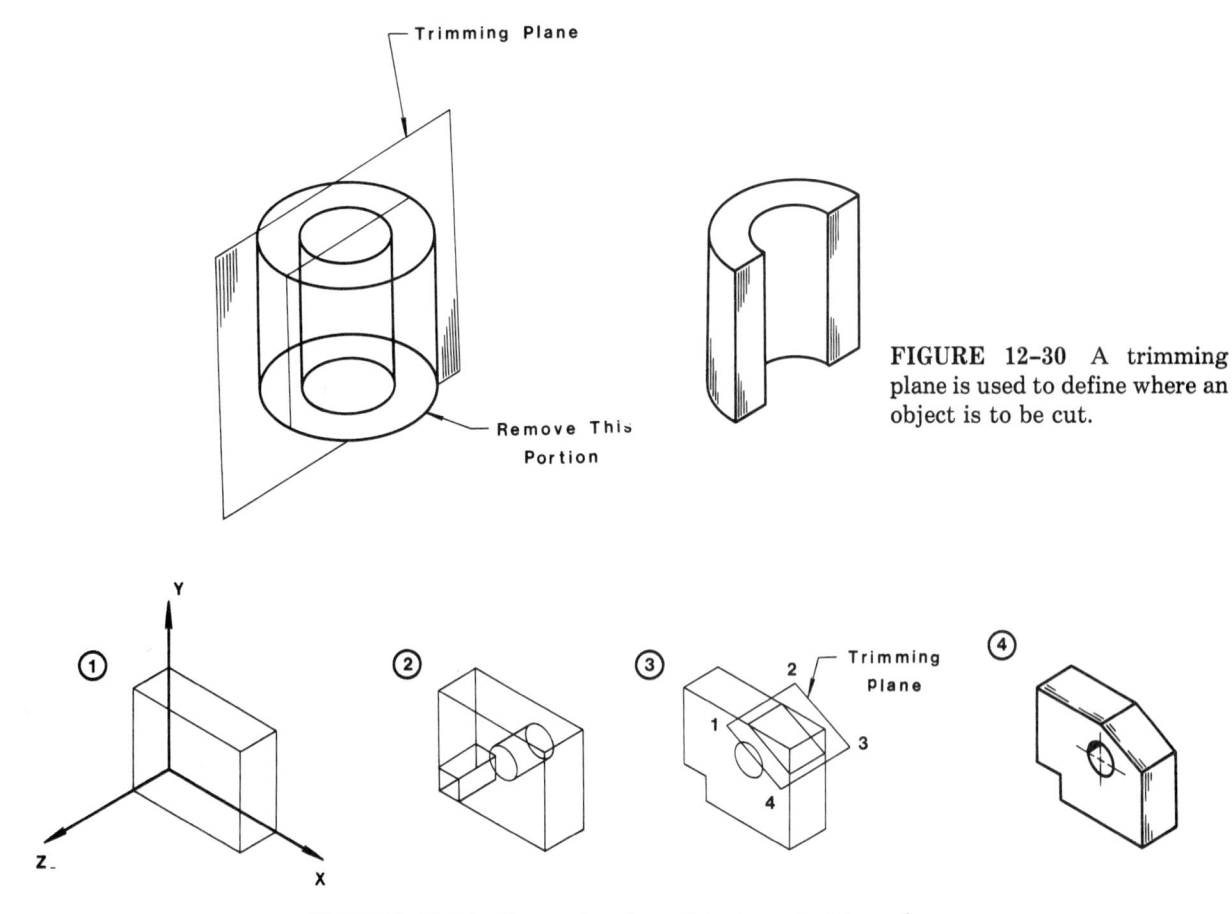

FIGURE 12-30 A trimming plane is used to define where an object is to be cut.

FIGURE 12-31 Example of an object created by subtracting other solids and by trimming.

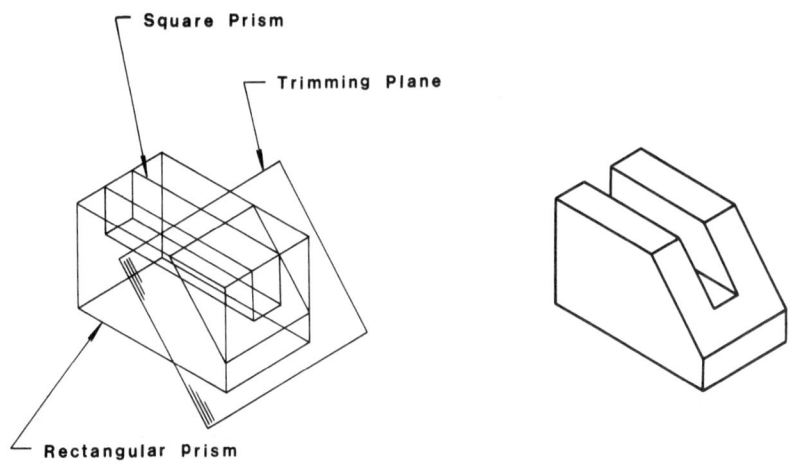

FIGURE 12-32 Example of an object created by subtracting a solid and by trimming.

12-13 ROUNDED THREE-DIMENSIONAL SURFACES

Figure 12-33 shows objects with a rounded three-dimensional surface. Computer graphic systems vary greatly in the techniques and input requirements needed to create a curved surface. Some systems have menu functions that create rounded corners directly given a location and a radius value. These functions can have one of several different names: corner, fillet, round, or arc are common. Direct menu functions are only available on larger systems (Figure 12-34).

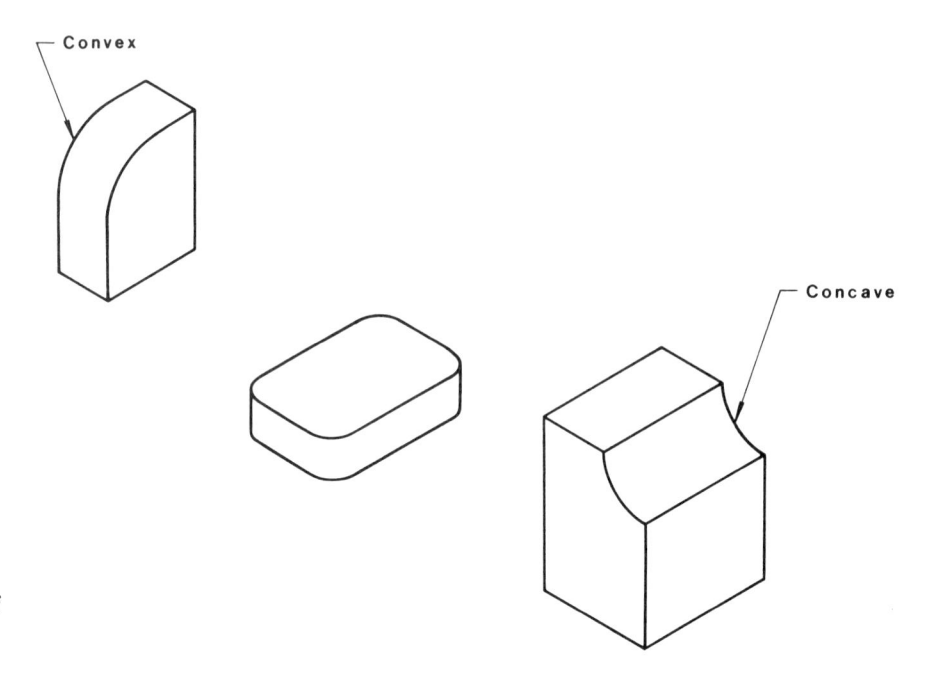

FIGURE 12-33 Examples of curved surfaces.

FIGURE 12-34 Some larger systems can create rounded corners directly.

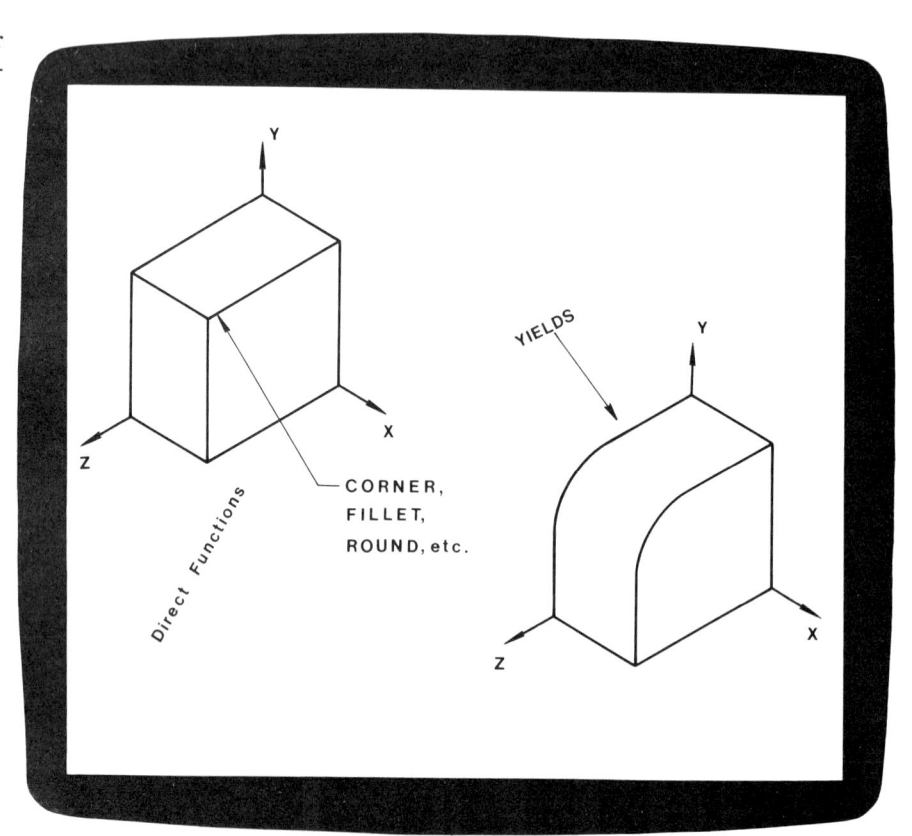

Sec. 12-14 Preparing Three-Dimensional Drawings from Orthographic Views   369

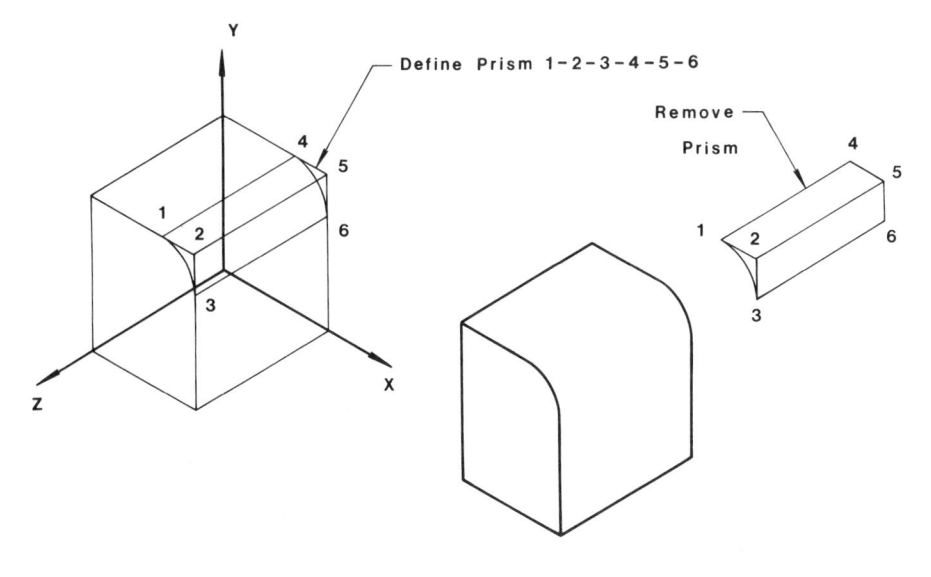

FIGURE 12-35 Example of a rounded corner created by subtracting a prism.

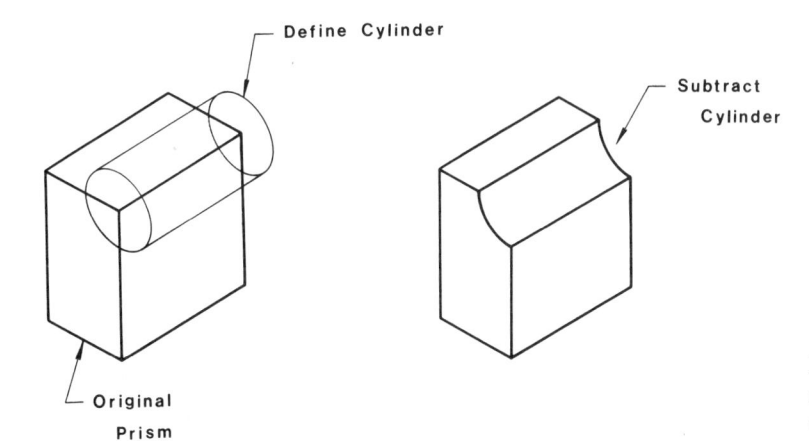

FIGURE 12-36 An example of a concaved surface created using a cylinder.

Figure 12-35 shows the procedure used to create a corner by defining a prism with a curved surface and then removing the prism. In Figure 12-35 a finite plane 1-2-3 is defined. Line 1-3 of the plane is a curved line. Prism 1-2-3-4-5-6 is defined based on the finite plane 1-2-3. Once the computer recognizes prism 1-2-3-4-5-6 as an individual entity, it can be subtracted or removed from the original rectangular prism.

Figure 12-36 shows how a curved concaved surface can be created by subtracting a cylinder from the original rectangular prism. The upper right corner line 1-2 was used as an axis of rotation for the cylinder.

12-14 PREPARING THREE-DIMENSIONAL DRAWINGS FROM ORTHOGRAPHIC VIEWS

Dimensional values given on orthographic views may be transferred directly to three-dimensional axis systems if, and only if, they are parallel to one of the principal axis lines. Slanted, oblique, and curved lines must first be defined in terms of the principal axis lines and then transferred. An exception to this can be found in some of the larger systems that recognize angular values defined relative to a three-dimensional axis.

In Figure 12-37, all edge lines in the object are parallel to one of the principal axis lines. These lines are called *normal lines*. They may be transferred directly to either the cartesian or isometric axis as shown. The length dimension 3 is drawn as 3 on the three-dimensional axis—similarly with the height dimension of 2, and all other dimensions.

Figure 12-38 shows an object that has a 30° angular dimension for the slanted surface. If a cartesian coordinate system is used as shown in example 1 of Figure 12-38 and the object is oriented as shown, the 30° angle dimension may be used directly. However, if the object is oriented to a cartesian coordinate system as shown in example 2 or to an isometric system as shown in example 3, the 30° dimension cannot be transferred.

Figure 12-39 shows a similar object with a 30° slanted surface. Instead of transferring the 30° angle to the isometric and cartesian axis systems shown, the slanted surface was redimensioned. The 30° dimension was replaced by a second linear dimension (8.3). The linear dimension, which is parallel to the vertical axis, was transferred to the three-dimensional axis to define the limits of the slanted surface. This

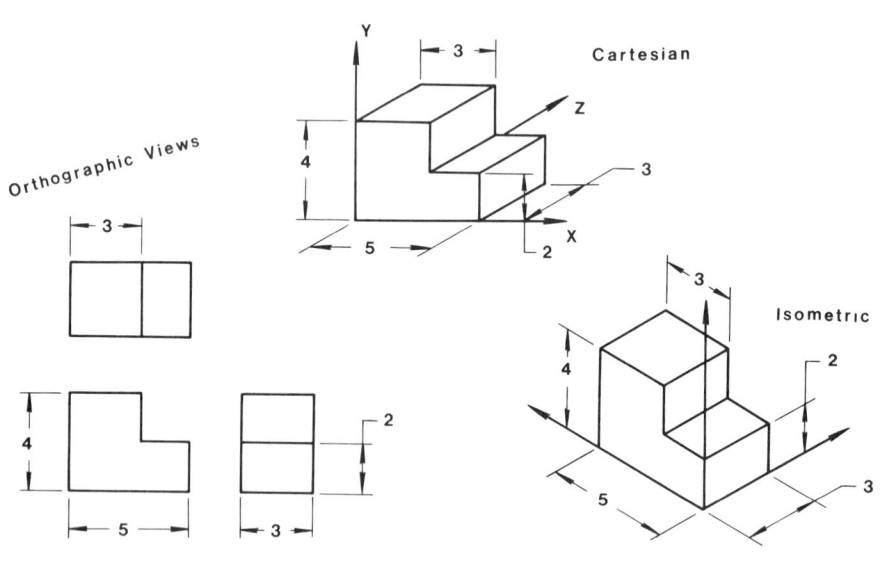

FIGURE 12-37 Examples of orthographic views and the equivalent objects drawn using a Cartesian and isometric axis system.

FIGURE 12-38 Angular dimensions can be used directly in three dimensional drawings only if the slanted surface is aligned with a 90° axis.

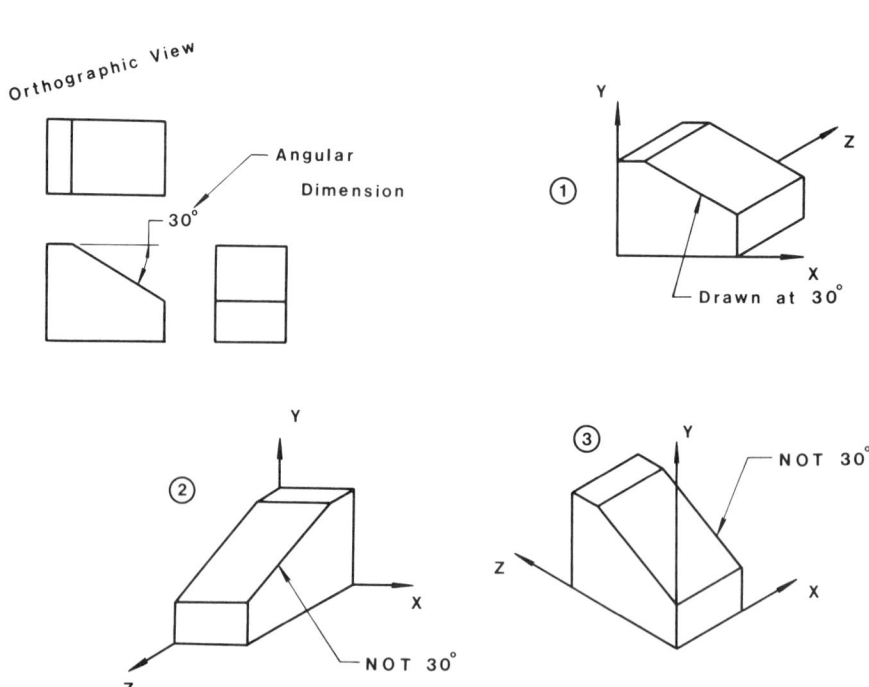

Sec. 12-14 Preparing Three-Dimensional Drawings from Orthographic Views   371

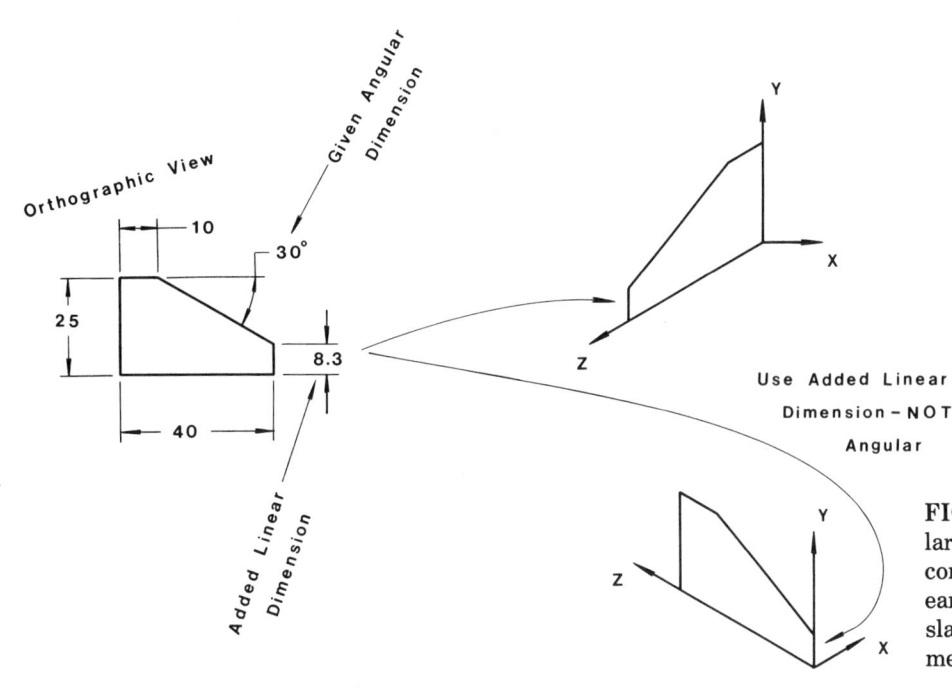

FIGURE 12-39 Convert angular dimensions to their linear components, and use the linear components to define the slanted surface on the three-dimensional axis.

procedure is not exactly correct from a manufacturing standpoint, where the tolerance values may vary according to the type and location of dimensions, but is generally considered acceptable for creating pictorial drawings.

Figure 12-40 shows how the linear dimensions are created. Given a 30° angular dimension, have the computer dimension the vertical linear distance. Once dimensioned, use the linear value in the three-dimensional drawing. In this example a value of 8.3 was derived. This approach relies on the given 10° dimension along the top surface to help define the slanted surface.

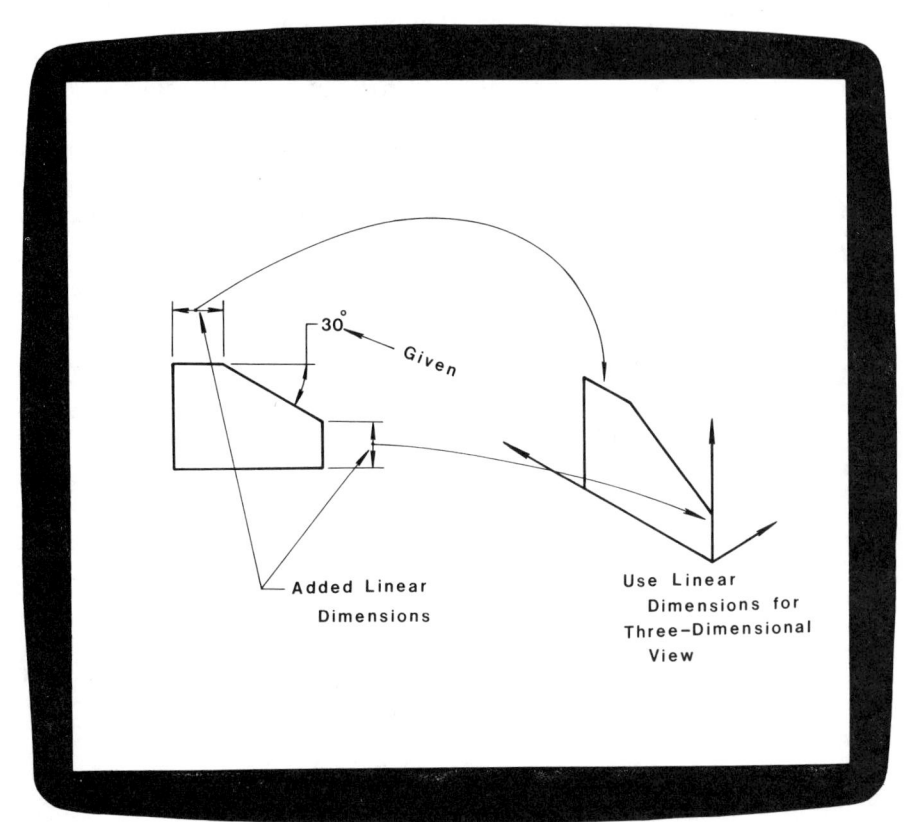

FIGURE 12-40 Linear components of an angular dimension used to define a slanted surface on an isometric axis.

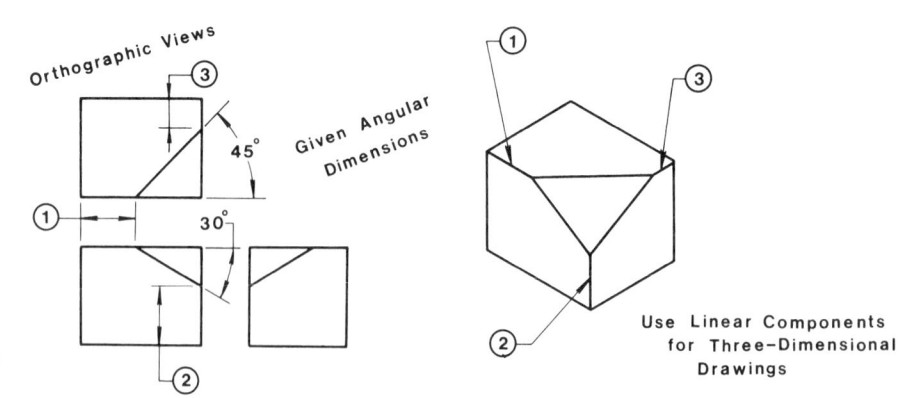

FIGURE 12-41 Oblique surface.

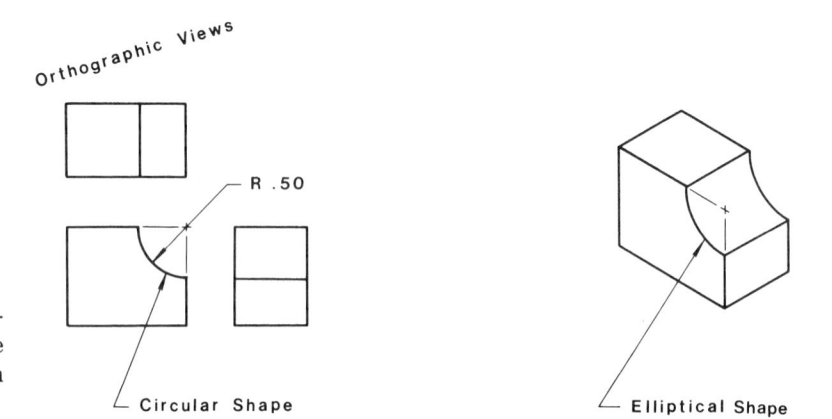

FIGURE 12-42 Curved surfaces of constant radius are shown as elliptical shapes in three dimensional drawings.

A second approach would be to change the 30° value to two linear values—one horizontal and one vertical—and then use these values to define the slanted surface. In this example, the two linear components of the 30° angular dimension are 40 and 16.7

Figure 12-41 shows an object that contains an oblique surface. The transfer procedure requires each of the angular dimensions to be converted into their linear components, which are, in turn, transferred to the three-dimensional axis.

Figure 12-42 shows an object with a curved surface. Three-dimensional drawings of curved surfaces can be created by treating the surfaces as arcs or by subtracting cylinders as explained in Section 12-13.

Holes are drawn in three-dimensional drawings as negative cylinders; by direct input, if it is within the system's capability; or by creating ellipses or splines as shown in Figures 12-43 and 12-44, respectively. Circular shapes cannot be drawn directly because the axis lines used to represent the three-dimensional axis system are not at 90° to each other.

The procedure for drawing an ellipse on the three-dimensional axis is as follows (Figure 12-43):

1. Define the centerpoint for the ellipse using centerlines.
2. Lay out the boundaries of the ellipse by using the radius value for the circle as shown.
3. Construct an ellipse about the centerpoint formed by the intersection of the horizontal and vertical lines. Fit the ellipse so that it is tangent to the boundary lines.

Sec. 12-14 Preparing Three-Dimensional Drawings from Orthographic Views 373

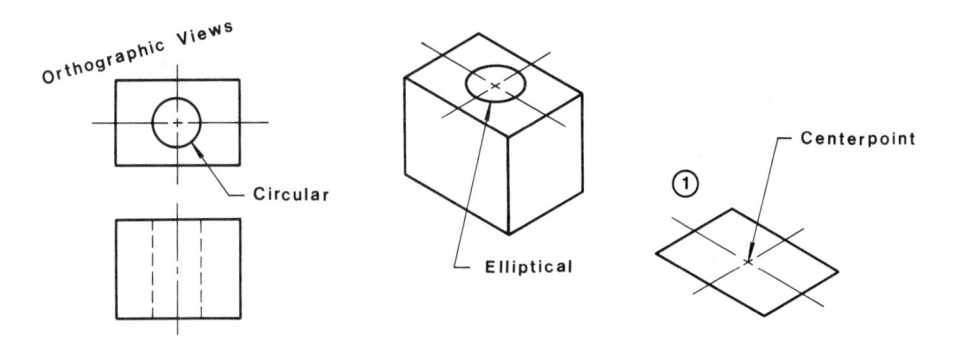

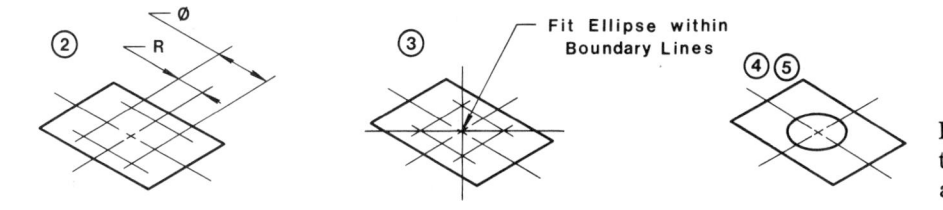

FIGURE 12-43 How to define the boundaries of an ellipse on a three-dimensional surface.

4. Draw the ellipse using the derived major and minor axis.
5. Erase any excess lines.

The procedure for drawing a spline that looks like an ellipse on a three-dimensional axis is as follows (Figure 12-44):

1. Define the centerpoint for the ellipse using centerlines.
2. Lay out the boundaries of the ellipse by using the radius value for the circle as shown.
3. Define the intersection points of the centerlines and the boundary lines as points 1, 2, 3, 4, as shown.
4. Draw a closed spline using points 1, 2, 3, 4.
5. Erase any excess lines.

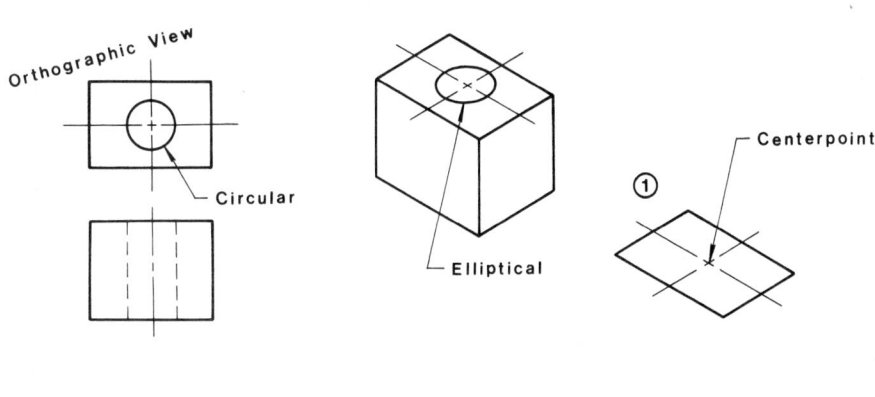

FIGURE 12-44 How to define the points for a spline used on a three-dimensional surface to represent a circle.

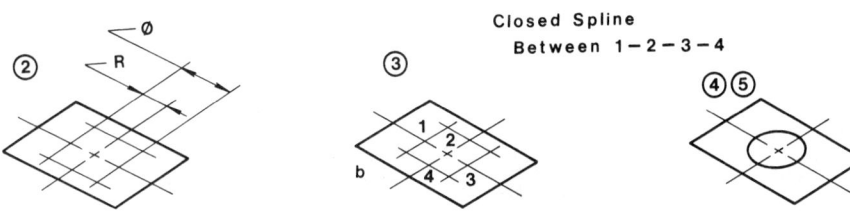

12-15 THREE-DIMENSIONAL WINDOWED DRAWINGS

Figure 12–45 shows the general format for a three-dimensional windowed drawing. The screen is divided into four separate areas or windows. Three of the windows are used for the standard front, top, and right-side orthographic views. The fourth window is used for a pictorial drawing. The idea is to be able to view both the orthographic views and the pictorial drawing simultaneously.

Computer systems vary greatly in how they create and modify objects using windowed formats. The most advanced systems interconnect all four windows, meaning that a change in one window is automatically incorporated into the other three windows. The smaller systems treat each window as a separate entity, unrelated to the other three windows. Changes in this type of format must be made within each individual window.

The advantage of the windowed format is that it allows the drafter to view, in three dimensions, the object being created. This reduces the need for visualization of orthographic views. The disadvantage to the windowed format is that unless used carefully, this can create some very confusing objects. Two-dimensional drawings contain stacks of lines, that is, lines over lines. If the object shown in Figure 12–46a is to be modified with a slanted surface and the designer adds a slanted line to the front view in the windowed drawing, but forgets to modify the rear surface, the results will be as shown in Figure 12–46b—not what the drafter originally intended. This is very simplistic and the error is obvious, but for more complex objects the errors are more subtle and not always obvious.

FIGURE 12–45 Computer graphics system that shows orthographic views and a three-dimensional view simultaneously.

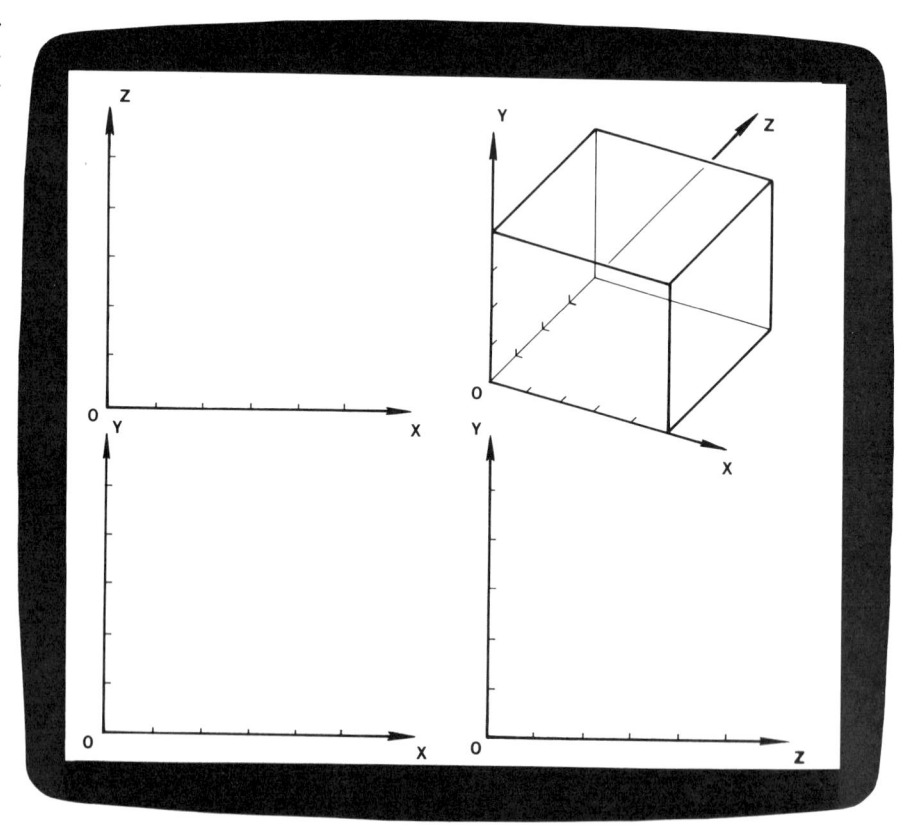

Sec. 12-15 Three-Dimensional Windowed Drawings   375

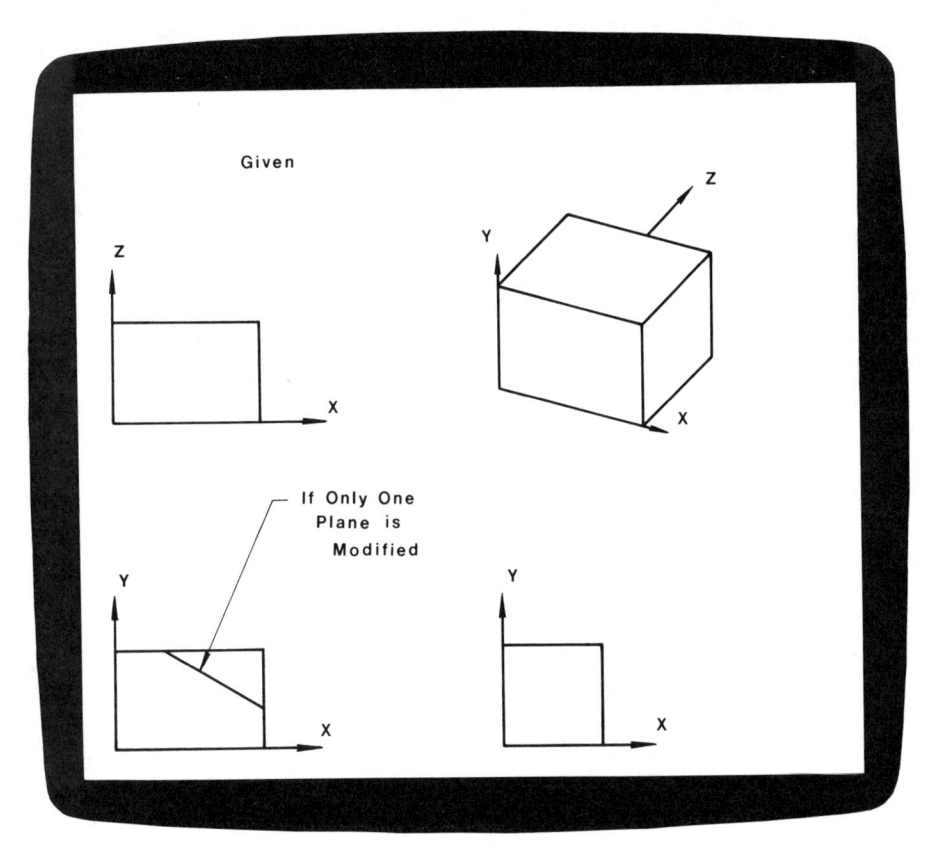

FIGURE 12-46(a) Example of an error created when trying to add a slanted surface to an existing rectangular prism. The front view is modified by adding just one slanted line. [See Figure 12-46(b).]

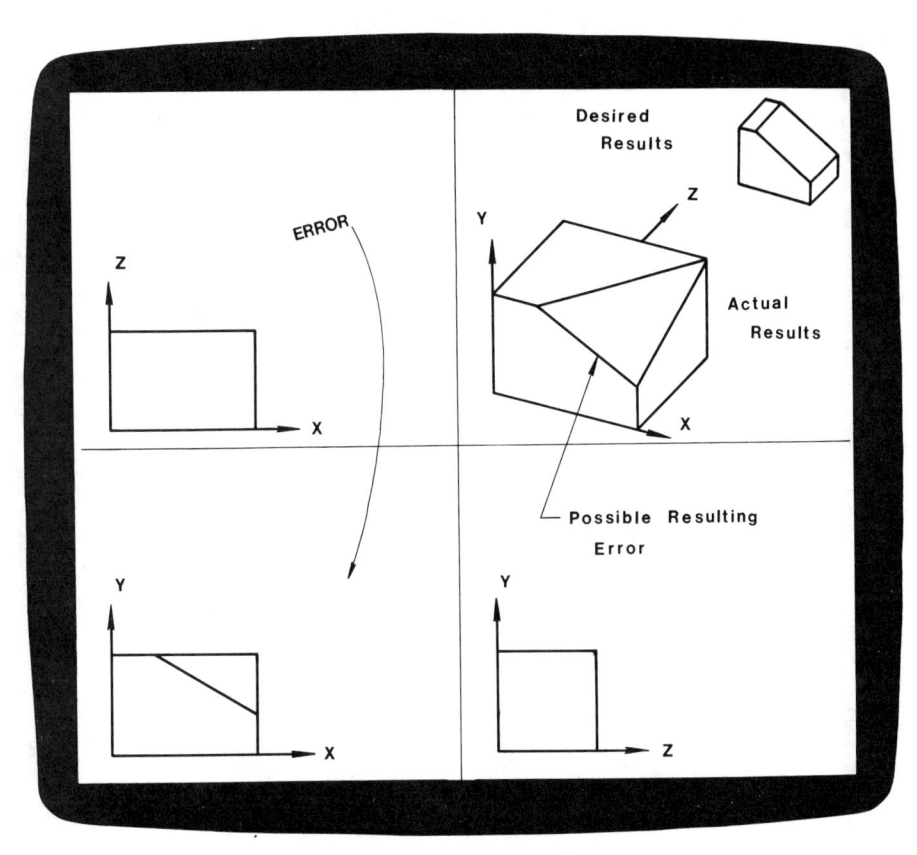

FIGURE 12-46(b) The result of the error created in Figure 12-46(a) will generate an oblique surface, not the slanted surface desired.

12-16 THREE-DIMENSIONAL DRAWINGS CREATED USING TWO-DIMENSIONAL SYSTEMS

Figure 12-47 shows a pictorial drawing that was created using a two-dimensional drawing system. It looks like a three-dimensional drawing but is in fact a series of individual lines. This means that if we attempt to treat the lines as a complete object, it will not respond. For example, the object cannot be rotated as a whole. Each line must be rotated separately.

The pictorial drawing shown in Figure 12-47 was created by first drawing a square and a circle, including centerlines, using the procedure outlined in Chapter 2 for two-dimensional objects. The points at the corners of the square are defined. The back corners of the cube are defined using either coordinate values or by drawing three slanted lines from the front corners, all at the same angle. In this example, 30° angles were used. Points 4, 5, and 6 are defined and then connected with straight lines.

Figure 12-48 shows another example of a two-dimensional drawing that looks like a three-dimensional drawing. The front face of the object, including the circle, is drawn first, then given the illusion of depth by adding slanted receding lines. In this example a slanted line is also drawn from the hole's centerpoint on the front surface to define the hole centerpoint on the rear surface. A second circle is then drawn about the centerpoint on the rear surface to see if any part of the circle on the rear surface can be seen through the hole on the front surface. In this example, part of the rear circle can be seen, so it is included in the final drawing. The unseen portion of the rear circle is erased.

FIGURE 12-47 Example of a three-dimensional drawing created using just two dimensions.

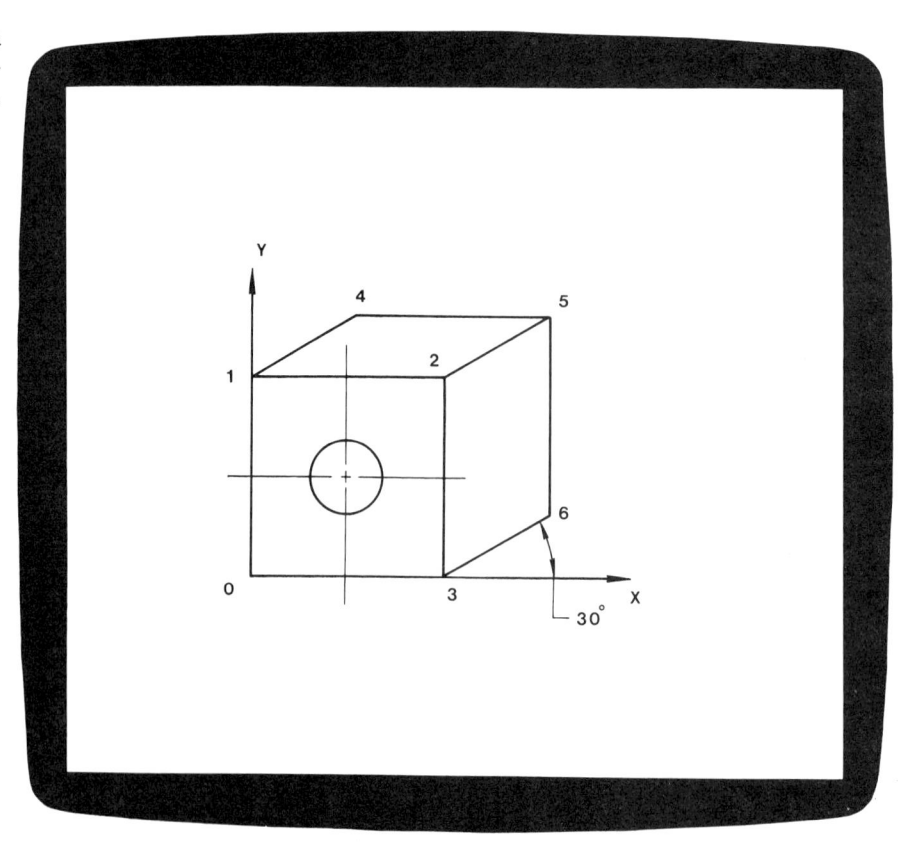

Sec. 12-16   3-D Drawings Created Using 2-D Systems

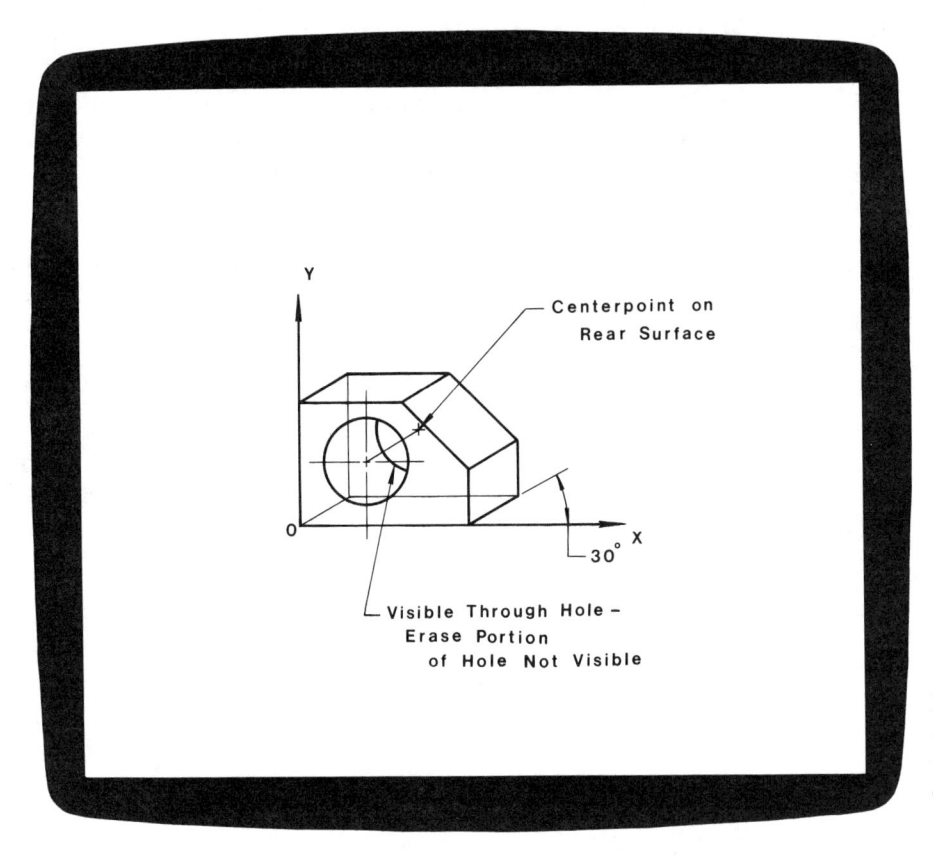

FIGURE 12-48 Draw a circle on both the front and rear surfaces to determine if a portion of the rear circle is visible through the front circle.

Figure 12-49 shows an object drawn using two sets of receding lines, in imitation of an isometric axis. The receding lines are drawn 30° to the horizontal. Holes in this type of drawing, or any axis system where the planes are not drawn at 90° to each other, are not drawn as a circle but as an ellipse, as shown in Figure 12-43.

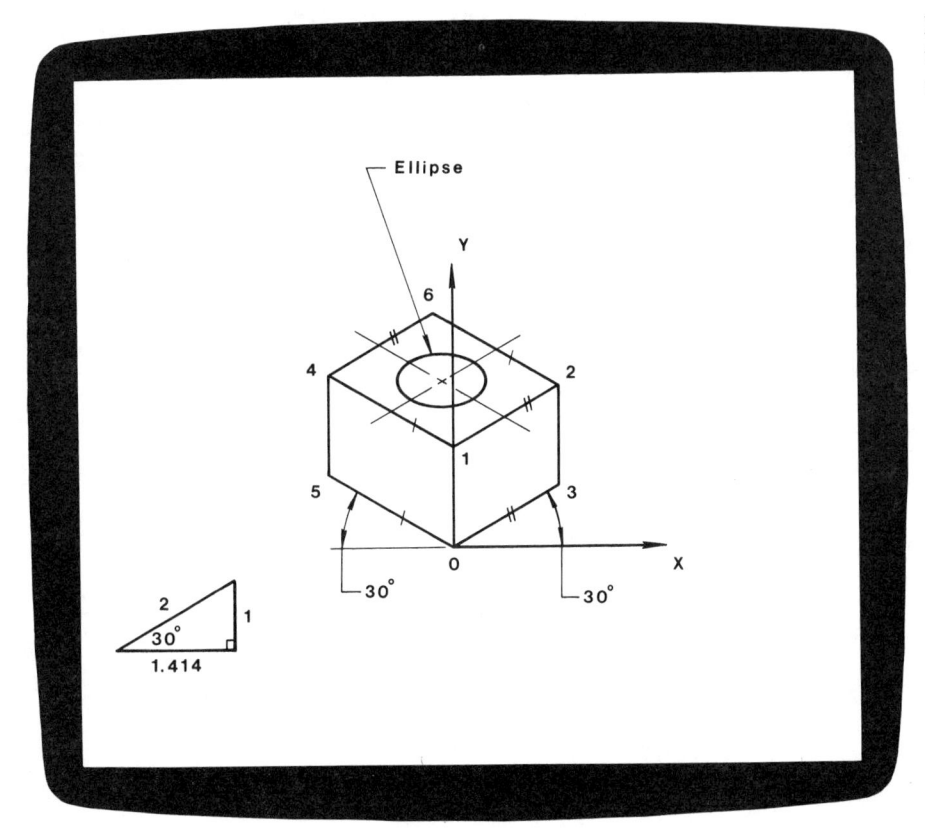

FIGURE 12-49 Example of a three-dimensional drawing created using just two dimensions.

12-17 EXPLODED DRAWINGS

Exploded drawings are three-dimensional assembly drawings. Each part of the assembly is positioned as if the assembly had come apart in space. Exploded drawings make excellent visual instructions for assembling parts.

The exploded drawing shown in Figure 12-50 shows a bolt, a nut, two washers, and an object. The drawing is really no more than a composite of prisms and cylinders aligned along a common centerline. It is important that centerlines be included in exploded drawings, as they give direction to the assembly of the parts.

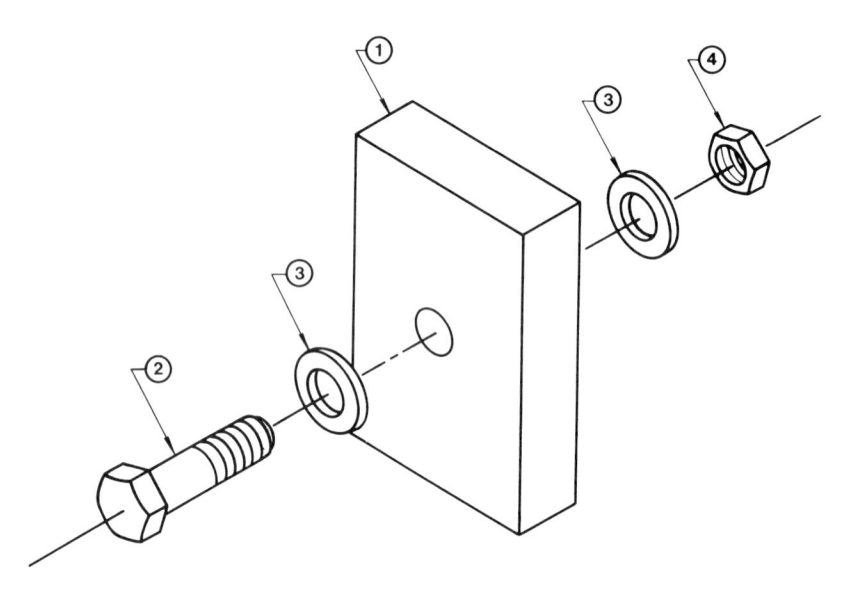

FIGURE 12-50 Example of an exploded drawing.

PROBLEMS

All dimensions for Problems P12-1 through P12-17 are in screen units and may be interpreted as either inches or centimeters.

P12-1 Draw a cartesian coordinate system as shown in Figure P12-1 and add the following points.
1. 6, 0, 6
2. 8, 6, 0
3. 0, 4, 4
4. 1, 5, 1
5. 4, 5, 7

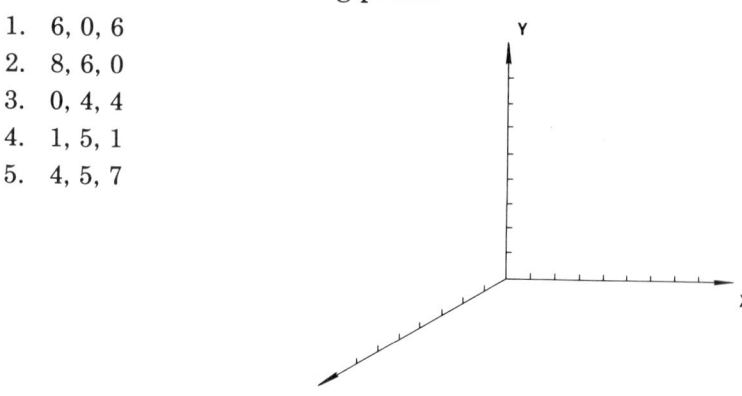

FIGURE P12-1

Chap. 12   Problems

P12-2   Draw a cartesian coordinate system as shown in Figure P12-2 and add the following points.

1. 6, 6, −2
2. 1, 4, −3
3. −4, 2, −3
4. −6, 1, −1
5. −6, −3, 2
6. −3, 4, 4
7. 5, −2, 3
8. 3, −6, 1
9. −3, −5, −2
10. 0, 0, 0

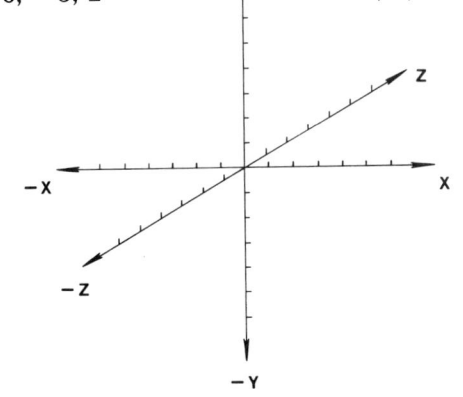

FIGURE P12-2

P12-3   Draw an isometric axis as shown in Figure P12-3 and add the following points.

1. 6, 0, 6
2. 8, 6, 0
3. 0, 4, 4
4. 1, 5, 1
5. 4, 5, 7

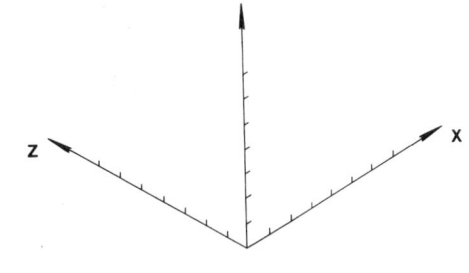

FIGURE P12-3

P12-4   Draw an isometric axis as shown in Figure P12-4 and add the following points.

1. 6, 6, −2
2. 1, 4, −3
3. −4, 2, −3
4. −6, 1, −1
5. −6, −3, 2
6. −3, 4, 4
7. 5, −2, 3
8. 3, −6, 1
9. −3, −5, −2
10. 0, 0, 0

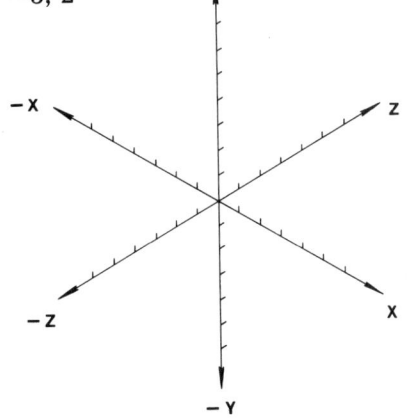

FIGURE P12-4

P12-5 Draw the rectangular prism shown in Figure P12-5. The size values are as follows.
  a. $X = 4, Y = 2, Z = 3$
  b. $X = 1, Y = 4, Z = 1$
  c. $X = 2, Y = 6, Z = 2$

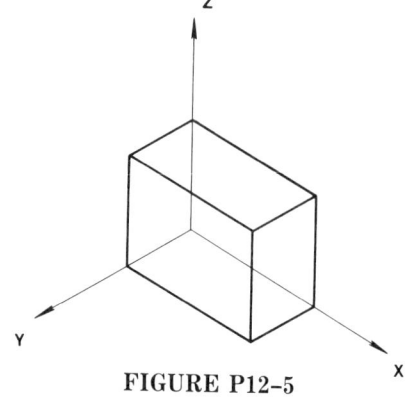

FIGURE P12-5

P12-6 Draw the three rectangular prisms shown in Figure P12-6 in the same positions shown. The size values are as follows.
  a. $X = 6, Y = 5, Z = 2$
  b. $X = 4, Y = 4, Z = 4$
  c. $X = 5, Y = 2, Z = 1$

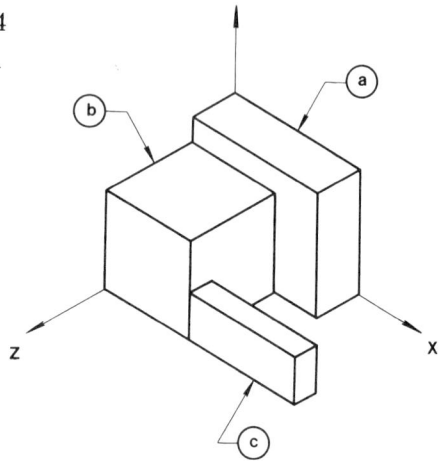

FIGURE P12-6

P12-7 Draw the three rectangular prisms shown in Figure P12-7 in the same positions shown. The size values are as follows.
  a. $X = 8, Y = 8, Z = 1$
  b. $X = 6, Y = 6, Z = 2$
  c. $X = 2, Y = 2, Z = 6$

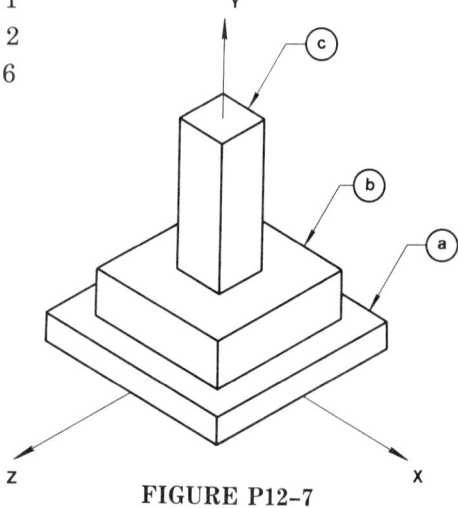

FIGURE P12-7

Chap. 12   Problems

P12-8   Draw the three rectangular prisms shown in Figure P12-8 in the same positions shown. Each prism has a size value equal to 2 × 2 × 5.

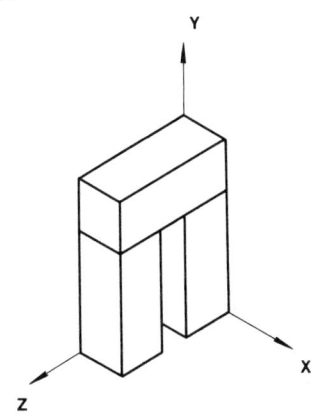

FIGURE P12-8

P12-9   Draw the prisms shown in Figure P12-9. Use the size values and orientation shown.

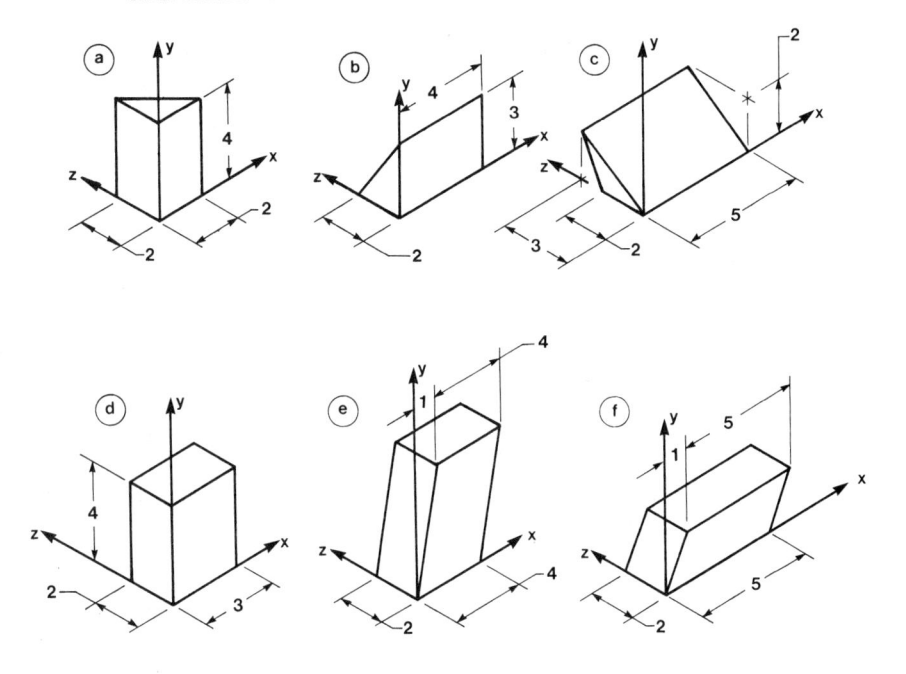

BOTH HEXAGONS ARE 3 ACROSS THE FLATS

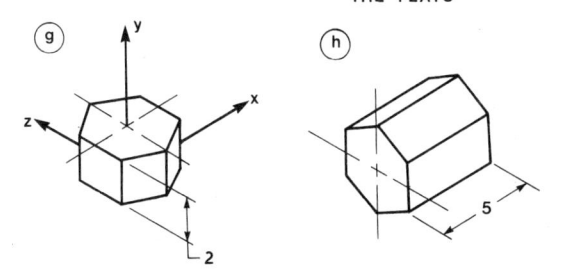

FIGURE P12-9

P12-10 Draw the cylinders shown in Figure P12-10. Use the size values and orientation shown.

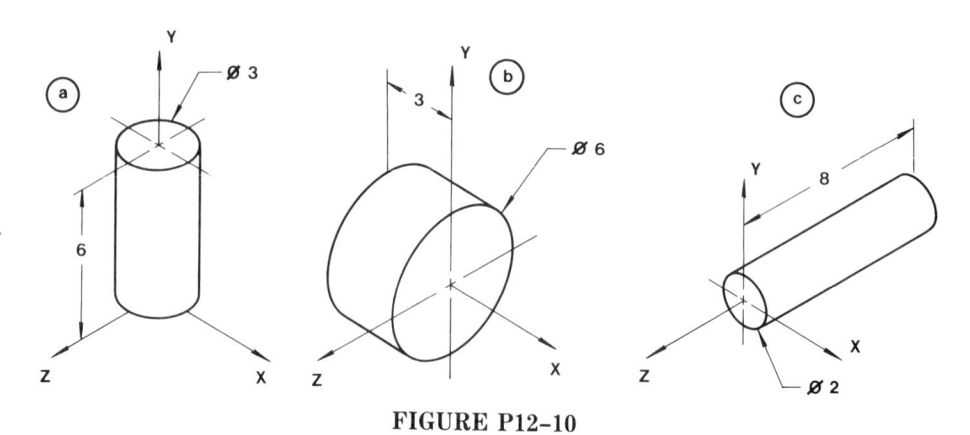

FIGURE P12-10

P12-11 Draw the three cylinders as shown in Figure P12-11 in the same positions shown. The size values are as noted below (ϕ = diameter, H = height).

  a. $\phi = 2, H = 4$
  b. $\phi = 4, H = 1$
  c. $\phi = 6, H = 2$

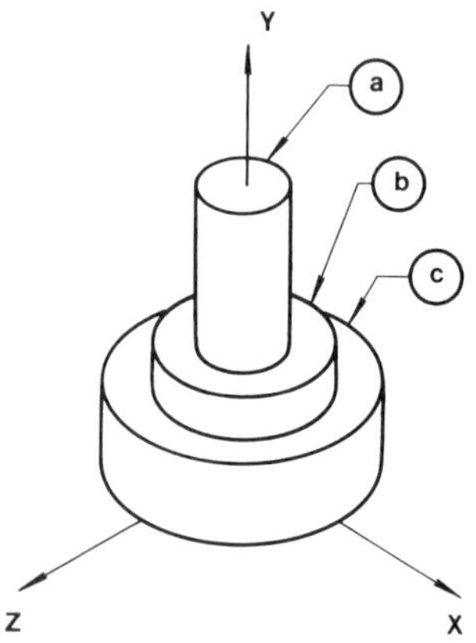

FIGURE P12-11

P12-12 Draw the oblique cylinder shown in Figure P12-12.

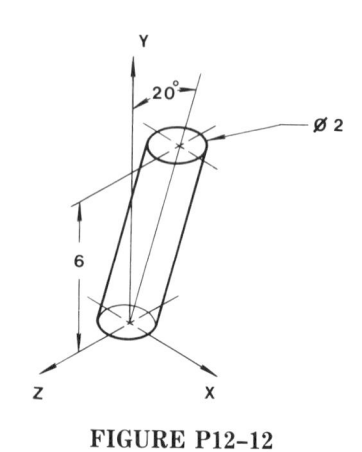

FIGURE P12-12

Chap. 12   Problems   383

P12-13   Draw the pyramids shown in Figure P12-13. Use the size values and orientation shown.

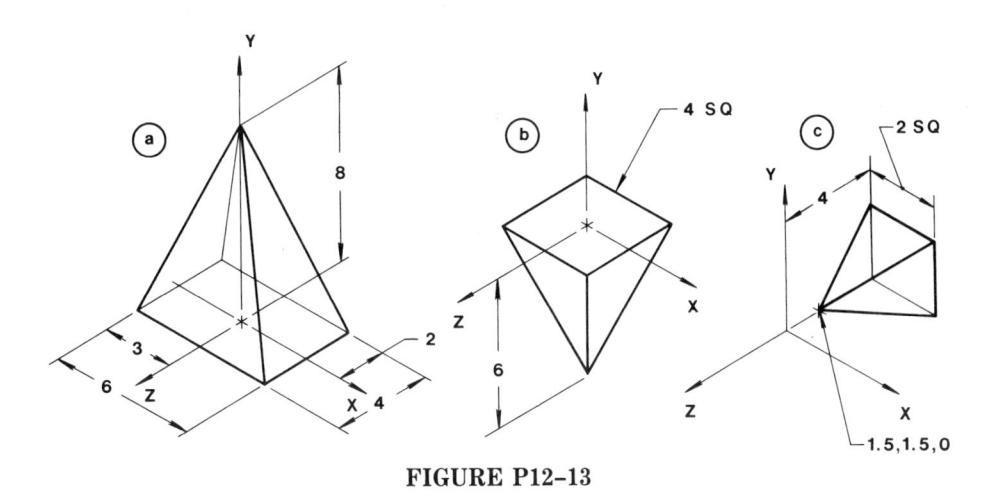

FIGURE P12-13

P12-14   Draw the cones shown in Figure P12-14. Use the size values and orientation shown.

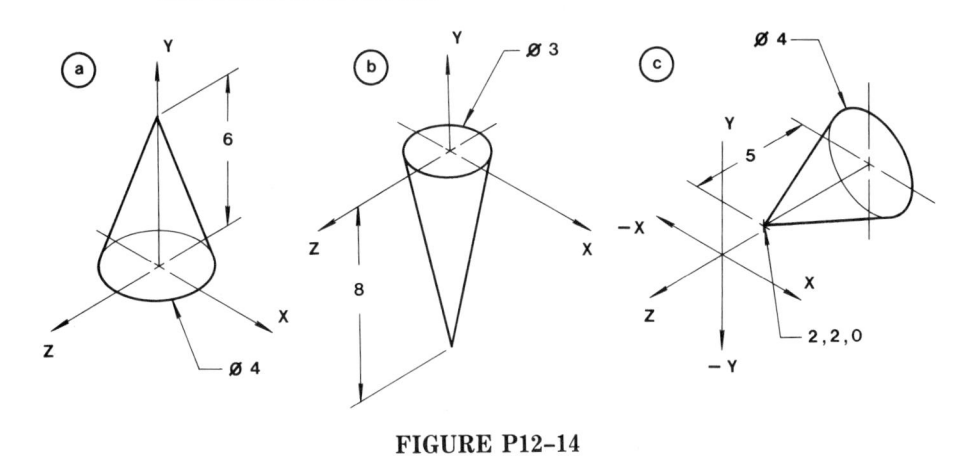

FIGURE P12-14

P12-15   Draw the offset pyramid shown in Figure P12-15. Use the size values and orientation shown.

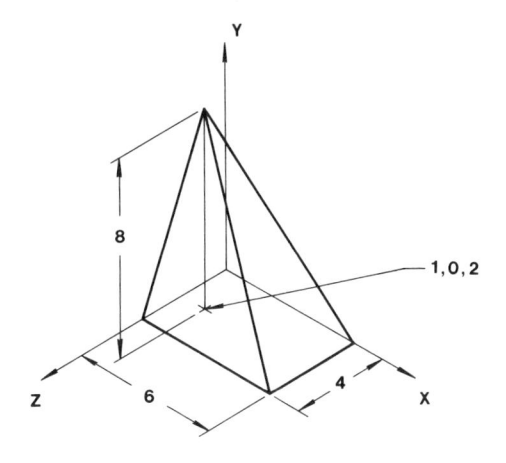

FIGURE P12-15

P12-16 Drawn the oblique cone shown in Figure P12-16. Use the size values and orientation shown.

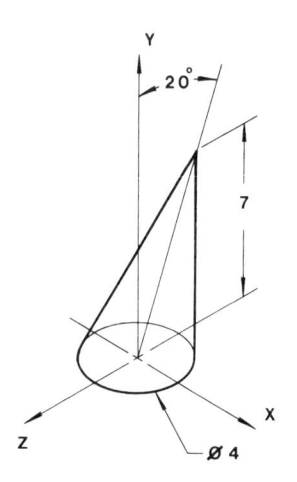

FIGURE P12-16

P12-17 Draw the spheres shown in Figure P12-17. Use the size values and vertex locations shown.

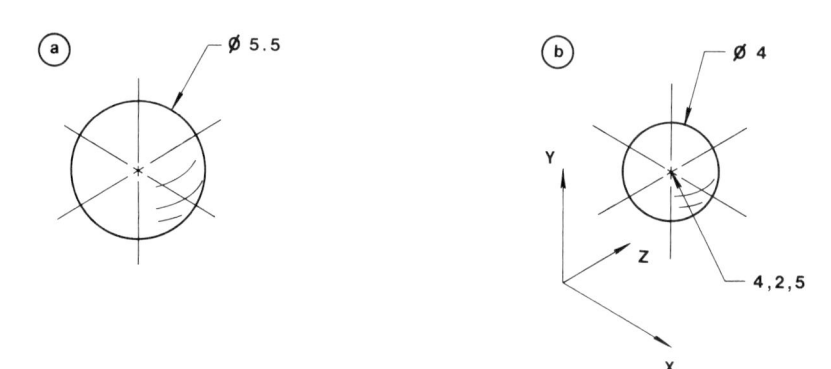

FIGURE P12-17

P12-18 through P12-28 Draw the shapes shown in Figures P12-18 through P12-28. Unless otherwise specified, all dimensions are in millimeters.

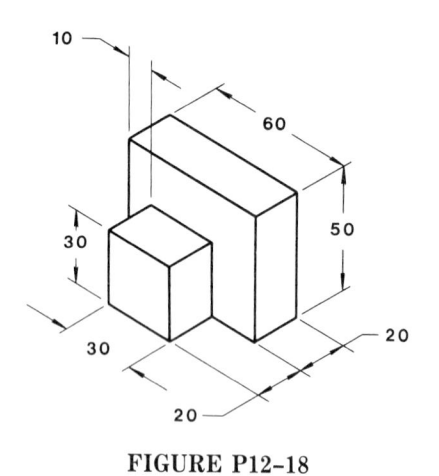

FIGURE P12-18

FIGURE P12-19

Chap. 12   Problems

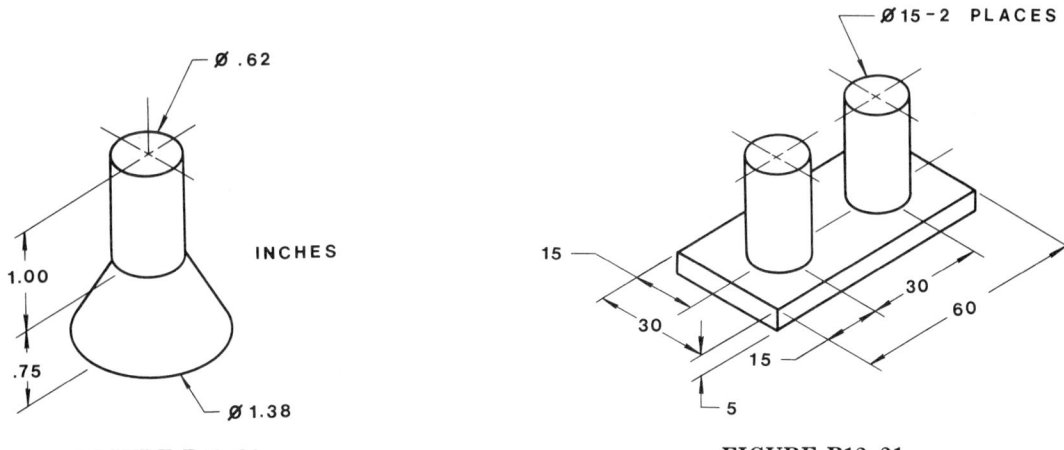

FIGURE P12-20

Ø .62
1.00
.75
Ø 1.38
INCHES

FIGURE P12-21

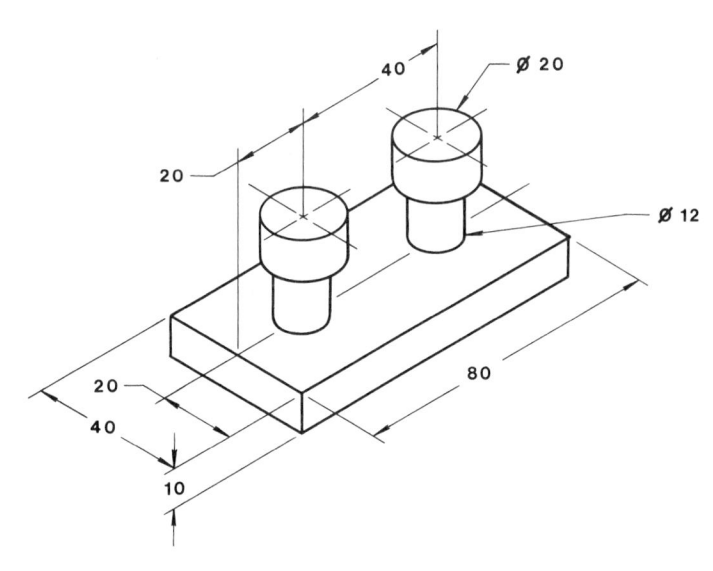

Ø 15 – 2 PLACES
15
30
30
15
60
5

FIGURE P12-22

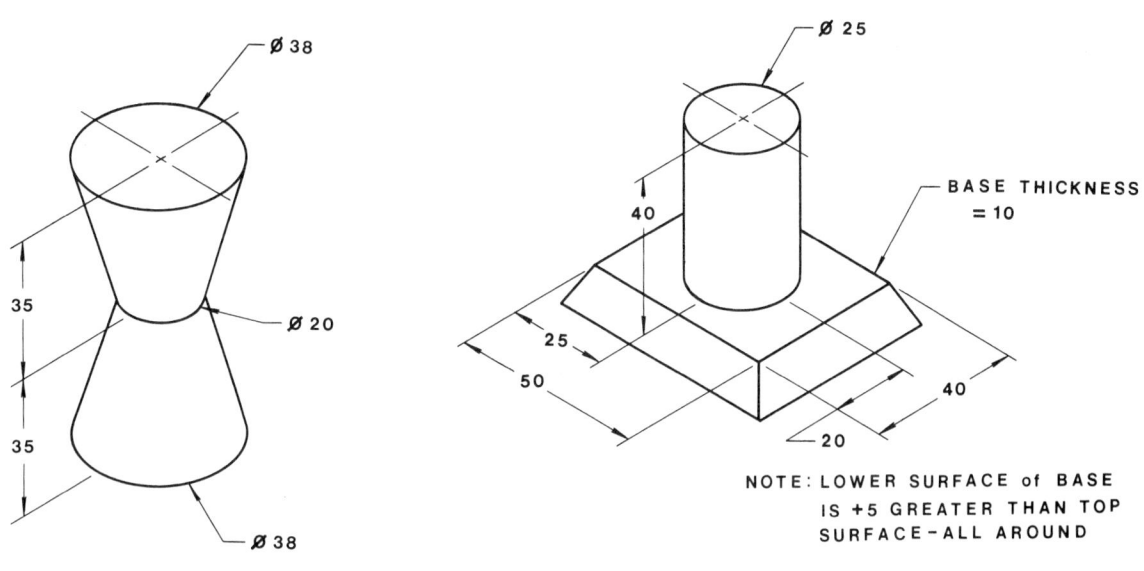

40
Ø 20
20
Ø 12
20
40
80
10

FIGURE P12-23

Ø 38
35
Ø 20
35
Ø 38

FIGURE P12-24

Ø 25
BASE THICKNESS = 10
40
25
50
40
20

NOTE: LOWER SURFACE of BASE IS +5 GREATER THAN TOP SURFACE – ALL AROUND

FIGURE P12-25

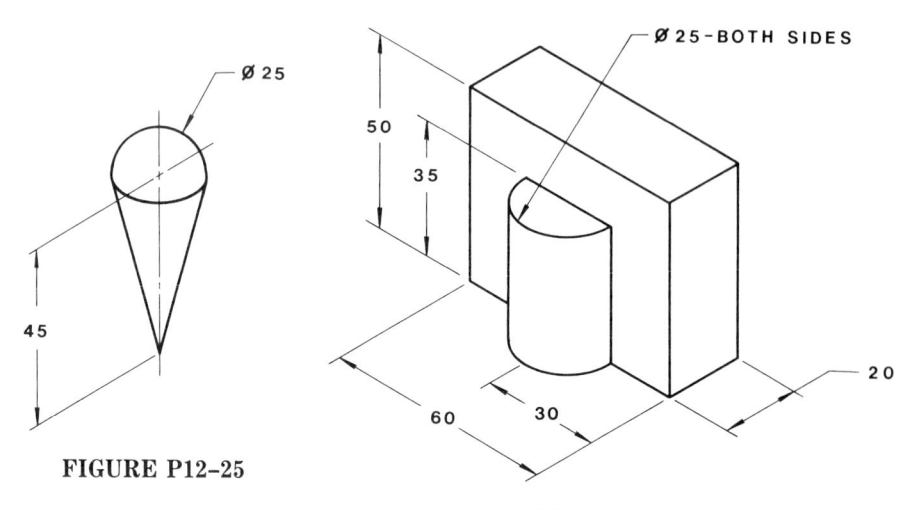

FIGURE P12-26

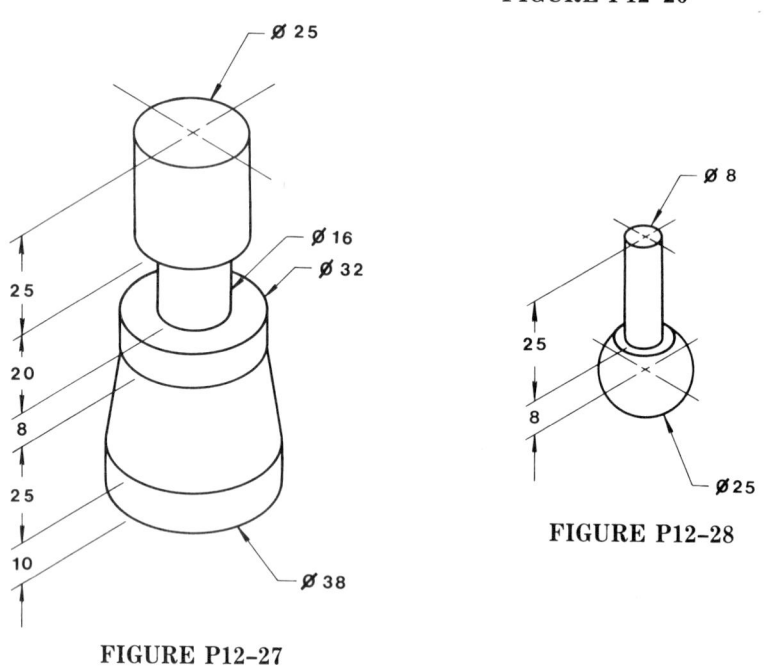

FIGURE P12-27

FIGURE P12-28

P12-29 through P12-40 Draw the truncated and modified shapes shown in Figures P12-29 through P12-40. Unless otherwise specified, all dimensions are in millimeters.

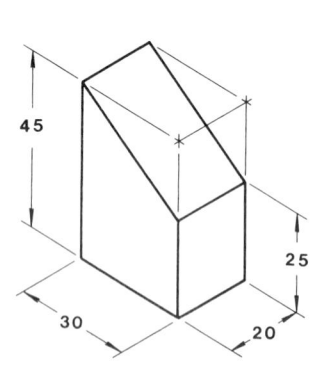

FIGURE P12-29

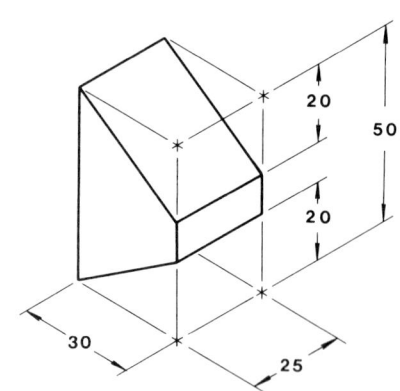

FIGURE P12-30

Chap. 12 Problems

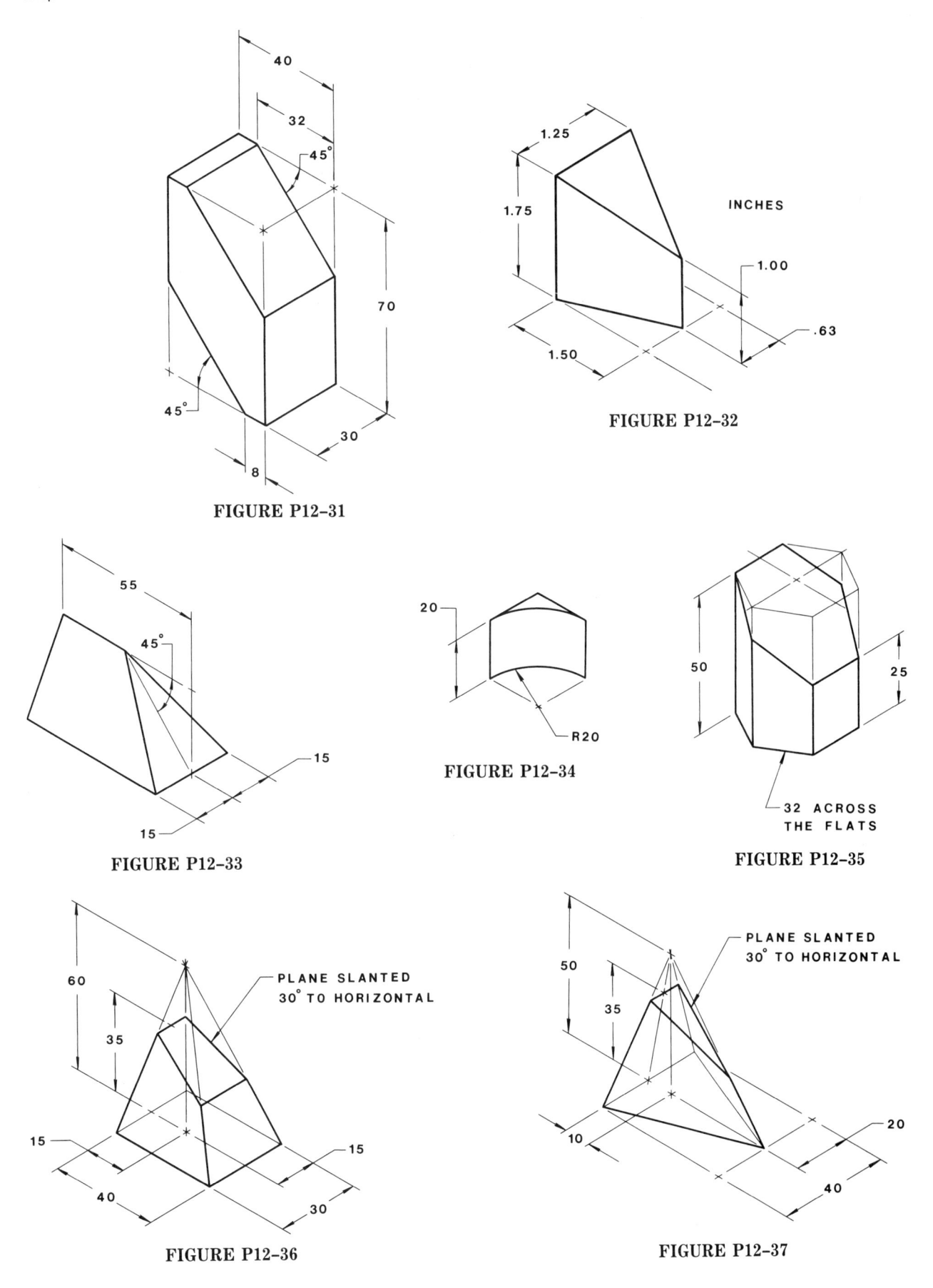

FIGURE P12-31

FIGURE P12-32

FIGURE P12-33

FIGURE P12-34

FIGURE P12-35

FIGURE P12-36

FIGURE P12-37

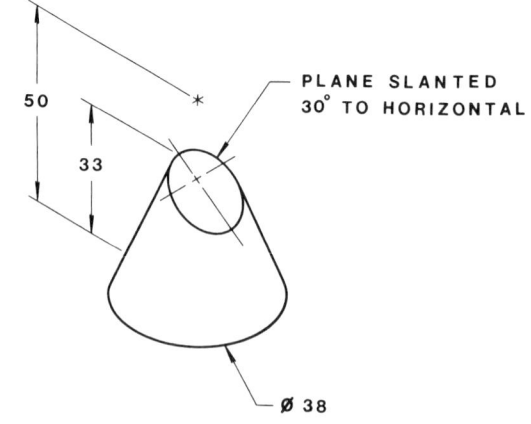

FIGURE P12-38

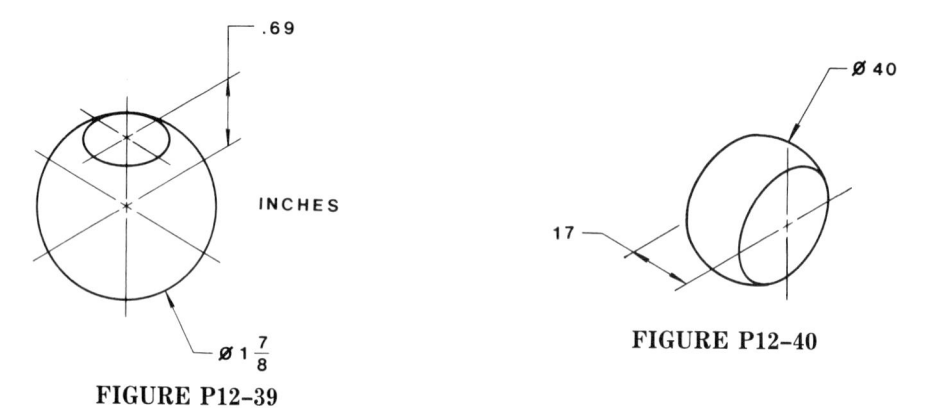

FIGURE P12-39

FIGURE P12-40

For Problems P12-41 through P12-50, redraw the three-dimensional shapes shown in Figures P12-41 through P12-50. The units for the dimensions are as noted below.

P12-41	Inches	**P12-46**	Millimeters
P12-42	Inches	**P12-47**	Millimeters
P12-43	Inches	**P12-48**	Inches
P12-44	Inches	**P12-49**	Millimeters
P12-45	Inches	**P12-50**	Millimeters

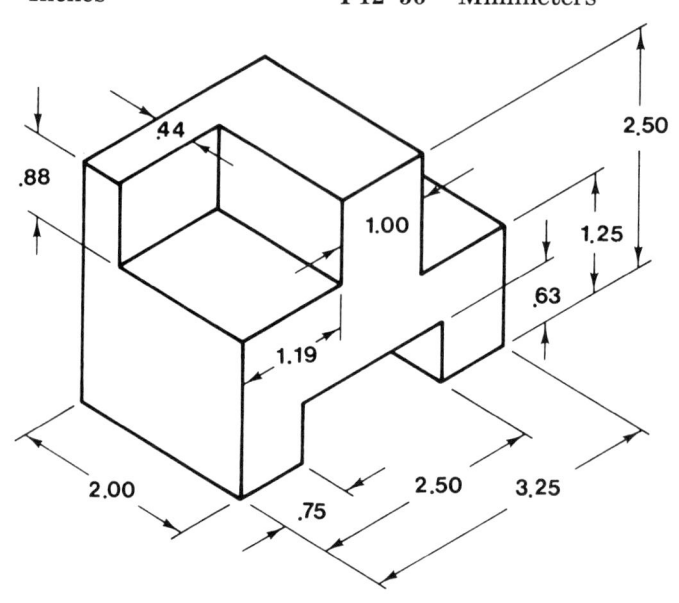

FIGURE P12-41

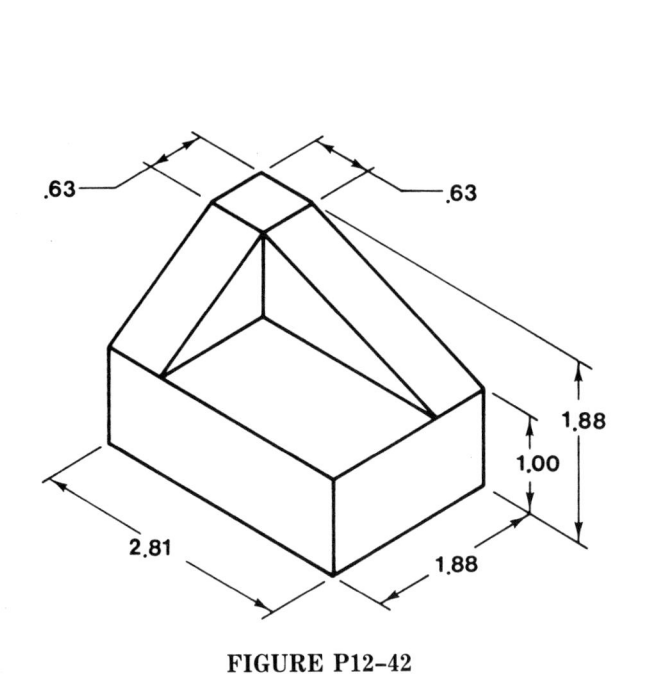

Chap. 12   Problems

FIGURE P12-42

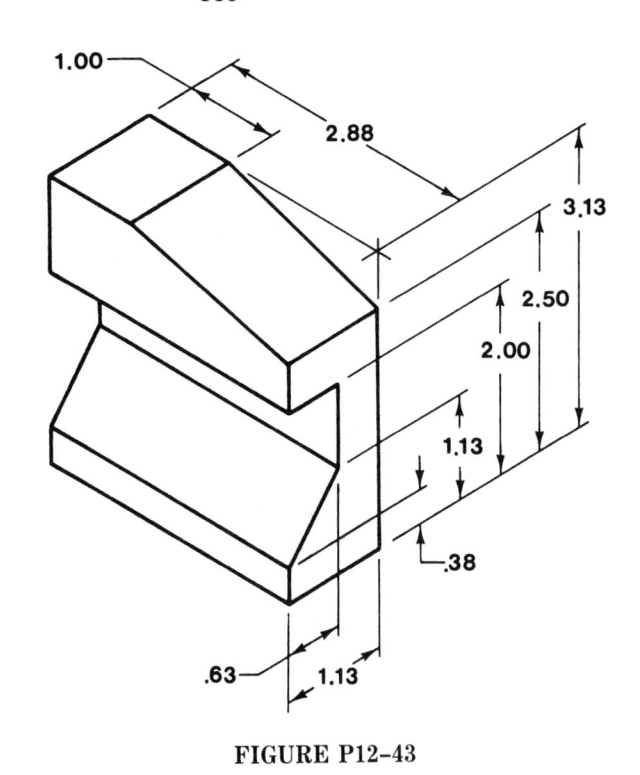

FIGURE P12-43

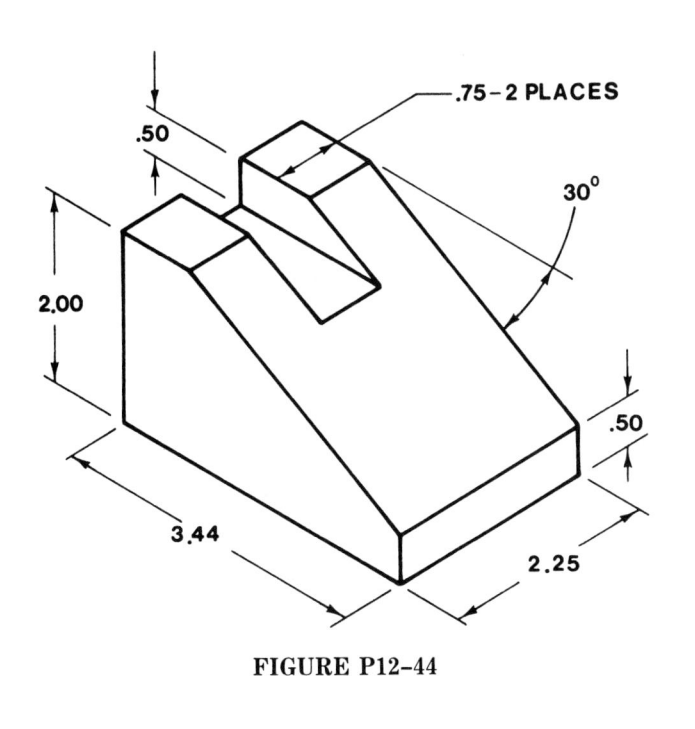

FIGURE P12-44

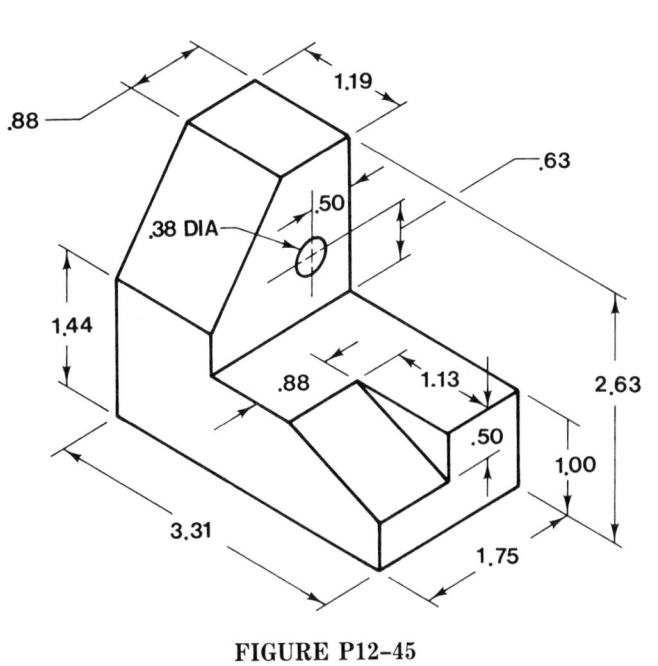

FIGURE P12-45

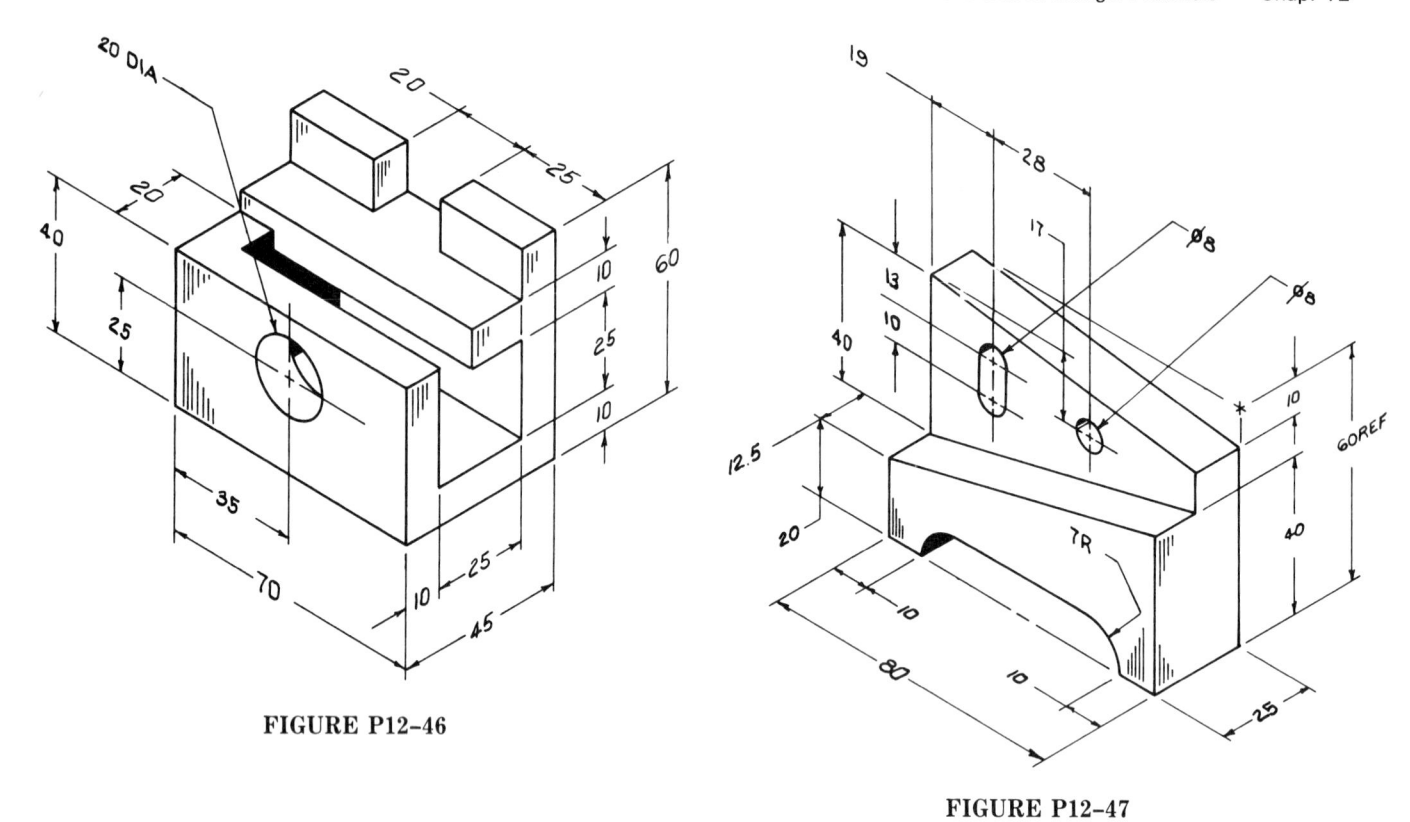

FIGURE P12-46

FIGURE P12-47

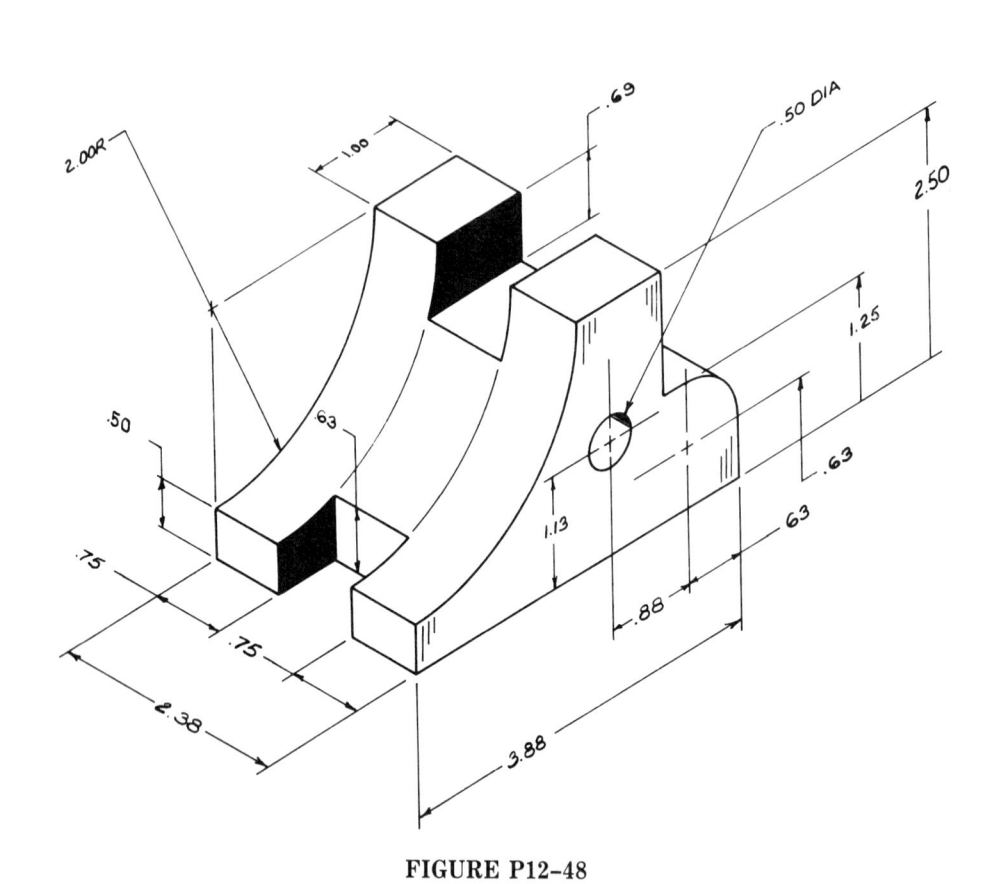

FIGURE P12-48

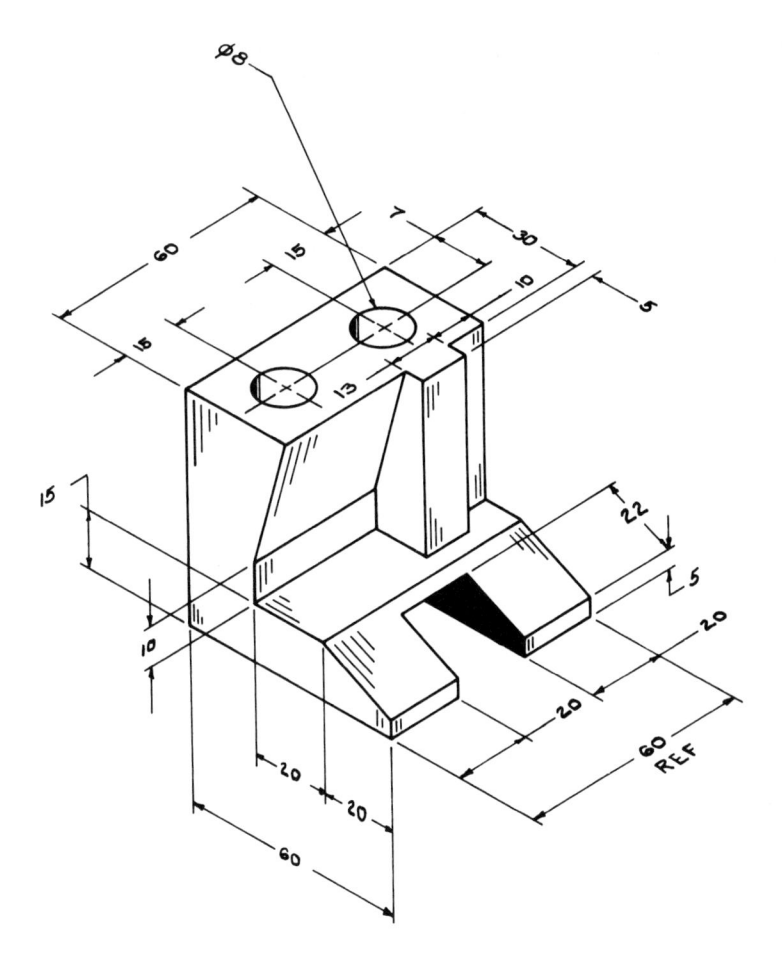

FIGURE P12-49

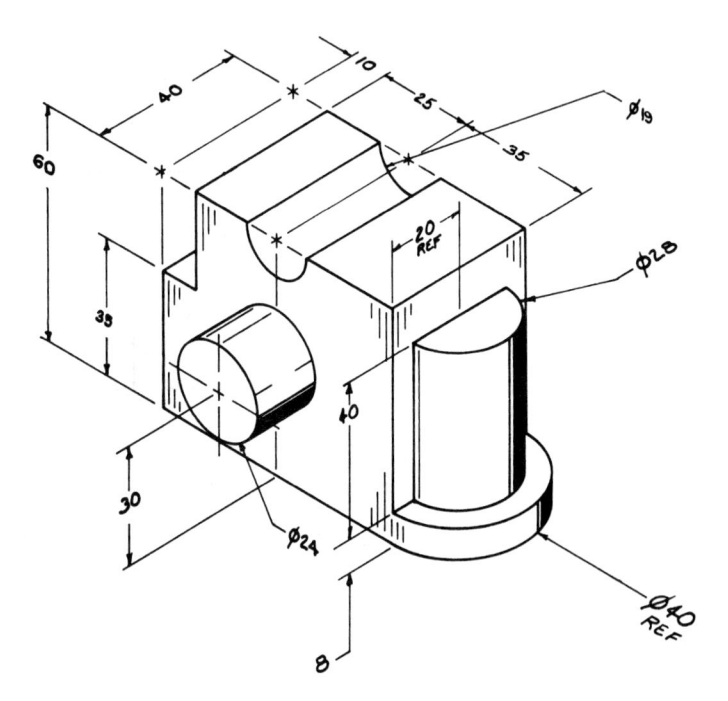

FIGURE P12-50

For Problems P12-51 through P12-57, draw three-dimensional drawings from the orthographic views shown in Figures P12-51 through P12-57. The units for the dimensions are as noted below.

P12-51   Inches
P12-52   Inches
P12-53   Inches
P12-54   Inches

P12-55   Millimeters
P12-56   Millimeters
P12-57   Inches

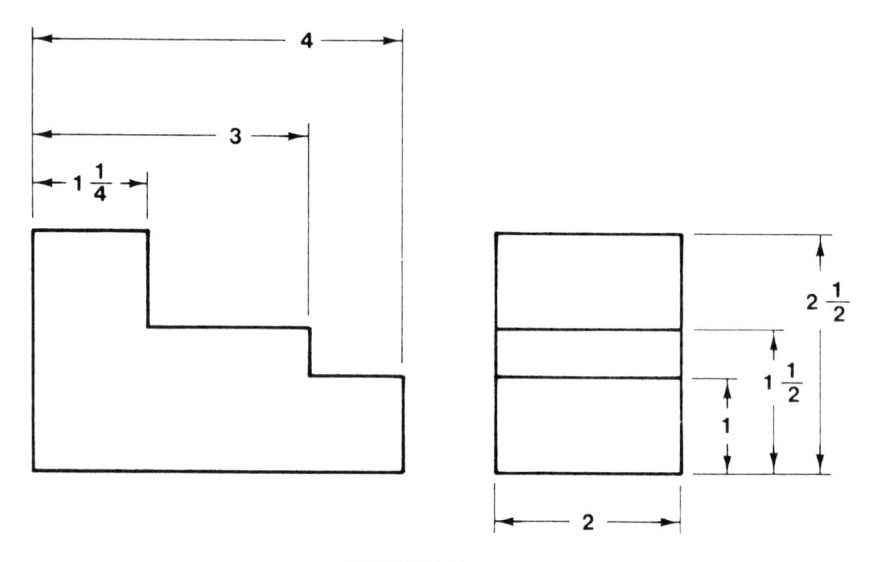

FIGURE P12-51

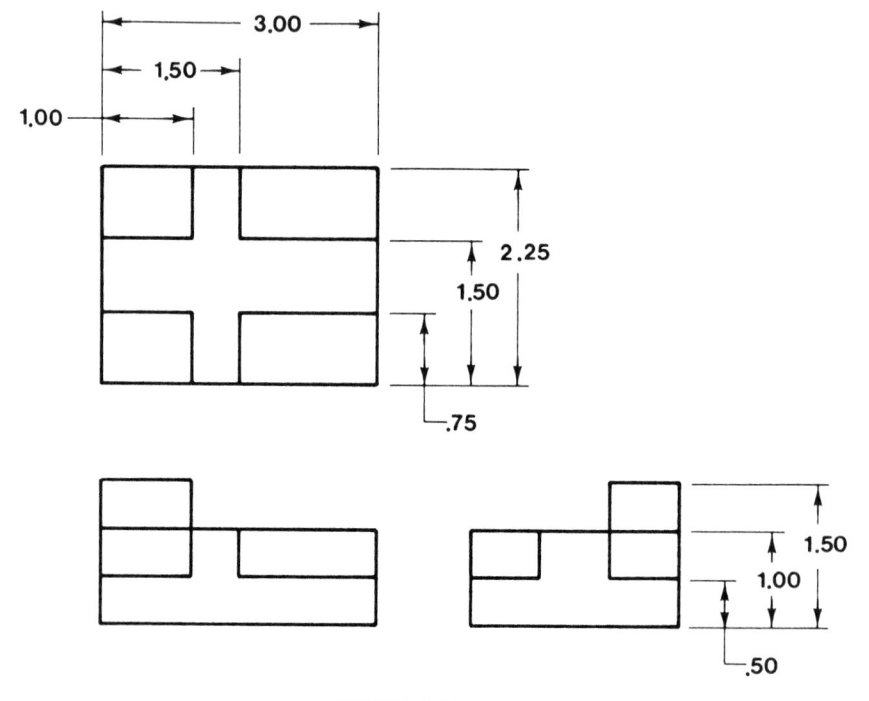

FIGURE P12-52

Chap. 12 Problems

FIGURE P12-53

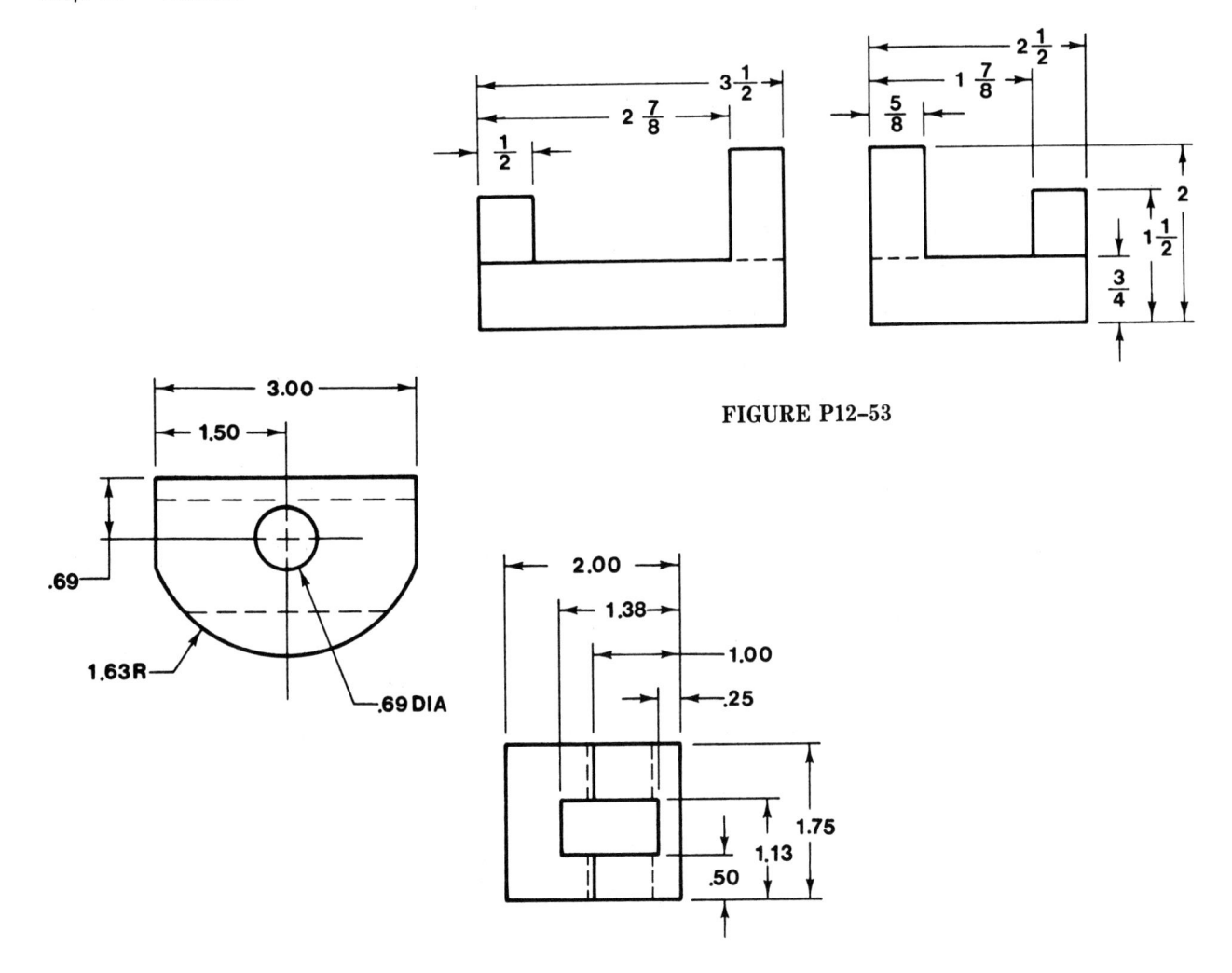

FIGURE P12-54

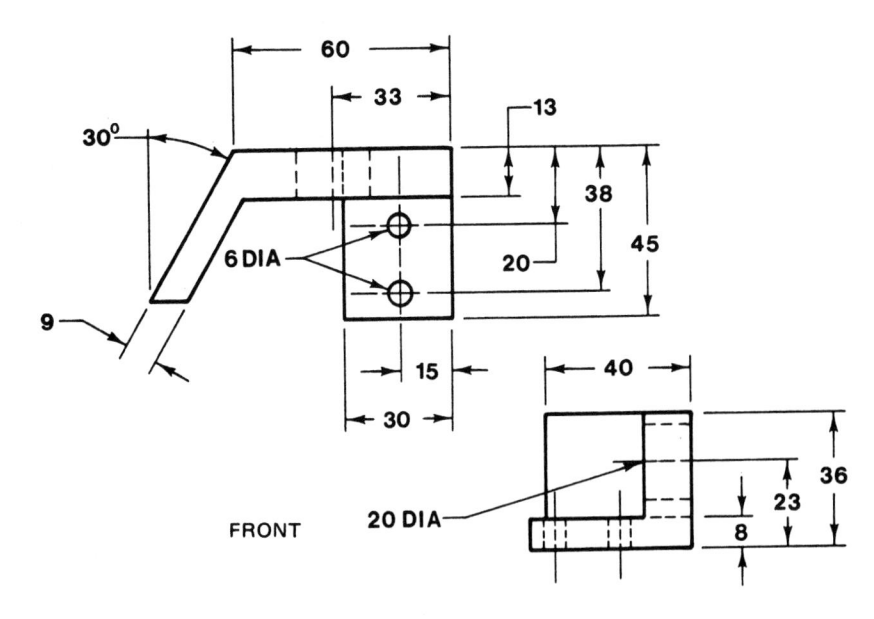

FRONT

FIGURE P12-55

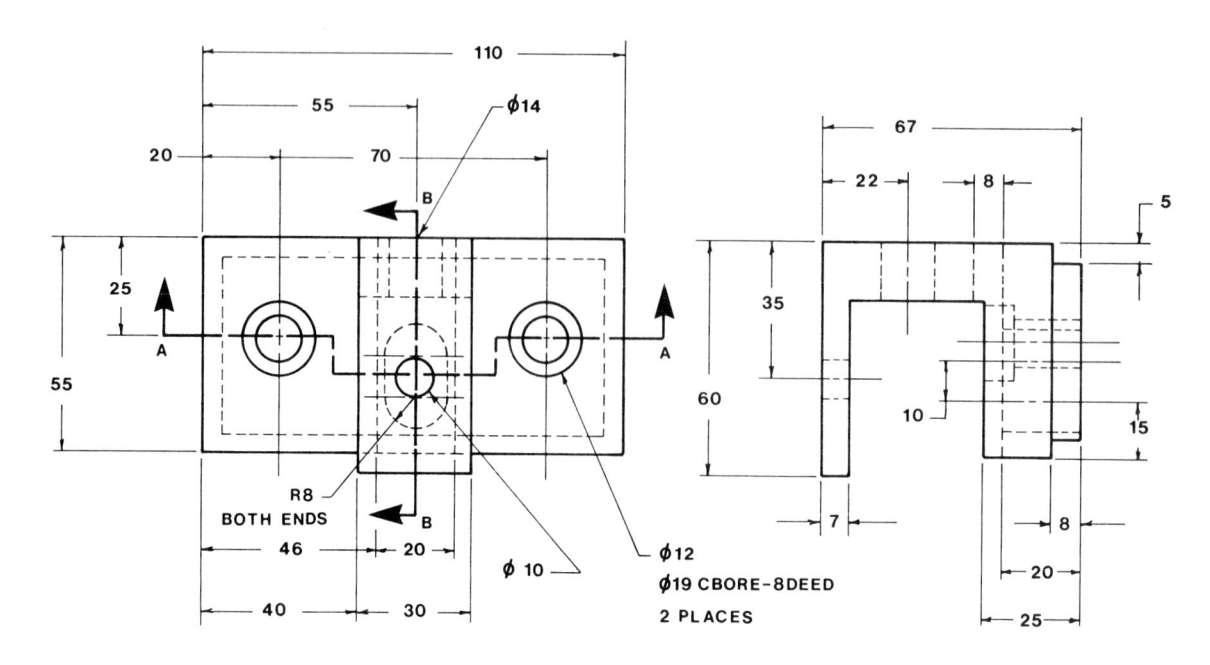

FIGURE P12-56

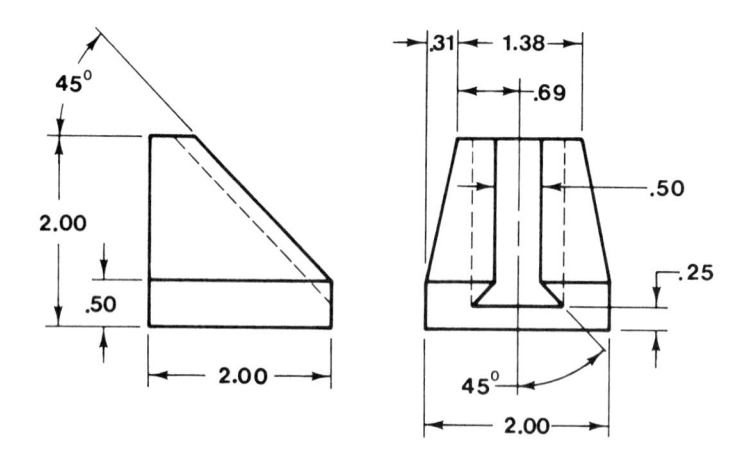

FIGURE P12-57

Chap. 12   Problems

P12-58   Draw an exploded drawing based on the information given in Figure P12-58. All dimensions are in inches.

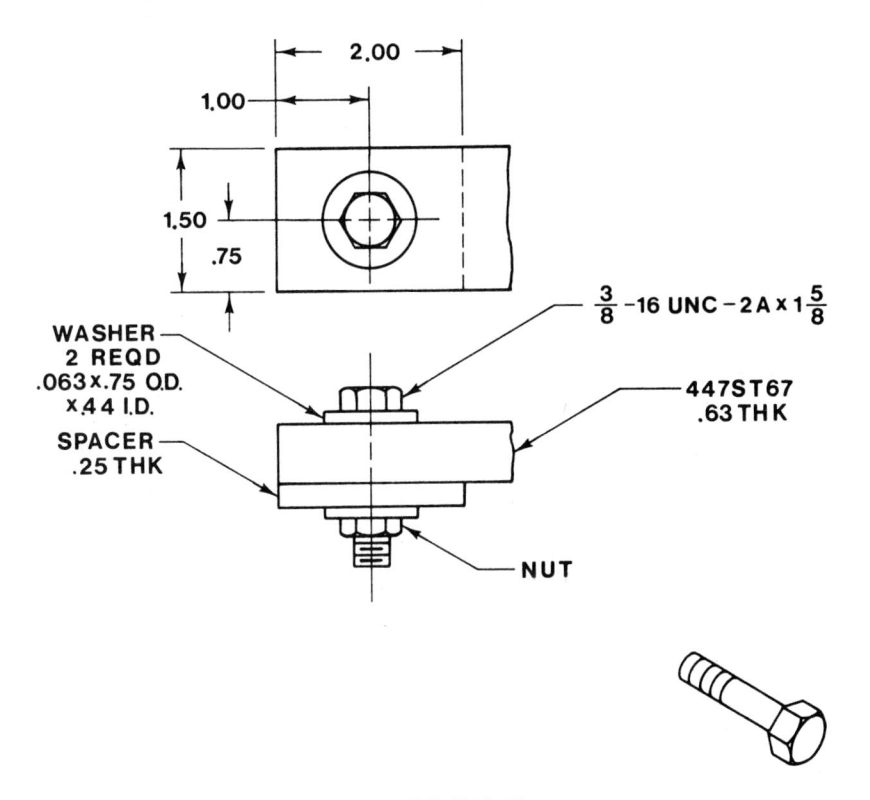

FIGURE P12-58

APPENDICES

A STANDARD THREAD SIZES

Whenever possible, drafters should call for standard thread sizes in their designs. Standard threads may be purchased from many different manufacturers, are completely interchangeable and are relatively inexpensive when compared to "special" thread sizes.

Tables A-1 and A-2 are the UNC and UNF standards. To find the standard size for a given diameter, look up the diameter under the desired thread (UNC or UNF) and read the standard thread size adjacent to it. For example, a $\frac{1}{2}$-diameter thread UNC has 20 threads per inch. The drawing callout would be

$$\frac{1}{4}\text{-20 UNC}$$

A $1\frac{1}{4}$ UNF has 12 threads per inch and would be called out on a drawing as

$$1\frac{1}{4}\text{-12 UNF}$$

The size numbers at the top of the tables are for small diameter threads. For example, a No. 4 UNF has a diameter of 0.112 and 48 threads per inch. The drawing callout would be

$$\#4(0.112)\text{-48 UNF}$$

Tables A-3 and A-4 define the 8 and 12 National (N) series thread. In each case, all diameters in the series are made with the same number of threads. All 8 series threads have 8 threads per inch. All 12 series threads have 12 threads per inch. For example, a $1\frac{7}{8}$ diameter series 8 thread would have the drawing callout

$$1\frac{7}{8}\text{-8 UN}$$

App. A   Standard Thread Sizes

TABLE A-1
UNC

Diameter	Threads per inch, P
1 (0.073)	64
2 (0.086)	56
3 (0.099)	48
4 (0.112)	40
5 (0.125)	40
6 (0.138)	32
8 (0.164)	32
10 (0.190)	24
12 (0.216)	24
$\frac{1}{4}$	20
$\frac{5}{16}$	18
$\frac{3}{8}$	16
$\frac{7}{16}$	14
$\frac{1}{2}$	13
$\frac{1}{2}$	12
$\frac{9}{16}$	12
$\frac{5}{8}$	11
$\frac{3}{4}$	10
$\frac{7}{8}$	9
1	8
$1\frac{1}{8}$	7
$1\frac{1}{4}$	7
$1\frac{3}{8}$	6
$1\frac{1}{2}$	6
$1\frac{3}{4}$	5
2	$4\frac{1}{2}$
$2\frac{1}{4}$	$4\frac{1}{2}$
$2\frac{1}{2}$	4
$2\frac{3}{4}$	4
3	4
$3\frac{1}{4}$	4
$3\frac{1}{2}$	4
$3\frac{3}{4}$	4
4	4

TABLE A-2
UNF

Diameter	Threads per inch, P
0 (0.060)	80
1 (0.073)	72
2 (0.086)	64
3 (0.099)	56
4 (0.112)	48
5 (0.125)	44
6 (0.138)	40
8 (0.164)	36
10 (0.190)	32
12 (0.216)	28
$\frac{1}{4}$	28
$\frac{5}{16}$	24
$\frac{3}{8}$	24
$\frac{7}{16}$	20
$\frac{1}{2}$	20
$\frac{9}{16}$	18
$\frac{5}{8}$	18
$\frac{3}{4}$	16
$\frac{7}{8}$	14
1	12
$1\frac{1}{8}$	12
$1\frac{1}{4}$	12
$1\frac{3}{8}$	12
$1\frac{1}{2}$	12

TABLE A-3
Series 8

Diameter	Threads per inch, P
$1\frac{1}{8}$	8
$1\frac{1}{4}$	8
$1\frac{3}{8}$	8
$1\frac{1}{2}$	8
$1\frac{5}{8}$	8
$1\frac{3}{4}$	8
$1\frac{7}{8}$	8
2	8
$2\frac{1}{8}$	8
$2\frac{1}{4}$	8
$2\frac{1}{2}$	8
$2\frac{3}{4}$	8
3	8
$3\frac{1}{4}$	8
$3\frac{1}{2}$	8
$3\frac{3}{4}$	8
4	8
$4\frac{1}{4}$	8
$4\frac{1}{2}$	8
$4\frac{3}{4}$	8
5	8
$5\frac{1}{4}$	8
$5\frac{1}{2}$	8
$5\frac{3}{4}$	8
6	8

TABLE A-4
Series 12

Diameter	Threads per inch, P
$\frac{1}{2}$	12
$\frac{5}{8}$	12
$1\frac{1}{16}$	12
$\frac{3}{4}$	12
$1\frac{3}{16}$	12
$\frac{7}{8}$	12
$\frac{15}{16}$	12
$1\frac{1}{16}$	12
$1\frac{3}{16}$	12
$1\frac{5}{16}$	12
$1\frac{7}{16}$	12
$1\frac{5}{8}$	12
$1\frac{3}{4}$	12
$1\frac{7}{8}$	12
2	12
$2\frac{1}{8}$	12
$2\frac{1}{4}$	12
$2\frac{3}{8}$	12
$2\frac{1}{2}$	12
$2\frac{5}{8}$	12
$2\frac{3}{4}$	12
$2\frac{7}{8}$	12
3	12
$3\frac{1}{8}$	12
$3\frac{1}{4}$	12
$3\frac{3}{8}$	12
$3\frac{1}{2}$	12
$3\frac{5}{8}$	12
$3\frac{3}{4}$	12
$3\frac{7}{8}$	12
4	12
$4\frac{1}{4}$	12
$4\frac{1}{2}$	12
$4\frac{3}{4}$	12
5	12
$5\frac{1}{4}$	12
$5\frac{1}{2}$	12
$5\frac{3}{4}$	12
6	12

B WIRE AND SHEET METAL GAGES

Gage	Thickness	Gage	Thickness
000 000	0.5800	18	0.0403
00 000	0.5165	19	0.0359
0 000	0.4600	20	0.0320
000	0.4096	21	0.0285
00	0.3648	22	0.0253
0	0.3249	23	0.0226
1	0.2893	24	0.0201
2	0.2576	25	0.0179
3	0.2294	26	0.0159
4	0.2043	27	0.0142
5	0.1819	28	0.0126
6	0.1620	29	0.0113
7	0.1443	30	0.0100
8	0.1285	31	0.0089
9	0.1144	32	0.0080
10	0.1019	33	0.0071
11	0.0907	34	0.0063
12	0.0808	35	0.0056
13	0.0720	36	0.0050
14	0.0641	37	0.0045
15	0.0571	38	0.0040
16	0.0508	39	0.0035
17	0.0453	40	0.0031

C PAPER SIZES

Size	Dimensions (in.)
A	$8\frac{1}{2} \times 11$
B	11×17
C	17×22
D	22×34
E	34×44
J	Roll size

D FIT TOLERANCES

CLEARANCE FITS - Metric   HOLE BASIS

BASIC SIZE		LOOSE RUNNING HOLE SHAFT FIT H11 c11	FREE RUNNING HOLE SHAFT FIT H9 c9	CLOSE RUNNING HOLE SHAFT FIT H8 f7	SLIDING HOLE SHAFT FIT H7 g6	LOCATIONAL HOLE SHAFT FIT H7 h6
1	Max	1.060 0.940 0.180	1.025 0.980 0.070	1.014 0.994 0.030	1.010 0.998 0.018	1.010 1.000 0.016
	Min	1.000 0.880 0.060	1.000 0.955 0.020	1.000 0.984 0.006	1.000 0.992 0.002	1.000 0.994 0.000
1.2	Max	1.260 1.140 0.180	1.225 1.180 0.070	1.214 1.194 0.030	1.210 1.198 0.018	1.210 1.200 0.016
	Min	1.200 1.080 0.060	1.200 1.155 0.020	1.200 1.184 0.006	1.200 1.192 0.002	1.200 1.194 0.000
1.6	Max	1.660 1.540 0.180	1.625 1.580 0.070	1.614 1.594 0.030	1.610 1.598 0.018	1.610 1.600 0.016
	Min	1.600 1.480 0.060	1.600 1.555 0.020	1.600 1.584 0.006	1.600 1.592 0.002	1.600 1.594 0.000
2	Max	2.060 1.940 0.180	2.025 1.980 0.070	2.014 1.994 0.030	2.010 1.998 0.018	2.010 2.000 0.016
	Min	2.000 1.880 0.060	2.000 1.955 0.020	2.000 1.984 0.006	2.000 1.992 0.002	2.000 1.994 0.000
2.5	Max	2.560 2.440 0.180	2.525 2.480 0.070	2.514 2.494 0.030	2.510 2.498 0.018	2.510 2.500 0.016
	Min	2.500 2.380 0.060	2.500 2.455 0.020	2.500 2.484 0.006	2.500 2.492 0.002	2.500 2.492 0.002
3	Max	3.060 2.940 0.180	3.025 2.980 0.070	3.014 2.994 0.030	3.010 2.998 0.018	3.010 3.000 0.016
	Min	3.000 2.880 0.060	3.000 2.955 0.020	3.000 2.984 0.006	3.000 2.992 0.002	3.000 2.994 0.000
4	Max	4.075 3.930 0.220	4.030 3.970 0.090	4.018 3.990 0.040	4.012 3.996 0.024	4.012 4.000 0.020
	Min	4.000 3.855 0.070	4.000 3.940 0.030	4.000 3.978 0.010	4.000 3.988 0.004	4.000 3.992 0.000
5	Max	5.075 4.930 0.220	5.030 4.970 0.090	5.018 4.990 0.040	5.012 4.996 0.024	5.012 5.000 0.020
	Min	5.000 4.855 0.070	5.000 4.940 0.030	5.000 4.978 0.010	5.000 4.988 0.004	5.000 4.992 0.000
6	Max	6.075 5.930 0.220	6.030 5.970 0.090	6.012 5.996 0.040	6.012 5.996 0.024	6.012 6.000 0.020
	Min	6.000 5.855 0.070	6.000 5.940 0.030	6.000 5.978 0.010	6.000 5.988 0.004	6.000 5.992 0.000
8	Max	8.090 7.920 0.260	8.036 7.960 0.112	8.022 7.987 0.050	8.015 7.995 0.029	8.015 8.000 0.024
	Min	8.000 7.830 0.080	8.000 7.924 0.040	8.000 7.972 0.013	8.000 7.986 0.005	8.000 7.991 0.000
10	Max	10.090 9.920 0.112	10.036 9.960 0.260	10.022 9.987 0.050	10.015 9.995 0.029	10.015 10.000 0.024
	Min	10.000 9.924 0.080	10.000 9.924 0.080	10.000 9.972 0.013	10.000 9.986 0.005	10.000 9.991 0.000
12	Max	12.110 11.905 0.315	12.043 11.956 0.136	12.027 11.984 0.061	12.018 11.994 0.035	12.018 12.000 0.029
	Min	12.000 11.795 0.095	12.000 11.907 0.050	12.000 11.966 0.016	12.000 11.983 0.006	12.000 11.989 0.000
16	Max	16.110 15.905 0.315	16.043 15.950 0.136	16.018 15.984 0.061	16.018 15.994 0.035	16.018 16.000 0.029
	Min	16.000 15.795 0.095	16.000 15.907 0.050	16.000 15.966 0.016	16.000 15.983 0.006	16.000 15.989 0.000
20	Max	20.130 19.890 0.370	20.052 19.935 0.169	20.033 19.980 0.074	20.021 19.993 0.041	20.021 20.000 0.034
	Min	20.000 19.760 0.110	20.000 19.880 0.065	20.000 19.959 0.020	20.000 19.980 0.007	20.000 19.987 0.000
25	Max	25.130 24.890 0.370	25.052 24.935 0.169	25.033 24.980 0.074	25.021 24.993 0.041	25.021 25.000 0.034
	Min	25.000 24.760 0.110	25.000 24.883 0.065	25.000 24.959 0.020	25.000 24.980 0.007	25.000 24.987 0.000

CLEARANCE FITS - Metric   SHAFT BASIS

BASIC SIZE		LOOSE RUNNING HOLE C11	SHAFT h11	FIT	FREE RUNNING HOLE D9	SHAFT h9	FIT	CLOSE RUNNING HOLE F8	SHAFT h9	FIT	SLIDING HOLE G7	SHAFT H6	FIT	LOCATIONAL CLEARANCE HOLE H7	SHAFT h6	FIT
1	Max	1.120	1.000	0.180	1.045	1.000	0.070	1.020	1.000	0.030	1.012	1.000	0.018	1.010	1.000	0.016
	Min	1.060	0.940	0.060	1.020	0.975	0.020	1.006	0.990	0.006	1.002	0.994	0.002	1.000	0.994	0.000
1.2	Max	1.320	1.200	0.180	1.245	1.200	0.070	1.220	1.200	0.030	1.212	1.200	0.018	1.210	1.200	0.016
	Min	1.260	1.140	0.060	1.220	1.175	0.020	1.206	1.190	0.006	1.202	1.194	0.002	1.200	1.194	0.000
1.6	Max	1.720	1.600	0.180	1.645	1.600	0.070	1.620	1.600	0.030	1.612	1.600	0.018	1.610	1.600	0.016
	Min	1.660	1.540	0.060	1.620	1.575	0.020	1.606	1.590	0.006	1.602	1.594	0.002	1.600	1.594	0.000
2	Max	2.120	2.000	0.180	2.045	2.000	0.070	2.020	2.000	0.030	2.012	2.000	0.018	2.010	2.000	0.016
	Min	2.060	1.940	0.060	2.020	1.975	0.020	2.006	1.990	0.006	2.002	1.994	0.002	2.000	1.994	0.000
2.5	Max	2.620	2.500	0.180	2.545	2.500	0.070	2.520	2.500	0.030	2.512	2.500	0.018	2.510	2.500	0.016
	Min	2.560	2.440	0.060	2.520	2.470	0.020	2.506	2.490	0.006	2.502	2.494	0.002	2.500	2.494	0.000
3	Max	3.120	3.000	0.180	3.045	3.000	0.070	3.020	3.000	0.030	3.012	3.000	0.018	3.010	3.000	0.016
	Min	3.060	2.940	0.060	3.020	2.975	0.020	3.006	2.990	0.006	3.002	2.994	0.002	3.000	2.994	0.000
4	Max	4.145	4.000	0.220	4.060	4.000	0.090	4.016	4.000	0.024	4.016	4.000	0.024	4.012	4.000	0.020
	Min	4.070	3.925	0.070	4.030	3.970	0.030	4.004	3.988	0.010	4.004	3.992	0.004	4.000	3.992	0.000
5	Max	5.145	5.000	0.220	5.060	5.000	0.090	5.028	5.000	0.040	5.016	5.000	0.024	5.012	5.000	0.020
	Min	5.070	4.925	0.070	5.030	4.970	0.030	5.010	4.988	0.010	5.004	4.992	0.004	5.000	4.992	0.000
6	Max	6.145	6.000	0.220	6.060	6.000	0.090	6.028	6.000	0.040	6.016	6.000	0.024	6.012	6.000	0.020
	Min	6.070	5.925	0.070	6.030	5.970	0.030	6.010	5.988	0.010	6.004	5.992	0.004	6.000	5.992	0.000
8	Max	8.170	8.000	0.260	8.076	8.000	0.112	8.035	8.000	0.050	8.020	8.000	0.029	8.015	8.000	0.024
	Min	8.080	7.910	0.080	8.040	7.964	0.040	8.013	7.985	0.013	8.005	7.991	0.005	8.000	7.991	0.000
10	Max	10.170	10.000	0.260	10.076	10.000	0.112	10.035	10.000	0.050	10.020	10.000	0.029	10.015	10.000	0.024
	Min	10.080	9.910	0.080	10.040	9.964	0.040	10.013	9.985	0.013	10.005	9.991	0.005	10.000	9.991	0.000
12	Max	12.205	12.000	0.315	12.093	12.000	0.136	12.043	12.000	0.061	12.024	12.000	0.035	12.018	12.000	0.029
	Min	12.095	11.890	0.095	12.050	11.957	0.050	12.006	11.982	0.016	12.006	11.989	0.006	12.000	11.989	0.000
16	Max	16.205	16.000	0.315	16.093	16.000	0.136	16.053	16.000	0.061	16.024	16.000	0.035	16.018	16.000	0.029
	Min	16.095	15.890	0.095	16.050	15.957	0.050	16.016	15.982	0.016	16.006	15.989	0.006	16.000	15.989	0.000
20	Max	20.240	20.000	0.370	20.117	20.000	0.169	20.053	20.000	0.074	20.028	20.000	0.041	20.021	20.000	0.034
	Min	20.110	19.870	0.110	20.065	19.948	0.065	20.020	19.979	0.020	20.007	19.987	0.007	20.000	19.987	0.000
25	Max	25.240	25.000	0.370	25.117	25.000	0.169	25.053	25.000	0.074	25.028	25.000	0.041	25.021	25.000	0.034
	Min	25.110	24.870	0.110	25.065	24.948	0.065	25.020	24.979	0.020	25.007	24.987	0.007	25.000	24.987	0.000

TRANSITION AND INTERFERENCE FITS – Metric
HOLE BASIS

BASIC SIZE		LOCATIONAL TRANSITION HOLE H7 / SHAFT k6 / FIT	LOCATIONAL TRANSITION HOLE H7 / SHAFT n6 / FIT	LOCATIONAL INTERFERENCE HOLE H7 / SHAFT p6 / FIT	MEDIUM DRIVE HOLE H7 / SHAFT s6 / FIT	FORCE HOLE H7 / SHAFT u6 / FIT
1	Max	1.010 1.006 +0.010	1.010 1.010 +0.006	1.010 1.012 +0.004	1.010 1.020 −0.004	1.010 1.024 −0.008
	Min	1.000 1.000 −0.006	1.000 1.004 −0.010	1.000 1.006 −0.012	1.000 1.014 −0.020	1.000 1.018 −0.024
1.2	Max	1.210 1.206 +0.010	1.210 1.210 +0.006	1.210 1.212 +0.004	1.210 1.220 −0.004	1.210 1.224 −0.008
	Min	1.200 1.200 −0.006	1.200 1.204 −0.010	1.200 1.206 −0.012	1.200 1.214 −0.020	1.200 1.218 −0.024
1.6	Max	1.610 1.606 +0.010	1.610 1.610 +0.006	1.610 1.612 +0.004	1.610 1.620 −0.004	1.610 1.624 −0.008
	Min	1.600 1.600 −0.006	1.600 1.606 −0.010	1.600 1.606 −0.012	1.600 1.614 −0.020	1.600 1.618 −0.024
2	Max	2.010 2.006 +0.010	2.010 2.010 +0.006	2.010 2.010 +0.004	2.010 2.020 −0.004	2.010 2.024 −0.008
	Min	2.000 2.000 −0.006	2.000 2.004 −0.010	2.000 2.006 −0.012	2.000 2.014 −0.020	2.000 2.018 −0.024
2.5	Max	2.510 2.506 +0.010	2.510 2.510 +0.006	2.510 2.512 +0.004	2.510 2.520 −0.004	2.510 2.524 −0.008
	Min	2.500 2.500 −0.006	2.500 2.504 −0.010	2.500 2.506 −0.012	2.500 2.514 −0.020	2.500 2.518 −0.024
3	Max	3.010 3.006 +0.010	3.010 3.010 +0.006	3.010 3.012 +0.004	3.010 3.020 −0.004	3.010 3.024 −0.008
	Min	3.000 3.000 −0.006	3.000 3.004 −0.010	3.000 3.006 +0.012	3.000 3.014 −0.020	3.000 3.018 −0.024
4	Max	4.012 4.009 +0.011	4.012 4.016 +0.004	4.012 4.020 0.000	4.012 4.027 −0.007	4.012 4.031 −0.011
	Min	4.000 4.001 −0.009	4.000 4.008 −0.016	4.000 4.012 −0.020	4.000 4.019 −0.027	4.000 4.023 −0.031
5	Max	5.012 5.009 +0.011	5.012 5.016 +0.004	5.012 5.020 0.000	5.012 5.027 −0.007	5.012 5.031 −0.011
	Min	5.000 5.001 −0.009	5.000 5.008 −0.016	5.000 5.012 −0.020	5.000 5.019 −0.027	5.000 5.023 −0.031
6	Max	6.012 6.009 +0.011	6.012 6.016 +0.004	6.012 6.020 0.000	6.012 6.027 −0.007	6.012 6.031 −0.011
	Min	6.000 6.001 −0.009	6.000 6.008 −0.016	6.000 6.012 −0.020	6.000 6.019 −0.027	6.000 6.023 −0.031
8	Max	8.015 8.010 +0.014	8.015 8.019 +0.005	8.015 8.024 0.000	8.015 8.032 −0.008	8.015 8.037 −0.013
	Min	8.000 8.001 −0.010	8.000 8.010 −0.019	8.000 8.015 −0.024	8.000 8.023 −0.032	8.000 8.023 −0.037
10	Max	10.015 10.010 +0.014	10.015 10.019 +0.005	10.015 10.024 0.000	10.015 10.032 −0.008	10.015 10.037 −0.013
	Min	10.000 10.001 −0.010	10.000 10.010 −0.019	10.000 10.015 −0.024	10.000 10.023 −0.032	10.000 10.028 −0.037
12	Max	12.018 12.012 +0.017	12.018 12.023 +0.006	12.018 12.029 0.000	12.018 12.039 −0.010	12.018 12.044 −0.015
	Min	12.000 12.001 −0.012	12.000 12.012 −0.023	12.000 12.018 −0.029	12.000 12.028 −0.039	12.000 12.033 −0.044
16	Max	16.018 16.012 +0.017	16.018 16.023 +0.006	16.018 16.029 0.000	16.018 16.039 −0.010	16.018 16.044 −0.015
	Min	16.000 16.001 −0.012	16.000 16.012 −0.023	16.000 16.018 −0.029	16.000 16.028 −0.039	16.000 16.033 −0.044
20	Max	20.021 20.015 +0.019	20.021 20.028 +0.006	20.021 20.035 0.000	20.021 20.048 −0.014	20.021 20.054 −0.020
	Min	20.000 20.002 −0.015	20.000 20.015 −0.028	20.000 20.022 −0.035	20.000 20.035 −0.048	20.000 20.041 −0.054
25	Max	25.021 25.015 +0.019	25.021 25.028 +0.006	25.021 25.035 −0.001	25.021 25.048 −0.014	25.021 25.061 −0.027
	Min	25.000 25.002 −0.015	25.000 25.015 −0.028	25.000 25.022 −0.035	25.000 25.035 −0.048	25.000 25.048 −0.061

TRANSITION AND INTERFERENCE FIT - Metric SHAFT BASIS

BASIC SIZE		LOCATIONAL TRANSITION HOLE K7 / SHAFT h6 / FIT	LOCATIONAL TRANSITION HOLE N7 / SHAFT h6 / FIT	LOCATIONAL INTERFERENCE HOLE P7 / SHAFT h6 / FIT	MEDIUM DRIVE HOLE S7 / SHAFT h6 / FIT	FORCE HOLE U7 / SHAFT h6 / FIT
1	Max	1.000 1.000 +0.006	0.996 1.000 +0.002	0.994 1.000 0.002	0.986 1.000 -0.008	0.982 1.000 -0.012
	Min	0.990 0.994 -0.010	0.986 0.954 -0.014	0.984 0.994 -0.016	0.976 0.994 -0.024	0.972 0.994 -0.028
1.2	Max	1.200 1.200 +0.006	1.196 1.200 +0.002	1.194 1.200 0.000	1.186 1.200 -0.008	1.182 1.200 -0.012
	Min	1.190 1.194 -0.010	1.186 1.194 -0.014	1.184 1.194 -0.016	1.176 1.194 -0.024	1.172 1.194 -0.028
1.6	Max	1.600 1.600 +0.006	1.596 1.600 +0.002	1.594 1.600 0.000	1.586 1.600 -0.008	1.582 1.600 -0.012
	Min	1.590 1.594 -0.010	1.586 1.594 -0.014	1.584 1.594 -0.016	1.576 1.594 -0.024	1.572 1.594 -0.028
2	Max	2.000 2.000 +0.006	1.996 2.000 +0.002	1.994 2.000 0.000	1.986 2.000 -0.008	1.982 2.000 -0.012
	Min	1.990 1.994 -0.010	1.986 1.994 -0.014	1.984 1.994 -0.016	1.976 1.994 -0.024	1.972 1.994 -0.028
2.5	Max	2.500 2.500 +0.006	2.496 2.500 +0.002	2.494 2.500 0.000	2.486 2.500 -0.008	2.482 2.500 -0.012
	Min	2.490 2.494 -0.010	2.486 2.494 -0.014	2.484 2.494 -0.016	2.476 2.494 -0.024	2.472 2.494 -0.028
3	Max	3.000 3.000 +0.006	2.996 3.000 +0.002	2.994 3.000 0.000	2.986 3.000 -0.008	2.982 3.000 -0.012
	Min	2.990 2.994 -0.010	2.986 2.994 -0.014	2.984 2.994 -0.016	2.976 2.994 -0.024	2.972 2.994 -0.028
4	Max	4.003 4.000 +0.011	3.996 4.000 +0.004	3.992 4.000 0.000	3.985 4.000 -0.007	3.981 4.000 -0.011
	Min	3.991 3.992 -0.009	3.984 3.992 -0.016	3.980 3.992 -0.020	3.973 3.992 -0.027	3.969 3.992 -0.031
5	Max	5.003 5.000 +0.011	4.996 5.000 +0.004	4.992 5.000 0.000	4.985 5.000 -0.007	4.981 5.000 -0.011
	Min	4.991 4.992 -0.009	4.984 4.992 -0.016	4.980 4.992 -0.020	4.973 4.992 -0.027	4.969 4.992 -0.031
6	Max	6.003 6.000 +0.011	5.996 6.000 +0.004	5.992 6.000 0.000	5.985 6.000 -0.007	5.981 6.000 -0.011
	Min	5.991 5.992 -0.016	5.984 5.992 -0.016	5.980 5.992 -0.020	5.973 5.992 -0.027	5.969 5.992 -0.031
8	Max	8.005 8.000 +0.014	7.996 8.000 +0.005	7.991 8.000 0.000	7.983 8.000 -0.008	7.978 8.000 -0.013
	Min	7.990 7.991 -0.010	7.981 7.991 -0.019	7.976 7.991 -0.024	7.968 7.991 -0.032	7.963 7.991 -0.037
10	Max	10.005 10.000 +0.014	9.996 10.000 +0.005	9.991 10.000 0.000	9.983 10.000 -0.008	9.978 10.000 -0.013
	Min	9.990 9.991 -0.010	9.981 9.991 -0.019	9.976 9.991 -0.024	9.968 9.991 -0.032	9.963 9.991 -0.037
12	Max	12.006 12.000 +0.017	11.995 12.000 +0.006	11.989 12.000 0.000	11.979 12.000 -0.010	11.974 12.000 -0.015
	Min	11.988 11.989 -0.012	11.977 11.989 -0.023	11.971 11.989 -0.029	11.961 11.989 -0.039	11.956 11.989 -0.044
16	Max	16.006 16.000 +0.017	15.995 16.000 +0.006	15.989 16.000 0.000	15.979 16.000 -0.010	15.974 16.000 -0.015
	Min	15.988 15.989 -0.012	15.997 15.989 -0.023	15.971 15.989 -0.029	15.961 15.989 -0.039	15.956 15.989 -0.044
20	Max	20.006 20.000 +0.019	19.993 20.000 +0.006	19.986 20.000 -0.001	19.973 20.000 -0.014	19.967 20.00 -0.020
	Min	19.985 19.987 -0.015	19.972 19.987 -0.028	19.965 19.987 -0.035	19.952 19.987 -0.048	19.946 19.987 -0.054
25	Max	25.006 25.000 +0.019	24.993 25.000 +0.006	24.986 25.000 -0.001	24.973 25.000 -0.014	24.960 25.000 -0.027
	Min	24.985 24.987 -0.015	24.972 24.987 -0.028	24.965 24.987 -0.035	24.952 24.987 -0.048	24.939 24.987 -0.061

RUNNING AND SLIDING FITS - Inches
HOLE BASIS

ALL VALUES SHOWN BELOW ARE IN THOUSANDS OF AN INCH
(for example 0.5 = 0.0005 inches)

NOMINAL SIZE	Class RC1			Class RC2			Class RC3			Class RC4			Class RC5		
Over - To	Cl	Hole H5	Shaft g4	Cl	Hole H6	Shaft g5	Cl	Hole H7	Shaft f6	Cl	Hole H8	Shaft f7	Cl	Hole H8	Shaft e7
0 - 0.12	0.1 / 0.45	+0.2 / 0	-0.1 / -0.25	0.1 / 0.55	+0.25 / 0	-0.1 / -0.3	0.3 / 0.95	+0.4 / 0	-0.3 / -0.55	0.3 / 1.3	+0.6 / 0	-0.3 / -0.7	0.6 / 1.6	+0.6 / 0	-0.6 / -1.0
0.12 - 0.24	0.15 / 0.5	+0.2 / 0	-0.15 / -0.3	0.15 / 0.65	+0.3 / 0	-0.15 / -0.35	0.4 / 1.12	+0.5 / 0	-0.4 / -0.7	0.4 / 1.6	+0.7 / 0	-0.4 / -0.9	0.8 / 2.0	+0.7 / 0	-0.8 / -1.3
0.24 - 0.40	0.2 / 0.6	+0.25 / 0	-0.2 / -0.35	0.2 / 0.85	+0.4 / 0	-0.2 / -0.45	0.5 / 1.5	+0.6 / 0	-0.5 / -0.9	0.5 / 2.0	+0.9 / 0	-0.5 / -1.1	1.0 / 2.5	+0.9 / 0	-1.0 / -1.6
0.40 - 0.71	0.25 / 0.75	+0.3 / 0	-0.25 / -0.45	0.25 / 0.95	+0.4 / 0	-0.25 / -0.55	0.6 / 1.7	+0.7 / 0	-0.6 / -1.0	0.6 / 2.3	+1.0 / 0	-0.6 / -1.3	1.2 / 2.9	+1.0 / 0	-1.2 / -1.9
0.71 - 1.19	0.3 / 0.95	+0.4 / 0	-0.3 / -0.55	0.3 / 1.2	+0.5 / 0	-0.3 / -0.7	0.8 / 2.1	+0.8 / 0	-0.8 / -1.3	0.8 / 2.8	+1.2 / 0	-0.8 / -1.6	1.6 / 3.6	+1.2 / 0	-1.6 / -2.4

NOMINAL SIZE	Class RC6			Class RC7			Class RC8			Class RC9		
Over - To	Cl	Hole H9	Shaft e8	CL	Hole H9	Shaft d8	Cl	Hole H10	Shaft c9	Cl	Hole H11	Shaft
0 - 0.12	0.6 / 2.2	+1.0 / 0	-0.6 / -1.2	1.0 / 2.6	+1.0 / 0	-1.0 / -1.6	2.5 / 5.1	+1.6 / 0	-2.5 / -3.5	4.0 / 8.1	+2.5 / 0	-4.0 / -5.6
0.12 - 0.24	0.8 / 2.7	+1.2 / 0	-0.8 / -1.5	1.2 / 3.1	+1.2 / 0	-1.2 / -1.9	2.8 / 5.8	+1.8 / 0	-2.8 / -4.0	4.5 / 9.0	+3.0 / 0	-4.5 / -6.0
0.24 - 0.40	1.0 / 3.3	+1.4 / 0	-1.0 / -1.9	1.6 / 3.9	+1.4 / 0	-1.6 / -2.5	3.0 / 6.6	+2.2 / 0	-3.0 / -4.4	5.0 / 10.7	+3.5 / 0	-5.0 / -7.2
0.40 - 0.71	1.2 / 3.8	+1.6 / 0	-1.2 / -2.2	2.0 / 4.6	+1.6 / 0	-2.0 / -3.0	3.5 / 7.9	+2.8 / 0	-3.5 / -5.1	6.0 / 12.8	+4.0 / 0	-6.0 / -8.8
0.71 - 1.19	1.6 / 4.8	+2.0 / 0	-1.6 / -2.8	2.5 / 5.7	+2.0 / 0	-2.5 / -3.7	4.5 / 10.0	+3.5 / 0	-4.5 / -6.5	7.0 / 15.5	+5.0 / 0	-7.0 / -10.5

CLEARANCE LOCATIONAL FITS - Inches
HOLE BASIS

All Tolerance Values are in 0.001 Inches

Nominal Size Over - to	Class LC1 Cl	Class LC1 Hole H6	Class LC1 Shaft h5	Class LC2 Cl	Class LC2 Hole H7	Class LC2 Shaft h6	Class LC3 Cl	Class LC3 Hole H8	Class LC3 Shaft h7	Class LC4 Cl	Class LC4 Hole H10	Class LC4 Shaft h9	Class LC5 Cl	Class LC5 Hole H7	Class LC5 Shaft g6	Class LC6 Cl	Class LC6 Hole H9	Class LC6 Shaft f8
0 - 0.12	0 / 0.45	+0.25 / 0	0 / -0.2	0 / 0.65	+0.4 / 0	0 / -0.25	0 / 1.0	+0.6 / 0	0 / -0.4	0 / 2.6	+1.6 / 0	0 / -1.0	0.1 / 0.75	+0.4 / 0	-0.1 / -0.35	0.3 / 1.9	+1.0 / 0	-0.3 / -0.9
0.12 - 0.24	0 / 0.5	+0.3 / 0	0 / -0.2	0 / 0.8	+0.5 / 0	0 / -0.3	0 / 1.2	+0.7 / 0	0 / -0.5	0 / 3.0	+1.8 / 0	0 / -1.2	0.15 / 0.95	+0.5 / 0	-0.15 / -0.45	0.4 / 2.3	+1.2 / 0	-0.4 / -1.1
0.24 - 0.40	0 / 0.65	+0.4 / 0	0 / -0.25	0 / 1.0	+0.6 / 0	0 / -0.4	0 / 1.5	+0.9 / 0	0 / -0.6	0 / 3.6	+2.2 / 0	0 / -1.4	0.2 / 1.2	+0.6 / 0	-0.2 / -0.6	0.5 / 2.8	+1.4 / 0	-0.5 / -1.4
0.40 - 0.71	0 / 0.7	+0.4 / 0	0 / -0.3	0 / 1.1	+0.7 / 0	0 / -0.4	0 / 1.7	+1.0 / 0	0 / -0.7	0 / 4.4	+2.8 / 0	0 / -1.6	0.25 / 1.35	+0.7 / 0	-0.25 / -0.65	0.6 / 3.2	+1.6 / 0	-0.6 / -1.6
0.71 - 1.19	0 / 0.9	+0.5 / 0	0 / -0.4	0 / 1.3	+0.8 / 0	0 / -0.5	0 / 2.0	+1.2 / 0	0 / -0.8	0 / 5.5	+3.5 / 0	0 / -1.1	0.3 / 1.6	+0.8 / 0	-0.3 / -0.8	0.8 / 4.0	+2.0 / 0	-0.8 / -2.0

Nominal Size Over - to	Class LC7 Cl	Class LC7 Hole H10	Class LC7 Shaft e9	Class LC8 Cl	Class LC8 Hole H10	Class LC8 Shaft d9	Class LC 9 Cl	Class LC 9 Hole H11	Class LC 9 Shaft c10	Class LC 10 Cl	Class LC 10 Hole H12	Class LC 10 Shaft	Class LC 11 Cl	Class LC 11 Hole H13	Class LC 11 Shaft
0 - 0.12	0.6 / 3.2	+1.6 / 0	-0.6 / -1.6	1.0 / 2.0	+1.6 / 0	-1.0 / -2.0	2.5 / 6.6	+2.5 / 0	-2.5 / -4.1	4.0 / 12.0	+4.0 / 0	-4.0 / -8.0	5.0 / 17.0	+6.0 / 0	-5.0 / -11.0
0.12 - 0.24	0.8 / 3.8	+1.8 / 0	-0.8 / -2.0	1.2 / 4.2	+1.8 / 0	-1.2 / -2.4	2.8 / 7.6	+3.0 / 0	-2.8 / -4.6	4.5 / 14.5	+5.0 / 0	-4.5 / -9.5	6.0 / 20.0	+7.0 / 0	-6.0 / -13.0
0.24 - 0.40	1.0 / 4.6	+2.2 / 0	-1.0 / -2.4	1.6 / 5.2	+2.2 / 0	-1.6 / -3.0	3.0 / 8.7	+3.5 / 0	-3.0 / -5.2	5.0 / 17.0	+6.0 / 0	-5.0 / -11.0	7.0 / 25.0	+9.0 / 0	-7.0 / -16.0
0.40 - 0.71	1.2 / 5.6	+2.8 / 0	-1.2 / -2.8	2.0 / 6.4	+2.8 / 0	-2.0 / -3.6	3.5 / 10.3	+4.0 / 0	-3.5 / -6.3	6.0 / 20.0	+7.0 / 0	-6.0 / -13.0	8.0 / 28.0	+10.0 / 0	-8.0 / -18.0
0.71 - 1.19	1.6 / 7.1	+3.5 / 0	-1.6 / -3.6	2.5 / 8.0	+3.5 / 0	-2.5 / -4.5	4.5 / 13.0	+5.0 / 0	-4.5 / -8.0	7.0 / 23.0	+8.0 / 0	-7.0 / -15.0	10.0 / 34.0	+12.0 / 0	-10.0 / -22.0

TRANSITION FITS - Inches
HOLE BASIS

All Tolerance values are in 0.001 inches.

NOMINAL SIZE Over - To	Class LT1 Fit	Class LT1 Hole H7	Class LT1 Shaft js6	Class LT2 Fit	Class LT2 Hole H8	Class LT2 Shaft js7	Class LT3 Fit	Class LT3 Hole H7	Class LT3 Shaft k6	Class LT4 Fit	Class LT4 Hole H8	Class LT4 Shaft k7
0 - 0.12	-0.12 +0.52	+0.4 0	+0.12 -0.12	-0.20 +0.8	+0.6 0	+0.2 -0.2						
0.12 - 0.24	-0.15 +0.65	+0.5 0	+0.15 -0.15	-0.25 +0.95	+0.7 0	+0.25 -0.25						
0.24 - 0.40	-0.2 +0.8	+0.6 0	+0.2 -0.2	-0.3 +1.2	+0.9 0	+0.3 -0.3	-0.5 +0.5	+0.6 0	+0.5 +0.1	-0.7 +0.8	+0.9 0	+0.7 +0.1
0.40 - 0.71	-0.2 +0.9	+0.7 0	+0.2 -0.2	-0.35 +1.35	+1.0 0	+0.35 -0.35	-0.5 +0.6	+0.7 0	+0.5 +0.1	-0.8 +0.9	+1.0 0	+0.8 +0.1
0.71 - 1.19	-0.25 +1.05	+0.8 0	+0.25 -0.25	-0.4 +1.6	+1.2 0	+0.4 -0.4	-0.6 +0.7	+0.8 0	+0.6 +0.1	-0.9 +1.1	+1.2 0	+0.9 +0.1

NOMINAL SIZE Over - To	Class LT5 Fit	Class LT5 Hole H7	Class LT5 Shaft n6	Class LT6 Fit	Class LT6 Hole H7	Class LT6 Shaft n7
0 - 0.12	-0.5 +0.15	+0.4 0	+0.5 +0.25	-0.65 +0.15	+0.4 0	+0.65 +0.25
0.12 - 0.24	-0.6 +0.2	+0.5 0	+0.6 +0.3	-0.8 +0.2	+0.5 0	+0.8 +0.3
0.24 - 0.40	-0.8 +0.2	+0.6 0	+0.8 +0.4	-1.0 +0.2	+0.6 0	+1.0 +0.4
0.40 - 0.71	-0.9 +0.2	+0.7 0	+0.9 +0.5	-1.2 +0.2	+0.7 0	+1.2 +0.5
0.71 - 1.19	-1.1 +0.2	+0.8 0	+1.1 +0.6	-1.4 +0.2	+0.8 0	+1.4 +0.6

INTERFERENCE LOCATIONAL FITS - Inches
HOLE BASIS

All Tolerance Values are in 0.001 inches

NOMINAL SIZE Over - To	Class LN1 Int	Class LN1 Hole H6	Class LN1 Shaft n5	Class LN2 Int	Class LN2 Hole H7	Class LN2 Shaft p6	Class LN3 Int	Class LN3 Hole H7	Class LN3 Shaft r6
0 - 0.12	0 0.45	+0.25 0	+0.45 +0.25	0 0.65	+0.25 0	+0.45 +0.4	0.1 0.75	+0.4 0	+0.75 +0.5
0.12 - 0.24	0 0.5	+0.3 0	+0.5 +0.3	0 0.8	+0.5 0	+0.8 +0.5	0.1 0.0	+0.5 0	+0.9 +0.6
0.24 - 0.40	0 0.65	+0.4 0	+0.65 +0.4	0 1.0	+0.6 0	+1.0 +0.6	0.2 1.2	+0.6 0	+1.2 +0.8
0.40 - 0.71	0 0.08	+0.4 0	+0.8 +0.4	0 1.1	+0.7 0	+1.1 +0.7	0.3 1.4	+0.7 0	+1.4 +1.0
0.71 - 1.19	0 1.0	+0.5 0	+1.0 +0.5	0 1.3	+0.8 0	+1.3 +0.8	0.4 1.7	+0.8 0	+1.7 +1.2

FORCE and SHRINK FITS – Inches
HOLE BASIS

ALL VALUES SHOWN BELOW ARE IN THOUSANDS OF AN INCH
(for example 0.5 = 0.0005 inches)

Nominal Range Over — To	Class FN 1 INT	Class FN 1 Hole H6	Class FN 1 Shaft	Class FN 2 INT	Class FN 2 Hole H7	Class FN 2 Shaft s6	Class FN 3 INT	Class FN 3 Hole H7	Class FN 3 Shaft t6	Class FN 4 INT	Class FN 4 Hole H7	Class FN 4 Shaft u6	Class FN 5 INT	Class FN 5 Hole H8	Class FN 5 Shaft x7
0 – 0.24	0.05 / 0.5	+0.25 / 0	+0.5 / +0.3	0 / 0.2	+0.4 / 0	+0.85 / +0.6				0.3 / 0.95	+0.4 / 0	+0.95 / +0.7	0.3 / 1.3	+0.6 / 0	+1.3 / +0.9
0.12 – 0.24	0.1 / 0.6	+0.3 / 0	+0.6 / +0.4	0.2 / 1.0	+0.5 / 0	+1.0 / +0.7				0.4 / 1.2	+0.5 / 0	+1.2 / +0.9	0.5 / 1.7	+0.7 / 0	+1.7 / +1.2
0.24 – 0.40	0.1 / 0.75	+0.4 / 0	+0.75 / +0.5	0.4 / 1.4	+0.6 / 0	+1.4 / +1.0				0.6 / 1.6	+0.6 / 0	+1.6 / +1.2	0.5 / 2.0	+0.9 / 0	+2.0 / +1.4
0.40 – 0.56	0.1 / 0.8	+0.4 / 0	+0.8 / +0.5	0.5 / 1.6	+0.7 / 0	+1.6 / +1.2				0.7 / 1.8	+0.7 / 0	+1.8 / +1.4	0.6 / 2.3	+1.0 / 0	+2.3 / +1.6
0.56 – 0.71	0.2 / 0.9	+0.4 / 0	+0.9 / +0.6	0.5 / 1.6	+0.7 / 0	+1.6 / +1.2				0.7 / 1.8	+0.7 / 0	+1.8 / +1.4	0.8 / 2.5	+1.0 / 0	+2.5 / +1.8
0.71 – 0.95	0.2 / 1.1	+0.5 / 0	+1.1 / +0.7	0.6 / 1.9	+0.8 / 0	+1.9 / +1.4				0.8 / 2.1	+0.8 / 0	+2.1 / +1.6	1.0 / 3.0	+1.2 / 0	+3.0 / +2.2
0.95 – 1.19	0.3 / 1.2	+0.5 / 0	+1.2 / +0.8	0.6 / 1.9	+0.8 / 0	+1.9 / +1.4	0.8 / 2.1	+0.8 / 0	+2.1 / +1.6	1.0 / 2.3	+0.8 / 0	+2.3 / +1.8	1.3 / 3.3	+1.2 / 0	+3.3 / +2.5
1.19 – 1.58	0.3 / 1.3	+0.6 / 0	+1.3 / +0.9	0.8 / 2.4	+1.0 / 0	+2.4 / +1.8	1.0 / 2.6	+1.0 / 0	+2.6 / +2.0	1.5 / 3.1	+1.0 / 0	+3.1 / +2.5	1.4 / 4.0	+1.6 / 0	+4.0 / +3.0
1.58 – 1.97	0.4 / 1.4	+0.6 / 0	+1.4 / +1.0	0.8 / 2.4	+1.0 / 0	+2.4 / +1.8	1.0 / 2.8	+1.0 / 0	+2.8 / +2.2	1.8 / 3.4	+1.0 / 0	+3.4 / +2.8	2.4 / 5.0	+1.6 / 0	+5.0 / +4.0
1.97 – 2.56	0.6 / 1.8	+0.7 / 0	+1.8 / +1.3	0.8 / 2.7	+1.2 / 0	+2.7 / +2.0	1.3 / 3.2	+1.2 / 0	+3.2 / +2.5	2.3 / 4.2	+1.2 / 0	+4.2 / +3.5	3.2 / 6.2	+1.8 / 0	+6.2 / +5.0

E STANDARD TWIST DRILL SIZES

STANDARD TWIST DRILL SIZES

by Number, Letter, and Fraction (inches)

SIZE	DIA	SIZE	DIA	SIZE	DIA
40	.098	11	.191	R	.339
39	.0995	10	.1935	11/32	.3438
38	.1015	9	.196	S	.348
37	.104	8	.199	T	.358
36	.1065	7	.201	23/64	.3594
7/16	.1094	13/64	.2031	U	.368
35	.110	6	.204	3/8	.375
34	.111	5	.2055	V	.377
33	.113	4	.209	W	.386
32	.116	3	.213	25/64	.3906
31	.120	7/32	.2188	X	.397
1/8	.125	2	.221	Y	.404
30	.1285	1	.228	13/32	.4062
29	.136	A	.234	Z	.413
28	.1405	B	.238	27/64	.4219
9/64	.1406	C	.242	7/16	.4375
27	.144	D	.246	29/64	.4531
26	.147	1/4(E)	.250	15/32	.4688
25	.1495	F	.257	31/64	.4844
24	.152	G	.261	1/2	.5000
23	.154	17/64	.2656	9/16	.5625
5/32	.1562	H	.266	5/8	.625
22	.157	I	.272	11/16	.6875
21	.159	J	.277	3/4	.750
20	.161	K	.281	13/16	.8125
19	.166	9/32	.2812	7/8	.875
18	.1695	L	.290	15/16	.9375
11/64	.1719	M	.295		
17	.173	19/64	.2969		
16	.177	N	.302		
15	.180	5/16	.3125		
14	.182	O	.316		
13	.185	P	.323		
3/16	.1875	21/64	.3281		
12	.189	Q	.332		

NOTES FOR TWIST DRILL SIZES - INCHES

1. This is only a partial list of standard drill sizes.
2. Whenever possible, specify holes sizes that correspond to standard drill sizes.
3. Drill sizes are available in 1/64 increments between .5000 and 1.2500.
4. Drill sizes are available in 1/32 increments between 1.2500 and 1.5000.
5. Drill sizes are available in 1/16 increments between 1.5000 and 2.0000.

STANDARD TWIST DRILL SIZES
(millimeters)

DIA	DIA	DIA	DIA	DIA
0.40	2.30	6.00	10.00	22.00
0.42	2.35	6.10	10.20	22.50
0.45	2.40	6.20	10.50	23.00
0.48	2.40	6.30	10.80	23.50
0.50	2.45	6.40	11.00	24.00
0.55	2.50	6.50	11.20	24.50
0.60	2.60	6.60	11.50	25.00
0.65	2.70	6.70	11.80	25.50
0.70	2.80	6.80	12.00	26.00
0.75	2.90	6.90	12.20	26.50
0.80	3.00	7.00	12.20	27.00
0.85	3.10	7.10	12.50	27.50
0.90	3.20	7.20	12.80	28.00
0.95	3.30	7.30	13.00	28.50
1.00	3.40	7.40	13.20	29.00
1.05	3.50	7.50	13.50	29.50
1.10	3.60	7.60	13.80	30.00
1.15	3.70	7.70	14.00	30.50
1.20	3.80	7.80	14.25	31.00
1.25	3.90	7.90	14.50	31.50
1.30	4.00	8.00	14.75	32.00
1.35	4.10	8.10	15.00	32.50
1.40	4.20	8.20	15.25	33.00
1.45	4.30	8.30	15.50	33.50
1.50	4.40	8.40	15.75	34.00
1.55	4.50	8.50	16.00	34.50
1.60	4.60	8.60	16.25	35.00
1.65	4.70	8.70	16.50	35.50
1.70	4.80	8.80	16.75	36.00
1.75	4.90	8.90	17.00	36.50
1.80	5.00	9.00	17.25	37.00
1.85	5.10	9.10	17.50	37.50
1.90	5.20	9.20	18.00	38.00
1.95	5.30	9.30	18.50	40.00
2.00	5.40	9.40	19.00	42.00
2.05	5.50	9.50	19.50	44.00
2.10	5.60	9.60	20.00	46.00
2.15	5.70	9.70	20.50	48.00
2.20	5.80	9.80	21.00	50.00
2.25	5.90	9.90	21.50	

INDEX

A

Algorithm, 8
Aligned system, 101
Analog, 8
Apex, 361
Arcs, 42, 79
Auxiliary views, 212-37
  oblique surfaces, 229
  partial, 223-28
  primary, 215-23
  rounded shapes, 224-28
Axis:
  axonometric, 352
  isometric, 354, 370
  orientation, 355
  rotation, 358
  three dimensional, 352

B

Baseline method, 109
Basic hole system, 261
Basic shaft system, 262, 268
Batch processing, 8
Bill of materials, 338
Binary system, 6
Bit, 6, 8
Blanking, 8
Bolts, 297

Boss, 163
Buffer, 8
Byte, 6, 8

C

CADAM, 39
Castings, 162
Centimeter, 13
Chain system, 109
Chamfers, 114
Character, 8
Chips, computer, 3, 8
Circles, 39
Clipping, 8
Cone, 357, 363-64
Coordinates:
  absolute, 23
  cartesian, 352-53, 370
  polar, 20-21
  rectangular, 17-25
  relative, 23
  rotated, 19-20
  three dimensional, 21-22
Corner, 42, 82-85, 368
Counterbores, 118
Counterdrills, 119
Countersinks, 117
Cylinder, 152, 357, 358-60

D

Decameter, 13
Decimeter, 13
Digital system, 8
Digitizing board, 6
Dimensions, 99-122
  angles, 107
  angular, 252
  arc, 106
  base, 252
  baseline, 253
  chain, 252
  circular, 104
  direct, 252
  double, 121, 253
  dual, 274-76
  hole patterns, 109-11
  slanted features, 103
  small distances, 109
Dot matrix, 346
Drawing:
  assembly, 331
  detail, 334, 335
  exploded, 378
  notes, 345
  oblique, 353
  paper sizes, 400
  perspective, 352
  pictorial, 351-78
  production, 331
  revisions, 340
  titles, 336
  top, 333
  windowed, 374
  zones, 342, 343
Drill sizes, 410, 411

E

Element, 8
Ellipse, 85, 153
Engineering change orders, 342
EPROM, 8
Error message, 8

F

Fasteners, 290-320
Fillet, 42, 163, 368
Fit Tolerances, 258-61, 401-9
Floppy disks, 8

G

Gages:
  sheet metal, 400
  wire, 400
Gate, 8

H

Hard copy, 8
Hardware, 8
Hectometer, 13
Hexagon, 74
Holes, 154-55, 200

I

Identification numbers, 338
Image processing, 8
Integrated circuit (IC), 8
Interactive, 8
Irregular curves, 44
Irregular features, 119
Irregular shapes, 156-61

K

Keys, 116, 307
Keyseats, 116
Kilometer, 13
Knurls, 114

L

Lay symbols, 272-73
Light pen, 5
Limits, 258-61
Lines:
  cutting plane, 186, 190-95
  dimension, 100
  divided, 63
  extension, 99
  hidden, 136-38
  horizontal, 30
  object, 100
  parallel, 67
  perpendicular, 60, 63
  sectional, 186
  slanted, 37
  tangent, 65

true length, 141, 212-15
vertical, 30
Local area network, 8
LOGO, 39
LSI, 8

M

Megameter, 13
Memory, 8
Metric system, 13
Microcomputer, 8
Micrometer, 13
Microprocessor, 8
Millimeter, 13
Mode, 9
Modem, 9
Modifying phrases, 336
Monochromatic screen, 9
Mouse, 5

N

Nanometer, 13
Noun phrase, 336
Number crunching, 9
Nuts, 300

O

Octagons, 77
On-line, 9
Operator, 9
Orthographic views, 128-65

P

Painting, 9
Pan, 343
Parabola, 85-86
Part number, 338
Parts list, 338
Pentagons, 72
Perpendicular bisect, 60
Pixel, 4, 9, 14
Plan views, 138
Plotters:
    drum, 346
    flatbed, 346

Points, 17-25
Primitive, 9
Printers:
    impact, 346
    nonimpact, 346
Prism, 357, 360-61
Profile view, 138
Program, 9
Pyramids, 357, 361-63

R

RAM, 2, 9
Raster screen, 9
Resolution, 9, 14
Rivet, 308
ROM, 2, 9
Round, 42, 163, 368
Rounded ends, 115
Runout, 162

S

Screen units, 14-17
Screws, 297-300
Sectional views:
    broken-out, 196
    half, 198
    revolved, 197
    rotated, 197
    thin part, 198
Setscrew, 305
Sheet metal object, 161, 199
Slotted hole, 116
Software, 9
Sphere, 357, 364
Spline, 44-45, 156
Spotface, 118, 163
Spring, 309
Square, 70
Standard part, 339
Stud, 305
Surfaces:
    finish, 269-73
    normal, 140
    oblique, 143
    rounded, 150
    slanted, 141

T

Threads, 290-320
  American standard, 292-93
  metric, 294
  standard, 398-99
  symbols, 294-97
  terms, 291
  UNC, UNF, 293
Thumbscrews, 5
Time sharing, 9
Title block, 337
Tolerances, 249-76
  accumulated, 252
  bilateral, 250
  studies, 254
  symbols, 262
  unilateral, 251
Triangles, 68

U

Unidirectional system, 101
User, 9

V

Visual display unit (VDUs), 4
VLSI, 9

W

Washers, 304
Window, 9

Z

Zoom, 9, 343